THE
YEAR'S WORK IN
ENGLISH STUDIES

VOLUME XLII

1961

EDITED BY

BEATRICE WHITE
D.Lit., F.S.A., F.R.Hist.S., F.R.S.L.

AND

T. S. DORSCH, M.A.
(Assistant Editor)

Published for
THE ENGLISH ASSOCIATION
by
OXFORD UNIVERSITY PRESS
LONDON
1963

Oxford University Press, Amen House, London E.C.4

GLASGOW NEW YORK TORONTO MELBOURNE WELLINGTON
BOMBAY CALCUTTA MADRAS KARACHI LAHORE DACCA
CAPE TOWN SALISBURY NAIROBI IBADAN ACCRA
KUALA LUMPUR HONG KONG

PRINTED IN GREAT BRITAIN

PREFACE

THE present volume of *The Year's Work* bears ample testimony to the healthy state of English Studies. The well-tilled field yields a yearly crop of sturdy and almost riotous growth which shows no signs of a diminishing harvest. Articles and books from all over the world are dealt with in these pages, the very number of which is a pointer to the vigorous activity of scholars dedicated to the cause of English language and literature.

The list of contributors to this volume contains three changes. Dr. Haddakin is replaced by Mr. J. Chalker, M.A., and Mr. John Gross, M.A., by Mr. B. C. Southam, M.A., B.Litt., and Miss Betty Hill, Ph.D., joins Dr. Macdonald in the preparation of Chapter IV.

Offprints of articles, together with relevant works in foreign languages, should be sent to The Secretary, English Association, 8 Cromwell Place, London, S.W. 7, for distribution to the contributors.

BEATRICE WHITE
T. S. DORSCH

ABBREVIATIONS

ABC	*American Book Collector*
AL	*American Literature*
A Ling	*Archivum Linguisticum*
Ang	*Anglia*
AQ	*American Quarterly*
Archiv	*Archiv für das Studium der Neueren Sprachen*
AS	*American Speech*
ATR	*Anglican Theological Review*
AUMLA	*Journal of Australasian Universities Modern Language Association*
BC	*The Book Collector*
BJRL	*Bulletin of the John Rylands Library*
B.M.	British Museum
BMQ	*British Museum Quarterly*
BNYPL	*Bulletin of the New York Public Library*
BSL	*Bulletin de la Société Linguistique*
BUSE	*Boston University Studies in English*
C	*Critique*
CE	*College English*
CL	*Comparative Literature*
CLA	*College Language Association Journal*
CQ	*Critical Quarterly*
DR	*Dalhousie Review*
DUJ	*Durham University Journal*
Ea	*Études anglaises*
EC	*Essays in Criticism*
EDS	*Essays by Divers Hands*
E.E.T.S.	Early English Text Society
EFT	*English Fiction in Transition*
EG	*English and Germanic Studies*
EJ	*English Journal*
ELH	*Journal of English Literary History*
ELT	*English Language Teaching*
E.P.N.S.	English Place-Name Society
ES	*English Studies*
ESA	*English Studies in Africa*
E & S	*Essays and Studies*
Ex	*Explicator*
HLB	*Harvard Library Bulletin*
HLQ	*Huntington Library Quarterly*
HR	*Hudson Review*
HTR	*Harvard Theological Review*
JEGP	*Journal of English and Germanic Philology*
JHI	*Journal of the History of Ideas*
JWCI	*Journal of the Warburg and Courtauld Institutes*
KR	*Kenyon Review*
KSJ	*Keats–Shelley Journal*
L	*Language*
Lib	*The Library*
LLM	*Les Langues Modernes*

LS	*Language and Speech*
MÆ	*Medium Ævum*
MCR	*Melbourne Critical Review*
MD	*Modern Drama*
MFS	*Modern Fiction Studies*
MLJ	*Modern Language Journal*
MLN	*Modern Language Notes*
MLQ	*Modern Language Quarterly*
MLR	*Modern Language Review*
MP	*Modern Philology*
MR	*Massachusetts Review*
MS	*Mediaeval Studies*
N	*Neophilologus*
NCF	*Nineteenth Century Fiction*
NEQ	*New England Quarterly*
NM	*Neuphilologische Mitteilungen*
NMS	*Nottingham Medieval Studies*
NQ	*Notes and Queries*
NS	*Die Neueren Sprachen*
O.E.D.	*Oxford English Dictionary*
PBA	*Proceedings of the British Academy*
PBSA	*Papers of the Bibliographical Society of America*
PMLA	*Publications of the Modern Language Association of America*
PQ	*Philological Quarterly*
QQ	*Queen's Quarterly*
QR	*Quarterly Review*
REL	*Review of English Literature (Leeds)*
RES	*Review of English Studies*
RI	*Rice Institute Pamphlets*
RLC	*Revue de Littérature Comparée*
RMS	*Renaissance and Modern Studies*
RN	*Renaissance News*
RP	*Renaissance Papers*
R.S.L.	Royal Society of Literature
S	*Speculum*
SAQ	*South Atlantic Quarterly*
SB	*Studies in Bibliography*
Sew	*Sewanee Review*
Sh J	*Shakespeare Jahrbuch*
Sh Q	*Shakespeare Quarterly*
Sh S	*Shakespeare Survey*
SL	*Studia Linguistica*
SN	*Studia Neophilologica*
SNL	*Shakespeare Newsletter*
SP	*Studies in Philology*
S Ren	*Studies in the Renaissance*
S.T.C.	*Short Title Catalogue*
T	*Traditio*
TCF	*Twentieth Century Fiction*
TCL	*Twentieth Century Literature*
TLS	*Times Literary Supplement*
TPS	*Transactions of the Philological Society*
TQ	*Texas Quarterly*
TSE	*Tulane Studies in English*
TSL	*Tennessee Studies in Literature*

UKCR	*University of Kansas City Review*
TSLL	*Texas Studies in Language and Literature*
UMSE	*University of Mississippi Studies in English*
UTQ	*University of Toronto Quarterly*
UTSE	*University of Texas Studies in English*
VS	*Victorian Studies*
YDS	*Transactions of the Yorkshire Dialect Society*
YW	*The Year's Work in English Studies*
ZAA	*Zeitschrift für Anglistik und Amerikanistik*

CONTENTS

I. LITERARY HISTORY AND CRITICISM: GENERAL WORKS

By T. S. DORSCH

1. Histories of Literature and Reference Works

THE appearance of a revised and enlarged edition of *Annals of English Literature*,[1] which was first published in 1935, will be generally welcomed. Many corrections have been made to the section which ends at 1900, and the section from 1900 to 1925 has been reset to make possible the inclusion of more entries, especially those relating to Commonwealth and American literature. An entirely new section has been added to bring the record down to 1950—it previously ended with 1925. The work of revision was mainly done by the late R. W. Chapman, whose labours have been co-ordinated by Mrs. W. K. Davin.

Another reference book whose reappearance in an expanded form will be welcomed is *The Concise Cambridge History of English Literature*.[2] In its eleven printings in the course of the last twenty years this work has established itself so firmly that there is no need to describe the bulk of it here. The expansion takes the form of a sensible and reasonably comprehensive chapter on 'The Age of T. S. Eliot', by R. C. Churchill; this replaces George Sampson's shorter final chapter, which with a few exceptions excluded writers born later than 1890 as not yet having 'passed into history'. Churchill, also with a few exceptions, brings the qualifying birth-date forward by twenty years; it is a pity that he has not brought it a little farther forward, for by excluding practically all writers who are not yet in their fifties he is excluding some who may be felt already to have won their spurs. However, his survey of the literature of the present century is, as far as it goes, competent enough, and the volume is certainly the more useful for having been brought more up to date.

A Critical History of English Literature,[3] by David Daiches, was not available for notice last year. It is a work of solid and well-pondered erudition, and weighty also in the physical sense. Well stocked with reliable information, it will make a useful reference book; but Daiches has aimed at 'the maximum ease of reading compatible with sound scholarship and intellectual responsibility', and has therefore avoided a pedantic accumulation of facts and left undiscussed the conflicting views of his predecessors. As his title indicates, his purpose is critical as well as, perhaps even rather than, historical, and the opinions he expresses are his own. Exception has been taken to the proportions of the work, the relatively long or short treatment

---

[1] *Annals of English Literature, 1475–1950: The Principal Publications of Each Year together with an Alphabetical Index of Authors with Their Works.* Second Edition. O.U.P. pp. vi+380. 25s.

[2] *The Concise Cambridge History of English Literature*, by George Sampson. Second Edition, with a chapter on 'The Age of T. S. Eliot', by R. C. Churchill. C.U.P. pp. xv+1071. 25s.

[3] *A Critical History of English Literature*, by David Daiches. Secker & Warburg, 1960. Two vols.: pp. viii+1–534; iii+535–1169. £5.

that Daiches gives to particular authors; but in a one-man work of this kind allowance must surely be made for the writer's personal preferences. He might, indeed, have begun at some time in the Middle English period, since the twenty-seven pages that he gives to Old English literature are too sketchy to have much interest, but otherwise it is one of the merits of the volume that it bears the stamp of a single mind; a mind, moreover, of great sensibility, and one that has been nourished on the literature of many periods, as Daiches's many previous publications testify. It may be added that the readability at which he aims is greatly increased by his generous use of quotation and analysis.

Josef Raith's *Geschichte der englischen Literatur*,[4] now issued in a revised and expanded edition, is rather a short encyclopedia of English and American literature than the history that its title implies. It opens, indeed, with a historical survey of thirty-three pages, and thereafter it presents its authors in chronological order, but it does no more than list the writings (sometimes only the major writings) of these authors with a certain amount of annotation and an occasional critical comment. Shakespeare receives a page and a half, but otherwise the average length of the entries is about half a page. In English literature the volume ranges from *Beowulf* to Dylan Thomas, and in American from Washington Irving to Thomas Wolfe. It is generously illustrated with portraits and prints.

The final volume of the Pelican Guide to English Literature,[5] which covers the literature of this century,

follows the pattern of its predecessors. It opens with chapters on 'The Social and Intellectual Background' (by G. H. Bantock) and 'The Literary Scene' (by John Holloway). Chapters on individual writers and movements are as follows: 'Henry James: The Drama of Discrimination', by Henry Gifford; 'From *Heart of Darkness* to *Nostromo*: An Approach to Conrad', by Douglas Brown; 'Hardy, de la Mare, and Edward Thomas', by H. Coombes; 'The Literature of the First World War', by D. J. Enright; 'The Later Poetry of W. B. Yeats', by Graham Martin; 'The Irish Contribution', by Grattan Freyer; 'Shaw and the London Theatre', by T. R. Barnes; 'The Comedy of Ideas: Cross-currents in the Fiction and Drama of the Twentieth Century', by R. C. Churchill; 'The Prose of Thought', by E. W. F. Tomlin; 'Mr. Forster's Good Influence', by G. D. Klingopulos: 'Virginia Woolf: The Theory and Practice of Fiction', by Frank W. Bradbrook; 'L. H. Myers and Bloomsbury', by G. H. Bantock; 'D. H. Lawrence and *Women in Love*', by W. W. Robson; 'The Consistency of James Joyce', by Arnold Kettle; 'Ezra Pound's *Hugh Selwyn Mauberley*', by Donald Davie; 'T. S. Eliot: Poet and Critic', by L. G. Salingar; 'Criticism and the Reading Public', by Andor Gomme; 'The Poetry of W. H. Auden', by R. G. Cox; 'Novelists of Three Decades: Evelyn Waugh, Graham Greene, C. P. Snow', by Graham Martin; 'Metaphor and Maturity: T. F. Powys and Dylan Thomas', by David Holbrook; 'The Twentieth-Century Best-Seller', by P. N. Furbank; 'Mass Communications in Britain', by Richard Hoggart; 'Poetry Today', by Charles Tomlinson; and 'The Novel Today', by Gilbert Phelps. The volume closes with a helpful bibliography, compiled by Joy Samuel.

H. M. Green's *History of Australian*

---

[4] *Geschichte der englischen Literatur*, von Josef Raith. München: Hueber. pp. viii + 184. DM. 8.80.
[5] *The Modern Age*. Volume 7 of the Pelican Guide to English Literature, ed. by Boris Ford. Penguin Books. pp. 559. 7s. 6d.

Literature,[6] in two massive volumes, is an extremely important contribution to the study of Commonwealth literature. As its sub-title shows, its scope is very wide: 'A critical review of all forms of literature produced in Australia from the first books published after the arrival of the First Fleet until 1950, with short accounts of later publications up to 1960.' It would seem surprising that there could be omissions in so thorough-going a study, but perhaps one may be noted 'for the record'. Green writes admirably on the Australian newspapers, some of which have had a life of more than a century and a half; in order to illustrate the speed with which printing was established in Australia, he might have mentioned that the presses on which the Adelaide *Register* began its distinguished career (now, alas, ended) were set up on the beach at Glenelg before the first shipload of South Australian colonists had built their first homes. Otherwise a sample reading suggests that very little is missing, from the earliest annals and surveys printed in New South Wales to the work of the fine poets and novelists of today and the scientific publications, especially notable in the field of anthropology, which are now appearing in ever-increasing numbers. More rapidly than other Commonwealth countries, Australia has produced a literature, both light and serious, which is distinctively her own, and Green's history of this literature in all its facets will long remain a standard work of reference.

The Commonwealth Pen,[7] edited by A. L. McLeod, is a work on a very

much smaller scale. It is a collection of essays, the longest of fewer than thirty pages in length, outlining the history of the literature of ten Commonwealth countries. Each of the authors is a national of the country he discusses, and an authority on its literature. Australia is covered by McLeod himself and H. J. Oliver; Canada by F. W. Watt; New Zealand by J. C. Reid; South Africa by Randolph Vigne; Ceylon by Yasmine Dias Bandaranaike; India by K. R. Srinivasa Iyengar; Pakistan by S. Sajjad Husain; West Africa by K. E. Senanu; the West Indies by G. R. Coulthard; and Malaya and Singapore by J. M. Hardman. In the space at their disposal the authors can, of course, offer no more than very brief outlines of the more important literary movements; for example, living Australian poets, who include such considerable figures as Judith Wright, Kenneth Slessor, and A. D. Hope, are dismissed in a couple of dozen lines, and about the same number of pages deals with the whole of Anglo-Indian literature in the last century and a half. What is interesting and valuable about the book is that it provides in brief compass a clear conspectus of a group of literatures which have a common background, but in which new themes and techniques are constantly being explored, often with very impressive results.

One of the most important works of the year is Bernard Weinberg's *History of Literary Criticism in the Italian Renaissance.*[8] It is very much more comprehensive and thorough than previous books on the subject, being based on a wider and more intensive scrutiny of the available documents, including many manuscripts untouched by the earlier historians, and it will

[6] *A History of Australian Literature, Pure and Applied,* by H. M. Green. Angus & Robertson. Two vols.: pp. xxix+1–842; vii+843–1469. £8. 8s.

[7] *The Commonwealth Pen: An Introduction to the Literature of the British Commonwealth,* ed. by A. L. McLeod. Cornell U.P. and O.U.P. pp. xi+243. $3.50. 28s.

[8] *A History of Literary Criticism in the Italian Renaissance,* by Bernard Weinberg. Chicago U.P. Two vols.: pp. xv.+1–634; iii+635–1184. $20. £8.

long remain the standard work on its field. Only a very general indication of Weinberg's treatment can be given here. After preliminary chapters on the classification of Poetics among the sciences and 'The Methodology of the Theorists', four chapters are devoted to the tradition of Horace's *Ars Poetica*, with full discussion of the earliest commentaries, of the confusion with Aristotle, and the application of Horace's precepts to practical criticism—in each case with copious reference to the relevant Italian writings. There follow two chapters on Platonism, and five on the tradition of Aristotle's *Poetics*, and the treatment of these two authors and of works based on their views is as thoroughgoing as that of Horace and his disciples and antagonists. Next the new 'Arts of Poetry' are considered, those of Vida, Trissino, Minturno, and the rest. Part II, 'Practical Criticism', deals with the various controversies relating to the works of Dante, Speroni, Ariosto and Tasso, and Guarini. The work ends with an extremely valuable bibliography of forty-five pages. This large and complex subject could hardly have been more reliably and competently handled than it has been in Weinberg's excellent study.

Although not nearly as comprehensive as J. T. Shipley's *Dictionary of World Literary Terms* (*YW* xxxvi. 9), the short paper-back *Dictionary of Literary Terms*,[9] compiled by Sylvan Barnet, Morton Berman, and William Burto, is both handy and reliable. It compresses a good deal of information into its larger entries on such topics as drama, epic, or versification, and saves a good deal of space by a careful system of cross-references. Moreover, it gives useful advice on further reading; for example, the two-page entry on the Renaissance ends with references

to five excellent standard works on Renaissance literature.

2. *Annual Publications and General Criticism*

As most of the articles in *Essays and Studies, 1961*,[10] are noticed in other chapters, little more is required here than a general survey of the contents. S. C. Roberts opens the volume with some lively reminiscences of R. W. Chapman, referring particularly to his services in the field of Johnsonian scholarship. C. P. Snow contributes a short biographical and critical study of Italo Svevo, an 'attractive and idiosyncratic' writer whose novels have affinities with those of William Cooper and Kingsley Amis. In the next article, a species of postscript to C. P. Snow's *The Two Cultures and the Scientific Revolution*, S. Gorley Putt recalls his association at Cambridge with Snow, F. R. Leavis, and Sir Arthur Quiller-Couch, discusses their outlooks, and concludes that 'The scientist in Snow, the critic in Leavis, the worldly wisdom of "Q", all have for us the same lesson: that the enemy of our culture is not another kind of culture, but rather that *both* cultures of the Rede Lecture are threatened by that drab confusion of ends and means which passes nowadays by the name of technique.' R. W. Burchfield gives an interesting account of the problems confronting the editors of the new supplement to *O.E.D.* that is being prepared, and of the progress of the work. Edmund Blunden's essay, 'On Regency Fiction: A Fragment', takes in, among others, Scott, Jane Austen, Maria Edgeworth, Godwin, Mrs. Radcliffe, Anne Maria Porter and her sister Jane, Amelia Opie, and Maturin. A. C. Ward reflects on various uses of language as a means

[9] *A Dictionary of Literary Terms*, by Sylvan Barnet, Morton Berman, and William Burto. Boston: Little, Brown & Co., 1960. pp. 96.

[10] *Essays and Studies, 1961*. N.S. Vol. XIV. Collected for the English Association by Derek Hudson. Murray. pp. v+114. 13s. 6d.

of communication in modern life. Beatrice White provides some fascinating glimpses of English travellers to Iceland in the late eighteenth and the nineteenth centuries, and appraises their writings. Finally, Derek Hudson offers a study of Algernon Blackwood and his works.

Four items in the 1961 *Proceedings of the British Academy*[11] relate to English studies. Donald Davie's Chatterton Lecture on an English Poet is on 'The Poetry of Sir Walter Scott'. Scott has long been underrated as a poet, and Davie has no difficulty in showing, by means of well-chosen quotation and analysis, that he deserves much warmer praise than he commonly receives; 'in subject and mood, vocabulary and metre, and also in morality, Scott is a poet, not merely a novelist who also wrote verse'. The Sarah Tryphena Phillips Lecture, delivered by Carl Bode, concerns 'The Sound of American Literature a Century Ago'. Bode outlines the activities of the American Lyceum, a series of literary institutes inaugurated by Josiah Holbrook in 1826; he goes on to show, with special reference to the writings of Emerson, Thoreau, Mark Twain, and Bayard Taylor, many of which were originally read aloud in these institutes, how 'reading to an audience trains an author's ear' and gives him a feeling for style. In his interesting Shakespeare Lecture, 'Shakespeare and the Players', Richard David draws together the most important verified facts relating to the organization of the Elizabethan companies of players, particularly that for which Shakespeare wrote. The Warton Lecture on English Poetry, entitled 'Some Themes and Variations in the Poetry of Andrew Marvell', is by J. B. Leishman. Leishman finds Marvell a very versatile poet, one who

was ready 'to accept, to exploit, and to recombine, to Marvellize and seventeenth-centurify, anything that had ever made poetry enjoyable'. Other lectures published in the volume are 'The Metamorphosis of Metaphysics', by John Wisdom; 'The Excavations at Surkh Kotal and the Problem of Hellenism in Bactria and India', by Daniel Schlumberger; 'The Colour Question in the Portuguese Empire, 1415–1825', by C. R. Boxer; 'Hume's Doctrine of Space', by C. D. Broad; 'The Welsh Metrical Treatise Attributed to Einion Offeiriad', by Thomas Parry; 'Felice Feliciano *Antiquarius*', by Charles Mitchell; and 'Some Alexandrian Forgeries', by P. M. Fraser.

The 1961 volume of *Studies in Bibliography* is noticed later in the section headed *Bibliographical Studies* (see note 39).

A new journal instituted at Osmania University under the title *Osmania Journal of English Studies*[12] deserves a welcome. It is edited by Shiv K. Kumar, and is to be published once a year. It opens with the first instalment of a study by V. K. Gokak entitled ' "Progress" in Language Viewed in Relation to Literary Expression'—an attempt to discover whether, 'aesthetically speaking', English has become 'less expressive or more expressive, less beautiful or more beautiful', as a result of such developments as the decay in inflexions and the dropping of gender distinctions. In 'Hopkins and T. S. Eliot—A Study in Linguistic Innovation' B. N. Joshi aims at showing that each of these poets uses a 'heightened language' of a special kind, and that the poetic art of each has 'become a highbrow exclusiveness, demanding a sensibility that is the product of a

[11] *Proceedings of the British Academy, 1961.* Vol. XLVII. O.U.P., 1962. pp. xvii + 428. 84s.

[12] *Osmania Journal of English Studies: A Journal of English Language, Literature and Philology*, ed. Shiv K. Kumar. Asst. Editor, V. A. Shahare. Hyderabad: Osmania Univ. pp. iii + 80. Rs. 2.50. 4s. 50c.

sophisticated culture'. H. N. L. Sastri examines *The Song Celestial*, Sir Edwin Arnold's translation of the *Bhagavad-Gita*, and finds that, although it has felicities, it lacks scholarly precision and often seriously misrepresents the original. V. Madhusudan Reddy studies 'The Concept of Time in T. S. Eliot's *The Four Quartets*'. V. A. Shahare's subject is the influence of Henry James on E. M. Forster; he comes to the conclusion that, although this influence is fairly considerable, Forster is in almost all respects inferior to James. Finally, Kumar writes on 'Joyce and Bergson's "Mémoire Pure" ', expressing the view that, 'interpreted in terms of Bergson's *mémoire pure*, much of the work of Joyce acquires a new coherence and significance'. The volume also contains book reviews.

Abstracts of English Studies,[13] now in its fourth year, has again extended its range, and now covers almost all journals in the western world that are of interest to students of English, as well as some from Commonwealth countries and from the Orient. It digests articles in sufficient detail to enable one to decide whether those which have appeared in comparatively inaccessible journals are worth tracking down, and is therefore of value as a means of saving time.

Dissertation Abstracts[14] continues its very useful career, and extends its range with every year of its life—nearly 120 American universities now co-operate in its production. As readers of *YW* will know, it provides digests

of doctoral theses presented in these universities and available in microform, and every number contains a valuable section on language and literature. It is becoming increasingly well known in this country, and probably every university teacher of English now consults it or directs his research students to its pages.

The second series of *English Studies Today*[15] brings together twenty-three of the papers read at the fourth international conference of Professors of English, which was held at Lausanne and Berne in August 1959. Limitations of space will allow only a brief outline of its contents. In the opening lecture, 'Switzerland and the English-Speaking World', Heinrich Straumann gives an interesting account of the centuries-long connexions, both historical and cultural, that have existed between Switzerland and England. Herbert Read makes a timely attack, none the less effective for its courtesy, on a disturbing phenomenon of the past fifty years, that is, 'a total rejection of style as a criterion of literature, and a scornful refusal to observe its requirements in the course of criticism'. He himself believes that 'style is the best index to the purpose or intention of the critic'. In 'The Novelist and the Narrator' Angus Wilson draws on his own experience in order to describe 'the process of narrating as it goes on when one is actually composing or writing a novel'. René Wellek's subject is 'Literary Theory, Criticism and History'. Reviewing recent tendencies in criticism, he concludes that 'we must return to the task of building a literary theory, a system of principles, a theory of values which will necessarily draw

[13] *Abstracts of English Studies*. Vol. IV. Editor-in-Chief, Lewis Savin. Univ. of Colorado. In 12 monthly parts, pp. 576. Annual Subscription $4.

[14] *Dissertation Abstracts: Abstracts of Dissertations and Monographs in Microform*. Ann Arbor: University Microfilms, Inc. In 12 monthly parts. Vol. XXI, Nos. 7–12, pp. 1677–3907, with Indexes; Vol. XXII, Nos. 1–6, pp. 1–2119, with Indexes and Author Index to Vol. XXI. Annual subscription $27.50 (U.S.A.), $30 (Abroad).

[15] *English Studies Today, Second Series: Lectures and Papers Read at the Fourth Conference of the International Association of University Professors of English Held at Lausanne and Berne, August 1959*, ed. by G. A. Bonnard. Berne: Francke Verlag. pp. 322.

on the criticism of concrete works of art and will constantly invoke the assistance of literary history'—though 'the three disciplines are and will remain distinct'. In 'Modern Bibliography and the Literary Artifact' Frederick W. Bateson takes up arms against Fredson Bowers, and argues that 'analytical bibliography is a discipline in its own right, but its findings are likely to be of only marginal interest to the student of literature', and that 'formalist criticism must be taken more seriously than bibliography because its concern is with meanings'. Then follow a dozen papers on literary topics. Kemp Malone discusses 'Symbolism in *Beowulf*'. He suggests, for example, that Heorot symbolizes 'imperial power and with it the glories of this world'. The life led in the hall represents an ideal worldly society, and Grendel the enemy of society; and Malone attaches symbolic significances to other persons and events in the poem. R. Derolez considers the Latin background of Old English poetry, and voices the hope that Latin scholars will contribute towards its study. Przemyslaw Mroczkowski takes ' "The Friar's Tale" and its Pulpit Background' as his subject, and brings forward evidence that the tale has its roots in the *exempla* of the preaching tradition. George Ian Duthie's analysis of *Macbeth* leads him to style it 'A Study in Tragic Absurdity'; Macbeth displays 'a pitiful lack of intelligence', and at the end of the play, if his courage 'is admirable in itself, it is nevertheless being absurdly misapplied'. Jean Jacquot illustrates from *Bussy D'Ambois* Chapman's conception of tragedy. Clifford Leech's paper is a stimulating discussion of 'The Dramatic Style of John Fletcher', and is especially interesting on *The Faithful Shepherdess*. Pierre Janelle ranges widely over 'Devotional Literature in the XVIth and XVIIth Centuries', paying special attention to

Andrewes, Cosin, Laud, and Anthony Stafford, the last of whom stands 'at the extreme apex of the Catholicizing movement in the Church of England'. Recalling that 'it was above all from the epistolary writers that Jane Austen had learnt to write a novel', Ian Jack discusses her use of letters in her own novels, and finds it of considerable interest. With the notable exception of R. W. Chapman's edition of Jane Austen, there are no reliable editions of our great novelists. In 'Editing a Nineteenth-Century Novelist' John Butt puts forward 'Proposals for an Edition of Dickens' which will be worthy of a novelist of his stature. Under the title 'Innocence in the Novels of George Eliot', Irène Simon provides an excellent study both of the innocence and of the guilt and evil that exist in the world of George Eliot's novels. David Daiches speaks of 'Imagery and Mood in Tennyson and Whitman', and draws a contrast between Tennyson's 'imagery of introspection' and Whitman's 'imagery of association'. Theodore Dreiser is usually regarded as a naturalistic writer. Roger Asselineau explores a side of him on which very few critics have touched, namely, his transcendentalism; this indeed he believes to be 'the true source of his greatness'. Three papers are concerned with translation. Drawing on his own experience, Josip Torbarina considers some of the difficulties of translating Shakespeare into another tongue. Speaking on 'What Modern Translators May still Learn from the Old', Rudolf Sühnel concludes that 'a genuine translation will be a balanced fusion of old and new, of native and foreign'. Gay Wilson Allen compares several translations of Whitman's poems in order to illustrate 'The Problem of Metaphor in Translating *Leaves of Grass*'. The last three papers are on linguistic topics. R. W. Zandvoort explores ways in which grammatical

terminology might be simplified, but
decides that on the whole the study
of English syntax will be best served,
'not by a wholesale destruction of
traditional terms, but rather by their
re-interpretation to fit the facts of
modern English'. Simeon Potter's subject is 'Problems of Word Order'; he
illustrates, and suggests means of
avoiding, various kinds of ambiguity
and stylistic infelicity. An extremely
interesting mixed bag of papers concludes with one by Frank Behre on
'The Principle of Connecting Elements of Speech in Contemporary
English'.

The substantial *Festschrift*[16] presented to Theodor Spira on his seventy-
fifth birthday reflects the breadth of
Spira's interest in English and American literature, ranging from the Anglo-
Saxon to the modern period. Amos N.
Wilder opens the collection with translations from Hölderlin and Rilke. In
the Anglo-Saxon division Heinrich
Christoph Matthes offers a study of
Hygd, the wife of Hygelac, to which he
adds a detailed commentary on *Beowulf* 1925–62. Kemp Malone notes
about 350 variant readings in the texts
of *Judith* prepared by A. S. Cook, E. V.
K. Dobbie, and B. J. Timmer, and discusses them in the light of his own
study of the text in MS. Cotton Vitellius A. XV. Karl Schneider considers
the form and some of the pagan
religious elements in a group of Anglo-
Saxon Charms. Willi Erzgräber contributes an interpretation of *The
Wanderer*, together with an analysis of
its structure; and the section ends with
a short note on *Deor* by Karl Jost. Two
studies of Chaucer, the one, by Ewald
Standop, relating to the allegorical
significance of *The Nun's Priest's Tale*,
the other, by Henry Lüdeke, to the passage on Zenobia in *The Monk's Tale*,

[16] *Festschrift zum 75. Geburtstag von
Theodor Spira*, ed. by H. Viebrock and W.
Erzgräber. Heidelberg: Winter. pp. 405.

are noticed in Chapter V. Wolfgang
Schmidt-Hidding discusses the place
of the ballad *Edward, Edward* among a
group of ballads with kindred themes.
Several articles are devoted to Shakespeare and other Elizabethans. Horst
Oppel makes a careful analysis of the
scene (III. iii), in the Second Part of
Henry VI, in which Cardinal Beaufort
dies; Franz H. Link considers Shakespeare's dramatic handling of remorse
and repentance; and Walther Fischer
examines the relationship between *The
Tempest* and *The Rare Triumphs of Love
and Fortune*. Siegfried Korninger coun-
ters the commonly accepted view that
Marston to some extent presents himself in the persons of his malcontents.
From K. L. Klein come some observations on the authorities on rhetoric and
the poetic theorists of the Elizabethan
age, and from Kuno Schuhmann
a survey of the background of the
Character writings of the seventeenth
century, with special reference to
rhetorical theory. Ludwig Borinski reviews some Puritan and Anglican outlooks that are reflected in the literature
of the Commonwealth period. Taking
as his text Wordsworth's line, 'And
Nature deepens into Nature's God',
Helmut Viebrock analyses some passages, mainly from *The Prelude*, in
order to bring out the relationship
between God and Nature in Wordsworth's poetry. Gerhard Müller-
Schwefe's subject is Gerard Manley
Hopkins, whom he considers to be in
many respects a typical Victorian. H.
W. Häusermann casts light on the
literary controversies in the 1920's
between W. J. Turner and H. G. Wells
and Arnold Bennett. In the next section Amos Wilder writes on American
literature and its religious archetypes;
Hans Galinsky attempts an interpretation of the late seventeenth-century
Virginian poem *Bacon's Epitaph, made
by his Man*, which he sees as an example of 'Colonial Baroque'; and

Hertha Marquardt gives an account of Margaret Fuller's projected biography of Goethe. Several articles deal with linguistic problems. Karl Brunner traces the development of the modern English pronunciation of -al- in such words as *calf*, *half*, and *calm*. Herbert Koziol shows how certain types of English idiom have evolved, using such examples as *iron steed, middlebrow, blackout*, and *iron curtain*. Friedrich Schubel studies the nuances of meaning of the word *bealu* in the Anglo-Saxon *Christ*, I–II. Hans Marchard discusses the prefix *anti-* in such modern compounds as *anti-aircraft, anti-missile protection*, and the like. Fritz Meinecke's paper is a highly technical account of English accentuation. The volume closes with an essay by Edgar Mertner on tradition and reform in English universities in the eighteenth century.

Elizabeth Jennings's interesting book *Every Changing Shape*[17] is 'concerned with three things—the making of poems, the nature of mystical experience, and the relationship between the two'. Among the earlier writers considered are St. Augustine, Julian of Norwich, Herbert, Vaughan, and Traherne, and the later include Hopkins, Rilke, Edwin Muir, T. S. Eliot, David Gascoyne, Wallace Stevens, and Hart Crane. Where they are prose writers, she has studied them largely 'at the highest peaks of their writing, at those moments when prose most nearly resembles poetry'. On the whole she finds that the prose mystics are able to tell us more about their experiences than the poets, partly 'because the ultimate experience of mysticism is so difficult to capture in words that mystical writers often have to satisfy themselves with detailed accounts of the thoughts, feelings and events which preceded that experience'. Miss Jennings realizes that such a task as she has undertaken

demands 'a bold humility and a disinterested intelligence'; she herself displays these qualities, and, though she does not claim to have said the final word about the mysticism of any of the writers she discusses, she has done much to clear the ground for others who may follow her.

Martin Turnell's Lauriston Lectures for 1959 have been published under the title *Modern Literature and Christian Faith*.[18] Turnell's aim is 'to describe the effect on writers of changes in belief which have taken place during the past four hundred years'. Within the space of three lectures he has necessarily to be selective. He begins by comparing the opening of Chaucer's *Prologue* with that of *The Waste Land*, and observes that 'while Chaucer's is a poetry of acceptance, Eliot's by comparison is a poetry of refusal and as such represents the modern outlook as Chaucer's represents the medieval'. He goes on to consider the poetry of Donne, Crashaw, Patmore, and Hopkins, relating each to the general climate of belief in his age. D. H. Lawrence, E. M. Forster, and Virginia Woolf are the principal subjects of the second lecture; Turnell sets them against the background of twentieth-century thought, and notes, among other things, that the characters of their novels are 'examples of what Edwin Muir called "the Natural Man" as opposed to "the Christian Man"'. In the final chapter he turns to Claudel, Mauriac, and Graham Greene, and finds on every page of their works reminders 'that human beings, however vile, have immortal souls; that the alternatives salvation-damnation are the greatest reality, indeed the only reality, in the World'. Turnell's approach is interesting, and his book contains some sensible criticism.

[17] *Every Changing Shape*, by Elizabeth Jennings. André Deutsch. pp. 240. 25*s*.

[18] *Modern Literature and Christian Faith*, by Martin Turnell. Darton, Longman and Todd. pp. vii+69. 12*s*. 6*d*.

Laurence D. Lerner's *English Literature: An Interpretation for Students
Abroad*,[19] first published in 1954, now
appears in a second and corrected
edition. As its sub-title suggests, it does
not claim to go very deeply into critical
questions. However, it is well adapted
to its purposes. In the first two chapters,
'Literature and Language' and 'Literature and Society', Lerner discusses
some important aspects of style and of
the relations of literature to life. In the
remainder of the book he illustrates
some critical approaches to poetry, to
the novel, and to the plays of Shakespeare, with analysis of representative
passages. The book should prove very
helpful to the students for whom it is
designed.

3. Studies of Particular Forms and Genres

James Reeves's *Short History of
English Poetry*[20] is intended for general
readers and students who may want to
get a 'brief historical perspective' of
English poetry from Chaucer to the
present day. However, recognizing
that a history of poetry runs the risk of
being 'everything about it which is unimportant', Reeves illustrates his survey with a great deal of quotation, and,
without losing his sense of balance, he
writes about the poets of whom he is
particularly fond with an infectious
enthusiasm. Having no sympathy with
those critics who would divorce a poet's
verse from his life and background, he
provides as much biographical and
historical information as his space
allows. He finds room for a surprising
number of minor poets, on some of
whom his criticism is first-rate—in his
seven pages on Skelton, for example,

and his shorter sketches of Lady
Winchilsea, Christopher Smart, or
John Clare. But as is inevitable in a
'short history', his main concern must
be with the great poets, and his quality
as a critic is seen at its best in his
sections on such poets as Chaucer,
Wordsworth, Milton, and Spenser,
where he is always concise, concrete,
and to the point.

How to Read a Poem,[21] by Roy
Thomas, is addressed to the general
reader, with the hope, however, that it
may prove useful to 'students in the
Sixth Form and to intending teachers
of English'. It may well appeal to these
classes of reader, for, without being
profound or breaking new ground, it is
full of practical good sense. Thomas
begins by trying to answer the question
'What is Poetry?' Having reviewed
various answers that have been given to
this question in the past, he selects for
his purposes that which describes
poetry as an art which 'is continually
offering us new ways of "seeing" our
environment and our experiences',
achieving concentration 'through the
fullest exploitation of the resources of
language'. Chapter II, 'Reading a
Poem', discusses poetic techniques.
The central section of the book is an anthology of twenty poems, each accompanied by a sensible commentary. In
his final chapter Thomas considers the
kinds of pleasure that poetry gives,
advises the reader to approach it with
humility, and suggests that, while recognizing that 'the best is the enemy of
the good', he should often be prepared
to lower his sights.

A book with a similar aim, but
addressed to students at the undergraduate level, is *Poetry: An Introduction to Its Form and Art*,[22] by Norman

[19] *English Literature: An Interpretation for
Students Abroad*, by Laurence D. Lerner.
O.U.P., 1960. pp. viii+198. 8s. 6d. in
boards; 5s. limp.

[20] *A Short History of English Poetry, 1340–
1940*, by James Reeves. Heinemann. pp.
xvi+228. 21s.

[21] *How to Read a Poem*, by Roy Thomas.
Univ. of London Press. pp. 144. 6s.

[22] *Poetry: An Introduction to Its Form and
Art*, by Norman Friedman and Charles A.
McLaughlin. New York: Harper. London:
Hamish Hamilton. pp. xvii+197. 17s.

Friedman and Charles A. McLaughlin. The treatment is fuller and deeper than Thomas's. Chapter by chapter the authors illustrate and explain the various techniques associated with the writing and with the criticism of poetry, progressing from outward form and diction to larger problems of style, artistic purpose, organic unity, and total effect. Each section is followed by about a dozen poems to which the student may apply the critical methods about which he has just been reading. By the end of the volume he should have acquired a sound knowledge of critical techniques and terminology and a familiarity with about a hundred admirably chosen poems.

Frank M. Whiting's *An Introduction to the Theatre*,[23] first published in 1954, now appears in a revised edition in which, among other changes, the sections on the modern drama have been substantially rewritten and expanded. Although the opening chapters are historical, the book is a very helpful study of almost all 'the numerous arts and crafts that comprise the complex fabric of stage art'. There are chapters on directing, acting, costuming and make-up, theatre architecture, scenic design, stage-lighting, and the various technical devices used in a modern theatre; and a final section deals with 'The Theatre as a Profession'. The method throughout is partly historical and partly descriptive. The book is profusely and excellently illustrated with plates depicting not only famous players, settings, and theatres, but also the technical appurtenances of the theatre.

The second, and revised, edition of Milton Marx's *The Enjoyment of Drama*,[24] which first appeared in 1940, is published in the Goldentree Books paperback series. In this work Marx discusses in a sensible and practical way such topics as the purpose, the aim, and the nature of drama, its form and structure, the essential qualities of tragedy, comedy, and other types of play, and dramatic criticism. The most important changes in the revised edition are the inclusion of new material on the conflict in drama, references to plays which have been produced since 1940, and some consideration of television.

In her Presidential Address to the English Association, *Approaches to Drama*,[25] Clemence Dane considers the attitude of modern cinema, radio, and television audiences, most members of which desire to be entertained without the need for thought on their part; she herself insists that it is the 'thinking audience which today and always is the theatre's necessary partner', and recalls the spirit in which audiences of the past have approached the drama. Turning to the work of some recent playwrights, she suggests that 'if the plays of the present decade fade ... without any major harvesting, the reason may well be that the present approach to drama is too grievance-ridden, too class-conscious and too fond of a "private language", and that the main characters ("hero" is a dated word) strike us as insignificant'. However, she notes occasions in these plays when a 'transference from the personal to the universal' manifests itself.

This year has produced the customary crop of books on tragedy. Feeling that most books on tragedy, though they may provide helpful definitions, fail to get down to first principles, Elder Olson sets out, in *Tragedy*

[23] *An Introduction to the Theatre*, by Frank M. Whiting. (Revised edition.) New York: Harper. London: Hamish Hamilton. pp. xxi+369. 60s.
[24] *The Enjoyment of Drama*, by Milton Marx. Second edition. (Goldentree Books.) New York: Appleton-Century-Crofts. pp. vii+167. $1.50.
[25] *Approaches to Drama*, by Clemence Dane. (Presidential Address to the English Association, 1961.) O.U.P. for the English Association. pp. 12. 5s.

and the Theory of Drama,[26] to dis-cover what kind of response the various components of drama, especially of tragic drama, aim at awakening in the audience or the reader. To this end he examines in turn such elements as plot, incident, character, dialogue, dramatic form, and total dramatic effect. When the time comes for him to sum up the results of his analysis, he finds it impossible to define tragedy in any but the most general terms; he describes it as 'drama which proposes the exhibition of an action of the ut-most seriousness and the utmost signi-ficance'. Olson then turns to the detailed criticism of three tragedies, Aeschylus's *Agamemnon*, Shakespeare's *King Lear*, and Racine's *Phèdre*. Here his method is largely descriptive, and it cannot be said that he adds much to our understanding of the plays. Indeed, the book as a whole, though it is sen-sible enough, is rather thin, and comes no nearer to reaching first principles than the common run of books on tragedy.

Indeed, the next book to be noticed, *A Definition of Tragedy*,[27] by Oscar Mandel, is much more thorough and penetrating. One of its merits is that it constantly relates tragedy to human experience. After a preliminary review of previous definitions, from Aristotle to our own day, Mandel puts forward his own definition: 'A work of art is tragic if it substantiates the following situation: A protagonist who com-mands our earnest good will is impelled in a given world by a purpose, or under-takes an action, of a certain seriousness and magnitude; and by that very pur-pose or action, subject to that same given world, necessarily and inevitably meets with grave spiritual or physical suffering.' It is a largely Aristotelian

view of tragedy, but Mandel lays parti-cular stress on the last part of it, main-taining that 'the hero's fall must be unconditionally determined from the instant his purpose or action begins'. He goes on to discuss, among other things, the ethical and emotional impact of tragedy, and the question of 'tragic pleasure', and he writes well on the tragic hero, the 'pathetic victim', and such topics as free will and tragic guilt. He illustrates his findings with refer-ence to a wide range of tragic dramas.

Prosser Hall Frye's *Romance and Tragedy*[28] has been well known for more than half a century (published in 1908); it is now issued as a paperback by the University of Nebraska Press. Frye begins with an attempt to define the terms 'classic' and 'romantic', realizing, of course, that they do not lend themselves to short and clear-cut definition. However, for his own pur-poses he takes 'classic' to refer, not only to such things as Sophoclean tragedy and Virgilian epic, 'but also to such qualities, wherever found, as are characteristic of these works—notably an extreme susceptibility to the moral significance of the subject, resulting externally in a sense for order, balance, moderation, measure, and the like—in short, to a certain easily recognizable manner of conceiving and rendering life'. Romanticism is marked by 'a sus-ceptibility to irregular beauty, a fond-ness for the striking and the unusual even at the expense of regularity and order, a preference for fascinating detail above symmetry and proportion, a predilection for the coruscation of style—for the glittering word and phrase, for the exotic and exquisite epithet, for everything that touches and thrills and dazzles, a hunger for

[26] *Tragedy and the Theory of Drama*, by Elder Olson. Wayne State U.P. pp. vii+269. $6.95.
[27] *A Definition of Tragedy*, by Oscar Mandel. New York U.P. pp. lx+178. $4.50.

[28] *Romance and Tragedy: A Study of Classic and Romantic Elements in the Great Tragedies of European Literature*, by Prosser Hall Frye. (Bison Books.) Nebraska U.P. pp. xiii+372. $1.25.

sensation, even when these desires lead to a dissipation of the attention'. In the light of these definitions he discusses the tragedies of the Greeks, of the German Romantics, of Corneille, Racine, and Calderon. Of greatest relevance to readers of *YW* is the remaining chapter in which Frye compares the tragedy of Shakespeare and of Sophocles from the point of view that the one is 'popular and natural', the other 'humane and moral'.

George Steiner's thesis in his admirable book *The Death of Tragedy*[29] is that tragedy implies a special vision of man and his place in the universe, and that the rarity of great tragedies in the western world of the last three centuries is largely due to the loss of this vision. In his opening chapters Steiner establishes, as he sees it, the nature of the tragic vision, which is one of the great legacies of the Greeks to modern civilization. It arises from the belief 'that the forces which shape or destroy our lives lie outside the governance of reason or justice. Worse than that: there are around us daemonic energies which prey upon the soul and turn it to madness or which poison our will so that we inflict outrage upon ourselves and those we love.' These conceptions are intrinsic to western life from the time of Aeschylus to that of Shakespeare. But after the seventeenth century these beliefs, and concepts such as grace, damnation, purgation, blasphemy, or the chain of being, 'which are everywhere implicit in classic and Shakespearean tragedy', lose their vitality. Moreover, the spread of realistic prose is inimical to the expression of those high passions which form so much of the stuff of tragedy. Conditions in the world of today would seem favourable to the rebirth of tragedy; but it is an art 'which requires the intolerable burden of God's presence', and it

is 'now dead because His shadow no longer falls upon us as it fell on Agamemnon or Macbeth or Athalie'. Steiner keeps his argument concrete by means of plentiful illustration and some excellent analysis, and he seems equally at home in the literatures of ancient Greece and Rome and of England, France, Germany, and Italy.

The first three chapters of Lionel Stevenson's 'panorama' of the English novel[30] deal with the development of prose fiction before 1740, the year in which, with the publication of *Pamela*, Stevenson believes the novel proper to have come into being. Beginning with Malory and Mandeville, he quickly moves on to the sixteenth century, and gives a short but competent survey of Elizabethan prose fiction. In the seventeenth and early eighteenth centuries the qualities which he demands of a true novel—the illusion of reality, individualized characters, unity of structure, and the rest—emerge more frequently and begin to be more successfully combined, and he finds himself compelled to be more expansive; to Defoe, for example, he gives a dozen pages. However, it is with Richardson that he embarks on the body of his book. In the 450-odd pages that remain to him he naturally gives most attention to the major novelists, allowing himself space to summarize as well as to comment on many of their novels; but his work is remarkably inclusive, and he manages to give a page or two to writers of the stature of, say, Robert Bage, Charlotte Smith, and Lady Caroline Lamb. He carries his history through to L. P. Hartley, Angus Wilson, and Iris Murdoch, though he finds the contemporary novel 'deficient in momentum'. The book ends with a useful bibliography and a 'chronological summary'.

[29] *The Death of Tragedy*, by George Steiner. Faber. pp. viii+355+xii. 30s.

[30] *The English Novel: A Panorama*, by Lionel Stevenson. Constable. pp. iv+539. 32s. 6d.

Richard Church's *The Growth of the English Novel*,[31] first published in 1951, has now been included in Methuen's University Paperbacks series. It is a work on a much smaller scale than Stevenson's, covering much the same span of years in about a quarter of the length; but it is an interesting survey, and everywhere shows the perceptiveness of a practising novelist and poet. However, it is too well known to need a full description here; it is enough to say that its appearance in a cheap edition will be warmly welcomed.

The Novel and the Reader,[32] by Katherine Lever, was noticed last year (*YW* xli. 21), when it appeared in the Goldentree Books paperback series. It is now published in hard covers by Methuen.

First published in 1939, *The English Novel, 1740–1850*,[33] by Andrew Block, now appears in a revised edition. In this work are listed, under the names of authors arranged alphabetically, all the novels, prose romances, short stories, and translations of foreign fiction, as far as Block has been able to trace them, that were published in England between 1740 and 1850. Under each entry are provided the title, the sub-title, the date of publication, and other bibliographical data relevant to the book named. Reviewers have drawn attention to a few slight inaccuracies, chiefly relating to the location of copies; clearly, however, these will not seriously mar the value of this work for any student of the English novel in the first century of its development.

An Experiment in Criticism,[34] by C. S. Lewis, is an attempt to find a new way of judging literature which will better help us to appreciate good writing than do current types of evaluative criticism. Lewis is suspicious of these forms of criticism because in their various ways they interfere with our own response to what we are reading, and are sometimes based on false notions of what is good taste or bad taste. He believes that it should be possible to judge literature according to the way in which it is read. A good book, whether in prose or verse, actively encourages us to find pleasure in its content, structure, and use of language; it can be often re-read, and continually offers fresh sustenance for the mind and the ear. A bad book offers no such encouragement, nor is it likely to be read more than once. A fondness for the first kind of book is the mark of the 'literary' reader, who 'receives' literature; an addiction to the second denotes the 'unliterary' reader, who merely 'uses' literature—to fill a vacant hour, to read himself asleep, or to project himself into an unreal world of false values. Literature, says Lewis, is above all else an art, and is to be *enjoyed* as an art; our surrender to it 'has something in common with love, with moral action, and with intellectual achievement'. As in everything that Lewis writes, the argument is clear, concrete, and persuasive; and though it is doubtful whether the application of his 'experiment' would for long remain very different from the methods of the evaluative critics, the way in which he expounds it makes it sound promising as a new approach to criticism.

In *Some Mythical Elements in English Literature*[35] E. M. W. Tillyard uses the

[31] *The Growth of the English Novel*, by Richard Church. (University Paperbacks.) Methuen. pp. ix+179. 6s.

[32] *The Novel and the Reader*, by Katherine Lever. Methuen. pp. 120. 12s. 6d.

[33] *The English Novel, 1740–1850: A Catalogue Including Prose Romances, Short Stories, and Translations of Foreign Fiction*, by Andrew Block. Dawsons of Pall Mall. pp. xv+349. £7. 10s.

[34] *An Experiment in Criticism*, by C. S. Lewis. C.U.P. pp. v+143. 15s.

[35] *Some Mythical Elements in English Literature, Being the Clark Lectures, 1959–60*, by E. M. W. Tillyard. Chatto & Windus. pp. 143. 16s.

word 'myth', not in its most generally accepted sense, but to denote a story, a person, a place, or an event which has become 'a communal possession, the agreed and classic embodiment of some way of thinking and feeling'—as during the war the survival of St. Paul's Cathedral in the midst of a devastated area came to embody the Englishman's belief in final victory. One such myth which was current especially in the Middle Ages is that of the Harrowing of Hell, and Tillyard discusses its treatment in our medieval religious drama and in *Piers Plowman*. Two somewhat later myths that he brings within the scope of his lectures are those which were fostered by King Henry VII: that the ancient virtues of King Arthur were reincarnated in the House of Tudor, and that the Tudors had been divinely appointed to lead England out of an unspeakable tyranny into happiness. These myths form an important part of the background of such works as *The Faerie Queene*, Warner's *Albion's England*, Drayton's *England's Heroical Epistles*, and Shakespeare's *Richard III*. Tillyard also discusses, with appropriate illustration, the popular eighteenth-century myth of 'retirement from the busy world to a retreat, preferably in the country, from which to study the glories of God as revealed in nature and to contemplate the approach of death', and the belief that a love of liberty is 'the great English characteristic'. The book explores interestingly some of the by-paths of literature, and makes good reading.

Under the auspices of the Colston Research Society, a symposium on the subject of metaphor and symbol was held at the University of Bristol in the summer of 1960, and the papers read on this occasion have now been published.[36] Metaphor and symbol were chosen 'because they are typical forms of non-literal expression in poetry and creative literature generally, and to discover more about them is to discover more about the creative imagination'. Philip Wheelwright's paper on 'Semantics and Ontology' is a tentative exploration of 'the interrelated rôles of imagination, imitation, and participation'. In 'The Hinterland of Thought' D. W. Harding, illustrating his approach with quotations from Shakespeare, Wordsworth, and Shelley, expresses the hope that psychologists will be able to find out more about 'the pre-cognitive ordering of incipient thought'. M. C. Bradbrook's 'The Image of the Delinquent in Literature, 1955–60', is an excellent study of the various kinds of 'Anti-Hero' in recent English and American literature. George Wingfield Digby's paper is an interesting treatment of the problems of 'Content and Communication in the Visual Arts', illustrated by reproductions of a variety of paintings, sculptures, and other works of art. Owen Barfield provides a penetrating discussion of 'The Meaning of the Word "Literal"'. In 'Imagination and Experience' H. D. Lewis considers 'the problem of mental images and the importance which imagination, in this form, has for our understanding of ourselves and the world around us'. H. H. Price's subject is 'Paranormal Cognition and Symbolism'. D. G. James's admirable paper is entitled 'Metaphor and Symbol'; its main thesis is that I. A. Richards's distinction between the scientific and the emotive use of language will not stand up to close examination. In 'The Function of Symbols in Religious Experience' F. W. Dillistone discusses some of the 'insights' of religious experience, and the symbols 'through which the conflicts between love and hate, life and death, power and

[36] *Metaphor and Symbol: Proceedings of the Twelfth Symposium of the Colston Research Society*. Butterworth, 1960. pp. xi + 150. 30s.

weakness, hope and despair, begin to find their resolution'. Stressing various 'points of resemblance between rituals and works of the literary imagination', John Holloway considers 'The Concept of Myth in Literature'. Finally, L. C. Knights shows what light the writings of Coleridge throw upon the subject of 'Idea and Symbol'. Most of the papers are accompanied by the discussions which followed their delivery, and these add considerably to the value and interest of the volume.

A Short Guide to English Style,[37] by Alan Warner, is primarily written for those who, though they have a pretty good command of English, were not brought up to use it as their mother tongue; it could be read with profit, however, by many people who have never used any other language—they will soon discover that Warner's advice is much sounder than might be suggested by such facetious chapter-headings as 'Please Do Not Spit', or 'Don't Mix Your Drinks'. Part I, 'How to Write Clean English', discusses section by section various current perversions and adulterations of style—genteel euphemism, verbosity, circumlocution, journalistic jargon, and the like—and ends with some samples of 'clean' modern English style. Part II is a concise and sensible history of English prose style from Chaucer to the Victorians. In the third Part Warner returns to contemporary English, and gives advice, with appropriate illustration, on such matters as colloquialism, the proper use of Americanisms, and the language of specialists.

Essentials of Effective Writing,[38] by Vincent F. Hopper and Cedric Gale,

aims at providing for 'the potential writer an expert command of the fundamentals of good English usage and the basic skills required for effective writing'. Beginning with descriptions of the parts of speech and rules of accidence, syntax, and punctuation, it moves on to consider some aspects of style, and ends with practical advice on the preparation of material for the press. An accompanying volume provides exercises on the matter of the main volume. It is difficult not to feel that 'the potential writer' should have got through almost everything contained in this work long before he left school; but no doubt it has been written in answer to a demand that exists somewhere.

4. *Bibliographical Studies*

Some of the articles in the 1961 volume of *Studies in Bibliography*[39] are noticed in other chapters, and only a general indication of their subject-matter is called for here. In 'Proof-reading Lockhart's *Scott*: The Dynamics of Biographical Reticence' Francis Russell Hart makes a careful examination of Lockhart's corrected proof-sheets; he shows, not only that Lockhart assembled his heterogeneous materials with considerable skill, but also that this biography, 'which contemporary readers found distressingly candid', would have been even more so had Lockhart not yielded to the pressure of friends and advisers. Cyprian Blagden describes some of Thomas Carnan's skirmishes with the Stationers' Company, and in particular his partially successful campaign, at the end of the eighteenth century, to deprive the Company of its monopoly in the publication of Almanacks. Cyrus

---

[37] *A Short Guide to English Style*, by Alan Warner. O.U.P. pp. viii+198. 12s. 6d.

[38] *Essentials of Effective Writing: A Practical Grammar and Handbook of Basic Writing Techniques.* pp. xiii+203. *Practice for Effective Writing.* pp. ix+160. By Vincent F. Hopper and Cedric Gale. New York: Barron. Each $1.50.

[39] *Studies in Bibliography: Papers of the Bibliographical Society of the University of Virginia.* Vol. XIV. Ed. by Fredson Bowers. Charlottesville: Bibliographical Soc. of the Univ. of Virginia. pp. iv+291. $10.

Hoy presents the sixth instalment of his study of 'The Shares of Fletcher and his Collaborators in the Beaumont and Fletcher Canon'. H. W. Jones considers some 'Literary Problems in Seventeenth-Century Scientific Manuscripts'. Following up the article which, with R. P. Doig, he published in *SB* xii, Robert Hay Carnie contributes 'Scottish Printers and Booksellers 1668–1775: A Second Supplement (I)'. C. William Miller discusses the printing and publication of Benjamin Franklin's 'Poor Richard' Almanacks. Richard Beale Davis describes Thomas Jefferson's fine collection of Virginiana. Hannah D. French's subject is the career of Andrew Barclay, the eighteenth-century American bookbinder. Ralph M. Aderman identifies and lists all but a handful of the contributors to the *American Quarterly Review*, 1827–33. James B. Colvert discusses and prints the forty-one letters which, between 1897 and 1930, Ellen Glasgow wrote to her literary agent, Paul Revere Reynolds, and which throw light on her methods and development as a novelist. Joseph X. Brennan offers a bibliographical note on the *Grammaticae Artis Institutio* of Joannes Susenbrotus. William Ringler argues persuasively that the I. S. who in 1559 published Lydgate's prose work *The Serpent of Division* was John Stow. Jack Stillinger outlines the bibliographical history of E. K.'s glosses to *The Shepheardes Calender*. From evidence drawn from the recently discovered first two half-sheets of a 24to Book of Common Prayer, Giles E. Dawson describes a printing-house practice with regard to 'Guide-Lines in Small Formats (about 1600)'. Franklin B. Williams, Jr., gives examples of methods of altering incorrect title-pages to which 'penny-pinching printers' of the sixteenth and seventeenth centuries resorted instead of cancelling the pages. I. A. Shapiro examines the two extant copies of the first edition of Greene's *Quip for an Upstart Courtier*, and concludes, among other things that in the variant sheet F. Greene's original text is to be found rather in the Bodleian than in the Huntington copy. Robert K. Turner, Jr., contributes 'Notes on the Text of *Thierry and Theodoret* QI'. T. C. Duncan Eaves and Ben D. Kimpel describe the contents of a little-known volume of 'Richardsoniana' in the Forster Collection at the Victoria and Albert Museum. G. E. Bentley, Jr., prints a letter by Thomas Taylor, the Platonist who may have influenced several of the Romantic poets, which establishes Taylor's authorship of the article on him in *Public Characters of 1798*. As an appendix to an article in *SB* xi, David V. Erdman, Lucyle Werkmeister, and R. S. Woof publish 'Unrecorded Coleridge Variants: Additions and Corrections'. David Bonnell Green prints two letters from Elizabeth Barrett to Shelton Mackenzie. A. N. L. Munby draws attention to an unrecorded tract, Elias Burling's *Call to Back-sliding Israel*, printed in New York in 1694, and recently acquired by the Cambridge University Library. By comparing the printed texts of some of Hawthorne's short stories with the manuscripts, Seymour L. Gross and Alfred J. Levy show that the editorial alterations were not as serious as Hawthorne seems to have felt them to be. Matthew J. Bruccoli and Charles A. Rheault, Jr., discuss the use of imposition figures and plate gangs in the printing of Conrad's *The Rescue*. The volume closes with a selective check list of bibliographical scholarship in 1959 compiled by Rudolf Hirsch and Howell J. Heaney.

Geoffrey Ashall Glaister's *Glossary of the Book*[40] will be of considerable

[40] *Glossary of the Book*, by Geoffrey Ashall Glaister. Allen & Unwin, 1960. pp. xv+484. £6. 6s.

value to students of bibliography, to librarians, and to anyone connected with the book trade. Its sub-title gives a pretty clear indication of its scope: 'Terms used in paper-making, printing, bookbinding and publishing, with notes on illuminated manuscripts, bibliophiles, private presses, and printing societies.' And indeed it is as comprehensive as this suggests. In some 450 double-column pages it gives nearly 3,000 definitions and descriptions, varying in length from several pages on the more complex processes of printing to a line or two defining a tool or a material. There are useful appendixes listing Latin place-names used in the imprints of early printed books, proof-correction symbols, and the like, discussing contemporary private presses, and giving specimens of type-faces. The book is generously and interestingly illustrated.

Allan Stevenson's *Observations on Paper as Evidence*[41] is a plea for a closer and more systematic study of paper as evidence in the dating of early books and the discovery of other bibliographical facts about them. All too few scholars, he feels, have any knowledge of the subject, or any notion of its potential value. He cites many occasions when the nature of the paper used, or the unusual location or use of watermarks, or 'sewing dots' have enabled him to make interesting bibliographical discoveries.

Kenneth R. Shaffer's *The Book Collection*[42] is a textbook on the problems of policy that may confront the librarian of a public or academic library. Twenty-five 'cases' are presented in the form of chatty narratives

or exchanges of letters, and the student is required to answer questions on the matters of policy involved. For a work intended to be used in schools of librarianship the method looks a little strange to an English reader, but it should have the desired effect of making the student think for himself.

To commemorate his eightieth birthday, two friends of John Dover Wilson have compiled a bibliography of his published writings.[43] It makes a very impressive record, listing more than thirty books in addition to the volumes of the New Shakespeare, and close on 200 articles, ranging in subject from 'The Aims and Methods of the Social Revolutionary Party in Russia' (1906, under the pseudonym Wildover Johnson) and educational methods to abstruse bibliographical problems. Wilson's friends and admirers all over the world will rejoice to see his great services to scholarship honoured in this way.

Another very fine scholar has been similarly honoured. On the occasion of his eighty-fifth birthday, friends, colleagues, and pupils of Eilert Ekwall, nearly 300 of whom are listed at the beginning of the volume, have joined together to present to him a bibliography of his writings,[44] which has been compiled by Olof von Feilitzen. More than 350 books, articles, and reviews are recorded, most of them relating to the field of language and place-name studies in which Ekwall has done such distinguished work.

S. B. Liljegren has written two

[41] *Observations on Paper as Evidence*, by Allan Stevenson. Univ. of Kansas Libraries. pp. vi+28.

[42] *The Book Collection: Policy Case Studies in Public and Academic Libraries*, by Kenneth R. Shaffer. Hamden, Conn.: Shoestring Press. pp. xxi+147. $4.75.

[43] *A List of His Published Writings Presented to John Dover Wilson on His Eightieth Birthday, 13 July 1961*, compiled by John Butt and J. C. Maxwell. C.U.P. pp. 32. 3s. 6d.

[44] *The Published Writings of Eilert Ekwall: A Bibliography*, compiled by Olof von Feilitzen. (Lund Studies in English 30.) Lund: Gleerup, and Copenhagen: Munksgaard. pp. 52. Sw. kr. 15.

pamphlets[45] of rather specialized interest. In *Canadian Studies in Sweden* he tells how he was led to Canadian literature by his studies in American English; he has read widely in this literature, and is well fitted to describe how it has been taken up as a subject of study in Sweden. His fondness for Irish literature has extended over half a century, and he is the founder of a centre of Irish studies in Sweden. In *Irish Studies in Sweden* he describes the growth of these studies.

In an off-print from *Acta Universitatis Debreceniensis* entitled 'Twentieth Century English Literature in Hungary from 1945 to 1959', Anna Katona surveys the translations of English works that have appeared in Hungary since the Second World War. As might be expected, novels easily take the first place; a great many novels have been translated, the majority of them dating from before the war, although some as recent as *Lucky Jim* have also appeared. Among post-war plays are *A Taste of Honey* and *Look Black in Anger* (*sic*). Several verse anthologies have been compiled, and literary journals welcome English verse in translation; the most popular poets appear to be Eliot, Yeats, Auden, and MacDiarmid.

5. *Anthologies*

The most agreeable anthology of the year is C. Day Lewis's collection of English lyrics,[46] published in boards by Chatto and Windus and as a paperback in the Goldentree Books series, the only differences lying in the titles and the arrangement of the indexes. Apart from a few anonymous medieval lyrics,

it covers the four centuries from 1500 to 1900, and is confined to the poetry of Great Britain. Spelling and punctuation are modernized, which is probably an advantage in a volume designed to appeal to a great variety of readers. In order to give the book some structure, Lewis has divided it into sections representing his view of the principal uses of the lyric form—Songs, Story Lyrics, Lyrical Poems (far the longest section), and Devotional Lyrics. He has included a certain number of poems which it would be mere eccentricity to omit, but on the whole he has avoided the obvious anthology-pieces, and has thus given his collection an unusual freshness. Particularly well represented are the less well-known lyrics of the sixteenth and seventeenth centuries.

Four volumes are devoted to modern verse. The most interesting is Elizabeth Jennings's *Anthology of Modern Verse, 1940–1960*.[47] Although it covers only twenty years, the contributors range from Walter de la Mare, born in 1873, and Andrew Young and Edwin Muir, both born in the mid-80's, to a number of poets born in the 1930's, of whom the youngest, Dom Moraes, was born in 1938. This mixture of the mature wisdom of the elderly with the sometimes perplexed questing of the very young provides a pleasant variety of approach. As is also to be seen in the three volumes to be noticed after this one, the poetry of recent years is especially notable for its meticulous craftsmanship and for the alertness of mind and intellectual honesty of those who write it. Thomas Blackburn's *45–60*[48] covers a slightly shorter period than Miss Jennings's anthology, and

[45] *Canadian Studies in Sweden*. pp. 39. *Irish Studies in Sweden*. pp. 40. By S. B. Liljegren. Upsala: A.-B. Lundequistska Bokhandeln. Each Sw. kr. 10.
[46] *A Book of English Lyrics*, ed. by C. Day Lewis. Chatto & Windus. pp. 256. 15*s*. *English Lyric Poems, 1500–1900*, ed. by C. Day Lewis. (Goldentree Books.) New York: Appleton-Century-Crofts. pp. xviii+ 249. $1.45.

[47] *An Anthology of Modern Verse, 1940– 1960*, chosen and with an introduction by Elizabeth Jennings. Methuen. pp. 299. 11*s*. 6*d*.
[48] *45–60: An Anthology of English Poetry, 1945–60*, chosen by Thomas Blackburn. Putnam. pp. 176. 18*s*.

presents the work of far fewer poets. It is, however, rather more adventurous in its choice of poets and poems. Whereas Miss Jennings rarely strays from the beaten track, Blackburn includes poems by a few poets who rarely reach the anthologies, such as J. C. Hall and Zofia Ilinska.

The second volume of the *Albemarle Book of Modern Verse for Schools*,[49] edited by F. E. S. Finn, is an unusually enterprising sixth-form anthology. It is a stiff mixture of English, American, and Commonwealth poems which makes few concessions to the youth of the pupils. However, provided that the teacher uses the book sensibly, this is as it should be, and the sixth-former who has both sensibility and intelligence, and who has previously been brought up on the first volume of the anthology, should leave school well equipped to tackle any modern poet.

The fourth volume of *The Guinness Book of Poetry*[50] follows the same pattern as its predecessors. It represents 'a short list chosen from among some 3,000 poems published between July 1959 and July 1960 when they were considered for the Guinness Poetry Awards by the judges appointed for the period, who were Patrick Kavanagh, John Press, and Stephen Spender'. The volume opens with the four poems which won the awards, by Thomas Blackburn, David Wright, Louis MacNeice and R. S. Thomas. These are followed by the poems which won the Guinness prizes for unpublished verse at the Cheltenham Festival—poems by Mark Richards, Alastair W. Thomson, W. S. Merwin, and A. E. Wylde. The remainder of the volume consists of about sixty-five 'runner-up' poems,

some of them by poets who have not yet won their spurs, but the majority by poets with established reputations.

Two volumes edited by James Reeves which have not previously been available for notice require mention here. Both are collections of English traditional verse. *The Idiom of the People*[51] contains about 120 songs or pieces of verse collected in the early years of the century, mostly from elderly people, by Cecil J. Sharp. Most of them carry the unmistakable stamp of 'the people', and many have considerable charm. Where variants occur, they are recorded. Reeves gives an interesting account of the folk-song movement in England of the last three-quarters of a century, describes the activities of Sharp and discusses his manuscripts, and provides some excellent criticism of the verse he prints. *The Everlasting Circle*[52] is a companion volume based on the manuscript collections made by Sabine Baring-Gould, one of the great pioneers of the movement, and by H. E. D. Hammond and George B. Gardiner. It contains about 140 songs. Once again Reeves supplies biographical and bibliographical notes and some criticism. The two volumes provide a fascinating record of the songs of some of our mute inglorious Miltons, and Reeves deserves our gratitude for the scholarship he has put into the task of editing them.

In recent times poetry and science have been commonly regarded as mutually antipathetic activities. Rightly rejecting this view, W. Eastwood has

[49] *The Albemarle Book of Modern Verse for Schools, Volume 2,* ed. by F. E. S. Finn. Murray. pp. xxi+197. 7s.
[50] *The Guinness Book of Poetry, 1959/60.* Putnam. pp. 138. 10s. 6d.
[51] *The Idiom of the People: English Traditional Verse,* ed. with an introduction and notes by James Reeves from the manuscripts of Cecil J. Sharp. Heinemann, 1958. pp. xii+244. 21s.
[52] *The Everlasting Circle: English Traditional Verse,* ed. with an introduction and notes by James Reeves from the manuscripts of S. Baring-Gould, H. E. D. Hammond, and George B. Gardiner. Heinemann, 1960. pp. xv+303. 25s.

compiled *A Book of Science Verse*[53] in order to demonstrate that poets of all ages have written great poetry about scientific facts and theories. As he points out, 'poet and scientist are alike concerned with the ordering of experience, and to both the imagination is all-important'—he might indeed have mentioned that the early Greek cosmologists and natural scientists presented their theories to the world in the form of poems, though later poets have usually had to accept their scientific facts at second hand. His selection begins with extracts from Lucretius in A. D. Winspear's recent translation and from Dante in Cary's translation, and brings us down to John Wain's 'Poem Feigned to have been written by an Electronic Brain'; in between come more than a hundred poems and extracts whose authors include almost all the great English poets—among them Chaucer, Shakespeare, Donne, Milton, Dryden, Pope, Wordsworth, and Shelley, not to mention a good many of the best modern poets. The book makes good reading, and convincingly upholds Eastwood's belief in the close relations that exist between poetry and science.

Like comic verse, parody can be tiresome in large quantities, and Dwight Macdonald's volume of *Parodies*[54] (more than 550 pages of them) must be sipped, not gulped. Many of the items, such as Wordsworth's 'Stuffed Owl' and Dickens's description of Little Nell's death (and indeed the whole section headed 'Self-Parodies—Unconscious'), are not in fact parodies, and some are quite straightforwardly comic; but the greater number are genuine parodies, from Chaucer's 'Sir Thopas'

down to Henry Reed's admirable 'Chard Whitlow (Mr. Eliot's Sunday Evening Postscript)'. Macdonald has not stinted himself of space. He has included the whole of Jane Austen's *Love and Freindship*, about sixty pages from Beerbohm's *A Christmas Garland*, many of Joyce's parodies in *Ulysses*, and several passages of the length of Hogg's 'The Flying Tailor: Further Extract from "The Recluse", a Poem'. He closes the volume with 'Some Notes on Parody'.

Mention must be made here of a delightful little 'anthology' entitled *A Leaden Treasury of Poesie*,[55] which is recorded for the gramophone by Jupiter Recordings, Ltd. It consists of two poems by Thomas Haynes Bayly, 'Oh ask me not for sportive lays' and 'Toujours le même'; Longfellow's 'Excelsior'; 'Incident at the battle of Minden', by Erasmus Darwin; 'The Female Friend', by Cornelius Whur; and 'The death of Lord and Lady Dalhousie', by the Homer of the North, William McGonagall. The poems are read by Alec Guinness with a mock-seriousness which admirably brings out their bathos, and are introduced by appropriate harp music improvised by Osian Ellis. It is to be hoped that further records will be added to this anthology; the next might well be drawn from *The Oxford Book of English Verse*, and opened with 'At her Window' by Frederick Locker-Lampson.

The Power of Eloquence,[56] edited by Andrew Scotland, is an anthology of famous English speeches. The volume is dominated by the twin themes of patriotism and liberty—perhaps inevitably, since threats to our freedom have always called out the noblest

[53] *A Book of Science Verse: The Poetic Relations of Science and Technology*, sel. by W. Eastwood. Macmillan. pp. xvi+279. 21s.

[54] *Parodies: An Anthology from Chaucer to Beerbohm—and After*, ed. by Dwight Macdonald. Faber. pp. xxiii+575. 30s.

[55] *A Leaden Treasury of Poesie*, read by Alec Guinness. Jupiter Recordings, Ltd. One seven-inch record, jep OC 24.

[56] *The Power of Eloquence: A Treasury of British Speech*, sel. and ed. by Andrew Scotland. Cassell. pp. ix+255. 21s.

eloquence of our leaders. The note is struck from the first with Queen Elizabeth's speech at Tilbury in 1588, and is carried through to the six war-time speeches of Sir Winston Churchill that are included. However, some diversity is provided by one of Donne's sermons, Macaulay's speech on literature to the Edinburgh Philosophical Institution, Newman's sermon at Oxford on the work of the Christian, the Duke of Edinburgh's 1951 Presidential Address to the British Association, and by the themes of a few other of the forty-odd speeches that the volume contains.

Most of us were brought up on the earlier volumes of *One-Act Plays of Today* published by Harrap, and the appearance of a seventh volume in the series,[57] edited by Hugh Miller, must not pass unnoticed. It contains *The Laughing Mind*, by Harold Brighouse; *The Will*, by J. M. Barrie; *The Bet*, by Miles Malleson; *E. & O.E.*, by Eliot Crawshay-Williams; *Sunday Costs Five Pesos*, by Josephina Niggli; and *The Road to Damascus*, by Margaret Wood. Miller provides helpful notes on acting and stagecraft.

6. *Translations*

Richmond Lattimore's *Greek Lyrics*[58] has in its second edition been expanded to include more than a hundred poems and fragments. In order to form a representative collection of Greek lyrical poetry, it has of course been necessary to use a good many fragments, since most of the poets are known at first hand only by passages from their writings quoted by later authors. Happily many of the fragments are of some length, as, for

example, are those of Sappho, two of which, indeed, appear to be complete or all but complete poems; where only short fragments exist, Lattimore has selected those which reveal something of their authors' quality even when divorced from their context. A couple of dozen poets are represented, about half of them in complete poems or long fragments, and they have been translated in their own metres, or in as close an approximation to these metres as the differences between the languages permit. Lattimore is an experienced and accomplished translator, and probably this little volume will come closer than any other to giving the Greekless reader some idea of the nature of Greek lyric.

Philip Vellacott, whose version of the *Oresteia* appeared in the Penguin Classics about five years ago, has now translated the remaining four extant plays of Aeschylus in a companion volume.[59] As in his previous translations of Greek tragedy, he has used a loose six-stressed line for the episodic parts, and lyrical measures for the choruses. He has not quite succeeded in reproducing the dignity and gravity of Aeschylus's dialogue—indeed, it would be difficult in the English of today to do this without sounding stilted—nor the rich splendour of his choruses; but he has achieved a dignity of his own, and his translations read very well.

Of the projected fifteen-volume Loeb edition of Plutarch's *Moralia*, the tenth volume to be published is Volume IX,[60] containing the Table

[57] *One-Act Plays of Today, Seventh Series*, ed. with notes on acting and stagecraft by Hugh Miller. Harrap. pp. 196. 6s.

[58] *Greek Lyrics*, translated by Richmond Lattimore. Second edition, revised and enlarged. (Phoenix Books.) Chicago U.P. pp. xvii+81. $1.35. 8s. 6d. (Also available clothbound.)

[59] *Aeschylus*. '*Prometheus Bound*'; '*The Suppliants*'; '*Seven Against Thebes*'; '*The Persians*', translated with an introduction by Philip Vellacott. Penguin Books. pp. 159. 3s. 6d.

[60] *Plutarch's 'Moralia'*. *Volume IX* (697c–771e), with an English translation by Edwin L. Minar, Jr., F. H. Sandbach, and W. C. Helmbold. (Loeb Classical Library.) Heinemann and Harvard U.P. pp. xii+454. 18s. $3.50.

Talk and the 'Dialogue on Love'. These works are translated into easy, natural modern English by Edwin L. Minar, Jr., F. H. Sandbach, and W. C. Helmbold. Apart from the intrinsic interest of the *Moralia*, students of Shakespeare and other Elizabethan writers will be glad that it is being made available in an authoritative modern version.

Also in the Loeb Classical Library, the seventh of eight volumes of Lucian's writings has appeared.[61] This is a particularly interesting volume, since it contains the Dialogues of the Dead, of the Sea-Gods, of the Gods, and of the Courtesans, which are delightful in themselves and have provided models for several English writers. The translation, by M. D. Macleod, is good. The Lucianic strain is well marked in English literature, from Sir Thomas More to Max Beerbohm, and a reliable modern translation is to be welcomed.

Paul Turner's admirably racy versions of selected writings of Lucian[62] should also give a great deal of pleasure. Most of them are taken from various of Lucian's books of dialogues, but they include also the *Alexander* ('the bogus oracle') and that wonderful satire on the lying travel-writers of his day (or any day), *The True History*.

Saint Augustine's *Confessions* have appeared in the Penguin Classics in a new translation by R. S. Pine-Coffin.[63] Translators of the *Confessions*, even the most recent, seem mostly to think it necessary to use archaic forms of expression. There is nothing of this about the present version, which is written in good modern literary English, and is likely to attract many people to the reading of the *Confessions*.

Nine Icelandic sagas have been translated for the World's Classics by Gwyn Jones.[64] They are 'Hen-Thorir', 'The Vapnfjord Men', 'Thorstein Staff-Struck', 'Hrafnkel the Priest of Frey', 'Eirik the Red', 'Thidrandi Whom the Goddesses Slew', 'Authun and the Bear', 'Gunnlaug Wormtongue', and 'King Hrolf and His Champions'. There are occasional awkwardnesses of expression, but for the most part Jones has managed to catch an easy and appropriate style for his translations.

Burton Raffel's *Poems from the Old English*[65] contains most of the poems that one would expect in such a collection—'The Seafarer', 'The Wanderer', 'The Dream of the Rood', 'The Battle of Maldon', a few of the Riddles, and the like. The translations cannot be highly commended. Raffel has omitted metaphors for which a little patient thought would have enabled him to find satisfactory renderings, and has added images not in the originals 'in order to explain something not otherwise intelligible, or in order to sustain the verse line or emphasize what for an Anglo-Saxon reader would have needed no emphasis'. His free four-beat line sounds very thin beside the Anglo-Saxon measure, nor has he considered carefully enough how a judicious use of alliteration might help him to recapture the feel of the original.

[61] *Lucian. Volume VII*, with an English translation by M. D. Macleod. (Loeb Classical Library.) Heinemann and Harvard U.P. pp. xi+476. 18s. $3.50.

[62] *Lucian. Satirical Sketches*, translated with an introduction by Paul Turner. Penguin Books. pp. 320. 3s. 6d.

[63] *Saint Augustine. 'Confessions'*, translated with an introduction by R. S. Pine-Coffin. Penguin Books. pp. 347. 5s.

[64] *'Eirik The Red' and Other Icelandic Sagas*, selected and translated with an Introduction by Gwyn Jones. (The World's Classics.) O.U.P. pp. xix+318. 8s. 6d.

[65] *Poems from the Old English*, translated, with an Introduction, by Burton Raffel. (Bison Books.) Nebraska U.P. pp. xxx+59. $1.

Also from America comes a translation of the prose romance of Perceval,[66] by Dell Skeels. The accuracy of Skeels's version cannot be judged by one who has no acquaintance with the original; as translation it reads easily and fluently, and brings out well the spirit of Arthurian romance.

The republication of John Jay Parry's translation of Andreas Capellanus's *The Art of Courtly Love*[67] will be welcomed, as will the fact that it is now readily available in England. The merits of this translation are too well known to require emphasis here. It is preceded by an introduction in which Parry relates the work to Ovid's poems on love and to the growth of the medieval doctrines of courtly love.

Although it is a 1962 publication, this seems an appropriate point at which to mention the appearance of a second edition of Felix Schlösser's book on Andreas Capellanus.[68] This is a very thorough study of Andreas's place in medieval literature, of his importance in the development of the courtly love convention, and of the twelfth-century world for which he was writing.

A new translation of Machiavelli's *Prince*[69] has been made for the Penguin Classics by George Bull. It is one of the happiest of the many translations of this work, and gives a very good impression of the directness, the vigour,

and the spontaneity of Machiavelli's writing. In an interesting introduction Bull sets Machiavelli against the background of the age in which he lived, and estimates the importance of *The Prince* in the history of political thought.

This year the Oxford University Press have produced the first five volumes in their Library of Italian Classics. The first is Dante's *Inferno*,[70] translated by Warwick Chipman. On the whole Chipman manages to reproduce the simple gravity of the original. He rightly uses *terza rima*, in common with most recent translators, but by the total exclusion of feminine endings he fails to capture the Dantesque movement of the line which was so successfully recaptured by Dorothy Sayers.

J. R. Hale's volume of *The Literary Works of Machiavelli*[71] is especially welcome. Hale's translation of *Mandragola* has been noticed in a previous number of *YW* (xxxix. 36), and this admirable comedy has twice been produced in London during the past quarter of a century in Ashley Dukes's adaptation; but *Clizia*, Machiavelli's other comedy of manners, is virtually unknown in this country, and it is good to have it now in an excellent English version. Hale's volume also contains *Belfagor*, a witty tale of a devil who discovers 'the evils which women bring with them into the home', the *Dialogue on Language*, and a selection of Machiavelli's private correspondence.

Also to be welcomed is a volume containing three comedies by Goldoni.[72]

[66] *The Romance of Perceval in Prose.* A Translation of the E Manuscript of the Didot Perceval, by Dell Skeels. Seattle: Univ. of Washington Press. pp. xi+98. $3.50.

[67] *The Art of Courtly Love, by Andreas Capellanus*, translated, with an Introduction and Notes, by John Jay Parry. New York: Ungar, 1959. London: Christopher Johnson. pp. xi+218. $5. 35s.

[68] *Andreas Capellanus: Seine Minnelehre, und das christliche Weltbild des 12. Jahrhunderts*, von Felix Schlösser. Bonn: Bouvier, 1962. pp. 386. DM. 27.

[69] *Niccolo Machiavelli. 'The Prince'*, translated with an Introduction by George Bull. Penguin Books. pp. 154. 3s. 6d.

[70] *'The Inferno', from 'La Divina Commedia', of Dante Alighieri*, translated by Warwick Chipman. O.U.P. pp. xxix+151. 12s. 6d.

[71] *The Literary Works of Machiavelli*, edited and translated by J. R. Hale. O.U.P. pp. xxvi+202. 16s.

[72] *Carlo Goldoni. Three Comedies*, introduced by Gabriele Baldini. O.U.P. pp. xxvii+293. 16s.

Mine Hostess (*La Locandiera*) is translated by Clifford Bax, *The Boors* (*I Rusteghi*) by I. M. Rawson, and *The Fan* (*Il Ventaglio*) by Eleanor and Herbert Farjeon. These are all accomplished translators, and their versions would probably act very well.

Alfieri's *Memoirs*[73] are published in an anonymous translation of 1810, completely revised by E. R. Vincent. This remarkable autobiography has many kinds of interests—among others, as the reflections on his art of a great tragic dramatist, as an account of (mainly amorous) intrigues, and as a record at first hand of life in revolutionary Paris.

Italian Regional Tales of the Nineteenth Century[74] contains a dozen short stories, each of which has been entrusted to a different translator. There is plenty of variety in the volume, in which we find cheek by jowl such tales as Sacchetti's *Wedding Eve*, Verga's *Cavalleria Rusticana*, Giacomo's *Pasquino*, and a couple of stories by D'Annunzio.

To the average English mind Nietzsche's *Thus Spoke Zarathustra*[75] is an unattractive and often repellent work, but it is probably right that a book which did so much to shape the Nazi philosophy should be as easily available as its inclusion in the Penguin Classics will make it. R. J. Hollingdale has translated it well, but at least one reader will not be persuaded to approve of it by the approval that he himself seems to express in an introduction that is otherwise informative and helpful.

The first four of Michael Meyer's translations of Ibsen's plays were noticed last year (*YW* xli. 30). This year he has added two more to the series, *Little Eyolf* and *The Master Builder*.[76] As before, Meyer has constantly borne in mind the requirements of the theatre, and has therefore omitted tautologous phrases and a certain amount of matter which might sound bathetic in an English rendering. For the rest, his versions read well, and some of them have already proved themselves on the stage.

Maxim Gorky's *Childhood*[77] has been added to the World's Classics in a translation made by Margaret Wettlin and revised by Jessie Coulson. It is a very good translation, and it is to be hoped that its appearance in a cheap edition will draw many people to read this memorable account of a Russian childhood, and thus, among other pleasures, to make the acquaintance of Gorky's delightful grandmother.

[73] *Vittorio Alfieri. 'Memoirs'.* The anonymous translation of 1810, revised by E. R. Vincent. O.U.P. pp. xx+310. 16s.
[74] *Italian Regional Tales of the Nineteenth Century*, selected and introduced by Archibald Colquhoun and Neville Rogers, and translated by various hands. O.U.P. pp. xv+268. 16s.
[75] *Nietzsche. 'Thus Spoke Zarathustra'*, translated with an Introduction by R. J. Hollingdale. Penguin Books. pp. 343. 5s.
[76] The Plays of Henrik Ibsen, translated by Michael Meyer. *Little Eyolf*, pp. 87. *The Master Builder*, pp. 127. Hart-Davis. Each vol. 10s. 6d.
[77] *Maxim Gorky. 'Childhood'.* Translation by Margaret Wettlin, revised by Jessie Coulson. (The World's Classics.) O.U.P. pp. xii+330. 7s. 6d.

II. ENGLISH LANGUAGE

By R. M. WILSON

CHRISTINE MOHRMANN, A. Sommerfelt, and J. Whatmough edit a useful account of trends in linguistics during the last thirty years,[1] and if the stress is more particularly on the contributions of American scholars, this is not surprising in the circumstances. Of particular interest are chapters by W. G. Moulton on 'Linguistics and Language Teaching in the United States 1940–1960', which describes also the development of the teaching of English as a second language, and that by C. C. Fries on 'The Bloomfield "School"'. In addition, M. Joos discusses 'Linguistic Prospects in the United States', while W. Plath, H. Hoijer, H. Spang-Hansen, and E. P. Hamp respectively deal with 'Mathematical Linguistics', 'Anthropological Linguistics', 'Glossematics', and 'General Linguistics—The United States in the Fifties'. A less satisfactory chapter on 'Comparative Linguistics in America 1930–1960' by S. Andrews, Jr., and J. Whatmough is no doubt due to the fact that it had to be taken over from the original author at a comparatively late date. In the revised and enlarged edition of H. A. Gleason's excellent introduction to descriptive linguistics[2] the basic plan of the work remains unchanged, though the original chapter on syntax has been rewritten as 'Immediate Constituents' and 'Syntactic Devices'. New chapters are included on 'Transforma-

tions', 'Language and Grammars', and 'Phonemic Field-Work', with new sections in the chapter on 'Inflectional Categories', and a revision of the notes and bibliography. The result is a book with all the virtues of the original edition, and even more information. A. Upton's *Design for Thinking*[3] is an introduction to a philosophic study of language, an attempt to show how semantics, as compared with formal grammar and linguistics, can lead to a sounder interpretation of the written and spoken word, and to an enhanced capacity for solving complex problems by critical analysis. L. F. Brosnahan[4] tests the hypothesis that genetic factors influence the sounds of speech, and concludes that its basis would appear to be sound. In a number of cases the distribution of sound features in Europe shows what would seem to be a non-fortuitous patterning that corresponds in some respects with the type of clinal distribution of genes which present-day observation and our knowledge of the genetic history of Europe would lead us to expect. He investigates various other factors, and suggests some lines of inquiry which should be fruitful in the further development of the subject. H. Kurath, 'Phonemics and Phonics in Historical Phonology' (*AS*), points out that the techniques of synchronic, diachronic, and area linguistics are applicable to language without reference to the culture and history of the speech com-

[1] *Trends in European and American Linguistics 1930–1960*, ed. by Christine Mohrmann, A. Sommerfelt, and J. Whatmough. Utrecht: Spectrum. pp. 299.

[2] *An Introduction to Descriptive Linguistics*, by H. A. Gleason. Revised edition. New York: Holt, Rinehart & Winston. pp. viii+503. $7.

[3] *Design for Thinking*, by A. Upton. Stanford U.P. pp. xi+240. $5.

[4] *The Sounds of Language*, by L. F. Brosnahan. Cambridge: Heffer. pp. vi+250. 25s.

munity. But historians of language, comparativists, and dialectologists need to relate their purely linguistic findings to the culture and history of the peoples who use the language, and for such problems the phonemic point of view is essential. The way in which the phonic character of phonemes may change is illustrated from the findings of the *Linguistic Atlas of the Atlantic States*, and it is claimed that areal and social linguistics can thus make a substantial contribution to our understanding of historical processes in phonology. Similarly, R. I. McDavid, Jr., points out some of the similarities and differences of aims and methods between 'Structural Linguistics and Linguistic Geography' (*Orbis*). According to A. McIntosh, 'Patterns and Ranges' (*L*), grammarians tend to be concerned with establishing and describing allowed patterns, but some distinction between grammar and lexis is necessary here since lexical factors may rule out sentences which conform to rules of grammatical pattern. Words may have only a certain potential of collocability, and collocations may be acceptable according to certain criteria of pattern which can be called *range*. Meanings of words are associated with our experience of them in a variety of contexts and associations, and while dictionaries record the combined lexical habits of many people, they do not accept anything that falls below a certain generality of experience. In present-day English there is enormous range-drift, and just as *pattern* is used of the structure of a sentence, so *range* should be applied to the collocations out of which sentences are made. In 'Grammaticality' (*Word*) A. A. Hill argues against the belief that convergent rejection of all ungrammatical sentences can be used to build a theory of grammaticality. Experiments with various illustrative sentences taken from Chomsky's *Syntactic Structures*

show that many of the statements there are not borne out, and that the intonation pattern influences acceptance or rejection of grammaticality. An article by N. Chomsky, 'Some Methodological Remarks on Generative Grammar' (*Word*), replies to these and other criticisms of his methods.

W. P. Lehmann, in 'A Definition of Proto-Germanic: A Study in the Chronological Delimitation of Languages' (*L*), argues that Proto-Germanic may be defined as that stage of Germanic spoken between the time of the Germanic accent shift and the loss of /e a/ when final and weakly stressed, and notes some disputed questions which such a definition may clarify. E. H. Antonsen, 'Germanic Umlaut Anew' (*L*), beginning with Hockett's proposed phonemic structure for pre-Anglian Old English, describes the phonemic-allophonic structure of proto-Germanic, and sets up phonemic systems for Icelandic, pre-Anglian Old English, West Saxon, and Middle English. Various conclusions follow: that *u*-umlaut does not entail labialization, that Old English 'breaking' and velar umlaut are both organically related to Old Icelandic *u*-umlaut, and that the term '*o/a*' umlaut is a misnomer. It is claimed that the system makes it possible to describe more accurately the sounds represented by the medieval spellings, and that the assumption that mutation proceeded through medial syllables is rendered obsolete. 'Der Umlaut im Englischen und Deutschen: Ein historisch-grammatischer Vergleich' (*ZAA*) is also dealt with by V. Schirmunski, who takes in turn umlaut due to inflexional endings, and umlaut in word formation. In 'Scribal Practice: Some Assumptions' (*L*) R. P. Stockwell and C. W. Barritt reaffirm their belief that in early Old English the short diphthongs represented allophones of the front vowels /i/, /e/, /æ/, that *ea* remains an allophone whereas the others later became phonemes, and they question some of Hockett's assumptions about scribal practices. S. M. Kuhn, 'On the Syllabic Phonemes of Old English' (*L*), gives an account of the phonemic system of Old English from the point of view of the traditional linguist, dealing first with the Old English vowels and diphthongs as they existed *c*. 700, and then with Mercian, Northumbrian, West Saxon, and Kentish. In 'A Note on "Hw" in Old English' (*NQ*) N. F. Blake shows that two developments appear, since, apart from *hw* itself, the group is sometimes represented by *h*, sometimes by *w*.

The current numbers of the *Middle English Dictionary*[5] contain a comparatively large number of words appearing only in a single author, but on the whole fewer learned words than usual. Moreover, some of those included are hardly Middle English, e.g. *crucifige*, *decempedes*, *dealbacioun*, *dentifricie*, while others look more like scribal errors, e.g. *depointed* (*depeinted*) *delakke* (*the lakke*), *dereful* (*drereful*), *descrie* (*crie*), *despien* (*despisen*), *devoiden* (*deviden*). Not all the explanations are convincing: *croucheman* 'dweller near a cross' is perhaps rather 'cross-bearer', *Dicoun* as a personal name is more probably from *Dick* than 'deacon', *denesone* is as likely to be *denizen* as 'dean's son', there is no reason to connect the name of Elias Defling with 'deaf', and it seems doubtful that *deis* was used as a surname. H. H. Carter[6] includes in his dictionary a good many common words which are occasionally used with reference to music, but the value of their inclusion is doubtful. The more technical terms

are carefully defined, illustrated by quotations, and the etymology given. All the obvious sources have been used, along with others not so obvious, and since the author is able to deal with the words in some detail, his work will be found useful by those interested in the history of music as well as by linguists. H. Käsmann[7] gives a judicious account of the linguistic situation in England between 1100 and 1350, and notes previous investigations of the Middle English vocabulary. He groups the different words according to subject, gives the Latin word along with the Middle English equivalents, and discusses the occurrence of these in the different texts. The work has been carefully carried out, and the result is much useful information on one aspect of Middle English vocabulary. P. Grierson surveys the etymologies which have been suggested at different times for 'Sterling',[8] and has no difficulty in disposing of them. Since the word originally implied 'English coin', the question is what differences existed between these and contemporary continental or earlier Anglo-Saxon coins that would have given rise to a special name. Anglo-Norman coins were substantially heavier than the majority of the later Anglo-Saxon issues, and were much more stable in weight. Consequently, Grierson suggests derivation from an OE. **stēre*, **stīere* 'strong, rigid, fixed', an etymology which would satisfy both linguistic and historical requirements, and explain what the word originally meant and how it came to be used. J. Gerritsen, 'A Ghost-Word: *crucethūs*' (*ES*), claims that the *Peterborough Chronicle* really reads *crucethur* which

[5] *Middle English Dictionary: Parts D 1, 2, and 3*, by H. Kurath and S. M. Kuhn. Michigan U.P. pp. 767–894, 895–1022, 1023–1150. $3 each part.

[6] *A Dictionary of Middle English Musical Terms*, by H. H. Carter, edited by G. B. Gerhard. Indiana U.P. pp. xv+655. $5.

[7] *Studien zum kirchlichen Wortschatz des Mittelenglischen 1100–1350*, by H. Käsmann. Tübingen: Niemeyer. pp. viii+380. DM. 40.

[8] In *Anglo-Saxon Coins. Studies Presented to F. M. Stenton on the Occasion of his 80th Birthday*, ed. by R. H. M. Dolley. pp. xv+296. 16 plates. 63s.

he derives from L. *cruciator*. In 'A Note on Two Expressions contained in the Manuscript B.M. Royal 13 A xviii: "En le mene temps, en poynt devis"' (*MLR*), occurring in an Anglo-Norman chess treatise, B. Kenyon suggests that since the former appears to have been current in insular French before 'in the meantime' was used in English, it is possible that the Middle English phrase was modelled on the Old French expression. The second may have been originally a chess term, 'on the appointed square', which was adopted as a metaphor and passed into the everyday vocabulary with a change of meaning to 'precisely, with extreme nicety or correctness'. N. Davis, 'The Earliest "Do Not"' (*NQ*), points out that the appearance of *do* in a 'negative declarative' sentence in the Laud version of the legend of St. Scholastica is certainly an error, and since the other manuscripts read *dorre*, this isolated example should not be regarded as a genuine forerunner of the construction. Bridget James suggests connexion of '"Pernyng" in "Sir Gawain and the Green Knight", Line 611' (*NQ*) with dialectal *pirn* 'reel, bobbin', the word being used here in the sense 'flitting', and R. T. Lenaghan, 'A Note on OE. "Melcan"' (*NQ*), takes the appearance of *molken* twice in a brief passage in Caxton as evidence for the survival of OE. *melcan* after the Conquest.

J. Šimko's analysis of 'Some Aspects of the Transition from the Impersonal to the Personal Construction in English' (*Fililogia Közlöny*) rests on the alliterative *Morte Arthure*, the Winchester Malory and Caxton's Malory. At this period the usage of the construction was evidently still unsettled, but the two later texts make it clear that the personal construction was rapidly gaining ground, the change being closely connected with the stabilization of the word-order in

English. L. F. Brosnahan examines the use of 'The Apostrophe in the Genitive Singular in the 17th Century' (*ES*), and notes that it appears to have originated in the last years of the sixteenth. During the first two or three decades of the seventeenth century it becomes a little more common, especially in words ending with -*a* or -*o*, but there is considerable variation from text to text. Between 1630 and 1670 there is a clear increase in the frequency of use, and though at first restricted almost entirely to the names of persons or their occupations, by the end of the century the apostrophe comes to be used in the genitives of simple common nouns. In addition, H. Koziol, 'Zum Gebrauch des Demonstrativums anstelle des unbestimmten Artikels' (*NM*), gives examples of the variation from Middle English and Spenser.

K. Brunner, 'Sprachlehrbücher im Mittelalter',[9] includes descriptions of some English books on the subject between Ælfric and Palsgrave. *English Examined*[10] contains a series of passages on various aspects of the English language from Camden to Cobbett. The authors quoted are not only philologists or schoolmasters, but also historians, poets, dramatists, and philosophers, and while some of them are accurate, others are wildly inaccurate even for their own time, but all alike give important evidence of the development of the study of the language. Many of the sources are not easily accessible, so that the student will welcome this scholarly and convenient collection of key passages on the development, nature, and use of language during a particularly important

[9] In *Language and Society. Essays Presented to Arthur M. Jensen on his Seventieth Birthday*. Copenhagen: Det Berlingske Bogtrykkeri. pp. 203. Abbreviated below as *L & S*.
[10] *English Examined*, by Susie I. Tucker. C.U.P. pp. xix+154. 22*s*. 6*d*.

period of its history. Some of those whose writings can easily be found are absent, or represented only briefly, but Appendix I gives a list of important passages and the books in which they are available. A good introduction points out the different kinds of evidence on such subjects as pronunciation, usage, vocabulary, &c., provided by the different writers, brief details of whom are given in Appendix II. This excellent anthology gives evidence of the editor's wide and appreciative knowledge of the subject, and should prove invaluable to the student, while the general reader will also find in it much to interest and amuse him. J. L. Rosier investigates 'The Sources and Methods of Minsheu's *Guide into the Tongues*' (*PQ*). This was the first English dictionary based on etymology, the first to make extensive citations of sources, and the first to recognize the lexicographical significance of Old and Middle English. Rosier indicates the influence of the work on later lexicographers, and describes and illustrates Minsheu's sources and methods.

Chatto's Modern Science Dictionary[11] has been revised for English readers by W. Abbott. Comprehensiveness would perhaps be an impossible ideal for such a dictionary, but nevertheless it contains some 16,000 words dealing with the main branches of science. These are defined as simply as the subject allows, and the book is intended essentially for the layman rather than the scientist. The lack of etymologies is perhaps of little importance, but some indication of pronunciation would have been useful. *A Glossary of Geographical Terms*[12] is limited to those used in current geographical literature written in English, but ordinary words used in such writings with their normal meanings have not been included, and foreign words are present only if they are in use in their original form. Within these self-imposed limitations, the glossary is remarkably comprehensive, covering all the several branches of geography. Wisely, no attempt has been made to give an agreed definition of the various terms, though when there is no doubt of the meaning, the definition is quoted without comment from one of the standard authorities. Where words have extended or changed their meanings, this is shown by quotations illustrating the change, and where necessary a final comment is added, either by a member of the committee or by an expert who has been specially consulted. New terms, or those defined in recent years, have wherever possible been traced back to their originators, and the original definition given. Appendixes list the Greek and Latin roots commonly used in the construction of such words, the foreign words which have been absorbed into English, and stratigraphical terms. It is safe to say that this glossary will certainly establish itself as an indispensable reference book. M. M. A. Schröer and P. L. Jaeger[13] continue their useful English–German dictionary, while E. Partridge has made a skilful abridgement of his own *Dictionary of Slang and Unconventional English*[14] by excluding all material which was obsolete by 1900, by omitting most of the language of the underworld, and by perhaps too strict a bowdlerization. The result is a useful selection of such terms, but one that can hardly replace the original

[11] *Chatto's Modern Science Dictionary*, compiled by A. Hechtlinger, edited by W. Abbott. Chatto & Windus. pp. 559. 25s.
[12] *A Glossary of Geographical Terms*, prepared by a Committee of the British Association for the Advancement of Science and edited by L. Dudley Stamp. Longmans. pp. xxx+539. 63s.

[13] *Englisches Handwörterbuch*. Lieferung 19: Bogen 91–95, by M. M. A. Schröer and P. L. Jaeger. Heidelberg: Winter. DM. 8.90.
[14] *Smaller Slang Dictionary*, by E. Partridge. Routledge. pp. ix+204. 18s.

work. *Theatre Language*[15] contains over 3,000 words and phrases, with full definitions, referring in the main to the legitimate stage, but including also some of the closely allied fields. Obsolete terms from the Elizabethan period onwards are included, with an indication of their period of use, but no etymologies are given, though an explanation of the origin of slang terms sometimes appears. The emphasis is mainly on American theatre language, but a good many distinctively British terms appear, and the result is a useful collection of such words which is more comprehensive than anything on the subject that had been previously available. R. W. Burchfield, 'O.E.D.: A New Supplement' (*E & S*), emphasizes the necessity for this, and indicates the sources available. It will contain antedatings for many words already treated, and some revised definitions will also be needed. Many new words and new senses will appear: dialectal words have made their way into the standard language, numerous American ones, a few from the Commonwealth, with others from French, German, and the more exotic languages. One of the main features will be an increase in the number of words formed from initials; by-forms and shortenings of common words are as prominent as ever, along with nouns used as verbs, phrasal verbs, and new formations using common affixes. But despite all the advances in etymology, there will still be a number of words of obscure or disputed etymology, e.g. *boffin*, *cagey*, *gimmick*, *wog*. In 'Einige Grundsätze für die Gestaltung deutsch-englischer und englisch-deutscher technischer Fachwörterbücher' (*ZAA*) R. Walther gives useful and necessary advice on the rendering of technical words from one language into the other, with some indication of the particular problems involved, while J. Vachek writes 'A Propos de la Terminologie Linguistique et du Système de Concepts Linguistiques de l'École de Prague' (*Philologica Pragensia*).

J. Warburg[16] defines the best-chosen English as 'English which communicates as effectively as possible the meanings the sayer intends to communicate', whether or not these meanings are themselves the best, or the less than best chosen. A discussion of the question of choice in English is followed by descriptions of some of the different kinds of English now being investigated by the Communication Research Centre which plans to produce handbooks of them, to be followed by an attempt to discover whether the English they use in fact communicates the intended meaning. R. Quirk[17] emphasizes the extent to which contemporary ideas on language were anticipated by R. G. Latham, professor of English at University College, 1839–45. He goes on to point out the deficiencies in our knowledge of contemporary English which it is hoped that the Survey of Educated English, now being carried on at University College, London, will help to remedy. R. A. Hall, Jr.,[18] makes a reasoned criticism of the 'look and say' method of teaching children to read. He discusses the relation of spelling to sound, describes the phonemes and graphemes of American English, and shows that the spelling is far more regular than its critics suppose. Few words are wholly capricious in spelling;

[15] *Theatre Language*, by W. P. Bowman and R. H. Ball. New York: Theatre Arts Books. pp. xii+428. $6.95.

[16] *The Best-Chosen English*, by J. Warburg. Communication Research Centre, University College, London. pp. 35. 6s.
[17] *The Study of the Mother-Tongue*, by R. Quirk. Published for University College, London, by H. K. Lewis & Co. Ltd. pp. 23.
[18] *Sound and Spelling in English*, by R. A. Hall, Jr. New York: Chilton Company. pp. 34. $1.

most irregular spellings are irregular only in the representation of one or two of the phonemes contained in the group, and even so they fall to a large extent into certain sub-sets which are consistent within themselves. He argues that a properly planned series of reading texts should be based on the principle of graded selection of words in terms of their difficulty. All this is reasonable enough, but it is surprising to find that the irregularities of English spelling are ascribed to a deliberate plot by the nobles and intellectuals of the late Middle Ages who wished to keep the art of reading and writing as their private possession.

A number of books on English are addressed particularly to the teachers.[19] That by D. Holbrook gives a depressing picture of the present state of the subject in the secondary school, and provides a practical handbook on the teaching of various aspects of English. The aims are laudable, the book is written with refreshing enthusiasm, and it contains much good advice along with some useful if rather out-of-date book-lists. Unfortunately there is also a complete ignorance of language and the way it works, an uncritical admiration for so-called folk art, and a complete inability to realize that there are other worth-while subjects than English literature. E. H. Sauer deals in turn with the history of the language, different levels of English, traditional grammar and the value of structural linguistics, advice on the setting and marking of essays, &c. He then considers the teaching of poetry, drama, and different kinds of prose, includes a reconsideration of the literary programme in the High School, and outlines a syllabus for the gifted child. The author shows clearly the interrelation of the various aspects of English, and provides a practical book on the subject which teachers will find useful. G. W. Stone reprints a series of articles on the subject arranged under different headings. Part I, 'Issues and Problems', includes an article on the basic issues in the teaching of English, and reports from conferences held in 1940 and 1942. Part II, 'Language and Writing', has two chapters from the *American English Grammar* of C. C. Fries, and two from J. B. Greenough and G. L. Kittredge, *Words and their Ways in English Speech*, along with an article on 'Cultural Levels and Functional Varieties of English' by J. S. Kenyon. Part III, 'Literature', gives an extract from De Quincey's essay on Pope, an appreciation of the Authorized Version by J. L. Lowes, and a passage from E. Auerbach's *Mimesis*, while Part IV contains a suggested programme of action. The collection contains much of interest and value, but it is not clear that it really makes the kind of book promised by the title. A. Bernstein's book is illustrated by a number of case histories, and each section followed by a brief annotated bibliography which provides a useful guide to other materials on the subject. The usual subjects are dealt with, as well as problems of discipline and the planning of lessons. Anyone beginning a teaching career will find here much useful practical advice and information, presented in a stimulating and interesting way. R. B. Long describes in detail the structure of standard American English, and, while necessarily paying

---

[19] *English for Maturity*, by D. Holbrook. C.U.P. pp. xii+255. 21s. *English in the Secondary School*, by E. H. Sauer. New York: Holt, Rinehart & Winston. pp. ix+245. $3.75. *Issues, Problems, and Approaches in the Teaching of English*, by G. W. Stone, Jr. New York: Holt, Rinehart & Winston. pp. x+246. $2.50. *Teaching English in High School*, by A. Bernstein. New York: Random House. pp. vi+470. $5.95. *The Sentence and its Parts*, by R. B. Long. Chicago U.P. pp. 528. $6. *Teaching the Mother Tongue in Secondary Schools*, by P. Gurrey. Longmans. pp. x+219. 12s. 6d.

most attention to the written language, considers also the spoken word. He tries to avoid too sharp a break with the traditional grammar, but is at the same time fully aware of recent advances and techniques and makes good use of them. The very full treatment of the subject is particularly valuable for its numerous lists and for the richness of its illustrative material drawn from present-day idiomatic usage, but the addition of a glossary of grammatical terminology was only too necessary since there is perhaps a tendency to use too many unfamiliar terms. The book by P. Gurrey will be found particularly useful by the student in training. He deals with the principles on which the teaching of English should be based, with the aims that the teacher should have in mind, and with the reasons for limited plans and procedures. More specific problems are then dealt with, and there is a particularly useful chapter on the teaching of English to technical students in which some of the suggested methods should rouse interest.

So far as the usual textbooks on English are concerned,[20] the first deals clearly and concisely with the usual subjects, and also provides a survey of composition types from the paragraph to the essay, with a chapter which gives useful hints to the student on the various types of examination. In the second, there are sections on abbrevia-

tions, proof-correction, and the use of the dictionary. The examples in it avoid the usual artificial appearance, and the numerous exercises, interspersed with the text rather than segregated at the end of the chapters, do their work well, but the Glossary of Usage is too brief and elementary to be worth the space. D. A. Conlin aims to synthesize the most useful elements of the traditional and the linguistic viewpoints. He points out the limitations of the traditional grammar and the practical applications of linguistics to grammar, but in fact most of the book, apart from differences of terminology, follows a fairly conventional pattern. D. W. Lee's combination text and work-book succeeds in living up to its title, and presents the essentials of English briefly and lucidly. The definitions are clear, rules of usage are interpreted with an eye to the facts rather than to the statements of prescriptive grammar, and new material is included, especially in the short chapter on the main sentence patterns. F. E. Foden's book is in general a briefer and more compact version of almost any textbook on the writing of English, the only difference being that examples are usually taken from scientific subjects, and problems of specifically technological description are included in the exercises. S. Pit Corder gives a useful survey of the possibilities of television in the teaching of English, an appraisal of its advantages and defects, and an indication of the most suitable methods of taking advantage of it.

Of the books on composition,[21] the

[20] Heath Handbook of English, by H. I. Christ, M. M. Starkey, and J. C. Tressler. Boston: Heath & Co. pp. xii+436. $2.85. Practical English Handbook, by F. C. Watkins and E. T. Martin. Boston: Houghton Mifflin Co. pp. xxii+450. $3.75. Grammar for Written English, by D. A. Conlin. Boston: Houghton Mifflin Co. pp. xiii+341. $2.50. English Essentials, by D. W. Lee. Englewood Cliffs, N.J.: Prentice-Hall. pp. iv+124. $1.95. Efficient English for Technical Students, by F. E. Foden. University of London Press. pp. 205. 7s. 6d. English Language Teaching and Television, by S. Pit Corder. Longmans. pp. iv+107. 7s. 6d.

[21] English Composition, by C. H. Vivian and B. M. Jackson. New York: Barnes & Noble. pp. xxxv+451. $2.50. Mastering English Composition, by Nina Walter. New York: Holt, Rinehart & Winston. pp. viii+279. $2.50. Handbook for Basic Composition, by A. R. Kitzhaber and D. W. Lee. Englewood Cliffs, N.J.: Prentice-Hall. pp. xv+464. $4.50. Rhetoric for Exposition, by R. D. Chittick and R. D. Stevick. New York:

first begins with a bibliography of standard textbooks on the subject and a table showing the pages in these books in which the topics here treated are dealt with. General advice on composition and clear thinking is followed by sections dealing in turn with the whole composition, with shorter expository and non-expository themes, and with the research paper. A chapter on diction includes advice on the use of the dictionary, while that on spelling gives lists of homonyms and of words frequently mispronounced or misspelled. The second deals in ascending order of difficulty with spelling, punctuation, grammar, and sentence structure. Each lesson begins with a concise account of the particular subject, and is followed by exercises. The *Handbook for Basic Composition* describes the technique of essay writing, from the selection of a subject, through its organization, to paragraph, sentence, and the choice of words. The grammar is dealt with more briefly, but particularly useful here is the careful definition of grammatical terms and a detailed chapter on spelling. *Rhetoric for Exposition* defines the type of writing in which skilful use of rhetorical forms can be used to advantage, presents traditional forms of definition, and deals with logical and non-logical forms of rhetoric. Most of the chapters contain an essay by some standard author which is then analysed in terms of its principal rhetorical interest. A. Warner tries to do too much in too brief a

space. His practical advice on the writing of clear English tends to be too dogmatic and has some contradictions, while in his outline of the development of English prose, the section on Old and Middle English is too brief to be of any value and has some bad mistakes. The third part gives examples of the different levels of style in use today, with indications of their particular uses. D. W. Lee and W. T. Moynihan present a selection of essays and passages, in the main from twentieth-century writers, which offers examples of good prose. The passages are so arranged that the student passes from the simpler to the more complex style. Each passage is preceded by a short biography of the author, and followed by numerous exercises. The other two both give a series of extracts from writers ranging from Bacon to the present day, but with the main accent on contemporary authors, and arranged under various headings. In the former, each section has a short introduction dealing with the qualities of that type of writing, and is followed by a note on the author and by questions on style and matter. The latter has a minimum of commentary, usually little more than a note on the source of the passage.

Of the books on the teaching of English as a second language,[22] H. G. Wayment presents a report of the proceedings of a conference held in December 1960 on training and research in the teaching of English as a second language. With some excep-

---

Appleton-Century-Crofts. pp. x+208. $2.50. *A Short Guide to English Style*, by A. Warner. O.U.P. pp. viii+198. 7s. 6d. *Using Prose*, by D. W. Lee and W. T. Moynihan. New York: Dodd, Mead & Co. pp. xix+620. $4.95. *University Readings*, by L. G. Locke and H. W. Wilson. New York: Holt, Rinehart & Winston. pp. viii+358. $2.25. *The Craft of Writing*, by D. Colville and J. D. Koerner. New York: Harper. pp. x+382. $4.75.

[22] *English Teaching Abroad and the British Universities*, by H. G. Wayment. Methuen. pp. 63. 6s. *Teaching English in Difficult Circumstances*, by M. West. Longmans. pp. viii+136. 10s. 6d. *The Techniques of Language Teaching*, by F. L. Billows. Longmans. pp. xi+259. 15s. *Language Testing*, by R. Lado. Longmans. pp. xxiii+389. 32s. 6d. *The English we Use*, by R. A. Close. Longmans. pp. x+221. 6s. *Conversational English*, by A. Paratore. Englewood Cliffs, N.J.: Prentice-Hall. pp. xii+83. $1.50.

tions, the two introductory speeches to each session are printed, along with a few shorter contributions. In general, they are too short for much beyond vague generalities to emerge, and with each speaker urging the pre-eminent importance of his own speciality. The undoubted value of the conference hardly emerges here. M. West has had much experience of teaching English in difficult circumstances, i.e. in an unsuitable class-room to an overlarge and ill-assorted class, and he here puts forward some methods for dealing with the problems involved. Useful devices for the large class are suggested, hints given on the teaching of reading and pronunciation, and on the construction of reading material. Anyone compelled to teach in such circumstances will profit much from this short but valuable book. F. L. Billows, too, has had experience, not only in the teaching of English as a second language, but also in the training of teachers, and he writes a sensible and stimulating book on the problems and techniques involved. He knows the latest work on psychology and descriptive linguistics, and takes advantage of the results without accepting all of them uncritically. The usual subjects are dealt with, and anecdotes from the author's varied experience help to drive home his points and keep the reader's interest. From R. Lado comes a valuable account of the construction and use of foreign-language tests which, of course, applies also to the teaching of English as a second language. A general discussion of the theory of language testing is followed by a description of the special techniques for the different elements of language: pronunciation, grammatical structure, and vocabulary. Other sections deal with the testing of the integrated skills, with possible ways of testing cross-cultural understanding, and with the refining and use of language tests. Dr.

Lado is thoroughly at home with the subject; he knows the particular difficulties involved, and points out clearly the ways in which many of the usual tests miss the point. R. A. Close's book consists of a series of short passages taken from the *Listener*. Some provide training in the comprehension of continuous speech, while others are intended for textual study, for use as a source of discussion and free composition, and as material for speech training. A. Paratore provides a series of lessons which give practice in speaking and hearing the language for those with some knowledge of English. The lessons are carefully designed, and emphasize more particularly the many constructions and idioms which employ auxiliary verbs.

S. R. Levin[23] examines the language of poetry from the point of view of structural linguistics. This discloses certain structures peculiar to the language of poetry, known as *Couplings*, defined as two forms which may be equivalent in respect to some extra-linguistic factor. Levin shows how such couplings serve to unify a poem, considers what degree of coupling is desirable in poetry, and suggests some of the combinations that may constitute too great a concentration. He then examines Shakespeare's *Sonnet 30*, and points out the integral and thoroughgoing role that coupling plays in the organization of the poem. J. Levý, 'On the Relations of Language and Stanza Pattern in the English Sonnet',[24] offers an example of the complex relations into which a prosodic form enters if transferred into a foreign literature, since the concrete forms a stanza pattern takes on are determined by the prosody of the language. Metre is chiefly dependent

---

[23] *Linguistic Structures in Poetry*, by S. R. Levin. 's-Gravenhage: Mouton & Co. pp. 64.
[24] In *Worte und Werte: Bruno Markwardt zum 60. Geburtstag*. Berlin: De Gruyter.

on the phonemic qualities of the word, while a stanza is under stronger influence from the phonemic qualities of the sentence. Elsewhere, the same author discusses 'The Development of Rhyme-Scheme and of Syntactic Pattern in the English Renaissance Sonnet' (*Acta Universitatis Palackianae Olmucensis, Philologica IV*).

J. Vachek, 'Some Less Familiar Aspects of the Analytical Trend of English' (*Brno Studies in English*), summarizes and revises earlier articles, and discusses in detail various points which provide evidence of this analytical character: the status of the word, the possessive case, the sentence, the opposition of quantity and quality in the vowels, of voice and tension in paired consonants, and the loss of medial *h*. These provide evidence of the mutual interdependence linking various planes of language, and of the necessity for regarding the analytical trend of English as a principle which affects all planes of language. In 'Principles of Morphological Analysis' (*Philologica Pragensia*) B. Trnka lists, with observations, some of the fundamental concepts and assumptions found useful or indispensable in the area of structural morphology. D. Bolinger, 'Syntactic Blends and Other Matters' (*L*), criticizes the transformational approach. The more evidence the transformational grammarian brings himself to consider, the more he is likely to find that his formulas are hedged in, the more restrictions he must apply to make them fit the evidence, and the closer he gets to the point of diminishing returns. Three particular weaknesses in the method are illustrated in some detail: a tendency to base generalizations on insufficient evidence, the existence of syntactic blends which make it difficult and perhaps impossible to single out *the* transformational origin of certain constructions, and the fact that the entire grammatical structure is permeated by threads of idiom. 'A Class of Complex Modifiers in English' (*L*) by Carlota S. Smith is an exercise in generative grammar in which a rule is formulated that will most simply produce the sentences in question, and the rule is then related to the rest of the grammar in such a way that a place in the ordered sequence of rules can be assigned to it. Generalizations are made to account for sentences containing adjectival modifiers, and rules formulated to produce only the acceptable sentences. Comparative adjectives are then dealt with, and it is shown how they fit into the rules already formulated. R. B. Lees also makes a 'Grammatical Analysis of the English Comparative Construction' (*Word*), and formulates a set of rules to generate such constructions, while the same author describes the formal features of 'The Constituent Structure of Noun Phrases' (*AS*).

An important study on the verb[25] defines the units on which any syntactical analysis of the language could be based, and since criteria for isolating them must be found at other than syntactical levels, the isolation of the 'sentence' is sketched at the phonological and orthographical levels. The minimum language unit correlated with a definable object is said to be a number of *concretes*, the behaviour of which can be described by taking into account the way in which they combine with other units. One result of the isolation of concretes is that, along with the traditional verb, certain complex structures can also be considered, e.g. not only *fight* and *look*, but also *be a fighter* and *have a look*. Various chapters deal with the minimum opera-

[25] *On the Syntax of the English Verb with Special Reference to* Have a Look *and Similar Complex Structures*, by Y. Olsson. Gothenburg Studies in English 12. Stockholm: Almqvist & Wiksell. pp. 246. Sw. kr. 25.

tion unit, with the major verb paradigm, with complexes as structures, and with the contextualization of the major verb paradigm. J. Firbas, 'On the Communicative Value of the Modern English Finite Verb' (*Brno Studies in English*), shows that although the verb remains the most adequate conveyer of the predicative categories of tense and mood, and so sets up definite limits to the shift towards nominal expression, nevertheless it shows considerable losses in communicative value. These losses notably change the position of the verb within the structure of the language and affect its role in the very act of communication, but do not impair the communicative efficiency of the sentence in particular and of the utterance in general. 'Co-existing Negative Preterite Forms of *dare*' (*L & S*; see note 9) by R. Quirk and Anne P. Duckworth records the result of an experiment involving the translation by students of a passage from the *Dream of the Rood* containing three occurrences of *ne dorste* (*ic*)+the infinitive. The dominant forms in the translations were *dared* and *did+dare*, but it was clear that the individual's natural repertoire of negative preterite forms freely comprehended all combinations of the main forms, and these could be exploited for stylistic reasons. In 'Pseudo-subjunctive *Were*' (*AS*) W. M. Ryan gives examples of the hypercorrect substitution of *were* for *was* in *if* clauses in the indicative mood in some modern American writers.

T. Kanekiyo surveys previous interpretations of 'The Conjunction-Headed Phrase' (*ES*), the name given to a single word or word-group introduced by a conjunction and with the resultant construction having the same function as a dependent clause, and concludes that it is not to be explained by any hard and fast rule. A. A. Boersch, 'On the Use of Conjunctions'

(*AS*), suggests a classification into one-way connectors—those which always connect the subject-predicate group of which they are a part to another subject-predicate group to the left of theirs, e.g. *and, or, but*—and two-way connectors which connect the subject-predicate group to another which may be either to the right or left of theirs, e.g. *when, although, because*. In 'Notes on the Situational Adverbs in English and Czech from the point of view of Functional Sentence Perspective' (*Sborník prací filosofické fakulty Brněnské University*) Eva Dvorakova inquires into the differences displayed by English and Czech in regard to the sentence position of situational adverbs, i.e. of words and phrases that function as modifiers of the verbal notion as to time, place, or cause, and J. Firbas adds to it 'Another Note on the Position of the Situational Adverbs in English and Czech', providing a wider setting for such problems. H. Spitzbardt traces the history and deals with the syntax of '(US.) *I rather* (*that*) +Konjunktiv' (*Philologica Pragensia*), while B. Jacobsson, in 'An Unexpected Usage: "ahead", "alive", and the like before Nouns' (*Moderna Språk*), points out that the almost exclusively predicative use of such words can be explained as due to their meaning, to euphony, or to the fact that the word requires a complement. Since the most important of these factors is probably meaning, a purely formal approach cannot provide an enlightening account of grammatical problems of this kind. Eleven papers which appeared at various dates between 1939 and 1959 have been collected together and published in honour of the sixty-fifth birthday of F. Behre.[26] The only one not previously

---

[26] *Papers on English Vocabulary and Syntax*, by F. Behre. Gothenburg Studies in English. Göteborg: Almqvist & Wiksell. pp. xix+170. Sw. kr. 18.

available, '"It Cannot be; It is Impossible"', takes the particular meaning of these phrases in Shakespeare, and from there traces the earlier use of the idiom and its predecessors in Old and Middle English. In addition, some of the other papers were originally published in periodicals which are not easy to obtain in this country, so that it is useful to have them available here. The same author, in 'A Question of Linguistic Predictability' (*L & S*; see note 9), takes an idiomatic construction consisting of initial *that* (commutable by *the fact that*) plus *should* (commutable by the indicative), and attempts to discover whether the expression following it is predictable. It would seem that such a sequence can only be followed by one or other of the following types: 'it is surprising', 'is natural', 'is proof of', 'is due to'. R. W. Zandvoort, 'Varia Syntactica' (*L & S*; see note 9), shows that the split genitive of the type *Ælfredes sweostor cyninges* survived into the first half of the eighteenth century. He gives examples from otherwise careful writers of the use of a plural subject with a singular verb and vice versa, and of hyphened verb-adverb combinations which indicate that a pronunciation with single stress now takes precedence of one with a double stress. In '"I found myself walking"' (*ELT*) the same scholar notes a number of variations of the construction, and emphasizes the inadequacy of our present documentary evidence for the variation of syntactic patterns in English.

S. Hagen, 'Note on the Pronunciation of "ex" in English' (*Moderna Språk*), describes the different pronunciations of the prefix, according as to whether it is stressed or unstressed. In 'System Status of Obscured Vowels in English' (*L*) L. S. Hultzén points out that while some scholars recognize a reduced vowel /ə/ occurring only in unstressed syllables, others would assign examples of it to phonemes which are represented in stressed syllables. Both interpretations lead to difficulties, and a simpler operation would be to set up a sub-system of vowels occurring only in unaccented syllables. A. A. Hill, 'Suprasegmentals, Prosodies, Prosodemes. Comparison and Discussion' (*L*), compares the analytical procedures of J. R. Firth with those of one American linguist—himself. He finds a good deal of agreement disguised by differences of terminology, and much that is stimulating in Firth's theories, along with a certain vagueness and lack of adequate definition. C. F. Hockett, 'Linguistic Elements and their Relationship' (*L*), discusses some of the theories of relationship between phonemes and morphemes, and K. Malone's 'Glides, Diphthongs, and Boundaries' (*ES*) deals with criticisms by A. A. Hill of Malone's paper on 'The Phonemes of Current English'.

A number of severely technical studies in *LS* includes Frieda Goldman-Eisler's 'A Comparative Study of Two Hesitation Phenomena' in which she measures and compares the duration of filled pauses with those of unfilled pauses, while the same writer, in 'Continuity of Speech Utterance, its Determinants and its Significance', measures pause frequency and word length in speech sequences uttered without a break. Eva Sivertsen, 'Speech Inventories for Speech Synthesis', claims that speech synthesis from stored segments provides a means of checking certain theories about linguistic structure, and phonetic statements about the nature of speech. But its value lies less in the new data on language and speech that it may provide, and more as a check on data and hypotheses derived by other means. In L. S. Harms, 'Listener Comprehension of Speakers of Three Status

Groups', such listeners attempt to re-construct spoken messages of speakers of the three groups. The not surprising conclusion is that speakers of high status were most comprehensible, but that listeners achieved highest relative comprehension when speaker and listener status coincided. S. W. Becker, A. Bavelas, and Marcia Braden, 'An Index to Measure Contingency of English Sentences', define contingency in this context as reconstructability. Several indexes were constructed, the best form of index was then selected and retested, and it was concluded that the index is a valid initial approxima-tion to a measure of contingency. In addition, A. Liberman, Katherine S. Harris, P. Eimas, L. Lisker, and J. Bastian deal with 'An Effect of Learn-ing on Speech Perception: The Dis-crimination of Durations of Silence with and without Phonemic Signi-ficance', while J. W. Black discusses 'Relationships among Fundamental Frequency, Vocal Sound Pressure, and Rate of Speaking'.

A textbook on intonation by J. D. O'Connor and G. F. Arnold[27] is mainly taken up with a series of intona-tion drills. The preface gives a com-pact and lucid account of English intonation, and is followed by a section on intonation and meaning in which the authors show the importance of the speaker's attitude and of the sentence pattern in determining in-tonation pattern. The drill sentences are followed by eleven dialogues for practice, and four records are available containing a representative sample of the drills and the first six dialogues. A. Vanvik[28] considers that stress is best considered as a linguistic dif-ferentiating concept, since no single

phonetic or gestural feature, or set of such features, is always present in the stressed syllable. D. L. Bolinger, 'Con-trastive Accent and Contrastive Stress' (L), notes the primary role of pitch in contrastive accent, but questions whether the latter is really a special kind of accent or only a particular way in which a more general kind of pitch contrast happens to be used at the moment. The same author reports some 'Ambiguities in Pitch Accent' (Word) in noun compounds consisting of verb plus adverb.

Shift of Meaning[29] is concerned more particularly with words whose meaning has changed but of which the form remains the same. J. R. Copley takes some 250 such words which are liable to be misunderstood because of this; under each he gives the etymology with special emphasis on meanings that have now disappeared, illustra-tive quotations taken from a wide range of authors, and usually a short note on the later developments to the modern sense. A good idea has been well carried out, and the book should prove useful to all students of English literature, not only by the actual examples given, but as a warning of the possibility of still other changes of meaning which are not here docu-mented. Popular books about words are common, and usually competently enough written, but it would be a pity if, on that account, John Moore's book[30] should be missed. It is excel-lently done; he uses the best autho-rities, and not only makes interesting and readable the information they provide, but adds a contribution from his own knowledge of dialect. All the usual subjects are dealt with—change of meaning, euphemism, the varied sources of the English vocabulary,

[27] Intonation of Colloquial English, by J. D. O'Connor and G. F. Arnold. Longmans. pp. viii+270. 10s. 6d.

[28] On Stress in Present-Day English, by A. Vanvik. Oslo: Norwegian Universities Press. pp. 108.

[29] Shift of Meaning, by J. R. Copley. O.U.P. pp. ix+166. 6s. 6d.

[30] You English Words, by John Moore. Collins. pp. 288. 21s.

dialect, &c.—but they are dealt with freshly and imaginatively, with many new and unhackneyed illustrations. The author has his prejudices, but realizes that they may be linguistically unjustified; he has many amusing anecdotes and apposite quotations, and the result is one of the best books on the subject to appear for some time. From Eric Partridge come a dozen pleasantly written and scholarly articles,[31] mostly short, on various aspects of the language. Some deal with etymology, and these are of particular interest when concerned with slang words such as *phoney* or *tanner*. Others are concerned with problems of semantics or with folk-etymology, including one on 'learned' folk-etymology. The author calls this 'a light-hearted excursion', but it contains a good deal of useful information interestingly expressed. Ivor Brown's *Words in Season*[32] is made up of the usual series of pleasantly written and discursive brief essays on a number of common and uncommon words. This time the words are linked by a continuing subject, and follow the seasons from spring to winter, though the theme is treated freely enough. Something is said about etymology and meaning, but the greater part of each article treats of the ideas which the word gives rise to in the author, with frequent quotation, especially from the poets. A second[33] book contains a selection from his various works on the subject. Readers who enjoyed his amusing and erudite articles will welcome the reappearance of this selection in Penguin Books. In 'The "Linguistic" Theory of Usage' (*The Journal of the Canadian Linguistic Association*) R. J.

Baker argues that modern linguists are guilty of inconsistency in that when dealing with words that arouse social disapproval, they abandon the contextual theory of meaning and substitute one based partly on translation and partly on reference to extra-linguistic events. It is not true, for example, to say that *ain't* has the same meaning as *isn't, haven't,* &c., since people react differently to the different words, and when a speaker uses a word that produces an effect quite different from the one he intended, we are entitled to say that he has used the 'wrong' word. J. M. Berman, 'Contribution on Blending' (*ZAA*), comments on a few recent examples of this method of word-formation, while K. Hansen, 'Makkaronische Sprachformen — Hybride Wortbildungen' (*ZAA*), notes some modern words of this type, and G. Langenfelt, 'Land and Country and Equivalents' (*L & S*; see note 9), discusses the endings used to form the names of countries or districts, whether real or fictitious, and traces something of their individual meanings in compounds. In 'Polysemantic Extensions of *Dog* and Allied Terms' (*AS*) T. B. Haber includes *bitch, cur, hound, pup, whelp*. These, along with *dog*, are often employed outside their original senses to describe new referents which fall into two groups denoting 'holding, gripping', and 'pursuit', and the various senses are classified and listed. P. Zaic, 'Zur Geschichte der Bedeutung des Suffixes *-ite* im Englischen und Amerikanischen' (*Orbis*), traces the history and meaning of the suffix as added to proper names, while J. M. Skrebnev writing 'Zum Problem der semantisch-stilistischen Analyse der englischen Phraseologie' (*ZAA*) finds that metaphor is easily the most important stylistic element, followed by metonymy, with others such as hyperbole, oxymoron, and alliteration, comparatively rare.

[31] *Adventuring Among Words*, by E. Partridge. Deutsch. pp. 70. 10s. 6d.
[32] *Words in Season*, by Ivor Brown. Hart-Davis. pp. 159. 15s.
[33] *Chosen Words*, by Ivor Brown. Harmondsworth, Middlesex: Penguin Books. pp. 284. 5s.

H. W. Bailey and A. S. C. Ross examine the etymology of 'Path' (*TPS*), and conclude that the sense 'valley' occurring in the *Lindisfarne Gospels* is adequately attested in Old English and in later northern English and Scottish, as well as in other languages. The form *pad*, found in English dialects, is due to Verner's Law, and they conclude that the word is an Iranian loan into Germanic. B. D. H. Miller, '"Mala Medicamenta, viz. Yele Syne"' (*NQ*), takes *syne* to be OE *sind* 'draught', *yele* as OE *geld* 'barren', and translates 'a useless medicine'. B. Foster contends that Shakespeare's image in '"The Seamy Side"—A Popular Etymology' (*NQ*) has been misunderstood, and that the word is really *seamy* 'greasy', while L. A. Goodman, 'Notes on the Etymology of Serendipity and Some Related Philological Observations' (*MLN*), discusses the etymology of *Serendip* 'Ceylon', the appearance of the word in English, and the change in meaning from Walpole's 'accidental sagacity' to the modern sense. A. F. Moe traces the history and use of the phrase '"Tell That (It) to the Marines"' (*AS*), W. A. Heflin investigates the history of 'Astronautics' (*AS*), and I. W. Russell, 'Among the New Words' (*AS*), lists, with quotations, new additions to the vocabulary.

The usual corrections to *O.E.D.* include Alison Hanham, 'The Cely Papers and the Oxford English Dictionary' (*ES*), who illustrates the use of thirty-six words not recorded in *O.E.D.* and of some ninety-seven words, forms, or senses first quoted by *O.E.D.* from a later date. In addition, the following articles appear in *NQ*: B. D. H. Miller, '"Dame Sirith" and the O.E.D.'; N. Davis, '"Coal-House"'; R. J. Schoeck, 'Inns of Court Nomenclature: "Moots" and "Mootable"'; G. Cross, 'Some Notes on the Vocabulary of John Marston'; R. Hall,

'John Locke's Unnoticed Vocabulary', and 'Shaftesbury: Some Antedatings and New Words'; P. Dixon, ' "The Man of Manners" and O.E.D.'; Susie I. Tucker, 'Predatings from Samuel Richardson's "Familiar Letters"', and 'Pre-Datings and Additions'; C. J. Rawson, '"Finisher" 1771: An O.E.D. Antedating'; Marghanita Laski, 'Words from Betsy Sheridan's Journal', 'Words from Mrs. Gaskell', and 'Words from "Robert Elsmere"'; J. C. Maxwell, 'Words from "Popanilla"', 'Words from "Vivian Grey"', 'The Swinburne Letters and O.E.D.'; Marghanita Laski, C. Newman, R. Hall, D. J. Barr, 'O.E.D.: Earlier Quotations'; P. J. Wexler, 'The Great Nomenclator: Whewell's Contributions to Scientific Terminology'; D. J. Barr, '"Heart goes Out"'.

An excellent introduction to the study of place-names comes from K. Cameron.[34] A chapter on the technique, including a good account of the materials available, is followed by a clear description of the various types of place-name formations, and the different contributions to English place-names: Celtic, Anglo-Saxon, Scandinavian, and French. Later chapters show something of the light thrown by place-names on such subjects as archaeology, religion, settlement, political, social, and economic history, with an account of the particular problems involved in the treatment of street and minor names. An appendix gives a list of common elements in English place-names, and a good bibliography is included. The particular value of the book lies in the clear description of the various problems, the very large number of names mentioned with no loss of readability, and the excellently chosen and reproduced maps. The English Place-Name Society has needed six volumes to deal

[34] *English Place Names*, by K. Cameron. Batsford. pp. 256. 30*s*.

with the place-names of the West Riding,[35] and the fact that these have all appeared within the year is a tribute to the energy of the editor. The introduction is still to appear, and until it does, it is not easy to evaluate the mass of information provided by these volumes. Even so, it is clear that there is here much new and valuable material on political and social history, on historical geography, archaeology, lexicography, and dialect. Evidence for the extent of woods and marsh at the various periods of settlement is provided, and it is possible to delimit the British kingdom of Elmet, even though it seems to have left no particular number of Celtic names. There is a considerable Scandinavian element, and in the dales some distinctively Norwegian-Irish names. New words are added to the dictionary, e.g. OE *nōst-lǣd* (Nostell), while Ferrybridge carries back the word *ferry* for a further three and a half centuries, and *beonet* in the sense 'rushes' is taken back to the beginning of the thirteenth century. Particularly noticeable is the mass of minor names and the comparative rarity of early forms, so that it is not surprising that some of them remain obscure. The suggested etymologies are usually convincing, but *Spen* remains an enigma, and although the legends surrounding the etymology of Halifax are disposed of, no obvious one can be suggested. Professor Smith has now completed his survey of the place-names of Yorkshire, and it is clear that only he could have dealt so successfully with the problems and difficulties of the three ridings, and in particular with those of the West Riding. In addition, in a review of some recent books on the subject,

B. Dickins describes 'The Progress of English Place-Name Studies since 1901' (*Antiquity*).

Over 300 Indian place-names survive in Maryland, and in the introduction to his survey of them H. Kenny[36] comments on the ethnology and migrations of the tribes concerned, discusses some of the more fantastic explanations that have been suggested, and describes briefly his etymological methods. Most of the tribal names are identical with river names, but since these are usually primarily descriptive, it seems clear that the tribes took their names from the rivers and not vice versa. The names are dealt with in alphabetical order, and under each important one are included the modern pronunciation, its location, early spellings, the opinions of earlier writers with commentary, and the author's own explanation. In most cases he is able to suggest a plausible etymology, though some, e.g. Allegheny and Antietam, remain obscure. Names such as Oldfield, Oldtown, and those in which an Indian is prefixed to an ordinary English word, should perhaps not have been included, and some of the genuine Indian names are later importations, e.g. Klondike, Ohio, Oklahoma. An appendix lists a number of extinct, misspelled, and scantily documented names which are apparently Indian, and an adequate map is included. In 'Pacific Place Names and the History of Discovery' (*AS*) E. V. K. Dobbie deals with the origin of some of the Spanish, French, and English names on the Pacific coast.

A. W. Reed[37] includes in his dictionary all the best known and more important of the Maori place-names,

---

[35] *The Place-Names of the West Riding of Yorkshire, Parts I-VI*, by A. H. Smith. E.P.N.S., vols. xxx-xxxv. C.U.P. pp. xi+346; xi+321; xiii+278; xii+262; xii+222; xii+274. 35s. each vol.

[36] *The Origin and Meaning of the Indian Place Names of Maryland*, by H. Kenny. Baltimore: Waverly Press. pp. xix+186. $7.

[37] *A Dictionary of Maori Place Names*, by A. W. Reed. Wellington: A. H. & A. W. Reed. pp. 144. 12s. 6d.

along with some not now in use. The names are broken up into their various components, the meanings given, and if possible a meaning suggested for the whole word, though it is emphasized that this can rarely be more than tentative, and that not infrequently more than one is possible. Occasionally the English name of the place is given, and an appendix lists such names with reference to the Maori ones. The book will prove useful to the place-name scholar as showing something of the types of names in use, but a map should have been given.

W. N. Francis, 'Some Dialectal Verb Forms in England' (*Orbis*), using information gathered for the linguistic atlas of England, plots on maps the different dialectal forms of various verbs, and compares some of the distributions with those described for the eastern United States.

Three of the articles in H. Galinsky's work on American English[38] deal with the language. In the first, American English is used to show the connexion between the language and the history of the settlement, while the other two deal with aspects of the relations between British and American English. O. L. Abbott, 'The Formal Subjunctive in Seventeenth-Century American English' (*AS*), gives examples of its use; L. Kissane notes instances of 'Dangling Constructions in Melville's "Bartleby"' (*AS*), and H. Koziol, in 'Zu Neubildungen und Lehnwörtern im amerikanischen Englisch' (*Orbis*), describes the development of a number of new phrases of the type *up-and-down*, new formations in *-age, -ee*, &c., a number of blends, and some loanwords from German.

An important work on the language of the eastern states[39] deals with the

source material, discusses the problem of interpreting the phonic record in phonemic terms, and gives an outline of the vowel system which has been set up. Eight of the main dialects of the area are outlined briefly, and an appendix gives details of the 157 informants. The regional and social differences in the pronunciation of the vowel phonemes are described, along with any positional allophones, and with a full discussion of the vowels before tautosyllabic and intersyllabic *r*. A description of the regional and socially varying incidence of vowel and consonant phonemes in the vocabulary is followed by the maps. The first four of these are general, giving the location of the informants, the speech areas, density of population at various periods, and the glides of the high and mid vowels. The remainder show the distribution of most of the illustrative examples used in the preliminary description. When cultivated usage differs more or less strikingly from that of the middle and lower classes, the latter is shown in an inset, and in addition, English dialect usage is sometimes given on a small-scale map of the southern counties. This is a particularly important work; one which has drawn on all the resources of modern dialectology, and presents the results lucidly and clearly in an excellently produced volume in which the numerous maps are particularly striking. T. H. Wetmore[40] analyses and describes, with numerous maps and diagrams, the low-central and low-back vowels, their phonic characteristics, and their incidence, in eight selected areas of the eastern United States, while in 'The "New

Atlantic States, by H. Kurath and R. I. McDavid. Michigan U.P. pp. xi+182. 180 maps. $15.

[38] *Sprache und Sprachkunstwerk in Amerika*, by H. Galinsky. Heidelberg: Quelle & Meyer. pp. 208. DM. 11.

[39] *The Pronunciation of English in the*

[40] *The Low-Central and Low-Back Vowels in the English of the Eastern United States*, by T. H. Wetmore. Publication of the American Dialect Society Number 32. pp. ix+131. $4.

England Short o": A Recessive Phoneme' (L) W. S. Avis shows that if usage in a given community is divided for a particular word, the recessive phoneme /e/ usually occurs, alone or beside /o/, in the speech of the older and less educated, and the innovating phoneme /o/, alone or beside /e/, in the speech of the younger and better educated. G. R. Wood[41] deals with the regional distribution of selected Midland and Southern words in the states of the interior South. The resulting maps provide evidence of likely major linguistic boundaries in the region, and explain the distribution in terms of settlement history. In 'Lexical Usage in Southern Louisiana'[42] M. Babington and E. Bagby Atwood are mainly concerned with six Louisiana parishes in the heart of the Acadian area. They give a short account of the settlement, compare the words found in Louisiana with those which occur also in the eastern states and the different responses of older and younger informants, and note the survival of French terms. A. L. Hench, 'A Southern Geographical Word List' (AS), gives a list of earlier or previously unrecorded words. C. T. Hankey, 'Semantic Features and Eastern Relics in Colorado Dialect' (AS), illustrates some interesting semantic developments that accompany the more clearcut dialectal characteristics of pronunciation, grammar, and vocabulary, along with some eastern dialect items that are rare in Colorado and may be regarded as relics. In 'The Pronunciation of English in the Pacific Northwest' (L) C. E. Reed points out that varieties of American English spoken in this area are largely derived from eastern sources. Items of widespread

occurrence in the Atlantic states are common here, where also Northern and North Midland forms are strongly represented. Midland forms are in a minority generally, but are more prominent in eastern Washington, Oregon, and Idaho, while Northern forms are particularly frequent in the Puget Sound area, where too the old New England settlement area preserves a number of New England relic forms. C. E. Reed, 'Double Dialect Geography' (Orbis), points out some of the problems of dialectology when combined with those of bilingualism, as in the south-eastern section of Pennsylvania, and J. A. Drake investigates 'The Effect of Urbanization on Regional Vocabulary' (AS), the region chosen being Cleveland. In the 'Phonological Rules of a Subdialect of English' (Word) by J. R. Applegate, the dialect in question is that of three children, and it is claimed that the description of their special language provides an insight into the development of language. In addition, T. G. Lish gives a 'Word List of Construction Terms',[43] restricted to those common to all classes of workers in the heavy construction trade.

The first part of Jamaica Talk[44] deals with history, pronunciation, and grammar, the second with vocabulary. Jamaicanisms are first defined and classified according to their types, and then considered under the various aspects of life with which they deal. The American Indian element in the vocabulary is slight and comes mainly through Spanish and Portuguese; there is a wider range of original Spanish and Portuguese words, little French influence, and contributions from Dutch and oriental languages are almost negligible. Of non-British

[41] Word Distribution in the Interior South, by G. R. Wood. Publication of the American Dialect Society Number 35. pp. 27.
[42] In Publication of the American Dialect Society Number 36.
[43] In Publication of the American Dialect Society Number 36.
[44] Jamaica Talk, by F. G. Cassidy. Macmillan. pp. ix+468. 30s.

influences African is easily the largest, though even so, the whole of the non-British element including mixed compounds is less than 10 per cent. The British element has often been altered in form, and of particular interest here is the large number of words, obsolete in British and American English, which are still in use in Jamaica. So far as pronunciation and grammar are concerned, there has been a powerful negative influence from African, while peculiarities of intonation are also to be traced to African influence. This is a thorough and scholarly study of the subject, containing a mass of information about many aspects of Jamaican life skilfully woven into an interesting narrative. In 'South African English Pronunciation' (*English Studies in Africa*) D. Hopwood illustrates and explains various differences between British and South African English. The latter can be seen as a more or less unified derivative of English dialects (chiefly Cockney and Northern English), which is being increasingly modified by contact with Afrikaans.

Mention should also be made of a bibliography of the writings of E. Ekwall,[45] and of an interesting description of 'English Studies at the Moscow State University' (*ZAA*) by O. S. Akhmanova and E. M. Mednikova.

[45] *The Published Writings of Eilert Ekwall*, compiled by O. von Feilitzen. Lund Studies in English 30. Lund: Gleerup. pp. 52.

III. OLD ENGLISH LITERATURE

By R. M. WILSON

THE Saxon Shore is one of the most interesting of the problems connected with the transition from Roman Britain to Saxon England. D. A. White[1] examines available evidence on the subject and concludes that the forts were erected by the usurpers Carausius and Allectus to defend themselves against an expected counter-attack by Roman forces. They had no connexion with the Saxons, and the name only appeared during the fourth century when the forts were reactivated to meet the threat of the Saxon invasions. C. Brooke[2] gives a clear description of English history from the reign of Alfred to that of Henry III. The introduction deals judiciously with the sources, archaeological and artistic as well as literary, and contains also a good account of medieval ideas and of the similarities and contrasts between medieval life and that of the present day. The next four chapters deal with the Anglo-Saxon period and the Conquest, the political and military history being described briefly, and with the stress on social and economic affairs. The author is fully at home with his subject, up to date with his information, and he writes well and interestingly. Excellently chosen illustrations and good maps help to make this a good general history of the period which students will find useful, and which may lead them on to the more detailed studies listed in the bibliography. An authoritative work on the

Vikings comes from H. Arbman.[3] The main stress is on archaeology, but the political, economic, and social history of the period is also covered, and particularly interesting are the chapters dealing with the expeditions of the Swedish Vikings to Russia, and with Viking art. The book has been well translated by A. L. Binns who also contributes a valuable introduction on Viking ships and weapons. P. Compton[4] gives a good popular account of the last Saxon king, making use of the standard literary authorities, both primary and secondary. Our information is scanty, and there are many gaps which the author is wisely content to accept, but no attempt is made to assess the differing value of the sources for the various events, perhaps because this would hinder the free flow of the narrative. Certainly, the result is an imaginatively written narrative which the reader can accept as a fair portrait of Harold, and a vivid description of the period.

In an interesting and learned book Margaret Deanesly[5] deals in detail with the pre-Conquest church from the first appearance of Christianity during the Roman period to the reign of the Confessor. She makes good use of all the various types of evidence: archaeology, literature, official documents, place-names, and coins, but some of the conclusions are perhaps more doubtful

[1] Litus Saxonicum, by D. A. White. Madison: The State Historical Society of Wisconsin for The Department of History, University of Wisconsin. pp. iii+122. $3.50.
[2] From Alfred to Henry III, by C. Brooke. Nelson. pp. xii+276. 21s.
[3] The Vikings, by H. Arbman, translated by A. L. Binns. Thames and Hudson. pp. 212. Plates 67. 30s.
[4] Harold the King, by P. Compton. Hale. pp. 191. 21s.
[5] The Pre-Conquest Church in England, by Margaret Deanesly. A. & C. Black. pp. vii+374. 38s.

than she suggests, and not all the material included is strictly relevant. Professor Deanesly has a wide knowledge of the Anglo-Saxon and Latin manuscripts of the period, and is particularly good on the contributions of the Celtic church to religion and art. All aspects of the subject are dealt with: religious organization, the liturgy, art, architecture, literature, and the influence of Christianity on the language. The book gives a fascinating if rather disorganized account of Anglo-Saxon church history, and succeeds also in fitting it into the wider context of religious life on the continent.

The value of coin evidence for our knowledge of the Anglo-Saxon period has only comparatively recently been recognized. Much remains to be done, but the articles in an excellently produced volume of essays[6] will form an invaluable foundation for a future definitive study of Anglo-Saxon coinage. As is to be expected, most of them are strictly technical; they establish the chronology of the issues of various kings, discuss Byzantine influence on the coinage, the connexion of the boroughs with the mints, and the metrology of the late Anglo-Saxon penny. Of more general interest is Dorothy Whitelock's article on 'The Numismatic Interest of an OE Version of the Legend of the Seven Sleepers', though in fact the apparent numismatic interest turns out to be merely an attempt by the translator to make sense out of a corrupt original. Nevertheless, the OE text does provide three otherwise unrecorded minting terms. But the whole volume, with its excellent series of plates and maps, is an important contribution to our knowledge of Anglo-Saxon England. The second volume of the *Sylloge of Coins*

of the British Isles[7] deals with the Hunterian and Coats collections of Glasgow University which between them contain over 1,200 Anglo-Saxon coins. The introduction describes briefly the formation and history of the collections, and then follow the plates. The opposite page contains a brief introduction to the coins of each king, information on the individual coin, its weight in grammes and in grains; the die position is indicated, and the legends and descriptions of the coins are given as fully as possible. Indexes of kings, archbishops, mints, moneyers, and find spots are also included.

R. C. Alston[8] provides a competent, concise, and well-presented introduction to Old English. The opening chapter deals with the usual subjects— the Old English dialects, orthography, pronunciation. In the grammar the paradigms are given in bold-face type, but the simplification of the noun declensions goes perhaps too far, and it is difficult to see why *stān, dæg, tungol, sunu, guma*, should all be included in the one masculine declension. Syntax and word-order are dealt with in much greater detail than usual, as also the phonology. A number of elementary exercises are given, along with various texts, divided more or less equally between prose and poetry, in which the author has wisely avoided the temptation to normalize the spelling. Notes, glossary, a selective bibliography, and three maps complete a good introduction to the subject in which the sections on syntax, word-order, and phonology are particularly well done. Here, too, should be

[6] *Anglo-Saxon Coins. Studies Presented to F. M. Stenton on the Occasion of his 80th Birthday*, edited by R. H. M. Dolley. Methuen. pp. xv+296. 16 Plates. 63s.

[7] *Sylloge of Coins of the British Isles: Hunterian and Coats Collections, University of Glasgow. Part I, Anglo-Saxon Coins*, by Anne S. Robertson. O.U.P. and Spink & Son for The British Academy. pp. viii+88. 42 Plates. 63s.

[8] *An Introduction to Old English*, by R. C. Alston. Toronto: The Copp Clarke Publishing Co. pp. xii+167. $4.25.

mentioned a fourth edition of Clark Hall's invaluable dictionary.[9] This is a reprint of the third, but with a twenty-page supplement by H. D. Meritt containing some 1,700 additional words and, equally important, pointing out that over 200 words or meanings appearing in the earlier editions have no justification and should be deleted. Much of the new material comes from Meritt's own work on the glosses, but the different contributions to Anglo-Saxon lexicography made by other scholars are also recorded. H. A. Benning[10] investigates certain elements of the Old English vocabulary, his three sections dealing respectively with the words for 'heaven', 'earth', and 'world', while appendixes consider words of related meanings, *wynn, cnēo, cynn, feorh, fierhþ, ielde,* and *ealdor.* In every case the etymology of the particular word is discussed, and its different meanings given, along with its appearance in various contexts in Old English poetry.

D. M. Zesmer's guide to Old and Middle English literature[11] is factual, clear, and concise. The illustrative quotations, usually given in translation, are well chosen, there are some useful maps and illustrations, and the annotated bibliographies compiled by S. B. Greenfield are particularly good. Within the space available only the more important works can be dealt with at any length, and for the others only brief accounts are possible, though even here occasional illuminating remarks are not infrequent. The

Old English section is introduced by a competent survey of the historical and linguistic background, while the poetry in general, and *Beowulf* in particular, is well described, with a useful indication of recent scholarship. The prose is treated much more briefly and perhaps hardly gets its fair share of attention.

In 'Some Notes on Anglo-Saxon Poetry'[12] F. P. Magoun, Jr., points out that while the religious poets were able to adapt much of the traditional diction, the traditional themes could only rarely be appropriated. However, in addition to 'the beasts of battle', two such themes appear at least twice, 'the grateful recipient' and 'the gesture of the raised shield and/or brandished spear'. Examples of these are given, and it is also noted that the device of 'the temporary misinterpretation of a sight or sound creating suspense and then surprise', though found in Old English only in the opening lines of the *Finnesburg Fragment,* is common in the *Kalevala,* and may also be traditional. A final note suggests that the excellence of *Maldon* may to some extent depend on the fact that it is the work of a poet dealing with just the kind of material for which most of the diction was originally created. R. E. Diamond, 'Theme as Ornament in Anglo-Saxon Poetry' (*PMLA*), analyses the use of some themes in the poetry, including from *Elene* the theme of battle and that of a sea voyage, the latter of which turns up also in *Christ II* and in *The Gifts of Men.* Other themes include that of exile occurring in *The Death of Eadgar* and in *Andreas,* in the second of which it appears as a component of the themes of comitatus loyalty and battle. Similarly, other passages are in effect a blend of two

[9] *A Concise Anglo-Saxon Dictionary,* by J. R. Clark Hall. Fourth edition with a Supplement by H. D. Meritt. C.U.P. pp. xv+452. 40s.

[10] *'Welt' und 'Mensch' in der Altenglisch Dichtung,* by H. A. Benning. Beiträge zur englischen Philologie 44. Bochum-Langendreer: Pöppinghaus. pp. ii+241. DM. 30.

[11] *Guide to English Literature. From Beowulf through Chaucer and Medieval Drama,* by D. M. Zesmer. New York: Barnes & Noble. pp. xi+397. $2.25.

[12] In *Studies in Medieval Literature in Honor of Professor Albert Croll Baugh,* ed. by MacEdward Leach. Pennsylvania U.P. pp. 344. $7.50.

or more themes, and if more of the poetry had survived we might be able to work out in detail how the various themes are related to each other. Because of this interrelation of theme, the more we understand about the way in which the poems were put together, the less certainly we can pronounce on the relationships of them to each other.

An examination of *Beowulf* in conjunction with the various Scandinavian analogues leads G. V. Smithers[13] to conclude that the poet received the two main episodes in a combined form, and did not himself combine two distinct stories. The dragon was evidently identical with the 'last survivor'—though possibly the poet has not understood this—and clearly belongs to the same order of beings as Grendel and his mother. Hence 'the central fable of Beowulf is *aesthetically* a unity, so far as this kind of unity may be supposed to depend on the homogeneity of the two main parts of the story'. Further examination of the dragon episode suggests that, like the first part, this too represents an already advanced stage in the transmission of a traditional tale, but the ending of the poem in the death of the hero may well be the author's own alteration of the inherited ending. There is much more of interest in the article, but these are perhaps the main conclusions. As argued here they are not entirely convincing; there is a tendency to use only the evidence which supports his own view and to ignore that which does not, but the promised book on the subject may be able to deal more fully with objections that must be ignored in a comparatively short article. In 'The Diction of *Beowulf*' (*PMLA*) W. Whallon believes that the formulaic theory is not incompatible with other theories of origin. In comparison with the *Iliad* and the *Odyssey* Anglo-Saxon

poetry appears to have no comparable amount of repetition; its diction is much less completely stereotyped, and on this basis *Beowulf* may be taken to represent an earlier stage in the development of an oral poem than do the Homeric poems. J. Taglicht, '*Beowulf* and Old English Verse Rhythm' (*RES*), claims that the various theories divide on the question of whether Old English verse had a 'musical' or 'non-musical' rhythm. But in dealing with such theories we must beware of relying on deductions from alleged general principles of rhythm which are in reality mere generalizations from our own habits and predilections. Sievers and Bliss are taken as examples of those advocating a rhythmical interpretation, but while Bliss concentrates on rhythmical distinctions which are relevant to the metre and which Sievers tends to gloss over, he achieves this only at the cost of obscuring the fundamental regularity of the structure behind a mass of detail. On the other hand, none of the methods of scansion based on the division of the verse into bars or measures of equal duration is free from serious weaknesses. It would seem clear that the metre has a quantitative or chronometric framework, and that the verse rhythm is based essentially on the rhythm of speech. Consequently, the measures of Old English alliterative verse are most likely to have been of equal length, and a system of scansion is proposed based on these considerations, in which the half-lines are divided into five main classes with various subdivisions of the first three. As usual, the criticism of established theories carries more conviction than Taglicht's own classification. An interesting article on 'Das Zeitgefühl im altenglischen *Beowulf*-Epos' (*Antaios*) comes from T. Finkenstaedt, while S. Einarsson, in 'Beowulfian Place Names in East Iceland'

[13] *The Making of Beowulf*, by G. V. Smithers. Durham U.P. pp. 26. 2s. 6d.

(*MLN*), notes a few place-names which might have some possible connexion with the *Beowulf* story, but in all cases the connexion, if any, is very slight.

F. L. Henry, '*Beowulf* Cruces' (*Zeitschrift für vergleichende Sprachforschung auf dem Gebiete der Indogermanischen Sprachen*), deals with (i) the epithets used of Beowulf's sword Nægling. *Ærgōd* is taken to mean 'good of old', *unglēaw* 'very bright', with a junction of Celtic meaning and English form, while *incgelāfe* may be a form of *inga lāf* 'remnant of (battle)-straits', with *ing* as a borrowing from Celtic. (ii) *eoletes* is derived from Northumbrian *ēo* 'water' and non-WS *geletes*, hence 'water course, sea passage', while (iii) the second element of *ealuscerwen* (*Beowulf*), *meoduscerwen* (*Andreas*) is taken to represent Old Irish *seirbe* 'bitterness'. From an original meaning 'the bitterness of the chieftain's ale to men who have to pay with their lives for it', the compound came to have the sense 'dire distress', and references are given from Welsh and Old English in support of such a meaning. K. Malone, 'A Note on "Beowulf" 489-90' (*MLR*), takes *meoto* in these lines as the imperative of *metgian* 'meditate, reflect', *sæl* as 'success', and reads *sige Hreðsecgum*, translating, 'Sit down now to the feast and think to your heart's content on success, victory for the Geats'. In 'Folklore and Beowulf's Defense of Heorot' (*ES*) D. H. Reiman notes parallels between this and a Celtic folk story of 'The Hand and the Child' type, suggesting that the fight with Grendel owes much to this motif, whereas the descent into Grendel's cavern derives from a variant of 'The Bear's Son Tale'. E. Adelaide Hahn believes that in the phrase 'Wæs Hrunting nama' (*L*) the word for 'name' was originally in partitive apposition with the word denoting the

owner of the name, and brings forward objections to the theory that the word for 'name' is used in apposition with the proper name, while H. C. Matthes, 'Hygd',[14] gives a general survey of the problems connected with the episode, and a detailed commentary on lines 1925-62 of the poem, and R. Willard reads for '*Beowulf* 2672b: līg ȳðum fōr' (*MLN*) in place of Pope's *līg ȳ ðum fōr*, with the translation 'flame advanced in waves'.

A revision of K. Malone's standard edition of *Deor*[15] takes into account work on the poem since the original publication, adds three new conclusions to the survey of the poem, and greatly expands the bibliography. In addition, a number of unobtrusive changes in the introduction and notes bring the new edition completely up to date and greatly increase its value to students of Old English. G. Langenfelt, 'Foreign Names in Old English: A Comparison between Alfred's "Orosius" and "Widsith"' (*NM*), assumes that the *Widsith* poet was unlettered and had been listening to a lector who read out of a book or told stories, hence some of the confusing names in the poem. He lists various names from Alfred's *Orosius* which would be difficult to explain if it were not for the Latin, classifies the different types of change illustrated, and concludes that, in comparison with Alfred, the *Widsith* poet did comparatively well. A note is added on *Iringes weg*, a name for the Milky Way in the *Epinal Glosses*. This is taken to be a scribal error for *Sciringes weg*, the first element of which is to be connected with Alfred's *Sciringes heal*.

Three of the most difficult of the Old English poems have been admirably

[14] In *Festschrift zum 75. Geburtstag von Theodor Spira.* Heidelberg: Winter. pp. 405.
[15] *Deor*, by Kemp Malone. 3rd edition. Methuen. pp. viii+40. 8s. 6d.

edited by R. F. Leslie.[16] All three contain enough detail to suggest that they may form parts of some larger story, and the result has been the elaboration of many theories on the subject. The editor deals judiciously with these, and in particular points out that those assuming a connexion between *The Wife's Lament* and *The Husband's Message* require us to supply much of the plot ourselves without any explicit justification from the texts. The introduction includes an analysis of each of the poems, discussion of their sources, and appreciations of their literary qualities. A good case is made out for the traditional identification of *The Ruin* with Bath, and it is suggested that the description would hardly have been applicable later than the first half of the eighth century. In fact, it would seem that all three were probably composed sometime during that century and in an Anglian dialect —probably Mercian. The texts themselves have been edited from the manuscript, and the textual notes are full and informative, especially in syntactical matters, the critical acumen of the editor being particularly evident in his discussion of suggested emendations. R. W. V. Elliott, 'Form and Image in the Old English Lyrics' (*EC*), claims that the Anglo-Saxon poets possessed a definite sense of form, and if this is best demonstrated in the shorter secular lyrics, some of the characteristics illustrated here appear also in the longer poems. He makes use of the elegies to show that the poets display a far surer sense of form and a more developed architectonic skill than they are often credited with. There are interesting suggestions here, but not all are equally convincing, and some of the interpretations

would hardly command general agreement.

In 'Cædmon and English Poetry' (*MLN*) K. Malone emphasizes Cædmon's originality as the first to change the inherited formulas of heroic verse so as to make them applicable to the Christian God.

In recent years a good deal of work on *Andreas* has appeared, more especially the publication of the Latin versions of the legend. The time was ripe for a new edition of the poem, and this, along with one of *The Fates of the Apostles*, has been most ably carried out by K. R. Brooks.[17] A brief introduction deals capably with the usual subjects. Brooks would put the *Andreas* later than the signed poems of Cynewulf, with whom he sees no reason to connect it. The language indicates a date for the originals not much later than the middle of the ninth century, and provides no evidence to show that the poem ever existed in a West Mercian or even an Anglian original. In general, the editor maintains a cautious attitude, and is unwilling to go further than the evidence will allow—which is not very far. More on the literary qualities of the poem would have been welcome, but in the main we are referred to Krapp for this. A complete glossary adds something to the standard dictionaries, and the commentary is particularly helpful, whether by the translation of difficult passages or by the judicious explanation of particular problems. The text has been treated as conservatively as possible, and the textual apparatus reduced to a minimum without omitting anything of value. N. F. Blake, 'Originality in "The Phoenix"' (*NQ*), points out that the Old English poet was not the first to christianize the *Carmen de ave phoenice*, but was probably following a tradition which

[16] *Three Old English Elegies*: The Wife's Lament, The Husband's Message, The Ruin, by R. F. Leslie. Manchester U.P. pp. xii+86. 12s. 6d.

[17] Andreas *and* The Fates of the Apostles, by K. R. Brooks. O.U.P. pp. liv+184. 38s.

interpreted the Lactantian poem in a Christian way, several of the features claimed as original being found already in the ninth-century *Life of St. Eligius*.

In 'The Heroic Style in *The Battle of Maldon*' (*SP*) E. B. Irving divides the poem into two parts, the first dealing with the beginning of the battle to the death of Byrhtnoth, the second with the individual speeches and actions of the surviving retainers. The first part is dominated by a plain, concrete style which contrasts with the epic style of tradition, there being a marked tendency in *Maldon* for the two styles to alternate. Epic diction becomes noticeably more frequent as the poem goes on, and has the result of raising a historical event to a higher level of significance. An analysis of the poem shows that the author has not been able to use many of the resources of the epic poet—the romantic glamour of antiquity, or the use of familiar plot and heroes—but he has nevertheless known instinctively how to use a style to suggest this epic world and to make it function as part of his own poem.

Janet M. Bately, 'King Alfred and the Latin MSS of Orosius' *History*' (*Classica et Mediaevalia*), from a careful examination of the Latin manuscripts of Orosius's *History*, is able to define the relationship of Alfred's version to the two groups of manuscripts of the Latin text distinguished by Zangemeister, and to reconstruct some of the major features of the Latin text lying immediately behind the Old English translation. It then becomes possible to distinguish a large number of errors in Alfred's exemplar from those which may have been introduced by Alfred himself or by some later scribe. A realistic examination of Alfred's treatment of his source, and especially of the proper names in it, can then be made, though it is emphasized that there can never be absolute certainty as to which corruptions occurred already in the Latin and which are to be attributed to Alfred himself. A. L. Binns, 'Ohtheriana VI: Ohthere's Northern Voyage' (*EG*), examines the account of this in the light of the experience of modern Hull trawler skippers, and concludes that, although some features remain puzzling, Ohthere deserves our admiration as an extremely prudent and skilful mariner who in the light of a vague general knowledge of the area, and a very good knowledge of the wind system of the North Sea and the Norwegian coast, chose the only conditions for his voyage in which it could reasonably be carried through.

In an earlier article (*YW* xxxix. 53) S. R. Levin had argued that the contracted forms of verbs with the negative particle were distinctively West Saxon. From this point of view, in an article 'On the Authenticity of Five "Wulfstan" Homilies' (*JEGP*), he examines Napier I, XL, XLIII, XLIV, XLV. Since there are no examples of uncontracted forms in the homilies generally agreed to be by Wulfstan, the presence of them in these five renders them suspect. Barbara M. H. Strang, 'Two Wulfstan Expressions' (*NQ*), provides evidence to show that Wulfstan's frequent appeal to the authority of unspecified books is to be taken as referring to the Bible, and that *stric* in the same author probably has the sense 'violence'. C. L. Smetana, 'Ælfric and the Homiliary of Haymo of Halberstadt' (*T*), shows that whilst Ælfric specifically mentions Haymo as a source in two of his homilies, in addition another twenty-five owe something to the same author, ranging from literal translations, sometimes quite lengthy, through illustrations and explanations from Scripture to mere Scriptural allusions or quotations, so that Ælfric's debt to Haymo is clearly much greater than had previously been recognized. In addition, R. L. Collins

(*TLS*, p. 201) announces the acquisition by the Lilly Library at Indiana University of a fragment of Ælfric's *Grammar* (Ker, No. 384) which was originally part of the same codex as Ker, No. 242, and E. Colledge notes 'An Allusion to Augustine in Ælfric's Colloquy' (*RES*). K. Malone collates, with comments, 'Readings from Folios 94 to 131, MS. Cotton Vitellius A XV'[18] with the edition of these texts by Rypins for the E.E.T.S.

On the glosses, H. D. Meritt prints a number of 'Old English Glosses, Mostly Dry Point' (*JEGP*) from eighteen manuscripts of varying dates. He corrects also two quotations in the Bosworth–Toller *Supplement*, and provides evidence to show that *flustriende*, glossing *plectentis*, may have the meaning 'flattering, blandishing'. J. J. Quinn, 'Ghost Words, Obscure Lemmata, and Doubtful Glosses in a Latin-Old English Glossary' (*PQ*), discusses sixteen words found on ff. 76r–117r of Cotton Cleopatra A III and printed in Wright–Wülcker. He solves a number of lemmata and glosses which had given difficulty, and shows that some of the glosses have resulted in ghost-words. G. C. Britton, 'Aldrediana IV: The E- and I-Diphthongs' (*EG*), summarizes Luick's conclusions, which are apparently still valid, as to the fate of IE *eu* in the *Lindisfarne Gospels*, and comments upon some of the apparent confusions, but adds little to what was already known. R. L. Thomson, 'Aldrediana V: Celtica' (*EG*), deals with a small group of words, peculiar in form or meaning to the Aldredian texts, in each of which Celtic influence may be suspected. These include *assald, biscop, carchern, diouol, ceaul, Iordanen, cursað/cursung*. A. S. C. Ross, 'Aldrediana XIV: *Felle-*

Read' (*NM*), argues that the word is a mistake for *pelleread* but that for some reason this was not recognized by Aldred who consistently altered it. Barbara Raw prints 'A Latin–English Word-List in MS. Arundel 60' (*EG*) written in a mid-fourteenth-century hand in the margins of ff. 8–11 of the manuscript. She concludes that the writer seems to have been working from a glossed Psalter of the Anglo-Saxon period.

An important work on the Old English charters comes from H. P. R. Finberg.[19] The introduction indicates the main sources of the material dealt with, and is followed by a calendar, with critical and explanatory notes of some 400 documents relating to the West Midlands before 1066. The relative authenticity of each document is shown, former identifications are not infrequently corrected, and two hitherto unpublished boundary surveys and a charter are printed, translated, and commented on. The second part consists of eight articles dealing with some of the particular problems on which light is thrown by the charter material, and includes also the publication of a further five previously unpublished charters. The discussions deal with the early history of Gloucester Abbey, the princes of the Hwicce, Offa of Essex, the Hallow–Hawling charter, St. Mildburg's testament, the princes of the Magonsæte, Bishop Athelstan's boundary, and a delineation of the ancient shire of Winchcombe. The first part of this work will prove indispensable to students of Anglo-Saxon history, while in the second the author shows something of the information which a historian as well equipped as he is himself can draw from such materials. 'Old English *scipsteall*' (*SN*) occurs only once, in a

[18] In *Studies in Medieval Literature in Honor of Professor Albert Croll Baugh*, ed. by MacEdward Leach. Pennsylvania U.P. pp. 344. $7.50.

[19] *The Early Charters of the West Midlands*, by H. P. R. Finberg. Leicester U.P. pp. 256. 50s.

charter of Edgar dated 962. R. Fors-
berg produces evidence to indicate
that the word denotes here some kind
of landing-place, and is to be distinguished from *sceapstall* 'place for
sheep' which is common in place-
names where it has similar forms.

On runes, R. I. Page examines the
evidence for 'The Old English Rune
ear' (*MÆ*), and decides that there is
no justification for the theory that it
was a comparatively late development.
It would seem that when Germanic
au was monophthongized in Anglo-
Frisian, a new rune, patterned on those
of the Anglo-Frisian runes for *a* and *o*,
was created to represent the monophthong. This rune did not survive
in Frisian because there the monophthong developed to *a* and came to
be represented by the *a*-rune. In Old
English the monophthong was diph-
thongized, the *ear*-rune being used for
the diphthong thus developed and then
for the other diphthongs which fell in
with it.

IV. MIDDLE ENGLISH, EXCLUDING CHAUCER

By A. MACDONALD and BETTY HILL

IN these days of extreme specialization it is most unusual to encounter a book covering so large a period as the Middle Ages; yet that is what Professor W. T. H. Jackson, of Columbia University, has bravely attempted.[1] Jackson's aims are quite clearly stated in his introduction; his work is intended for the general literate reader, it is not a history of medieval European literature (it concentrates on the twelfth and thirteenth centuries), it is selective even during these centuries, and it makes no claim to novelty of treatment or material. The reader is given a voluminous bibliography in order to pursue his study further. Having made this clear, Jackson proceeds to a discussion first of the survival and influence of the Classics, the reasons for writing literature, the audience for medieval literature, and the literary types, then gives six chapters devoted to a study of the various genres, the romance, *chanson de geste*, drama, &c. These are not all of equal worth, but one may recommend in all sincerity the three general chapters which initiate the genre discussions. The huge bibliographies must be used with caution; the reader in England has access to many paper-backed editions which apparently Jackson has not seen, or at any rate does not mention.

A few articles have appeared during the year on the debatable land between Old and Middle English. In 'A ghost-

word: *crucethūs*' (*ES*), Johan Gerritsen observes that in the important account of Stephen's reign in the *Peterborough Chronicle sub* 1137, the MS. correctly reads *crucethur*, a *hapax legomenon*. He provisionally accepts the etymology *cruciator*, after noting that it has not been explained 'why a word which, if applied to an instrument of torture at all, could be applied to all and any of them should describe this particular torture box'.

The interpretation of *areʒe* as 'coward, dastard, sneak' or 'arrow' and the use of *will* to express futurity are the main points in the *Proverbs of Alfred* discussed by O. Arngart, '*Seiʒe þu it noht þe areʒe* PA(M) 204', and G. Storms, '*Ne say þu hit þin areʒe* PA(T) 204' (both *ES*).

A. Macdonald, in 'An Anglo-Saxon Survival?' (*NQ*), draws an interesting parallel between the duties of Christina, the noble twelfth-century recluse of Markyate, as cup-bearer at the Gild merchant banquet, as described in the fourteenth-century Latin MS. (*YW* xl. 66) and those of Hroðgar's queen and daughter mentioned in *Beowulf*.

Two notes have appeared on the *Ancrene Riwle*; in 'The Titles of "MSS. A B"' (*MLN*) William J. Stevens remarks on the agreement of the uncommon titles of MSS. CCCC 402 (MS. A, *Ancrene Riwle*) and Bodley 34 (MS. B, *Katherine Group*), which sets these manuscripts apart from others of the *Ancrene Riwle* and *Katherine Group* and offers further proof of their surprisingly close relationship; C. A. Ladd, in 'A Note on

[1] *The Literature of the Middle Ages*, by W. T. H. Jackson. Columbia U.P. pp. xvi+ 432. 48s.

the Language of the *Ancrene Riwle*'
(*NQ*), considers the linguistic forms to
be assumed for the original version of
the text. The distribution of *mid* and
wið common to MS. A (CCCC 402),
G. (Gonville & Caius), and C (Cleopatra) must go back to a common
original. It is difficult to assume that in
these instances the Nero MS. (which
is not textually independent of the
group represented by G, C, and A and
shows particular kinship with G) best
preserved the language of the original.
E. J. Dobson, in 'A New Edition of
The Owl and the Nightingale' (*NQ*),
includes a stimulating discussion of
the rhyme evidence which suggests a
dialect bordering on Kent but not
Kentish itself, syntactic innovations
which characterize the poet's language
and reveal his preference for preposi-
tional constructions, metrical practice,
rhyming technique, and textual interpretation. Dobson's commentary reveals seven instances where the 'Jesus'
text is semantically, stylistically, or
metrically superior to the 'Cotton' text.

The phrase *we ne doz . . . breke* in the
Laud MS. of the *Early South-English
Legendary* (E.E.T.S., o.s. 87, 198/23)
has been twice listed as the earliest
example of the negative periphrastic
use of *do*; but Norman Davis suggests,
in 'The Earliest "Do Not" ' (*NQ*), that
doz is a scribal misreading of *dorre*
which the other early manuscripts of
the text have, and that the sense required is 'we dare not'. The scribe may
have thought of *doz* as a causative 'we
do not cause . . to be infringed'.

In a study which clarifies the 'Classical threads in *Orfeo*' (*MLR*), Constance Davies points out that in
Fairyland the *ympe-tre* has a significance differing from that in the first
part of the *lai*, where it is part of those
conditions reminiscent of the ritual
sacrifice demanded for sacrilege. The
tree's reappearance in the fairy king's
courtyard, in a passage unparalleled in

fairy lore, and the mingling of the kingdom of the Dead with that of Fairy,
can be explained with reference to the
classical strain. She draws instructive
parallels between the fairy king and
Dis, in the seasonal myth of Dis and
Proserpina, and between details in
the *lai* and the Celtic seasonal myth,
which took the form of the abduction
story represented by *Culhwch and
Olwen* and the *Vita Gildae*, but 'Orpheus and Eurydice' alone explains the
lack of motive for Heurodis's abduction. A comparison with the *Aeneid* vi.
273–86 reveals parallels between the
visual experiences of Aeneas in Hades
and Orfeo in Fairyland, the linking of
sleep with the idea of Death's kingdom,
and between the *ympe-tre* and Virgil's
ominous Elm of Dreams. D. M. Hill,
in 'The Structure of *Sir Orfeo*' (*MS*),
sees the *lai* in three parts (1–56, 57–476,
477–604) rather than Bliss's four (*YW*
xxxv. 47). A solution for *& wiþ a begger
her in y-nome*, '*Sir Orfeo*, l. 565',
(*Archiv*), is put forward by D. Gray;
in y-nome 'took lodging' is strikingly
paralleled in other romances and compares with ON. *taka (sér) inni* in the
late *Mariu Saga*; *her* may be objective
genitive or dative 'for her', though the
reading of the Ashmole MS. *ouer-jn*
could represent an original *oure in*.
Both would fit the context.

The only general work on the
Arthurian legend which has been published during this year is Richard
Barber's *Arthur of Albion*,[2] which the
author tells us was written in its
original form at Marlborough College.
He does not say how long this was
before publication, but one presumes
it was not too long, in view of the insistence in the blurb and the foreword
on Barber's youth. It is quite a remark-

[2] *Arthur of Albion.* An Introduction to
the Arthurian Literature and Legends
of England, by Richard Barber. London:
Barrie and Rockliff with the Pall Mall Press.
pp. xiv+218. 30s.

able feat to produce a book of this kind as, one supposes, a college essay; and one is always sympathetic towards any attempts to popularize the Arthurian legend in our time; one may therefore allow (with certain reservations) the blurb's description of the work as 'valuable', while rejecting its claim of originality. It would be extremely difficult in these days to produce anything 'original' on the Arthurian legend, or for that matter for anyone to write with authority on the whole of the legend in England (see *YW* xli. 66). One can sum the work up by saying that Barber has used the normal sources for information, and has written freshly on his subject; it is a book for the general reader, not the specialist.

William Matthews's work *The Tragedy of Arthur*[3] falls into an entirely different category, for here we have the true professional working for the benefit of his fellow professionals. As he points out, it is remarkable that the alliterative *Morte Arthure*, ranked among the great poems of the fourteenth century, and now shown to be an important source for Malory, should have attracted so little attention. Yet since the discussion of the poem's attribution to Huchown of the Awle Ryale culminating in the book by George Neilson (1902) remarkably little on it has appeared in print. At last, however, we have a full-scale study of the poem, its literary links and its genre. After a preliminary comparison of the poem with the chronicles of Wace, Geoffrey of Monmouth, and Laȝamon, Matthews postulates that many of the additions to the Arthurian story credited to the author of the *Morte Arthure* are adapted from the story of Alexander the Great as it was known in the later Middle Ages. This

thesis Matthews sustains by arguments which have certainly convinced at least one reader; one can scarcely doubt that the author of the alliterative *Morte Arthure* was acquainted with some form of *Les Vœux du Paon* and *Fuerres de Gadres*, and some version of the story of Alexander similar to the *Historia de Prœliis* (to this section of Matthews's work, especially p. 61, one might add that in at least one version of the Alexander story a number of the monstrous tribes encountered by him bear a remarkably close resemblance to those found in Mandeville). Matthews continues with a useful account of the rise and fall of the fame of Alexander in the fourteenth and fifteenth centuries, and of the varying attitudes to him—admiration for his vast achievements, associated with the traits of an ideal ruler, compared with criticism, even downright hostility (he omits the Scottish poet Henryson in this connexion). Matthews illustrates these from English literature, then the critical attitude of the author of *Morte Arthure*, going on from that to an analysis of the structure and genre of *Morte Arthure*, which he concludes to be a tragedy (in the medieval sense, like Chaucer's *Troilus and Criseyde*), not so much an account of the fall of a great man by means of Fortune as the story of someone who falls because of some fault in him—in Arthur's case the worst of the Seven Deadly Sins, pride. Later chapters attempt to relate *Morte Arthure* to other Arthurian works like *Awntyrs of Arthure, Golagros and Gawane*, and Malory's *Le Morte Darthur*, and finally suggest that the topic and attitude of the poem may have been prompted by the career of Edward III of England. Readers of this book must not neglect the notes, some of which are extremely full and satisfying.

Two articles on the Arthurian tradition have appeared in *MÆ*; in 'King

[3] *The Tragedy of Arthur.* A Study of the Alliterative 'Morte Arthure', by William Matthews. Univ. of Calif. Press and C.U.P. pp. xii+230. 40s.

Arthur in the Old Swedish Legendary', J. E. Cross gives an interesting account of Arthur's saintly appearance, with two popes, among the late fifth-century material in this oldest Swedish text in literary prose, composed 1276–1307 by a Dominican from Götaland. Cross usefully re-edits, with translation, the relevant passage which derives from the redaction of 1276 of Martinus Oppaviensis's *Chronicon Pontificum et Imperatorum*, and then considers how the Swedish author adds to his source from current Arthurian tradition. The combination of chronicle and legendary material in the mind of the Dominican author gave rise to an opinion of Arthur unique in early literature, for he includes an apparently original exemplum in which Arthur's actions are denigrated to point a moral on worldly vanity. Perhaps like Alcuin warning against Ingeld, the friar questions 'What has Arthur to do with Christ?' A. J. Bliss, in 'Celtic Myth and Arthurian Romance', indicates his disagreement with V. J. Harward's evidence (in *The Dwarfs of Arthurian Romance and Celtic Tradition*) for the existence of dwarfs in early Celtic (and in particular medieval Welsh) tradition.

Pride of place in work on the Gawain poet must go to the essay by Hans Schnyder[4] on *Sir Gawain and the Green Knight*, where he develops more fully his interpretation of the whole poem, on the lines suggested in 1959 (*YW* xl. 68–69), where he considered the Beheading episode in relation to the character of King Arthur. Schnyder takes the poem to be an allegory, whose theme is the same as Bunyan's *Pilgrim's Progress*, i.e. the pilgrimage of the life of man. From this point of view Gawain is to be regarded as the

one member of King Arthur's court who has not been corrupted by prosperity and pride, and is therefore alone capable of taking up the challenge of the Green Knight. Gawain's journey through the wilderness for the 'return match' symbolizes first his happiness, when he feels secure in the Word of God, then his despair in being in the waste land of his own soul, far away from charity or the love of God in the wilderness of Wirral. The enemies he fought and defeated—beasts, satyrs, giants—were symptomatic of the temptations which oppressed him but which he escaped. But now, on his arrival at the castle, he is faced with a more difficult task, a battle against his own heart; or, if you like, having faced a test of (mainly) physical endurance his next ordeal is to test his moral strength. Bercilak and the two ladies of the castle then represent different manifestations of God's Will or Divine Providence, and Gawain's temptations represent a not abnormal pattern of theological ideas. His stay in the castle ended, the wheel of Fortune turns, and he is again in adversity, and his journey to the Green Chapel is in effect a 'descensus Averni'. (At this point one may take up a small section of Schnyder's argument (p. 68), namely that Gawain's guide insists, in his description of the Green Knight, on the latter's punishment of the proud— 'Whosoever passes proudly in his arms is clubbed to death by the giant of the valley'—a statement linked up in the essay with the degeneration of Arthur's court in sinful pride. But this argument is surely based on a misreading of the text; the guide is trying to frighten Gawain, and described the 'frightfulness' of the Green Knight who is bigger than any four in Arthur's house, and so fierce that no one passes by that place, *however proud in his arms* that he does not kill him (ll. 2104–5); he would not spare churl or chaplain, monk or mass-

[4] *Sir Gawain and the Green Knight*. An Essay in Interpretation, by Hans Schnyder. (The Cooper Monographs 6.) Berne: Francke Verlag. pp. 81. Sw. fr. 9.50.

priest, so merciless is he; and so the guide argues that Gawain would be well advised to flee. This may well be a temptation, but not of the kind that Schnyder suggests.) The cut on Gawain's neck still symbolizes the sin of which Arthur's court is to be cleansed, and the references to the falls of Adam, Samson, Solomon, and David through the evil influence of women (often regarded as a lapse in artistry on the part of the author) now show Gawain seeing his own experiences as part of the universal story of the human fall. And so his insight into the true nature of his adventures causes him to wear the green girdle for ever, to cure his pride. And the court likewise acknowledge their sin by wearing the same sign (though they were remarkably lighthearted about it: ll. 2513 ff.). Such an argument is very difficult to refute; it may indeed lead to a new kind of evaluation of the poem; but it does depend to some extent upon proving that the author was familiar with the theological ideas Schnyder discusses.

In a useful summary article, 'Sir Gawain and the Green Knight: An Appraisal' (PMLA), Morton W. Bloomfield contends that the poem has complexities and puzzles not previously recognized; he relates them to present and past work (on dialect, meaning, authorship, milieu, theme, and sources and poetic intention) and suggests some possible solutions. He stresses the need for philological study as the basis of all sound literary work, reconsideration of the theory of common authorship of the poems in MS. Cotton Nero A x, caution in associating the dialect with the location of Bercilak's castle and the Green Chapel, consideration of the exact meaning of the work in terms of fourteenth-century culture, and an examination of the ninefold division of the poem in the manuscript to clarify the formal and stylistic principles.

The 'short version' of Le Livre de Caradoc was long ago rejected as a direct source of Gawain before the long and prose redactions were known. In a close study of 'The Source of the Beheading Episode in Sir Gawain and the Green Knight' (MP), Larry D. Benson compares the three versions of Caradoc with Gawain. Where the long and prose texts disagree with the 'short version' they agree with Gawain in important details and contain suggestions for many important passages in the English poem. He draws further parallels between the long and prose Caradoc and Gawain in the account of the return blow and the outcome of the tests, which is a disturbing self-discovery. Perhaps, he says, the reason for Morgan's presence in Gawain can be found in the close agreement between the conclusions of this poem and Caradoc. He concludes with reference to the Irish features, that the long prose Caradoc and Gawain do not derive from a common source. The direct and principal source of the beheading scene in Gawain is a lost long redaction of Caradoc, containing additional details which survive only in the prose edition of 1530.

J. F. Kiteley, in 'The De Arte Honeste Amandi of Andreas Capellanus and the Concept of Courtesy in Sir Gawain and the Green Knight' (Ang), discusses the lady's concept of courtesy, which differs from that of Gawain, and implies a clear connexion between 'talkyng noble' and 'luf-talkyng', coincident with the ideas of De Arte. A comparison between the behaviour of the lady and that advised in De Arte shows that in using the Courtly Love motifs she sometimes takes the initiative, thus reversing the Courtly Love situation. Kiteley thinks that the poet implies criticism of courtesy, which is the outcome of Courtly Love and not important as an end in itself, as is the true Christian virtue of courtesy. In

NQ Bridget James relates ' "Pernyng" in *Sir Gawain and the Green Knight*, Line 611' to the dialect noun *pirn*, 'reel, bobbin', giving the sense 'flitting', while P. J. Frankis suggests in '*Sir Gawain and the Green Knight*, Line 35: With Lel Letteres Loken' that the meaning is 'embodied in truthful words' and does not refer to alliterative verse technique.

A critical assessment of 'Landscape and Rhetoric in Middle English Alliterative Poetry' (*MCR*) is made by Ralph W. V. Elliott. Although the functional and beautiful use of description recommended by Matthew of Vendôme was deliberately aimed at, the popularity of the *Roman de la Rose*, which set the pattern of poetic landscape, and the claims of episodic narrative often produced irrelevance and tediousness in late fourteenth-century alliterative poetry. Among those poems, where, it is shown, landscape description is effectively handled, *Sir Gawain and the Green Knight*, to which Elliott devotes almost half his discussion, stands out. The Gawain-poet's scenic descriptions, sometimes primarily evoking mood, sometimes creating a vivid picture of a strongly particularized landscape, are made integral parts of the story, its moods, and moral meaning.

From his analysis of the poet's typological structure, which clarifies the association between the day, the place and the vision, William J. Knightley, in '*Pearl*: The "hy3 seysoun"' (*MLN*), concludes that the poet experienced his vision at the festival time of the Transfiguration. The harvest metaphors of the opening not only recall the last harvest but suggest that the symbolic scheme of the herber reproduces the scheme of the last harvest. The herber is used as a structural *repetitio* to introduce the theme of the vision, the revelation of the maiden's transfiguration, by calling to mind the last harvest when the Transfiguration,

which typifies not only the glory of Christ but that also of the saints, shall take place. A sermon of Peter the Venerable is quoted, where the scriptural figures of the last harvest are used to explain the spiritual senses of the Transfiguration, and the scene of the Transfiguration used to explain the senses of the scene of the last harvest. The methods of the Venerable Peter and the *Pearl*-poet correspond if the *hy3 seysoun* is taken as a metaphor of the Transfiguration, and the herber as an emblem of the last harvest. In '*Patience*: A Study in Poetic Elaboration' (*SN*) Normand Berlin considers how the poet, in adapting the Vulgate narrative for instruction and entertainment, reveals his success in translation, paraphrase, and pictorial elaboration.

One book on *Piers Plowman*, by David C. Fowler,[5] appeared during 1961. Fowler candidly admits to a belief in the multiple-authorship theory, and naturally enough his arguments in this work are coloured by that belief. In the main he is concerned with the relationships between the A and B versions of the second part of *Piers Plowman*, the Vita de Do-Wel, Do-Bet, and Do-Best; and by a closely argued comparison he suggests that they were by different authors taking up different points of view. He admits that some of the arguments might well be taken as supporting single authorship, however. He claims that one passage in the B text is based on a Cornish *Origo Mundi*, on what for the reader may seem inadequate evidence, and on the Cornish link thus forged would seem to be based largely his tentative attribution of the authorship of the B text to John of Trevisa. Elisabeth M. Orsten discusses *Piers Plowman* B. Prol. 146–209 'Belling the Cat' in 'The Ambigui-

---

[5] *Piers the Plowman. Literary Relations of the A and B Texts*, by David C. Fowler. Seattle: Univ. of Washington Press. pp. xiv + 260. $5.75.

ties in Langland's Rat Parliament' (*MS*). The cryptic lines 150–5 of 'Patience's Riddle, *Piers Plowman* B, XIII' are explained in the light of their traditional associations by Ben H. Smith, Jr. (*MLN*). In l. 151 *ex vi transicionis* means 'by the principle of grammatical transitivity'; Langland's *half a laumpe lyne in latyne* 'Latin half-line containing a reference to a lamp' becomes the first half of Psalm iv. 7 which, glossed transitively, is a synecdoche for the great acts of Creation and Redemption. Smith puts forward four possible interpretations of ll. 150–1, any or all of which the poet may have had in mind. In ll. 153–4, 'Saturday that first set the calendar' is translated into the seventh day of creation and Wednesday to the fourth, which in medieval *Hexamera* were respectively correlated with charity and wisdom. But the solution to the poet's reference not to the fourth day of creation but to the fourth day of next week lies again in the transitive gloss to Psalm iv. 7. After some further discussion, Smith suggests that in ll. 153–5 'the *might* of both the sign of the Saturday and the wisdom of the next Wednesday springs from the full moon, [and] seems to mean that neither the Creation, completed on the seventh day, nor the Passion, represented by the fourth day of next *week*, has any ultimate meaning from the human point of view without the Resurrection'. Smith finally discusses Patience's statement that Dowel is bound up with love and wisdom.

R. H. Bowers, in ' "Foleuyles Lawes" (*Piers Plowman*, C. xxii. 247)' (*NQ*), suggests that 'Foleuyle', which Skeat in his Oxford edition of 1886 printed as a proper name but was unable to identify, refers to the five notorious Folville brothers of Ashby-Folville, Leics., and Teigh, Rutland. They appear in records in 1326 and for almost twenty years afterwards as professional strong-arm men, but were approved by contemporaries as performing a rough kind of justice. The occurrence of 'Folville's Law' in a eulogistic context suggests that the expression had gained currency and registered a popular doctrine of 'justifiable redress'. Amendments to Skeat's list of 'Quotations from the Bible (Vulgate version)' (E.E.T.S., o.s. 81) are given by Anne Havens Fuller in 'Scripture in *Piers Plowman* B' (*MS*).

Even a short addition to the corpus of Middle English love-lyrics is welcome. In 'A Middle English love poem and the "O-and-I" refrain-phrase' (*MÆ*) R. L. Greene quotes and discusses a six-line love lyric in informal style, probably the first stanza of a poem. It is written in a fifteenth-century hand on the back flyleaf, f. 129^v, of Huntington Library MS. HM 503. Its most interesting feature is its refrain-phrase 'With an Y and an O' which renders this text additional to a group of ten vernacular lyrics listed by Greene. These likewise begin the fifth line of a six-line stanza with 'With an O and an I' or a close variant of it, and have an identical rhyme-scheme. Greene suggests that the explanation of the 'O-and-I' phrase is to be found in Dante's *Inferno*, xxiv, 97–102, where the poet uses as a term of comparison for great speed the quickness with which a scribe writes an 'O' or an 'I', and interprets the refrain-phrase as 'Indeed and without delay'. In *NQ* Peter Dronke communicates his elucidation of hitherto illegible or inaccurate readings in 'The Rawlinson Lyrics', while D. Gray, 'A Middle English Epitaph', discusses the poetic handling of the traditional form and content of *Farewell, this World is but a Cherry Fair* and the use, as an epitaph, of its final stanza. *Dame Sirith* is the subject of two notes by B. D. H. Miller (*NQ*). In '*Dame Sirith*: Three Notes' he discusses the interpretation of *as hende, setten spel on ende* (61–62), *somer driuen* (247), which he suggests refers to a type of rough justice administered from Classical times and paralleled in *Havelok*, but which would seem here to be a unique vernacular reference to such treatment of a procuress, and (*leue*) *nelde* (415). The textual history of the *fabliau* ('*Dame Sirith* and the O.E.D.') suggests that it may well date from 1250 or before.

There continues to be a steady flow of material on mystical and devotional prose, headed by a general work on *The English Mystical Tradition*[6] by the Regius Professor of Modern History in Cambridge. The substance of the book was given as lectures at Aberystwyth in 1959–60, and supplants an earlier book on the English mystics published as long ago as 1928. The core of the work is Knowles's chapters on Rolle, *The Cloud of Unknowing*, Hilton, Julian of Norwich, and Margery Kempe, all of whom are discussed with great acumen; but the earlier chapters on what is meant by mysticism, and its evolution, cannot be ignored by any reader. It is a book for the general reader, but the specialist might well learn from it. Yet another translation of *The Cloud* has been published, the translator Clifton Wolters.[7] This is a much more colloquial translation than that of Ira Progoff (*YW* xl. 71) (which incidentally Wolters does not mention among his 'Books that Might be Helpful' on pp. 39–40). Unlike Progoff, who cast a wide net in dealing with the religious aspects of the work, Wolters in his introduction concentrates mainly on interpreting the text to the modern Catholic reader. On the whole it reads well, though in a few places one seems to detect a false note in the translation. The publication of MS.

Bodley 959 (*YW* xl. 71) has continued under the editorship of Conrad Lindberg;[8] this volume contains the work of the second scribe. Yet another Biblical text has been edited by a Scandinavian scholar, this one Elis Fridner,[9] who has produced a carefully edited version of MS. Harley 874 with variants in footnotes. There is a copious introduction, from which it is clear this manuscript is East Midland, and dated 1340–70; and it is, of course, linked with the Wycliffite controversy. In Henry Hargreaves's study of 'The Marginal Glosses to the Wycliffite New Testament' (*SN*) he discusses the systematic glosses, confined to two manuscripts, which are the basis of sporadic glosses in other manuscripts and some textual glosses, and derive chiefly from the Postils of Nicholaus of Lyra, the fourteenth-century commentator. The systematic glosses, it is shown, were intended to accompany the most revised and most idiomatic form of the *E*(arlier) *V*(ersion) of the New Testament represented, among others, by *V* (New College, Oxford MS. 67). *V* and the marginal catchwords from the text agree with *EV* against *L*(ater) *V*(ersion) in vocabulary, *V* and catchwords frequently with *LV* against *EV* in grammatical constructions. Although the glosses did not originate in *V* itself, they are closer to the original than are those of the other manuscript in which they occur. The fact that Nicholaus's Postils were used to accompany the *V*-type text shows that the Wycliffite commentator turned to his work earlier than supposed, and

[6] *The English Mystical Tradition*, by David Knowles. London: Burns & Oates. pp. viii+197. 25s.

[7] *The Cloud of Unknowing*. A New Translation by Clifton Wolters. Harmondsworth: Penguin Books. pp. 144. 3s. 6d.

[8] MS. Bodley 959. Genesis–Baruch 3. 20 in the Earlier Version of the Wycliffite Bible. Vol. 2: Leviticus–Judges 7.13, ed. by Conrad Lindberg. (Stockholm Studies in English, VIII.) Stockholm: Almqvist & Wiksell. pp. 281. Sw. kr. 25.

[9] *An English Fourteenth Century Apocalypse Version with a Prose Commentary*. Ed. from MS. Harley 874 and ten other MSS. by Elis Fridner. (Lund Studies in English, 29.) Lund: Gleerup. pp. lviii+290. Sw. kr. 32.

that the final revision of the New Testament, which produced *LV*, was later than the composition of the marginal glosses. Hargreaves finally discusses the glosses (not in *V*) to the Gospels in Longleat MS. 5 (*LV*), which differ from the others in nature and source. The Gospel glosses, which were not composed for the Longleat text, derive probably from the *Glossed Gospels* and from the longer commentary of the *Glossed Gospels*. Greene (see above) notes, on ff. 1–128ᵛ of Huntington Library MS. HM 503, an unpublished version of the prose tract *The Clergy May Not Hold Property*, Wycliffite in sentiment but probably not by Wycliff, which differs appreciably from the printed Lambeth version (E.E.T.S., o.s. 74).

Mandeville's Travels are the subject of two articles by M. C. Seymour. In his investigation of 'The Origin of the Egerton Version of *Mandeville's Travels*' (*MÆ*) he suggests that the maker of the Egerton Version used, as far as *the Egypt Gap*, a somewhat fuller Defective Version than that now extant. He shows how, for *the Egypt Gap* and subsequent material, the maker of the Egerton Version was indebted to the lost English translation (of the Latin version in MS. Royal 13 E ix and related manuscripts) from which the Bodley Redaction was abridged. After *the Egypt Gap* the maker of the Egerton Version used, in conjunction with the lost English translation, a manuscript belonging to sub-group A of the Defective Version. From a comparison of the Bodley Redaction with the Latin manuscript from which it ultimately derives, Seymour shows, in 'A Medieval Redactor at Work' (*NQ*), how the Bodley Redactor successfully abridged and rearranged his material to produce a narrative of marvel calculated to attract the unlettered layman.

With regard to Lydgate, it is pleasing to be able to record the publication of an English edition of W. F. Schirmer's work,[10] originally reviewed in this chapter in 1952 (*YW* xxxiii. 83–84). Like its predecessor, this is a handsome piece of publishing. Alain Renoir has written 'On the Date of John Lydgate's Mumming at Hertford' (*Archiv*), 'The Immediate Source of Lydgate's *Siege of Thebes*' (*SN*), and 'Attitudes Toward Women in Lydgate's Poetry' (*ES*). In the last he discusses previous judgements on Lydgate's verse and then, towards a re-evaluation of his work, selects for study his attitude towards women in the secular poems. He finds three distinct attitudes—the courtly (*pro*), the clerical (*anti*), and the poet's own (individual merit considered) and that Lydgate's expression of them 'reveals an uncommon versatility of talent, ranging from the most satirical to the most deeply moving'. It is argued by J. Norton Smith, in 'Lydgate's Metaphors' (*ES*), that the 'knot' images have an organization that does not quite agree with Renoir's description (*YW* xxxviii. 88). He reconsiders the *Gentlewoman's Lament* 17–28 and the *Temple of Glas* 1229–30. His interpretation of the last seems to depend on the theory of the 'undesirable husband' based on a passage (extant in two manuscripts), which Renoir (*ES* above) rejects as an interpolation.

One general book on medieval drama has appeared in 1961. *The Drama of Medieval England*[11] is addressed to the general reader, not the specialist, and is a survey of the way in which most people believe drama developed in this country. What perhaps distinguishes this book from other popular works on the subject is that Williams constantly approaches it

[10] *John Lydgate*. A Study in the Culture of the XVth Century, by Walter F. Schirmer. London: Methuen. pp. xiv+303. 42s.
[11] *The Drama of Medieval England*, by Arnold Williams. East Lansing, Mich.: Michigan State Univ. Press. pp. vi+186. $5.00.

from the point of view of a modern theatre-going, television-watching reader. Periodical publications on the drama have been confined to the Towneley cycle. E. Catherine Dunn, accepting Sepet's view 'that the *Processus prophetarum* became, through elaboration and reorganization, the Old Testament cycle plays', suggests, in 'Lyrical Form and the Prophetic Principle in the Towneley Plays' (*MS*), that the old-age laments of the patriarchs are a lyrical extension of the prophetic utterances of the *Processus prophetarum*. She finds the presence of the *planctus* in all three strata of composition strong evidence that it formed part of the earliest version, and suggests that as a structural principle in the cycle's formation the *planctus* was retained or imitated by subsequent redactors. In *The Scourging* ll. 12–13 (Towneley play XXII), Pilate states that he is named by the clergy *As mali actoris*. Sister Nicholas Maltman puts forward an admirable case for the emendation of this corrupt reading to *os malleatoris* in 'Pilate—*os malleatoris*' (*S*). Her title is taken from Isidore of Seville's etymology 'Pilate—the mouth of the hammerer', an interpretation which became an exegetical commonplace. SS. Gregory and Bernard, among others, refer to the devil as 'hammerer', an idea not unknown in fourteenth-century England. Pilate's boast that the clergy name him *os malleatoris* is true, and this description, 'the mouth of the devil, the hammerer', not only clarifies the whole passage but fully harmonizes with Pilate's character throughout the Towneley cycle where he is the antagonist of Christ.

One peripheral work published within the year is J. C. Dickinson's *Monastic Life in Medieval England*,[12] which

[12] *Monastic Life in Medieval England*, by J. C. Dickinson. London: Black. pp. xvi+160. 38s.

also is intended for the general reader. It falls into three parts, which describe respectively the monastic buildings, the history of the monastic orders, and the dissolution of the monasteries. To cover so much ground in so little space has necessarily meant compression and generalization, with their attendant dangers. For instance, Dickinson's statement (p. 2) that the church 'was normally of stone' does not hold for a considerable time in Northern England at least, and when he says (p. 4) that the wealthiest English monasteries 'in their heyday had between fifty and a hundred brethren' he must be thinking only of post-Conquest times, as Bede records (in his *Lives of the Abbots*) that when Abbot Ceolfrith set off on pilgrimage to Rome he left in Wearmouth and Jarrow about 600 brethren. The author goes sadly astray (on p. 26) in his siting of the shrine of St. Cuthbert in Durham Cathedral, and is rather tentative in his discussion of the military orders. The select bibliography has some obvious omissions. Leaving out these minor points, it must be stressed that this is a useful and informative work, very well illustrated. If one had to pick out an outstanding part of it, one would select the chapter called 'The Aftermath', where Dickinson gives an admirably succinct account of the treatment meted out to monastic furnishings, &c., after the Dissolution.

To the two short couplet versions of *Titus and Vespasian* in MSS. B.M. Add. 10036 and Pepys 2014, Curt F. Bühler, in 'The New Morgan Manuscript of *Titus and Vespasian*' (*PMLA*), adds a third, lacking the first leaf, in the recently acquired MS. Pierpont M 898. It is of the early to mid-fifteenth century. The Morgan text, which derives from the common ancestor of MSS. B and P and is in closer agreement with P than B, is nevertheless unique. For the romance is divided into eighteen chapters with appropriate headings, and short prose summaries, which Bühler quotes, are included in the text. These rubrics indicate the form of the story acceptable to a fifteenth-century reader. The short version, which is not an abridgement of the longer version, often provides the smoother rendering.

In 'Tradition and the Interpretation of the *Kingis Quair*' (*RES*) John MacQueen discusses the interpretation of the conventional elements and their context. The attitude of the poem is basically that of the *Roman de la Rose*, the theme, closely related to Boethius's *De Consolatione*, is the liberation of Youth by Love and Philosophy (Minerva) from servitude to Fortune, who is seen as the central figure in the context of divine government and is finally, for the poet, reconciled with Nature. The poet reveals how his own experience counterpoints that of Boethius in that a youth, not dedicated to Philosophy and so in thrall to Fortune, may yet come to a happy acceptance of his place in an ordered Christian universe. The poem is, in effect a *Remedium Fortunae* in a form most closely associated with courtly love visions. By assuming scribal error in the unique manuscript, Carl E. Bain clarifies the interpretation of *renewe* (stanza 125) and *all oure hath* (stanza 196) in ' "The Kingis Quair" : Two Emendations' (*NQ*).

In 'Usk's "Knot in the Hert" Again' (*ES*), Claes Schaar defends and extends his interpretation of this phrase (*YW* xxxvii. 86).

V. MIDDLE ENGLISH: CHAUCER

By JOYCE BAZIRE

1. General

IN *Chaucer's Verse*[1] Paull F. Baum maintains a sensible attitude towards the poetry and does not try to force upon the lines exact conformity to a set pattern, particularly since variants complicate the picture. It is the sound of the line, not the system, that is important, and this is emphasized by many references to earlier writers on the subject and their—in some cases—mechanical theories of versification, for always the distinction must be made between what may have been Chaucer's intent or practice and what actually is the editor's. Further, it is important to distinguish between rhythm and metre.

The chapter on metre covers with many examples metrical variations, liberties and licences, and also rhymes. The chapter on prosody (which Baum regards as the more important part of the study, since the sound is bound up with the meaning) deals with alliteration, and its extension beyond the initial sound (though Baum admits that the latter may be accidental rather than significant), Chaucer's rhyming habits and his means of achieving various metrical effects—all liberally illustrated. Some of these means, effective in certain lines, have in others turned into practically meaningless patterns.

Its title, 'Art Poetical', indicates the content of the third chapter. Passages, which in Baum's opinion illustrate Chaucer's art, are selected for examination, always with the findings of the

previous two chapters in mind. Particular attention is paid to the *Parlement of Foules*, which is 'purple all through'.

In summing up his findings, Baum concludes that Chaucer gives a 'steady level of competence', preferable in narrative poetry to displays of virtuosity, though occasionally the poet demonstrates what he can do when the occasion arises. As appendixes 'the rhythmical or four-beat heresy' and the Canon's Yeoman's *Prologue* and *Tale* are discussed in the light of points made earlier in the book.

F. P. Magoun's *A Chaucer Gazetteer*[2] represents in the main a conflation made by Ojars Kratins of Magoun's three articles, already noticed in *YW* (see xxxiv, xxxv, xxxvi) when they appeared in *Mediaeval Studies*. Although it is useful to have the papers together, they have unfortunately not been corrected, nor have their forewords been included. [Reviews: R. T. Davies, *NQ* ix, N.S. (1962), 159; J. Burrow, *RES* xiii, N.S. (1962), 216–17; Joyce Bazire, *MLR* lvii (1962), 299–300.]

About half of Rolf Berndt's book, *Einführung in das Studium des Mittelenglischen*,[3] is devoted to material concerned with Middle English in general, but, in the second part, under the heading, *Mittelenglische Sprachproben*, he turns his attention to Chaucer. First he discusses the poet's technique in writ-

[1] *Chaucer's Verse*, by Paull F. Baum. Duke U.P., C.U.P., Burns & MacEachern. pp. viii+145. $6, 48*s*., $7.75.

[2] *A Chaucer Gazetteer*, by F. P. Magoun, Jr. Uppsala: Almqvist & Wiksell. pp. 173. Sw. kr. 16.

[3] *Einführung in das Studium des Mittelenglischen unter Zugrundelegung des Prologs der 'Canterbury Tales'*, by Rolf Berndt. Halle (Saale): Max Niemeyer Verlag. 1960. pp. xviii+398. DM. 35.30.

ing verse, and then gives the text of the *General Prologue* (the Manly-Rickert version) with a phonetic transcript of the first 78 lines. Berndt next provides an account of Chaucer's life and works (the *Equatorie* is not mentioned as a possible work), the chronology of the latter, and the various influences on Chaucer at different periods.

The *Canterbury Tales* are the object of most of Berndt's attention, and his study covers the essential points of such a survey: plan, effects achieved, characters of the pilgrims, sources, themes, &c. A brief description follows of the historical background itself and of its reflection in Chaucer's writings; and then this part is concluded with some illustration of his contemporaries' opinions of the poet. The comprehensive glossary does not contain simply the meanings of words found in the *Prologue*—no line-references are given —but the etymology (in some instances quite detailed) and the Modern English equivalent are generally cited, and in addition there are found notes regarding constructions, or other necessary explanatory comments.

David M. Zesmer's section on Chaucer in *Guide to English Literature*[4] provides valuable summaries of and a commentary on the poet's works. Within the limits imposed by considerations of space, Zesmer manages to take cognizance of the findings and arguments of scholars who have preceded him, even recently. The section is well furnished with references, and is also supplemented by a useful annotated bibliography compiled by Stanley B. Greenfield.

Most of the second volume of *Chaucer Criticism*[5] is devoted to articles

on *Troilus*, though four are concerned with the minor poems, and the first— Dodd's 'The System of Courtly Love' —provides a background to them all. In the Preface the editors summarize the articles, explaining also the purpose of their selection, how they are connected and how they show divergent interpretations and evaluations. All have previously appeared in print, apart from Kaske's, and most have already been noticed in *YW*. It is useful to have them collected in this way.

Kaske's contribution, 'The Aube in Chaucer's *Troilus*', a paper originally read to the Chaucer Group in Chicago, compares the aube as found in *Troilus* with its source in Boccaccio and with the motifs exemplified in other works, particularly the numerous *Tagelieder*.

Tatlock and MacKaye's *The Modern Reader's Chaucer*,[6] which first appeared in 1912, is now issued as a Macmillan Paperback.

Russell and Russell have reissued the English translation, made in 1913 by L. Lailavoix, of Legouis's book, *Geoffrey Chaucer*.[7] Lailavoix also supplied a Preface describing Chaucer studies in France.

The first of the five studies centring on Chaucer,[8] in *Studies in Medieval Literature*,[9] is R. S. Loomis's 'Was Chaucer a Free Thinker?', which defends the thesis that, although

[4] *Guide to English Literature*. From Beowulf through Chaucer and Medieval Drama, by David M. Zesmer. College Outline Series, No. 53. New York: Barnes & Noble. pp. xi+397. $2.25.

[5] *Chaucer Criticism II; Troilus and Criseyde & The Minor Poems*, ed. by Richard J. Schoeck and Jerome Taylor. Notre Dame U.P. pp. x+293. $1.95.

[6] *The Modern Reader's Chaucer*, by John S. P. Tatlock and Percy MacKaye. Macmillan Paperbacks. New York: The Macmillan Company. pp. xi+596. $2.35 and 18s.

[7] *Geoffrey Chaucer*, by Emile Legouis, translated into English with a Preface by L. Lailavoix. New York: Russell and Russell Inc. pp. xxxvi+220. $6.50.

[8] The others are noticed in their appropriate places.

[9] *Studies in Medieval Literature*. In Honor of Professor Albert Croll Baugh, ed. by MacEdward Leach. Pennsylvania U.P. and O.U.P. pp. 344. $7.50.

Chaucer was a devout and orthodox Christian, he, like many of his contemporaries, had his periods of scepticism, reflected in certain heterodox opinions expressed by his characters. It is not without significance that Chaucer introduced such passages where his source gave no warrant for them.

L. D. Benson presents a clear account of 'Chaucer's Historical Present' (*ES*). The great majority of examples indicates continuing action in the past which is usually ended by a preterite; some without the preterite suggest conditions which obtain over a long period. Other—but fewer—examples occur in cases of indirect quotation, apostrophe, &c. About a hundred examples remain which Benson cannot fit into a group, and he admits that along with these there are other relevant points which have not been explained.

In a chapter in his book, *Sieben Meister des literarischen Humors in England und Amerika*,[10] Wolfgang Schmidt-Hidding reviews the work of Chaucer as a humorist. He passes from the self-irony in the poet's portraits of himself to the development of humour which is to be traced from his early works up to *Troilus*, 'das erste humoristische Werk der europäischen Literatur'. This work is discussed at length, and particularly the character of Pandarus, who is not only represented as humorous, but has humour himself. Schmidt-Hidding deals somewhat with the structure of the *Canterbury Tales*—the constancy of characters, whether in the *General Prologue*, *Tale* or *Link*, the antithesis of characters, the Marriage Group—before pointing out how the humorous effect is achieved, and that through humour sympathy is evoked, even for the rogues. For this 'all-com-

prehending, loving humour' Chaucer has a religious basis.

Kenneth Kee's article, 'Two Chaucerian Gardens' (*MS*), reviews the conventional aspects of the garden setting in medieval literature, its associations with courtly love, and its connotation of the earthly paradise. The gardens in the Merchant's and Franklin's *Tales* serve as illustrations of Chaucer's use of such implications to give added meaning to his descriptions.

There is little overlapping with A. A. Dent's 'Chaucer and the Horse' (*YW* xli) in John H. Fisher's 'Chaucer's Horses' (*SAQ*), as the latter writer discusses links between riders and their mounts, and also Chaucer's use of equine imagery, subjects barely touched on by Dent.

The circumstances of the three occasions on which Chaucer identifies the date as 3 May suggest a connexion with the feast day of Flora when—as John P. McCall notes in 'Chaucer's May 3' (*MLN*)—'the effects of irrational love . . . are keenly felt'.

In 'A Postscript to Chaucer Studies' (*ES*) Claes Schaar provides answers to some critics of his two books (see *YW* xxxv and xxxvi).

Neil D. Isaacs concludes that ' "Furlong wey" in Chaucer' (*NQ*) cannot be defined more precisely than 'a short time'.

2. Canterbury Tales

Charles A. Owen's interesting article, 'The Twenty-Nine Pilgrims and the Three Priests' (*MLN*), contains the proposal that the Monk and the Friar were substituted in the *Prologue* for two of the priests, though the deletion of the priests was left for a later revision.

John M. Steadman suggests in 'Chaucer's Thirty Pilgrims and Activa Vita' (*N*) that the number may have had the symbolism, conventional in medieval exegesis, of the *activa vita*—

---

[10] *Sieben Meister des literarischen Humors in England und Amerika*, by Wolfgang Schmidt-Hidding. Heidelberg: Quelle & Meyer, 1959. pp. 168.

'the practice of the moral virtues in the civil life'—as this concept of the active life has a bearing on the *Canterbury Tales*.

'Chaucer's Gentry in the Historical Background'[11] by Toshinori Hira contains comments in some cases on the possible reality of certain 'members of the gentry' in the *Canterbury Tales*, and in others on the characteristics of some of their particular callings in real life, followed by an historical account of the positions of such gentry.

W. H. French, in 'General Prologue 74: Horse or Horses?' (*MLN*), rejects Garland Ethel's interpretation (*YW* xli) on the ground that *goode* must be plural.

E. E. Ericson's article, 'Pulling Finches and Woodcocks' (*ES*), supports Kittredge's interpretation of the phrase as a reference to cases of fornication.

In 'A Maner Latyn Corrupt' (*MÆ*) J. Burrow affirms his belief that this description of Custance's speech had its origin in Isidore and may have had double significance.

Theodore Silverstein's article, 'Wife of Bath and the Rhetoric of Enchantment: or, how to make a Hero see in the Dark' (*MP*), provides a commentary on the *Prologue* and *Tale*, beginning with the Wife's successful skirmishing with certain other members of the company. Silverstein debates the reason for the introduction of the rape, and then points out that we, as well as the hero, learn much through his quest. Three other versions of the theme are compared with the Wife's treatment of it, particularly with regard to the important 'lesson' after the marriage, and reference is made throughout to the variations and introductions which suit the Wife's purpose. Silverstein finally considers

what kind of picture is created of the Wife through her *Tale*, and denies that she is a pathetic figure.

Robert A. Pratt's theme, 'The Development of the Wife of Bath' (*Studies in Medieval Literature*; see note 9), provides an intricate but well-argued article. He shows how Chaucer's conception of her developed from a fairly straightforward personage, to whom the present *Shipman's Tale* was well suited. Pratt suggests that the three main segments of her *Prologue* were not composed consecutively, and that their final arrangement led to alterations in the positioning of the Wife's *Tale* among the other *Tales*; this enlivened her personality and also extended her relationship with the other pilgrims. Details now developing in the Wife's character necessitated inclusions in her portrait in the *General Prologue*. But it was not until the completion of the Wife's *Prologue* that Chaucer gave her a new tale, the heroine of which can in many ways be identified with Alice. Pratt finally discusses certain later insertions in the Wife's *Prologue* and their significance, and then sums up the character with which we are finally presented.

Paul E. Beichner's article, 'Baiting the Summoner' (*MLQ*), shows how the *Friar's Tale* not only fits the teller, 'but especially the teller's purpose in relating it', and leaves the Summoner in the position that whether he retaliates or keeps silence, he will be the loser in the contest. Already in their passage before the actual *Tale*, the Friar seems to have come off better, and when telling the *Tale*, he soon makes the Summoner involve himself in the story. As Beichner points out, by various means the oblique attack is cleverly sustained throughout, culminating in the refusal of the Friar's Summoner to repent, and the Friar's request to the pilgrims that they should pray for the conversion of the summoners.

[11] In *Essays in English and American Literature*. In Commemoration of Professor Takejiro Nakayama's Sixty-First Birthday. Tokyo: Shohakusha. pp. 348.

Przemysław Mroczkowski, who writes on 'The Friar's Tale and its Pulpit Background',[12] finds the inspiration for the Tale in the 'sermon tradition of the High Middle Ages and its loci communes', though not 'pulpit rhetoric in its formal aspect'. Mroczkowski regards it as 'basically a study in greed'—which would be highly suitable for a mendicant—though there are some deviations to other topics; and for evidence he devotes his attention mainly to a few particular works. He considers the Tale in detail in the light of his proposed thesis.

Using this article as a starting-point, Adrien Bonjour writes on 'Aspects of Chaucer's Irony in "The Friar's Tale"' (EC). Chaucer puts in the Friar's mouth ironical comments on the archdeacon, and, because of the latter's connexion with summoners, Chaucer's Summoner is reached. Furthermore, the denunciation is put in the mouth of a person of not dissimilar habits.

Janette Richardson, writing on 'An Ambiguous Reference in Chaucer's Friar's Tale' (Archiv), believes, unlike Robinson, that this somonour refers to the Friar's protagonist.

Although the Merchant may consider that he, unlike January, is no longer suffering from the blindness of marital concupiscence, yet he fails to realize his tale's relevance to his own position as merchant. So Paul A. Olson believes in 'Chaucer's Merchant and January's "Hevene in erthe heere"' (ELH). January's avarice is revealed in that he really wanted May as a possession, and his locking her up in the garden reflects the Merchant's locking-up (or remaining silent about) his possessions. January, by choosing May as his earthly good, attaches himself to Fortune's wheel and must inevitably fall; and, even when his eyes are

opened, he fails to see. And thus is the fragility of the Merchant's world paralleled and illuminated.

'Afterthoughts on the Merchant's Tale' (SP), by Bertrand Bronson, shows that if the Tale is examined in its own right, and unrelated to the Merchant, it appears in a different light. The audience to whom it was directed was rather Chaucer's courtly audience, not the Canterbury pilgrims. It is linked by means of paradoxes with Melibeus and the Wife's Prologue, as though written about the same time. All in all, if taken independently, it is not 'beyond the pale of traditional anti-feminist japery'. However, when it was assigned to the Merchant, the Prologue had to fit it to the teller, since the portrait in the General Prologue was no preparation for it; but the Merchant's misogyny then gave to the whole a 'mordant venom' not previously present.

Donald C. Baker joins a minority of writers when in 'A Crux in Chaucer's Franklin's Tale: Dorigen's Complaint' (JEGP) he defends Chaucer against the charge of prolixity and disorganization in the complaint. Dorigen is trying to steel herself to suicide: first her exempla deal with suicide before rape, then the possibility of suicide afterwards is introduced. The final exempla reflect her own despair and indecision; and so the decision is to be left to Arveragus. So beneath the apparent confusion lies Chaucer's carefully worked-out plan.

'The Deadliest Sin in The Pardoner's Tale' (TSL), by Eric W. Stockton, comprises in the main a discussion of the Tale in the light of what its author considers the outstanding crime of the three revellers, who in their pride 'blasphemously wish to usurp the role of Christ Himself', that is, in killing Death.

In 'Chaucer and Don Juan' (Philological Papers: West Virginia University Bulletin) Armand E. Singer

---

[12] In English Studies Today. Second Series, ed. by G. A. Bonnard. Berne: Francke Verlag. pp. 322.

considers it unlikely that the *Shipman's Tale* had any influence in Spain on the Don Juan theme, but likely that it had influence in England.

Paul E. Beichner investigates the properties of 'The Grain of Paradise' (*S*), and concludes that it was such a 'grain' that the Virgin placed most appropriately on the tongue of the *litel clergeon*.

NQ contains an article on the *Prioress's Tale* by Raymond Preston, 'Chaucer, his Prioress, the Jews and Professor Robinson', and a note by M. Domnitz on Hugh of Lincoln.

Commenting in 'Chaucers persische Zenobia'[13] on Chaucer's ascription to Persian sources of information concerning Zenobia (B 3438), Henry Lüdeke thinks that Chaucer misread in Boccaccio a contraction for *priscis* as *persis*.

Ewald Standop approaches his subject in 'Zur allegorischen Deutung der *Nonnes Preestes Tale*' (*Festschrift zum 75. Geburtstag von Theodor Spira*; see note 13) by way of a commentary on previous interpretations of the *Tale*, and these he does not find satisfactory. He himself believes that the protagonists represent the combination of an animal with a human characteristic, though considerable complexity is achieved. Chauntecleer and Pertelote also represent a courtly couple, and, in another light, a bourgeois couple. From a religious-allegorical standpoint an earthly paradise is shown. More structural questions are also discussed—the function of the introduction in the farmyard, and the identity and character of the narrator.

In order to answer the question, 'Does the Nun's Priest's Epilogue contain a Link?' (*SP*), Leger Brosnahan first reviews the article (*YW* xxxv) by

R. F. Gibbons, with whom he is to a certain extent in agreement. His own careful analysis of the disputed passage, comparing it with other lines in Chaucer, decides him against its authenticity.

In 'The *Canon's Yeoman's Prologue and Tale*' (*MP*) Judith S. Herz studies various aspects of that work; the metaphor of alchemy in characterization and structure; the Yeoman's illusory view of life, contrasted with his recollections of reality; his method of telling his *Tale*, and what it reveals of him. She also discusses his use of the diction of Romance and its function in the *Tale*, and eventually concludes that the flaw in the work is that, although the work is important because of its 'literary uniqueness', the Yeoman speaks out of character at the end of his *Tale*.

Richard Hazelton provides, with a full commentary, parallel excerpts concerned with the *remedia* from the *Parson's Tale*, *Moralium dogma*, and *Romanz de moralitez* to illustrate his belief that Chaucer, in using *Moralium dogma*, 'relied on both a Latin text and a French translation' of it. Further study may reveal more precisely the manuscript relationship of the three texts. Hazelton, in the conclusion of his article, 'Chaucer's *Parson's Tale* and the *Moralium dogma philosophorum*' (*T*, 1960), challenges the belief that Peraldus's *Summa de viciis* is a source of the *Tale*.

'Chaucer's Retraction: A Review of Opinion' (*Studies in Medieval Literature*, see note 9), by James D. Gordon, summarizes the trend of opinions throughout the ages concerning the Retraction, together with various comments by Gordon; but a more detailed treatment would have been of greater value.

3. *Troilus and Criseyde*

Troilus and Criseyde is one of the works examined in John Bayley's *The*

[13] In *Festschrift zum 75. Geburtstag von Theodor Spira*, ed. by H. Viebrock and W. Erzgräber. Heidelberg: Carl Winter: Universitätsverlag. pp. 405.

Characters of Love.[14] This section is introduced by some discussion of Courtly Love, together with Chaucer's observance of the 'rules' of rhetoric, both in this poem and in parts of the *Canterbury Tales*, and the effects he thereby produces. Bayley believes that *Troilus* is neither true tragedy nor a psychological novel; but to prove that, although he does not analyse or moralize, Chaucer is as sophisticated and highbrow as Proust or George Eliot, Bayley makes a detailed study of the poem, noting that its 'moral climax' is reached when Criseyde is to be sent from Troy, and that the tragic aspect is here intensified through the Code. Inevitably much of the commentary covers well-known ground, but it is not without new and interesting remarks. [Review: W. J. Harvey, *EC* xii (1962), 95–97.]

Joseph A. Longo traces 'The Double Time Scheme in Book II of Chaucer's *Troilus and Criseyde*' (*MLQ*) and shows that there is a purpose in the apparently inconsistent use of time references, the one type concerned with the short periods of Pandarus's machinations, the other with an indeterminate period covering the growth of Criseyde's love for Troilus. These suggest a 'rapid but not hasty consummation' of their love.

Sister Mary Charlotte Borthwick's article, 'Antigone's Song as "Mirour" in Chaucer's *Troilus and Criseyde*' (*MLQ*), shows that, just as there is a glittering surface on a mirror, but also an opaque background, so in several respects behind the apparently pure joy of love in Antigone's song, lie hints of other aspects of love. It shows love 'as it is' and also 'as it should be', love both earthly and heavenly. Sister Mary Charlotte finally argues that Antigone's song can be regarded as a de-

[14] *The Characters of Love*, by John Bayley. Longman's (Toronto) and London: Constable. 1960. pp. 296. $4.25 and 21s.

tailed reply to Criseyde's objections to love.

F. L. Utley provides a scene-analysis in 'Scene-division in Chaucer's Troilus and Criseyde' (*Studies in Medieval Literature*; see note 9), prefaced by an exploration of the ways in which this 'helps us to grasp some of the complexity of this long and closely textured poem'.

Under the title, 'Chaucer's *Troilus*, iv. 1585: A Biblical Allusion?' (*MLN*), Albert C. Baugh and E. Talbot Donaldson separately reject L. G. Evans's interpretation of that line (*YW* xl), the one on literary grounds and the other on linguistic.

In his article, 'From Gorgias to Troilus' (*Studies in Medieval Literature*; see note 9), Hardin Craig comments on the relationship between these two texts and also on their connexion with Boethius's *Consolatio*.

In Tatyana Moran's '*The Testament of Cresseid* and *The Book of Troylus*' (*Litera*, 1959), some attention is paid to Chaucer's poem for comparative purposes.

4. *Other Poems*

'Geffrey' in the *House of Fame* is generally regarded as a comic figure, but in several respects David M. Bevington in his interesting article, 'The Obtuse Narrator in Chaucer's *House of Fame*' (*S*), looks at the comedy from a slightly different angle. He doubts that Chaucer actually left the poem incomplete, and seeks clues to the lost ending in the development of the narrator, a self-caricature of the author, particularly with regard to his 'bookishness and thickheaded naïveté'. As 'Geffrey's' 'child-like faith' is not destroyed by his 'literary experience' in the first part of the poem, he must have his eyes opened—albeit unwillingly—to all sorts and conditions of men in the second. Bevington believes that the news of the *man of gret auctorite* would be of a general rather than a particular nature.

John M. Steadman points out the significance of the use of the desert of Libya where the eagle picked up Chaucer in 'Chaucer's "Desert of Libye", Venus, and Jove (*The Hous of Fame*, 486–87)' (*MLN*). It has links with both Jove and Venus.

R. C. Goffin in ' "Tidings" in the "Hous of Fame" ' (*NQ*) interprets 'tidings' as 'stories' rather than as 'news'.

Donald C. Baker begins 'The Poet of Love and the *Parlement of Foules*' (*UMSE*) with an annotated review of aspects of previous studies of the poem. His own contribution is concerned with Chaucer's development of twin themes—'the nature and function of love in a Boethian universe' and 'the nature and function of the Poet, particularly the love-Poet'—in explicit statements and in imagery and allusions. In view of the philosophical nature of the question, the use of the *Somnium* and of Scipio as guide is not inappropriate, but the occasion of St. Valentine's Day is not neglected. All falls into place under Cytherea, who has much wider powers than the Venus of the temple, and with whom Nature is partially equated. She presides over the garden which serves as a 'microcosmic figuration of the world and of man's life', and this is particularly reflected in the parliament. The roundel would seem to be the answer to the Poet's twofold quest.

In 'Meter and Rhyme in Chaucer's "Anelida and Arcite" ' (*UMSE*) A. Wigfall Green continues his analyses as indicated in the title, to lend support to Lounsbury's contention that the poem contains 'unusual metrical forms' and 'daring experiments in versification'.

Charles Dahlberg's 'Macrobius and the Unity of the *Roman de la Rose*' (*SP*) is not without interest for Chaucerians.

VI. THE RENAISSANCE

By B. E. C. DAVIS

A LUMINOUS point of departure for this chapter is provided in *The Horizon Book of the Renaissance*,[1] an Anglo-American production, published by Collins in conjunction with the publishers of *Horizon*. This handsome volume, in respect both of content and production, has much to offer readers of widely differing tastes and interests, presenting 'a panorama of that magnificent age', an age of genius which 'has never in all its variety ceased to entrance generations of men and women'. The main text, by J. H. Plumb, consists of ten chapters, between which are interspersed essays, biographical and critical, by Morris Bishop, Garrett Mattingly, Kenneth Clark, Ralph Roeder, J. Bronowski, Iris Origo, H. R. Trevor-Roper, Denis Mack-Smith, and Maria Bellonci. The illustrations, about a third of which are in colour, present a visual running comment on the text and on related topics such as Renaissance weapons of war, rules for gentlemen, and the drawings of Leonardo. While interest is focused primarily on the Renaissance in Italy, the subjects covered and the mode of treatment bear relevant application to the movement elsewhere. Thus the sections on Machiavelli, neo-Platonism, education, the position of women, and the theatre contain much that is pertinent to sixteenth-century English literature, which is treated more specifically in the last chapter, dealing with 'The Spread of the Renaissance'. Though designed primarily for the benefit of the general reader rather than the specialist, this is a book to be read and not merely looked at, notwithstanding the wealth of its illustrations. For this due credit must be given to the editor, who has done full justice to a great theme. At the same time the interspersed essays, apart from some descents into 'popular' idiom and style, are of a level to be expected of the contributors. The black and white illustrations as a whole are excellent, though this cannot be said, without qualifications, of those in colour, the quality of which is distinctly uneven. Nevertheless *The Horizon Book of the Renaissance* should prove a welcome addition to any library.

Studies in the Renaissance,[2] edited by M. A. Shaaber, includes several essays within the scope of this chapter. S. K. Heninger, Jr., writing on 'Some Renaissance Versions of the Pythagorean Tetrad', discusses the vogue and influence throughout the Renaissance era of Pythagorean theories with respect to metempsychosis, mathematics, and cosmography. This influence is shown to extend to writers as widely separated in time and interest as the early neo-Platonists, Reuchlin, Copernicus, and Henry More. The application of the Pythagorean tetrad to theology and natural philosophy is indicated by illustrations from contemporary printed books, and an appendix lists the first editions of major Pythagorean works until 1700. Aldo Scaglione's article on 'The Humanist as Scholar and Politian's Conception of the *Grammaticus*' touches upon several major interests of Renaissance humanists,

---

[1] *The Horizon Book of the Renaissance*, by J. H. Plumb and the Editors of *Horizon Magazine*. Collins. pp. 431. £5. 5s.

[2] *Studies in the Renaissance*. Volume VIII. The Renaissance Society of America. pp. 299.

more especially the precise nature of the return to antiquity, the concept of *humanitas*, the distinction between mystical and philological 'philosophy'. Politian's fame and success as teacher and commentator are attributed to his liberal notion of *grammaticus*, which differentiates his principles and methods from neo-Platonism on the one hand and Ciceronianism on the other. Irving D. Blum, examining 'The Paradox of Money Imagery in English Renaissance Poetry' from Wyatt to Herbert, notes, by means of illustrative quotations, the wide divergency between the conventional treatment, through imagery, of money as a symbol, at one extreme, of sordid, earthy existence, and, at the other, of the good and beautiful. Walter J. Ong, writing on 'Ramist Method and the Commercial Mind', relates the Ramist view of knowledge and of the educational process with the development of typography, which 'brought western man to react to words less and less as sounds and more and more as items deployed in space'. Discussing the significance of Ramist logic and rhetoric in education, he notes the distinction between the Ramist way of organizing discourse and disputation between rival parties, and indicates features in the Ramist method which would account for its appeal to burghers and artisans of the sixteenth century possessed with desire for order rather than experimentation. George B. Parks, under the title 'The First Italianate Englishmen', traces the fluctuation in taste and fashion regarding the Italianate type and Italianization from glowing eulogy like that of William Thomas to the uncompromising denigration of Elizabethan and Jacobean writers. He notes as the earliest use in print of the word 'Italianate' a reference in the second edition of Wilson's *Arte of Rhetorique* (1560), where, however, the objection to Italianization is not moral, but rhetorical. The current

tag on 'Inglese italianato' cited by Ascham is shown to have been anticipated in a quotation from Sir William Paget, applied to English officers aping the manners of Italian mercenaries during the French war of 1545–6. Even Thomas had sprinkled in his general praise some dispraise of Venetian noblemen, but Ascham's views regarding the moral danger occasioned through travel in Italy was probably influenced by Cheke, the reaction against it being doubtless intensified by the fact that it was favoured by disaffected Catholics. Subsequently, during the Catholic revolts of the later sixteenth century, 'Italianate became the particular term of opprobrium for traitors', and its implications are applied by Archbishop Parker to his predecessor, Pole, in his *De antiquitate Britannicae ecclesiae*. This paragraph may suitably conclude with reference to two contributions to *RN*. P. O. Kristeller writes on 'The Platonic Academy of Florence', with special reference to the writings and methods of Ficino, the basis of his teaching in the central concept of contemplation, and its relation to ethics, metaphysics, and cosmology. Vera L. Bullough supplies a list, with comments, of medical works in the library presented by Duke Humphrey to the University of Oxford.

The University of Wisconsin has published a group of papers read at a symposium held in the University to commemorate the centenaries of Voigt's *Wiederbelebung des classischen Alterthums* and J. Burckhardt's *Cultur der Renaissance in Italien*.[3] The common object of the contributors is to examine and to evaluate Renaissance scholarship of the last hundred years within the fields of politics and diplomatic history, philosophy, science, art, and

[3] *The Renaissance. A Reconsideration of the Theories and Interpretations of the Age*, ed. by Tinsley Helton. Wisconsin U.P. pp. xiii+160. $4.

literature. Garrett Mattingly stresses
the importance of diplomatic history,
neglected by most historians since
Burckhardt, as a key to proper understanding of the conditions governing
Renaissance principates and republics,
relations between the peoples of Western Europe, and the political notions
of Machiavelli, a revaluation which un-
dermines Burckhardt's over-simplified
concept of 'the State as a Work of Art'.
P. O. Kristeller summarizes the achievement since Burckhardt of research
work on Renaissance philosophy, in
particular that of Gentile, Cassirer,
Baron, Toffanin, and Bush, showing
how far this has entailed reinterpretation of Renaissance Platonism,
Aristotelianism, and humanism. Earl
Rosenthal discusses changing views of
Renaissance art as related, on the one
hand, to that of antiquity and of the
Middle Ages, and, on the other, to the
development of realism, mannerism,
and baroque. Edward Rosen devotes
his paper mainly to the work of Pierre
Duhem, 'the arch-opponent of Burckhardt' in consequence of the latter's indifference to science both of the Middle
Ages and of the Renaissance. Bernard
Weinberg traces the course of reaction
against the romantic-historical attitude
to literature and culture typified in
Burckhardt and Symonds through the
more specialized studies of Toffanin
and Lanson, the expansion of the term
'Renaissance' by Wölfflin and others
towards mannerism and baroque, and
the rehabilitation of the Middle Ages
effected by Gaston Paris and Bédier.
Harry Levin examines distinctive features of the Renaissance in England,
noting especially the predominance of
the Christian, 'Hebraic' spirit in contradistinction to 'Hellenic' paganism in
other countries, the consequent pursuit
of Biblical and patristic scholarship,
the educational basis of English humanism, Elizabethan political ideas as reflected particularly in the works of

Spenser and Shakespeare, and the
development of character in Elizabethan drama. A bibliography is
appended to each paper, and the collection as a whole is both searching and
suggestive, providing an up-to-date
background to Renaissance studies.

The same can be said of Denys Hay's
*The Italian Renaissance in its Historical
Background*,[4] a survey designed to demonstrate the relation of Renaissance
culture to Italian history of the fourteenth and fifteenth centuries, and to
the diverse conditions of politics, society, and education throughout this
period. Recognizing the concurrence of
medieval features derived from northern France with new orders in politics,
intellectualism, and art predominantly
Italian, Hay accepts the idea of Renaissance, urging the replacement of the
traditional twofold division of European history, medieval, modern, by a
threefold division, medieval, the new
period, modern. Special problems of
Italian history, reflected in the works
of successive historians, are related to
the geography of the peninsula, incessant strife between Papacy and
Empire, the rivalry of local communes,
and the accidents of public life. Over
all these contending forces, distinct in
each of the city states, Renaissance
culture is shown to have exercised
something of a unifying influence,
though the reception and evaluation of
Renaissance ideas differed, to some degree, in the different states according to
local conditions. In the last chapter,
dealing with the reception of the Renaissance in the north, Hay discusses
the reasons why the process of dis-
semination should have been so long
delayed, attributing this largely to the
lack of urban life comparable with that
of Italy, and showing the means whereby the new culture was transmitted

⁴ *The Italian Renaissance in its Historical
Background*, by Denys Hay. C.U.P. pp.
xii+218. 30s.

through mutual efforts of Italians in the north, and northerners in Italy, all alike stimulated through the invention of printing. The appeal of his book, for every type of reader, is considerably enhanced through the attractive illustrations and maps.

An article, by J. Gordon Eaker, in the *Bucknell Review*, entitled 'The Quest for the Historical Renaissance', deals with some aspects of the movement similar to those treated in several of the works already reviewed. The author seeks to distinguish different tendencies, religious, philosophical, political, economic, and scientific with view to reassessing the conclusions of authoritative historians, in particular Burckhardt, Symonds, Burdach, Baron, Toynbee, and Bush. The survey entails examination of changing interpretations of the Renaissance, at first conceived as a glorious age of freedom and exuberance, and of the culture which it induced. Eaker concurs with Bush as to the predominantly Christian character of humanism, the 'atheistic' Machiavelli being 'no more typical than the orthodox Hooker'. 'Humanism was a precarious balance between classical wisdom and Christian faith that could never be achieved by many, and it broke up along various paths.' The break-up of humanism is attributed to the replacement of international by national faith, the pressure of sceptical, naturalistic philosophy, and the following of the letter rather than the spirit of the classics. 'The historian rightly insists that we give attention to the political basis of the Renaissance and the problem left by the formation of national states.' The mind of man would seem to have been diverted from its Christian heritage to 'a sort of Jungian realm of impersonal collective consciousness'. What, then, can humanism, a minority in the world today, contribute to this crisis? The humanist need not lose heart. 'Hooker is convinced

that humane values can never be submerged by any triumph of naturalistic science.' The classics, the Church, and the Bible are still speaking; one can base one's life on an unseen reality as Plato and Cicero did.

An important contribution to general studies of the Renaissance has been made by Roland Mousnier in the third edition, revised and enlarged, of his *Les XVIe et XVIIe siècles*,[5] which traces the process of expansion in Europe and of decline in the east through different branches and aspects of intellectual development and scientific discovery. The first part deals with 'new structures' of sixteenth-century civilization, classified as mental, economic, and religious. On this basis it is argued that the scientific revolution of the seventeenth century had been anticipated long before through advancement in mathematics, geographical discovery, and Protestant attacks on Catholicism. The general trend of thought 'proved Plato right against Aristotle', Paduan rationalism, exemplified in Pomponazzi, being superseded by the scientific vision of Leonardo and Copernicus. Thus, throughout the earlier phases of the movement, *devotio moderna*, inspiring the effort of individual man in his approach to God, preserved a strain of mysticism, as shown in the devoutness of Vasco da Gama, submitting his enterprise to divine direction. Discussing the term Renaissance and the different meanings attached to it by historians, Mousnier cites Vasari as one of the earliest writers to put the underlying concept to practical account through transferring the ideas of Petrarch to the fine arts, the development of which reflects in turn the reaction against Gothic and Byzantine, the

[5] *Les XVIe et XVIIe siècles. Les progrès de la civilisation européenne et déclin de l'Orient (1492–1715)*, by Roland Mousnier. Paris P.U.F. pp. 671. 40 NF.

development of realism, the idea of perfection fostered by neo-Platonism, and the recognition of the divine in man as suggested in Castiglione's *Courtier*. The diversity of new structures in religion and politics is attributed to the individuality of leading reformers, Erasmus, Luther, Calvin, and Zwingli, and to concepts of state widely different, at one extreme that of the Paduan school, fulfilled in Machiavelli, at the other that of the English constitutional monarchy.

A paper by Rudolf Wittkower, read in September 1960 at the first meeting of the International Society for the History of Ideas held in Cambridge, deals with 'Individualism in Art and Artists' (*JHI*). The treatment of the subject turns upon the relative values attached to the artist and his work, which raise separate problems of individualism in both. The break-up of the gild monopoly during the sixteenth century is represented as the main cause of a new individualism in the artist, as seen in the demand for solitude by Leonardo and Michelangelo, the association of art with madness, and the melancholic artist, such as Federico Barocci. The depiction of the artist as an eccentric by Boccaccio and Sacchetti is confirmed more seriously by Cardanus, who describes painters as 'fickle, of unsettled mind, melancholic, and changeable in their manners'. Further confirmation to the same effect is given in Timothy Bright's detailed analysis of melancholy (1586), which gives a clue to many current views of the artist, including the association of artistic genius with melancholic disposition. Wittkower discusses how far the sense of individuality was dependent upon new or traditional modes of thought, and how far influenced by philosophical and literary conventions, concluding that the Renaissance, in raising art from a mechanical to an intellectual level, 'first raised the artist's personality upon a lofty pedestal'. His paper offers a lucid exposition of a theme clearly relevant to a balanced assessment of Renaissance art, and he draws interesting, though disputable, analogues between the Renaissance fight for liberation from the encumbrance of the gilds and the romantic fight for liberation from the ties of the academy, suggesting that, paradoxically, 'the untrammelled individualism of the twentieth-century *avant-garde*, their personality and social problems were ultimately derived from the Italian Renaissance, the period in history on which they heaped the fullness of their scorn'. Another article of *JHI*, by S. K. Heninger, Jr., deals with 'The Renaissance Perversion of Pastoral' from its original classical form to satire, moral allegory, and sentimental narrative. The revival of pastoral he attributes to sociological rather than literary influences, to a sense of art as compensation for what culture lacks rather than as expression of what culture has achieved. From this aspect Renaissance pastoral, though attempted by most major writers, must be regarded as a state of mind rather than as a literary genre. For poets ignored the original purpose of the form, 'perverting' it to other ends, as instanced in the moral, religious, and satiric eclogues of Petrarch, Mantuan, Marot, and Spenser, as well as in the replacement of the eclogue by other forms such as pastoral drama and romance. On this argument, pastoral, unlike tragedy, 'never realized its potentiality', failing to achieve greatness 'when the humanistic poet could have given substance to its wavering vision of man's nature'. This, clearly, is a matter of individual taste, since many readers may find in Renaissance pastoral, as in other revived classical forms, no perversion, but rather fulfilment, through quickening into new forms adapted to the life and fashions of a later age.

Of bibliographical and related studies, the most distinctive, within the context of this chapter, is the lecture, by F. C. Francis, given at the University of Glasgow on the David Murray Foundation, entitled *Robert Copland: Sixteenth-Century Printer and Translator*.[6] Copland is shown to have been closely associated with Wynkyn de Worde, first, in 1508, as translator, and subsequently, between 1514 and 1535, the year of de Worde's death, as printer, thereafter continuing to work in both capacities until 1547, when Andrew Boorde described him as 'the eldest printer in England'. As a printer he failed to rise above the relatively low standard of his contemporaries in this country. As a translator, while conforming with current practice in apologies for his deficiencies, he would appear to have been ready to undertake any work which came to hand, even when it entailed the rendering of hard, technical terms. Most of the works which he printed or translated contain original contributions in the form of prefaces, additions, or postscripts either in prose or verse, which are characterized by a strongly personal note and an addiction to moralizing. Several of his pieces, including a dialogue between 'Copland' and 'Quidam', throw light on current printing and publishing practice. From the appearance of Copland's name as 'the Printer' in several books under de Worde's name, and Copland's use of de Worde's address for his own publications, Francis concludes that the two were in partnership, presumably sharing both the costs and the profits of their business. Between 1522 and 1530 Copland appears to have been printing independently, the books which he printed during this period including several devotional works. After 1530 his activities, not

merely as a printer but also as a man of letters, seem to have increased, a noteworthy instance of his efforts at authorship being a verse preface to de Worde's edition of *The Parliament of Fowls*. 'Because of his practice of writing something of himself in all his books, he presents a curiously consistent picture, whether in his capacity as translator, editor, printer, or publisher.'

The quatercentenary of the English Geneva Bible is commemorated in an article (*Lib*), by M. H. Black, entitled 'The Evolution of a Book-form: The Octavo Bible from Manuscript to the Geneva Version'. The subject entails consideration both of the way in which the early printer set about turning manuscript into type, and of the influences which affected his choice of conventions, topics which, we are told, have hitherto been unduly kept apart in consequence of the distinctive specialized fields of palaeography and bibliography. The Bible in octavo presents special problems, in view of its length and small dimension, which presented peculiar difficulties to the scribe and to the printer producing a traditional book in a new medium, and which would account for some of the differences between early Bibles printed from manuscript and those of today. Yet printing is generally firm, clear, and consistent, and by the end of the fifteenth century the tendency towards uniformity is 'almost certainly international'. A series of plates serves to illustrate changes in production, and incidentally for comparison between the work of Froben and of Estienne. The tempo quickened in the 1550's, which is 'the crucial decade in the history of bible-design'. In the Geneva English Bible the only feature which now seems slightly unusual is the size of the capitals used for the first lines of book-headings. The article concludes with reference to John Legate's Bible, printed at Cambridge in 1591,

---

[6] *Robert Copland: Sixteenth-Century Printer and Translator*, by F. C. Francis. Glasgow, Jackson. pp. 44. 7s. 6d.

'a Geneva version in the Geneva style', and with a survey of the influence of Estienne, who 'had the foresight to produce the most imaginative and superb bibles ever printed'.

This section may suitably close with reference to three other contributions within the field of bibliography. In the 'Eighty-sixth Critical Bibliography of the History of Science and its Cultural Influences (to 1 January 1961)' (*Isis*), by Harry Woolf, Phyllis Brooks Bosson, and Carol B. Hewitt, fifteen pages are allotted to works on the Renaissance and the Reformation. Part 1 of 'A Selective Check List of Bibliographical Scholarship for 1959', by Rudolf Hirsch and Howell J. Heaney (*SB*), relates to 'Incunabula and the Early Renaissance'. 'Lydgate's *Serpent of Division*, 1559, Edited by John Stow' is the theme of a short article, by William Ringler (*SB*). Stow appears to have had a lifelong interest in Lydgate, whose only known prose work is *The Serpent of Division*. He owned, or made copies, of many Lydgate manuscripts, appended Lydgate's *Siege of Thebes* to his 1561 edition of Chaucer, and contributed an extensive bibliography of Lydgate's works, including *The Serpent of Division*, to Speght's 1598 Chaucer. For the text of his edition of *The Serpent of Division*, Stow did not use 'The Auctours old copy', notwithstanding his statement to this effect on the title-page, but the print of Peter Treverys, which was followed by H. N. MacCracken in his edition of 1911.

The outstanding work of the year on English history during this period is *The Fifteenth Century*, by E. F. Jacob, the latest addition to *The Oxford History of England*.[7] The last chapter, entitled 'The Peaceful Arts', gives a compact, yet comprehensive survey of acts and monuments reflecting the earliest phases of the Renaissance in England,

[7] *The Fifteenth Century, 1399–1485*, by E. F. Jacob. O.U.P. pp. 775. 38s.

achievements, which, as in other countries, appear on the surface to be strangely at variance with the political turmoil and civil disorder of the age. Noting the connexion between economic prosperity, especially in the woollen industry, and the splendour of English architecture and stained glass, Jacob suggests that this was the age of the carver rather than of the sculptor, in wood and alabaster as much as in stone. The close proximity between warlike and peaceful activities is indicated by the fact that *Le Morte Darthur* was printed in the year of Bosworth Field, and that the knightly redactor composed most of his work in prison, drawing parallels between King Arthur and Henry V, and adapting the traditional itinerary of Arthur in France to correspond with the route taken by Henry. For Malory's concern with Arthur is that of an artist, a superb storyteller, which, presumably, would account for the fact that his language is not typical, or characterized by the anomalies of variant usage recorded by Caxton. Other topics discussed include the extent of the reading classes, their reading habits, the effect of the book trade upon 'utilitarian learning', instanced by that of William Kingsmill the scrivener, the growth of libraries and of educational foundations. Restriction of space probably accounts for the rather brief attention given to the achievement of Duke Humphrey as a book-collector, his benefaction at Oxford, his dealings with Italian scholars, and the first Italianate Englishmen stimulated by his initiative, all of which topics have, in fact, been treated at fair length, if not exhaustively, in more specialized works; but due emphasis is laid upon the growth of literacy, reflected in an increasing hunger for books, and in the foundation of colleges, grammar-schools, and song-schools. As might be expected, the libraries of noble and knightly classes seem to have been better stocked than those of merchants, particularly with histories. The universities, while anxious to encourage liberal arts, lacked the means to endow them, and a library containing both humanistic and scholastic works, such as that presented to Balliol College by William Grey, was probably exceptional. The chapter concludes with a critical note on Reginald Pecock, 'a publicist, a literary figure pure and simple, for whom "cleer witt" meant the employment of syllogistic logic in English philosophical language. . . . Perhaps the most cogent reason why Pecock was frowned upon was that the English Church needed not syllogism, but ardour and conviction.'

Great Britain to 1688,[8] by Maurice Ashley, is intended to indicate a new attitude towards history, consistent with the modern mind and the contemporary scene. 'We are now looking at matters in the light of the Nuclear Age in which we live, and are reading history books not in the buoyant, confident world before the first German war, but books written in what many of us in England regard as the Age of Guilt.' The projected novelty of interpretation is not evident in the section, comprising about a hundred pages, which deals with the early Renaissance. Ashley concurs with historians who regard the English Renaissance as more native than foreign in origin, accepting Tillyard's conclusion that much of the picture of Elizabethan world order is painted on medieval lines. He refers briefly to fifteenth-century Chaucerians, Caxton, the early humanists, antiquarians, and chroniclers, noting the damage to education resulting from the dissolution of monasteries. Discussing the forces most influential in the development of sixteenth-century English politics and society, he attributes it mainly to the Protestant Reformation, the broadening of the middle classes, and the rise of the House of Commons. Though none of these conclusions is either startling or original, as a popular textbook this may well serve its purpose.

A few contributions, of historical rather than literary interest, call for brief notice. *A Tudor Tragedy: The Life and Times of Catherine Howard*,[9] by Lacey Baldwin Smith, is offered, in contradistinction to the traditional romance of 'the rose without a thorn', as 'an exercise in historical causation, encompassing "the entire sink and puddle" of palace politics and backstairs bickering, which throve so abundantly within the garden of Henry VIII's government'. Nurtured within a world of violence and moral laxity, Catherine appears as the passive, though by no means guiltless, victim of circumstance, entangled fatally in a hornet's nest of political, religious, and personal intrigue. Martin Biddle surveys the history of Nonsuch Palace, suggesting the probability of rivalry in the building of royal mansions between Henry VIII and Francis I, who was continually embellishing the palace of Fontainebleau (*History Today*). *The Art of War in Renaissance England*,[10] by John R. Hale, is the first of a series of booklets projected by the Folger Library to describe various aspects of the cultural history of the sixteenth and seventeenth centuries for the benefit both of the research worker in history and literature, and for the non-specialist. It consists of a brief introduction, followed by a series of plates reproduced from books of the period, with accompanying critical comments, concerned with military training, tactics,

[8] *Great Britain to 1688: A Modern History*, by Maurice Ashley. Michigan U.P. pp. 441. Cresset P. £2. 10s.

[9] *A Tudor Tragedy: The Life and Times of Catherine Howard*, by Lacey Baldwin Smith. Cape. pp. 222. 21s.
[10] *The Art of War in Renaissance England*, by John R. Hale. Folger Shakespeare Library. pp. 59.

and strategy. The revolution in the art of war resulting from the invention of gunpowder necessitated the reduction of heavy armed cavalry, and its replacement by infantry, changes which entailed new methods of fortification, battle formation, and recruiting. The visual effect of these changes is vividly represented in the excellent illustrations of this attractive booklet.

BJRL includes a useful and substantial article, by Sydney Anglo, entitled 'The *British History* in Early Tudor Propaganda. With an Appendix of Manuscript Pedigrees of the Kings of England, Henry VI to Henry VIII'. Anglo cites evidence connecting the History of Geoffrey of Monmouth with 'a problem central to the study of early Tudor propaganda—the British descent of the Tudor dynasty'. Propaganda on these lines, which dates back to the projected address to Henry VII on his entry into Worcester in 1486, is composed of four elements, the allegedly Trojan descent of the British kings, the Prophecy to Cadwallader of ultimate victory over the Saxons, the greatness of King Arthur, and the symbolical significance of the Red Dragon. The descent of Henry VII from British kings is noted by several of his contemporary supporters, most impressively by Bernardus Andreas, though Henry VIII seems to have been little concerned to preserve the claim of British ancestry. Other evidence to the same effect is to be found in royal ceremonial and pageant scenes, for instance in the greeting of Henry by Ebranus at York, the inclusion of Arthur as one of the Nine Worthies in the *Coventry Leet Book*, and the name, Arthur, given to Henry's eldest son, the significance of which was duly stressed in the pageants presented at the Prince's marriage. Though King Arthur apparently does not figure in other early Tudor pageants, he has a prominent place in the battle over Geoffrey's *History* waged by Leland and other antiquarians. John Rastell, who was closely associated with Court festivities, was highly critical of the *History*, concerning which he would 'let euery man be at his lyberte to beleue ther in what he lyste'. The comparatively recent assignment of the Red Dragon as a badge to Cadwallader, and the supposed significance of the Dragon's prophecy were readily utilized in armorial and symbolic propaganda, a red dragon being included in the standard presented by Henry at St. Paul's soon after his accession.

Examination of 'Internal Chronology in Malory's *Morte Darthur*' has led Charles Moorman (*JEGP*) to oppose Vinaver's case for separate tables, and to offer 'a somewhat more detailed chronology than has been offered, and to propose two general points concerning the structural unity and method of composition of Malory's book based on that chronology'. The scheme of chronology deduced from the text, and demonstrated by means of a chart, shows that the difficulties and inconsistencies in the time-scheme are confined to the early part of the story, analysis of which indicates a deliberately planned chronology, with cross references and retrospective narrative. Avoiding the 'tapestry technique' of his French originals, Malory chose 'a method of presentation which blocked out its episodes in structural and thematic units'. On this premiss *Morte Darthur* is presented in terms of theme rather than time, for it was necessary to take great liberties with chronology, 'lest a strict chronological rendering obscure the thematic pattern'. An incidental piece of evidence, also supporting the case for planned unity in *Morte Darthur*, is cited by Victor Angelescu in connexion with 'The Relationship of Gareth and Gawain' (*NQ*), the apparent inconsistency in Gawain's character and behaviour, it is argued, being more readily understood if the work is viewed as a unified whole.

An earnest of the projected Yale edition of the complete works of Thomas More is provided in *St. Thomas More: A Preliminary Bibliography of His Works and of Moreana to the Year 1750*,[11] compiled by R. W. Gibson with the assistance of J. Max Patrick. The bibliography is published by the St. Thomas More Project, Yale University, under the auspices of Gerard L. Carroll and Joseph B. Murray, Trustees of the Michael P. Grace, II, Trust. Gibson has closely followed the method of bibliographical description used in his bibliography to the works of Bacon (1950). The title-pages are either reproduced in facsimile, or given in transcription, together with sizes, collations, and contents. Opening with a frontispiece of representative signatures of More in chronological order, the volume is divided into eleven sections, six of which provide bibliographical descriptions relating to *Utopia*, Separate Works, Collected Works, Lucian, with More's translations, Prayers, and Lives of More. The other sections list letters to and from More, allusions to More and his works, Utopiana, fictitious publishers' imprints using Utopian addresses, and portraits of More that appear in works included in the Bibliography. The section entitled *Utopiana*, supplied by J. Max Patrick, comprises an extensive selection of Utopias and Utopian literature. In view of the vast number of works within this category written between 1500 and 1750, the task of making such a selection is clearly a formidable one, and we are not surprised to be told that 'the works considered for this bibliography, but

rejected, far outnumber those included'. Fortunately, the compiler's interpretation of a 'proper Utopia' and its derivatives is liberal, and his compilation generous; it is therefore surprising that, while making three references to Swift, including the latter's glowing tribute to More, and listing both *The Fable of the Bees* and *Le Nouveau Gulliver*, he should have excluded reference to *Gulliver's Travels*, an omission presumably deliberate. In substance, however, the Utopiana section supplies a mine of information over a wide range of literature, which should prove invaluable to any worker within this field, and the same must be said of the Bibliography as a whole. All readers will appreciate the wisdom and consideration of the editors in thus making immediately available a store of useful material systematically arranged, in full recognition of the fact that this bibliography is only preliminary, and subject to enlargement during the next ten years while work on the Yale edition is in progress.

The English Department of Rice University has founded a new quarterly periodical, entitled *Studies in English Literature*,[12] the first number of which appeared in the winter of 1961. One issue will be devoted annually to each of the four following subjects: Renaissance Poetry and Prose (including Milton), Elizabethan Drama, Restoration and Eighteenth-Century Literature, Romanticism and Victorian Literature. Each issue is to include a review article, similar in scope to *YW*, covering important work on the relevant period published during the preceding year. To judge from the first of these, 'Recent Studies in the English Renaissance', by Arthur E. Barker, the series should prove a timely addition to critical-bibliographical surveys now

[11] *St. Thomas More: A Preliminary Bibliography of His Works and of Moreana to the Year 1750*, compiled by R. W. Gibson with a Bibliography of Utopiana compiled by R. W. Gibson and J. Max Patrick. Yale U.P. pp. xx+499. $12.50.

[12] *Studies in English Literature 1500–1900. The English Renaissance*. Rice U.P. pp. ii+157. $1.50.

available. Though English scholars may well be envious of the resources already provided by American learned periodicals, the potential material for publication far exceeds available space, and this new enterprise should therefore be well received. The first number contains an article, by Rainer Pineas, on 'Sir Thomas More's Controversy with Christopher Saint-German', discussing the background to More's *Apologie*, and a probable influence upon his technique as a controversialist. St. German's *Diuision . . . betwyxte the spiritualitie and the temporalitie* (1532), against which much of the *Apologie* is directed, seems to have struck More as particularly dangerous on account of its ostensibly mild and impartial spirit. His reply to More's criticism, entitled *A dialogue betwyxte . . . Salem and . . . Bizance*, was countered by More in *The Debellacyon of Salem and Bizance*, both works relating to the rival priorities of canon and civil law. Through illustration from the pamphlets of both writers Pineas demonstrates how palpably and deliberately More adopts St. German's controversial devices, such as the generalization 'they say', left-handed compliment, and complaints of his opponent's inconsistencies, More's object being to tear down St. German's façade of impartiality in the conviction that behind it lay a ruthless desire to destroy the Church, and discredit the clergy. If More was, in fact, thus paying back his opponent in the latter's own coin, this was probably intentional. More was already a practised controversialist, and had made earlier use of generalized statement, as a form of irony, in *Richard III*. Both More and St. German obviously were drawing on modes of ironical statement derived from the common stock of rhetorical art. In another article (*SP*) Pineas discusses 'Thomas More's Use of Humor as a Weapon of Controversy'. Having

illustrated different uses of humour as a popular weapon for theological disputation from the work of Erasmus, Luther, Tyndale, and others, he proceeds to examine modes and features of More's humour as exemplified in his replies to Simon Fish and Tyndale, as well as to Saint German. One of his favourite artifices, employed to rebut Fish's statistics of clerical and monastic wealth, is to invert his opponent's argument by means of *reductio ad absurdum*. More subtle than this is the introduction, in the *Dialogue*, of a messenger, ostensibly arguing against More on behalf of the reformers, a device clearly allowing unlimited scope for the use of dramatic irony, in which More was a past master. Another artifice, exploited both in the *Dialogue* and in the *Confutacion*, is the introduction of a 'merry tale', which serves both to relieve monotony, and to divert attention from the main point at issue. In short, throughout More's controversial works humour frequently takes the place of direct refutation, irony and *reductio ad absurdum* doing service for argument. In common with other writers, More deemed it necessary to defend his use of humour in religious controversy, though not, like some of the reformers, by citing precedents from Scripture, but rather as a human characteristic, in keeping with his role as a layman, unwilling to assume false gravity and solemnly preach to his readers. His humour in controversy derives from the sense of fun colouring much of his behaviour in life, echoes of which are to be found throughout his writings, including non-controversial works such as *Utopia* and *Richard III*. 'It is obvious that More felt one of the best methods of fighting those who were attacking the Church was to laugh at them.'

In 'More and his Detractors' (*The Month*), John McAleer seeks to refute charges levelled against More, first of persecuting heretics and justifying his action, secondly of inconsistency between such action and the toleration practised in Utopia. The allegation that More suffered heretics to be beaten, tortured, and martyred in his own house is shown to be a fiction, first disseminated by Foxe, but based on nothing beyond garbled report and idle hearsay. There is no reason to doubt the statement of Erasmus to the effect that no man was put to death for heresy during More's Chancellorship, or More's assertion that no one who came into his hand ever had 'any stripe or stroke given them, so much as a fillip on the forehead'. Beneath the rhetorical severity of the *Dialogue concerning Heresies* 'there is the greatest gentleness, concern, and love for those who have lost the true religion'. But More does not advocate toleration at any cost, the Utopian policy, in this respect, being one not of principle but of expediency, an alternative to controversy, which could only destroy good and evil together. Violent religious propaganda in Utopia was punished by bondage, 'and bondage in Utopia meant death, if the bondman continued to be violent'. The legend of More's violence towards heretics was maintained, to some degree, even by reputable historians, at least until the date of his canonization, 1935. Anyone still disposed to believe the legend reading this article may well be persuaded to think again.

'The Vocation of St. Thomas More', as treated by Catherine Jarrot (*American Benedictine Review*), poses a number of questions. Was More the last great medievalist, forced through political circumstances to play a role he did not desire, or the first offspring of the English Renaissance, asserting the value of secular concerns against an outmoded otherworldliness? Wishing to be a monk, how was it that he became England's Chancellor? What was his attitude to the active and to the contemplative life? The statements of More's early biographers all go to confirm the assumption of his early vocation to the cloister, which he could not reconcile, however, with his desire for the married state. But as a layman he consistently submitted himself to the discipline of asceticism, and in several works he suggests how the layman may secure for himself a contemplative life, for instance by having 'some secret place in his own house to which he might withdraw'. The life of More, 'the King's good servant, but God's first', may be summed up as 'essentially contemplative, but superabundantly active'.

Under the title 'The Dialogue in *Utopia*: Two Sides to the Question' (*SP*), David M. Bevington examines More's use of dialogue in the first part of *Utopia* as a means of presenting a balanced, middle view of the topics under discussion by allowing the speakers to express conflicting opinions on current problems, which are deliberately left unsolved. He compares this with the dramatic use of dialogue in the interludes of Medwall and Rastell, as contrasted with the controversial *Dialogue concerning Heresies*. As the conversation with Hythloday is supposed to have taken place twenty years before the publication of *Utopia*, several of the topics discussed are no longer relevant, and More's presentation of himself is a fictitious *persona* More rather than directly self-expressive. On this premiss 'Hythloday and *persona* More represent the two polarities of More's own mind, by an analysis of *Utopia* in terms of its genre and its historical perspective'. The dialogue form offers a means of surveying with fairness and impartiality questions which More could not resolve concerning the true nature of the reigning monarch and his policy, foreign, fiscal, and domestic. Similarly, the account of Utopia is an impartial survey of problems which preoccupied his inquiring mind concerning the ideal form of political and social organization. An allusion by More in his conversation with Hythloday to Seneca's disputation with Nero in *Octavia* is discussed in a short article, entitled 'More and Seneca', by John Crossett (*PQ*), who considers that More must have been greatly impressed by the passage, which voices some of the central ideas in *Utopia* and in Hythloday's comments, particularly with respect to the advantages of retirement from civic responsibilities and the virtues of the Golden Age contrasted with present abuses. At the same time, More pleads for a philosophy more 'civil' in the prince's court than one of 'rigorous sapience'. 'As one cannot mix literary genres without destroying the play, so one cannot be too sternly philosophical without destroying life.'

Studies on the Origin and Early Tradition of English Utopian Fiction,[13] by S. B. Liljegren, presents *Utopia* against the background of earlier travel literature, classical and medieval, and as an analogue to the ideal commonwealths of Bacon, Hartlib, and Harington. Believing earlier treatment of the subject to be unsatisfactory, the author sets out to 'distinguish between definite influence, and the inspiration occasioned by the existence of events, books, and ideas obvious to More and his contemporaries'. The formative influences discussed are, on the one hand, the tradition of travel literature, and, on the other, the contemporary spirit of geographical discovery and adventure, surviving belief in unknown western islands, sites of an Earthly Paradise or El Dorado, fanciful notions of remote regions disseminated by medieval travellers like Marco Polo and Sir John Mandeville, and conflicting ideas of happiness as related to riches, climate, soil, leisure, and spiritual welfare. Parallelism between *Utopia* and the records of Columbus are sufficient to suggest some direct borrowing, Hythloday's association with Vespucci being attributable to the latter's greater reputation, the consequence of his ability as 'a gifted pretender with a knack at writing exciting stories . . . where he also copied the narratives of others, and pretended that he himself had achieved the feats in question'. But notwithstanding More's obvious interest in the records of contemporary voyagers, his humanity reacted against the attitude and conduct of conquistadors, in particular their thirst for gold, their enslavement of conquered natives, and the competitive lust for power stimulated through their discoveries. This is a fresh and useful study, but seriously impaired through lack of an index. An outstanding masterpiece of Utopian fiction is treated by John Traugott in 'A Voyage to Nowhere with Thomas More and Jonathan Swift: *Utopia* and *The Voyage to the Houyhnhnms*' (*Sew*) which traces points of affinity both in the two works and in their authors. Swift's detestation of Henry VIII was equalled only by his admiration for More, whom he eulogized as 'a person of the greatest virtue this kingdom has ever produced'. 'Like More, Swift played the fool only north north-west', they are comparable not only as masters of irony but in their 'Utopian mentality', and, irony apart, 'Houyhnhnms and Yahoos have the same sort or reality as the inhabitants of More's *Utopia*'.

English Bibles of the sixteenth and seventeenth centuries are treated as fully as space permits in F. F. Bruce's *The English Bible. A History of Trans-*

[13] *Studies on the Origin and Early Tradition of English Utopian Fiction*, by S. B. Liljegren. Uppsala: A-B Lundequistska Bokhandeln. Copenhagen: Ejnar Munksgaard. pp. 151. 25s.

lations,[14] a scholarly survey from the eighth century to 1961. Religious literature is the theme of some articles, three of which call for notice. Wilfred O. Cross, writing on 'Doctrine of the Church in Tudor and Caroline Writings' (*Hist. Mag. Prot. Episc. Church*), shows that, despite the emphasis on continuity and catholicity in the Church, Anglican theology of the sixteenth century was deeply tinged with the doctrines of Calvin, whose *Institutes* influenced both 'Puritans', like Cartwright, and 'Anglicans' like Whitgift. 'Anglican authors from 1550 to 1660 should be read, when they discuss the Church, in the light of two very closely allied principles of interpretation, viz. the Incarnational doctrine of the relationship between grace and nature, as expressed in the sacramental principle, and the allied teaching that all being is a composite substance of form and matter.' P. A. Sawada discusses 'Two Anonymous Tudor Treatises on the General Council' (*Journal of Ecclesiastical History*), one of which is extant in a single manuscript at Hatfield (no. 46), the other in two extant copies of the printed version, published in 1538 as *A Treatise concernynge generall councilles. . . .* The first attacks papal sovereignty by appealing to the canons of the Church, supported by traditional authorities and councils. The second defends the divine origin of kingly powers, and exposes the usurpation of these powers by the Pope. Earlier historians attributed the authorship of the first treatise to Cranmer, suggesting that it was addressed to the House of Lords, or to Thomas Cromwell in 1533 or 1534. Sawada dates it at least a year later in view of the topics discussed, which were preoccupying Cranmer and other prelates early in 1536. He suggests that the authors of the two treatises were, respectively, Henry Cole and Alexander Alesius, both of whom are referred to by Henry VIII in connexion with the proposed Council of Vicenza. 'Thomas Becon and Literary Studies' is the theme of a paper by A. G. Newell (*Evangelical Quarterly*). Its purpose is to gather 'what evidence Becon's works afford for a consistently held attitude to literature on the part of early English Protestantism'. The evidence cited is confined to Becon's *Catechism*, 'set forth Dialoge-wise in familiar talke between the father and the son . . . not six years'. His concern in this work is the need for the Christian education of children, which means knowledge of the Scriptures, particularly of the Psalms, and safeguarding against the pernicious influence of pagan and medieval authors as well as all contemporary literature savouring of filthiness or idle jesting. Such classics as he allows are to be carefully selected, and 'interlaced' with godly comment and interpretation. Here, it is suggested, Becon assumes the role of 'popular expositor of the practical aspects of Protestantism'. His attitude to literary studies 'is consistent, and, for an "incipient Puritan", it is liberal'.

The Word 'Irony' and its Context,[15] by Norman Knox, is designed as a continuation of the earlier history of the word by G. G. Sedgewick through examination of its development and usage in England during the Renaissance and neo-classical periods. The second chapter, comprising about one-quarter of the book, consists of a quotation-dictionary illustrating irony as pretence, deception, blame-by-praise and its converse, understatement, indirection, fictional elaboration, mock-serious discourse, derisive attack, and dramatic artifice. Other chapters cover

[14] *The English Bible. A History of Translations*, by F. F. Bruce. Lutterworth Press. pp. 234. 25s.

[15] *The Word 'Irony' and its Context, 1500–1755*, by Norman Knox. Duke U.P. C.U.P. pp. xi+258. 60s.

the original uses of the word by ancient writers, methods of blame-by-praise, criticism of the art of irony, raillery, and banter. The earliest known use of 'yronye' in English occurs in *Thordynary of Crysten men* (1502), where it translates *ironia* as used by Quintilian and later rhetoricians. 'But throughout the century the Latin or French form of the word was as likely to turn up in an English context as the English form.' Thus, Coverdale cites *ironia* from a statement of his adversary John Standish in the sense of 'ironical concession'. Although irony was recognized and freely exercised as a rhetorical device, the word itself was not at first in frequent or easy use, remaining 'esoteric and technical'. It did not become common until its resources were more fully exploited during the neo-classical period, while serious criticism of the art of irony did not develop before the end of the eighteenth century. Knox's book is a useful contribution within a field of study not yet overworked. It is fully documented, but the arrangement of the documentation is such as to make it, in places, difficult to see the wood for the trees.

Richard Sherry's *A Treatise of Schemes and Tropes* (1550),[16] reproduced in facsimile, with an introduction and index by Herbert W. Hildebrandt, renders accessible a pioneer textbook which, within its limitations as 'a highly organized dictionary of ancient, medieval, and Renaissance schemes and tropes', anticipates the more liberal and literary 'arts of rhetoric' by Wilson, Peacham, and Puttenham. 'The Significance of Elyot's Revision of the *Gouernour*', by Elizabeth Holmes (*RES*), shows, by comparison of the

editions of 1531 and 1537, a marked change in Elyot's use of neologism and archaism, which suggests recognition of his prolixity with a developing sense of English syntax, attributable, probably, to his association with the 'ink-horn terms' controversy, the compilation of his Latin–English dictionary, and his experience in translation. Summarily, 'Elyot's changes point in one major direction, that he wished to modernize, to simplify, to clarify, and to make his style more vivid'. Harold H. Davis calls attention to 'An Unknown and Early Translation of Seneca's *De Beneficiis*' (*HLQ*), namely, that of Nicholas Haward, whose *Line of Liberalitie* (1569), a translation of the first three books of Seneca's work, anticipates Golding's translation of 1577–8. By means of quotation he compares the style of Haward's with versions of Golding and Lodge.

The Autobiography of Thomas Whythorne,[17] edited by James M. Osborn, is the first reproduction from manuscript of a work which the author describes as 'A book of songs and sonetts, with longe discoorses sett with them . . .', 'discourses' which give an account of his childhood, youth, and later years, intermingled with anecdotes, moralizing, and proverbs. About a quarter of the book is in verse, poems being 'the heart of the autobiography', to which much of the prose is an appendage. Set out with a new 'orthografye', based upon that of John Hart, published in 1569, it can fairly be described as the first known autobiography in English, telling in detail the story of Whythorne's early life as composer, executant, and teacher of music, his numerous fairly innocent love-affairs, ending in marriage at the age of 49, his sojourns in Oxford, Cambridge, and abroad, his pro-

[16] *A Treatise of Schemes and Tropes by Richard Sherry and his Translation of the Education of Children by Desiderius Erasmus.* A Facsimile Reproduction with an Introduction and Index, by Herbert W. Hildebrandt. Gainsville, Florida. pp. x+238. $7.50.

[17] *The Autobiography of Thomas Whythorne*, ed. by James M. Osborn. O.U.P. pp. lxvi+328. 45s.

fessional career from pupillage under John Heywood to the post of Master of Music in the Chapel of Archbishop Parker. Though Whythorne had the distinction of publishing the first set of English madrigals in 1571, his music was unknown or underrated until the publication of an appreciative study by Philip Heseltine in 1925, since which its value has been generally recognized. The autobiography reveals an engaging personality, responsive alike to the grave and gay things in life, keenly interested in the society he encounters, and devoted to the art and practice of music, to which he devotes an extensive historical survey near the end of the work, particularly interesting in its reference to the music of his age. The editor has fulfilled his task admirably, supporting the text with introduction, notes, and appendixes fully adequate, yet not excessive. The excellent illustrations include photographic reproductions of portraits, title-pages, a page from Whythorne's song-book, and a specimen of his handwriting. The last appendix gives an index to all Whythorne's known poems, together with a few other verses found in his Autobiography. Osborn promises an edition in modern spelling, and has published a lecture on Whythorne delivered at the Clark Library Seminar.[18]

'Tradition and the Interpretation of the *Kingis Quair*' (*RES*), by John MacQueen, is a revaluation of the poem, stressing its dependence upon tradition and convention rather than realism or self-expression. On this premiss the theme is related to that of *De Consolatione Philosophiae* and *The Pilgrimage of the Life of Man*, figuring the liberation of Youth by Love and Philosophy from its bondage to For-

tune. There is no account of the lovers' meeting or relationship, no clear indication of 'emotion recollected in tranquillity'. The poet is not telling his own love story, but showing how his experience is a counterpart to that of Boethius. 'The conclusion, in fact, is the unconditional and happy acceptance by the individual of his place in an ordered universe that is Christian, at least in terms of the naturalistic Platonism of Bernard Sylvestris, Alain of Lille, and the school of Chartres.' Two emendations, in stanzas 125 and 196 of *The Kingis Quair*, are proposed by Carl E. Bain (*NQ*). D. Duncan, discussing Henryson's *Testament of Cresseid* (*EC*), joins issue with the generally accepted view that the poem satisfies poetic justice, finding this to be incompatible with the designation 'tragedie'. He suggests that in the horror and repulsive details of Cresseid's state Henryson is depicting a contemporary reality, the plague in Scotland treated in his *Prayer for the Pest*. The poem is a vision of hopelessness, experience temporarily overturning faith. As in the *Fables*, 'there is the strength of independence as well as orthodoxy in Henryson's thought, toughness as well as gentleness in his humanity'.

Sir Richard Roos, Lancastrian Poet (*c. 1410–1482*),[19] by Ethel Seaton, is a long and copiously documented work, setting forth the writer's conclusions concerning the obscure individual whose name appears on the Harleian manuscript of the English version of Chartier's 'La Belle Dame Sans Merci'. At the outset Miss Seaton argues that the author of this piece was not, as generally assumed, the younger son of Thomas Lord Roos, but his uncle, Sir Richard Roos, Lord Roos's younger brother. She devotes her first chapter to an account of the Roos family,

[18] *The Beginnings of Autobiography in England.* A paper delivered at the Fifth Clark Library Seminar 8 August 1959, by James M. Osborn. California U.P. pp. 25.

[19] *Sir Richard Roos, Lancastrian Poet* (*c. 1410–1482*), by Ethel Seaton. Hart-Davis. pp. 592. 63*s*.

constructed from contemporary records, and the second to a hypothetical
biography of Sir Richard Roos, embodying the few recorded facts relating
to him, amplified by many more un-
proven deductions, a story most of
which is narrated, inevitably, in the
conditional tense or the subjunctive
mood. The theory that Roos wrote an
extensive collection of poems under the
patronage of Duke Humphrey and his
circle is supported by an array of
evidence, deduced from supposed
cryptograms and acrostics hiding the
names of these patrons, and alleged
to recur throughout a large body of
fifteenth-century poetry. On the strength
of these assumptions, the Cambridge
University MS. of 'La Belle Dame Sans
Merci' is termed 'the Roos scrap-book',
as 'containing many lyrics, short poems
and fragments of Roos's composition'.
Far more startling than this claim are
the arguments advanced and the conclusions reached concerning the 'Canon'
of Roos's works, which, we are asked
to believe, includes *The Legend of Good
Women*, the Chaucerian *Romaunt of
the Rose*, most of the lyrics within the
present Chaucer canon, *The Black
Knight, The Parliament of Love, The
Flower and the Leaf*, and a large proportion of the pieces assigned to Wyatt,
Surrey, and 'Uncertain Authors' in
Tottel's *Miscellany*. The energy and
fertility of such a poet, if he existed,
must have equalled his ingenuity in
devizing complex word-puzzles, the
reading of which supplies the sole
evidence for the 'Canon', linguistic and
kindred difficulties being ignored. If
the theory advanced in this book is
valid, the history of English poetry
from the fourteenth to the sixteenth
century, as hitherto accepted, must be
radically revised and rewritten. If not,
most of the effort devoted to re-estab-
lishing this 'Lancastrian poet' is mis-
spent.

*Music and Poetry in the Early Tudor
Court*,[20] by John Stevens, is a fresh,
interesting study revolving around the
three surviving song-books of this
period, the Fairfax MS., the MS. of
Henry VIII, and the Ritson MS., the
contents of which are examined against
the perspective of other lyrical poetry,
medieval and contemporary. Perusal of
these books raises questions concerning their origin, authorship, environment, and intention. The paucity of
such manuscripts still extant, even
allowing for Reformation vandalism,
suggests that during the early Tudor
period, as in the later Middle Ages, the
public for verses was much larger than
that for written music, and that music
manuscripts, apart from plain-song,
were never very numerous. The variety
of styles represented, alike in subject-
matter and musical form, reflect a
corresponding variety of origin, in
medieval Latin poetry, Chaucerian
love-lyric, and popular carol. The two
different styles of love-poetry, ornamental and simple, seem to be echoed
in musical settings, though about this
it is dangerous to be dogmatic, in view
of the complex and inexplicit character
of musical notation. Stevens is critical
of popular assumptions as to the close
association between poetry and music,
believing them to have arisen through
failure to distinguish between the
musical culture of the Elizabethan
period and that of the early sixteenth
century. He argues that the natural
union between poetry and music broke
up during the fourteenth century, the
former having become a branch of *ars
rhetorica*, the latter an independent
form of art, objective and highly complex. Such natural union survived only
in folk-song, and while poetry still
provided musicians with forms for
their compositions, practitioners in
each art were virtually indifferent to the

[20] *Music and Poetry in the Early Tudor
Court*, by John Stevens. Methuen. pp. xi+
483. 63s.

other. Tudor song-books are anterior to the 'great divide', which made it axiomatic that music should 'express' moods signalized in the words of a song, a notion encouraged by the Reformation custom of setting simple, sacred words to emotive music. Analysis of the song-books and of lyrics set to music shows that the music bears no relation to the words, apart from forms, while few of the courtly lyrics have tunes extant, or were necessarily intended for music, apart from those derived from popular songs. On this assumption, the conventional view of Wyatt as a maker of songs is mistaken, apart from the fact that it conflicts with contemporary descriptions of him as 'weighty' and 'depe-witted'. The poetry of the courtly makers is to be related rather with traditional courtly love-poetry, with conventions, images, and 'language of love' never intended to be mere words on a page, but forming rather part of a social drama or game. Accordingly, Stevens devotes the last part of his book to examination of music in ceremonies, entertainments, and plays played both by amateurs and professionals. The texts of the three song-books are printed in an appendix, followed by an index of songs, and a full bibliography. This is a challenging study, and in opposing accepted views the author, in places, is inclined to overstate his case. But he presents it forcefully, with the support of wide scholarship and judicious comment, and his work contains much to interest both the musicologist and the literary critic.

J. Hollander, in *The Untuning of the Sky*,[21] directs attention to 'certain beliefs about music rather than music itself'. These beliefs, during the fifteenth and early sixteenth centuries, are shown,

by means of quotations, to range between outright, or implied disapproval, through association of music with worldly vanity, and interest in the philosophical and educational elements of music, both theoretical and practical. Thus, 'mirth and melody' are preoccupations of Flesh in *The Castle of Perseverance*, the craft of music and minstrelsy are of no avail in the *Dance of Death*, and Barclay, after Brant, in *The Ship of Fools* condemns drunkards, 'syngynge theyr folysshe songes of rybawdry'. At the other extreme is the presentation, in the *Court of Sapience*, of Dame Musyk discussing with Dame Philosophy the origins and ethics of her art in conventional school terms, the careful evaluation of music, celestial and classical, in Douglas's *Palace of Honour*, and Henryson's picture of Orpheus completing his musical education within the heavenly spheres. Skelton's detailed references to musical instruments and technique are cited as a valuable source of information on music at the early Tudor court, and references in works of the courtly poets as anticipating the more extensive use of music and musical imagery by the Elizabethans. As a study designed to be impressionistic and selective rather than systematic this book can be recommended.

Skelton and Satire,[22] by A. R. Heiserman, is a detailed study of Skelton's major satires, taking into account his use of conventions and other forms of literary tradition. Kenneth Muir has edited a selection of poems from the Blage MS. in Trinity College Dublin, an anthology of poems written between 1530 and 1550,[23] including pieces by Wyatt and Surrey, with both of whom the original owner,

[21] *The Untuning of the Sky. Ideas of Music in English Poetry, 1500–1700*, by John Hollander. Princeton U.P. pp. xiv+467. $8.50.

[22] *Skelton and Satire*, by A. R. Heiserman. Chicago U.P. pp. 326. $6.50.
[23] *Unpublished Poems*, ed. from the Blage Manuscript by Kenneth Muir. Liverpool U.P. pp. xviii+91. 12s. 6d.

Sir George Blage, was acquainted. Muir's selection consists of fifty poems, together with two printed in Ault's anthology, and sixteen previously published poems of Wyatt. Two of the fifty pieces are ascribed to Wyatt in the manuscript, and Muir assigns to him several others from evidence of style, vocabulary, and metre. Comparison of the text of Wyatt's poems in the Blage MS. and in other sources shows that the former is superior to all other texts except the Egerton MS. As Blage was a close friend of Wyatt, he might well have been in a better position to collect Wyatt's poems in a reliable text than the unknown compiler of the Devonshire MS., which contains many poems of uncertain authorship. The anonymous poems in *The Court of Venus* and *Songes and Sonnettes* are generally inferior to those in the Blage MS., which suggests that either Blage's taste was finer, or his opportunities greater than those of other compilers. The specimen poems printed abound in the conventional images and word-play characteristic of *Songes and Sonnettes*, and show considerable variety in metrical form. Among the best are some in stanzas of short lines, typical of Wyatt, and not unworthy of him. Muir's suggestion that Wyatt was the author of the lament on the execution of Lord Rochford and other alleged paramours of Queen Anne gains support from the inscription 'Viat' against no. XLIII, presumably written at about the same time, when Wyatt was imprisoned in the Tower. Over and above the possibility of attributing to Wyatt some of the poems now published and of thus enlarging the Wyatt canon, the collection makes some interesting additions to the corpus of works by Tudor courtly makers.

In 'Un nuovo contributo sulla prima esperienza petrarchesca in Inghilterra' (*Italica*) Marco Pecoraro traces affinity and differences between the introspec-

tion of Petrarch and the melancholic spirit of Wyatt, which he attributes to a life much disturbed by unhappy events, and which is traceable in Wyatt's satires and translations from the Psalms as well as in his lyrics. He notes distinctive features in Wyatt's renderings of Petrarch, in particular the elimination of visual imagery, the trend towards realism, and the replacement of abstract by concrete motifs. Albert S. Gérard, replying to an earlier article by D. Hainsworth on Wyatt's 'They fle from me' (*EC*), suggests that the poem refers to the general theme of woman's inconstancy rather than cynical philandering, or emotional lust for revenge, the poet pondering in wry humour and detachment on the moral implications of the situation he presents. Florence H. Ridley, examining 'Surrey's Debt to Gawin Douglas' (*PMLA*), concludes that Douglas contributed little to the form, but greatly to the content of Surrey's translation, the proximity, extending even to the use of Scottish words, being so close as to suggest that Surrey had Douglas's version before him. Her analysis of Surrey's translation shows 465 lines in Book II, and 346 in Book IV directly dependent upon Douglas.

A new edition of John Hall's *Court of Virtue* (*1565*)[24] is the first reprint in full of 'the most encyclopaedic' of early Tudor anthologies. The text followed is that of the Huntington Library copy, corrected by reference to the British Museum copy, with some typographical modernizations, including transcriptions of musical settings. Hitherto such notice as has been paid to Hall's miscellany has been focused on his moralized versions of poems in *The Court of Venus* and *Songes and Sonnettes*, which he parodies both in the

[24] *John Hall. The Court of Virtue* (*1565*), ed. with an Introduction by Russell A. Fraser. Routledge and Kegan Paul. pp. xxv+424. 56s.

title and in the Prologue, adapted from the Prologue to *The Court of Venus* with substitution of ethical for secular allegory. His redacting of poems by Wyatt, for instance 'My penne take payne' and 'Blame not my lute', are textual curiosities, if nothing more, and other poems are probably redacted from secular originals no longer extant. His metrical versions of psalms, canticles, and other passages from sacred writings offer a variety of specimens of poetry adapted for popular consumption from Protestant liturgical sources and of different verse-forms to which such poetry was set. Though the general level of his poetry is not high, it expresses an intensity of conviction, which, his editor considers, renders him 'capable in flashes of fine verse'. Apart from its relation to earlier poetry, *The Court of Virtue* is interesting historically, revealing the observations of an intelligent medical practitioner upon many different facets of sixteenth-century life and thought, including religion, education, costume, entertainment, roguery, botany, astronomy, and magic. Hall has been well served by his editor, who has produced his work in a form both readable and scholarly, supported by a compact introduction, notes, glossary, bibliography, and index.

Alan Stephens has edited *Selected Poems*[25] of Barnabe Googe, whose works have not been generally available, except in anthologies, for nearly a century. In the introduction he relates Googe's poems to the native tradition, the study of rhetoric, and the poetry of Tottel's *Miscellany*, noting characteristic features in prosody and diction, which, at strategic points, 'becomes cleanly literal and plain', revealing 'a modulated power and hard clarity not available to any other kind of writing'.

Footnotes are provided, identifying the persons addressed, defining archaic words and obsolete usage, and offering brief comments. Paul E. Parnell, under the title 'Barnabe Googe: A Puritan in Arcadia' (*JEGP*), finds in Googe's pastorals the reaction of a sturdy Protestant against the pastoral, which was not suited to sixteenth-century English mentality. Googe's treatment of Mantuan shows that he must have read Italian pastorals with mixed feelings, and wrote the Eclogues 'as a sort of refutation of the pastoral tradition', his antipaganism leading him to be 'anticlassical and antiaesthetic as well'.

Four brief contributions on dramatic works deserve mention. J. H. P. Pafford supplies 'Two Notes on Bale's "King John" ' (*MLR*). The first is an emendation of 'apared crowne' (l. 1291) to 'a pared crowne', a 'broken head', possibly in the sense of 'a shaven tonsure'. The second discusses Bale's reference to 'maister Morres' (l. 1851), which Pafford thinks likely to have been derived from Giraldus Cambrensis. Two papers read at the first Congress of the Société des Anglicistes de l'Enseignement are summarized in *Ea*. Jean Jacquot, discussing 'Les Tragédies de Sénèque et le théâtre élizabéthain', notes the diffusion of 'Senecanism', apart from direct imitation, and the marked care for problems of government and civil law in Senecan plays not acted, especially associated with the circle of the Countess of Pembroke. Paul Bacquet, in 'L'Influence de Sénèque sur *Gorboduc*', examines the distinctive themes, structure, characterization, and style of the play, all of which, he considers, reveal a work that is something more than mere Senecan imitation.

The Founding of English Metre,[26] by John Thompson, is an analysis of the

[25] *Selected poems of Barnabe Googe*, ed. with an Introduction by Alan Stephens. Alan Swallow, Denver. pp. 61. $2.50.

[26] *The Founding of English Metre*, by John Thompson. Routledge and Kegan Paul. pp. ix+181. 32s.

techniques and development of the iambic line in English poetry from Tottel's *Miscellany* to *Astrophel and Stella*. English metre, it is argued, 'developed out of internal necessities in the English language'. Metre adds to language 'the elements of imitation that makes the two, when they are joined, the art of verse'. The principle underlying this theory is applied to sixteenth-century poetry from Wyatt to Spenser. The effect of the speaking voice in the original versions of Wyatt's satires is contrasted with the enforced metrical 'correctness' imposed upon the versions printed by Tottel. The monotony of Surrey's blank verse is attributed to its remoteness from speech rhythm rather than to metrical regularity. In that 'extraordinary museum of metre', *The Mirror for Magistrates*, Dolman's 'Hastings' is preferred to all the other contributions, including those of Sackville, on the ground that Dolman 'varies the relation of the metrical pattern of his language according to his dramatic intention'. Gascoigne is justly praised for making a major advance both in poetics and poetic technique. *The Shepheardes Calender* represents the culmination of metrical tendencies developed since Tottel's *Miscellany*, 'not the beginning of a new way in metre, but a turning round at a dead end'. In the poetry of Sidney, on the other hand, 'the metrical system of modern English reaches perfection for the first time'. The general impression conveyed by this study is one of potentiality rather than fulfilment. Some of the metrical analyses, with the comments accompanying them, are difficult to follow, owing partly to unfamiliar terminology. The relation between speech and verse, admittedly a basic principle of prosody most significant during the sixteenth century, cannot adequately be treated through analysis of the iambic line alone, to the exclusion of other types of verse, particularly those of popular poetry.

VII. SHAKESPEARE

By T. S. DORSCH

1. Editions

No edition of the complete works or complete plays has been produced this year, nor have there been any additions to such standard undergraduate series as the Arden or the Cambridge New Shakespeare.

One paperback edition, however, calls for mention. This is The Laurel Shakespeare,[1] of which twenty-one volumes have so far appeared. The text is that of C. J. Sisson. The general editor of the series is Francis Fergusson, who provides for each play a critical introduction which includes textual notes and suggestions for further read-

[1] The Laurel Shakespeare. General Editor, Francis Fergusson. *The Taming of the Shrew*, commentary by Margaret Webster. pp. 190. *Romeo and Juliet*, commentary by W. H. Auden. pp. 221. *Richard III*, commentary by Stuart Vaughan. pp. 254. *The Merchant of Venice*, commentary by Morris Carnovsky. pp. 188. *Macbeth*, commentary by Flora Robson. pp. 188. *Twelfth Night*, commentary by E. Martin Browne. pp. 191. *Othello*, commentary by John Houseman. pp. 252. *As You Like It*, commentary by Esme Church. pp. 192. *The Winter's Tale*, commentary by D. A. Traversi. pp. 224. *Henry IV, Part 1*, commentary by Sir Ralph Richardson. pp. 219. *A Midsummer Night's Dream*, commentary by Lincoln Kirstein. pp. 159. *Much Ado about Nothing*, commentary by Virgil Thomson. pp. 191. *The Sonnets*, commentary by C. L. Barber. pp. 224. *The Tempest*, commentary by Jean Rosenthal. pp. 189. *All's Well that Ends Well*, commentary by Dorothy Jeakins. pp. 221. *Henry V*, commentary by Joseph Papp. pp. 224. *Richard II*, commentary by J. A. Bryant, Jr. pp. 191. *Measure for Measure*, commentary by Robert H. Chapman. pp. 223. *Antony and Cleopatra*, commentary by William Troy. pp. 254. *Hamlet*, commentary by Maurice Evans. pp. 255. *Julius Caesar*, commentary by Philip Lawrence. pp. 188. New York: Dell. Each vol. 35c.

ing; Fergusson is also responsible for the informative essay in every volume on Shakespeare's career and the theatres and theatrical conditions of his day. H. H. Smith has prepared the helpful glossaries, which cover classical and literary allusions as well as unfamiliar words and usages. The type used (Times Roman) is unusually clear and readable, much more so, indeed, than the type faces used in the vast majority of editions of Shakespeare. What lends a special interest to the series, however, is the commentaries on the individual plays written by well-known American and English actors and producers. These cannot all be dealt with here; a few examples must serve to indicate their nature. Margaret Webster writes of *The Taming of the Shrew* as a play in which 'there is little need for respectful orthodoxy' on the part of producers and actors; she goes on to describe the 'whole bag of tricks' that she has used in her own productions. In her notes on playing the role of Lady Macbeth, Dame Flora Robson ascribes Lady Macbeth's fall to overweening ambition coupled with lack of imagination; 'Macbeth has an excess of imagination; she has none'; and this has to be conveyed to the audience. To Sir Ralph Richardson, Falstaff is a character who 'has received a plenary indulgence, which is rarely extended in Shakespeare's world'; his part must be played accordingly. Virgil Thomson discusses illuminatingly the music that should be used in a production of *Much Ado About Nothing*; and Maurice Evans provides 'Comments on Playing the Role of Hamlet' in which he describes the Gloomy Dane, the Princely Dane, the Intellectual Dane, and the Soldierly Dane, as the part has been re-created by famous actors, he himself favouring the Soldierly Dane. The commentaries on the other plays are similarly un-academic and fresh, and each adds something to our feeling for the play with which it deals.

Other editions of single plays are listed in the invaluable *Sh Q* bibliography for 1961, which this year is published in the 1962 Summer number.

This bibliography also lists well over a hundred translations into a great variety of tongues, including Frisian, Korean, Lettish, Urdu, Ethiopian, Javanese, and Punjabi. With the appearance of its last three volumes, the new eight-volume translation by various hands of the complete works into Russian has been completed under the editorship of A. Smirnov and A. Anikst (Moscow: Iskusstvo). Cesare Vico Lodovici's translation into Italian has also been completed, in three volumes (Turin: Einaudi); and the third volume of Carlo Ruscini's Italian translation brings up to twelve the number of plays he has so far issued (Rome: Editrice italiana di cultura). In French the second volume of François-Victor Hugo's version adds thirteen to the dozen plays of the first volume (Paris: Éditions Garnier). Another translation of the complete works now concluded is that of Luis Astrana Marin into Spanish (Barcelona: Vergara).

2. *General Studies*

First published in 1951, *The Meaning of Shakespeare*,[2] by Harold C. Goddard, now appears in the Phoenix Books paperback series. So well known a book requires few words here. It is a study of the plays as poetry—'not merely as poetry in the romantic meaning of that term but as works of the Imagination in the widest and deepest sense'. At the same time Goddard believes that the poems and plays ought to be considered 'integrally, as chapters, so to speak, of a single work'. He therefore treats them in chronological order, and aims at tracing through them the development of Shakespeare as a poet and dramatic artist. Goddard is a perceptive and clear-headed critic, and the wider circulation now assured to this work of his is to be welcomed.

At her death Una Ellis-Fermor left behind her the plan of a book on Shakespeare on which she had been engaged for some years, and of which she had completed, or almost completed, several chapters. Under the title *Shakespeare the Dramatist*,[3] these chapters, edited by Kenneth Muir, have now been published, together with other papers which might have formed part of the book, or which are relevant to or illustrative of its approach to Shakespeare. This approach is to a large degree summed up in Miss Ellis-Fermor's well-known British Academy Lecture, 'Shakespeare the Dramatist', which was designed as the opening chapter of the projected book, and which now holds that position. It is followed by a chapter in which, by comparing a passage from Ibsen's *Ghosts* with one from *Macbeth*, Miss Ellis-Fermor demonstrates that it is the function of dramatic character, as 'an image on the grand scale', to evoke in our minds 'certain perceptions, realizations, emotions, which are themselves aspects of an underlying reality', and not 'an abstract from that perceived reality'. This idea is developed further in the next chapter, 'Shakespeare and the Dramatic Mode'. Later

[2] *The Meaning of Shakespeare*, by Harold C. Goddard. (Phoenix Books.) Chicago U.P., 1960. Two vols.: pp. xiii+394; v+300. Each vol. $1.95. 15s.

[3] '*Shakespeare the Dramatist*' and Other Papers by Una Ellis-Fermor, ed. by Kenneth Muir. Methuen. pp. xvi+188. 25s.

chapters deal with '*Coriolanus*', 'The Nature of Plot in Drama' (see *YW* xli. 13), 'Communication in Thought', 'Some Functions of Verbal Music in Drama', and 'Shakespeare and Ibsen as Dramatic Artists'. Muir's notes indicate how these chapters were intended to fit into the scheme of the whole book, had it been completed. The volume ends with studies of *Timon of Athens* and *The Two Noble Kinsmen* which bring out the 'imperishable and eternal significance' that earlier sections of the book have aimed at teaching us to find in great drama. Miss Ellis-Fermor's sensitivity and good sense are everywhere apparent in these papers, and we must be grateful to the editor and the publishers for having made them available.

The Sense of History in Greek and Shakespearean Drama,[4] by Tom F. Driver, deals with more fundamental dramatic problems than its title might suggest. Driver sees drama as 'an art that reflects basic understandings about time, space, and history. The representative drama of a given period reflects that period's "sense of history".' In order to establish the difference between the Greek and the Elizabethan conceptions of history, Driver makes a study of four Greek and four Shakespearian plays, comparing *The Persians* with *Richard III*, the *Oresteia* with *Hamlet*, *Oedipus Tyrannus* with *Macbeth*, and *Alcestis* with *The Winter's Tale*. His analyses lead him to the conclusion that recent attempts to identify Shakespeare's view of tragedy with that of the Attic playwrights are ill-conceived, for the different sense of history of the two periods presupposes different conceptions of destiny and different ways of confronting destiny. Moreover, 'the culture of the Greeks . . . was oriented toward an under-standing of nature in its recurrences, structures, and laws. Its bias was "anti-historical", and its drama reflected the fact with great power.' On the other hand, the Elizabethan popular drama 'provides enactments which represent to the audience something of the people's deepest understanding of itself. . . . That is to say, it will reflect the historical consciousness.' Driver's book contains some sensible criticism, and adds to our knowledge of Shakespearian (and general Elizabethan) outlooks.

J. A. Bryant, Jr., has given the eccentric title *Hippolyta's View*[5] to his book on 'some Christian aspects of Shakespeare's plays' because he believes that Shakespeare's treatment of the Scriptures, in the words that Hippolyta uses of the lovers' tales, 'grows to something of great constancy'. The Elizabethans, says Bryant, were accustomed to typological interpretations of the Scriptures, and 'Shakespeare's references to the data of Elizabethan Christianity and his frequent recourse to Biblical analogies have in addition to [the] ordinary power of metaphor the extraordinarily vital shaping power of typology'. Bryant analyses a dozen of the plays in order to trace the typological patterns that he thinks Shakespeare incorporated in them and reinforced by means of Biblical allusions and analogies. As an example, he finds in *Richard II* and *Hamlet* references to the story of Cain and Abel which seem to him to add new depths of meaning to these plays. Bryant writes well about some of Shakespeare's Christian allusions and themes; but he often overstates his case, or reads too much into the analogies he discerns, as when, on the strength of a single Biblical reference, he asserts that the pattern by which Antony and Cleopatra rise to tragic

[4] *The Sense of History in Greek and Shakespearean Drama*, by Tom F. Driver. Columbia U.P., 1960. pp. ix+231. $5. 40s.

[5] *Hippolyta's View: Some Christian Aspects of Shakespeare's Plays*, by J. A. Bryant, Jr. Kentucky U.P. pp. xi+239. $6.50.

grandeur 'makes complete sense only when viewed from the Christian perspective that Antony's allusion to the Messianic psalms explicitly invites'.

Leo Kirschbaum has published two interesting lectures on Shakespeare[6] which he has delivered at a number of British universities and in Jerusalem and Moscow. The subject and approach of the first are indicated by its title, 'In Defense of Guildenstern and Rosencrantz'. Kirschbaum believes that these two characters have been unfairly treated by the critics; their only crime is 'the vile sin of loyalty to their King', and they are the victims of Hamlet's 'constantly misdirected hatred of his father's murderer'. The thesis developed in '*The Tempest*—Apologetics or Spectacle?' may be summed up in Kirschbaum's own words: 'Of all Shakespeare's plays, *The Tempest* is the most obviously theatrical. Of all Shakespeare's plays it is the most profoundly religious. I would like to show how both are aspects of a theatrically successful unity.'

Early Shakespeare,[7] edited by John Russell Brown and Bernard Harris, is an extremely interesting collection of essays relating to Shakespeare's early career. The volume opens with 'The Profession of Playwright', an excellent survey, by R. A. Foakes, of 'the development of a regular professional theatre and a professional drama drawing on the best talents of the time'— just the kind of setting in which Shakespeare and his most gifted contemporaries might exploit to the full their dramatic and poetic genius. From Norman Sanders comes a sensible appraisal of the comedy of Greene and

of the influence it may have exerted on that of Shakespeare. Harold Brooks writes illuminatingly on 'Themes and Structure in *The Comedy of Errors*'. Already in this very early play he finds an astonishing command of the elements of dramatic construction, both on the large scale and in the control of details. Most interestingly and organically developed of the themes are those of relationship and of the contrast between appearance and reality. J. P. Brockbank's subject is the three Henry VI plays, which 'express the plight of individuals caught up in a cataclysmic movement of events for which responsibility is communal and historical, not personal and immediate, and they reveal the genesis out of prolonged violence of two figures representing the ultimate predicament of man as a political animal—Henry and Richard, martyr and machiavel'. In 'Dramatic Techniques and Interpretation in *Richard II*' R. F. Hill writes well on the artificial and stylized diction of the play, and relates it to Shakespeare's presentation of the characters. John Lawlor sets *Romeo and Juliet* against the medieval and Renaissance traditions of tragedy, and aims at showing that it is 'profoundly consistent with the longer run of the Shakespearian imagination'. Gareth Lloyd Evans sees in the two Henry IV plays 'the emergence of new dimensions in Shakespeare's plays' and a dramatic method that 'makes of history much more than a chronicle tapestry. It implies an attitude towards the dramatic presentation of life that sees things not in terms of one-dimensional narrative, varied by dissociated areas of comic and tragic action and character, but strictly as a unity of comical-tragical-historical.' In a paper illustrated by a number of plates, W. Moelwyn Merchant discusses stage-settings, pictorial representations, and adaptations of *A Midsummer Night's*

[6] *Two Lectures on Shakespeare: In Defense of Guildenstern and Rosencrantz; 'The Tempest'—Apologetics or Spectacle?*, by Leo Kirschbaum. Oxford: Blackwell. pp. 41. 7s. 6d.

[7] *Early Shakespeare*, ed. by John Russell Brown and Bernard Harris. (Stratford-upon-Avon Studies, 3.) Arnold. pp. 232. 25s.

Dream in order to demonstrate the changes that have taken place through the years in the critical assessment of this play and in the tastes of its audiences. John Russell Brown's approach to Shylock is both theatrical and interpretative; he outlines Shylock's stage-history from Charles Macklin's portrayal in 1741 to Sir John Gielgud's in 1938, and then considers what the text of the play suggests should be the manner of his presentation. Finally, Frank Kermode briefly discusses Shakespeare's development as a comic playwright between *A Midsummer Night's Dream* and *Twelfth Night*.

John W. Draper's *Stratford to Dogberry*[8] is a collection of thirty essays on about a dozen of Shakespeare's earlier plays, down to and including *Much Ado*. The first six essays are general, treating such topics as mistaken identity in the comedies, the contrast between court and country life, or Shakespeare's handling of bastardy. The remaining papers deal with special aspects of individual plays—the dating of *A Midsummer Night's Dream*, for example, or the mercurial temperament of Richard II. Five relate to *Romeo and Juliet*, three to *The Merchant of Venice*, half a dozen to Falstaff and his associates. A final group is devoted to the mature comedies, and includes studies of Beatrice and Benedick and of Dogberry's function as a satirical portrait of 'all minor officialdom'. The essays are uneven in quality, but the volume as a whole contains much good sense, especially where Draper interprets incidents in the plays against the background of Elizabethan life.

In comparison with the numerous books written about Shakespearian tragedy, general studies of the comedies are few and far between. In *Wand-*

lungen der Shakespeareschen Komödie,[9] an extended version of a lecture delivered to the Shakespeare-Gesellschaft in 1959, Ernst Th. Sehrt describes the changes of mood and technique that Shakespearian comedy underwent in its course from *The Comedy of Errors* to *The Tempest*. His main approach is by way of the element of play or sport ('Spiel'), and he examines the comedies chronologically in order to determine what this element contributes to the fabric of each. In the earliest comedies men are shown largely as the playthings of fortune, sported with rather than themselves directing the sport; but gradually, as is first clearly apparent in *Love's Labour's Lost*, they assume control of the sport of fun and wit and intrigue by which many of Shakespeare's best comic effects are achieved. At this time, too, Shakespeare with ever-increasing success embodies the play-element in courtly young gentlemen possessing both wit and worth, but needing to have these attributes guided into the right channels. At the same time he blends serious themes with the comic matter of his stories. In the 'dark' comedies play becomes the property of the minor characters, and the main characters become involved in sombre and near-tragic circumstances which have nothing of the comic about them except in their happy endings. Cheerfulness and farce return in the romances, combined, however, with serious moral issues treated in something of a religious spirit. Sehrt's thesis is developed more broadly than this outline might suggest, and he makes plenty of interesting comments on individual plays.

Robert Ornstein has edited a collection of essays[10] on the so-called

[8] *Stratford to Dogberry: Studies in Shakespeare's Earlier Plays*, by John W. Draper. Pittsburgh U.P. pp. viii+320. $3.

[9] *Wandlungen der Shakespeareschen Komödie*, von Ernst Th. Sehrt. Göttingen: Vandenhoeck & Ruprecht. pp. 60. DM. 2.40.

[10] *Discussions of Shakespeare's Problem Comedies*, ed. with an introduction by Robert Ornstein. Boston: Heath. pp. ix+111.

'problem' comedies. As most of them are well known, the volume requires no extended notice here. It opens with studies of *Troilus and Cressida* by Coleridge, F. S. Boas, D. A. Traversi, Una Ellis-Fermor, and Ornstein himself. The next five essays are concerned with *All's Well*: two, by E. K. Chambers and Hazelton Spencer, appear under the title of the play; the other three are 'The Role of Helena', by Edward Dowden, 'Dramatic Emphasis in *All's Well that Ends Well*', by Harold S. Wilson, and 'The Theme of Ambition in *All's Well that Ends Well*', by Clifford Leech. The last eight essays relate to *Measure for Measure*: the first four, having as titles the name of the play, are by A. W. Schlegel, Walter Pater, Sir Walter Raleigh, and Sir Arthur Quiller-Couch; these are followed by M. C. Bradbrook's 'Authority, Truth and Justice in *Measure for Measure*', W. M. T. Dodds's 'The Character of Angelo in *Measure for Measure*', Arthur Sewell's 'The Character of Angelo', and William Empson's 'Sense in *Measure for Measure*'; one might have expected also R. W. Chambers's influential British Academy lecture, and perhaps an extract from Mary Lascelles's excellent book on the play. The value of this collection is that it enables one to trace the changing fortunes of these three plays in the criticism of the last century and a half.

The Cease of Majesty,[11] by M. M. Reese, is much more than the 'study of Shakespeare's history plays' that its subtitle declares it to be; it is a thorough and highly informative study of the Tudor conception of history, and it is not until more than half way through that individual plays of Shakespeare are examined, though numerous references to them appear earlier. In the first half of the book Reese describes

Shakespeare's 'artistic inheritance' in the field of history by means of an admirable survey of Tudor historical literature in which, both from the professed historians and from the poets and playwrights who used historical material, he traces the development of the Tudor Myth and brings out the nature of the didacticism which was so important a part of these writings. He also discusses influences from outside, such as that of Machiavelli. He is able to show that, broadly speaking, outside his artistic purposes, Shakespeare accepted the common view of his age that it was 'the poet-historian's mission to interpret the past for the practical enlightenment of the present; and the lesson he chiefly taught was the old and familiar one that order means prosperity and bad or hesitant government means confusion'. Broadly speaking, for, as Reese demonstrates in his analyses of the plays, however much the characterization and the values of the histories may be determined by political orthodoxy, 'the universalising pattern is always large enough to contain individual variations'. Reese deals with many other aspects of the histories, and among other things he stresses Shakespeare's interest in 'the ideal social relationship in which king and people were united in a conception of their mutual duty'.

L. C. Knights's pamphlet[12] on four of Shakespeare's histories opens with a chapter in which Shakespeare's approach to history is, as in Reese's book but on a very much smaller scale, related to 'the major themes and assumptions of English historical writing in the sixteenth century'. The four plays he treats are *Richard III*, *King John*, *Richard II*, and *Henry V*.

[11] *The Cease of Majesty: A Study of Shakespeare's History Plays*, by M. M. Reese. Arnold. pp. ix+350. 35s.

[12] *William Shakespeare. The Histories:* '*Richard III*'; '*King John*'; '*Richard II*'; '*Henry V*', by L. C. Knights. (Writers and Their Work.) Longmans, for the British Council and The National Book League. pp. 55. 2s. 6d.

Although he discusses them from various points of view, especially in their political bearings, his main thesis is summed up in his words: 'What gives Shakespeare's early political plays their distinctive quality is the fact that they are part of the same continuous, and continually deepening, exploration of the nature of man that includes the great tragedies.'

H. B. Charlton's *Shakespearian Tragedy*[13] has become widely known since its publication in 1948; its inclusion in a reasonably priced paperback edition will bring within the compass of the average student's income a work of sound scholarship which will serve as a useful corrective to the type of criticism which is deplored in the next book to be noticed, and which all too many undergraduates uncritically echo.

The Story of the Night,[14] by John Holloway, contains extremely interesting studies of Shakespeare's major tragedies. The introduction is a timely and well reasoned exposure of the ill-conceived and often confusedly presented criticism of some recent Shakespearian commentators—of what Holloway calls 'the current coin of Shakespeare criticism'—exemplified in the elaborate search for extra-dramatic significances of such critics as G. Wilson Knight, D. A. Traversi, and, at times, L. C. Knights and F. W. Bateson. He himself sees a Shakespearian play as, first and foremost, 'a momentous and energizing experience', and in Shakespearian criticism he would like to see modernistic over-ingenuity replaced by 'discussion which puts the stress on interpretation'. His own criticism illustrates the value of the methods he advocates, as when, for example, he shows how much the

dramatic effect of *Hamlet* depends on 'an incessant play and thrust of frenzied intrigue, of plot and counter-plot, and on the surface of this, as its overt counterpart, a scintillating texture of intelligence and wit'. The final chapter of the book is an interesting examination of the partial resemblances between Shakespeare's tragedies and certain scapegoat ceremonies that have been widespread in human societies.

In his pamphlet[15] on the four great tragedies Kenneth Muir draws no generalizations on Shakespearian tragedy, for, though all the tragedies have something in common, their differences are, in his view, more important than their similarities. In contrast to most critics, he believes it more fruitful to approach *Hamlet* through the relationships between the characters than to concentrate on the Prince, and he shows what a study of these relationships adds to our understanding of the play. In *Othello* he lays particular stress on the theme of jealousy, which recent critics have tended to play down, and which he considers to be more important and more pervasive than even the older critics allowed. His studies of *Lear* and *Macbeth* are clear statements of orthodox viewpoints.

For his inaugural lecture as Joseph Cowen Professor of English at Newcastle, Peter Ure took as his subject *Shakespeare and the Inward Self of the Tragic Hero*.[16] The Shakespearian tragic hero, says Ure, has two 'selves'; he is the outward man whom the other characters in his drama see, and he is the inward man, the 'real self', whom the reader or audience alone is privileged to see. After a glance at Richard III, Hamlet, and Macbeth, Ure deals

[13] *Shakespearian Tragedy*, by H. B. Charlton. C.U.P. pp. ix+246. 10s. 6d.
[14] *The Story of the Night: Studies in Shakespeare's Major Tragedies*, by John Holloway. Routledge & Kegan Paul. pp. x+187. 21s.
[15] *Shakespeare. The Great Tragedies*, by Kenneth Muir. (Writers and Their Work.) Longmans, for The British Council and The National Book League. pp. 46. 2s. 6d.
[16] *Shakespeare and the Inward Self of the Tragic Hero*, by Peter Ure. Univ. of Durham. pp. 22. 2s. 6d.

more fully with the inward selves of Richard II, Othello, Lear, and Coriolanus. Richard's inward self is annulled, Othello's remains unchanged, Lear's is radically transformed, and Coriolanus's is revealed as it really is beneath deceptive outer appearances. What happens to these inward selves is directly related to the outcomes of the four tragedies which, says Ure, 'combine to make one of the mighty Shakespearian *arpeggii*; if all else perished, it would be possible to reconstruct from them a substantial portion of the whole mind of Europe'.

The sub-title of Maurice Charney's *Shakespeare's Roman Plays: The Function of Imagery in the Drama*[17] requires elucidation. Following the practice of many recent critics, Charney extends the meaning of the word 'imagery'. Although he accepts it in its normal usage (a verbal image generally presented as some form of metaphor, simile, or personification), he is more interested in 'nonverbal or "presentational" imagery', that is, 'the large body of images that is not part of the spoken words of the text, but directly presented in the theater'. For example, throughout *Antony and Cleopatra* there is verbal imagery of serpents suggesting evil and death, but Cleopatra's suicide by the agency of the asp is a presentational image. In *Julius Caesar* the dominant imagery of this kind is to be found in the storm and its portents, in blood, and in fire; in *Antony and Cleopatra* 'the world theme', the symbolic contrast of Egypt and Rome, the 'heightening' of Cleopatra, and the tragedy of Antony; in *Coriolanus* food and eating, disease, animals, acting and the theatre, and isolation. While some of Charney's interpretations seem rather to refer to thematic structure than to imagery in his sense of the term, his approach is sensible and fresh, and

takes us into the heart of the plays he is discussing.

Kenneth Muir's *Last Periods of Shakespeare, Racine, and Ibsen*[18] contains the text of four lectures delivered at Wayne State University in 1959. Although the last work of some authors reflects failing powers—that of Shaw, for example—Muir believes that others 'acquire a new profundity, a new understanding, in making a last attempt to solve the enigma of life'. After preliminary comments on Sophocles, Euripides, and Strindberg, he examines in some detail the last plays of Shakespeare, Racine, and Ibsen. In *Pericles, Cymbeline, The Winter's Tale*, and *The Tempest* he sees none of the signs of poetic or dramatic deterioration that some critics have attributed to these plays, nor can he regard them as 'merely an old man's consolation, an escape from reality', for in spite of their happy endings they do not deny or evade the tragic realities of life. The last plays of Shakespeare, Racine, and Ibsen are not, perhaps, the greatest single plays of any one of the three playwrights, but in their wisdom, humanity, and poetic art they 'round off the work of their respective authors in such a way that their total achievement seems to be greater than the sum of their individual plays'.

Most of the articles in this year's *Shakespeare Survey*[19] are concerned with Shakespeare in relation to his contemporaries, the main topic of discussion at the Shakespeare Conference at Stratford in 1959. The volume also contains international notes; a list of productions in the United Kingdom in 1959; a critique, by John Russell Brown, of productions at

[17] *Shakespeare's Roman Plays: The Function of Imagery in the Drama*, by Maurice Charney. Harvard U.P. pp. xi+250. $4.75.

[18] *Last Periods of Shakespeare, Racine, and Ibsen*, by Kenneth Muir. Liverpool U.P. pp. vii+117. 15s.

[19] *Shakespeare Survey, 14: An Annual Survey of Shakespearian Study and Production*, ed. by Allardyce Nicoll. C.U.P. pp. viii+180. 27s. 6d.

Stratford by Peter Hall and Michael Langham, and at the Old Vic by John Neville; a conspectus of the year's contributions to Shakespearian study in which critical studies are reviewed by Bernard Harris, studies of Shakespeare's life, times, and stage by W. Moelwyn Merchant, and textual studies by James G. McManaway; and a survey of 'Studies in Elizabethan and Jacobean Drama since 1900' by Arthur Brown. The nature of another item is indicated by its title and sub-title: 'Stratford-upon-Avon a Hundred Years Ago: extracts from the travel diary of the Reverend William Harness'. The gist of the remaining articles may be given fairly briefly. Herbert Howarth considers what there was about Shakespeare, whether in his life or in his art, that prompted Ben Jonson to speak of him as 'My gentle Shakespeare'. In 'Shakespeare v the Rest: The Old Controversy' T. J. B. Spencer reviews the fluctuating fortunes of Shakespeare's contemporaries in criticism from Dryden to the Mermaid editions. The influence of Marlowe on Shakespeare is discussed by Nicholas Brooke; Brooke describes Marlowe as a 'provocative agent' in that he was for Shakespeare the creator of 'something initially alien which he could only assimilate with difficulty, through a process of imitative recreation merging into critical parody'. I. A. Shapiro claims that Anthony Mundy would repay closer study than he has received; a fuller knowledge of his work in the last two decades of the sixteenth century would probably illuminate various aspects of Shakespeare's early work. Michel Grivelet demonstrates, with special reference to *The English Traveller*, that Heywood is anything but simple or thoughtless. However, for 'continuity of imaginative thought' he depends too much on ingenuity of construction, while Shakespeare embodies his thought in 'a coherent, if

complex, fable'. In 'The Tragedy of Revenge in Shakespeare and Webster' Harold Jenkins contrasts the approaches and techniques of the two playwrights, noting, among other things, that the 'fundamental contest' in *Hamlet* is between good and evil, whereas in Webster's plays it is between life and death. Ivor Morris expresses the belief that Fulke Greville's tragic vision, though much simpler, has resemblances to Shakespeare's, and that it suggests questions that we should ask in relation to Shakespeare. Finally, R. K. Das Gupta tries to show that Milton's admiration for Shakespeare is to a large extent a modern fiction.

Shakespeare Quarterly,[20] the admirable journal of the Shakespeare Association of America, prints numerous articles and notes of interest to students of Shakespeare; these are noticed in the relevant sections of the present chapter. It also reviews books and productions; and it is interestingly illustrated. Of particular value is the excellent annotated bibliography in the Spring number, this year edited by Robert W. Dent, and covering books and articles on Shakespeare published in 1960 in almost every country from China to Peru.

Although several of the ten articles in *Shakespeare Jahrbuch*[21] are concerned with questions of style, they are not as closely bound together by a central theme as those of some recent numbers. Max Lüthi studies the techniques by which Shakespeare persuades his hearer or reader to accept as real, for his dramatic purposes, conceptions or manifestations which are themselves

[20] *Shakespeare Quarterly*. Published by the Shakespeare Assn. of America, Inc. Annual subscription $8. Each number $2.50.
[21] *Shakespeare Jahrbuch*, ed. for the Shakespeare-Gesellschaft by Hermann Heuer, assisted by Ernst Theodor Sehrt and Rudolf Stamm. Vol. 97. Heidelberg: Quelle & Meyer. pp. 390.

unreal—false appearances, false report, self-deception, supernatural phenomena, and other things invisible or intangible. Helmut Viebrock shows how greatly the poetic theory of Coleridge and Keats was influenced by their reading of Shakespeare, and how their views moulded the image of Shakespeare for later generations. Kleinschmit von Lengefeld and Patrick Cruttwell consider whether Shakespeare is a baroque artist, as is sometimes claimed, and by different routes they come to much the same conclusion—that, although most of the qualities accepted as baroque are found in Shakespeare, they are more than offset by other qualities which make the total effect something that is not essentially baroque. Ludwig Borinski isolates medieval elements in some verse and prose styles of the sixteenth century, and shows how they become fused with or superseded by new forms of composition that have little in common with the medieval. Dieter Mehl follows the development of the play-within-a-play convention in Elizabethan drama. Horst Oppel offers some interesting comments on the effects that Shakespeare achieves by the use of contrast and of counterpoint. Gustav Kirchner surveys recent work done on the language of Shakespeare. Finally, there are short papers from Cardinal Frings, Archbishop of Cologne, who compares *Othello* with Verdi's opera derived from it, and from Robert Thonon, who supports the emendation 'skill' for *still* in the twelfth line of Sonnet 106. As usual, about half the volume is devoted to reviews of productions, books, and articles, the annual bibliography (for 1960), and Association notes.

The Shakespeare Newsletter,[22] now in its eleventh year, and still edited by

Louis Marder, provides digests of books, articles, and lectures, gathers together notes on a variety of Shakespearian topics, and publishes a few short original articles. The subjects of its brief biographies, prepared by John J. McAleer, are this year Colley Cibber, Edmond Malone, Edmund Kean, Edward Dowden, and Richard Grant White. Doris Peterson Franklin offers a tribute to Elmer Edgar Stoll, who died in 1959. Among the contributions of the editor is a plea for a more systematic approach to Shakespearian criticism.

Ashland Studies in Shakespeare[23] is an annual volume produced as an ancillary to short courses accompanying the Oregon Shakespeare Festival. It presents critical articles on the plays chosen for the Festival, and reprints source materials, literary and graphic, from Renaissance works and from theatre history. The 1961 volume, which deals with *Hamlet*, *All's Well*, *Henry IV, Part 1*, and *A Midsummer Night's Dream*, is well up to the standard of its predecessors. It opens with an extract from *The Dissent of the Lorde Percis*, a somewhat crude, ballad-like poem written by William Pears, secretary to the first Earl of Northumberland; the extract includes a vigorous account, from one who probably knew him personally, of the character and exploits of Harry Hotspur. In '*Hamlet*: A Kydian Revenge Play' John David Ratliff discusses Elizabethan revenge tragedies from *The Spanish Tragedy* to *Bussy D'Ambois*, laying special emphasis on the consolidation of the type by Kyd and its refinement by Shakespeare in *Hamlet*. There follows *An Acte Concernynge Artificers & Labourers*, a statute passed early in the reign

[22] *The Shakespeare Newsletter*, ed. and published by Louis Marder. Kent State Univ., Ohio. Six issues annually, $1.50.

[23] *Ashland Studies in Shakespeare, 1961*, ed. by Margery Bailey. Privately issued and sold by the Oregon Shakespeare Festival Assn., Inc., Ashland, Oregon. pp. vii+99+x. $2.

of Henry VIII which throws light on the portrayal of the mechanicals in *A Midsummer Night's Dream*. Appended to this are a couple of stanzas from the poor tiler's song which may have been sung in *Tom Tyler & His Wife*. Francis D. Haines, Jr., contributes a paper on 'The Tragedy of John of Gaunt', an admirable account of the career of a man who had, it seems, all the requisites of greatness but was debarred by political circumstances and his own loyalty and integrity from reaching the high position for which his talents fitted him; this paper contains interesting sections on Bolingbroke. The next item, of relevance to *All's Well*, is the instructions drawn up by Lord Burleigh for the housing of Queen Elizabeth and her large retinue of noblemen when she honoured him with a five-day visit at Theobalds in 1583. This is followed by the pleasant verses which Burleigh wrote to his wife on making her a New Year's gift of a spinning wheel. Finally, as a long footnote to *A Midsummer Night's Dream*, Marcia Belsher Thayer describes some Elizabethan dances, especially those which are appropriate to this play. The volume contains about a dozen excellent reproductions of prints and paintings which are relevant to the plays of the season.

In his *Shakespeare in Warwickshire*[24] Mark Eccles adds nothing new to what is known of Shakespeare's life, but as a well-ordered and very carefully documented presentation of the known facts of his life at Stratford the book will be of service to future biographers. It begins with his ancestry and family connexions, and goes on to recount all that can be discovered about his school and about his marriage to Anne Hathaway. The second half of the book is concerned with Shakespeare's later part in the life of Stratford, after his purchase of New Place. All these facts are obtainable elsewhere, though not always so clearly presented. What adds a special interest to the book is the mass of information that Eccles has collected about Shakespeare's neighbours and possible friends in and around Stratford. Not only does this information give perspective and life to Shakespeare's Warwickshire background; it also suggests lines of research which may lead to further knowledge of Shakespeare himself.

The early parts of F. E. Halliday's *Life of Shakespeare*[25] will not do. The kind of reader who is likely to be interested in Shakespeare's life will not nowadays expect to have the lean years for which few or no facts are available padded out with meaningless speculation. Once Shakespeare has reached London, the documentary evidence thickens, and on the whole Halliday deals with it fairly competently. But his book is not nearly as comprehensive, reliable, or interesting as M. M. Reese's *Shakespeare: His World and His Work* (1953—see *YW* xxxiv. 115), of which he makes no mention in a bibliography which contains the lives by Sidney Lee, Ivor Brown, and even (*horresco referens*) Hesketh Pearson.

Nor can much be said for Dorothy Macardle's *Shakespeare, Man and Boy*,[26] which, almost completed at the time of her death, was given final touches and seen through the press by George Bott. Miss Macardle's object is to present Shakespeare's plays to senior schoolchildren against the background of his life, and thus to relate his artistic development to his development as a man. To this end she recounts the main events of his career, and at appropriate points introduces the plays and poems,

[24] *Shakespeare in Warwickshire*, by Mark Eccles. Wisconsin U.P. pp. ix+182. $4.50.

[25] *The Life of Shakespeare*, by F. E. Halliday. Duckworth. pp. x+248. 25s.

[26] *Shakespeare, Man and Boy*, by Dorothy Macardle. Faber. pp. 260. 18s.

suggesting how they reflect his circumstances while he was writing them. It is a sensible enough idea, but its execution is spoilt by many questionable and erroneous assumptions: to give only two or three examples, that Shakespeare's wife was 'out of sympathy with all that made up his work and reputation'; that in the Sonnets he unlocked his heart; that only 250 copies of the Folio were printed—but indeed, Miss Macardle would have been well advised to keep clear of all bibliographical topics. Where the verified facts of Shakespeare's life are concerned she is safe enough, but it is difficult to see where her book could be used in a school, or to what other class of reader it is likely to be of service.

Christopher Whitfield, in 'The Kinship of Thomas Combe II, William Reynolds, and William Shakespeare' (*NQ*), explores the probable friendship of Shakespeare with a number of families in various Cotswold villages. In an article in *Sh Q* Frederick J. Pohl makes a careful comparison of the bust in Stratford Church and the death-mask which is called Shakespeare's. He decides that there can be no doubt that they represent the same man, nor any reasonable doubt that the bust, though later tampered with, was modelled from the mask.

Albert Howard Carter writes 'On the Meaning of Characters' Names in Shakespeare' (*Mississippi Quart.*), warning us that, although Shakespeare must often have chosen his names with an eye to 'their meaning, connotation, or potentiality for punning', we must not make any unwarrantable assumptions about them.

C. J. Sisson's *New Readings in Shakespeare*[27] was published in 1956 (see *YW* xxxvii. 114), and fairly soon went out of print. It has now been taken over by new publishers and reprinted. Though many of Sisson's readings have not won acceptance, his book remains a valuable contribution to Shakespearian textual scholarship, and its reappearance is to be welcomed.

The findings of Hardin Craig's *A New Look at Shakespeare's Quartos*[28] cannot be briefly summarized. The book is essentially a plea for the application of rational and well-tried principles and techniques to the bibliographical problems of the Shakespearian quartos. Craig believes that some of the current methods of determining Shakespeare's original texts or the relationship between quarto and folio texts depend on the 'construction of more or less ingenious invented causes' of error. He will have nothing to do with what he regards as 'special hypotheses to account for unsolved problems', for example, the theory of reporting or of memorial reconstruction, which presupposes a reporter 'always conveniently at hand for the removal of almost any obstacle that stands in need of removal'. He has based his own study of the quartos on 'ordinary and customary processes', and maintains that most of the 'bad' quartos are either Shakespeare's foul papers or revised versions of the originals which Shakespeare made in the light of theatrical experience. Whether or not the conclusions he reaches about individual quartos are accepted, his book will have done good service if it persuades less cautious bibliographers to ponder deeply on 'customary processes' and any known facts relating to their problems before they formulate their hypotheses.

In the ten years or so since Charlton Hinman first described the photographic process by which he was collating the Folger copies of the First

[27] *New Readings in Shakespeare*, by C. J. Sisson. Dawsons. Two vols.: pp. ix+218; vii+300. 50s. the set.

[28] *A New Look at Shakespeare's Quartos*, by Hardin Craig. Stanford U.P. and O.U.P. pp. ix+134. $3.50. 28s.

Folio (see *YW* xxxiv. 114), he has from time to time published some of the results of this collation. In a lecture delivered in 1960 at the University of Kansas and now published,[29] he gives further information about his findings. Having completed the collation of the eighty-odd Folger copies, he has found just over 500 variants—a very different matter from the 15,000 to 18,000 that E. E. Willoughby's researches in the 1930's suggested as a possible number. Of these variants only a few dozen involve substantive error, and only two involve error which was indisputably corrected by reference to copy. Hinman discusses half a dozen fairly trivial variants in order to illustrate the way in which the Folio proof-reader worked; he seems to have been far more interested in getting rid of obvious typographical blemishes than in the faithful reproduction of the copy.

In a letter from George Chapman to Sir George Buc Elias Schwartz (*Sh Q*) sees evidence that Buc possessed real power and authority to license for the press, and that his position as licenser was not, as Greg thought, merely advisory.

In 'Stylistic Contrast in Shakespeare's Plays' (*West Virginia Univ. Bull., Philological Papers*) John W. Draper examines a number of the plays in order to demonstrate that, 'as his art matured, Shakespeare became a master both of melodious variety and of dissonant, even strident, contrasts of dramatic style'.

In another paper, 'Shakespeare and Barbary' (*Ea*), Draper shows that Shakespeare pays little attention to 'the local color of Barbary'; however, his presentation of characters from this part of the world becomes increasingly realistic, from Aaron to the Prince of Morocco, and from Morocco to Othello.

W. H. D. Rouse's excellent edition of Arthur Golding's *The XV Bookes of P. Ouidius Naso, entytuled Metamorphosis* was published in a small limited edition by the de la More Press in 1904. It has long been unobtainable, and many libraries are without a copy. It is very welcome news that a facsimile of Rouse's edition[30] has now been produced in a handsome volume by the Centaur Press. This edition is a reprint of the first edition (1567) from a copy in the Cambridge University Library. The original spelling has been retained, with certain exceptions, such as the correction of obvious misprints, the expansion of abbreviations, and the separation of words wrongly run together, such changes being recorded in the textual notes; punctuation has been altered only where it is likely to mislead a modern reader. Rouse's admirable bibliographical introduction has been kept. The Centaur Press deserves our gratitude for making this work once more available.

The Spring number of *Sh Q* contains the following notes on rather specialized aspects of Shakespearian study: 'A Signed American Binding on the First American Edition of Shakespeare', by Edwin Wolf IInd—the edition being that of Mountford, Bioren, & Co. (1795–6); 'Shakespeare in Early American Decorative Arts', by Marian S. Carson; 'Shakespeare in Marble in Colonial America', by Hanford Henderson; 'The First American Engraving of Shakespeare', by James G. McManaway—an unsigned engraving of the Westminster Abbey statue published in 1787 in *The Columbian Magazine*; 'Shakespeare and America's Revolutionary Leaders', by Ernst J. Schlochauer; and 'Shakespeare and Science Fiction', by Robert E.

---

[29] *Six Variant Readings in the First Folio of Shakespeare*, by Charlton Hinman. Univ. of Kansas Libraries. pp. ii+17. 50c.

[30] *Shakespeare's Ovid: Being Arthur Golding's Translation of the 'Metamorphoses'*, ed. by W. H. D. Rouse. (Centaur Classics.) Centaur Press. pp. xviii+321. £5. 5s.

Morsberger, who notes that the plot of the motion picture *Forbidden Planet* is based on *The Tempest*. In the Summer number Robert D. Monroe describes an engraving of Shakespeare by Abraham Wivell.

Other general articles worthy of mention are Robert Fricker's 'Vom Wirken der Providenz bei Shakespeare' (*Ang*), and R. S. Berman's 'Power and Humility in Shakespeare' (*SAQ*).

The year has produced the usual crop of nonsense about the non-Shakespearian authorship of the plays. Those who have no better use for their time may, with the help of the *Sh Q* bibliography, seek out a number of articles by 'anti-Stratfordian' cranks.

3. *Studies of Individual Plays and Poems*

As in the past the plays are treated in the order in which they are printed in the First Folio. Criticism of the comedies is very scanty this year, and several, including the first three in the Folio, are not represented in individual articles.

Measure for Measure

In 'Scenic Design in *Measure for Measure*' (*JEGP*) Anthony Caputi claims that most criticism of the play, especially that which approaches it as 'a dark intellectual puzzle', disregards the fact that it is first and foremost a dramatic structure; its dramatic pattern is clearer than is sometimes realized. Among other things, this pattern puts the marriages at the end 'in a reasonable perspective . . . in which they . . . serve quite simply and effectively to support the affirmation of faith in civilization on which the play closes'. Gunnar Sjögren argues (*RLC*) that the Vienna of the play is Vienne, in France. Together with evidence from other plays, this, he thinks, makes it likely that Shakespeare visited France, prob-

ably in about 1585. '*Measure for Measure* and the Protestant Ethic' is the title of a paper in *EC* in which Raymond Southall describes the play as 'a fierce criticism of the forces making for social decay, of the breach in the medieval order which was being effected by Protestantism'.

Much Ado About Nothing

'Comic Awareness, Style, and Dramatic Technique in *Much Ado About Nothing*' (*BUSE*), by Charles A. Owen, Jr., is largely a study of Beatrice and Benedick as they 'pursue a journey into self-knowledge'. The other characters adopt conventional attitudes and conventional forms of utterance. The comic awareness of Beatrice and Benedick, 'an expression of the freshness and vivacity of their minds, has not only protected them from the vanities of self-assertion; it has given them a sense of appropriate conduct and appropriate utterance in the vicissitudes of their fellows'. Barbara Everett contributes to *CQ* an article in which she asserts that in *Much Ado* Shakespeare for the first time attempted a serious and complex treatment of the clash between the different worlds of man and woman.

The Merchant of Venice

John D. Hurrell, in 'Love and Friendship in *The Merchant of Venice*' (*TSLL*), puts forward the view that Antonio's sadness at the beginning of the play, far from being that of the conventional 'melancholic', arises largely from some feeling that Portia is a rival who will deprive him of Bassanio's affection; this, says Hurrell, is an important 'interior' theme of the play. In 'Shylock: "Devil Incarnation" or "Poor Man . . . Wronged"?' (*JEGP*) John Hazel Smith reaches the scarcely novel conclusion that this 'complex, developing character' is neither tragic nor comic, but reveals himself as both 'villain and human'. Discussing 'The Trial Scene in *The Merchant of Venice*' (*REL*), E. M. W. Tillyard declares that in one of her aspects Portia represents 'Justice and Mercy reconciled'. She knows that she possesses 'the infallible means of rescuing Antonio according to the letter of the law'; but Christian mercy is concerned with the souls of all men, and when Portia lectures Shylock on mercy she is not, like everyone else, thinking merely of Antonio, but of the salvation of Shylock's soul. In ' "Loneliness" in *The Merchant of Venice*' (*EC*) M. G. Deshpande takes exception to views on the play expressed last year by Graham Midgley (see *YW* xli. 110). In a later issue of the journal Tillyard, with some qualifications, supports Midgley.

As You Like It

Hugh M. Richmond suggests, in 'To his Mistress' Eyebrow' (*PQ*), that Jaques's words (ii. vii. 148) may be an allusion to the type of verse made popular by Clément Marot; if this is so, Shakespeare was interested in things French before he became a member of a Huguenot household in 1602.

All's Well That Ends Well

John F. Adams argues (*Sh Q*) that 'the problem of sex and procreation' is a central theme in *All's Well*, underlying and unifying other strains, such as a preoccupation with the nature of honour and 'the responsibilities of youth to the past'.

Twelfth Night

In 'Mistakes in *Twelfth Night* and Their Resolution' (*PMLA*) Porter Williams, Jr., suggests that the many mistakes in the play are more than merely elements of the plot; they are thematically important as well. 'The wise and the generous . . . survive their

foolish mistakes, and profit', and 'the inner life of the play reveals that only blemishes of the heart destroy'. Melvin Seiden, in 'Malvolio Reconsidered' (*Univ. of Kansas City Rev.*), describes Malvolio as 'a scapegoat sacrificed to the amoral bacchanalian gods of comedy'; however, these gods are themselves sacrificed at the end of the play when Sir Toby is chastised. John Russell Brown observes, in 'Directions for *Twelfth Night*, or What You Will' (*Tulane Drama Rev.*), that in this play 'the characters, the situations and the speeches are protean', lending themselves to a great variety of interpretations. However, it should be possible, by intelligent use of the text and of the arts of the theatre, to devise a production 'answering more fully than before to Shakespeare's text and combining the strength of many interpretations'. Brown suggests ways of working towards such a production.

The Winter's Tale

J. H. P. Pafford contributes to *NQ* a valuable typographical study of the Folio text of *The Winter's Tale*; it includes an analysis of the work of the two compositors and a careful examination of the entry and exit directions.

Richard II

Peter G. Phialas considers (*Sh Q*) the 'extremely attractive' view, put forward by E. M. W. Tillyard in *Shakespeare's History Plays*, that *Richard II* is Shakespeare's picture of medieval life. He argues that much of the play emphasizes a contrast between the state of England under Richard and under his predecessor, and that this makes Tillyard's view unacceptable. In 'Shakespeare and Richard II' (*History Today*) Harold F. Hutchison contrasts Shakespeare's treatment of Richard's fall with the way in which it actually came about. The real Richard, he says, was not the 'mumbling neurotic' portrayed by Shakespeare.

Henry IV, Parts 1 and 2

In 'The Composition of Shakespeare's Lancastrian Trilogy' (*TSLL*) Robert Adger Law compares the plays with their sources in Holinshed and *The Famous Victories*, and comes to the conclusion that 'differences in conception of the three plays make their composition as a single unit improbable'.

Hugh Dickinson considers 'The Reformation of Prince Hal' (*Sh Q*) from the point of view of a producer. The theme of the play is 'the education of a prince to a realization of his duty and acceptance of the burden it imposes'. By 'redeeming the time' Prince Hal unifies the action; he stands against a 'panorama of disorder', and demonstrates that the supreme attribute of kingship is 'not honor, but self-sacrifice'. George Burke Johnston suggests, in 'Camden, Shakespeare, and Young Henry Percy' (*PMLA*), that it may have been from Camden's *Britannia* that Shakespeare and Daniel took their picture of a Harry Percy a good deal younger at the time of his death than he was in history. In a note on 'Shakespeare's *1 Henry IV*, III. iii. 91–97' (*Ex*) Ruth S. Perot expresses the view that Falstaff may have included among his knaveries the trick of 'ring-dropping', as it is described by John Awdeley in *The Fraternity of Vagabonds* (1561).

Paul A. Jorgensen discusses (*PMLA*) 'The "Dastardly Treachery" of Prince John of Lancaster' when, in *2 Henry IV*, he 'tricks the rebels into an armistice', and then arrests their leaders and causes his troops to 'pursue the scatter'd stray'. Nothing comparable with this is done by any other of Shakespeare's generals, and Jorgensen thinks that it must reflect changing policy in Elizabethan warfare, especially as it was practised in Ireland.

Henry V

Most critics have assumed that Shakespeare's attitude to the French nobles whom he depicts in *Henry V* was one of contempt and ridicule. In 'Shakespeare's *Henry V* and the French Nobility' (*TSLL*) Haldeen Braddy sets out to show that, in spite of their apparent triviality, the French are regarded by the English as worthy and courageous opponents, and that 'the valiant Dauphin' is the logical successor to Hotspur as a foil to King Henry. In 'Henry V and Germanicus' (*Sh Q*) George R. Price suggests that Shakespeare may have taken hints for Henry's conduct during the night before Agincourt from the account of one of Germanicus's battles in Richard Grenewey's translation of Tacitus's *Annales* (1598). From the Folio reading 'his nose was as sharpe as a Pen, and a Table of greene fields' (II. iii. 16–18), Robert F. Fleissner (*Sh Q*) seizes upon *greene* as the most significant word, and contends that, 'instead of being *pathetic*, Falstaff's death is really *bathetic*—a humorous, ironic descent of the Knight from the sublimity of a carefree existence to the absurdity of a death resulting, directly or indirectly, from "a kind of male green sickness" '.

Richard III

In 'The Relationship of *Richardus Tertius* to the Main Richard III Plays' (*BUSE*) Robert J. Lordi aims at showing that, though Shakespeare may have known *Richardus Tertius*, the three-part Latin tragedy written by Thomas Legge, there is no clear evidence that he drew on it for his own play. Louis E. Dollarhide maintains (*Mississippi Quart.*) that the episode in which Richard overcomes the opposition of Queen Elizabeth (IV. iv. 198 ff.), though it is a fine rhetorical set-piece, comes too late to be compatible with the structure of the play. G. A. Wilkes directs attention (*Sh Q*) to a known, but strangely disregarded, early allusion to *Richard III*. It occurs in a satire of Sir John Davies, probably written in 1594, in which there are echoes of Richard's opening soliloquy; and it strengthens the possibility that the play had been acted by the end of 1594.

Henry VIII

'Why did Shakespeare write Henry VIII?' asks E. M. W. Tillyard (*CQ*). He suggests that Shakespeare, perhaps for a special occasion, dramatized material from Hall that he had long had in his mind—dramatized it skilfully enough, but without his earlier creative energy. Fletcher's participation in *Henry VIII* has been questioned in recent years. Marco Mincoff sets out (*Sh Q*) to rehabilitate him as Shakespeare's collaborator or co-author. He claims that all the positive evidence resulting from 'ten objectively measurable and essentially independent indicators' points to Fletcher as Shakespeare's partner, and that no convincing evidence against this view has been produced. No source has been found in the chronicles for the vision which comes to Katherine of Aragon as a token of approaching death. However, the funeral oration for Queen Margaret of Navarre mentions that her death was heralded by just such a dream, and E. E. Duncan-Jones suggests (*NQ*) that Shakespeare may have transferred the episode from the one queen to the other.

Troilus and Cressida

One reason why critics are puzzled by *Troilus and Cressida*, says William W. Main, is that Shakespeare's characters are not types, like those of his contemporaries. In 'Character Amalgams in Shakespeare's *Troilus and Cressida*' (*SP*) Main asserts that the characters are complex mixtures of types designed to arouse 'ambivalent sympathies'. Cressida, for example, represents four roles current in Elizabethan love plots, 'a romantic modest maid, a satiric forward maid, a satiric shrew, or a pathetic penitent'; and similarly Hector represents current conceptions of both hero and villain. Two articles on *Troilus and Cressida* appear in *Sh Q*. David Kaula examines in Augustinian terms the philosophies of life of Troilus and Ulysses, who represent 'the idealistic and realistic, passional and rational'; neither rises above the pursuit of a 'strictly human excellence', and both of their ways of life are equally ineffectual. It is 'the nihilism of Thersites and the predatory anarchism of Achilles which finally prevail over the shattered earthly city'. In 'Order and Confusion in *Troilus and Cressida*, I. iii' F. Quinland Daniels argues that in this scene Agamemnon's opening speech betokens a floundering mind, in contrast to the logic and precision of Ulysses, and that his limited military attitude is the sickness from which the Greek cause is suffering. Inge Leimberg provides a note (*Ang*) on III. iii. 145 ff., tracing the image of time used by Ulysses to its source in Harington's *Ariosto*, or, perhaps more immediately, in *The Return from Parnassus*.

Coriolanus

Describing *Coriolanus* as 'a tragedy of youth', F. H. Rouda claims (*Sh Q*) that 'the idealism of the young is for Coriolanus that blind spot—that ignorance of some vital, fundamental truth —that every tragic hero has as the source not only of his downfall but of the sublime imprudence that sends him frequently where angels fear to tread'.

Titus Andronicus

Titus Andronicus bristles with problems that have so far defied solution, and in his full-scale study of the play[31] Horst Oppel, like his predecessors, often finds himself at a loss. In his opening chapter, for example, where he sums up admirably the conflicting results of earlier research into the authorship, the date of composition, and the sources of the play, he reaches no clear-cut conclusions of his own; though one feels that he would like to attribute the whole work to Shakespeare, he remains troubled by the first act, noting that different methods of assessing its authorship produce contradictory results. In the next two chapters he relates *Titus* to the Elizabethan convention of the tragedy of blood, and considers its debt to the plays of Marlowe. In an excellent chapter on the argument he describes the play as Shakespeare's first approach to the theme of 'man's inhumanity to man', and discusses his handling of its two dominant motifs, honour and suffering. There follow an analysis of the banquet scene and a useful study of the diction and the imagery of the work as a whole. Finally, in an attempt to relate the play to Shakespeare's development as a dramatic artist, Oppel discusses its characterization and its structure. This is a thoughtful and sensible book which should be of some value to future students of *Titus Andronicus*.

Arun Kumar Dasgupta provides 'A Note on *Titus Andronicus*, II. i. 1–11' (*Sh Q*), in which he finds more poetic and dramatic interest than previous commentators. Also in *Sh Q*, John J. Enck observes of IV. ii. 22–23 ('O, 'tis a verse in Horace; I know it well: / I read it in the grammar long ago') that

[31] *Titus Andronicus: Studien zur dramengeschichtlichen Stellung von Shakespeares früher Tragödie*, von Horst Oppel. Heidelberg: Quelle & Meyer. pp. 122. DM. 12.

'Chiron indulges himself in a tested gag, which, rather than Titus' trick, prompts Aaron's speech' about 'no sound jest'.

Romeo and Juliet

In 'Christianity and the Religion of Love in *Romeo and Juliet*' (*Sh Q*) Paul N. Siegel compares Shakespeare's play with other Elizabethan adaptations of *novelle* that tell of lovers whose families are at enmity, and who finally die for love. In these others he finds 'a crudely mechanical mixture of a glorification of passionate love and a Christian moralistic condemnation of it'. In *Romeo* 'the ideas of the religion of love and those of Christianity . . . are interwoven into a unified artistic pattern'. In ' "Sirrah, Go Hire Me Twenty Cunning Cooks" ' (*Sh Q*) Gunnar Sjögren draws on the correspondence of a fifteenth-century Italian merchant in order to show that Shakespeare deliberately portrayed Capulet as 'an easily recognizable caricature of an Italian nobleman with an attitude to household affairs very different from the one obtaining among the English upper classes'.

Timon of Athens

E. A. J. Honigmann makes a close study (*Sh Q*) of *Timon of Athens* in relation to its sources, and finds that it owes much more to Plutarch's life of Marcus Antonius than has been recognized, and something also to the life of Coriolanus. He believes that the likeliest source of Shakespeare's knowledge of Lucian's dialogue *Timon, or the Misanthrope* is Filbert Bretin's *Les Œuvres de Lucian* (1582/3), and that the debt to Lucian is also more extensive than commentators have realized. Finally, he argues that some of the textual difficulties of *Timon* are due rather to compositorial tampering than to the state of Shakespeare's manuscript. In '*Timon of Athens* and its Dramatic Descendants' (*REL*) G. Wilson Knight shows that the play 'has exerted a strong appeal on creative writers'; its themes have often been reworked by later playwrights.

Macbeth

The view developed by Julian Markels, in 'The Spectacle of Deterioration: *Macbeth* and the "Manner of Tragic Imitation" ' (*Sh Q*), is that *Macbeth* illustrates the importance to the tragic playwright of 'both the choice of episodes to render and the visual machinery which is intrinsic to the rendering'. Aristotle, says Markels, underestimated the importance of both aspects of 'manner'. The authenticity of the Porter scene is not seriously questioned today. John B. Harcourt (*Sh Q*) finds in this scene several significant thematic links with other parts of *Macbeth*, and considers the implications of the Porter's vision of the gates of Inverness Castle as the Gate of Hell. Geoffrey Carnall (*REL*) sees De Quincey's essay on the knocking at the gate as 'obviously the work of a nineteenth-century critic, an admirer of Wordsworth, a connoisseur of murder'. It tells us little about the play, but 'helps us to understand what *Macbeth* really meant to the London theatregoer of the early nineteenth century'. In 'A Missing Scene in *Macbeth*' (*JEGP*) Daniel A. Amnéus notes several details, especially in III. ii. 8–22, which seem to him to point to the loss of a scene. He believes that Simon Forman was right in describing the banquet as having taken place on the night after Banquo's murder. In a note on 'Shakespeare's *Macbeth*, III. iv. 122–6 and IV. i. 90–94' (*Ex*) William Joseph Free interprets these passages as showing that Macbeth's 'moral imagination' has been blinded by the Witches, and ironically he 'fails to see that the same power which moved stones to expose murder may move a forest for the same reason'.

Hamlet

J. Dover Wilson's well-known study *What Happens in 'Hamlet'*[32] is now published in a paper-back edition. Controversial as some of Wilson's conclusions are, the book is something of a landmark in *Hamlet* criticism, as well as being extremely readable, and students of Shakespeare will be very glad that it is being kept in print, and at a price which will bring it within the reach of a wide circle of readers.

In 'I know not "seems" ' (*REL*) J. Swart develops the view that sincerity is a central theme in *Hamlet*. 'The variations on the theme are omnipresent, from the slight subterfuge to essential malignity, but its centre is found in Hamlet, whose tragedy is that, caught by his willing co-operation in the web of pretence, he is inevitably involved until he cannot extricate himself and becomes the exponent of the vice he fights.' Raymond H. Reno's thesis, in 'Hamlet's Quintessence of Dust' (*Sh Q*), is that, although his vision of man as dust does not dissuade Hamlet from his revenge, 'it does in a way adjust his task to the universal perspective offered by the graveyard', and reconciles him to death. It also prepares us for his new mood of resignation in the last act of the play. From Sister Miriam Joseph, C.S.C., comes the suggestion (*PMLA*) that Shakespeare knew 'the theory of the discernment of spirits' and 'used it as the rationale for discerning the ghost' of Hamlet's father; the four witnesses test the apparition according to the three steps prescribed in this theory. Sister Miriam further argues that the abode of the ghost and his character fit

[32] *What Happens in 'Hamlet'*, by J. Dover Wilson. C.U.P. pp. xxii+357. 13s. 6d. $1.95.

descriptions of a purgatorial spirit, that the command of the ghost is just, and that the command is properly qualified in Christian terms.

Hamlet, says Richard Foster, in 'Hamlet and the Word' (*UTQ*), contains many symbols of the 'Word motif'; in one aspect it is 'an articulation of the mystery of the Word in the country of profanation'. Hamlet is a kind of 'messianic custodian of the Word', and it is through his sensibility and intelligence that redemption from the effects of the Fall is promised. *Hamlet* seems to have a fatal attraction for the psychoanalytical critics. The latest 'psychoanalytical-symbolic' interpretation is that of A. Andre Glaz, who argues (*American Imago*) that the play is Shakespeare's 'Personal catharsis'. In 'Das Spiel im Spiel: Formen dramatischer Illusion bei Shakespeare' (*Archiv*) Wolfgang Iser considers the different ways in which Shakespeare uses the play-within-the-play in *Hamlet* and *A Midsummer Night's Dream*.

In 'Rhetorical Patterns in *Hamlet*, III. i. 56–60' (*NQ*) D. McElroy analyses the opening lines of the 'To be, or not to be' soliloquy in terms of rhetorical theory, and claims that his analysis supports those who think that Hamlet is here both 'debating suicide, and . . . trying to decide whether to pursue his revenge'. In '. . . Some Enterprise That Hath a Stomach In't . . .' (*Sh Q*) Vlas Kozhevnikov argues that the word 'stomach' in this line does not mean 'courage' or 'resolution', as it is usually glossed, but refers to secret intentions on the part of Fortinbras. Dissatisfied with existing glosses on I. ii. 187, David Barrett (*NM*) believes that he has found the true meaning of the phrase 'all in all'. A passage in Richard Carew's *The Excellencie of the English Tongue* (*c.* 1595), supported by 1 Cor., xv. 28, and a further passage from Stubbes, suggests that it means something like 'a model of perfection'.

King Lear

Sigurd Burckhardt claims (*Minnesota Rev.*) that a 'verbal' reading of the first scene of *King Lear* explains Lear's fall, and indicates 'the specific kind and direction and even depth of his fall'. The second scene gives the same kind of information about Gloucester. In 'Cordelia and the Fool' (*Sh Q*) Thomas B. Stroup allies himself with those who believe that the parts of Cordelia and the Fool were written for the same boy actor; this would afford 'a reasonable explanation for the unusual preparation for the first entrance of the Fool, for the omission of IV. iii, and for other cuttings from the Folio'. It would also enable us to find a double meaning in 'And my poor fool is hang'd'. James O. Wood draws attention (*Sh Q*) to 'A Special Cadence in *King Lear*'. This is Lear's habit of beginning lines with four monosyllables, often so accented as to produce a spondaic effect, as in 'No, I'll not weep', or 'Didst thou give all?'. Charles H. Gold examines (*NQ*) the Q/F variant at I. i. 151, and decides that the F reading, 'When Maiesty falls to folly', 'is more consistent with the totality of meanings and implications which belong to the play' than the Q 'stoops' for 'falls'.

Arthur M. Sampley finds (*Sh Q*) 'Two Analogues to Shakespeare's Treatment of the Wooing of Cordelia' in Dekker's *Old Fortunatus* and the anonymous *The Wisdom of Doctor Dodipoll*, both printed in 1600, some years before the probable date of *Lear*. In 'Poor Tom in "King Lear"' (*TLS*, 15 Dec.) Charles Garton shows that Shakespeare retained from the cries of the Bedlam beggars such phrases as 'Poor Tom's a-cold' and 'Bless thy five wits'. Barbara Everett's article in *CQ* last year, 'The New King Lear' (see *YW* xli. 116), has provoked a correspondence in the same journal in which John F. Danby, John Holloway,

William Empson, Emrys Jones, and Kenneth Muir have taken part.

Othello

According to its sub-title, *The Masks of Othello*,[33] by Marvin Rosenberg, is 'the search for the identity of Othello, Iago, and Desdemona by three centuries of actors and critics'. Beginning with Richard Burbage's 'grieved Moor, made jealous by a slave', Rosenberg has combed theatrical records in order to do full justice to the interpretations of the leading parts by famous actors and actresses of the last three centuries —Betterton, Booth, Garrick, Macready, Irving, and Paul Robeson, Mrs. Siddons, Ellen Terry, and Sarah Bernhardt, to name only a few of the most memorable. He then turns to the critics, and discusses a large variety of approaches to *Othello*, from that of Rymer, who regarded it as 'a bloody farce, without salt or savour', to that of G. Wilson Knight, who reads far too much into the play. Rosenberg has done a useful job in assembling and trying to reconcile so many interpretations of this complex tragedy.

Othello, says Terence Hawkes, in 'Iago's use of Reason' (*SP*), is 'fundamentally concerned with an attack of Evil on Good'. The Nominalist-Baconian advocacy of the 'lower' or discursive reason, as opposed to the 'higher' or intuitive reason of Scholasticism, was regarded by churchmen as Satanic pride; Iago embodies this pride, and Othello's fall to his assault parallels Adam's.

Three notes in the April number of *NQ* relate to *Othello*. From documents in the Public Record Office W. E. Miller finds that there were negroes living in London four or five years before the composition of *Othello*, so

that Shakespeare might have had opportunities of getting to know negroes at first hand. Ned B. Allen notes that critics interested in the source of *Othello* have ignored the head-link of the tale in the *Hecatommithi* from which Shakespeare took his story; Allen believes that Shakespeare was influenced by the attitude towards adultery expressed in this head-link, and that he also drew some phrases from it. In 'Othello's Name' F. N. Lees suggests that the name may have been derived, with the addition of the diminutive suffix, from Othoman, the founder of the Ottoman empire, whose exploits are described in Richard Knolles's *Generall Historie of the Turkes* (1603). Lees finds other interesting resemblances between Knolles's history and *Othello*; he thinks that the relationship between the two might repay study.

In 'The Alienated City: Reflections on *Othello*' (*Encounter*) W. H. Auden makes a psychoanalytical study of Iago and other characters in the play. Lawrence J. Ross suggests, in ' "Marble", "Crocodile", and "Turban'd Turk" in *Othello*' (*PQ*), that the course of Othello's spiritual battle with the devil is reflected in his diction. The line 'That turn'd your wit the seamy side without' (IV. ii. 147) is usually taken as a reference to the seam inside a garment or piece of cloth. In ' "The Seamy Side"—A Popular Etymology?' (*NQ*) Brian Foster argues that *seamy*, as it is used here, is paralleled in 'bastes his arrogance in his own seam' (*Troil.* II. iii. 197), and 'the rank sweat of an enseamed bed' (*Ham.* III. iv. 92), and means 'greasy'; Emilia is alluding to 'the greasiness of Iago's nature, and hence to his turpitude and evil, obscene thoughts'.

Antony and Cleopatra

At *Antony and Cleopatra*, III. xiii. 76–78 Kenneth Muir (*Sh Q*) gives good

---

[33] *The Masks of Othello: The Search for the Identity of Othello, Iago, and Desdemona by Three Centuries of Actors and Critics*, by Marvin Rosenberg. California U.P. and O.U.P. pp. xii+314. $5. 40s.

grounds for proposing an emendation of the Folio text to give the reading, 'there to kneele, / Till, from his all-obeying breath, I heare / The doome of Egypt'.

Cymbeline

The view put forward by Emrys Jones, in 'Stuart Cymbeline' (*EC*), is that *Cymbeline* blends its romantic elements, not altogether satisfactorily, with a nationalistic theme to which King James I in his role as a peace-maker is the clue.

The Two Noble Kinsmen

In 'The Date of *The Two Noble Kinsmen*' (*Sh Q*) Paul Bertram, after a careful review of the evidence, assigns the composition of the play to 1613, in time for performance in the November of that year.

The Poems

M. A. Palmatier considers 'A Suggested New Source in Ovid's *Metamorphoses* for Shakespeare's *Venus and Adonis*' (*HLQ*). He believes that Adonis's 'scorn and hardness of heart' may derive from *Met*. x. 503–28, where Adonis's birth is described.

Harold R. Walley believes (*PMLA*) that *The Rape of Lucrece* has been undervalued. He himself regards it as an important key to Shakespeare's development, and in particular it foreshadows many of the great qualities of the later tragedies.

The thesis that Daniel Seltzer develops in ' "Their Tragic Scene": *The Phoenix and Turtle* and Shakespeare's Love Tragedies' (*Sh Q*) is that '*The Phoenix and Turtle* is a lyric statement of truths which the tragedies set forth dramatically, constructed so as to reveal not only the inevitable doom of "the sovereignty of nature" when it achieves the pure essence of love, but also to describe in some measure the emotional effects of such action'.

The Sonnets

Themes and Variations in Shakespeare's Sonnets,[34] by J. B. Leishman, is the most penetrating study of the Sonnets to have appeared for many years. Leishman's main approach is by means of comparison with the works of other poets, a fruitful method of criticism largely neglected by previous commentators. He is chiefly interested in Shakespeare's handling of the themes of time, beauty, and love, and the first section of the book is a considerably amplified form of an earlier paper (see *YW* xl. 123) in which he compares Shakespeare's treatment of 'Poetry as Immortalization' with that of various poets from Pindar and Horace down to the Elizabethans. Section II is concerned with 'devouring time and fading beauty', and again Leishman draws illuminating comparisons between Shakespeare and other poets who have exploited these themes; especially interesting are some resemblances he sees with the sonnets that Michelangelo addressed to Tommaso de' Cavalieri and Vittoria Colonna. In the last section, devoted to the Dark Lady sonnets, Leishman concerns himself chiefly with what he calls Shakespeare's 'un-Platonic hyperbole' and with the 'religiousness' of his love. Here the comparison is with Donne and Herbert, and Leishman finds 'a continual oscillation between doubt at the heart of assurance and assurance at the heart of doubt'. He finds also 'an intensity of inner vibration such as we do not receive from Donne's love-poems', though there is something like it in some of his religious poems.

Parturient montes, nascetur ridiculus mus. Rudolf Melander Holzapfel's

---

[34] *Themes and Variations in Shakespeare's Sonnets*, by J. B. Leishman. Hutchinson. pp. 254. 35s.

Shakespeare's Secret,[35] an expensively and beautifully produced edition of most of Shakespeare's Sonnets, earns a mention in *YW* as the silliest book on Shakespeare for 1961. The sub-title (printed below) gives some indication of its method. Its thesis is that the first 126 of the Sonnets, addressed to William Herbert, third Earl of Pembroke, are—but perhaps Holzapfel should be allowed to reveal Shakespeare's secret in his own manner: 'I may astound you; I may be ridiculed by layman and expert—and yet I must tell you: William Herbert, third Earl of Pembroke, poet, courtier, Knight of the Garter and Lord Chamberlain, and whom Gardiner correctly describes as "the Hamlet of the English Court", *was Shakespeare's own son.*' It should perhaps be mentioned, in explanation of this astonishing circumstance, that Shakespeare, a page at Wilton, was at the age of fifteen seduced by the Countess of Pembroke (Sidney's sister, Pembroke's mother), who was at that time seventeen years of age. It is probably unnecessary to add that the Countess is the Dark Lady of the later sonnets.

The argument put forward by R. P. Blackmur, in 'Poetics for Infatuation' (*KR*), is that the order in which the Sonnets are printed in Thomas Thorpe's volume of 1609 gives shape to the theme of infatuation—'its initiation, cultivation, and history, together with its peaks of triumph and devastation'.

Sonnet 110 is often interpreted as an expression of Shakespeare's disillusion with the stage and all it represents ('made myself a motley to the view, . . . sold cheap what is most dear', &c.). By means of close paraphrase and analysis, Virginia L. Radley and David C. Redding aim at showing (*Sh Q*) that it has nothing to do with the stage, and that its theme is the poet's transgressions against ideal love. Hans Combecher offers (*NS*) a new interpretation of Sonnet 116 ('Let me not to the marriage of true minds . . .'). In 'Iconic Organization in Shakespeare's Sonnet CXLVI' (*ES*) Albert S. Gérard argues that this sonnet is 'a remarkable example of Renaissance organization both in structure and in imagery'.

4. *Shakespeare and the Theatre*

The reissue of John Cranford Adams's *The Globe Playhouse*,[36] first published in 1942 by the Harvard University Press, will be generally welcomed. Though Adams's description of the Globe is controversial in some of its details, it remains one of the most comprehensive expositions of the traditional view of the Elizabethan playhouse, and it serves as a corrective, where correction is required, to some more adventurous recent views. In this edition Adams has revised the opening section on early maps and views, following the discovery of two panoramic views of London of about 1600, has made a few alterations in the text in other chapters, has added photographs of a model of the Globe based on his conclusions, and has tried to reconstruct the original staging of *Lear* in order to illustrate Elizabethan theatrical techniques.

Toby Lelyveld's *Shylock on the Stage*[37] follows the history of Shylock as a stage figure from the time when he was first presented, possibly by Will

[35] *Shakespeare's Secret: A new & correct interpretation of Shakespeare's Sonnets, which are now for the first time fully explained, with a word-for-word interpretation of each Sonnet & a running commentary proving the continuity of the first 126 Sonnets and a re-arrangement of the 'Dark Lady' Sonnets*, by Rudolf Melander Holzapfel. Dublin: The Dolmen Press. pp. xxiv+160. 42s.

[36] *The Globe Playhouse: Its Design and Equipment*, by John Cranford Adams. Second Edition. New York: Barnes & Noble. pp. xv+435. $8.50.

[37] *Shylock on the Stage*, by Toby Lelyveld. Routledge & Kegan Paul. pp. x+149. 21s.

Kempe, but more probably by Richard Burbage, down to Peter O'Toole's portrayal at Stratford in 1960. Dr. Lelyveld has no doubt that in the earliest performances of *The Merchant of Venice* Shylock was played, and was intended to be played, unsympathetically, in accord with the general Elizabethan feeling against the Jews, and she looks askance at recent productions which have endowed him with a certain tragic dignity. Her book interestingly illustrates the changes of taste and outlook in Shakespearian audiences that have occurred in the three and a half centuries since Shylock was created.

Finding it difficult to believe that so climactic a scene as *Othello* v. ii would have been played 'in as restricted a space and as far back on the Globe stage as theories presuming a permanent "inner stage" must suppose', Lawrence J. Ross, in 'The Use of a "Fit-Up" Booth in *Othello*' (*Sh Q*), argues that 'some sort of booth-like curtained structure, projecting forward from the tiring house façade into the main acting area, served as or contained the bed'.

In the Autumn number of *Sh Q* Virgil K. Whitaker reviews the twelfth season of the San Diego National Shakespeare Festival; Robert L. Perkin the fourth Colorado Shakespeare Festival; Robert D. Horn the 1961 Festival at Ashland, Oregon; Claire McGlinchee the 1961 Festival at Stratford, Connecticut; Robert Speaight the 1960–1 season at Stratford upon Avon and at the Old Vic; Edward Hubler a Shakespeare season held at Princeton after a gap in the use of the McCarter Theatre for serious drama; Jerry H. Bryant the Festival at Phoenix, Arizona. The *Sh Q* bibliography lists about 140 further reviews, articles, and notes concerned with productions on stage, screen, television, radio, or gramophone.

Florence Warner Brown, in 'Shakespeare and Gielgud, Co-Authors of Men' (*Sh Q*), praises Sir John Gielgud as the actor most capable of identifying himself with Shakespeare's men, disciplining himself 'to speak the antiquated patterns with sufficient skill and intuition to make them live again'.

Richard David's British Academy Shakespeare Lecture, 'Shakespeare and the Players' (*PBA*), is noticed in Chapter I (see p. 13, note 11).

5. *Shakespearian Scholarship. Echoes and Allusions*

Bernard Shaw reviewed many a production of Shakespeare, and many comments on Shakespeare occur in his other writings—in articles, prefaces, and letters. Drawing on all these sources, Edwin Wilson has compiled an extremely interesting anthology entitled *Shaw on Shakespeare*.[38] Although Shaw's criticism of Shakespeare often seems perverse, it is never so from ignorance; and there are occasions, especially when he is speaking of Shakespeare's word-music, when he shows himself to be an extraordinarily sensitive and penetrating critic. Wilson's collection, grouped under the headings of the individual plays, will be of value to students both of Shakespeare and of Shaw.

Gordon W. Couchman suggests (*PMLA*) that Shaw's hostile criticism of Shakespeare's Antony resulted from his having fallen victim 'to what we might call the subjective convention'. In 'Reflections on the Sentimentalist's Othello' (*CQ*) Barbara Everett criticizes F. R. Leavis's essay on *Othello* in *The Common Pursuit*.

In 'Shakespeare in Peru' (*Sh Q*) C. E. Zavaleta describes the growing interest

---

[38] *Shaw on Shakespeare: An Anthology of Bernard Shaw's Writings on the Plays and Production of Shakespeare*, ed. and with an Introduction, by Edwin Wilson. New York: Dutton. pp. xxiii+284. $1.75.

in Shakespeare in Peru over the last century or so. Shakespeare has been much translated by Peruvian writers, and has influenced some Peruvian poets, but has not attracted much critical attention.

Joseph Frank draws attention (*Sh Q*) to a reference to Falstaff in a drinking song printed in 1654 in John Crouch's scurrilous journal *Mercurius Fumigosus*. James G. McManaway (*NQ*) finds reminiscences of *Hamlet* in Thomas Jordan's broadside poem of 1660, *A Speech Made to His Excellency The Lord General Monk*. Ralph Haven Wolfe briefly discusses (*NQ*) the use made by Wordsworth and De Quincey of the phrase from *Hamlet*, 'like a guilty thing'. D. Biggins believes that Scott's *Heart of Midlothian* was significantly influenced by *Measure for Measure*. He notes (*Ea*) some close linguistic parallels, similarities in the moral trials of Jeanie Deans and Isabella, and some resemblances between characters.

Jules C. Alciatore (*MLN*) finds a possible echo of *Cymbeline* or *Lear* in a phrase used by Stendhal, 'a pris par terre la mesure d'un sot'. R. E. C. Houghton (*Sh Q*) observes parallels between Hardy's *The Return of the Native* and *King Lear*. In 'The Iago of *Brave New World*' (*Western Humanities Rev.*) William M. Jones discerns signs of the influence of *Othello* on Huxley's novel.

The following books, which arrived too late for inclusion in this chapter, will be noticed next year: *Shakespeare: A Biographical Handbook*, by Gerald Eades Bentley (Yale U.P.); *Stratford Papers on Shakespeare, 1961*, edited by B. W. Jackson (Toronto: Gage); *Angel with Horns and Other Shakespeare Lectures*, by A. P. Rossiter (Longmans); *Hamlet: A Tragedy of Errors*, by Weston Babcock (Purdue University Studies); and *The Case for Shakespeare's Authorship of 'The Famous Victories'*, by Seymour M. Pitcher (State Univ. of New York).

VIII. LATER ELIZABETHAN AND EARLY STUART DRAMA

By ARTHUR BROWN

SIR WALTER GREG'S masterly edition of Henslowe's *Diary* (1904) has long been out of print, and second-hand copies, not often available, have been commanding prices beyond the reach of the average scholarly purse. At the same time the *Diary* is indispensable for any serious student of this period, and it is welcome news indeed that a new edition, edited by R. A. Foakes and R. T. Rickert, is now available from the Cambridge University Press.[1] 'The main purpose of this edition', we are told, 'is to make available again the text of the chief source for theatrical history between 1590 and 1604, Henslowe's *Diary*, and the fragments and manuscripts associated with it, in as convenient a form as possible.' The editors have made a fresh transcript of the material, and have taken the opportunity to reconsider the meaning of Henslowe's entries and Greg's detailed interpretation of them. Their hopes that this new edition will encourage further scrutiny of the evidence will certainly be fully realized. They have themselves indicated certain new interpretations which will need to be considered seriously: the meaning of Henslowe's 'ne' attached to the titles of certain plays; the truth about Henslowe's alleged 'illiteracy'; the nature of his relation with the players; and the extent of his dealings with other dramatic companies of the time. There is not the space to consider any of these matters here; attention may be drawn, however, to a review of this volume by K. M. Lea (*Lib*, June 1962), in which some of the important differences between this and Greg's edition are admirably summarized.

Wolfgang Clemen's *Die Tragödie vor Shakespeare* was noted in *YW* xxxvi. 125. The book is now available in an excellent English translation by T. S. Dorsch, under the title *English Tragedy before Shakespeare*.[2]

Reprinted last year by Barnes and Noble of New York, Lily B. Campbell's *Scenes and Machines on the English Stage during the Renaissance*, first published by C.U.P. in 1923, is now being distributed in this country by Constable.[3] Inevitably some of the material has become a little out of date during the intervening thirty-seven years, and it seems a pity that no attempt should have been made to overcome this drawback; even the addition of a bibliography of more recent studies would have been useful— at present there is no bibliography at all, and the reader is left to fight his way through sources mentioned only in the footnotes. Yet the book, with its four main sections on 'The Classical Revival of Stage Decoration in Italy', 'Stage Decoration in England during the Sixteenth Century', 'Stage Decora-

[1] *Henslowe's Diary*, ed. with Supplementary Material, Introduction, and Notes, by R. A. Foakes and R. T. Rickert. C.U.P. pp. lix+368. 60s.

[2] *English Tragedy before Shakespeare: The Development of Dramatic Speech*, by Wolfgang Clemen. Translated by T. S. Dorsch. Methuen. pp. 301. 30s.

[3] *Scenes and Machines on the English Stage during the Renaissance*, by Lily B. Campbell. New York: Barnes and Noble, Inc.; London: Constable. pp. xii+302. 60s.

tion in England 1600–1650', and 'Stage Decoration in England after the Restoration', contains much that is of interest and value, and its reappearance is welcome.

Studies in the Elizabethan Theatre, edited by Charles T. Prouty,[4] contains three essays on subjects of some importance to students of this period. Morton Paterson writes on 'The Stagecraft of the Revels Office during the Reign of Elizabeth', making use of Feuillerat's edition of *Documents relating to the Office of the Revels in the time of Queen Elizabeth* to discuss such matters as the purpose of the Revels Office, the production schedule, costumes, scenery, properties and lighting, and the court audience. James Stinson writes on 'Reconstructions of Elizabethan Public Playhouses', and includes a number of illustrative plates. Robert K. Sarlos writes on 'The Development and Operation of the First Blackfriars Theatre', and the volume ends with a bibliography and index. It is fairly clear from Professor Prouty's brief introduction that the essays are aimed particularly at a non-scholarly audience, although it may be felt that he exaggerates the ignorance of the undergraduate, the graduate, and the teacher of the matters discussed. Is it, for example, really true that 'nowadays there are few undergraduate courses in Elizabethan Drama where the plays of Greene, Peele, Marlowe, and John Lyly are read' (p. x)? However, the essays have a certain value as brief summaries of our knowledge of these matters, even if one feels that Mr. Sarlos, when he adapts Gosson to remark that 'the virtue of "breuitie" will be our constant curse, compelling chroniclers to "ouer skippe" information that is of the greatest importance to us', is un-

consciously anticipating what many readers will feel about the book.

A more valuable collection of essays seems to be that edited by R. J. Kaufmann under the title *Elizabethan Drama: Modern Essays in Criticism*.[5] Kaufmann has brought together nineteen studies of various aspects of Elizabethan Drama, all of which have appeared before in separate books or journals, and in which the emphasis 'is on essentially critical rather than essentially scholarly writing'. Kaufmann goes on to say: 'Lacking the assistance of rich biographical and social materials to inform his inquiry, and confronted by these complex and maturely ironic poetic dramas, the most gifted student and general reader needs some help to direct his intelligence in order that the pleasures others have found in these plays may not be pointlessly denied him. These essays have been chosen with an eye to guaranteeing this help and assisting this pleasure.' Space forbids a listing of all nineteen, but one notes with especial pleasure the presence of F. P. Wilson on 'Elizabethan and Jacobean Drama', M. M. Mahood on 'Marlowe's Heroes', Samuel Schoenbaum on 'The Precarious Balance of John Marston', Ray L. Heffner on 'Unifying Symbols in the Comedy of Ben Jonson', and Helen Gardner on 'The Tragedy of Damnation'. To single out these for special notice is by no means to suggest that the others are less worthy; it is a rich and useful volume.

This year saw the appearance of the fourth volume of Fredson Bowers's *The Dramatic Works of Thomas Dekker*,[6] with which, we are told, 'the textual editor's assignment is completed'. In this volume we are given

[4] *Studies in the Elizabethan Theatre*, ed. by Charles T. Prouty. Hamden, Conn.: The Shoe String Press, Inc. pp. xi+198. $4.75.

[5] *Elizabethan Drama: Modern Essays in Criticism*, ed. by R. J. Kaufmann. (Galaxy Book No. 63.) O.U.P. pp. 372. 15s.

[6] *The Dramatic Works of Thomas Dekker*, ed. by Fredson Bowers. Volume IV. C.U.P. pp. viii+418. 45s.

the texts of two Lord Mayors' Entertainments (*Brittania's Honour* and
London's Tempe), the play *The Sun's
Darling* (which has always been part
of the Dekker canon, though Ford's
name shares the title-page with his),
and three plays which the editor has
selected from the list of those at various
times attributed to Dekker—*Lust's
Dominion*, *The Noble Spanish Soldier*,
and *The Welsh Ambassador*. These are
presented in accordance with the editorial principles described in the first
volume of the series, published in
1953. Professor Bowers is to be thanked
and congratulated most heartily on
the successful completion of his task,
in which he has set a new and very
high standard for work of this kind
in the future. The proposed volume of
commentary and more critical material
is eagerly awaited.

The second volume of a projected
three-volume edition of *The Life and
Works of George Peele* contains
Edward I, edited by Frank S. Hook,
and *The Battle of Alcazar*, edited by
John Yoklavitch.[7] In the case of
both plays, the introductions present
material on the authorship, dating,
and sources of the play concerned, a
discussion of textual problems, and an
account of the methods used to establish the present text. The texts retain
the old spellings, and variant readings
from early quartos (where these exist)
and from previous editors are given in
footnotes. Explanatory notes follow
the texts, and for *Edward I* we are
given the text of the ballad, *The
lamentable fall of Queene Elnor*, from
which Peele took some of his material.

The Revels Plays, under the General
Editorship of Professor Clifford Leech,
continue to flourish, and this year
Thomas Heywood's *A Woman Killed*

with *Kindness* was added to the series.[8]
In a long introduction the editor,
R. W. Van Fossen, provides a full
survey of previous scholarship on the
sources, theme, structure, characters,
and style, as well as a fresh interpretation of some aspects of the play, a concise stage history, and an investigation
of the considerable difficulties involved
in establishing a text. On this last point
at any rate he has the whole-hearted
sympathy of the present writer! Faced
with two quartos, one dated 1607 and
extant only in a single copy in the
British Museum, another dated 1617,
extant in at least a score of copies but
bearing on its title-page 'The third
edition', with no known edition either
appearing between the two or antedating both of them, and with no
clear indication of the relationship between the two, Van Fossen has done
his best to make the best of the situation. His text is, he admits, highly
eclectic, 'and not very scientifically
eclectic at that'. With some hesitation
he has chosen the 1607 quarto as his
copy-text, but since he finds evidence
for some independent authority in the
1617 quarto he has not hesitated to
accept readings from it when he
thought this desirable. His apparatus
is commendably full, and he prints as
an appendix the story of Salimbene
and Angelica from Painter's *Palace of
Pleasure*, which seems to have been the
source of Heywood's sub-plot.

The Malone Society published two
volumes this year, *The Bloody Banquet*
(1639) by T. D., edited on the basis of
a collation of ten of the known copies
of the quarto, and *Collections VI*,
Dramatic Records in the Declared
Accounts of the Treasurer of the
Chamber, 1558–1642.[9] The latter

[7] *The Dramatic Works of George Peele:
Edward I*, ed. by Frank S. Hook; *The Battle
of Alcazar*, ed. by John Yoklavitch. Yale
U.P. pp. x+373. 80s.

[8] *A Woman Killed with Kindness*, by
Thomas Heywood, ed. by R. W. Van Fossen.
(The Revels Plays.) Methuen. pp. lxxiii+
122. 18s.

[9] *The Bloody Banquet*, by T. D., ed. by
S. Schoenbaum, with assistance from G. E.

volume contains also a Supplement to Sir Walter Greg's edition of *Sir Thomas More* by Harold Jenkins. Greg's edition of the play was first published in 1911; since stocks were exhausted, the Malone Society has had the edition reprinted for the benefit of new members who wished to purchase it, and Professor Jenkins's Supplement was added to Greg's original introduction as a survey and an assessment of the work that has been done on the play since 1911. For the convenience of members who already possessed the original edition, the Supplement was included in *Collections VI*.

'Coinciding with the reign of Charles I', says R. J. Kaufmann, 'the plays of Richard Brome, written between 1629 and 1641, have been neglected by critics because they have shared the era with the work of Shakespeare, Milton, and Donne. However, his realistic comedies were extremely popular with Caroline audiences and were much admired by contemporary playwrights such as Ben Jonson. Together, Brome's fifteen plays form a unified and enlightened commentary on the life and drama of the period.' For these reasons Kaufmann has devoted an entire book to Brome,[10] emphasizing particularly the playwright's position 'at a time when changes in both society and the theatre were brought about by the early seventeenth century social revolution in England'. He points out that previous critical work on Brome has been

sparse and mainly poor in quality, and he has done his best to redress the balance by utilizing modern historical and critical knowledge. There is certainly much in the book that deserves to be more widely known; on the other hand there is perhaps a tendency to concentrate rather too much on the background at the expense of Brome himself, and the reasons for omitting from the discussion four of the fifteen plays are not entirely convincing (p. 16). If the man has been rather shabbily treated in the past, that is all the more reason for the fullest possible discussion of all his work now.

One of the most important articles to appear this year was Samuel Schoenbaum's 'Internal Evidence and the Attribution of Elizabethan Plays' (*BNYPL*), which should be made compulsory reading for all students of this period. Schoenbaum reviews with solid common sense and a dry humour some of the 'attributions' of the past, considers the weaknesses of the bases upon which they were made, and propounds, with adequate illustration, seven principles to be taken very seriously into account by 'canonical investigators'. These deserve to be reported in full, since the illustrative material of the rest of the paper is too long for summary. (1) External evidence cannot be ignored, no matter how inconvenient such evidence may be for the theories of the investigator. (2) If stylistic criteria are to have any meaning, the play must be written in a style. (3) The investigator must always work with reliable texts, preferably directly with the early editions or manuscripts. (4) Textual analysis logically precedes canonical analysis. (5) For any author proposed, a reasonable amount of unquestioned dramatic writing, apart from collaborations, must be extant. (6) Intuitions, convictions, and subjective judgements generally, carry no

Bentley and the General Editor. O.U.P. for the Malone Society. pp. xi+60. Issued to members only. *Collections VI: Dramatic Records in the Declared Accounts of the Treasurer of the Chamber, 1558–1642*, ed. by David Cook, with assistance from F. P. Wilson. O.U.P. for the Malone Society. pp. xxx+192. Issued to members only.

[10] *Richard Brome, Caroline Playwright*, by R. J. Kaufmann. Columbia U.P. pp. 193. $5.00.

weight as evidence. (7) Wherever possible, stylistic evidence should be
supplemented by textual evidence. It
is distressing that in this day and age
it should be necessary to call attention
to what one might hope would be
fundamental principles, hammered into
the mind of every scholar from his
first venture into his chosen field; yet
a regular survey of our periodical
literature shows how often they are
not only ignored, but might well never
have existed. Schoenbaum has done
great service in reminding us of them.
If only one could hope that in a year's
time it will not be necessary for someone else to repeat the reminder!

In 'Studies in Elizabethan and
Jacobean Drama since 1900' (Sh S),
Arthur Brown surveys the more important contributions to scholarship
during this period under the headings
of General Works, Dramatic Forms,
Textual Studies, General Editions,
Editions of Individual Authors, Studies
of Individual Authors, and Theatre
and Acting, and ends with some suggestions about the direction of research
in the future.

D. F. Foxon's *Thomas J. Wise and
the Pre-Restoration Drama* was noted
in *YW* xl. 137. This year Foxon and
W. B. Todd publish a Supplement to
this work (*Lib*) which gives the results
of an examination of certain volumes
in the Wrenn and Aitken collections
of the University of Texas, and the
sorry story of Wise's thefts of leaves
from British Museum copies of plays
is taken one stage further.

In 'The Enigmatic Elizabethan Stage'
(*English*) W. A. Armstrong surveys
briefly but sensibly 'the wide range of
evidence concerning the structure and
stagecraft of the Elizabethan public
theatres'. There are three main categories of evidence: pictorial (alas, all
too slight!), documentary (contemporary contracts, descriptions, and
references to the theatres in non-

dramatic literature), and dramatic
(dialogue and stage directions in those
editions of Elizabethan plays published
in the sixteenth and early seventeenth
centuries). Armstrong considers the
various interpretations of the evidence
by such writers as G. F. Reynolds,
J. C. Adams, G. R. Kernodle, C. Walter
Hodges, Leslie Hotson, and others,
but finds, quite properly, that few, if
any, firm conclusions can be drawn.
'The enigma', as he says, 'remains.'

An interesting and important article
by Allardyce Nicoll arrived too late
for notice in this chapter last year. It
is entitled '"Tragical-Comical-Histori-
cal-Pastoral": Elizabethan Dramatic
Nomenclature' (*BJRL*), and the author
discusses some of the problems involved
in the interpretation of the various
labels which have been attached to
plays. Starting with Polonius's catalogue, he asks first of all whether
Shakespeare was being strictly topical
in his use of these terms, or whether,
for the sake of a jest, he was per-
mitting his imagination to range. The
answer to this question 'must assume
a more complicated form than the
query from which it springs', but it is
interesting to note that *Hamlet* itself
seems to be the first play to which the
term 'tragical-historical' was applied,
being printed in 1603 and 1604 as *The
Tragicall Historie of Hamlet*. This in
turn raises the question how far
nomenclature emanated from the
dramatist himself, and how far it was
the responsibility of the printer, and
Professor Nicoll illustrates the matter
from a wide range of plays. He discusses too the vexed term 'interlude',
which suddenly disappears from title-
pages after 1576, a phenomenon which
he links up with the establishment of
the first permanent English playhouse.
'Comedy', 'tragedy', and 'history' are
all touched upon, and the result is a
fascinating survey of a topic which has
been sadly neglected in the past.

M. C. Bradbrook summarizes neatly enough most of what we know about the Children's Companies in '"Silk? Satin? Kersey? Rags?" The Choristers' Theatre under Elizabeth and James' (*Studies in English Literature, 1500–1900*). She pays particular attention to the men who were responsible for their activities, since 'children's troupes rise or decay with the appearance or disappearance of some talented and energetic promoter. Their history is the history of the men who trained the children.' This is true enough, but one must beware of assuming too much about these men. There is no firm evidence, for example, that Sebastian Westcott wrote *Liberality and Prodigality*, or any of the other plays that have been lightly attributed to him from time to time, nor can we be sure that John Heywood wrote plays for the Paul's Boys.

The first meeting of the newly formed Société des Anglicistes de l'Enseignement Supérieur was held at Bordeaux in April 1961. Although the papers read on that occasion have not been published in full, summaries of them appear in *Ea*; readers of this chapter will find 'Les Tragédies de Sénèque et le Théâtre Élisabétain' by Jean Jacquot, and 'L'Influence de Sénèque sur *Gorboduc*' by Paul Bacquet, of particular interest.

There seems to be no end to speculation about the nature of the 'discovery space' on Elizabethan stages. This year Albert B. Weiner writes on 'Elizabethan Interior and Aloft Scenes— A Speculative Essay' (*Theatre Survey*), and suggests that this discovery space was not an inner stage but possibly a platform hinged with two legs which, when not in use, could be raised and folded flush against the tiring-house wall immediately below the gallery. Such a device could serve as pavilion, balcony, tent, scaffold, or wall, and would help to explain a number of stage directions in Elizabethan plays.

In 'Interplay in Peele's *The Old Wives' Tale*' (*BUSE*) Herbert Goldstone shows how Peele's ability to handle material from different literary worlds and to make them interact one upon another leads to the success of the humour and to the unification of plot structure in this play.

Zdeněk Stříbrný contributes, in 'Christopher Marlowe, 1564–1593' (*Časopis pro moderní filologii*), a full-length study of the dramatist, summing up the major results of modern Marlovian research and attempting to suggest some new observations. Starting from the premiss that Marlowe was a highly subjective artist, in contrast to the supreme objectivity of the art of Shakespeare, Stříbrný deals first with some questions of Marlowe's life and early death, notes that Marlowe's humble origin seems to be reflected in the status of many of his dramatic heroes, then defines the Marlowe canon, and proceeds to analyse the plays in their probable chronological order.

John H. Crabtree, Jr., writes on 'The Comedy in Marlowe's *Dr. Faustus*' (*Furman Studies*). He seems to suggest that the authorship of the comic scenes need not concern us greatly, since, whether they come from Marlowe or from a collaborator, they were clearly intended to form an integral part of the play, to produce, with the more serious portions, a unified and coherent drama. Conventional comic characters, conventional sub-plot, and other theatrical resources, are all employed by the author or authors to this end.

There is an interesting study of *The White Devil* in H. Bruce Franklin's 'The Trial Scene of Webster's *The White Devil* Examined in Terms of Renaissance Rhetoric' (*Studies in English Literature, 1500–1900*). He points out how the dramatic techniques of the play compound 'all kinds of disguise, deceit, and false rhetoric', and it is on this last element that he concentrates his attention. The speeches of the trial scene are examined in detail, and we are shown how the lawyer's initial mass of 'inkhorn terms and grotesque sounds in a periphrastic and confused syntax', and Monticelso's euphuism, enthymeme, and rhetorical questions, both intended to impress the hearers and to crush Vittoria, are defeated by her wit, her brief retorts, and her abrupt questions which penetrate to the weakest part of the prosecution. Later in the scene Vittoria's own speeches also take on a more rhetorical tone, but it is made clear that she is much more in command of the various devices and ornaments of speech than her accusers are. After examining the rest of the scene in the same way, Franklin concludes that in Vittoria, Webster has created 'a rhetorician and a woman about whom it is not easy to make a simple absolute judgement. . . . She is not persuasive enough to prove that she is not evil and not a devil. But she is sufficiently eloquent to demonstrate that she is not the only devil, and that perhaps she is not the worst of the four devils on trial. The degrees of false rhetoric in the trial scene become part of the demonstration that "As in this world there are degrees of evils, / So in this world there are degrees of devils".'

In 'Webster's Italian Tragedies' (*Tulane Drama Review*) Irving Ribner sees *The White Devil* and *The Duchess of Malfi* as two powerful tragedies representing 'a search for moral order in the uncertain and chaotic world of Jacobean scepticism'. The former play presents 'the deception of appearances' and 'the shallowness of the conventional moral order', while the latter goes beyond the presentation of evil to show 'the possibility of a moral order'. It is a closely unified play, in which

mood, action, characterization, and poetry are all designed to show 'the effect on the debased world of . . . the spirit's triumph in spite of the body's destruction'.

Chapman has attracted a fair amount of attention this year, much of it concerned with the chronology of his plays. C. L. Barber discusses 'The Ambivalence of *Bussy D'Ambois*' (*REL*), and suggests that the play may be read in two ways—in terms of Christian morality or in terms of the code of honour. As a result the audience is left, to a certain extent, with certain unanswered questions. Bussy himself seems to represent the seventeenth-century conception of the man of honour in the private rather than in the public sense; this becomes apparent in his sensitivity to insult, in his private quarrels, and in the way in which he conducts an adulterous affair. At the same time the play may be interpreted as showing the triumph of passion over reason. Barber thinks that in offering this choice of interpretations, the play is perhaps a victim of the moral and political tensions of the early seventeenth century.

Elias Schwartz has three articles on Chapman. In the first, 'The Date of Chapman's Byron Plays' (*MP*), he refers back to his earlier article (see *YW* xl. 140) in which he had argued that these plays were in existence before 1606, and had dismissed evidence for a later date—their apparent dependence on Grimestone's *General Inventorie of the History of France* (1607)—by suggesting that Chapman had used some unknown source or the French originals rather than Grimestone's translation. Further study has now convinced Schwartz that Chapman did in fact use Grimestone, and he suggests, therefore, that Chapman saw Grimestone's work in manuscript before publication. Chapman was related to Grimestone, knew him personally, and was probably in France about the time that Grimestone was there. Schwartz also feels that Chapman's letter to Sir George Buc about the latter's reluctance to license the Byron plays for printing after the French Ambassador had objected to their performance, indicates that the plays had been 'allowed' for acting by the Privy Council in 1606, 1607, and 1608, which accords well with a composition date of 1605. Schwartz's second article concerns 'The Date of *Bussy D'Ambois*' (*MP*). This he wishes to place about 1596, and he is concerned to dispose of the arguments advanced against such a date. The reference in Henslowe's *Diary* to a garment worn by William Sly he interprets as to a garment bought from Sly; the play's jest on leap-year, taken by E. K. Chambers to refer either to 1600 or to 1604, could equally well refer to 1596; the reference to the 'old' queen means the 'aged' queen, not the 'late' queen, and 1596 was in any case a crucial year for Elizabeth; and the reference to Bussy as a 'knight of the new edition' need not refer to James's creation of knights, but could equally well apply to the sixty-six knights made at Cadiz by Essex and the Lord Admiral in June 1596. Some of the points made by Schwartz in these and earlier articles are disputed by Robert Ornstein in 'The Dates of Chapman's Tragedies once more' (*MP*). He concludes that while Schwartz may not necessarily be wrong, 'at the present time there is not sufficient evidence supporting the thesis of earlier dates to counterbalance the conservative scholarly arguments which support Parrott's dating of Chapman's plays'.

Moving from questions of chronology, Schwartz discusses Chapman's *Caesar and Pompey* in 'A Neglected Play by Chapman' (*SP*). Swinburne's censure seems to have been mainly responsible for the neglect of this play,

and it has been criticized mainly on the grounds that it is disunified and that Pompey is inconsistently characterized. Schwartz analyses the play scene by scene in considerable detail to show not only that these criticisms are unjustified, but that on the contrary the play is one of considerable power. Lack of unity can be alleged against it only if it is assumed, wrongly, that Cato is the protagonist. 'But Cato . . . has other dramatic functions: he is the focal point of opposition to Caesar, a guide to Pompey, and a choric figure, establishing the ethical norm of the play and fixing, by word and deed, its final meaning.' Inconsistent characterization of Pompey can be alleged only if it is assumed, wrongly, that he is a static character and that he is meant to be from first to last. But Pompey is the true protagonist of the play, developing gradually throughout the action. 'The progressive growth of Pompey, whose final status is as much a conquest of himself as of Caesar, enhances his viability as a tragic hero.'

In 'The Date of Composition of Chapman's *Caesar and Pompey*' (*RES*) J. E. Ingledew thinks that although 1612–13 is the generally accepted date for the play, it was probably composed earlier. The earliest possible date is 1599, and a passage in *The Teares of Peace* (1609) borrowed from the play indicates that it cannot be later than 1609. A passage containing a reference to the death of Tilney, the Master of the Revels, was probably written later. If the date of composition is in fact substantially earlier than 1612–13, we should have to revise many of our popular views of Chapman's development as poet, dramatist, and thinker.

Writing on 'The Dramatic Uses of Homeric Idealism: The Significance of Theme and Design in George Chapman's *The Gentleman Usher*' (*ELH*), Henry M. Weidner suggests that one can perhaps best understand the varying ideologies attributed to Chapman—Stoicism, Platonism, School of Night Marlovianism, Christian Humanism—'if one sees them reflected in the prism of Chapman's constantly expanding Homeric idealism. On the evidence of the plays it would seem that Homer looms larger in Chapman's thought as the 1590's draw to a close. At the turn of the century the great translator of Homer seems increasingly aware both of the complex evil in the world and of the compelling good found in the simplicity of epic heroism. The central issue in life becomes the relationship of man to evil as played against the normative vision of a Homeric golden age.' Weidner feels that the mature Chapman's 'rigidly dualized notion of good and evil' finds exceptionally rich expression in dramatic romance and satire, but is less satisfying in comedy and tragedy where his too-simple idealism clashes with the demands of *genre. The Gentleman Usher*, examined here in detail, is one of Chapman's almost perfect successes with complex materials. 'In general one may say that its basic structure lies in the contrast between the first two acts of misused, over-formalized ceremony, and the last two acts of properly employed, sensibly formalized ceremony. The third act serves partially as transition, partially as "comic relief" from the tensions found in the opening and closing segments. Ceremony is properly employed by those who act decorously with complex wisdom. These characters . . . Margaret . . . Stozza and Vince, are in correct relationship with reality. Those characters who cannot act with complexity in their implementation of "shews" and courtly masques become foolish absolutists. The greatest offender is the Duke, absolute in his lust . . . unable to distinguish love rivalry from treason.' The world of the play is a dramatically idealized one, and a change of attitude 'is enough to promote the cures for all the serious wounds of the flesh and the soul. This is the stuff of a dream world which is the symbolic norm for our real world.'

In '*Bartholomew Fair*: Comedy of Vapours' (*Studies in English Literature, 1500–1900*) James E. Robinson thinks that the general tone of the play is not so far removed as some critics have thought from the classical principles of construction apparent in Jonson's other plays. He proposes to show that 'the centre of the structure and meaning of *Bartholomew Fair* lies in the symbolism of vapours that pervades the play's imagery, characterization, and action. To explain the play as a comedy of vapours is to explain how the play is designed to fulfil classical concepts of dramatic unity, verisimilitude, and the function of comedy.' The function of 'vapours' is similar to that of 'humours', and drawn from the same source. They arose from 'bilious humours in unnatural heat because of physiological disorder or immoderate passions', and in rising clouded the brain and produced madness. By using this imagery, Jonson puts the characters of this play 'all in smoke from the impassioned humours of their lower natures and so exposes the beclouded state of their higher natures'. The symbolism of vapours is created in the atmosphere of the Fair itself, in the characterizations, in the special language and games of Captain Knockhum the horse trader, in the interaction of the two worlds of Fairers and Fairmen. 'It is in the fusion of imagery, character, scene, and action to produce a universal comic truth that the structure and unity of the play lies. Such a structure is compatible with Renaissance classical principles of dramatic unity.'

James D. Redwine, Jr., writes on 'The Moral Basis of Jonson's Theory of Humour Characterization' (*ELH*). Asper's long speech on humours in the induction to *Every Man Out of His Humour* is often separated from its context, and treated as if it were a learned digression on psychology or psychological characterization. This is the wrong way to approach it; the remarks are almost meaningless out of their context, and treated in that way give a false impression of Jonson's theory. They elucidate and are elucidated by the critical ideas that surround them. Asper is not a psychologist but a moralist, and to call Jonson's theory of humours a 'psychology' is to risk serious misunderstanding. Crites, in *Cynthia's Revels*, also describes the process of a humour in some detail, and in unmistakably moral terms; he conceives of a humour as the subjection of the spirit to the evil habit of the flesh, concupiscence. Contrition, confession, and satisfaction constitute the catastrophe of *Cynthia's Revels*. Those critics who have attempted to define the theory of humours in terms of psychology or of aesthetic decorum have failed to notice that both these, for the Renaissance, were elements of moral philosophy. Redwine quotes extensively from Thomas Wright's *The Passions of the Mind in General* (written 1597–8, pirated 1601, and seen through the press in a corrected edition by Wright in 1604), the authorized version of which opens with Jonson's tribute to the author and the book, in order to show the parallels in thought between the two writers.

In 'Some Notes on the Vocabulary of John Marston, XXI, XXII, XXIII' (*NQ*) Gustav Cross continues his series of studies of words used by Marston which are either unrecorded in the *O.E.D.*, or recorded there with a different shade of meaning or from a date later than their occurrence in Marston. Cross also writes on 'The Retrograde Genius of John Marston' (*REL*), pointing out that since T. S. Eliot did not do justice to Marston, most subsequent critics have not done so either. Cross sees him as a serious moralist, writing in the tradition of the hell-fire preacher. Possibly he had already begun to contemplate taking holy orders when, in *Sophonisba*, he tried to demonstrate the adequacies of Stoicism, a philosophy which he had previously attacked for its limitations.

Last year Christopher Ricks dealt with a group of words in *The Changeling* 'each of which has two meanings, one of them sexual', meanings which, by the end of the play, have become inextricable (see *YW* xli. 134). This year he writes on 'Word-Play in *Women Beware Women*' (*RES*), using a very similar group of words (*business, employ, service, spent, work, use*) and the same technique. Middleton achieves his important moral purpose in this play not only through action, character, and image, but through intensive word-play, sometimes involving puns, in which ordinary words, many of them carrying traditionally ambiguous meanings, reinforce the moral argument. Thus the theme of the corruption of life and love by money is emphasized by the use of words which draw together the ideas of sex and commerce.

Robert G. Lawrence publishes 'A Bibliographical Study of Middleton and Rowley's *The Changeling*' (*Lib*). The details of his investigation are too technical to be summarized here, but his conclusions are as follows: 'The above analysis of composition and printing shows that the text of *The Changeling* did not suffer seriously at the hands of its first printer. The quarto, printed presumably from a playhouse prompt-copy (or a transcript), offers no difficulties of interpretation which were the responsibility of the compositor and printer. There are a few minor verbal cruxes (most of them created by the authors), rather sketchy stage-directions, and much carelessness in the arrangement of lines of verse. Here the compositor was clearly trying to save space. Rowley was much more careless and casual than Middleton in his habits of versification and frequently made it difficult for the compositor to distinguish between verse and prose.'

The sixth instalment of Cyrus Hoy's 'The Shares of Fletcher and his Collaborators in the Beaumont and Fletcher Canon' (*SB*) is concerned with three plays: *The Captain*, in which Hoy finds that Beaumont probably contributed four scenes, although the greater part of the work is that of Fletcher; *Love's Cure*, the extant text of which is very largely the work of Massinger, but probably a revision by Massinger of a Beaumont–Fletcher original; and *Rollo Duke of Normandy*, which contains the work of Fletcher and Massinger, but perhaps also that of Chapman and Jonson.

'Notes on the Text of *Thierry and Theodoret* Q1' (*SB*) by Robert K. Turner, Jr., is perhaps also too technical for easy summary here. From a close examination of such bibliographical features as running-titles, spelling, type shortages, and broken and deformed types, he draws some inferences about the book's printing and about the kind of copy from which it was set up. He concludes that the single compositor concerned was perhaps an apprentice or a 'relief compositor', that he was setting from a composite fair copy written in the hands of the three collaborators (Beaumont, Fletcher, and Massinger) which may have been reviewed and slightly revised by Fletcher. There is nothing to suggest that this manuscript had served as a prompt copy, or that it had been annotated for transcription into prompt copy.

Previous critics of Heywood's *The English Traveller* have found little to praise in the relation between main plot and sub-plot, some indeed doubting if there is any worth-while connexion at all. Norman Rabkin, in 'Dramatic Deception in Heywood's *The English Traveller*' (*Studies in English Literature, 1500–1900*) suggests that in this play Heywood reaches the height of his achievement in comedy. 'His skill is manifest in the use of a double plot to convey a complex theme, the full implications of which are not seen until the independent plots have been brought to their conclusions and the two actions considered together.' A number of accepted dramatic conventions are manipulated in such a way that the audience is mystified and deluded for much of the time, their expectation of certain conventional developments being thwarted again and again. The 'supreme analogue' underlying both actions is the familiar theme of appearance and reality; in the main plot this theme is developed with respect to fidelity in love, while in the sub-plot it is generalized.

By a coincidence this theme is dealt with again by Michel Grivelet in 'The Simplicity of Thomas Heywood' (*Sh S*). He admits that at first sight the relation between the two plots in *The English Traveller* is not particularly clear, but he finds in the title of the play a first hint of what they have in common. It is during Geraldine's travels that he loses his childhood sweetheart first in marriage to Wincott, and next to the seducer Dalavill, and it is during Old Lionel's travels that his house is misused by his son and his companions. 'The house idea is as essential to Young Lionel as its counterpart, the travel idea, is to Young Geraldine', and the implications of the proper upbringing of a young man are present in both symbols. Further, the characters' names are pointers to a deeper, hidden meaning in the play: Dalavill is 'all devil', Geraldine is a 'dire angel', Reignald (in the sub-plot) is the almost exact anagram of Geraldine, 'and there is little doubt that Heywood wants us to look for some symmetry between the two characters. . . . Though very different and even opposed, Geraldine and Reignald play similar roles. . . . Little harm is done to his masters, young and old, by the wily and unscrupulous knave, whereas the ambiguous virtue of the English traveller proves deadly to the woman he loves.'

In 'Massinger's Use of his Sources for *The Roman Actor*' (*AUMLA*) C. A. Gibson points out that Suetonius, possibly supplemented by Dio Cassius, provides all the major events of the play. Two passages are provided by Tacitus (*Histories* and *Agricola*), and there are other borrowings from Juvenal, Ovid, Horace, and *Epitome de Caesaribus*. English sources include Jonson's *Sejanus* and Webster's *Duchess of Malfi*. In the manipulation of his sources, Massinger 'explores the implications and consequences to society of rule by a king whose will dominates his reason'.

A number of articles appearing in *Sh S* may be listed here as having some bearing on this chapter, although their main interest seems to be rather in Shakespeare: Marco Mincoff, 'Shakespeare and Lyly'; I. A. Shapiro, 'Shakespeare and Mundy'; Nicholas Brooke, 'Marlowe as Provocative Agent in Shakespeare's Early Plays'; Harold Jenkins, 'The Tragedy of Revenge in Webster and Shakespeare'; and T. J. B. Spencer, 'Shakespeare v. The Rest'.

IX. THE LATER TUDOR PERIOD, EXCLUDING DRAMA

By Patricia Thomson

Amongst this year's publications on Elizabethan history, the volume[1] presented to Sir John Neale stands out. The thirteen essays, of consistently high quality, are on a variety of subjects, and this review must be confined to a survey of contents. C. H. Williams provides a study of the queen's personality as understood by historians from her day to this. Conyers Read's posthumously published essay is on William Cecil's responsibility for public relations as exemplified chiefly in the government pamphlets which were put out to justify or explain policy. S. T. Bindoff writes on the making of the Statute of Artificers (which was by no means so consistent a thing as its preamble suggests) and on its passage through Parliament. Wallace T. Mac-Caffrey emphasizes the extent to which the Elizabethan monarchy rested on its capacity to reward its supporters, and examines the crown patronage together with Burleigh's influence upon it. Patrick Collinson studies John Field's influence on Elizabethan Puritanism in the 1570's and 1580's, and his non-separatist idea of reforming the Church of England and eliminating 'popish dregs'. W. G. Hoskins discusses the careers, finances, and standard of living of the Elizabethan merchants of Exeter. Marjorie Blatcher goes into the writ of Latitat (the writ to get a defendant into court, used after the writs of attachment and arrest

had failed). G. R. Elton describes the exchequer of Receipt (the pay-office department of the exchequer) and the thirty-year war which raged between its officers over their rights. A. H. Dodd outlines the career of Thomas Myddleton, a typical puritan merchant, who, after enriching himself in London, returned to his native Wales as a landowner. Gordon Donaldson writes on the long but steady process of *rapprochement* between England and Scotland preceding their union. R. Dudley Edwards studies Elizabethan Ireland and, particularly, its revelation of 'the conflicts of the traditional cultures with the new forces of Reformation and Counter-Reformation'. R. B. Wernham re-examines the charge that Elizabeth, in her war strategy, 'did all by halves', and, to a large extent, justifies her. Finally, Joel Hurstfield describes the succession struggle, giving special attention to Robert Cecil's skilful management of affairs c. 1603.

Albert J. Schmidt's booklet *The Yeoman in Tudor and Stuart England*[2] is addressed to the non-specialist, being 'one of a series planned by the Folger Library to describe various aspects of the cultural history of the sixteenth and seventeenth centuries'. It fulfils this purpose well, giving a balanced picture of the English yeoman, and emphasizing particularly his social mobility. This class was, generally, on the up-grade. A few members

---

[1] *Elizabethan Government and Society: Essays presented to Sir John Neale*, ed. by S. T. Bindoff, J. Hurstfield, and C. H. Williams. Athlone Press. pp. x+423. 50s.

[2] *The Yeoman in Tudor and Stuart England*, by Albert J. Schmidt. (Folger Booklets on Tudor and Stuart Civilizations.) The Folger Shakespeare Library. pp. 29+19 plates.

of it declined into the condition of labourers, but, for the enterprising, there were 'unprecedented opportunities' for the purchase of land and profitable production of foodstuffs and wool. Many yeomen, therefore, made their way into the gentry class, sent their sons to the university, built fine houses, and rested their weary heads on pillows instead of good round logs. Nevertheless, they did not always lose the traditional pride in their yeoman status. All this is illustrated from contemporary records, and the booklet concludes with 'Suggested Reading' and an array of delightful plates.

Charles and Katherine George have produced a scholarly book,[3] which, they emphatically insist, is not a history of the Reformation but an analysis of Protestant ideology between 1570 and 1640. They are interested in the relation between Protestantism in England and the outbreak of rebellion in 1640. A discussion of the historical ideas contained in this book would not be appropriate to a review of English literary studies. It need only be said that such an illumination of the Protestant mind has interest for all students of this period. Furthermore, the Georges' primary sources, mainly sermons and religious tracts, are as much the property of 'English' as of 'History'. A few of the writers whose work is used are Richard Hooker, Lancelot Andrewes, the 'Marprelate' pamphleteers, Joseph Hall, John Foxe, Richard Baxter, Thomas Becon, Myles Coverdale, John Jewel, John Preston, William Prynne, George Herbert, and John Donne.

An account of the life and work of the miniaturist Nicholas Hilliard (1547–1619) has great historical interest, for he was familiar with the courts of Elizabeth and James, and portrayed, besides many unknown ladies and gentlemen, a host of the most notable courtiers. Erna Auerbach's handsome volume[4] will perhaps be most valued for its illustrations: it contains 252 monochrome plates and seven in colour.

George B. Parks, in 'The First Italianate Englishmen' (*Studies in the Renaissance*), remarks on the characteristically Elizabethan ambivalence of feeling about Italy, and it is interesting to have this illustrated in *English Miscellany* in two contrasting studies. Jeannette Fellheimer writes on 'The "subtelty" of the Italians', which was, of course, one of the chief reasons for the Elizabethan distrust of Italy. The 'subtle Machiavell' became a by-word and bogey man. 'Subtle' was also used by Italians of their own compatriots, and, though most often it carries the pejorative sense of 'crafty', it can mean merely 'witty' or 'dexterous'. This article is illustrated with many quotations from the English and Italian literature of the Renaissance. Anna Maria Crinò's paper on seventeenth-century contacts between England and Tuscany includes a prefatory account of some Elizabethan tourists in Italy, such as the Earl of Oxford. 'A man who has not been in Italy is always conscious of an inferiority.' Johnson's remark, which is certainly applicable to the Elizabethans, aptly introduces this study.

There are a few other items on foreign relations. W. E. Miller and Eldred D. Jones both contribute, to *NQ*, evidence for the presence of Africans in Elizabethan England, while 'Welshmen in Shakespeare's London' (*Anglo-Welsh Review*) are dealt with by Raymond Chapman.

The Elizabethan letter-writer Rowland Whyte, employee of Robert

[3] *The Protestant Mind of the English Reformation*, by Charles H. & Katherine George. Princeton U.P. and O.U.P. pp. x+452. $8.50, 68s.

[4] *Nicholas Hilliard*, by Erna Auerbach. Routledge and Kegan Paul. pp. xxiv+352. £6. 6s.

Sidney, has always proved useful to historians because of his accounts of the events and personalities of his day. He himself has not, however, been much noticed, and accordingly Lisle C. John provides a biographical account (*Studies in the Renaissance*).

Libraries are dealt with in two articles, 'A Sixteenth-Century Inventory of the Library of Corpus Christi College, Cambridge' (*Transactions of the Cambridge Bibliographical Society*) by John M. Fletcher and James K. McConica, and Paul Kaufman's account (*NQ*) of 'the contents of the library of David Wedderburn of Dundee, as revealed by the titles of books lent to his friends, 1587–1630'.

Printing is the subject of several comments, mainly short notes. Giles E. Dawson, in 'Guide-Lines in Small Formats (About 1600)' (*SB*), writes of a printing-house practice which has escaped the notice of bibliographers. Franklin B. Williams's 'Penny-Pinching Printers and Tampered Titles' (*SB*) is on the Elizabethan printers' handling of title-pages. A. G. Watson (*Lib*) records two sets of verses, of penitential character, printed by Simon Stafford during the plague year, 1603, and not listed in *S.T.C.* William A. Jackson notes 'An English Printed Sheet-Number of 1579' (*Lib*) and Lloyd E. Berry 'Another Booklet of Thomas Charde' (*PBSA*). Also to be noticed is J. A. van Dorsten's book[5] on Thomas Bassoñ, the English printer in Leiden.

By way of introduction to this year's work on Elizabethan literature, it is a pleasure to welcome a new quarterly 'of historical and critical studies' from Rice University. *Studies in English Literature 1500–1900*[6] gets off to a

good start with a number devoted to the English Renaissance. Most of the articles are on particular authors or works, and those relevant to this chapter will be described in the appropriate places below. Meanwhile two 'general' ones can be noticed immediately. Arnold Stein writes 'On Elizabethan Wit', stressing the flexibility and comprehensiveness of the concept of wit, and illustrating his points from a variety of authors, notably Bacon. Arthur E. Barker gives an account of recent books and articles, noticing what still has to be done as well as what has been done in Renaissance English studies.

This year's weightiest contribution to the background of Elizabethan literature is John Leon Lievsay's thorough, detailed study[7] of Stefano Guazzo and his influence on English authors between 1575 and 1675. *La Civil Conversatione* (1574), though Guazzo's best-known work, is still not widely known, for it has been overshadowed by Castiglione's *Cortegiano* and, to a lesser extent, by Della Casa's *Galateo*. But, as Lievsay points out, Guazzo has in many ways a wider scope than Castiglione, being more practical and workaday, and less confined to the hot-house atmosphere of court. His is not a light book on 'amiable chit-chat', but a serious one on manners and social behaviour. It quickly acquired a European reputation and was much translated, the first complete English version, *The Civile Conversation* (1586) being the joint work of George Pettie and Bartholomew Young. Having dealt with these preliminaries, Lievsay goes on to show how far and in what aspects Guazzo was familiar to English authors. Lyly's ideas often correspond to

[5] *Thomas Basson 1555–1613: English Printer at Leiden*, by J. A. van Dorsten. Leiden U.P., for the Sir Thomas Browne Institute. O.U.P. pp. xii+126. 21s.

[6] Address for business communications: Rice University, P.O. Box 1892, Houston 1, Texas.

[7] *Stefano Guazzo and the English Renaissance 1575–1675*, by John Leon Lievsay. North Carolina U.P. and O.U.P. pp. xiv+344. $7.50. 60s.

Guazzo's, and Spenser shares his high seriousness, though in neither case is a direct debt absolutely proved. Guazzo is cited by Lodowick Bryskett and Gabriel Harvey. Greene made use of him. Rich filched whole passages. Merbury and Florio enriched their collections of proverbs from this source. Lievsay carries his study into the seventeenth century, concluding with an account of the manuscript translation of *La Civil Conversatione* by William Reymes. He omits the dramatists, whose debt to Guazzo might well provide the subject of an independent study.

The Italian influence on Elizabethan literature, especially on the poetry, is also brought out in Charles Dédéyan's 'Dante en Angleterre' (*Les Lettres Romanes*). His series of articles on this subject reaches, this year, Churchyard, Harvey, Greene, and Spenser, and involves much patient listing on lines similar to Paget Toynbee's.

Norman Knox's book[8] on the word irony includes material from Elizabethan literature, and should prove useful both for its ideas and as a scholarly reference book. Examples illustrating the various senses in which 'irony' was used in the period 1500–1755 are set out, with their classical precedents. The commentary reveals that the word was esoteric, technical, and erudite in the sixteenth century, gradually anglicized in the seventeenth, and not widely current till the eighteenth. Nevertheless, there is a good array of Elizabethan examples, the commonest meaning attached to irony being 'censure through counterfeited praise'.

John Hollander's book[9] on 'ideas of

music in English poetry 1500–1700' has a general relevance to this chapter since it explains and illustrates ideas with which the Elizabethans lived. It also contains some particular reference to Elizabethan authors. For example, to the traditional *encomium musicae* contributions, in prose or verse, are made by Richard Mulcaster, Thomas Lodge, John Case, and Sir John Davies. Musical images, especially those connected with instruments such as the lute, are much used by the Elizabethan sonneteers. Other favourite topics are the power of music to affect the hearer, its use in solemn praise of God, and in 'easy praise' of mistresses.

The theory of rhetoric, the theory of poetry, and the relation between them in sixteenth-century England is the subject of a paper[10] by Karl L. Klein, who illustrates his points from the statements of Thomas Wilson, Richard Sherry, Roger Ascham, Philip Sidney, George Puttenham, John Hoskins, and other authorities of the period. Of these, Puttenham, for example, is by no means exceptional in including the 'eloquence' of rhetoric in his theory of poetry. Many are the distinctions between true and false eloquence, the pleas for plainness and attacks on excessive ornament. The common criterion is that words and matter must correspond, and that the poet-rhetorician's 'discretion' will help him to see that they do so.

S. K. Heninger, Jr. (*JHI*), discusses the pastoral poetry of the Renaissance, touching on some English poets of the Elizabethan period. His opinion is that, on the whole, pastoral did not achieve greatness at this time. It was usually 'perverted to satire, moral allegory and sentimental narrative' and 'assumed modish, superficial forms'.

[8] *The Word 'Irony' and its Context, 1500–1755*, by Norman Knox. Duke U.P. and C.U.P. pp. xv+258. $7.50. 60s.
[9] *The Untuning of the Sky: Ideas of Music in English Poetry 1500–1700*, by John Hollander. Princeton U.P. and O.U.P. pp. xii+467. $8.50. 68s.
[10] 'Rhetorik und Dichtungslehre in der elisabethanischen Zeit', in *Festschrift zum 75. Geburtstag von Theodor Spira*, ed. by H. Viebrock and W. Erzgräber. Heidelberg: Winter. pp. 405. DM. 14.

In 'The Paradox of Money Imagery in English Renaissance Poetry' (*Studies in the Renaissance*), Irving D. Blum controverts the view that 'it is axiomatic . . . that commerce, trade, and coinage are unpoetic, and that Donne in using money imagery, is anti-Petrarchan, anti-Spenserian'. The Renaissance poet can write scornfully of the acquisition of money, but he also uses it in metaphor to describe things of beauty or tender emotions. To prove the point is a variety of examples from Wyatt, Gascoigne, Spenser, Sidney, Daniel, Shakespeare, and Chapman.

John Thompson[11] traces, in an admirably lucid and orderly way, the development of the iambic line from Tottel's *Miscellany* to *Astrophel and Stella*. Agreeing with the received opinion that it goes from a vigorous beginning (Wyatt), through a dull patch (Googe, Turberville, Gascoigne), to a splendid achievement (Sidney), he seeks chiefly to *explain* the development, 'to show how and why it took place in each of its major stages in accordance with a developing contemporary body of expressed and unexpressed principles of metre'. This is done largely through detailed metrical analysis of numerous examples. The first part of the book is reviewed above (see Chapter VI, note 26), while the second is the present concern. For Gascoigne the metrical pattern and the natural rhythm of the spoken language must coincide perfectly. He was stricter in this respect than any predecessor. The Spenser of *The Shepheardes Calender* breaks away. Thompson agrees that this work was new, and immediately recognizable as new, on its publication in 1579. It is, he also concedes, experimental. Where he differs from some earlier authorities is in his

belief that 'Spenser's variety, and his experiments, do not really add up to anything coherent'. The classical metres of the Sidney–Spenser–Harvey group are next considered. Thompson insists that we do not know what quantity meant to these men. (That Elizabethan quantitative verses are virtually impossible to judge would be agreed by R. L. Montgomery, whose book on Sidney is reviewed below.) But Thompson discerns something of value in the fact that this new, classical structure 'was not based on a complete correspondence of metrical pattern and language'. Consequently, as experiments they were important, much more so than *The Calender*. For Sidney and Spenser hereby learned that 'those two elements of verse could be joined without losing their separate identities'. Sidney, whose poetry is the subject of the last chapter, 'discovered how to maintain a maximum tension between the language of the poem and the abstract pattern of the metre'. His system is, in fact, the modern one. It is good to have Sidney's poetry valued historically, and, even more, valued for its perfection. Thompson's praise is kept within certain bounds, but he makes his own contribution to the current revaluation of *Astrophel and Stella*.

Thompson's investigation of his metre is only the first of this year's long list of Spenser studies, which range from a biographical note to critical accounts of particular themes or poems. First, a review article of recent books should be mentioned. It is by William R. Mueller (*TSLL*). He calls Pauline Parker's *The Allegory of "The Faerie Queene"* the book which he would 'most like to have written', a feeling which other reviewers would appreciate: Douglas Bush (*JEGP*), for example, has welcomed it as a labour of love, and the enthusiasm which characterizes it was mentioned in last

[11] *The Founding of English Metre*, by John Thompson. Routledge and Kegan Paul. pp. ix+181. 32s.

year's *YW* (xli. 150–1). But Mueller picks without hesitation on Ellrodt's *Neoplatonism in the Poetry of Spenser* (see *YW* xli. 148) as 'the most impressive piece of Spenserian scholarship over the past decade'. And here he has the support of C. S. Lewis, whose review article, 'Neo-Platonism in the Poetry of Spenser' (*Ea*), is also a contribution to the subject. William Nelson (*RN*) has also reviewed this book, and, though inclined to think Ellrodt unduly sceptical over the influence of Plato on Spenser, admires his logic and scholarship.

Charles E. Mounts (*Renaissance Papers* for 1958–60, published 1961) contributes to Spenser's biography a discussion of his relationship with the Earl of Essex. There is plenty of evidence that Spenser sought his patronage but none that he received any during his life. Why? Mounts conjectures that Essex blamed Spenser for putting the idea of his Irish posting into the authorities' heads.

Form and Convention in the Poetry of Spenser[12] is a collection of six essays, by different scholars, covering minor and major poems. These essays will be mentioned in the appropriate places below, but the thread connecting them deserves separate attention. All the contributors to this symposium are agreed on Spenser's complexity and concerned to analyse his structures. They oppose, in fact, those critics (from Dryden onwards) who have found Spenser planless.

That *The Shepheardes Calender* contains allusions to current affairs and personalities has long been recognized. Paul McClane has now produced the most thorough and complete account[13]

of the historical allegory, attempting to confirm some identifications made by other scholars and to suggest other wholly new ones. His is an excellent piece of detective work, based partly on anagrams and the hitherto neglected woodcuts, but largely on a close study of religious and political history in 1578, when Spenser was in Bishop Young's service, and in 1579, when he was in the Earl of Leicester's. He believes that Spenser includes serious reflections on events right up to the date of licensing, 5 December 1579, and that the date affixed to E. K.'s prefatory letter, 10 April 1579, is probably a protective fiction. Certainly he convinces us of the need for protective colouring of all kinds, for the queen was rabidly antagonistic to those who, like Spenser and the Leicester group, criticized her plan to marry Alençon. The *Calender*, then, is a weapon in a paper war, and this war is McClane's chief quarry. His identifications are of great interest, though it must be said that many are probable rather than certain, and that his whole case inevitably (for Spenser, after all, sought secrecy) lacks the perfection of absolute proof. Elizabeth is Rosalind, and also, as Mary Parmenter suggested, Dido, while Alençon (notice the anagram) is Menalcas. Leicester and Oxford as Oak and Briar is another new suggestion, while Aubigny and King James as Fox and Kid is again Miss Parmenter's, McClane adding the point that the Goat in this fable is James's tutor George Buchanan. Following the hints of various scholars, he identifies Bishop Young in Roffyn, Bishop Piers in Piers, Bishop Aylmer in Morrell, and Bishop Davies in Diggon Davie. He also adds the brilliant suggestion that Bishop Cooper is Thomalin, and surely even the most sceptical will follow the steps by which Thomas Cooper of Lincoln becomes Thom-a-lin. The later chapters deal

[12] *Form and Convention in the Poetry of Edmund Spenser: Selected Papers from the English Institute*, ed. by William Nelson. Columbia U.P. pp. x+188. $3.50. 30s.
[13] *Spenser's Shepheardes Calender: A Study in Elizabethan Allegory*, by Paul E. McClane. Notre Dame U.P. pp. xiii+370. $5.

with the personal allegory, that concerning Spenser's friends and fellow-poets. Harvey appears, as usual, as Hobbinol, but McClane has two new identifications to offer, finding Edward Dyer in the unrewarded poet Cuddie and Fulke Greville in that puzzle of puzzles, E. K. McClane has also published two articles on the same subject as his book: ' "Private Personage Unknowne" of Spenser's Letter to Harvey' (*MLN*) and 'Spenser's Chloris: The Countess of Derby' (*HLQ*). Other scholars have also been on his hunting-ground. Celeste Turner Wright (*PMLA*) investigates Edward Knight's claims to be taken as E. K. He was a writer who prefixed verses to Anthony Mundy's *Mirrour of Mutabilitie* (1575) and signed them 'E. K., Gentleman'. Hence, incidentally, Wright also investigates the connexions of Spenser and Mundy. The dedication of the *Calender* interests William Ringler (*RN*), and he suggests that traces of Spenser's original intention to dedicate the poem to Leicester survive in his use of 'his honor' as a term of address. The poem's glosses are reconsidered by Jack Stillinger (*SB*) who pleads for a preservation of their old order, or rather, their old disorder.

Epithalamion and *Prothalamion*, in respect of their influence, are the subject of a comment by Charles G. Osgood (*MLN*). He gives a useful list of the 'principal epithalamies' which reflect the Spenserian precedent, and another of 'certain details' common to *Epithalamion* and its successors. A. Kent Hieatt's essay on *Epithalamion*, in *Form and Convention* (see note 12), is an offshoot from his book, published last year (see *YW* xli. 149–50). There he attempted to illustrate the matching of the stanzas, in the first and second halves of the poem. Now he takes two pairs of matching stanzas (numbers 1 and 13 and numbers 3 and 15), and shows in more detail than before the

ways in which they correspond. In conclusion, he claims that we should see here 'a densely and deftly woven, flexible, economical web of associations and allusions'. In the same volume appears Hallett Smith's essay on the use of conventions in *Muiopotmos*, *Daphnaida*, *Epithalamion*, and *Prothalamion*. 'Whether he succeeds or fails artistically, Spenser seems always insistent upon handling a convention in such a way as to leave upon it the unmistakable stamp of his own mind and style.' *Muiopotmos* illustrates, particularly, his skill in handling the Ovidian metamorphosis. *Daphnaida* is a love-vision elegy in the tradition of *The Book of the Duchess*, and, Smith believes, less vulgar and ugly than has sometimes been supposed. *Epithalamion* is one of Spenser's most personal poems and yet, as a wedding-song, strictly conventional. *Prothalamion*, which needs little defence, combines motifs from the epithalamion and the 'river poem'.

Amoretti is the subject of a paper by Louis L. Martz also contributed to *Form and Convention*, a paper which will do something to enhance appreciation of Spenser's sonnets, so often found disappointing in comparison with Sidney's and Shakespeare's. He finds them more complex than they appear, and is particularly warm and convincing in appraising their comedy, humour, and lightness, the mistress's attractive character, and other generally neglected aspects. Another study of *Amoretti* is by Nobuyuki Yuasa (*Studies in English Literature*: Tokyo) who concentrates on its metaphors. He believes that Spenser's problem was to reconcile the metaphorical style characteristic of the sonnet with the allegorical style or 'style of simile' established in his own *Faerie Queene*. A single sonnet (*Amoretti* lxvii) is explained briefly and lucidly by William Bowman Piper (*CE*) who focuses mainly on its hunting metaphor.

A. C. Hamilton's *The Structure of Allegory in 'The Faerie Queene'*[14] is in line with modern Spenser criticism in that the Romantic idea of the poet as dreamer is repudiated and the allegory and meaning of the poem are taken seriously. It also purports to be new. Hamilton's approach 'involves a simple yet radical re-orientation', one towards Spenser's images instead of towards the ideas behind his images. In other words, the literal level of the story of *The Faerie Queene* has primacy. By focusing on image, the reader will understand its meanings. He should no longer have to read the poem twice, once for its story and once for its story's moral. Hamilton believes this approach to be an approximation to the Elizabethan, and he may well be right. There is too little Elizabethan comment on how readers then tackled and enjoyed allegory, but good use is made in this book of Sidney's *Apology* and Spenser's Letter to Raleigh. In Sidney's treatise Hamilton finds a method by which to read *The Faerie Queene* as 'an imaginatiue groundplot of a profitable inuention', while Spenser's letter outlines the 'Idea' of the poem. The letter is his chief prop and stay. He fights the view that the scheme described in it fails to fit the poem, drawing especially on Book I for support. He also gives useful studies of the 'structure of the allegory' in all the books, while always recalling that the whole poem is a single image of what Sidney called a 'golden world'. His argument will help to conquer any boredom with Spenser's allegory that still lingers, in spite of the recent wave of enthusiasm. Perhaps we are now on its crest.

Donald Baker (*MLN*) agrees in the

main with Hamilton's opinion that Spenser's letter is the best guide to the structure of *The Faerie Queene*, but he points to a few discrepancies between the letter and Book II.

Hamilton also contributes to *Form and Convention* (see note 12) an essay comparing *Piers Plowman* and *The Faerie Queene* and based on his previously published work (see *YW* xxxix. 101–2). This is useful in drawing attention to the neglected Langland tradition rather than to the much-stressed Chaucerian one. Particularly in Book I, Hamilton endeavours to show, Spenser's affinities are with Langland. Both poets use the quest form, and, though their structures are markedly different, they have a good deal of material in common.

Alastair Fowler (*NQ*) has made a study of marginalia in certain 1596 copies of *The Faerie Queene*, as a result of which he is able to say that 'a detailed, emblematic interpretation is historically completely justified'.

'The Structure of Imagery in *The Faerie Queene*' (*UTQ*) occupies Northrup Frye, who assumes, as a 'working hypothesis', that the 'six books we have form a unified epic structure'. The imagery supports the hypothesis, as detail taken from each book in turn illustrates.

Hans P. Guth and Millar Maclure have both tackled the perennially interesting subject of nature, art, and artifice in *The Faerie Queene*. Guth (*PMLA*) challenges the view that Spenser always uses art to suggest the artificial in its bad sense, and that nature, with him, is always good. Maclure (*ELH*) begins with a study of Spenser's use of the words 'nature' and 'art', and independently reaches conclusions similar to Guth's. In the second part of his long article he gives much detailed comment on passages from *The Faerie Queene* which cannot all be summarized here. He brings in

---

[14] *The Structure of Allegory in 'The Faerie Queene'*, by A. C. Hamilton. O.U.P. pp. 227. 35s.

Spenser's 'gardens', and on these Jim Corder also has some comments to offer in 'Colin Against Art Again' (*NQ*), a discussion of the use of Spenser's notions by the landscape gardeners of the eighteenth century.

An allied subject is Spenser's use of 'natural' or 'wild' men in *The Faerie Queene*. A. Sidney Knowles, Jr. (*Renaissance Papers* for 1958–60, published 1961), explores the ambiguity behind his 'salvages' who may be conceived on the one hand as ideal innocents and on the other as vile subhuman brutes. Herbert Foltinek (*Die Neueren Sprachen*) fills in the background, stressing the interest of both Middle Ages and Renaissance in wild men, satyrs, &c., their place in the folklore of Elizabethan England, and, in consequence, also stressing the fact that Spenser's motifs are built on those of his age.

In addition to these studies of aspects of the poem taken as a whole, there have been others of individual books of *The Faerie Queene*, or of parts of them. The allegory of the death of Error's children (*Faerie Queene* I) is related by Robert A. Bryan (*MLN*) to the somewhat similar descriptions of the death of Arius, and this underlines Spenser's moral, the self-destructiveness of falsehood, particularly of heresy. John M. Steadman (*NM*) also tackles Error, relating Spenser's idea of it to the Renaissance allegorical tradition, and noticing his 'happy innovation': Spenser combined two conventional mythological elements, hitherto kept separate, the forest-labyrinth and the serpent-woman.

In a 'continued allegory' the parts must obviously relate to the whole. Vern Torczon (*TSLL*) illustrates this by reference to the Orgoglio and Despair episodes (*Faerie Queene* I), and suggests that the maximum of sense and unity is obtained when Orgoglio is taken to mean 'presumption'.

Satyrane (*Faerie Queene* I) is the son of a satyr-father and nymph-mother, whose own father is Labryde, a name which J. M. Williams (*MLN*) has investigated. Irish mythology has a Gaelic god, Labraid of the Swift Hand on the Sword, and he would certainly prove a suitable ancestor for the blue-blooded and warlike Satyrane.

After an appreciative reference to A. Fowler's recent discussion of the name Guyon (see *YW* xli. 151), Susan Snyder (*RN*) puts forward another possible meaning. 'Gyon', she suggests, is *luctatio* (wrestling), and this is appropriate to the hero of *Faerie Queene* II, who 'wrestles' with incontinence and fights more than once with his bare hands. Fowler himself (*HLQ*) has also returned to *Faerie Queene* II, with a study of the tragedy of Mordant and Amavia and the miraculous washing of Ruddymane's hands. These 'present hieroglyphs of the human condition, which requires Guyon's ministration, and of the theological role of moral virtue in the regenerate life'. Fowler is concerned to emphasize Guyon's reliance on grace, and to check the tendency to regard his story as moral, instead of as moral and religious. Maurice Evans in 'The Fall of Guyon' (*ELH*) also contributes to this subject, criticizing F. Kermode's interpretation (see *YW* xli. 151) of the Cave of Mammon episode as an initiation. The allegory, he suggests, illustrates here not superhuman heroism but human weakness. C. R. Sonn too tends to emphasize the hero's weakness at this point in Spenser's story. 'Sir Guyon in the Cave of Mammon' (*Studies in English Literature 1500–1900*) focuses particularly on his limited perception and apprehension. This study also includes an interesting analysis of the whole Mammon episode, with comments on the interpretations of other scholars.

Robert C. Fox (*RES*) develops John Holloway's thesis (see *YW* xxxiii. 155) that 'the system of the Seven Deadly Sins provides a basic structure' for *Faerie Queene* II. It gives the book 'great variety in episodes and characters', though remaining 'subordinate to the dominant theme of temperance'.

M. A. Manzalaoui (*NQ*) notes a parallel between St. Augustine's *Confessions* and Spenser's description of the House of Alma (*Faerie Queene* II).

Harry Berger, Jr. (*UTQ*), quotes passages from Leonardo and Ficino which suggest 'two opposed sources of cosmic energy, one in chaos, the other in heaven' and, with these in mind, proceeds to the interpretation of the Garden of Adonis (*Faerie Queene* III).

Thomas P. Roche (*PMLA*) turns to the last episode in *Faerie Queene* III, in which Britomart liberates Amoret from the House of Busyrane. He shows how, because Busyrane represents the 'abuse of marriage', he is appropriately her chief adversary.

Books III and IV are taken up by Maurice Evans (*RES*) who believes that they are 'concerned with love as the Renaissance Platonists understood it', and that this can be illustrated from the story of Amoret. This study will be useful in checking any tendency to deny Spenser's Platonism altogether, such as might arise from too hasty a reading of Ellrodt's work (see above and *YW* xli. 148).

The use of classical mythology in the same two books is examined by Kathleen Williams (*ELH*), who concentrates chiefly on Venus and Diana, the two goddesses who, without being really at one, achieve a kind of false concord. This theme is developed by Spenser, who points the way to true *concordia*.

Harry Berger, Jr., gives, in *Form and Convention* (see note 12), a personal and subtle, if, for the reader, difficult, exposition of Spenser's imagination at work in *Faerie Queene* VI. His particular interest is in the poetic re-creation, in ancient, literary and ideal forms, of the raw material of modern life and actuality. Nearly allied to this is Berger's article 'The Prospect of the Imagination: Spenser and the Limits of Poetry' (*Studies in English Literature 1500-1900*). Here he considers 'the course of Spenser's poetry from the prospect of Mount Acidale' (*Faerie Queene*, VI. ix). The progress of his reflexive tendency and inward-turning up to their visionary climax is traced, and with it the 'conflict in the poet between the claims of the actual and of the imaginary'. Berger deals with both Spenser's response to the world and his retreat from it.

Also in *Form and Convention* is Sherman Hawkins's essay on the 'Mutabilitie Cantos'. Readers have often felt that Spenser, for all that he allows Nature to triumph over Mutability, was really in despair at the apparent universality of change. Sherman Hawkins, knowing that such pessimism is un-Spenserian, shows that Nature's case is a real one. Constancy does not mean changelessness, and, though all things do change, it is in accordance with a constant, providential law. The pageant of the months is a particularly fine revelation of 'the beauty of constancy within the wheel of change'.

Finally (and this will illustrate the lack of uniformity in current interpretations of Spenser), Graham Hough and Alastair Fowler join issue, in *EC*, on the subject of 'Spenser and Renaissance Iconography'. Hough attacks Fowler for having too great faith in contemporary iconography as a means of interpretation, whereat Fowler strikes back in self-defence.

Robert L. Montgomery, Jr., has filled a yawning gap in Sidney studies by providing an analysis[15] of the rhetoric of his poems. This is important because, as he rightly claims, Sidney 'epitomizes and illuminates the major forces in Renaissance lyric style'.

He therefore identifies and describes the two traditional styles, the ornate and plain, in the poems, but what gives his book added interest is the consistent attempt to relate style to mood and meaning. Thus, first, he describes poems (early pieces and the Psalms particularly) in which Sidney depends on formal rhetoric rather than on the demands of his subject, using an overemphatic beat or excessive symmetry. He goes on to Sidney's ornate structures, his use of Petrarchism and its influence on his own emotional extravagance and hyperbolic style. A study of Sidney's theory of artless style follows, after which Montgomery tackles, in his two final chapters, the poetry of *Astrophel and Stella*. This is taken as Sidney's peak achievement. That is no very revolutionary view. But this critic, unlike some of his predecessors, is at pains to emphasize that the poetry supposed to precede it (and the chronology, it should be remembered, cannot be precisely determined) is not all in the nature of an 'experimental prelude'. *Astrophel and Stella* illustrates a Sidney able to modify convention, to be witty and colloquial. Here his style is at its most flexible. Montgomery calls this 'thinking verse'. Acknowledging its variety, he nevertheless answers the question whether Sidney's sonnet sequence is a unity affirmatively. For him, the introspective pattern, especially, makes it so. The modernity and value of this book are thrown into relief by its whole emphasis. Sidney is not discussed, in the old-fashioned way, in terms of his personality, but in terms of his crafts-

manship, that of a rhetorician fully aware of the principles of his craft. With John Thompson's book (see note 11), this should do much to advance the study of Sidney's poetry. Also worth a glance are three items in *Ex*: Max Putzel's 'explication' of *Astrophel and Stella*, ix, and the comments of C. R. B. Combellack and Erhardt H. Essig on Clinton S. Burhans's interpretation (see *YW* xli. 152) of *Astrophel and Stella*, xxxi.

Walter F. Staton (*PMLA*) challenges various points in Harry Morris's article (see *YW* xl. 156), which attempted to show that Richard Barnfield was a member of the Sidney group of poets. In addition, he does not agree that there is evidence for the friendship or literary association of Thomas Watson and Abraham Fraunce.

Staton (*RN*) also shows that Thomas Lodge's 'In how contrarious formes haue I conuersed' is not, as generally believed, based directly on Desportes's *Diane* (i. 34), but on a madrigal of Watson's which itself derives from Desportes's sonnet.

An annotated edition of John Marston's poems has long been needed, for though Grosart's edition of 1879 threw some light on the numerous obscure references, for lack of time he inevitably left dark corners. Gratitude is due to the friends and colleagues of the late Arnold Davenport for seeing through the press the edition[16] he had completed at the time of his death. He was especially devoted to the Elizabethan satirists, and the new edition of Marston's poems admirably matches the one of Joseph Hall's, which he published in 1949. The text is beautifully printed (as we have come to expect of the Liverpool University Press). The main editorial problem was not so much the text itself as the

---

[15] *Symmetry and Sense: The Poetry of Sir Philip Sidney*, by Robert L. Montgomery. Texas U.P. pp. 134. $4.

[16] *The Poems of John Marston*, ed. by Arnold Davenport. Liverpool U.P. pp. xv + 393. 45s.

meaning of the text. Without explanatory notes Marston's satires will often strike the reader as a madman's ravings. Not only his allusions but his style is obscure. Davenport fortunately conceived his task as one of explication. His commentary will prove indispensable to serious students, for its interpretation of topical and literary allusions and its paraphrases of difficult passages, many of which have hitherto defied analysis. A few remain defiant and these are carefully noted along with others which have suggested only conjectural interpretations. The area of light has, however, been greatly increased. Davenport was prompted not only by the need to supply an edition. He also worked on Marston's poems because of a belief in their interest and value. If Hall's was the more polished manner, Marston's was the more interesting mind. To the mind revealed in *Pigmalion* and the satires Davenport devotes a most sympathetic introduction. The early poems, he believes, foreshadow Marston's plays. Particularly the poetic treatment of malcontentism anticipates his own, as well as Shakespeare's, handling of this theme in its specifically Jacobean form. Marston in 1598 already expresses the revulsion of Hamlet and the dilemma of Angelo. His use of gross physical terms in satiric contexts has, from his own day, been subject to severe criticism. Davenport suggests that it is the result, not, as has often been supposed, of irresponsibility, but of Marston's dismay at the miserable condition of humanity. His opinion of the aim of the controversial *Pigmalion* is also worth noticing. He agrees with the majority of critics that Marston did not write this Ovidian narrative with satiric intent. On the minority side are Douglas Bush and Hallett Smith, joined last year by Gustav Cross (see *YW* xli. 157), and this year by Anthony Caputi.

The first three chapters of Caputi's book[17] on Marston as satirist are given mainly to his non-dramatic poems. No great praise is lavished on *Pigmalion*, but *Certaine Satyres* and *The Scourge of Villanie* are given some dignity and importance. In fact, a main argument of this book is that Marston himself believed verse satire important. His efforts 'are most profitably seen in the context of an almost pretentious aim to elevate and dignify this "new" genre'. Caputi also deals with the relationship between Marston and the other satirists of the 1590's, the ways in which he differs from his enemy Hall, his satiric *persona*, his shifts of attitude, his use of types and *exempla*, and his style in general.

Gustav Cross continues his 'Notes on the Vocabulary of John Marston' (*NQ*), the examples being taken from both non-dramatic and dramatic works. His fellow satirist and opponent Hall is the subject of a note by John Crossett (*NQ*) on Pope's borrowings for the portrait of Atticus.

William Warner's vast historical epic *Albion's England* (1586) is one of six literary hulks, all popular in their day but now forgotten, which Dr. Robert Birley raised to the surface in his Clark lectures. These now appear in the form of a book.[18] The chapter on Warner's poem is defensive and appreciative. Birley believes that modern critics have been unduly stern in finding in it no more than a 'few good phrases'. He himself has no great love for Warner's rhyming fourteeners, but he readily puts himself in the place of an Elizabethan admirer of his sententiousness and, above all, of his story-telling. For this poet 'stands or falls as a story-teller'. In some cases, at

[17] *John Marston, Satirist*, by Anthony Caputi. Cornell U.P. and O.U.P. pp. xiii+ 289. $5. 40s.
[18] *Sunk Without Trace*, by Robert Birley. Hart-Davis. pp. 208. 25s.

least, he rises above 'the level of the ballad tale'. In addition he retains always an 'unjaded interest in the history of his country'. E. M. W. Tillyard was also interested in Warner's feeling for history, and gave some attention to *Albion's England* in his discussion of 'Two Tudor Myths',[19] the myth of 'Pedigree' and that of 'Divine Appointment'.

A scholarly edition[20] of the poems of a minor writer, Sir Francis Hubert (1568–1629), is the work of Bernard Mellor. *Edward the Second*, which he assigns to 1598–9, was suppressed for political reasons, but Hubert eventually revised and published it in 1629. It was followed by his Biblical paraphrase *Egypts Favorite*. Edmund Blunden, in his foreword, suggests that there may well be other poems by Hubert, as yet undiscovered.

Frank Kermode writes on 'The Banquet of Sense' (*BJRL*) in Renaissance literature with special reference to Chapman's *Ouids Banquet of Sence*. Is the author of this obscure poem writing to exalt the sublime Platonic or the bestial Ovidian love? Kermode believes that Chapman uses 'an erotic fiction in support of a philosophical scheme; but that scheme is itself an ironical sham, a learned defence . . . of the counter-Platonic Banquet, the Ovidian Banquet of sophisticated sensual indulgence'.

Two attractively printed and illustrated booklets[21, 22] provide the texts of one short love-poem apiece by the Earl of Oxford and Thomas Churchyard. Churchyard is also the subject of a note by W. H. Challen (*NQ*) stating that he is not identical with the husband of 'Patience Churchar', sister of the Countess of Nottingham.

In addition to the article (mentioned above) on Spenser, E. K., and Mundy, Celeste Turner Wright has provided two further accounts of Mundy and his friends. An article in *PQ* scrutinizes Mundy's connexion with the series of miscellanies published by John Bodenham, showing that he is the 'A. M.' who edited *Belvedere* (1600), that he may have influenced another editor, Francis Meres, and giving, besides, an interesting account of other members of Bodenham's staff. Wright also clarifies bits of literary history and illustrates the rougher side of the Elizabethan author's life in an account of 'Mundy and Chettle in Grub Street' (*BUSE*).

Daniel, like Shakespeare, depicted an unhistorically youthful Hotspur at the Battle of Shrewsbury. G. B. Johnston (*PMLA*) points out that both have the weighty authority of William Camden's *Britannia* (1586) behind them.

The remaining items on the Elizabethan poets must (regretfully) be reduced to a list. Thomas B. Stroup and H. Ward Jackson (*SP*) collaborate in an account of Gascoigne's use, in his satiric poem *The Steele Glas* (1576), of the ancient liturgical device of the bidding prayer. Lloyd E. Berry, continuing his studies of Giles Fletcher the elder, provides a bibliography of his works in *Transactions of the Cambridge Bibliographical Society*, and some biographical data, derived from his son Phineas Fletcher's account, in *JEGP*. Walter R. Davies (*MLQ*) gives a metrical analysis of several of Edmund Campion's lyrics from *A Booke of Ayres*. John W. Dickinson (*NQ*) notes the probable influence of Robert

[19] Chap. iii in *Some Mythical Elements in English Literature*, by E. M. W. Tillyard. Chatto & Windus. pp. 143. 16s.

[20] *The Poems of Sir Francis Hubert*, ed. by Bernard Mellor. Hong Kong U.P. and O.U.P. pp. xlvii+358. H.K. $42. U.S. $10. £3. 3s.

[21] *The Sheepheard's Commendation of his Nimph*, by Edward de Vere, Earl of Oxford. Pandora Press (48 Walton Street, Leicester). pp. 6. 5s.

[22] *Lovesong to an Inconstant Lady*, by Thomas Churchyard. Orpheus Press (48 Walton Street, Leicester). pp. 7. 4s. 6d.

Southwell's poetry on William Alabaster's, and, with further reference to Alabaster, comments (in *RLC*) on the sixteenth-century image of Christ's blood as ink. 'An Oxford Variant of Drayton's *Polyolbion*' (*Lib*) is noted by Bent Juel-Jensen. 'Unpublished Epigrams of Sir John Davies' (*RES*) in the Rosenbach Foundation Museum, Philadelphia, are described by James L. Sanderson. G. A. Wilkes (*TLS* 20 Oct.) suggests that William Ravenhill may be the 'W. R.' who produced the 1689 edition of Davies's *Nosce Teipsum*.

The most important contribution to this year's work on Elizabethan prose is Merritt E. Lawlis's edition[23] of Deloney's four novels. F. O. Mann's excellent edition of 1912 should not be left to gather dust, but unknown to him were two undated Folger fragments of *The Gentle Craft*, and these are used by Lawlis. This new edition is well printed, and things have been made easy for the reader: a minimum number of textual notes are placed at the foot of the relevant pages, important variant readings and explanatory notes at the back of the book. Lawlis has based his text on the earliest extant editions, as being the most authoritative, and collated his copy texts with other editions of the early and mid-seventeenth century. He provides a useful introduction, containing accounts of Deloney as a novelist, his use of the drama and jest-book, his characterisation and his life. This introduction is a brief restatement of the contents of Lawlis's monograph[24] on Deloney, published last year. Both contain warm appreciations of his work. Deloney is dramatic, humorous,

skilled in natural dialogue and truthful to the details of everyday life. He handles historical material well, and gives individuality even to his minor characters. With him the middle-class hero comes into his own in Elizabethan prose fiction. 'Magnanimitie and Knightly Prowesse, is not alwaies tyed within the compasse of Noble blood', as the General of the Gauls in *The Gentle Craft* says. Any reader unfamiliar with Deloney and sceptical of Lawlis's advertisement for a minor prose writer should turn at once to the text. He will soon find himself absorbed in a good story. *Jack of Newbury*, *The Gentle Craft* (I and II) and *Thomas of Reading* all have the same narrative virtues. They are racy and colloquial like Nashe's stories, only more temperate, less feverish. Above all they are humane and cheerful, giving the same pleasure as the comedies of Dekker. Lawlis's edition is useful and his appraisal of Deloney just. The review of the edition by C. William Miller (*RN*) is informative and favourable.

Two other new texts are also to be welcomed. Anthony Chute's *Tabacco*[25] (1595) has been reprinted for the first time this year. The new edition is the last of the Luttrell Society's reprints, a fact much to be regretted. F. P. Wilson has made a line for line reprint using the two known copies of the first edition, the one in the Huntington Library and the one in the Arents Tobacco Collection of the New York Public Library. His introduction provides information about its little-known author, who was the friend of Harvey and hence the object of Nashe's scorn. There follow accounts of Renaissance literature of tobacco and of Chute's debts to earlier authorities. *Tabacco*, an innocent eulogy of the 'diuine Hearbe' and the first English

[23] *The Novels of Thomas Deloney*, ed. by Merritt E. Lawlis. Indiana U.P. pp. xxxii+462. $12.50.
[24] *Apology for the Middle Class: the Dramatic Novels of Thomas Deloney*, by Merritt E. Lawlis. (Indiana University Humanities Series: no. 46.) Indiana U.P. 1960. pp. viii+165. $5.
[25] *Tabacco*, by Anthony Chute, ed. by F. P. Wilson. (Luttrell Society Reprints: no. 22.) Blackwell. pp. xxxix+9+54. 25s.

work on its subject, may well bring tears to the eyes of the modern addict. But before he indulges in nostalgia, he should be warned that Chute has nothing whatsoever to do with tobacco as a private indulgence or social pleasure. Like the majority of his contemporaries, he regards it as a medicinal herb and effective prophylactic against the plague. 'I speake of my selfe what I haue tried on my selfe.' The first part is given over to Chute's stories of the cure of headaches, coughs, tiredness, drunkenness, &c. Then he goes on to deliver opinions 'not of mine owne . . . but from the best Phisitions that haue written latest thereof'. Nicolas Monardes, Charles Estienne, and Jean Liébault are his chief sources for more stories of miraculous cures as well as for information about what the herb is like, how to grow it, and how to use it in pipe, brew, ointment, &c.

On reprinting Izaak Walton's *The Compleat Angler*, with Charles Cotton's sequel, in the World's Classics series, the publishers have taken the opportunity to append the anonymous *Arte of Angling* (1577)[26] which, very probably, influenced Walton, and which was discovered as recently as 1954. The text is a reprint of the modernized one already published (see *YW* xxxix. 166) by the Princeton University Library, which owns the only extant copy of the original edition. Six pages are lost, and the work, as it stands in the present edition, runs to only thirty-seven pages. It is less ambitious than *The Compleat Angler*, less learned and less anecdotal. The author shares Walton's practicality of purpose, and sticks doggedly to such subjects as how to make a float or fish from a boat, and what bait to use. He, or rather his mouthpiece 'Piscator', is a true English fanatic in the cause of his

favourite sport. 'I can tell you', says his wife, 'my husband hath cast off many, and that some of his chiefest acquaintances, for their jesting when he talketh of his cunning in angling.' Whether one is charmed or bored by Piscator depends on one's temperament. The book, which is in dialogue form, gives an impression of country life, manners, and conversation in the sixteenth century. The author seems to have been a less sophisticated man than Walton. Last year T. P. Harrison suggested that he might be a certain William Samuel (see *YW* xli. 144–5).

From Prague comes Jaroslav Hornát's 'Lyly's *Anatomy of Wit* and Ascham's *Scholemaster*' (*Acta Universitatis Carolinae*), written in English. He emphasizes Lyly's dependence on humanistic works on pedagogy and courtly conduct, and, particularly, on Ascham's book. Euphues himself is envisaged precisely as Ascham's 'quick wit', and this was, Hornát believes, certainly Lyly's source for the portrait of his clever and handsome, but unstable hero.

Another study by Hornát, 'The Literary Beginnings of Thomas Lodge' (*Časopis Pro Moderní Filologii*), is written in Czech, an English summary being provided at the end. The following works are covered: *Honest Excuses*, Lodge's reply to Stephen Gosson's attack on plays and poetry; *An Alarum against Usurers*, a moral treatise; *The Delectable Historie of Forbonius and Prisceria*, a euphuistic romance; and *Truths Complaint over England*, an allegorical poem. Thus the article surveys Lodge's 'beginnings' up to the year 1584.

Thomas Nashe's *The Terrors of the Night* (1594) mentions a visit to a house, 'some threescore myle' from London, in which he stayed one February night between 1592 and 1594. McKerrow left this unexamined and C. G. Harlow (*RES*) now tackles it.

---

[26] *The Compleat Angler*, by Izaak Walton and Charles Cotton, and *The Arte of Angling*, by an unknown hand. (World's Classics edition.) O.U.P. pp. xxiv+363. 7s. 6d.

He argues that Nashe was staying at Conington in the house of Sir Robert Cotton the antiquary in February 1593, and that part of *The Terrors* was written there, maybe even at the suggestion of Cotton, a sufferer from melancholia. Harlow makes a further investigation, in *NQ*, into Cotton's younger son William, to whom Nashe's one surviving letter is addressed.

The political satire in Nashe's *Pierce Penilesse* (1592) is elucidated by Anthony G. Pettie (*N*), who is inclined to read it as an attack on Burleigh and his son Robert Cecil. Pettie is not sure, indeed, that Nashe's 'Divill' is Burleigh, but, assuming that he is, traces a parallel between the two.

It has been known for some time that Robert Greene's novels are in debt to George Pettie's *A Petite Pallace*. Robert W. Dent (*HLQ*) investigates his plagiarism in *Gwydonius* (1584), and the parallel passages quoted in his article prove that whole passages are lifted from Pettie. Another inquiry into Greene's debts is made by Stanley Wells, whose 'Greene and Pliny' (*NQ*) traces the origin of a number of his euphuisms in *Planetomachia*. A final item on Greene concerns his *Quip for an Upstart Courtier* (1592). Only two copies, in the Bodleian and Huntington Libraries, of the first edition of this work survive. I. A. Shapiro (*SB*) reviews the variant readings in signatures E and F.

Phillip Stubbes's *Anatomie of Abuses* (1583) is constantly used to illustrate the Elizabethan social background, but 'rarely considered as a work of literary interest in its own right'. Terry P. Pearson (*MLR*) attempts to remedy this, discussing the bibliographical features of the book and its author's literary methods. She concludes that, with successive editions of his 'best seller', Stubbes's confidence increased. 'Imperfectly-sustained devices' and 'learned artificialities' disappear, and by 1595 he has lost his self-consciousness about his literary deficiencies.

Dale B. J. Randall (*Bulletin of Hispanic Studies*) discusses the debt of *The Troublesome and Hard Adventures in Love*, a prose romance of about 1594, by 'R. C.', to those most popular of Spanish source-books, the *Diana* of Montemayor and its sequels by Pérez and Gil Polo. He also denies Robert Codrington's claim to authorship, and, tentatively, puts forward Raffe Carr's.

Meyrick H. Carré (*History Today*) gives an account of Thomas Digges, the distinguished mathematician, and of the treatise published in 1576 in which he boldly supported the Copernican hypothesis and advanced beyond it with the suggestion that the firmament, and therefore the universe itself, are infinite.

James L. Rosier (*SN*) studies the vocabulary of Richard Stanyhurst's contributions, first printed in 1577, to the Irish Chronicle in 'Holinshed', noting particularly its colloquial vitality.

Facts relating to the 'last years' of William Baldwin, the minister and minor author, are provided by Arthur Freeman (*NQ*).

X. THE EARLIER STUART AND THE COMMONWEALTH PERIOD, EXCLUDING DRAMA

By AGNES M. C. LATHAM

A. ALVAREZ, writing on the metaphysical poets, would be the first to admit that his is a rearguard action, but there is room for skirmishing about the field in the wake of the heavy battalions.[1] Alvarez values metaphysical poetry for its intelligence, and deprecates the stress laid on imagery. Deliberately unliterary, it was poetry written by men of the world, who did not have to conform to the old Arts of Poetry, and did not produce new ones. It disappeared at the Restoration as quietly as it had come. The line of false wit was easily dismissed. A more profound alteration was effected by the shift in thinking which began with Bacon and ended with the Royal Society. A kind of poetry was condemned in the same breath as a kind of philosophy, when it was dubbed 'metaphysical', and there was no need for any literary challenge. Alvarez examines Donne, Herbert, Vaughan, Crashaw, and Marvell, trying to isolate the special qualities of each poet.

Margaret Willy makes up a single pamphlet from three brief essays on Crashaw, Vaughan and Traherne, with the addition of generous and up-to-date bibliographies.[2] She gives an account of the personality and experience of the three men, their poetic development and their distinctive gifts,

without attempting to characterize metaphysical poetry as such.

Jack Dalglish, in *Eight Metaphysical Poets*, has made a selection from Donne, Herbert, Carew, Crashaw, Vaughan, King, Marvell, and Cowley, with biographical and critical notes.[3] A general introduction says clearly and succinctly, and hence a little dogmatically, the things which are generally said of metaphysical poetry. This is not a book for scholars, but of its kind and for its purposes it is a pleasant book.

George Williamson's book, *The Proper Wit of Poetry*, is centred upon the seventeenth century, though it begins with Puttenham and ends with Addison.[4] In addition to illustrating and analysing the practice of the poets themselves, Williamson has made a valuable collection of contemporary comment, culled sometimes from periods when critical comment is disorganized and rare. He tries to discover what fashions reigned, how each generation defined wit and with what consistency, and traces the gradual separation of the serious and facetious, and of nature and fancy.

Mary Ellen Rickey, in a brief monograph, discusses Crashaw's use of rhyme, and shows how his practice increased in subtlety and originality.[5]

---

[1] *The School of Donne*, by A. Alvarez. Chatto and Windus. pp. 203. 18s.

[2] *Three Metaphysical Poets*, by Margaret Willy. Longmans for the British Council and the National Book League. pp. 48. 2s. 6d.

[3] *Eight Metaphysical Poets*, by Jack Dalglish. Heinemann. pp. viii+184. 9s. 6d.

[4] *The Proper Wit of Poetry*, by George Williamson. Faber. pp. 136. 21s.

[5] *Rhyme and Meaning in Richard Crashaw*, by Mary Ellen Rickey. Kentucky U.P. pp. 99. $3.00.

Rhyme words had for Crashaw very precise and important associations which they carry from stanza to stanza and from poem to poem. Hence his rhyming vocabulary is narrow and repetitive, but not because he allows himself to be carried away on a tide of vague emotion. His carefully planned rhyme-schemes are a way of imposing on his poems an orderly structure which actually controls their passion while preserving an appearance of spontaneity and lyrical abandon. A chapter is devoted to possible sources in contemporary verse for some of Crashaw's devices.

Russell M. Goldfarb, in 'Crashaw's *Suppose he had been tabled at thy teates*' (*Ex*), rejects Empson's interpretation of this epigraph, which does not refer to the Virgin Mary but to 'a certain woman' in Luke xi. 27.

John Press's pamphlet on Herrick apologizes to the taste of our time.[6] Herrick is not so trivial as it is fashionable to suppose, but he remains convicted of sometimes 'displaying a sensuality which we may term either sophisticated or unpleasant'. At his best, Press finds him subtle and delicate, with an acute organic sensibility, a playful, civilized wit, and a consummate technical skill. The classical background of his poems owes perhaps more to translations than to originals. He admired the aristocratic life of great country houses and responded readily to ceremonial and ritual. His deepest feeling is evoked by the transience of earthly things and the awareness of mortality. His *Noble Numbers* are too often dull and mechanical. Herrick is one of the easiest poets to illustrate by quotation (which partly explains the space allotted to him in *The Oxford Book*). Much of what he has to offer can be offered in its entirety,

as it is here, the unfamiliar and the familiar together, since there always seem to be pearls to be dredged from the bottom of the box.

Leo Spitzer, in 'Herrick's "Delight in Disorder" ' (*MLN*), disputes the interpretation of Herrick's poem as a plea for paganism and moral disorder. Herrick is not interested in a wanton Julia, but in 'art hiding behind apparent neglectfulness'.

Herbert Berry deals very competently with previously unpublished material relating to Suckling, from which it appears that the commonly accepted texts of Suckling's verse are by no means acceptable.[7] Berry is able to make a strong case for dismissing the supposition that *A Ballade upon a Wedding* was written for Roger Boyle, Lord Broghill, and prefers to join MS. Harleian 6917 in assigning it to the wedding of Lord Lovelace to the fifteen-year-old Lady Anne Wentworth on 11 July 1638. Transcripts of fourteen letters, four of them quite new, are printed and very fully annotated.

Stanley N. Stewart has selected for facsimile reproduction some pages from the one surviving copy, in the Huntington Library, of the poems of Anne Collins.[8] This unidentified writer composed pious verses to occupy her mind in sickness, thereby escaping any charge of wasting her time in vain pursuits. Her talent was small but she speaks with the authentic voice of her century.

Galbraith Miller Crump's edition of the poems of Thomas Stanley is not

---

[6] *Herrick*, by John Press, Longmans for the British Council and the National Book League. pp. 40. 2*s*. 6*d*.

[7] *Sir John Suckling's Poems and Letters from Manuscript*, by Herbert Berry. University of Western Ontario Studies in the Humanities, 1960. pp. 124. $3.00.

[8] *An. Collins. Divine Songs and Meditations* (1653). Selected with an Introduction, by Stanley N. Stewart. The Augustan Reprint Society, Number 94. William Andrews Clark Memorial Library: Univ. of California. pp. 30. Issued to subscribers.

noticed here since the publishers were unable to provide a review copy.[9]

Mario Praz, in 'Literary Resurrections' (*ES*), discusses the new reputation enjoyed by Vaughan and Carew, and recent attacks upon the rehabilitated Donne. He deals in particular with E. I. Selig, *The Flowering Wreath* (1958), and Clay Hunt, *Donne's Poetry* (1954).

Eleanor McCann treats 'Oxymoron in Spanish Mystics and English Metaphysical Writers' (*CL*).

Pamela Ulrey discusses 'The "One" in Donne's Poetry' (*RP* 1960), claiming that there is less division than critics suppose between Donne's earthly and spiritual loves. The completeness sought through earthly love, which demands a physical union, is none the less a religious experience. Elias Schwartz, in 'Donne's Elegie (*The Dreame*)' (*Ex*), rejects any platonic interpretation of the lady's image. It is merely a mental picture, such as the Elizabethans so often invoked, though without Donne's witty convolutions. In 'Donne and Dante: The Compass figure Reinterpreted' (*MLN*) Robert F. Fleissner wants the emphasis placed on the circle rather than on the instrument that draws it, and would relate it to Dante's picture of love occupying the very centre of a circle. Jay Arnold Levine makes a detailed examination of ' "The Dissolution": Donne's Twofold Elegy' (*ELH*), in which are fused the funereal and erotic modes. E. E. Duncan-Jones, in 'Donne's Praise of Autumnal Beauty: Greek Sources' (*MLR*), traces 'The Autumnall' to an anecdote by Claudius Ælianus and an epigram in the Greek Anthology. The effect may appear ungallant, but was not so meant by Donne nor so taken by Mrs. Herbert. S. A. Cowan, in 'Donne's The Legacie' (*Ex*), explains the heart's

corners and *colours.* If it has corners it falls short of perfection, symbolized by the circle, and if it has colours it is changeable and treacherous.

Stanley Archer, in 'Meditation and the Structure of Donne's "Holy Sonnets" ' (*ELH*), points out that the dramatic opening of the sonnets, allegedly derived from Ignatian techniques of meditation, is already to be found in many of Donne's secular lyrics, and even as early as the *First Satire*. It seems unlikely that he was introduced to anything so difficult as the *Spiritual Exercises* of Ignatius in his Catholic childhood. Where he found the threefold structure, if not in meditative technique, is a question still to be solved.

Discussing 'Donne's Holy Sonnet XIV' (*MLN*) Arthur L. Clements does not like to see the poem divided too rigidly into three quatrains, each reflecting the power of One Person of the Trinity. The Three Persons are concerned jointly with all the three actions. The heart of the poem is the Christian paradox of rebirth, expressed in the destructive, dividing imagery of war, and the uniting imagery of marriage, operative throughout. William R. Mueller, in 'Donne's Adulterous Female Town' (ibid.), interprets the same poem in relation to the Bible. The prophets often speak of the infidelity of communities rather than of individuals, and describe Israel going a-whoring after false gods. In particular Hosea, taking back his unfaithful wife, uses it as an image of God's mercy to unfaithful Israel.

A. B. Chambers, in 'Goodfriday, 1613. Riding Westward. The Poem and the Tradition' (*MLN*), traces the tradition that reason and passion in man move in opposite directions, like the circles of the fixed stars and of the planets in Plato's macrocosm. The one moves westwards, which is right, natural, and stable, reflecting God's will, and the other eastwards, which is wrong. In Christian symbolism, on the other hand, the east is the better quarter, presided over by the risen Christ. Donne plays elaborately with this paradox.

D. C. Allen, in 'Donne and the Ship Metaphor' (ibid.), follows the metaphors of the ship of salvation and the ship of love, from their classical originals to their use by Donne in prose and verse.

Irving Lowe supplies a note to *JHI* on 'John Donne: The Middle Way. The Reason-faith Equation in Donne's Sermons'. Donne, he argues, has been misunderstood. He believed, in accord with Catholic dogma, that natural reason can know the true God. His sermons frequently state this. Reason may appear subservient to faith but only because reason must assent to faith. Both are necessary. 'Mere reason apprehends the goal, rectified reason compasses the leap.' This does not mean that it is easy, and achieved without anguish. Donne brutally attacks human reason, but he does it as a preacher, to make us cherish a light which is at once so dim and so essential. This reason is not what the New Philosophy calls in doubt. That is finite knowledge, upon which vain reason so plumes itself and which is so unsure. Donne's universe was still theocentric.

Margaret Crum's 'Notes on the Physical Characteristics of some Manuscripts of the Poems of Donne and of Henry King' (*Lib*) examines the practice of King and his copyists, and looks at the best Donne manuscripts in the light of his friend's procedure, believing that his own was probably similar.

R. G. Howarth sends to *NQ* some 'Notes on Vaughan' (continued from ccv. 67). He claims that it is more than coincidence that a year after the publication of *Silex Scintillans* Cowley prefixed a statement to his *Poems* preferring divine poetry above all other. He says that Oldys, Henry Headley (1787), and Lamb show knowledge of Vaughan. He denies that Vaughan wrote 'Yet if his majesty'. James D. Simmonds, in 'Henry Vaughan: Imprisonment, Boethius, and Owen Felltham' (ibid.) corrects Howarth's earlier notes. He does not believe that Vaughan's translation of Juvenal's tenth satire (1646) was made while he was in prison in the Civil War and refers to the downfall of the King's cause. If Vaughan was imprisoned at all, and his reference to his 'Fellow-Prisoner' may well be figurative, there is no evidence that it was during the Civil War. Howarth's assumptions, he goes on, that Vaughan turned his attention to Boethius in 1650, and that his interest was awakened by Felltham, have no evidence to support them.

In 'Henry Vaughan's "To his Friends . . ." ' (ibid.), Simmonds claims that Hutchinson has misinterpreted Vaughan's translation of a poem by Ovid, assuming that Ovid (and Vaughan) are refusing to petition for release. What Ovid is saying is that since his friends will not back his appeal to Caesar it is useless for him to appeal any more. In 'The Problem of Henry Vaughan's Illness' (*Ang* 1960), Simmonds attempts to make more precise the date of the serious illness which Vaughan first mentions in the dedication of *Flores Solitudinis*, 1653. He favours some time between 17 April 1652 and 30 September 1654. Any influence on *Silex Scintillans* must be traced therefore in the second part. In *MLQ* Simmonds discusses 'The Identity of Henry Vaughan's Suppressed Poems'. He challenges the common identification of Vaughan's lascivious poems with the innocuous love poems in *Thalia Rediviva*, suspecting Vaughan of a more dissipated youth than his admirers will allow, and suggesting that a quantity of really objectionable poems has been lost. In *MLN* Simmonds considers 'The Publication of *Olor Iscanus*', and points out how openly and boldly Vaughan attacked the Puritans in such works as *The Mount of Olives* and *Flores Solitudinis*, which makes it unlikely that he had much to do with the subterfuges with which it is conjectured his friend Thomas Powell tried to veil his authorship of *Olor Iscanus*, with its anti-parliamentarian bias.

A. W. Rudrum, in 'Henry Vaughan's "The Book": a Hermetic Poem' (*AUMLA*), analyses the ideas pervading this poem as an instance of the extent to which Vaughan was indebted to hermetic philosophy. The doctrine that not only man but all created things will be made new at the resurrection, a Christian heresy, was held by Paracelsus. The very structure of the poem, in which Vaughan in imagination revives the different material elements of the book, owes something to the Paracelsan idea that 'the world exists as an exteriorisation of the imagination of God'. Paul A. Olson, in 'Vaughan's *The World*: the Pattern of Meaning and the Tradition' (*CL*), shows how the central figures in the poem accord with theological tradition, the lover illustrating the lust of the flesh, the statesman the pride of life, and the miser the lust of the eye. Beside their worldly desires (which the world can never satisfy), Vaughan symbolizes the love of God by the image of the Bridegroom, the Bride, and the great Ring of light. Fredson Bowers, in 'The Star Symbol in Henry Vaughan's Poetry' (*RP*), considers in some detail Vaughan's use of star symbols, always as reflected light and never as the direct source of light, images of faith and hope, breaking through obscuring clouds and bringing a divine message, but in the end to be transcended.

In 'Sacred "Parody" of Love Poetry,

and Herbert' (*S Ren*) Rosemond Tuve considers at some length the implications of Herbert's remaking a secular love lyric by Pembroke, and naming it 'A Parodie'. She invokes the time-honoured exchanges between secular and sacred music as evidence that a 'parody' need not be more than an imitation of purely formal, and hence neutral, elements in a work of art. 'Souls Joy' is not a conceptual parody of Pembroke's song. Though no tune has yet been found for it (Miss Tuve adapts one), it seems more than probable that it is a musical parody. In the seventeenth century a sacred song set to a secular tune did not necessarily remind the singer of the profane words for which the tune was first composed, did not deliberately play upon a tension between the two, and need not be interpreted as a criticism of secular love and its innocent songs. Jeffrey Hart, in 'Herbert's *The Collar* Re-read' (*BUSE*), indicates with great subtlety alongside the acknowledged pattern of rebellion a wider pattern, in which the vocabulary of rebellion, the fruit, wine, and corn for which the speaker longs, is used also to express the atonement and redemption, whereby these same things are offered to him in the Eucharist. Reaching for worldly fruit, he gathers supernatural fruit. Ronald Gaskell, in 'Herbert's "Vanitie"' (*CQ*), offers a brief appreciation of Herbert's poetical strategy in this poem, and the way he clarifies emotion by an exceptionally sensitive use of language.

M.-S. Røstvig, in ' "Upon Appleton House" and the Universal History of Man' (*ES*), seeks the meaning of the poem in the contrast between innocence and corruption, pursued through regional history, family history, and universal history. 'The regenerated state is marked by the supremacy of mind over body (a state reflected in the relationship between Fairfax and his house), and by mutual love not only between mind and body, but also between man and *res creatae*, and man and God. This is the ultimate truth revealed by Marvell's poem, a truth belonging neither to time nor space.' In ' "I was But an Inverted Tree": Notes toward the History of an Idea' (*SRen*) A. B. Chambers looks at Marvell's use, in *Upon Appleton House*, of the idea of man as *arbor inversa*. Plato described man as rooted in heaven by the divinest part of him, his head. Aristotle said that the roots of a plant were in effect its head, since it feeds itself through them. Both ideas were widely repeated and were in Marvell's mind. He was not thinking of fallen man as upside down, ruled by his lower powers, which was a current instance of topsy-turveydom.

George Williamson, discussing 'The Context of Marvell's "Hortus" and "Garden" ' (*MLN*), relates Marvell's poems to Cowley and other writers of the period who praise a retired life. R. H. Syfret, in 'Marvell's "Horatian Ode" ' (*RES*), considers recent commentary upon the very complex balance of attitudes in the Ode, and examines in detail Marvell's debt to Horace and Lucan. He draws on the experience of Horace, who was hoping much from an authoritarian régime after civil war, and of the later-born Lucan, who had seen such hopes dashed. Marvell's now famous impartiality covers a very deep involvement, on the whole unfavourable to Cromwell. He accepts him as a political necessity, hoping with Horace and fearing with Lucan. In 'The Early Seventeenth Century and the Tragic View of Life' (*RMS*) G. R. Hibbard touches on this poem, discussing its relation to Horace, and Marvell's perception of a parallel between England after 1649 and Rome after the Battle of Actium. He sees Marvell interpreting the events of his time as a tragic dramatist might have done, and the major

part of his essay is concerned with the interaction between life as presented by the dramatists and life as it was lived. Albert S. Gérard in '*Marvell's Horatian Ode upon Cromwell's Return from Ireland*' (*Ex*) argues that 'the spirits of the Shady Night', which Cromwell's sword will dispel, are not his bad dreams, but the enemies of God (as Cromwell conceived them), quelled by the cross hilt of the sword. Hibbard, on the other hand, thinks Cromwell was exorcizing blood guilt.

J. M. Wallace, in 'Marvell's "lusty Mate" and the Ship of the Commonwealth' (*MLN*), traces the literary origin of Marvell's simile in which Cromwell saves the ship of state in a tempest by seizing the helm, and discusses its use during the Civil War and the Commonwealth. L. N. Wall, in 'Marvell and Seneca' (*NQ*), notes some parallels.

Robert G. Collmer considers the central importance of a theme, in 'The Meditation on Death and its Appearance in Metaphysical Poetry' (*N*).

E. E. Duncan-Jones, in *NQ*, identifies some of the poems which are printed as new in J. P. Cutts's *Seventeenth Century Songs*. A. G. Watson, in 'Two Unrecorded Items of 1603' (*Lib*), reproduces two penitential ballads printed during the plague of 1603 by Simon Stafford. James L. Sanderson's 'The Posthumous Career of Peter Lambert' (*NQ*) is a note about the hanging of Peter Lambert in 1610 for murder and his subsequent exhumation, after a rumour that he had been seen alive in France. An anonymous poem in a Rosenbach manuscript treats the subject. In 'The Rebellion and "Flight of the Earls" in Verse' (*TLS*, 17 Mar.) Sanderson reproduces a contemporary ballad on Irish affairs from Rosenbach MS. 186.

To the four-hundredth anniversary of Bacon's birth, J. Max Patrick contributes a pamphlet upon Bacon as 'the supreme English exemplar of the Baroque Man'.[10] Most of the short space available is taken up with a list of Bacon's works and a very brief outline of his dominant ideas. Patrick considers that modern scientific method, by hypothesis and verification, is implicit in Bacon's recommendations, though he spent most of his time describing a procedure by tables and exclusions. In *The New Atlantis*, he points out, Bacon is careful to put checks upon the application of science, emphasizing the restraining factors of religion, home, and charity. He stresses the extraordinary flexibility and range which characterize Bacon's work, both in conception and execution. The apparent contradictions in his personality can be explained by the fervour with which he assumed the role of the moment.

In 'Francis Bacon: 1561–1626' (*QR*) Meyrick H. Carré, attempting to assess what was valuable in Bacon's work, insists that an original thinker must be appreciated in the circumstances of his age. Bacon indicated with great clarity and force the impediments to scientific thinking in his time. He never himself claimed that his procedures were perfect, and they were never, in any case, fully formulated. Utilitarian philosophies have been based on his work, but he himself always ranked the pursuit of truth before the pursuit of profit.

Frank B. Fieler (*RP* 1960) discusses 'The Impact of Bacon and the New Science upon Jonson's Critical Thought in *Timber*'. He sees Jonson's admiration of Bacon plainly reflected in his care to define terms, to put sense before style, to accept no one as dictator, and in his insistence that art must accord with nature. Jonson leaves 'what should be' to Sidney and concentrates on 'what is'.

The Proceedings of the American Philosophical Society record a number of papers contributed to a conference in honour of Bacon, which discussed the influence of science upon modern culture. In 'Bacon and Modern Physics: A Confrontation', Henry Margenau finds the modern mind unwilling to accept the idea of an ultimate unchanging truth, or of science as mere discovery, without involving human creativity. Bacon has been eyed askance for placing metaphysics at the apex of his pyramid of knowledge, but his own thinking would have been improved had he accorded the subject attention as well as respect. 'Man is no longer a passive, careful, and impartial spectator of nature, as Bacon would picture him, but a being who as an integral and active component of the universe can alter his own experiences and alter the objective world.' An instance is the theory of relativity.

Lewis Mumford, in 'Science as Technology', says that the danger to science now is not from the hostility of traditional institutions but from the patronage of contemporary ones. 'Science now makes all things possible, as Bacon believed: but it does not thereby make all things desirable.' Bacon must bear some blame for promoting a humanly impoverished mythology of power.

An interesting paper from Jaroslav Pelikan, 'Cosmos and Creation. Science and Theology in Reformation Thought', gives an account of Luther's attempt to describe the state of innocence as a historical fact, and the difficulties in which it involved him.

Lawrence A. Sasek makes a valuable inquiry into the Puritan attitude to literature and shows how various were the solutions to the problems it entailed.[11] In spite of the primacy of the

[10] *Francis Bacon*, by J. Max Patrick. Longmans for the British Council and the National Book League. pp. 43. 2s. 6d.

[11] *The Literary Temper of the English Puritans*, by Lawrence A. Sasek. Louisiana State University Studies. Humanities Series Number 9. L.S.U.P. pp. 131. $3.00.

Bible and the preacher, the presses had never turned out so much printed matter as under the Commonwealth. The two classes of literature most vocally banned were the immoral and the popular. The latter raised the whole problem of the right employment of leisure. All Puritans rejected the theatre, but they were not alone in this. Ministers of religion sensed the competition between the sermon and the play. Their attack could be extended to cover the whole of imaginative writing, but rarely was so extended. The advocacy of a plain style did not mean approval of what was rude or awkward. The stress was laid on brevity and clarity, and an absence of vain ostentation. If art was called upon, and there were Biblical precedents, it must be nothing less than the very best. Much of what the preachers condemned was what they thought of as trash. Puritans had no specialized theory of literature, for they accepted the standard criticism of the time. Their allegedly destructive effect upon the arts in the seventeenth century was less the result of their puritanism than of the conditions of the Civil War. There was a time when Milton himself exchanged poetry for ideology.

In 'The "High Churchmen" of the Earlier Seventeenth Century' (*RMS*) W. R. Fryer elucidates with great learning the position of the Caroline, or as he prefers to call them the Laudian divines. In spite of their exceptionally difficult situation, between the upper and nether millstones of Rome and Geneva, they contrived to be excellent historians of the early church, and to maintain a moderate, liberal, and tolerant attitude to the problems of the contemporary church. Unlike modern Anglo-Catholics, they would never have repudiated the name of Protestant, and readily claimed kinship with the Protestant churches abroad. Their great gift was their ability to hold an equal balance between apparent irreconcilables, making a place for reason and conscience without destroying authority and tradition.

In 'Richard Baxter and the Cromwellian Church' (*HLQ*) George R. Abernathy, Jr., considers Baxter's attempts to unite the major Protestant sects in a national church, in order to counter the excessive toleration permitted by Cromwell after 1648.

'An Ambitious Printing Project of the Early Seventeenth Century' (*Lib*) is described in Vivian Salmon's account of the patent granted by Charles I to Joseph Webbe in 1626 for publishing textbooks of a new method of language teaching. Webbe was not as successful as he had hoped. An article by Mrs. Salmon in *Bibliothèque d'Humanisme et Renaissance* supplies an account of Webbe's linguistic theories.

Allan Pritchard, in 'George Wither and the Somers Islands' (*NQ*), calls attention to a letter from Wither to Sir John Danvers, Governor of the Somers Islands Company, printed in a pamphlet of 1651. Wither is defending an outburst of royalist sympathy in Bermuda, after the execution of Charles I. The letter corroborates his claim (in 1646) that he was offered the governorship of the colony. His financial position did not permit of his accepting it. He had long had an interest in American colonization.

In 'Hebraic Synonymy in Sir Thomas Browne' (*ELH*) William Whallon argues with cogency and in impressive detail for the paramount influence of Hebrew poetry upon the 'majestic prolixity' and 'the *rime riche* of thought' in Browne's style. No other English stylist shows a comparable debt. In 'Wither's *Motto* and Browne's *Religio Medici*' (*PQ*) Allan Pritchard shows that Browne clearly had some lines from Wither's *Motto* in mind when he made what sounds like a purely personal confession in *Religio Medici*, and that his book may owe more than has been supposed to Wither's work, though it far surpasses it.

In 'Walton's *Angler* and Donne: A Probable Allusion' (*MLN*) Frank Manley suggests that Walton owes to Donne his theory of Solomon after his conversion turning his amorous disposition to God's service in the composition of the Song of Songs. He quotes a parallel passage from a sermon printed in 1661, perhaps available to Walton earlier. In 'The Age of Walton's Ancient Pike of Haylprunn' (*PQ*) Manley shows that Walton's story of an incredibly ancient fish, dated by an inscribed collar embedded in its neck, is an ancient and fishy story. There are many similar stories testifying to the immense age of stags, where the proof depends upon a collar and an inscription.

In 'Hobbes's "Table of Absurdity" ' (*Philosophical Review*) S. Morris Engel argues that the Table 'arose out of non-linguistic considerations and was meant to serve an extra-linguistic purpose'. Hobbes does not proceed from language to philosophy, but from his philosophy to certain facts about language which tend to support it. Thus the praise of Hobbes for his remarkable anticipation of modern ideas about logic and semantics is not very well placed.

Charles Blitzer gives an admirable account of the political theories of that admirable and ill-rewarded Commonwealthsman, James Harrington.[12] He reminds us that Harrington's *Oceana* was no utopian fantasy, but an eminently practical attempt to create a pattern for an 'equal Commonwealth' which could be adopted straightaway by an England that had beheaded the king he loved and that he saw sinking

daily deeper into anarchy and chaos. Retiring into his well-stocked library, he brooded upon the political thought of ancients and moderns, notably of Plato and Machiavelli, upon the history of past and present nations, and upon what his own eyes had actually seen of the functioning of modern states, notably of his native England, bent on ruin, and Venice which he admired beyond all the rest. It appears, however, that he was somewhat misled by Venetian historians as to the true history of Venice. Her constitution was less stable and her state less flourishing than he supposed.

Unlike Hobbes, Harrington saw no need to return to an absolute monarchy. The balance of power in England having come into the hands of the landed gentry, no monarch could ever again hope to be absolute. Hence Harrington's detached and rational plea for a well-organized Commonwealth, which was to be turned so cruelly against him at the Restoration. He was opposed, too, to Hobbes's abstract and deductive reasoning when applied to politics. Political science is much more like anatomy than geometry. The body politic is infinitely complex, but it is possible by studying it in a sample of recorded and living forms to discover the basic laws which govern it. A country may adopt what constitution it pleases, only if it observes these laws. No political system can possibly succeed that flies in the face of them.

Harrington's analysis of the nature and source of political power and the means to political stability, pursued in *Oceana* and many works which followed it, shows him to have had a real genius for investigations of this kind. His contemporaries were not on the whole impressed. They quibbled endlessly over alleged slights to religion (Blitzer agrees that Harrington's approach was profoundly secular), and

[12] *An Immortal Commonwealth. The Political Thought of James Harrington*, by Charles Blitzer. Yale Studies in Political Science 2. Yale U.P. pp. xv+342. $6.00.

they considered there was something inherently ridiculous in arm-chair politics and prefabricated constitutions. Subsequent centuries have made up for the neglect. Blitzer does not, however, deny that *Oceana*, swamped in administrative detail, is a dull as well as a great book.

In 'Penny-Pinching Printers and Tampered Titles' (*SB*) Franklin B. Williams, Jr., mentions some attempts of printers in the early seventeenth century to emend faults in title-pages without replacing them by new ones. Robert Krueger, in 'Manuscript Evidence for Dates of two *Short-Title Catalogue* Books' (*Lib*), reports that a commonplace book in the Bodleian confirms the date of 1606, suggested in *S.T.C.* for George Wilkins's *Three Miseries of Barbary*, and the date 'before 1609' suggested by Ruth Hughey and Philip Hereford for the third edition of Elizabeth Grymeston's *Miscelanea*. D. E. Rhodes, in 'The Authorship of The Life and Death of William Lawd, 1645' (*Lib*), attributes the work to Hezekiah (or Ezekias) Woodward (1590–1675) and not, as Wing and others have done, to Edmund Waller. John J. McAleer, in 'The King's Pamphlets' (*Lib. Chronicle, Univ. of Pa.*); gives an account of George Thomason and his great collection of seventeenth-century pamphlet literature.

The University of Nottingham recently acquired a manuscript copy of Rochester's famous Mountebank's Bill, published in broadside when he was using a period of enforced absence from the Court to practise in disguise as a quack. It has now been edited by Vivian de Sola Pinto,[13] with a full

account of the manuscript and of Rochester's escapade. The Nottingham copy was made by a former servant of Rochester, Thomas Alcock, as a New Year gift to the Earl's eldest daughter, Lady Ann Baynton. It agrees with the version printed by Tonson. There were two versions of the Bill, both of them, Pinto conjectures, with authority. He would date the Dr. Bendo affair between 1675 and 1676. The Bill is a brilliant and impudent parody of a true mountebank's bill, with an oblique reference to the mountebank tricks of politicians. Pinto recommends it as an early example of what he calls 'poker-face irony', later to be part of the stock in trade of Defoe and Swift.

Material on Milton is presented in the following order. (i) Life records. (ii) Thought and style. (iii) Poetry in chronological order. (iv) Prose. A notable store-house is the October issue of *JEGP*, devoted wholly to Milton topics, in honour of Harris Francis Fletcher.

(i) In Volume II of *The Intellectual Development of John Milton*,[14] Fletcher takes Milton through his Cambridge years, and supplies a picture of seventeenth-century university life and learning which is valuable in its own right, as well as being something which will be very much valued by Milton students. He uses documents unknown to Masson, notably Joseph Mead's accounts, which record books bought by undergraduates between 1614 and 1637, and Holdsworth's 'Directions for a Student at the University', of the same date.

Fletcher finds Milton an untypical student only in so far as he was a perfect student. He was all that a tutor dreamed of but rarely met, and college and university were proud of his achievements. In these years, with the

---

[13] *The Famous Pathologist, or The Noble Mountebank, by Thomas Alcock and John Wilmot, Earl of Rochester*, ed. with an introduction and commentary by Vivian de Sola Pinto. Nottingham University Miscellany Number 1. Sisson and Parker for the University of Nottingham. pp. 42. 5s.

[14] *The Intellectual Development of John Milton*, by Harris Francis Fletcher. Illinois U.P. pp. 693. $10.00.

help of common textbooks, he laid the
foundations of much of his theology
and cosmography, and what may
appear to be recondite knowledge in
Paradise Lost need often be traced no
farther than to Maginus's physics or to
the Ursinus catechism. The method of
teaching by disputation developed a
natural talent in Milton, and made him
a witty, bitter, and far from impartial
debater. His extant Exercises are of
their nature partisan, and should not
be read as his considered opinion upon
such subjects as the value of scholastic
philosophy or the alleged deterioration
of the world. The book concludes with
a careful chronological survey and an
evaluation of the verse which may be
assigned to the Cambridge period, including *L'Allegro* and *Il Penseroso*, a
product, Fletcher claims, of Milton's
deep interest in Italian poetry.

H. F. Fletcher and Alma DeJordy
have edited another book-list of this
period.[15] They print a transcript of a
manuscript in St. John's College, Cambridge, which they suppose to be itself
a transcript of lists compiled by Dr.
Thomas Barlow, Bishop of Lincoln,
who was Bodley's librarian from 1642 to
1460. Barlow's original papers are lost
and no record is as detailed as the
St. John's manuscript. The books are
almost all in Latin, printed on the Continent. They have been identified,
though not completely to the editors'
satisfaction, in a bibliographical index.
Barlow has made lists covering all
academic subjects for the use of young
Anglican divines with limited resources.
The texts that he recommends to them
are therefore in his opinion basic. He
expects them to be very widely read
and not confined to any one system, in

theology or in any other subject. The
method of teaching by disputation
required the student to meet a variety
of different points of view.

Edward S. Le Comte classifies and
makes easily available a great deal of
Milton scholarship in dictionary form.[16]
He promises to cover ' "hard" words
in Milton's verse and prose, capitalized
or uncapitalized, his allusions geo-
graphic and mythological, classical and
Biblical, literary and historical, his
characters, his correspondents and
named friends and opponents, his vocabulary archaic, obsolete, or special,
his puns and cruxes. Second, there is a
descriptive entry for each of Milton's
works, down to the smallest Latin and
Greek epigram and including Familiar
Letters. . . . Third, there are some fifty
entries, covering Milton, his mother
and father, his wives, his nephews, and
his biographers and editors and leading
critics. . . . References are located by
line numbers for the poems and by
page numbers of the Columbia edition
for the prose works.'

Ernest Sirluck, in 'Milton's Idle
Right Hand' (*JEGP*), inquires how
Milton was engaged in the not infrequent intervals between his prose
writings. Depression and ill-health,
and the labour of composing *Christian
Doctrine*, account for some of his later
time. The earlier gaps, Sirluck conjectures, were the result of his unhappy marriage. He conceives that
Milton, uneasy about his substitution
of a career as God's poet for that of
God's priest, had tried to clinch the
dedication of his gifts by adding a
pledge of celibacy. His tracts against the
bishops renewed his belief in himself as
a good servant of God, and he absolved
himself of his vow and married. The
failure of the marriage must have
seemed like a judgement on him, and

[15] 'A Library for Younger Schollers.'
Compiled by an English Scholar-Priest
about 1655. Ed. with Bibliographical Index
by Alma DeJordy and Harris Francis
Fletcher. Illinois Studies in Language and
Literature. Vol. 48. Illinois U.P. pp. xii+
149. $3.50.

[16] *A Milton Dictionary*, by Edward S. Le
Comte. Philosophical Library, New York.
pp. 358. $6.00.

not till physical blindness raised hopes in him of purification and inner enlightenment did he dare to speak again as God's poet.

In 'Some Recent Suggested Changes in the Chronology of Milton's Poems' (ibid.) Sirluck argues strongly against an early date for *Samson Agonistes*, against Parker's date for Sonnet VII, and against Masson's date for *Ad Patrem*. In 'The Chronology of Milton's Major Poems' (*PMLA*) John T. Shawcross disagrees with Ants Oras (*Studies in Milton*, ed. Patrick, 1953), who has claimed that the traditional chronology of Milton's major poems is supported by a close study of the blank verse. Shawcross finds that *Paradise Regained* was first planned as a drama. It lies near to but later than *Samson Agonistes*, and before *Paradise Lost* as we now know it. *Samson Agonistes* is early.

(ii) R. J. Beck stresses the affinities between Milton's thought and the more conservative trends of seventeenth-century opinion. In 'Milton and the Spirit of the Age' (*ES*) he examines the belief in the deterioration of man, in the superiority of Hebrew culture, and in pagan oracles as the voice of the fallen angels. In all these places Milton sides with orthodox opinion.

Don M. Wolfe considers 'Limits of Miltonic Toleration' (*JEGP*). Not only did Milton always strongly oppose toleration for the Catholics, but he failed to make his voice heard in the pleas for the readmission of Jews into England.

Michael F. Moloney, in 'Plato and Plotinus in Milton's Cosmogony' (*PQ*), considers Milton's debt to these philosophers and supposes that he may not have thought Plotinus, whom he never mentions, so separate from Plato as to merit individual mention.

In 'Milton's "On Time" and its Scholastic Background' (*TSLL*) O. B. Hardison, Jr., sees traces of Aristotelian studies. He argues that 'greet . . . with an individual kiss' means 'greet individually with a kiss' and that Milton had in mind the Christian doctrine that distinguishes between individual souls, some of whom may be saved and some damned, and the Averroist position which makes all souls an emanation of the active intellect, to which they return. The whole poem is Christian in asserting the corroding influence of time. Milton, though a natural Platonist, read Aristotle at the university, and Aristotle was running much in his head when he wrote his *Prolusions* and *On Time*.

Maurice Kelley, in 'Milton's Arianism again Considered' (*HTR*), rejects recent attempts to clear Milton of heresy, and asks why in any case there should be such anxiety to absolve the poet of his 'error of zeal'. Certainly he was no Socinian, and no Unitarian, but equally certainly he falls under the ban of Athanasius. In *Paradise Lost* he is generally quoting the words of Scripture and all depends on how he means them to be interpreted. It is not, however, likely that he thought one thing in *De Doctrina* and another in *Paradise Lost*, a synchronous work. He does state in so many words that God had 'no need' to beget the Son (*Paradise Lost* viii. 419–20) thus making the existence of the Son contingent.

D. C. Allen, in 'Milton and the Descent to Light' (*JEGP*), looks at Milton's use of the images of light and darkness, ascent and descent, which he found in the myths of Orpheus and Hercules. The Christian descends to rise, and enters darkness to see light. John Leon Lievsay's 'Milton Among the Nightingales' (*RP*) is a consideration of how Milton came to adopt the nightingale as a favourite image, a sweet singer in darkness, chaste and innocent, lonely and sad, the bird of true love echoing the harmony of the spheres.

Paul R. Sellin, in 'Sources of Milton's Catharsis: A Reconsideration', argues at length against Milton's debt to Minturno and Guarini and finds a much closer parallel in Daniel Heinsius. Milton valued tragedy for its moral effect. He gives a physical analogy, but it is an analogy only. The moral effect of tragedy is not the extirpation of the passions (purging), but their reduction and tempering (purification). Milton differs from Heinsius in allowing that though tragedy acts through pity and fear, it has its beneficial effect upon 'those *and such like* passions', whereas Heinsius seems to think of tragedy banishing only an excess of pity and fear (*JEGP*).

In 'Milton's Annotations of Euripides' (*JEGP*) Maurice Kelley and Samuel D. Atkins have distinguished three non-Miltonic hands in the Bodleian Euripides. One is the hand of Joshua Barnes, who acknowledged his use of Milton's copy when editing Euripides in 1694. The others, unidentified, seem to be later than Milton's time. Milton's own notes are subjected to careful scrutiny, from which he emerges as a competent scholar and an appreciative critic.

Morris Freedman's 'Milton and Dryden on Rhyme' (*HLQ*) associates Milton's views with those of Dryden and Sir Robert Howard.

Reasons for supposing that the Doni whom Milton met at Florence in 1639 was Niccoló Doni, and not the distinguished Greek scholar G. B. Doni, are supplied by Edith P. Hubbard in 'John Milton and Giovanni Battista Doni' (*NQ*).

(iii) In 'Milton's "L'Allegro" and "Il Penseroso"—Balance, Progression, or Dichotomy?' (*MLN*) Eleanor Tate sees the poems as offering a contrast rather than a steady progression. *Il Penseroso* rejects poetic fancies and enervating Lydian airs, and turns to a real world of pain and tragedy. Herbert

F. West, Jr., in 'Here's a Miltonic Discovery...' (*RP*), reviews Robert Graves's suggestion that sixteen lines of *L'Allegro* have been accidentally misplaced, and points out that both metrical tests and the correspondence between *L'Allegro* and *Il Penseroso* require them to remain where they are.

J. B. Broadbent's *Milton: Comus and Samson Agonistes* is the first of a new series of monographs upon books which are often prescribed texts for students.[17] It does not let the student off lightly. It is subtle and complex, devoted more to comprehension than enjoyment. It is doubtful whether Broadbent himself enjoys the texts as much as he enjoys criticizing them. He deals with the 'unrealistic kind' of *Comus*, which he aligns with Westerns and musicals; the pastoral form and its ambivalence (the lady shrinks from the 'loose unletter'd Hinds' and Milton is uneasy in the Dark Wood); magical virginity and Freudian explanations. He considers that Comus has better poetry than the Lady but we are not to deduce from this that his ethic is better. His arguments are very dubious, whereas the Lady is a good democrat who snubs the affluent society. The great moment of the poem is when the Lady abandons discursive reason and 'black magic is met by white, spirit by spirit'. *Samson*'s tougher fibre seems more congenial to the critic, but even here he finds that 'Milton excludes us most of the time from empathetic participation: we stand back from it to contemplate and, without much personal feeling, admire.'

Charles H. Shattuck, in 'Macready's *Comus*: A Prompt-Book Study' (*JEGP*), gives an account of the first attempt to stage a genuinely Miltonic *Comus*. Macready's version of 1843 was never printed but survives in the Folger Library. Milton's text is intelligently cut

[17] *Milton: Comus and Samson Agonistes*, by J. B. Broadbent. Arnold. pp. 63. 6s.

and supplemented by matter from other of his works. William Leahy's note, 'Pollution and *Comus*' (*EC*), answers Wilkinson's article (ibid., 1960). He points out that Milton could not make the Lady falter even for one moment, because she was the Lady Alice Egerton. Comus could be treated more realistically because he represented no one in the audience. John Arthos, in 'The Realms of Being in the Epilogue of *Comus*' (*MLN*), attempts an interpretation of the different spheres of existence in the Epilogue with reference to Ficino's commentary on Plato. In 'Milton's Haemony and Virgil's Amellus' (*NQ*) Arthos suggests that Milton took his description of the herb haemony from Virgil's amellus, described in the Fourth Georgic (271–8).

Michael Lloyd writes on 'The Two Worlds of "Lycidas" ' (*EC*). Milton is contrasting the self-absorbed life of this world with a life related to a world beyond. The poem is based upon an elaborate tissue of biblical texts, which Lloyd examines in detail. It is dramatized through the experience of the poet-speaker, who is gradually enlightened by divine voices. He publishes his new-found knowledge to those who are grieving within the limits of this world, a world whose insufficiencies need no longer be seen as motives for despair. 'A Possible Biblical Allusion in "Lycidas" 1', by David S. Berkeley (*NQ*), calls attention to the use of the expression 'Yet once more' in Hebrews xii. 26–27, signifying 'the removing of those things that are shaken, as of things that are made, that those things which cannot be shaken may remain'. Harris Fletcher discusses various identifications of 'Milton's "Old Damoetas" ' (*JEGP*) and concludes that the most probable original is William Chappell, who actually tutored both Milton and King. John T. Shawcross, in 'Division of Labor in *Justa Edovardo King Naufrago*

(1635)' (*Library Chronicle, Univ. of Pa.*), distinguishes two printers, probably Buck and Daniel themselves rather than their apprentices.

William B. Hunter, Jr., finds a date and an occasion for Milton's attempt to put the Psalms into simple diction and common metre. In 'Milton Translates the Psalms' (*PQ*) he relates that the Westminster Assembly was to prepare a metrical version, but failed to sponsor one that pleased. In 1647 the work was divided amongst four translators, and in April of 1648 more translators were appointed. The new committee took up the work at Psalm 80, which is where Milton's translations begin. He seems to have been familiar with most of the Puritan paraphrases and could have composed his lines without any reference to the Bible at all. His later versions of Psalms 1–8 are in a different style. John M. Steadman, in 'Milton's "Walls of Glass" (Psalm 136)' (*Archiv*), calls attention to patristic sources for the comparison of the parting of the Red Sea to walls of glass. Milton may have met the idea in the Geneva Bible, as well as in Du Bartas.

John T. Shawcross contributes 'Two Milton Notes: "Clio" and Sonnet 11' to *NQ*. He explains the references to Clio, in *Elegia IV* and *Ad Patrem*, by her function as 'guardian of man's individual history, that is, the guardian of what a man was given and what he was to become because of those talents'. He then gives reasons for thinking that the position of Sonnet XI ('I did but prompt the age'), in the Trinity College manuscript, is chronologically correct, dating it around September 1645. It indicates the reason why Milton retired for a time from public activity, despairing of the common man. In 'The Latona Myth in Milton's Sonnet XII' (*MLN*) Thomas E. Maresca inquires how Milton thinks himself related to Latona and her twin-born progeny.

In Bersuire's *Metamorphoseos Moraliz-atae*, Latona was 'faith or the Scripture, which from the beginning were pregnant with Phoebus and Diana, that is, with Christ and the Blessed Virgin'. Alexander Ross saw Apollo as Christ and Diana as His Church. The pearls cast before swine were generally glossed as the despised truths of the Gospel.

Ann Gossman and George W. Whiting challenge some recent interpretations, in 'Milton's First Sonnet on his Blindness' (*RES*). Milton's solution to his problem is simple resignation. It is not the realization of a deeper insight, nor the promise that all creative power is not lost. When he wrote the sonnet his talent *was* useless and he saw no prospect of using it again. Such is the plain meaning of the poem and the way it has always till now been interpreted. Milton, anything but optimistic, is digesting with pain a hard lesson. In reply (ibid.) Fitzroy Pyle points out that Milton makes patience answer an argument dismissed as 'fond', and at the end of the sonnet he is 'more bent' to use his talent and therefore still has hopes of using it. He has found a full and satisfying solution to his painful problem. 'The sonnet is a record of impatience recollected in a state of patience—a recurrent pattern of experience, it seems, at this time of crisis.' C. J. Morse discusses 'The Dating of Milton's Sonnet XIX' (*TLS*, 15 Sept.), toying momentarily with the idea that it may not be about his blindness at all since Milton did not supply the accepted title. He then considers and rejects the orthodox date of 1655, which depends upon the supposed chronological order of the printed sonnets, where 'On His Blindness' follows 'The Late Massacre in Piedmont'. Morse gives reasons why the sonnets need not necessarily be in precise chronological order, and argues for a date in 1652, when Milton became totally blind. In a letter of 6 October (ibid.) Émile

Saillens attempts to solve the riddle of 'ere half my days'. He thinks that some such vague allusion, suggesting that blindness has come almost before Milton has begun his day-labour, was an artistic necessity, not to be explained by reference to the Psalmist, to the age at which Milton's father died, or to Plato's span of a hundred years for the virtuous man. In 'Milton's Twenty-Third Sonnet' (*SP*) Thomas Wheeler, to avoid the insoluble and poetically irrelevant problem of which wife is intended, suggests that Milton was dramatizing his feeling of isolation and loss. The veiled figure is his ideal companion, whom he knows he can never see on this earth, but hopes to meet in heaven.

A provocative treatment of *Paradise Lost* and *De Doctrina* is William Empson's *Milton's God*.[18] His broadcast talks published last year in *The Listener* (*YW* xli. 170–1) gave the gist of his argument as it relates to the poem. The book is more outspokenly anti-Christian. Empson considers that Milton courageously battled with the primitive and repulsive idea of God which he derived from the Old Testament and the early church, and made the best that his broad and humane mind could of a very bad job. *Paradise Lost* goes at least some way towards justifying the ways of the Christian God to man, on the assumption that there is a great deal to be said for Adam, even more for Eve, and something on the score of rationality for Satan. God can be tolerated only in the belief that he will finally 'abdicate', having by ruthless but effective means brought the world to a point at which it can rule itself in joy and bliss for ever.

The book aroused considerable interest. Some reviewers objected that it was more relevant to Empson's own quarrel with Christianity than to

[18] *Milton's God*, by William Empson. Chatto and Windus. pp. 280. 25s.

Milton. Others found it stimulating, and felt that it brought into the open problems which trouble many readers. It treats *Paradise Lost* throughout as a more literal and more consistent poem than perhaps it is. Empson feels sure that Milton would honour his challenging approach to a challenging work, and rather too sure that Milton's mind jumps with his. He opposes C. S. Lewis's reading of the poem in the light of orthodox theology, and acknowledges a deep debt to Paul Phelps Morand (*De Comus à Satan*, 1939).

An earlier opponent of Lewis, A. J. A. Waldock, appears this year in a paperback.[19] In 1947 *Paradise Lost and its Critics* investigated some of the disconcerting elements in Milton's poem, its awkward literalisms and contradictions. Waldock, like Empson, sees Milton attempting to express values more humane than his grim commentary will own to.

T. Crehan's *Paradise Lost, Books I and II*, is edited as one of a series for students.[20] It gives a sober and sympathetic account of Milton's poem, stressing the Augustinian theology, and solving the problem of Satan by pointing out that he exists on two levels, in the story an apparently heroic leader, in the inner meaning of the poem a power of evil bent to destroy God's works. Milton's choice of an epic subject is explained as his response to the failure of the Commonwealth. It is a toughly optimistic, not a despairing response. The notes are full and helpful, directed to a simple reader, and avoiding ambiguities.

E. M. W. Tillyard, in 'On Annotating *Paradise Lost*, Books IX and X' (*JEGP*), considers what points most need elucidation for readers of school

age, and how they may benefit from a close study of the way a man like Milton uses words.

Douglas Bush, in 'Ironic and Ambiguous Allusion in *Paradise Lost*' (*JEGP*), gathers some instances of Milton's use of irony through veiled allusion, in which the primary meaning remains clear even to the reader who misses the secondary suggestion. The allusions would not, in fact, have offered much difficulty to an educated contemporary. H. F. Robins, in 'Satan's Journey: Direction in *Paradise Lost*' (ibid.), argues for the consistency and symbolic significance of Milton's cosmos, and the importance of direction in relation to God's position in Heaven. God is the physical as well as the metaphysical centre of the poem. On the other hand the entire cosmos is created for man, and the drama is his.

Merrit Y. Hughes, in 'Some Illustrations of Milton: the Expulsion from Paradise' (ibid.), examines pictures of the Expulsion, from which it appears that Milton's conception of Adam and Eve, led out by a gracious archangel in chastened hope, was in contrast to the common image of their anguish and God's vengeance. Modern illustrators have not accepted Milton's version, stressing 'cosmic violence and indifference' in place of a guiding Providence. William H. Marshall would assign some of the blame to Milton himself. In '*Paradise Lost: Felix Culpa* and the Problem of Structure' (*MLN*) he contends that the Fall is shown in action, and we respond emotionally to it, but that the Redemption is explained at second hand. Here Milton is didactic and intellectual and does not move us. Kester Svendsen, in 'John Martin and the Expulsion Scene of *Paradise Lost*' (*Studies in English Literature*), compares Martin with other illustrators of his period, especially Fuseli and Blake, and approves his clear vision of Milton's

[19] *Paradise Lost and its Critics*, by A. J. A. Waldock. C.U.P. 7s. 6d. $1.25.
[20] *Paradise Lost, Books I and II*, ed. with a critical commentary by T. Crehan. London U.P. pp. 160. 7s. 6d.

vast universe and the physical dis-advantage of Adam and Eve.

In 'Satan and the Narrative Structure of *Paradise Lost*: Some Observations' (*SN*) Calvin Huckaby contends that Milton has not erred in allowing Satan too much prominence at the beginning of the poem. He keeps man and his fate always before us, so that we eagerly expect the appearance of Adam and Eve.

Edgar F. Daniels, in 'Milton's "Doubtful Conflict" and the Seventeenth-Century Tradition' (*NQ*), discusses the growth of the tradition that there was a war in heaven before the rebellious angels were cast out, an idea not theologically acceptable to many commentators, but of use to Milton and other Christian poets. Milton wishes Satan to exercise a certain amount of free will, though he can oppose only the angels, not God Himself.

Allan Gilbert, in 'Form and Matter in *Paradise Lost*, Book III' (*JEGP*), thinks that when Milton rejects romantic epic and warlike themes, he is speaking as the preacher-poet rather than as himself, for he dearly loved romantic epic, and achieved some military passages even in *Paradise Lost* and *Paradise Regained*. Gilbert gives an appreciative account of Book III, in which he finds Milton's own deep feeling generating poetic energy. The speeches of the Father and the Son have as almost their only poetic ornaments an intricate verbal rhetoric. Inevitably, as persons in an epic story, they must be humanized, and they hold what is in effect a debate on royal policy. The reader need not accept Milton's theology to enjoy both the poem and the part theology plays in it. Here is a man reducing the world to order and comprehensibility, and a man of the seventeenth century, living in an unhappy world. He is not looking ahead to a remote utopia, but offering an explanation of things as they are and a hope of salvation.

John M. Steadman treats Milton's Christ, in 'The "Suffering Servant" and Milton's Heroic Norm' (*HTR*). Milton chose Christ as the hero of his epics because he is the archetypal pattern of Christian heroism. His ministry of redemption is beyond what any secular hero could hope to achieve, his supreme power lies in creation rather than destruction, and the climax is not his subjection to but His triumph over Sin and Death. Milton creates no epic of the passion and resurrection, perhaps because the Gospel accounts are too detailed. In any case, Vida had done it.

In '*Paradise Lost* and the "Tragic Illustrious"' (*Ang* 1960) Steadman inquires how far Milton was supported by renaissance poetic theory in according epic treatment to a tragic theme. Tasso would have disapproved, but older critics did not think Aristotle forbade the use of similar subjects to the epic and tragic poet. In 'Miracle and the Epic Marvellous' (*Archiv*) Steadman considers to what extent Milton consciously tried to arouse wonder, recommended by Aristotle and the Italians as proper to the heroic poem.

Ann Gossman contributes 'Two Milton Notes' to *NQ*. Firstly she relates 'darkness visible' to Plutarch's assertion that darkness is visible because rays are poured from the eyes of the beholder. Secondly, the iron rod and golden sceptre of *Paradise Lost*, II. 327–8 and V. 886–7 are related to Culverwel's description of Right Reason ruling with a golden sceptre and crushing with an iron rod. Culverwel claims to be quoting Plutarch. In 'Milton's *Paradise Lost*, II, 1013' (*Ex*) Gossman glosses Satan's upward springing 'like a Pyramid of fire' with reference to a contemporary derivation of pyramid from the Greek word for fire.

Doris P. Harding, in 'Milton's Bee-Simile' (*JEGP*), finds a source in Virgil's Fourth Georgic. She links

Virgil's comparison of the bees to the Cyclops with the way Milton compares the fallen angels to the insurgent giants of mythology.

Frank Manley, in 'Moloch and Demonic Motion' (*MLN*), says that Moloch's claim, that the fallen angels can easily return to heaven since their proper motion is upward, is deeply ironical. The only principle of upward motion in the universe comes from the love of God.

Florence L. Walzl, in 'Milton's *Paradise Lost*, III, 150–166' (*Ex*), shows how the lines spoken by Christ, 'For should Man finally be lost . . .', parallel in miniature the debate in Hell, and thus maintain the patterns of parallelism in Books II and III.

E. L. Marilla, considering 'Milton's "Paradise of Fools" ' (*ES*), finds Plato helpful, though in the myth of Er the aspiring souls that are rejected go to hell. Milton's fools are not guilty of great sins and they come to 'final dissolution'. This reflects Plato's belief that the immortality of the soul is dependent upon a noble existence in this world.

In 'Sin, Echidna and the Viper's Brood' (*MLQ*) John M. Steadman considers the way that Milton fuses two traditions, of the snake-woman and the snake that swallows its brood.

Douglas Day, in 'Adam and Eve in *Paradise Lost*, IV' (*TSLL*), claims that Book IV is the place to study the Fall in its embryonic stages, 'a masterfully subtle piece of dramatic foreshadowing'.

Frank Manley, in 'Milton and the Beasts of the Field' (*MLN*), describes some of the problems propounded by the story of creation when subjected to rational criticism. He thinks that Milton had filled Book VII of *Paradise Lost* with all the most controversial creatures simply to show that the truths of religion are mysterious and that scientific criticism, which requires

for instance an explanation of cross-breeds, is irrelevant to them. Milton solves the problems by ordering creation as he pleases, denying that there can be any difficulty, and by that very denial revealing that he himself knew of and felt the difficulty.

In 'Milton and the Love of Angels' (*MLN*) D. C. Allen quotes A. Piccolomini's *Della Institutione Morale* (1542) which says that whereas souls can perfectly unite and become one, bodies cannot, and souls enclosed in bodies cannot; only angels can and do. He supports a suggestion of Marilla that Raphael is speaking in terms of the ideal union of lovers, as in Donne's *Extasie*.

In 'Siloa's Brook, the Pool of Siloam, and Milton's Muse' (*SP*) George W. Whiting and Ann Gossman object to the tendency of recent criticism to equate Siloa's Brook with the Pool of Siloam and the miracle of the man born blind. The man cured at the pool is the type of spiritual blindness cured by baptism in Christ. Milton is not spiritually blind to begin with, and he is not conscious of any miracle worked especially on his behalf. He is invoking a divine muse in place of the pagan muse of Aganippe, and asking for a deeper spiritual insight, to be equal to his task.

In ' "Men of Renown": Heroic Virtue and the Giants of Genesis 6: 4 (*Paradise Lost*, XI, 638–99)' (*PQ*) John M. Steadman claims that Milton's commentary on the episode of the giants owes much to conventional interpretations of the biblical giants of Genesis, the 'mighty men that were of old'. The false hero he is supplanting, in favour of the just man, is not the classical hero only.

Stanley B. Greenfield, in 'Milton's *Paradise Lost*, XII, 629–632' (*Ex*), extends Svendsen's treatment of the passage (*Milton's Science*, 1936), indicating a structural unity in Book XII dependent on 'the counterpoise between expulsion-swiftness and home-coming-slowness'.

William Riley Parker's 'Notes on the Text of *Samson Agonistes*' (*JEGP*) makes a plea for a modern edition which will remove unnecessary archaisms while preserving everything which helps to indicate the sounds and rhythms Milton meant to be heard. He discusses in considerable detail the spelling and punctuation of the poem and the treatment accorded to it by modern editors.

In 'Milton's Treatment of Poetic Justice in *Samson Agonistes*' (*MLQ*) John Dale Ebbs makes a useful survey of interpretative criticism. He concludes that to Milton 'poetic justice' means God's Providence. Milton shows Samson fallen under the divine displeasure by exerting his free will in a way contrary to God's purpose, but regenerated by again exerting himself voluntarily, this time to submit with patience to his punishment, and to resist all temptations to rebel. Johnson perhaps came nearest to understanding *Samson* when he said that in all Milton's greatest poems the moral is 'essential and intrinsic'.

John M. Steadman, in 'Milton's Harapha and Goliath' (*JEGP*), thinks that Milton derived the name Harapha from the biblical father of Goliath, and that the situation in which Samson, handicapped and unarmed but strong in faith, daunts a scornful and heavily armed giant was suggested by the encounter between David and Goliath. Lee Sheridan Cox, in 'The "Ev'ning Dragon" in *Samson Agonistes*: A Reappraisal' (*MLN*), finds many connotations of *Dragon* in other works of Milton, in the Bible, and in *Apollonius of Tyana*, which make it applicable to Samson assailing the Philistines. We are not to think of a creeping snake but of a winged and fiery creature, the Greek 'seeing one', transfixing the fowls with the uncanny glitter in his eyes. Ann Gossman's 'Ransom in *Samson Agonistes*' (*RN* 1960) suggests analogues in Crito's offer to save Socrates, and in Priam ransoming Hector.

A. E. Dyson discusses 'The Meaning of *Paradise Regained*' (*TSLL*). He argues that the Miltonic virtue of 'obedience' is actually the final seal of pride. The obedient man, in control of himself, has no need for help from outside. 'He rises above society into the lonely, exalted heights of self-sufficiency.' The facts stand out most clearly in the less complex poem, in which Christ displays 'the arrogance of superior strength rather than . . . a truly moral insight and compassion'. Both Christ and Satan are conceived in heroic terms, and except that one is born to power and the other to subordination there is little to choose between them. Our mistake is to value as a great Christian poet a man who is truly a heroic poet, teaching us pride in victory, resilience in defeat, and offering inner discipline and integrity as the secret of greatness.

In 'Food-Word Imagery in *Paradise Regained*' (*ELH*) Lee Sheridan Cox offers some interpretations. He sees Satan's failure to recognize Christ as a warning to men. If they fail the same test, they too will fall. There is also a dreadful warning to sinners in the impossibility of Satan's having anything to do with love and compassion. Man may err and repent, but Satan *is* error. He cannot understand Christ, because he is Satan, and not because Christ speaks in riddles.

Richard J. Beck, in 'Milton and the Mirage. *Paradise Regained* IV. 40–2' (*New Scientist*), considers that Milton did not use the expression 'curious to enquire' in any derogatory sense. He was seriously offering possible explanations, in terms of optical science as he knew it, of the means whereby the devil could show Christ the kingdoms of the world from a mountain top. Beck further suggests that by 'Parralax' Milton perhaps meant mirage, a phenomenon known in his day, but not by our name, and not scientifically explained.

(iv) Douglas Bush, in 'The Complete Prose Works of John Milton' (*RN*), states the aims and policies of the Yale edition and defends it against charges of being too obvious or too minute. He sees a need for synthesis and reinterpretation. J. Milton French, in 'Some notes on Milton's *Accidence Commenc't Grammar*' (*JEGP*), comments favourably upon this instance of Milton's attempts to improve the world and do what others before him had failed to do. Kester Svendsen, in 'Milton and Alexander More. New Documents' (*JEGP*), brings evidence from Swiss records that Milton was particularly well informed as to More's career in Geneva, which is fully documented in the Council Registers there. He was right in according little value to the testimonials which More printed in self-defence.

Maurice Kelley writes on 'Milton and the "Nameless Discourse Written at Delft"' (*MLN*). In *Areopagitica*, Milton claims that Arminius 'was perverted merely by the perusing of a nameless discourse written at Delft'. This was *Responsio ad Argumenta quaedam Bezae et Calvini ex Tractatu de Praedestinatione in Cap. XI ad Romanos*, published in 1589 by Cornelisz and Donteclock, two divines of Delft. Asked to refute it in defence of Beza, Arminius was not led to embrace the doctrine it set out, but to formulate his own doctrine of predestination, much like Milton's in *De Doctrina*.

John M. Steadman thinks Milton may have been indebted to Becanus for the image of the torn body of Truth. In ' "Areopagitica" and the "Hieroglyphica" of Goropius Becanus' (*NQ*) he says that whereas Plutarch interprets the myth of Osiris in terms of the dispersal of the sacred writings, Milton and Becanus both apply it to the corruption of the true faith.

Robert W. Ayers, in 'A Suppressed Edition of Milton's *Defensio Secunda* (1654)' (*PBSA*), describes Vlacq's rare and previously unlocated reprint of *Defensio Secunda*, most of the sheets of which he seems to have held until he could add More's incomplete reply, *Fides Publica*. The bibliographical evidence now available supports Milton's own account of the affair at the beginning of his *Pro Se Defensio*.

Barbara Kiefer Lewalski discusses 'Milton on Learning and the Learned-Ministry Controversy' (*HLQ*). In *The Likeliest Way to Remove Hirelings*, Milton had to consider the education of the clergy. He stressed the primacy of the inner light, and then went on to treat human learning. He supported a literate clergy but not to the point of supporting tithes to pay for university courses.

XI. THE RESTORATION PERIOD

By V. DE S. PINTO

THE year under review has produced a rich crop of contributions to the study of Dryden. The present chapter begins with a survey of these contributions, and this is followed by notices of work on other poets, on the drama, on prose, and on miscellaneous subjects.

The natural starting-point is the new biography of Dryden by Charles E. Ward,[1] who has already produced a useful edition of Dryden's *Letters*. Ward's biography can be described as full, solid, generally reliable and well informed, but pedestrian and un-distinguished. It is a well-organized, well-documented catalogue of facts, a book of the sort that every specialist in the period must consult and every important library must possess. Ward acknowledges his debt to James M. Osborn, and his book incorporates the important additions to our know-ledge of Dryden made by Osborn, Bredvold, and others in the last quarter of a century. In his preface he expressly disclaims the intention of making any critical pronouncement on Dryden's works. Nevertheless, he quotes freely from them and makes a number of critical comments, which, if never very original, are generally apt and sensible. Much attention is paid to Dryden's work for the theatre, which is described perhaps more fully and competently than in any previous biography. The handling of the development of Dry-den's religious views is judicious and is largely based on the findings of Bred-vold. There are five appendixes, in-cluding a long and interesting one on

Albion and Albanius, and a rather un-satisfactory index from which several important names are omitted. On p. 251 Halifax, the great Trimmer, is strangely described as 'a staunch Tory and Anglican', and on the same page 'Jack Churchill' is wrongly identified with Lord Cornwallis.

Dryden and the Conservative Myth,[2] by Bernard N. Schilling, is a valuable and important book, though it suffers from verbosity and a plethora of erudition. Its main theme is indicated by its sub-title: 'A Reading of *Absalom and Achitophel*.' The first ninety-five pages are devoted to an exposition of 'The Myth and the Temper of Dryden'. The 'Myth' is the 'fiction' of Tory doctrine described as 'a force actively working to bind together English society at a time when it most needed cohesion, to "restore" the Restoration mood of 1660'. It is the myth of 'order', whether embodied in conservative politics or in neoclassic literary theory. 'Dryden's own temper' is analysed in an acute chapter leading to the con-clusion that the poet's mind was naturally fitted to the 'conservative myth': 'his conservatism is freely chosen, the natural and unforced result of what he was'. This introduc-tory section is followed by the complete text of *Absalom and Achitophel*. The rest of the book is occupied by a very long and elaborate 'reading' of the poem covering 181 pages. It is impos-sible even to attempt to summarize this very learned and widely ranging com-mentary in a short review. It is lavishly

[1] *The Life of John Dryden*, by Charles E. Ward. North Carolina U.P. and O.U.P. pp. vii+380. 45s.

[2] *Dryden and the Conservative Myth*, by Bernard N. Schilling. Yale U.P. pp. viii+329. 48s.

illustrated by reference to the ancient classics (notably Tacitus), contemporary poetry, pamphlets and sermons, and the whole range of Dryden's own writings in verse and prose.

A hearty welcome is to be given to a second, revised edition of Bonamy Dobrée's pamphlet *John Dryden* in the 'Writers and Their Work' series.[3] This is by far the most reliable, illuminating and up-to-date short introduction to Dryden's work at present available. In forty pages (followed by an admirable bibliography) Dobrée provides a vivid and masterly account of the man and the poet, illustrated by quotations which give delight in themselves and are well calculated to stimulate an appetite for a study of the complete texts of the poetry and prose of this most masculine of English writers. There is memorable and arresting criticism on every page: a fair specimen is this comment on the heroic plays: 'Artificial? of course, why not? Heroic drama is consciously artificed: and with Dryden you often feel that he is standing aside, and, with a twinkle in his eye, watching himself perform.'

In a long article in *PMLA* on 'Dryden's *Religio Laici*: An Anglican Poem', T. H. Fujimura makes a laborious attempt to refute the widely accepted view, supported by Louis I. Bredvold in his influential book *The Intellectual Milieu of John Dryden*, that *Religio Laici* is a 'Catholic poem in spirit' and essentially 'fideistic', forming 'a sort of prelude or introduction' to the frankly Romanist poem *The Hind and the Panther*. Fujimura argues that Bredvold's ideas on *Religio Laici* are 'completely unsound' and that Dryden's poem 'is, in most respects, a conventional work of Anglican apologetics'. This argument is pursued relentlessly through eleven pages

of double columns and buttressed by numerous quotations from famous Anglican divines, such as Hooker, Taylor, and Tillotson. Fujimura makes out a very strong case for Dryden's adherence to the latitudinarian brand of Anglicanism in 1682, but it seems a pity that he is so uncompromising. Surely Bredvold is right at any rate to the extent that there are some traces of a leaning towards fideism in *Religio Laici*, and that Dryden was already feeling the attraction of the authoritarianism of the Church of Rome. It is hard to believe with Fujimura that he was being 'ironical' when he wrote,

'Such an *Omniscient* Church we wish indeed,
'Twere worth *Both Testaments*, and cast in the *Creed*.'

There is not much that is original in Ira B. Davis's survey of Dryden's *The Hind and the Panther* contributed to *CLA Journal*. For the most part the article consists of a repetition of the commonplace judgements of the poem. Miss Davis believes that Dryden's attitude towards the Church of England changes in the course of the poem. 'In the first part of the poem', she writes, 'the Church of England is treated with much respect', but then the Hind's feelings towards the Panther undergo 'a sudden change'. This change is ascribed to the publication of the king's Declaration of Indulgence (here strangely called 'the Declaration of Conscience') at the beginning of April 1687.

HLQ contains three studies of aspects of Dryden's work. George McFadden, in 'Dryden's "Most Barren Period"— and Milton', describes *The State of Innocence* as 'an exercise on Dryden's part in developing a technique of internal reinforcement of sound in the manner of Virgil and Milton'. Dryden's 'barren period of 1672–1674' was, he contends, 'a period of intense study

[3] *John Dryden*, by Bonamy Dobrée. Longmans, for the British Council and the National Book League. pp. 48. 2s. 6d.

and experiment in versification'. At this stage he 'needed a new and better style in order to move into a higher rank as a poet', and he sought help from Virgil and Milton. McFadden's argument is supported by a close examination of a number of passages from Milton, Virgil, and Dryden. Morris Freedman, in a note on 'Milton and Dryden on Rhyme', connects Milton's well-known preface to *Paradise Lost* with the contemporary controversy on rhyme between Dryden and Sir Robert Howard, and especially with Dryden's remarks on rhyme in *An Essay of Dramatic Poesy*. Richard I. Cook, in 'Dryden's *Absalom and Achitophel* and Swift's Political Tracts, 1710–1714', points to resemblances between Dryden's poem and Swift's *History of the Last Four Years of the Queen*, with Queen Anne taking the part of King David and Marlborough that of Absalom, while Achitophel is paralleled by the 'Whig Lords' and their 'stock-jobber friends'.

EC contains two stimulating studies of Dryden's poetry under the title 'Two Approaches to Dryden'. In the first, entitled 'Dryden's Couplets: Wit and Conversation', McD. Emslie stresses the element of 'fine raillery' in Dryden's poetical satire: 'the fineness', he argues, 'is what was appreciated by the audience for which Dryden's satire was intended'. He illustrates the point by a detailed examination of the opening lines of *Absalom and Achitophel*, showing how Dryden uses the 'urbane descent' from the 'formality usual in the couplet' to the 'colloquial-urbane', the 'speaking voice of the Restoration Town-Gentleman'. Further illustrations are drawn from other parts of *Absalom and Achitophel* and *The Medal*. In the second study, entitled 'Dryden's Absalom', Christopher Ricks combats the commonly accepted view that Dryden treated Monmouth-Absalom with 'a kind of lenience'. He argues

that the apparent 'magnanimity does not *soften* the satire', but that it is strengthened by the show of impartiality. His argument is supported by a close and detailed examination of the language of the poem, in which stress is laid on the pervasive irony of the references to Monmouth. Ricks believes that his interpretation 'restores interest and force to great areas of the poem, and ... shows that [it] is alert and brilliantly knit'.

A brief article by Howard P. Schless in *PQ* makes an interesting contribution to our knowledge of the background of *Absalom and Achitophel*. Schless appears to be the first critic to draw attention to a manuscript poem of 1680 entitled 'A Dialogue between Nathan and Absolome' (B.M. Add. MS. 21094). He prints the text of this poem, which clearly refers to Monmouth and must have been written when that nobleman was at the height of his popularity in 1680. Schless does not claim that this anonymous poem had any 'direct influence' on *Absalom and Achitophel*, but he points to a number of interesting parallels between the two poems which suggest that Dryden may have known the 'Dialogue'.

'Charles II, Dryden's Christian Hero' is the title of an article by Albert Ball in *MP*. Ball provides a learned discussion of seventeenth-century views concerning the epic hero and of Dryden's interest in the subject. This leads to his contention that for Dryden a king was the ideal epic hero, and that this ideal was embodied in the figure of David in *Absalom and Achitophel*. Ball rejects the common view that Dryden 'had his tongue in his cheek when casting Charles II for divinity', and believes that Dryden was 'at his most serious' when he performed this remarkable feat.

A. Wallace Maurer in *Ex* provides a note on some words in *Absalom and*

Achitophel, ll. 745, 746, correcting in certain details the note on these words which he contributed to *Ex* in May 1959. The words in question are 'colored', 'pretense', and 'specious'. Maurer's argument turns on the 'positive' and 'pejorative' associations of these words.

J. E. Tanner in *MLN* discusses 'The Messianic Image in *Mac Flecknoe*'. A. L. Korn had suggested that there is a pattern in the poem 'in which Flecknoe and Shadwell emerge fleetingly as pseudo-messianic figures'. Tanner develops this suggestion and argues that Dryden in this poem shows Shadwell ironically as a Messiah (prophet, priest, and king) and Heywood and Shirley as 'Old Testament foreshadowings of Christ', whilst Flecknoe 'becomes John the Baptist'. In l. 87 of *Mac Flecknoe* Dryden exhibits 'ancient Decker' as the prophet of Shadwell, the 'mighty Prince' who was to be the 'scourge of wit, and flayle of Sense'. The recently published Oxford Dryden, ed. J. Kinsley, provides no note on this passage, but Scott and Noyes both point to Dryden's knowledge of Jonson's *The Poetaster* with its attack on Dekker. G. Blakemore Evans, in a note in *MLN*, suggests that Dryden was referring to two passages in Dekker's own play *Satiromastix*.

According to R. E. Hughes in an article entitled 'John Dryden's Greatest Compromise' and contributed to *TSLL*, Dryden's major satires are all based on a synthesis of history and rhetoric. He illustrates by quotation Dryden's view that 'history is not simply a question of the past, but it has a corrective bearing on present and future actions'. He contends that 'Dryden's view of history is rhetorical not only in the general sense of being persuasive, but in the special sense of being concerned with enthymeme, probability and time sequence', and that his 'attitude towards history concurs with Aristotle's definition of deliberative rhetoric'. He demonstrates that all Dryden's major satires, except *Mac Flecknoe*, are based on this rhetorical view of history. He describes *Mac Flecknoe* as a 'mock oratorical piece . . . parody within parody, mock rhetoric within mock epic'.

David D. Brown in a note in *MLR* supports Nichol Smith's contention that John Tillotson was the 'judicious and learned Friend' to whom Dryden tells us that he showed *Religio Laici* before it was published. In the absence of external evidence Brown shows that Tillotson was the only divine of the period living in or near London who had all the qualifications that fit in with Dryden's reference. He examines points on which Dryden is likely to have consulted Tillotson and refers to relevant passages in Tillotson's writings. The same writer contributes to *RES* an elaborate inquiry into the nature of Dryden's debt to Tillotson entitled 'John Tillotson's revisions and Dryden's "Talent for English Prose" '. Congreve's record of Dryden's emphatic acknowledgement of his debt to Tillotson has puzzled a good many critics. Nichol Smith thought the chief lesson that Dryden learned from Tillotson was to avoid ending a sentence with a preposition. Brown shows by a wealth of quotation that this supposition of Nichol Smith is not supported by the facts, as Tillotson, in fact, used the 'terminal preposition' with 'normal frequency'. By a careful consideration of Tillotson's writings he demonstrates that 'they have many qualities of which Dryden must have approved'. Moreover, a comparison between Tillotson's manuscripts and his printed sermons shows that he revised his prose very carefully when he prepared his works for the press. Brown thinks it likely that Dryden was personally acquainted with Tillotson and that when he spoke of having learnt a great

deal about English prose from reading Tillotson's writings, he meant that
'besides studying the printed works he
had seen the manuscript sermons of
the famous preacher' and talked with
the author about 'what was needed to
be done in preparing them for the
reading public: how to make speech
into prose, and prose sound like
speech'.

T. A. Birrell contributes to *ES* an
interesting article on 'Dryden's Pur-
chases at Two Book Auctions, 1680
and 1682'. The auctions in question
are the Digby Sale of 19 April 1680 and
the Richard Smith Sale of May 1682.
Birrell states that 'a consideration of
the two lists of books "convinces him"
that these are not the haphazard pur-
chases of a bookseller . . . but the
deliberate selection of a private pur-
chaser with certain specialized interests
which are consistent with what we
know of John Dryden, the poet'. He
lists the books which he believes were
bought by Dryden at the two sales.
They include works on philosophy,
theology, church government and
history, French and English translations of the classics, medical, chemi-
cal, and alchemical works (consistent
with Dryden's interest in the Royal
Society and the New Science), and five
courtesy books, 'throwing some light
on Dryden the *bourgeois gentilhomme*'.

A useful and attractive pocket edition
of *All for Love* has been added to
Barron's *Theatre Classics for the
Modern Reader*.[4] The editor, Benjamin
W. Griffith, Jr., provides a long and
competent introduction in which he
shows Dryden in this play as 'standing
between two ideological worlds. The
Renaissance man of feeling and the
imaginative Elizabethan on the one
side . . . on the other . . . the neo-

classical world of reliance on logic and
fact and the avoidance of emotionalism
and passion.' The introduction includes
an interesting and lively section on the
staging, with an account of the costumes used in eighteenth-century and
later productions and a sketch plan of
the Drury Lane stage, *c.* 1700. There is
a good bibliography and Tom Keogh
has contributed some striking designs
which might be helpful to a modern
producer. It is unfortunate, however,
that Dryden's own preface is omitted.

V. de S. Pinto believes that a number of Restoration poets have been
considerably and persistently undervalued, in particular the Earl of
Rochester. In 'Rochester and Dryden'
(*RMS*) Pinto suggests 'that the two
most interesting and significant poetic
personalities of the period were Dryden
and Rochester, and that the term
"minor" as applied to the latter poet
is quite inappropriate'. He discusses the
relationship between the two men,
and concludes that 'the impact of
Rochester's personality and poetry on
Dryden was an important, perhaps a
decisive, fact in the development of his
art and of Augustan poetry'. [T.S.D.]

Harold Whitmore Jones has performed a useful service to Dryden
studies by editing for the admirable
Scholars' Facsimiles and Reprints
series three of the contemporary replies
to *Absalom and Achitophel*.[5] All were
published anonymously in 1682. They
are *Absalom Senior: or Achitophel
Transpros'd*, ascribed on good authority to Settle, *Poetical Reflections*,
possibly by Edward Howard, and
Azaria and Hushai, probably by Por-
dage. Jones provides a short, competent
introduction including a list of variants
found in the second edition of *Absalom*

[4] *John Dryden. All for Love*, ed. by
Benjamin W. Griffith, Jr. (Barron's Educational Series.) Great Neck, N.Y.: Barron.
pp. 156. 65c.

[5] *Anti-Achitophel (1682): Three Verse
Replies to 'Absalom and Achitophel'*, ed. with
Introduction by Harold Whitmore Jones.
Gainesville, Fla.: Scholars' Facsimiles and
Reprints. pp. ix+112. $5.00.

Senior and a Table of Allusions containing identifications of the chief persons mentioned in the poems, some of which are derived from the annotated copies of *Absalom Senior* in the City of Manchester Public Library and Leeds University Library.

In 1717 Sir Samuel Garth published a composite translation of the *Metamorphoses* of Ovid. As this translation is largely by Restoration poets, notably Dryden, a new edition of it is appropriately noticed in this chapter. The edition is a very handsome one produced by the Heritage Press, New York.[6] It is introduced by a brilliant and delightful essay on Ovid and the *Metamorphoses* from the pen of Gilbert Highet, and Garth's own interesting preface is also reprinted. Graceful designs by Hans Erni are prefixed to each Book of the poem. For the student of English poetry there is much to learn from a comparison of the handling of the couplet by the different translators, ranging from the magnificent vigour of Dryden's versions to the polish and elegance of the contributions of Congreve and Pope, the liveliness and sparkle of Gay, and the undistinguished competence of Tate and Garth.

Until the year under review no edition of Sir Edward Sherburne's poems had appeared since 1819. This gap in English seventeenth-century studies has now been very competently filled by the Dutch scholar F. J. van Beeck.[7] Van Beeck's edition is scholarly, workmanlike, and unpretentious. He provides an admirably written and well-documented biographical and critical introduction, the text of the *Poems and Translations* of 1651, other verses from printed and manuscript sources, a very complete commentary and textual and bibliographical apparatus, an index of proper names, and a genealogical table. Mario Praz has shown fairly conclusively that Sherburne was 'purely a translator' and wrote hardly any original verse. Van Beeck, however, rightly points out that 'originality' in poetry is to a large extent a concept derived from the Romantic movement, and aptly quotes Edward Phillips's judgement that Sherburne was 'a discoverer of a more pure Poetical Spirit and Fancy, than many others can justly pretend to in their original works'. Nevertheless, van Beeck makes no excessive claims for Sherburne's poetry, and remarks that his verse 'is not to be judged by the standards of *poetical* history, but by those of the development of learning'. This is, perhaps, a little too severe. Sherburne had great metrical dexterity and command of a fine, racy, colloquial style used effectively in his delightful version of the 15th Idyll of Theocritus (pp. 38–44 in van Beeck's edition). A word of praise must be spared for the Dutch publisher and printer of this edition, who have done their work to perfection. The book is illustrated with a portrait of Sherburne and facsimiles of a manuscript and of title-pages.

Apart from F. W. Bateson in his *English Poetry* (1950), Waller's poetry has found few defenders in the present century. It is, therefore, refreshing to find a spirited attempt by H. M. Richmond in *SAQ* to revive interest in this once highly praised but now unjustly neglected poet. In his article entitled 'The Fate of Edmund Waller' Richmond makes some acute remarks about the reasons for the decline of Waller's reputation. He examines

---

[6] *Metamorphoses*: In Fifteen Books, Translated into English Verse Under the Direction of Sir Samuel Garth by John Dryden and Others. New York: Heritage Press. pp. li+520.

[7] *The Poems and Translations of Sir Edward Sherburne (1616–1702), excluding Seneca and Manilius*, ed. by F. J. van Beeck. Assen: Van Gorcum & Comp. N.V. pp. xlviii+202. Hfl. 16.50.

several of Waller's lyrics and argues that Waller 'is . . . by no means a trivial poet because he chooses to write lightly'. Waller's best verse, according to Richmond, is distinguished by 'a sharp sense of politely conversational exchanges'. Richmond confines himself to an examination of Waller's lyrical poetry; he might have strengthened his case by reference to the poems in the couplet, notably the resonant and impressive 'A Panegyric to My Lord Protector'.

James McManaway in *MLQ* (1940; see *YW* xxi. 181) published certain findings concerning the relationship between *The Seventh and Last Canto of Gondibert* (1685) and two dedicatory poems, 'Sir William Davenant to Mr Cotton', and 'To Sir William Davenant in Answer to the Seventh Canto of Gondibert', by Charles Cotton the Younger on behalf of his father, to whom the former poem was addressed. Alvin I. Dust, in an article entitled '*The Seventh and Last Canto of Gondibert* and Two Dedicatory Poems' contributed to *JEGP*, challenges McManaway's findings on the strength of a version of Cotton's poem to Davenant found in the newly discovered manuscript in Derby Borough Library containing a number of Cotton's poems. The upshot of Dust's argument is that the new evidence provided by the Derby manuscript shows that *The Seventh and Last Canto* is certainly Davenant's, that he was at work on it as early as 1658, and that the version of Cotton's poem printed in the surreptitious edition of 1689 was not, as McManaway supposed, a publisher's fabrication, but a fairly accurate reproduction of Cotton's own text, as it corresponds closely with the version in the Derby manuscript.

Margaret P. Boddy reports in *NQ* her identification of B.M. Sloane MS. 3208, ff. 96–128, as a holograph translation of parts of Virgil's *Georgics* by Richard Maitland, fourth Earl of Lauderdale. The text is almost the same as that which appears in the Dryden *Annual Miscellany* of 1694 and Lauderdale's *Works* of 1730.

Three Poems by Samuel Butler have been edited by Alexander C. Spence for the Augustan Reprint Society.[8] They are the Pindarick Ode 'To the Memory of the most renowned Du-Vall' from the edition of 1671, the 'Satyr' on the imitation of French customs, and 'The Elephant in the Moon', the two latter both from Thyer's edition of *The Genuine Remains* of 1759, where they were first printed. Spence in his introduction suggests that Butler's mock Pindarick is indebted to Walter Pope's prose Pamphlet *The Memoires of Monsieur Du Vall* (1670) and that the 'Satyr', because of 'various allusions within the text and the obvious affinity with the Duval Ode', was probably written about 1670. He labours rather unconvincingly to show that 'The Elephant in the Moon' is a satire, not on the Royal Society, but on the 'extravagances and dishonesty of certain individuals' who belonged to the Society.

Robert Etheridge Moore's very able and stimulating study of *Henry Purcell and the Restoration Theatre*[9] will be of the highest value both for musical specialists and for students of the Restoration drama. As Sir Jack Westrup notes in his foreword, 'It is a defect in most histories of opera that they do not sufficiently relate the music to the action. In the present book Mr. Moore treats both as equally important.' An introductory chapter entitled 'Backgrounds' provides a vivid and widely ranging account of the 'baroque ideal'

[8] *Samuel Butler. Three Poems*, ed. with an Introduction by Alexander C. Spence. (Augustan Reprint Society.) Los Angeles: Clark Memorial Library. pp. vi+25.

[9] *Henry Purcell and the Restoration Theatre*, by Robert Etheridge Moore. Heinemann. pp. xv+223. 30s.

in music, poetry, and painting, leading to descriptions of the heroic drama and the masque as forms that prepared the way for the Restoration 'dramatic opera': 'neither pure opera nor pure drama but something between the two, a typically English product'. The second chapter deals with *Dido and Aeneas*, described as 'the one opera before Gluck which succeeds triumphantly by the very standards of that master, the pioneer of modern opera', and 'the first modern opera, a music drama completely coherent and self-sufficient'. This is followed by a series of acute and well-illustrated studies of Purcell's great achievements, *King Arthur*, *The Fairy Queen*, *Dioclesian*, *Bonduca*, *The Tempest*, and *The Indian Queen*. A concluding chapter explains why the operas fell into disfavour in the eighteenth century when 'baroque outsize splendour was giving way to rococo refinement'. It also contains a plea for their revival on the modern stage, in spite of difficulties, which, 'dim before the compensations. For what can unroll before us is probably the richest vein in English culture of the baroque theatrical experience.' Illustrations to the book include a reproduction of a superb painting by Rubens and interesting 'Imaginary Landscapes' by Robert Robinson, 'an English decorator whose speciality was the painting of rococo *chinoiserie* long before that style properly came into being', and who may have designed the sets for *The Fairy Queen*.

Studies in English Literature 1500–1900: Restoration and Eighteenth Century (Rice University Press, Summer) contains one important article on a Restoration theme. This is a study by Rose A. Zimbardo of 'The Satiric Design in *The Plain Dealer*'. Beginning with a sensible rejection of the common practice of lumping together all the comic dramas of the period as 'Restoration Comedy', Miss Zimbardo argues that Wycherley is to be regarded as a satirist in the classical tradition, and that, in his last two plays, he is using the formal structure of Roman verse satire. This thesis is illustrated by a detailed and very acute analysis of *The Plain Dealer*. According to this view, Manly represents the satirist and Freeman the 'adversarius' or devil's advocate. The play shows 'the complete decline of Manly's character', giving the audience 'a vision of the vice-ridden world' and an example of virtue, but remaining 'open-minded'. At the end of her article Miss Zimbardo states that this study is 'part of a larger one on Wycherley's art'. Students of Restoration literature will look forward to the appearance of this 'larger study' of the work of a dramatist whose plays certainly deserve closer attention than they have hitherto received.

Another study of *The Plain Dealer* by K. M. Rogers appears in *ELH*. Rogers's view of the play is very different from that of Miss Zimbardo. Far from regarding it as showing 'the complete decline of Manly's character', he believes that, at the beginning of the play, Manly is a figure of fun, 'a comic butt', but 'by Act V, although his personality has not changed, Manly is almost wholly to be admired'. He makes some interesting comparisons between Wycherley's play and Molière's *Le Misanthrope*. Unlike Alceste in Molière's play, Manly 'cannot be dismissed to a life of solitary misanthropy'. In giving Manly Fidelia Wycherley, according to Rogers, 'was vicariously giving himself the absolute he longed for; the ending is a wish fulfilment'. 'The play', he concludes, 'is written from two incompatible moral viewpoints and two incompatible levels of morality.'

A manuscript copy of Davenant's operatic adaptation of *Macbeth* formerly in the Library of Kirkleatham Hospital and Free School in Yorkshire was acquired in 1953 by Yale University Library. This manuscript has now been edited by Christopher Spencer with an elaborate introduction and textual apparatus and a facsimile of four pages.[10] Eight printed texts of this Restoration *Macbeth* are extant. Davenant's name does not appear either in the Yale MS. or in the printed texts. It was, however, attributed to him by Downes, and there is every reason to believe that the attribution is correct. Spencer shows that the Yale MS. is not derived from any of the printed texts, and he believes that it was a fair copy used for the prompt-book and copied directly from Davenant's manuscript. A very interesting feature of the Yale text is that it does not appear to be founded on any known printed text of Shakespeare's play. Spencer gives reasons for supposing that Davenant used a pre-Restoration manuscript copy of *Macbeth* for his adaptation, and that this may have been Shakespeare's own manuscript adapted for use as a prompt-book for a special purpose. There are two songs in Davenant's adaptation which are not in the printed texts of Shakespeare's play. One of these is almost certainly by Davenant; Spencer thinks that it is likely that the other is by Shakespeare.

In a short article in *English Studies in Africa* entitled 'Congreve and Anne Bracegirdle', R. G. Howarth argues cogently against the views expressed in J. C. Hodges's *William Congreve, the Man* (1941, see *YW* xxii. 166) concerning the relationships of Congreve with Anne Bracegirdle and with the second Duchess of Marlborough. Howarth cites evidence to show that it is unlikely that Anne Bracegirdle was ever, as Hodges suggested, Congreve's mistress, or that the well-known poem 'False though she be to me and love'

[10] *Davenant's 'Macbeth' from the Yale Manuscript*, ed. by Christopher Spencer. Yale U.P. and O.U.P. pp. viii+225. 42*s.*

was in fact addressed to her. He also shows that it is highly improbable that there is any truth in the old allegation (repeated by Hodges and accepted without question in several recent books on Restoration comedy) that Congreve was the Duchess's lover and the father of her daughter.

Lucyle Hook contributes to *Theatre Notebook* an interesting study of 'Portraits of Elizabeth Barry and Anne Bracegirdle'. The portraits by which these actresses have hitherto been commonly known are the engravings in *The Biographical Mirrour* of 1795–1814 made from drawings by Silvester Harding. As Mrs. Hook points out, that of Elizabeth Barry in this collection is obviously unsatisfactory. Horace Walpole in his *Aedes Walpolianae*, describing the contents of the Common Parlour of Sir Robert Walpole's seat, Houghton Hall, mentions among them a sketch by Sir Godfrey Kneller for his equestrian portrait of William III at Hampton Court, and states that the two emblematic figures in the foreground of this picture are portraits of Elizabeth Barry and 'another actress'. Mrs. Hook brings evidence to show that the 'other actress' is Anne Bracegirdle. She has also examined the fine portrait sketch of Elizabeth Barry belonging to Mr. C. H. Hartmann, which legend ascribes to Kneller, and she suggests that this sketch was made by Kneller for the emblematic figure in the equestrian portrait of William III. She argues convincingly that the engraving in *The Biographical Mirrour* is actually 'a mediocre engraver's copy' of a copy by Silvester Harding of Mr. Hartmann's picture.

The great collection of tri-weekly newsletters sent to Sir Richard Newdigate and his successors at Arbury, Warwickshire, between 1674 and 1715, and used by Lady Newdigate-Newdegate in her valuable *Cavalier and Puritan in the Days of the Stuarts* (1901), is now in the Folger Library, Washington. J. H. Wilson has extracted from the newsletters all the items relating to theatrical performances and has published them in *Theatre Notebook* under the title 'Theatre Notes from the Newdigate Newsletters'. Wilson has also drawn attention in *NQ* to the incorrect attribution in Halkett and Laing's *Dictionary of Anonymous and Pseudonymous Literature* (new ed., 1928, iii. 364) of the authorship of *The Life of the Late Famous Comedian Jo. Hayns* (1701) to Thomas Brown. He shows that the author was Tobyas Thomas, a minor player with the Drury Lane Company who signed the dedication of the book.

Ola Elizabeth Winslow's *John Bunyan*,[11] like her earlier biography, *Master Roger Williams* (*YW* xxxix. 197), is competent, pleasantly written, and well informed. In her preface she disclaims any pretension to 'new discoveries of fact' or 'new unearthings of record'. Her book presents a vivid, sympathetic picture of the man Bunyan in the background of seventeenth-century England, and is divided into chapters with such colourful headings as 'Embattled Tinker', 'Field Preacher', and 'The Lord's Free Prisoner'. This is not a book for the scholar or student so much as for the intelligent 'Common Reader', for whom it would provide an excellent introduction to a reading of Bunyan's major works. Perhaps in her desire to make her narrative as picturesque as possible Miss Winslow has rather too many sentences containing the word 'probably' or some similar locution; however, this may be excused in a book which is obviously intended for a popular rather than a scholarly audience. Her criticism of Bunyan's famous works is genial, sensible, and quite unoriginal, but she

[11] *John Bunyan*, by Ola Elizabeth Winslow. New York: The Macmillan Company. pp. xi+242.

deserves commendation for devoting half a dozen pages to an appreciation of his admirable, but neglected, poems for children in *A Book for Boys and Girls*. Two of the illustrations in her book are reproductions of pages from the 1724 edition of this work, called *Divine Emblems of Youth*, with engaging woodcuts of beehives and a cackling hen.

That industrious and prolific writer John Ogilby is the subject of two interesting studies which go some way towards remedying the neglect of his works by modern criticism. Marian Eames contributes to *BNYPL* a lively and readable article entitled 'John Ogilby and his Aesop'. She provides a useful sketch of Ogilby's career, paying particular attention to his work as a translator and adapter of Aesop's Fables. Her article includes an account of Aesop and the fables ascribed to him and of the earlier English translations. She gives a detailed account of the illustrations to the various editions of Ogilby's *Aesop*, beginning with the rather crude pictures in the first edition, the 'mean quarto' of 1651, and going on to the pictures, mostly engraved by Hollar, in the second edition of 1664. Miss Eames believes that some of the drawings for these engravings are the work of Francis Barlow, who produced an *Aesop* under his own name in 1666. She also refers to the conjecture that Barlow had a considerable hand in the illustrations to Ogilby's *Aesopics*, a further collection of Fables which he published in 1668. Her article is well illustrated with reproductions, including one of the advertisement for Ogilby's first Lottery of 1665 and several of the illustrations to the various editions of his *Aesop*. She appends a checklist of the early editions of Ogilby's *Aesop* and *Aesopics* and a list of authorities consulted.

Janet R. Wadsworth contributes to the *Manchester Review* (Winter, 1961-2) a pleasant paper mainly devoted to a description of Ogilby's great work *Britannia* (1675). She emphasizes especially the importance of this book 'in measuring the main roads of England for the first time to the uniform measurement of seventeen hundred and sixty yards or eight furlongs to the mile and thus by 1675 giving the country a uniform mileage system'. Her paper includes a valuable bibliographical appendix listing 'Maps and Road Books of the British Isles first published before 1800' which are available in the Manchester Reference Library.

Walter Pope is one of the unjustly neglected minor authors of the Restoration period. The only work of his which is easily accessible to the modern reader is his admirable ballad, 'The Wish', a truncated version of which is printed in *The Oxford Book of Quotations* and *The Oxford Book of Seventeenth Century Verse*. His chief prose work, the Life of his friend and patron Seth Ward, Bishop of Salisbury, one of the most readable and amusing biographies of the seventeenth century, has now been edited for the Luttrell Society by J. B. Bamborough.[12] Bamborough's introduction to this edition contains the fullest account of Pope's life and works which has hitherto appeared, and includes the complete text of 'The Wish' from the edition of 1693. The Life of Ward is reprinted from the copy of the edition of 1697 in the Library of Wadham College, of which Pope was a Fellow, Bursar, and Sub-Warden. Bamborough states in his introduction that he has 'silently emended the obvious misprints' in the 1697 edition. He has, however, failed to emend one of the most glaring of them, which occurs on p. 196, where

the date of Ward's death is given as 1683. Ward actually died in 1688 (as correctly stated on p. 203).

Llewellyn Powys's excellent selection from *The Life and Times of Anthony à Wood*, first published in 1932 (*YW* xiii. 238), has now been re-issued in *The World's Classics*.[13] The new edition includes a very full index, which greatly enhances the value of the book.

The two racy and amusing dialogues called *The Humours and Conversations of the Town*, published anonymously in 1693, form a pleasant addition to the *Scholars' Facsimiles and Reprints* series.[14] They are edited by Brice Harris with a useful introduction and an index of names. Harris argues that the author of the dialogues was probably James Wright, whose rather similar *Country Conversations* appeared in 1694. Anthony à Wood, who disliked Wright, wrote in his notice of him in *Athenae Oxonienses* that, besides the works that he acknowledged, Wright published 'little trivial things of History and Poetry meerly to get a little Money, which he will not own'. *The Humours and Conversations* may well have been one of these 'little trivial things', but it is unfortunate that on the title-page of this reprint it should be stated categorically that they are 'by James Wright', when his authorship is only conjectural. In his introduction Harris suggests that the author of the dialogues is indebted to Bouhours, to whose *La Manière de bien penser dans les ouvrages d'esprit* (1687) Wright refers in the preface to *Country Conversations*. The vehement defence of the

[13] *The Life and Times of Anthony à Wood*, abridged from Andrew Clark's edition and with an Introduction, by Llewellyn Powys. (World's Classics.) O.U.P. pp. xxix+372. 8s. 6d.

[14] *The Humours and Conversations of the Town* (*1693*). A Facsimile Reproduction with an Introduction by Brice Harris. Gainesville, Fla.: Scholars' Facsimiles and Reprints. pp. ix+139. $5.

[12] *The Life of Seth Lord Bishop of Salisbury*, by Walter Pope, ed. by J. B. Bamborough. Published for the Luttrell Society by Basil Blackwell. pp. xxxv+206.

life of the country as opposed to that of the town in the *Humours and Conversations* is remarkable and recalls passages in Shadwell's plays, notably *Epsom Wells* and *Bury Fair* (see especially *Bury Fair*, III. i). The dialogues can be seen as part of the transition from the world of Etherege and Wycherley to that of Farquhar and Fielding.

It is pleasant to be able to record the first modern appearance of a satirical prose work by Rochester, the only prose of his that is known to survive apart from letters and a fragment of a comedy. Its title is *The Famous Pathologist, or The Noble Mountebank*,[15] and it takes the form of medical or pseudo-medical advice from a certain Dr. Alexander Bendo. It is edited by V. de S. Pinto, who in his introduction describes how the University of Nottingham in 1949 acquired the small manuscript book containing this scrap (it is only a dozen pages long), and how it was identified as the work of Rochester, showing also the hand of Thomas Alcock, who was at one time in Rochester's service. Pinto also provides a commentary and textual notes. [T.S.D.]

Sanford Golding in *PMLA* examines in some detail 'The Sources of the *Theatrum Poetarum*' of Edward Phillips (1675). He is at pains to refute the common belief that Milton had a considerable hand in this work of his nephew. As a result of 'a careful study of the sources and methods of composition' of the *Theatrum*, he has come to the conclusion that 'Milton had *no* hand in the work and that even his influence, if any, was negligible'. He demonstrates Phillips's debt to the *De Veterum Poetarum Temporibus* of Vossius, from which, he alleges, 'the first

book of the *Theatrum* is almost entirely derived'. He also examines the various authorities which Phillips used for the second book, while acknowledging that 'for some of the more famous English poets as well as for some of his contemporaries, he was able to write from first hand knowledge'. According to Golding, some of Phillips's errors have been perpetuated by Winstanley, Giles Jacob, and others, and survive in the British Museum General Catalogue and *The Short Title Catalogue*.

A thoughtful and erudite study entitled 'Latitude and Restoration Criticism', by Thomas A. Hanzo,[16] maintains the high standard of the publications in the series *Anglistica*. Its subject may be described as the relationship between the growth in the Restoration period of the ideas of 'latitude' and toleration in religion and philosophy and the similar attempts at compromise 'between the individual and authority' and 'between particular conditions and universal truth' in literary criticism. After an introduction in which the theme is defined and Arthur Lovejoy's *Parallel of Deism and Classicism* is cited as a starting-point of the argument, Hanzo passes in his first chapter to an account of the 'Argument for Latitude' in religion and philosophy as exemplified in the works of Bacon, Lord Herbert of Cherbury, the Cambridge Platonists, and Locke. The three subsequent chapters carry the argument into the field of literary criticism. The second chapter surveys the growth of 'Tolerance in Criticism 1650–1700' with particular reference to Davenant, Edward Phillips, Sir Robert Howard, and the controversy produced by Rymer's criticism. 'John Dryden and the Failure of Latitude' is

[15] *The Famous Pathologist, or The Noble Mountebank*, by Thomas Alcock and John Wilmot, Earl of Rochester, ed. by V. de S. Pinto. (Nottingham University Miscellany.) Sisson & Parker, Ltd., for the University of Nottingham. pp. 42.

[16] *Latitude and Restoration Criticism*, by Thomas A. Hanzo (*Anglistica*, vol. xii). Copenhagen: Rosenkilde & Bagger. pp. 153. Dan. kr. 27.50.

the subject of the third chapter, which contains an interesting and acute survey of Dryden's criticism. The fourth chapter deals with 'English Moderation in the Battle of the Books', and examines the contributions of Gildon, Temple, and Wotton to this controversy. In a short 'Conclusion' Hanzo points to the 'energetic' quality of the English criticism of this period, and remarks that 'out of the confusing struggle between neoclassical doctrine and vague descriptions of the subjective effects of literature comes not only the awkward compromise represented in the *Essay on Criticism* but the readiness to accept new interpretations of the literary essence'.

EA contains a learned and acute analysis by A. Mavrocordato of 'La Critique classique anglaise et la fonction de la tragédie (1660–1720)'. He examines especially the views of the nature of tragic enjoyment held by English critics of this period, and also their handling of the idea of poetic justice. The critics whose work he surveys include Dryden, Rymer, Dennis, Gildon, and Addison. His conclusion is that 'la critique classique anglaise, malgré un effort méritoire en vue d'expliquer la fonction du tragique, n'y a réussi qu'imparfaitement. Elle n'a pas su séparer les réactions que le théâtre éveille de celles qu'il devrait éveiller en nous.'

Jean Wahl contributes to the same periodical an article on Thomas Traherne, which is at once a review of Margoliouth's edition (see *YW* xxxix. 191) and an eloquent appreciation of Traherne's genius. The same issue also includes a notable study of 'Space and the Hero in the *Pilgrim's Progress*', by Henri Talon, in which he stresses the universality of the appeal of Bunyan's masterpiece: 'A man is never wholly the prisoner of his age. Everyman is seen in Christian as in every truthfully imagined character.'

Bernard N. Schilling has edited a stout volume containing an anthology of essays which are described as *Essential Articles for the Study of English Augustan Backgrounds*.[17] These essays are drawn exclusively from American periodicals, and the book, as the introduction indicates, seems to be intended primarily for the use of seminars in American universities. Schilling expresses the hope that it will relieve the pressure on volumes of learned periodicals in university libraries. There is also, surely, the danger that students will use it as a substitute for exploring original sources. The collection includes valuable articles by Morris Croll, R. F. Jones, Louis Bredvold, and Ruth Wallerstein. On the other hand, few English scholars are likely to regard as 'essential' Felix Schelling's outdated study of 'Ben Jonson and the Classical School' (from *PMLA*. 1898). The value of the book would have been greatly increased by the addition of an index.

S. Morris Engel in the *Philosophical Review* discusses 'Hobbes's Table of Absurdity' in chapter v of *De Corpore*. Engel argues against the view of a number of modern critics that Hobbes in the 'Table' 'anticipated modern techniques of logical analysis'. He believes that this view 'tends to falsify Hobbes and misrepresent his intentions'. This argument is supported by a close analysis of the Table leading to the conclusion that it 'is an attempt to lend added weight to a body of thought by subsuming it under a general schematic plan having the sanction and authority of language', and that 'it shows or proves nothing about the logic of language that that body of thought has not already assumed to have been proven and, therefore, discovers nothing about language that is

[17] *Essential Articles for the Study of English Augustan Backgrounds*, ed. by Bernard N. Schilling. (Archon Books.) Hamden, Conn.: The Shoe String Press. pp. 418. $8.50.

not already presupposed by that philosophy'.

Roland Hall contributed to *NQ* (May, June, July, September, November) five articles on 'John Locke's Unnoticed Vocabulary'. These articles contain lists of antedatings of the earliest *O.E.D.* quotations of various words and expressions, of words not found in the *O.E.D.* or Supplement, and certain other items from the writings of Locke. The lists include antedatings of 'Brahma', 'ill-nature', 'man of sense', and 'make a horse laugh'. In the last article of the series Hall corrects Cranston's statement in his *John Locke: a Biography* (1957; see *YW* xxxviii. 191) that it was 'only after Locke's death that Leibniz opened a correspondence with Lady Masham'. He shows that most of the correspondence occurred when Locke was still alive.

Locke's *An Essay concerning Human Understanding* (1690) evoked a number of replies and criticisms. The earliest of these, *Cursory Reflections upon a Book call'd An Essay concerning Human Understanding*, by John Norris of Bemerton, the Platonist, poet, and philosopher, was published in May 1690, and has now been edited for the Augustan Reprint Society with an introduction by Gilbert D. McEwen.[18] In his Introduction McEwen gives an interesting account of the relations between Locke, Lady Masham, and Norris. He points out that, unlike most of the early critics of the *Essay*, Norris 'questions Locke's epistemology rather than his theology'. In the *Cursory Reflections* he objects to Locke's failure to give an adequate definition of the term 'ideas', and, while agreeing with Locke that the 'ideas' are not innate,

he believes Locke gives the wrong reasons for coming to this conclusion. McEwen suggests that 'the great point of difference which seems to keep Locke and Norris from understanding each other is that Locke is working in a new way but using the traditional terminology of the Scholastics and Cartesians which both men had in common'.

TSL contains three essays which constituted the programme of a celebration of the tercentenary of the Restoration at the 1960 meeting of the South Atlantic Modern Language Association. The essays deal respectively with the 'Effects of the Restoration' on Prose Fiction, Drama, and Poetry. Short papers on such vast subjects are necessarily highly condensed, and, unless the writers are critics of outstanding ability, are unlikely to contain much that is memorable or distinctive. By far the best of the three papers is that of Benjamin Boyce on the 'Effect of the Restoration on Prose Fiction'. Boyce's paper is lively, informative, and illuminating, perhaps the best short description of Restoration prose fiction which has hitherto appeared. His remarks on the relationship of the different types of prose fiction of the period to contemporary patterns of conduct are particularly interesting and valuable. Cyrus Hoy's treatment of the drama is much less distinguished. He makes a few good points, but most of his paper consists simply of a repetition of the old *clichés*. The time-honoured practice of lumping all the 'comedies of manners' together reappears. Shadwell and Vanbrugh are not mentioned, and Farquhar is dismissed simply as the aftermath of Congreve. The weakest of the three papers is that of James E. Congleton on 'The Effects of the Restoration on Poetry'. Congleton devotes much space to a gossipy sketch of political and social history with the usual quotations from Pepys. The Restoration

[18] *John Norris. Cursory Reflections upon a Book call'd An Essay concerning Human Understanding*, ed. by Gilbert D. McEwen. (Augustan Reprint Society.) Los Angeles: Clark Memorial Library. pp. 44.

Court wits are labelled 'Cavalier Poets', and their poetry is dismissed as 'a glistening ripple on the river of English poetry'. The satires of Rochester and Oldham are ignored and the conventional tributes are paid to Dryden's 'smoothness', 'clarity', and mastery of the couplet.

XII. THE EIGHTEENTH CENTURY

By C. H. PEAKE and J. CHALKER

THE chapter proceeds as follows: (*a*) general studies of the century, or of the first half of it; (*b*) Defoe, Addison and Steele, Swift, Pope, Gay, Thomson, Johnson; (*c*) miscellaneous poetry, prose and drama to 1750 (excluding Collins, Gray, Richardson, and Fielding); (*d*) history of the theatre to 1750 [these sections are contributed by C. H. Peake]; (*e*) novelists and novels from 1750; (*f*) prose from 1750; (*g*) the drama from 1750; (*h*) poetry from 1750 [these sections are contributed by J. Chalker].

(*a*) Scott Elledge's two volumes of *Eighteenth-Century Critical Essays*[1] are of necessity highly selective, but they include quite enough to illustrate the intense critical activity of a century when most of the critical modes and methods familiar today were explored. Sensibly he has left out those works which are easily available elsewhere, such as *The Lives of the Poets, An Essay on Criticism, Conjectures on Original Composition*, and Morgann's *Essay on the Dramatic Character of Sir John Falstaff*. It was equally sensible to avoid, as far as possible, excerpts; and although for certain authors (Shaftesbury and Thomas Warton, for instance) this general rule had to be broken, the excerpts are of considerable length. It would be easy but unprofitable to object to the omission of this work or the inclusion of that; the choice has to be judged as a whole and on the principles by which it was guided. Here again Elledge has

shown good sense in selecting not only what seemed to him the 'best', but also those writings he considered 'most useful to an understanding of the variety of abilities and tastes of eighteenth-century critics': this second category accounts for the appearance of a specimen of the work of Joseph Trapp, 'first professor of poetry at Oxford, . . . the first professional academic critic', and a few other critical 'documents'. But what the ordinary reader will most welcome will be the texts of those critics who have for long been undeservedly ignored. To those who have never heard of Walter Whiter it will come as a pleasant surprise to find a late eighteenth-century critic anticipating recent discussions of the sources of Shakespeare's imagery, while those who missed the Augustan Reprint (1955) of Samuel Say's *Essay on the Harmony, Variety, and Power of Numbers* will be pleased to discover this careful study of a nonconformist clergyman who has been called 'one of the great metrical theorists of the whole English literary tradition'. The two volumes are full of criticism of first-rate importance (historical, intrinsic, or both) and one can only congratulate the editor on his selection as well as on the excellent introductory notes and annotations. Perhaps the summaries of the texts, intended to increase 'the usefulness of the book as a work of reference', might have been omitted to make room for more criticism, and some purists may object to the normalizing of the texts, but these are small objections to an admirably edited and well-produced collection.

A task almost as forbidding as that

---

[1] *Eighteenth-Century Critical Essays*, ed. by Scott Elledge. Cornell U.P. and O.U.P. 2 vols. pp. xxiii+570; xiii+571–1225. $12.50. £5.

which Scott Elledge faced confronts the compiler of a collection of modern scholarly and critical essays about the literature of this period. In 1959 J. L. Clifford's excellent selection was published (*YW* xl. 187), and this year Bernard N. Schilling has gathered *Essential Articles for the study of English Augustan Backgrounds*.[2] By 'Augustan', Schilling apparently refers to a period beginning with Dryden and ending with Pope, and most of the articles deal with the late seventeenth century, the chief exceptions being Louis Bredvold's 'A Note in Defence of Satire' and 'The Tendency toward Platonism in Neo-classical Esthetics', and H. T. Swedenberg's 'Rules and English Critics of the Epic, 1650–1800'. It can certainly be maintained that R. F. Jones's well-known studies of 'pulpit eloquence', 'science and English prose style', and 'science and criticism', though specifically concerned with the seventeenth century, provide an important background to the literature of Queen Anne's reign, but it is difficult to see why Ruth Wallenstein's essay on the development of the heroic couplet, 'Especially in 1625–1645', or Felix Schelling's 'Ben Jonson and the Classical School' (first published in 1898) are included in a collection with this title. Schilling says that he has chosen 'from the articles which time has sanctioned', but unfortunately on some of them time has left a deposit of dust. However, many of these articles are still of value, and it is convenient to have them in one volume, though it may seem that the price is rather high for the convenience provided.

Geoffrey Tillotson's *Augustan Studies*[3] is concerned with the period beginning with Pope and ending with Johnson. Some of these essays (for instance, 'The Manner of Proceeding in Certain Eighteenth- and Early Nineteenth-Century Poems' and the two discussions of 'Poetic Diction') will already be familiar to many readers, but the reprinted pieces have been revised, and five studies appear for the first time, including detailed examinations of Gray's *Ode on the Spring* and *Ode on the Death of a Favourite Cat*, and an introduction to Dyer's *Grongar Hill*, complete with annotated texts of the octosyllabic and Pindaric versions. Characteristically the essays combine scholarship with sensitive criticism, and close readings with challenging generalizations. Tillotson has too deep an understanding of the period to abandon his mind to the uncontrolled speculation which sometimes passes for interpretation, and, although some of his readings and generalizations are disputable, they are always plausible and interesting.

[Maren-Sofie Røstvig's *The Background of English Neo-Classicism, with some comments on Swift and Pope*[4] should be mentioned here, but as it has not been possible to see a copy, the book will be discussed in next year's volume.]

Arthur O. Lovejoy's new study in the history of ideas, *Reflections on Human Nature*,[5] starts from the incontestable assertion that 'there are few more important things to know about a writer than what his express view or his tacit but controlling assumptions concerning human nature and its dominant motives were, or to know about a period than what ideas on these subjects were prevalent in it'.

[2] *Essential Articles for the study of English Augustan Backgrounds*, ed. by Bernard N. Schilling. Hamden, Connecticut: Archon Books. pp. viii+418. $8.50.

[3] *Augustan Studies*, by Geoffrey Tillotson. Athlone Press and New York: O.U.P. pp. 266. 35s. $5.60.

[4] *The Background of English Neo-Classicism, with some comments on Swift and Pope*, by Maren-Sofie Røstvig. Oslo: Universitetsforl. pp. 110.

[5] *Reflections on Human Nature*, by Arthur O. Lovejoy. Johns Hopkins Press and O.U.P. pp. x+275. $4.75. 38s.

Lovejoy limits himself to the seventeenth and eighteenth centuries, and 'to a certain group of ideas about the dominant and distinctive motives of man which were extremely widely held and especially influential in that period'—more particularly, the concept of man's innate wickedness, the notion of self-love as the source of all specific human motives, and those manifestations of self-love expressed in the desire to win the approval of others or of oneself. The complexity of the argument cannot be briefly represented; as his title suggests, Lovejoy does not remain content to record the history of these ideas, but expounds at some length his own thoughts on the subject, ostensibly and legitimately in order to establish certain distinctions which were confused in the historical discussion, but also, one suspects, because he cannot resist joining in the debate. The result is an engrossing book which combines a learned investigation into the historical character of some crucial ideas with a lively discussion of human nature.

Louis I. Bredvold's *The Brave New World of the Enlightenment*[6] is rather less penetrating, but gives attractive and useful analyses of some of the ideas which occupied the philosophers of the same two centuries, such as the scientific view of man and society, sentimentalism, the concept of 'the noble savage', and 'Nature', and discusses their interplay and development. In 'The Idea of the Limitations of Science from Prior to Blake' (*Studies in English Literature*), William Powell Jones illustrates 'the highlights in English poetry after 1700 of the central idea that science, with all its glorious achievements proving the wisdom of God in nature, was unable to provide certain answers'; and James W. John-

son's 'That Neo-classical Bee' (*JHI*) shows how the writers of the early eighteenth century saw the bee as a symbol of universality, of moral choice and taste, of industry, and of social order, and thus 'turned the honey bee into a virtual paradigm of Neo-Classicism'.

Modern criticism and scholarship have become increasingly aware of the instability of terms and of the need to understand as fully as possible the particular complex of meanings and connotations associated with given words at given periods. Three studies this year are concerned with aspects of this problem. The most considerable is Norman Knox's *The Word 'Irony' and its Context, 1500–1755*,[7] which gives a brief history of the word, distinguishes between ten different meanings and fourteen sub-meanings during the period in question, and considers such related terms as 'raillery' and 'banter'. Knox demonstrates that the dominant meaning was 'censure through counterfeited praise', and that many of the modern refinements of the notion of irony have no relevance to the uses of the word in the eighteenth century. In ' "Beauty": Some Stages in the History of an Idea' (*JHI*) Jerome Stolnitz argues that the emergence during the eighteenth century of such terms as 'sublime' helped to 'displace "beauty" from the position it had enjoyed in classical and Renaissance thought'; and J. Dulck in a brief note on 'La Définition de *wit*, position du problème' (*Ea*) records a few of the meanings of the word.

Recent research and criticism are summarized in Erwin Wolff's 'Englische Literatur im 18. Jahrhundert: Ein Forschungsbericht (1950–1960)' (*Deutsche Vierteljahrsschrift für Literaturwissenschaft und Geistesgeschichte*); and

[6] *The Brave New World of the Enlightenment*, by Louis I. Bredvold. Michigan U.P. pp. 164. $3.95.

[7] *The Word 'Irony' and its Context, 1500–1755*, by Norman Knox. Duke U.P. and C.U.P. pp. xv+258. $7.50. 60s.

in more lively and provocative fashion in Donald J. Greene's 'Recent Studies in the Restoration and Eighteenth Century' (*Studies in English Literature*).

(*b*) The new *Moll Flanders*[8] in the World's Classics, unlike most modern reprints, follows the first edition instead of the 'corrected' third, Herbert Davis explaining in a 'Note on the Text' that he finds it difficult to accept that the corrections were made by Defoe. The point is disputable; what is not disputable is that a good reprint of the rare first edition at this price is extremely welcome. Bonamy Dobrée supplies an enthusiastic but judicious introduction which concludes: 'if we experience neither the absorption of tragedy nor the detachment of comedy, we get something that in its completeness is rarer and just as valuable, an insight as to how things really are with the vast majority of people'.

The only other Defoe text published this year is *Of Captain Misson*,[9] extracted from *A History of the Pyrates* (1728), the remarkable story of a deistic, radical, and unfortunately fictitious adventurer, who founded a settlement called Libertalia on egalitarian principles. A brief but useful introduction, relating the deistic and political notions to Defoe's other writings, is provided by Maximillian E. Novak, who is also responsible for five articles on Defoe. In 'Moll Flanders' First Love' (*Papers of the Michigan Academy of Science, Arts and Letters*) he interprets the first episode, that of the two brothers, as a

satirical presentation of the false values of society; 'Robinson Crusoe's "Original Sin" ' (*Studies in English Literature*) was, according to Novak, in abandoning his proper calling, against his father's wishes, thus involving himself in 'a sin against a specific religious-economic doctrine'; the article entitled 'Robinson Crusoe's Fear and the Search for Natural Man' (*MP*) examines the novel in the light of speculations about 'man's condition in the state of nature', and suggests that Defoe considered life in such a state wretched, and dominated by the emotion of fear; 'The Problem of Necessity in Defoe's Fiction' (*PQ*) illustrates Defoe's belief that a man could not be condemned for offences against the laws of society committed under the pressure of extreme necessity or motivated by the principle of self-preservation; and finally, in 'Colonel Jack's "Thieving Roguing" Trade to Mexico and Defoe's Attack on Economic Individualism' (*HLQ*), Novak points out that this trading venture was, in Defoe's eyes, an offence against trading morality and endangered the relations between England and Spain.

The only other articles on the major novels are Terence Martin's attempt to establish that 'The Unity of *Moll Flanders*' (*MLQ*) consists of 'a definable and coherent structural pattern of circumstances, resulting from Moll's different attempts to reach the same goal', that is, to achieve respectability and security; and an investigation of 'Chronology in *Robinson Crusoe*' (*PQ*) by Dewey Ganzel. Ganzel repudiates some objections made to details of chronology, but finds evidence of two distinct chronological schemes, the second, he believes, being introduced when Defoe was revising the novel.

Much the most important of the discussions of Defoe's minor works is the late Arthur W. Secord's 'Robert

[8] *The Fortunes and Misfortunes of the Famous Moll Flanders*, with an Introduction by Bonamy Dobrée and a Note on the Text by Herbert Davis. O.U.P. pp. xiii+394. 7s. 6d.

[9] *Of Captain Misson and His Crew* (1728), ed. with an Introduction by Maximillian E. Novak. (Augustan Reprint Society, No. 87.) Los Angeles: Clark Memorial Library, University of California. pp. iv+50. For members.

Drury's Journal' and Other Studies,[10] which, besides two long essays on the *Journal*, contains also examinations of 'The Origins of Defoe's *Memoirs of a Cavalier*' and 'Scarron's *Roman Comique* and its English Translators'. Secord produces fresh and convincing evidence that Robert Drury did in fact exist; that he was a member of the crew of the *Degrave* wrecked on Madagascar; that his account of his experiences tallies remarkably well with other records (notably those of the Dutch authorities at the Cape); and that the picture he gives of the geography and tribal organization of the island is generally reliable. Secord is led to conclude that Drury supplied Defoe with information, perhaps with a manuscript, though, as is admitted in the book, Defoe rehandled the material and introduced his own moralizings. In contrast, the *Memoirs of a Cavalier* are shown to have been compiled from histories and other sources, while the last essay demonstrates how freely eighteenth-century translators of Scarron borrowed (either at first or second hand) from 'the earliest and the only one that can be called an independent translation of the two parts by Scarron', John Bulteel's version of 1665.

In '*A New Voyage round the World*: Defoe's *roman à thèse*' (*HLQ*) Jane H. Jack notes some possible sources of Defoe's information, and maintains that the *New Voyage* was designed 'to enlist the sympathy of its readers for a serious scheme of colonisation and commerce'; Arthur H. Scouten's article, 'At that Moment of Time: Defoe and the Early Accounts of the Apparition of Mistress Veal' (*Ball State Teachers' College Forum*), shows that, although there were at least six earlier versions of the story, Defoe

carefully shaped the narrative to give greater human interest; and an account of Defoe's activities as a Whig pamphleteer is given by Jean Béranger in 'Defoe pamphlétaire, 1716–1720' (*Ea*).

This year, as last, Addison and Steele have received comparatively little attention. Apart from a discussion of the *Chevy Chase* papers in Albert B. Friedman's *The Ballad Revival*, and Robert Marsh's 'Akenside and Addison: The Problem of Ideational Debt' (*MP*) (both of which are considered in later sections of this chapter), there is only an article by William Kenney, entitled 'Addison, Johnson, and the "Energetick" Style' (*SN*), which contends that the old distinction between the energy of Johnson's style and the enervation of Addison's failed to allow for the differences in intention and purpose.

However, the two essayists appear in Bertrand Goldgar's book, *The Curse of Party: Swift's Relations with Addison and Steele*,[11] and although, as the subtitle suggests, Goldgar is principally interested in Swift, Addison's moderation and restraint show up well. Without offering new material or surprising insights, this book provides a thorough, sensible, and readable account of Swift's involvements in the political struggles of the last years of Queen Anne's reign, as well as of the relationship between the three men. Goldgar believes that the breach in their friendship was due not merely to politics but also to temperamental and intellectual incompatibility; here he is on what is necessarily speculative ground, and while he has little difficulty in showing that a lasting relationship between Swift and Steele was not likely to develop, it is dangerous to assume that friendship cannot survive even more striking differences of opinion and

[10] '*Robert Drury's Journal*' *and Other Studies*, by Arthur W. Secord. Illinois U.P. pp. 160. $4.50.

[11] *The Curse of Party: Swift's relations with Addison and Steele*, by Bertrand A. Goldgar. Nebraska U.P. pp. ix + 198. $4.

personality. In fact, Goldgar himself concludes that, once the political conflict diminished, Swift and Addison were able 'to reassert their mutual admiration and esteem'. Perhaps the weakest part of the book is the introductory section, where, in outlining the intellectual positions of the three men, Goldgar seems to confuse 'self-love' with 'selfishness'; of course, for Swift, as for Pope, 'self-love' was implanted in man by Providence for its own ends and was the source of all 'unselfishness' as well as of 'selfishness', in any moral sense of those terms.

The popularity of Swift's writings as a field for criticism is partly due to their extraordinary complexity, so that almost any careful approach to them is likely to produce interesting results. In *Swift's Classical Rhetoric*,[12] Charles Allen Beaumont subjects certain ironical pieces (in particular *A Modest Proposal, An Argument against Abolishing Christianity, A Vindication of Lord Carteret*, and *The Answer to the 'Craftsman'*) to close rhetorical analysis to reveal the skill with which Swift used such devices as 'ethical proof' (that is to say, the justification of the speaker's own moral and intellectual position), 'amplification', and 'diminution'. *A Modest Proposal* is in design, Beaumont claims, a complete classical oration. The danger of this kind of analysis is that of supposing that a writer of Swift's genius could not have arrived at the practice of these devices without help from the theoretical rhetoricians, whose labels and categories were derived from the study of great works of literature rather than productive of such works. Nevertheless, it is true that Swift was educated in a system dominated by classical rhetoric, and certainly Beaumont's thoughtful analyses often highlight subtleties and significances which could easily be overlooked.

Two critics have been concerned with Swift's religious position: John A. Yunck relates 'The Skeptical Faith of Jonathan Swift' (*Personalist*) to the beliefs of Dryden and Pascal, especially the concept of reason as a necessary guide for human behaviour but inapt for the unravelling of religious mysteries; and Phillip Harth's *Swift and Anglican Rationalism: The Religious Background of 'A Tale of a Tub'*[13] deals with the sources of the ideas and forms of attack in the religious satire of the *Tale*. This scholarly and level-headed book, instead of searching for improbable parallels, relates the nature and form of Swift's attacks on Catholics, Puritans, and certain metaphysical schemes to the seventeenth-century tradition of Anglican apologetics exemplified by the works of such writers as Henry More, Ralph Cudworth, and Joseph Glanvill. These Anglican rationalists rejected the deist belief that reason was a sufficient guide and the fideist position that 'reason ceases where religion begins', their contention being that both reason and revelation had their proper roles in religious matters. Harth convincingly demonstrates that on this and on other issues Swift shared the opinions of the Anglican rationalists, and that some of the basic notions of his satirical method (for instance, the treatment of the Puritans as madmen rather than as hypocrites) derived from the same tradition. The one place where Harth overstates his case is in the introductory chapter, where, partly to justify his separate treatment of the religious side of the *Tale* and partly to repudiate attempts to discover a structural unity in it, he asserts: '*A Tale of a*

---

[12] *Swift's Classical Rhetoric*, by Charles Allen Beaumont. Georgia U.P. pp. vii + 158. $2.50.

[13] *Swift and Anglican Rationalism: The Religious Background of 'A Tale of a Tub'*, by Phillip Harth. Chicago U.P. pp. 171. $5. 40s.

Tub, then, is a satire which deals with two separate subjects, in two separate groups of sections, by means of two separate satirical methods. In addition, the two parts of the book were written at two separate periods of time.' All this is true, but it is equally true that both parts were written by the same author, in a similar satirical spirit, and were combined by him and published as a single work. It is one thing to oppose attempts to foist on the *Tale* a modern concept of aesthetic unity, and quite another to imply that it consists of two entirely separate books rather carelessly shuffled together. But Harth's study places Swift's religious satire firmly in its proper context and illuminates the character and purpose of a part of the *Tale* which was from the beginning frequently misunderstood.

Other aspects of the same work are discussed by R. E. Hughes, who discovers an hierarchy of folly in 'The Five Fools in *A Tale of a Tub*' (*Literature and Psychology*), and by E. E. Duncan-Jones, whose note on 'Joseph's Party-Coloured Coat and *A Tale of a Tub*' (*NQ*) suggests that the passage about the covering of the brothers' coats with ornamental trimmings may be indebted to one of Thomas Fuller's sermons.

A few years ago good cheap texts of *Gulliver's Travels* were rare, but now there are several excellent paperback editions. To their number must be added Robert A. Greenberg's edition,[14] which provides a text based on Faulkner's, some explanatory footnotes, and a selection of critical essays and extracts, including a previously unpublished paper by R. S. Crane on 'The Rationale of the Fourth Voyage'. Crane disputes some current theories about the fourth voyage and maintains that it

has 'an argument, broadly moral and psychological rather than specifically Christian in its reference, worked out not allegorically but by means of a marvellous fable, and dependent, for its satirical point, on our taking Gulliver's misanthropy not as an error but as, in substance though not in degree, the natural and proper consequence of the experience he has had'. A more specialized collection of already published material is *A Casebook on Gulliver among the Houyhnhnms*,[15] edited by Milton P. Foster, which contains a text of the fourth voyage and twenty-six 'Evaluations and Interpretations'.

There are seven articles dealing specifically with the *Travels*: Maurice Johnson's 'Remote Regions of Man's Mind: The Travels of Gulliver' (*University of Kansas City Review*) treats Swift's book as though it were a series of Kafkaesque explorations of 'extreme mental situations' culminating in the narrator's 'frightful deviation into madness'; according to Clarence Tracey 'The Unity of *Gulliver's Travels*' (*QQ*) is manifested in contrasts, parallels, and interrelations, rather than in plot and character, the first three voyages satirizing in turn the world of action, the world of thought, and various abuses of reason, while the fourth presents a comparison between man's limited reason and Reason itself; John Traugott, in 'A Voyage to Nowhere with Thomas More and Jonathan Swift: *Utopia* and the *Voyage to the Houyhnhnms*' (*Sew*), compares the views and literary manners of the two writers, sees them both as politicians forced to compromise but 'maintaining an utopia in the back of the head as a measure of those compromises', and decides that 'the evidence that [Swift] drew heavily from More is overwhelming'; John D. Seelye believes there is a

[14] '*Gulliver's Travels': An Annotated Text with Critical Essays*, ed. by Robert A. Greenberg. New York: Norton. pp. viii+xiv+361. $1.95.

[15] *A Casebook on Gulliver among the Houyhnhnms*, ed. by Milton P. Foster. New York: Crowell. pp. xiii+319. $2.50.

connexion between 'Hobbes' *Leviathan* and the Giantism Complex in the First Book of *Gulliver's Travels*' (*JEGP*), Lilliput representing the Hobbesian state; in 'Swift's Fool: a Comment upon Satire in *Gulliver's Travels*' (*DR*), Warren Tallman considers Gulliver's behaviour as illustrating the folly of relying on human qualities rather than depending on God; Jim Corder's 'Gulliver in England' (*CE*) suggests that all the imaginary countries are distorted images of England; and George Sherburn gives reasons for supposing that 'The "Copies of Verses" about Gulliver' (*TSLL*), usually attributed to Pope, were written by the Scriblerians in collaboration.

George Mayhew has published 'Two Entries of 1702–3 for Swift's "Polite Conversation", 1738' (*NQ*) which show how long Swift was gathering materials for this work; and the same author prints some materials concerning Ormonde's campaign in Flanders which are among 'Swift's Notes for his *The History of the Four Last Years*, Book IV' (*HLQ*). Richard I. Cook observes some rather flimsy resemblances between the political situation in 'Dryden's *Absalom and Achitophel* and Swift's Political Tracts, 1710–1714' (*NQ*); John J. McAleer interprets a paragraph of *Some Free Thoughts upon the Present State of Affairs* as 'Swift's Letcombe Admonition to Bolingbroke' (*College Language Association Journal*), and unconvincingly relates it to a supposed escapade of Bolingbroke's in Greenwich Park; and W. U. McDonald, Jr., records 'A Letter of Sir Walter Scott on the Jeffrey-Swift Controversy' (*RES*) which praises William Scott for a pamphlet, usually attributed to Edward Berwick, defending Swift against Jeffrey's attack.

A new volume in the Twickenham edition is almost certain to be the chief event of any year in Pope studies. The latest to appear, *Pastoral Poetry*

and '*An Essay on Criticism*',[16] edited by E. Audra and Aubrey Williams, completes the edition as originally planned, but we are now promised four more volumes, two each for the *Iliad* and the *Odyssey*. The new volume contains the *Pastorals, Messiah, Windsor Forest, An Essay on Criticism*, and the early translations from Ovid, Statius, and Homer, besides *A Discourse upon Pastoral Poetry* and the 'Preface' to the 1717 edition of Pope's works. All the texts are based on first editions, corrected in the light of later versions, and although Pope's manuscripts exist for the two prose pieces and for many of the poems, the editors have wisely used them merely for clarification, and not for establishing the text, since Pope is known to have introduced corrections at proof stage. Like its predecessors in this splendid set, the volume combines reliable and well-presented texts with learned introductory essays and comprehensive and copious notes. Inevitably, a work such as this, including general assertions about the background of the poems, estimates of their literary value and importance, and explications of allusions and obscurities challenges disagreement; indeed, it is the function of such an edition to attract fresh critical and scholarly attention to the poems edited. It might, for instance, be argued that the sense of the word 'Nature' which is stressed in the 'Introduction' to the *Essay on Criticism* (the divinely ordered cosmic harmony) is not so directly relevant to an understanding of such lines as 'At once the Source, and End, and Test of Art', as the sense treated as primary in Tillotson's *Pope and Human Nature* (what is common to all men, at all times, and

[16] *Pastoral Poetry and 'An Essay on Criticism'*, ed. by E. Audra and Aubrey Williams. (Twickenham edition of *The Poems of Alexander Pope*, vol. I.) Methuen and Yale U.P. pp. xxiv+498. 55s. $8.50.

in all places). Or, on a point of detail, the editors' note on the difficult expression 'Equal Syllables' might be criticized. Other readers will find other points of disagreement, and the discussion of such points will be one of the services to Pope scholarship fulfilled by this excellent edition.

The second edition of another Twickenham volume, Epistles to Several Persons,[17] edited by F. W. Bateson, illustrates this service. Since its appearance in 1951, Bateson's volume has been the standard text for these poems, yet after ten years it has been 'drastically revised' in the light of critical comments, new material, and information derived from the other Twickenham editors. Bateson has also made good use of recent books and articles, and in particular of Sherburn's edition of the letters (1956). The 'Introduction' has been enlarged, a 'General Note on the Text' added, and some interesting material, including the text of A Master Key to Popery, appended. Particularly interesting are the reasons offered for identifying 'Atossa' as the Duchess of Buckingham instead of the Duchess of Marlborough, and the editor's unwillingness to accept that 'Cloe' was 'a portrait of Mrs. Howard'.

The useful series of Studies in English Literature includes an introduction to The Rape of the Lock by J. S. Cunningham.[18] The 'General Preface' to the series indicates that the intention is to provide 'close critical analyses and evaluations of individual works' for 'the advanced sixth former and the university student', and this little book serves that purpose admirably. Cunningham conveys clearly the poem's

brilliant balance of levity and seriousness, celebration and satire; he is ready to explicate subtleties of allusion, diction or antithesis; and he is not always content to be 'sound', but will suggest, for instance, that Ariel, 'a metamorphosed coquette in disguise', is engaged in 'undermining [Belinda's] moral position'. His account of the poem is greatly to be preferred to that given by Stanley Edgar Hyman in Poetry and Criticism: Four revolutions in Literary Taste,[19] where it is treated as a kind of ritual in order to make it fit into a simplified scheme of literary history. In 'The "Frail China Jar" and the Rude Hand of Chaos' (Centennial Review of Arts and Sciences) Murray Krieger contrasts the idyllic unreality of Belinda's world with the grim vision of reality in the Dunciad; and J. Copley notes some parallel contructions in 'The Rape of the Lock, II, 73–100' (MLN).

Articles dealing with other poems by Pope are, as usual, numerous. Kurt Schlüter's 'Pope's Windsor Forest, ein Ortsgedicht in Pastoraler Gestaltung' (Ang) observes some parallels in Virgil, and maintains that the unity of the poem is achieved by the elevated generalization of the details of scenery. John M. Aden presents 'The Doctrinal Design of An Essay on Criticism' (CE) as the centring of all the critical tenets upon 'the principle of Nature', but fails to discuss the precise range of meanings of the term 'Nature' appropriate to the poem. Henry Pettit finds in the use of 'Apposite Metaphor in Pope's Essay on Criticism' (Books Abroad) a 'discernible pattern' supporting the argument of the poem. Francis E. Litz, in 'Pope's Use of Derham' (JEGP), claims that the Essay on Man was considerably indebted to William Derham's Physico-Theology (1713) and Astro-Theology (1715), but

---

[17] Epistles to Several Persons (Moral Essays), ed. by F. W. Bateson. (Twickenham edition of The Poems of Alexander Pope, vol. III, ii.) Second edition. Methuen and Yale U.P. pp. lxv+201. 45s.
[18] Pope: The Rape of the Lock, by J. S. Cunningham. (Studies in English Literature, No. 2.) Arnold. pp. 64. 6s.

[19] Poetry and Criticism: Four Revolutions in Literary Taste, by Stanley Edgar Hyman. New York: Atheneum. pp. iv+178. $4.

the resemblances are of a kind that could hardly be avoided in two works on a similar subject; and Ernest Tuveson defends his attempt to establish the influence of Locke in the *Essay on Man* (*ELH* 1959) in '*An Essay on Man* and "The Way of Ideas": Some Further Remarks' (*PQ*). A careful account of the way in which Pope's 'moral commentary emerges from particular details of dramatised human behaviour' is given in ' "Reconcil'd Extremes": Pope's *Epistle to Bathurst*' (*EC*) by Thomas R. Edwards, Jr., who argues that the poem, though not 'openly doctrinal', presents the damage done to the proper relationship between man and his natural environment by the pressures of a money-dominated society. By an elaborate exegesis of 'Pope's *Ode for Musick*' (*ELH*), Earl R. Wasserman tries to show that the poem is a more complex and better-ordered whole than is usually allowed, but what learned ingenuity can read into a poem is not the same as what the poet has succeeded in making operative in his work. A similar ingenuity is displayed in David R. Hauser's 'Medea's Strain and Hermes' Wand: Pope's Use of Mythology' (*MLN*), which interprets these two references in the passage at the end of the *Dunciad* describing the advent of Dullness, in terms of allegorical readings of the myths, 'current in Pope's time', and purports to reveal that they 'serve as symbols of forces which are producing the destruction of civilized values and also as representatives of the very values being destroyed'. There is no controlling this kind of criticism, for when its investigations produce two blatant contradictions it merely takes them as evidence of rich poetic ambiguity. In 'Bishop Hall and Pope's Portrait of Atticus' (*NQ*) John Crossett asserts that Pope was influenced by Hall's prose sketch, 'Of the Envious'. More probably, N. W.

Bawcutt's 'Pope's "Duchesses and Lady Mary's": More Evidence' (*NQ*) suggests that the lines in the *Dunciad* concerning bawds who pass off their charges on the credulous as ladies of fashion are indebted to the *Spectator* No. 205.

Some important critical issues are raised in a stimulating article by Evan Jones, 'Verse, Prose and Pope' (*Melbourne Critical Review*). Starting from a comparison of some lines from Donne's fourth satire with Pope's version of them, Jones contends that, while the inner rhetorical structure of Pope's couplets has been minutely analysed and usually praised by modern critics, little attention has been given to what was lost by the use of heroic couplets: 'Poetry does not only tell us what a man might say (though that is important too) but shows us how a man might speak, how his speech might convey a sense of the commitment most proper to his ideas and beliefs. . . . It is this quality that Pope's verse not only lacks, but has lost the capability of.' This is to raise again, though in new form, some of the old objections to Pope's versification, and Jones's argument will certainly be strongly disputed, but at least this is a case worthy of dispute. Another aspect of Pope's versification is the subject of 'Pope and the Rules of Prosody' (*PMLA*), in which Jacob H. Adler compares the rules outlined in the letter to Henry Cromwell with current eighteenth-century opinion, and then, by comparing both with Pope's practice, shows that the poet never submitted fully to any such hard and fast notions. 'A New Pope Letter' (*RES*), discovered by Elizabeth Arlidge, is addressed to William Broome, and leads to an interesting discussion of a curious passage in Young's *Universal Passion* which may have been written by Broome and touched up by Pope. Another curiosity is considered by Nicolas J. Perella in 'Pope's Judgment of the *Pastor Fido* and a Case of Plagiarism' (*PQ*); passages from a letter by Pope (published in 1735) criticizing Guarini for departures from true pastoral simplicity were copied in the following year by Richard Fanshawe, the translator of the *Pastor Fido*, to make precisely the opposite point. *Pope's Iliad: An Examination by William Melmoth*,[20] edited by Grover Cronin, Jr., and Paul A. Doyle, reprints three 'letters' from Melmoth's *Letters of Sir Thomas Osborne* (1747–9) which are illustrative of well-informed mid-eighteenth-century opinion of the translation of the *Iliad*. Donald B. Clark explains that, despite 'The Italian Fame of Alexander Pope' (*MLQ*) in the eighteenth and early nineteenth centuries, interest was less in the poetry than in the 'benevolent optimism' of the *Essay on Man*, and, apart from *The Rape of the Lock*, none of the satires was translated into Italian.

It is extraordinary that a play so frequently referred to and of such distinguished authorship as *Three Hours After Marriage* should have been so little known and so difficult to acquire, but this year two editions of it have appeared, one by John Harrington Smith for the Augustan Reprint Society,[21] and one by Richard Morton and William M. Peterson as the first of a new series, *Lake Erie College Studies*.[22] Smith has chosen for his

reprint the five-act version printed in Dublin in 1758, while Morton and Peterson have based their text on the first edition of 1717, a three-act version, though, as Gay writes in the 'Advertisement', 'the Players in Compliance with the Taste of the Town broke it into five Parts in the Representation'. Smith defends his choice on a number of grounds, and supposes that the Dublin publisher 'had an authentic acting MS of the play', but his defence depends on conjecture, and the authority of the first edition is hardly shaken. One suspects that Smith has been influenced even more than he admits by the consideration that the Dublin version includes *A Key to the New Comedy; Call'd, Three Hours After Marriage* and *A Letter, &c. To the Publisher* 'giving an Account of the Origin of the Quarrel between *Cibber, Pope*, and *Gay*'. Nevertheless this Augustan Reprint is typical of the excellent and cheap publications of the Society, and Smith's introduction and notes are characterized by a pleasantly informal enthusiasm. Morton and Peterson also print the *Key*, as well as Parker's *Complete Key* (1717) and Breval's short farce *The Confederates*, in which the authors, the actors, and the publisher appear. These editors have room for a longer critical discussion of the play's merits and defects than was possible in Smith's introduction, and their 'Textual Apparatus' covers all the significant variants in eight early editions. (A facsimile edition of *The Beggar's Opera*,[23] edited by Louis Kronenberger and Max

---

[20] *Pope's Iliad: An Examination by William Melmoth*, ed. by Grover Cronin, Jr., and Paul A. Doyle. Catholic University of America Press, 1960. pp. vi+57. $1.95.

[21] *John Gay, Alexander Pope, John Arbuthnot: 'Three Hours After Marriage'*, ed., with an Introduction, by John Harrington Smith. (Augustan Reprint Society, No. 91–92.) Los Angeles: Clark Memorial Library, University of California. pp. 14+vi+139–222. For members.

[22] *'Three Hours after Marriage', by John Gay, Alexander Pope, John Arbuthnot, with 'The Confederates' and the Two Keys*, ed. by Richard Morton and William M. Peterson. (Lake Erie College Studies, vol. I.) Lake Erie College Press. pp. xvi+111.

[23] *'The Beggar's Opera' by John Gay: A Faithful Reproduction of the 1729 edition, which includes the words and music of all the airs, as well as the score for the Overture*, with Commentaries by Louis Kronenberger and Max Goberman on the Literary and Musical Background and with the Original Words of all the Airs that John Gay adapted for this work. Larchmont, N.Y.: Argonaut Books. pp. xxiv+viii+60 (text); 46 (music); xxv–liv. $10.

Goberman, also appeared in 1961 but no copy has been available.)

In 1958 Alan Dugald McKillop edited James Thomson's letters, and he has now followed this with another service to the poet, an edition of *The Castle of Indolence and Other Poems*.[24] McKillop is a painstaking editor; his texts are established with care and prudence, all important variants are recorded, and an extended introduction to each poem outlines its history and literary and social background. It is strange that a poem as famous and of such quality as *The Castle of Indolence* 'has never heretofore been critically edited or fully discussed and annotated', but this edition, with an introduction which places the poem in the mock-Spenserian tradition, and generally elucidates its theme and methods, compensates for earlier neglect. The book also contains reliable texts of the *Hymn on Solitude*, *A Poem Sacred to the Memory of Sir Isaac Newton*, *Britannia*, and *Rule, Britannia*, and should encourage a new interest in Thomson's lesser works.

The Life of Samuel Johnson, LL.D., by Sir John Hawkins, Knt.[25] has not been reprinted since the first and second editions of 1787. In 1960 Bertram H. Davis published a defence of this biography (see *YW* xli. 196), and now he has brought out an abridgement of it which retains the full portrait of Johnson but excludes many of the long digressions and quotations from Johnson's works. His introduction restates the case for considering Hawkins's *Life* as an account of Johnson which, different from Boswell's, is equally valid and in many

ways complementary to it. Biographical studies of Johnson are included in a collection of essays and papers by Russell Brain, entitled *Some Reflections on Genius and Other Essays*.[26] Brain writes about 'Dr. Johnson on Science', 'Dr. Johnson and the Kangaroo', 'The Dancing Bear', 'The Great Convulsionary', and 'A Postmortem on Dr. Johnson', and although there are occasionally traces of the old emphasis on Johnson as a great eccentric, the approach is usually lively and the expert medical opinion worth having. An account of 'Jonathan Swift: L'Enfant Terrible', which concludes somewhat glibly that Swift was 'an obsessional personality emotionally arrested at an immature stage of development', illustrates the danger of posthumous psycho-analysis, but there are good essays on Lord Monboddo and Christopher Smart. Other aspects of Johnson's life are dealt with by John H. Middendorf, who characterizes the relations between 'Dr. Johnson and Adam Smith' (*PQ*) as 'a state of uneasy truce marked by privately expressed dislike and by public civility occasionally broken', and by Alan G. Thomas, who describes Johnson's encounters with such booksellers as Osborne, Dodsley, and Davies in 'Dr. Johnson and the Book Trade' (*New Rambler*).

In his study of *Samuel Johnson the Moralist*,[27] Robert Brown Voitle, Jr., attempts to define Johnson's moral position by comparing his notions about reason and freedom with those of Locke, and by relating his utilitarian altruism to that of Richard Cumberland. This valuable discussion brings out clearly Johnson's recognition of

[24] *The Castle of Indolence and Other Poems*, ed. by Alan Dugald McKillop. Kansas U.P. pp. xi+222. $5.

[25] *The Life of Samuel Johnson, LL.D. by Sir John Hawkins, Knt.*, ed., abridged, and with an Introduction by Bertram H. Davis. New York: Macmillan and London: Cape. pp. xxxi+341. $5.95.

[26] *Some Reflections on Genius and Other Essays*, by Russell Brain. London: Pitman and Philadelphia: Lippincott. pp. 192. 30s. $4.50.

[27] *Samuel Johnson the Moralist*, by Robert Brown Voitle, Jr. Harvard U.P. pp. xvi+188. $4.25.

human limitations and his emphasis on man's duty to promote 'within his circle, however narrow, the happiness of others', and concludes by examining the bases of Johnson's morality and their relation to his religious beliefs. Bernard Knieger's article on 'The Moral Essays of Dr. Samuel Johnson' (*Personalist*) also concentrates on Johnson's concern with the practical side of morality, with due regard to man's limitations; and a short note by Maurice Quinlan deals with 'Johnson's Sense of Charity' (*New Rambler*). Three articles are concerned in different ways with Johnson's religion: the conflict between his sense of religious duty and his constitutional melancholy, so that 'the powerful inner compulsion to serve was frequently balked by psychological apathy', is the theme of 'Johnson's "Divided Self"' (*UTQ*) by Edward A. Bloom; in 'Johnson and the "Proofs" of Revelation' (*PQ*) Chester F. Chapin attributes both Johnson's desire for more certain evidence of the spiritual world and his hatred for the work of David Hume to a recurring uneasiness in his Christian faith; and the same author shows that 'Johnson's Prayer for Kitty Chambers' (*MLN*) apparently composed extempore, reveals his ability 'not only to recall at will particular phrases from the prayer book, but just those phrases, from just that part of the service, which happened best to suit his particular purpose at the time'.

Paul West examines Johnson's stoicism in 'Rasselas: The Humanist as Stoic' (*English*), and asserts that the book 'epitomized an abiding pessimism'; on the other hand, John M. Aden's '*Rasselas* and *The Vanity of Human Wishes*' (*Criticism*) protests against the usual identification of the themes of the two works on the grounds that 'far from being a prose version of *The Vanity of Human Wishes*, *Rasselas* seems rather a repudiation of the

pessimistic and melancholy doctrine of the poem'. A more general account of the moral and narrative schemes of the book is given by Paolo Casini in 'Rasselas o il mito della felicità' (*L'Approdo Literario*).

An address to the Johnson Society by Mary Lascelles presented 'Some Reflections on Johnson's Hebridean Journey' (*New Rambler*) which are chiefly concerned with the skilful use of transitions and changes of angle by which Johnson created 'a fabric of interlocking argument and narrative'; and the 1959 exhibition, in the Birmingham Library, of books known to Johnson was the occasion for a discussion of some of these books and their particular interest for Johnson in 'Johnson's Books and the Birmingham Library' (*New Rambler*) by Charles Parish.

Three articles have to do with possible sources: Robert C. Fox suggests that 'The Imaginary Submarines of Dr. Johnson and Richard Owen Cambridge' (*PQ*), appearing on the same day in the *Rambler* No. 105 and the *Scribleriad*, may both have been suggested by a series of articles on submarine experiments which had appeared in the *Gentleman's Magazine*; A. T. Elder asks if a stock anecdote from Plutarch which appears in both the *Spectator* and the *Rambler* is 'A Johnson Borrowing from Addison?' (*NQ*); and John M. Aden remarks on two couplets in *The Vanity of Human Wishes* as evidence of the influence of 'Pope's Horace in Johnson's Juvenal' (*NQ*). Gwin J. Kolb has come forward with 'More Attributions to Dr. Johnson' (*Studies in English Literature*), consisting of six short pieces in the *Gentleman's Magazine*, but the evidence offered is mainly stylistic and not very convincing.

The correspondence columns of *TLS* have printed several letters concerning Johnson: L. F. Powell corrects two points in his earlier letter about

Johnson's connexions with the South-well family; J. D. Fleeman attempts to identify the valley in the Highlands in which Johnson first thought of writing his *Journey*; Donald J. Greene points out that a witticism attributed to Johnson in Boswell's *Life* was printed in a jest-book in 1750; and a less-striking parallel is drawn by E. L. McAdam, Jr., between the crushing retort, 'Sir, your wife, under pretence of keeping a bawdy-house, is a receiver of stolen goods', and an ex-change in court reported in the *Annals of Newgate* (1776). Roger P. McCut-cheon's 'Samuel Johnson: 1709–1959' (*TSL*) comments briefly on the chief post-war events in Johnsonian studies.

(*c*) Two important but neglected authors have received some recogni-tion from abroad. In 'Illuministi inglesi: il paradosso Mandeville' (*Convivium*) Marco Saccenti compares Mandeville's work with that of Swift and Orwell, and Anna Maria Crino provides an introduction to *L'Opera Letteraria di Matthew Prior*[28] in a language into which none of Prior's poetry has as yet been translated. The book attempts no deep critical analyses, but considers separately and sensibly Prior's achieve-ments in the various poetic kinds and in prose, and indicates some of his indebtedness to Dryden and other seventeenth-century authors.

A selection of *The Works of Mr. Henry Needler*,[29] made and introduced by Marcia Allentuck, for the first time makes readily available some speci-mens of the writings of a minor poet whose work has recently received some critical attention; Michael Kelly has

[28] *L'Opera Letteraria di Matthew Prior*, by Anna Maria Crino. (Estratto dagli Atti dell'Accademia di Agricoltura, Scienze e Lettere di Verona, Serie VI, vol. XII.)

[29] *The Works of Mr. Henry Needler* (*1728*), selected, with an Introduction by Marcia Allentuck. (Augustan Reprint Society, No. 90.) Los Angeles: Clark Memorial Library, University of California. pp. iv+56. For members.

a discursive article on 'Sir Richard Blackmore in the Judgment of his Fellow-Writers' (*Journal of the History of Medicine*); J. E. Norton, in 'Some Uncollected Authors XXVII: Mary Astell, 1666–1731' (*BC*), gives a short biography and bibliography of a learned and pious lady who was a friend of Elizabeth Elstob and Lady Mary Wortley-Montagu; and Robert D. Horn discusses 'The Authorship of the First Blenheim Panegyric' (*HLQ*), and attributes it to James Smallwood, Marlborough's chaplain.

Shaftesbury is the principal concern of four articles this year. In 'Shaftes-bury's Theory of Poetry: The Impor-tance of "Inward Colloquy" ' (*ELH*) Robert Marsh argues that while certain stock notions about Shaftesbury's aesthetics have become current, the important idea of the self-examination or 'inward colloquy' by which a man could protect his innate moral and aesthetic taste against the corruptions of custom and fashion (an idea parti-cularly significant in Shaftesbury's dis-cussion of 'the nature and value of poetry and the poet') has been ignored. Irène Simon examines 'Shaftesbury and Eighteenth-Century Poetry' (*Revue des langues vivantes*) with particular reference to his influence on Pope and Thomson: 'It is certainly striking that the "moralist-poets" who owe most to Shaftesbury seem to have remembered nothing of the test of wit and humour. It looks as though his influence rather tended to encourage the kind of "gravity" that he so often ridiculed.' Jerome Stolnitz, in an article 'On the Significance of Lord Shaftesbury in Modern Aesthetic Theory' (*PQ*), claims that Shaftesbury originated 'the idea which, more than any other, marks off modern from traditional aesthetics. . . viz. the concept of "aesthetic disin-terestedness" '; and in another article 'On the Origins of "Aesthetic Dis-interestedness" ' (*Journal of Aesthetics and Art Criticism*) the same author describes the development of the idea from Shaftesbury to Burke.

A number of other articles can be briefly noted. C. J. Rawson disputes B. H. Bronson's claim that the capitalized word 'Rest' in 'Parnell's "Night-Piece on Death" ' (*NQ*) is a noun; J. A. Lavin quotes a popular ballad as 'The Source of Ramsay's "Nanny-O" ' (*NQ*); Michael Shugrue noted some references to 'Richard Savage in the Columns of "Applebee's Original Weekly Journal" ' (*NQ*), and prints some verses not previously included in Savage's writings; a compact account of Law's work as 'controversialist, moralist, and mystic' is given by Maurice Banting in 'William Law: Nonjuror, Writer, and Mystic' (*Theology*); while Eric W. Baker's 'William Law' (*London Quarterly and Holborn Review*) summarizes the stages in the development of Law's religious thought; in 'James Ralph in Berkshire' (*Studies in English Literature*) Alan D. McKillop publishes and discusses three letters concerning the activities in 1726 and 1727 of the American Grub Street writer; P. Dixon's ' "The Man of Manners" and O.E.D. ' (*NQ*) lists some unrecorded colloquial terms from an anonymous courtesy-book of the mid-1730's, and quotes some amusing comments on fashionable conversation; and Raymond Williamson explains the motives behind the scientific quarrels of the man who became the second Professor of Botany at Cambridge, in 'John Martyn and *The Grub-Street Journal*: With Particular Reference to his Attacks on Richard Bentley, Richard Bradley, and William Cheselden' (*Medical History*).

Several interesting studies of the background to eighteenth-century literature have appeared this year: Edward A. Bloom describes the 'Neoclassic "Paper Wars" for a Free Press' (*MLR*),

and maintains that these struggles, though often tawdry or venal, laid the foundations of the modern acceptance of the necessity for freedom of the press; in 'Glory or Gravity: Hutchinson vs. Newton' (*JHI*) Albert J. Kuhn outlines the history of Hutchinsonianism, which, stemming from John Hutchinson's numerous attempts 'to knock down Newton and set up Moses as the infallible guide to the natural and spiritual system of the universe', appealed to many believers in revealed religion as a way out of their difficulties until well into the nineteenth century; fresh information about 'The Early Life of John Partridge' (*Studies in English Literature*) is supplied by George P. Mayhew; a learned, detailed, and amusing account is given by S. A. Seligman of 'Mary Toft—The Rabbit Breeder' (*Medical History*); and Joseph M. Doggett describes early reactions to ' "A Strange Sort of Liquor Called Coffee" ' (*Forum*).

The following are mainly of bibliographical interest: William B. Todd's details about a copy of 'Philips's *Cyder*, 1708' (*BC*); notes on 'Two Poems by Susanna Centlivre' (*BC*) by Jacqueline Faure; Robert Hay Carnie's 'Scottish Printers and Booksellers, 1668–1775: A Second Supplement (I)' (*SB*); and *A Hand-List of Irish Newspapers, 1685–1750*[30] compiled by R. L. Munter.

(*d*) The second instalment of *The London Stage, 1660–1800*[31] to appear

[30] *A Hand-List of Irish Newspapers, 1685–1750*, by R. L. Munter. (Cambridge Bibliographical Society Monographs, no. 4.) Bowes and Bowes, 1960. pp. xiii+36.
[31] *The London Stage, 1660–1800: A Calendar of Plays, Entertainments & Afterpieces Together with Casts, Box-Receipts and Contemporary Comment compiled from the Playbills, Newspapers, and Theatrical Diaries of the Period*. Part 3, *1729–1760*, ed., with a Critical Introduction, by A. H. Scouten. Southern Illinois U.P. Vol. I: pp. clxxxviii+595+cxci–ccxxxiii; Vol. II: pp. xiv+597–1315+xvii–lii.

consists of two volumes, edited by A. H. Scouten, covering the years 1729–60. The importance of this 'Calendar of Plays, Entertainments & Afterpieces' for any study of the theatre of the period can hardly be exaggerated, and further encouragement to such study is given by Scouten's long, informative, and stimulating introduction, which covers all aspects of the theatre, and argues with enthusiasm that, had it not been for the Licensing Act of 1737, there might have been a new resurgence of the English drama, led by Fielding.

A more specialized study, Mary E. Knapp's *Prologues and Epilogues of the Eighteenth Century*,[32] illustrates the profit to be derived from intense work on a limited field. The book considers why there was a popular demand for these addresses to the audience, discusses some of the techniques of presenting them and some of the actors and actresses who delivered them, extracts from them information about eighteenth-century audiences and their expectations, and shows how the forceful wit of the Restoration period was succeeded by prologues and epilogues which ingratiatingly and humorously reflected daily life. A more theoretical examination of the drama of the early years of the century is made by A. Mavrocordato in 'La Critique classique anglaise et la fonction de la tragédie (1660–1720)' (*Ea*); Mavrocordato concentrates his attention on the critical notions concerning the proper ends of tragedy, particularly the ideas of catharsis and poetic justice, and suggests that they led to the favouring of 'happy endings'.

Alfred Schwarz's study of 'An Example of Eighteenth-Century Pathetic Tragedy: Rowe's *Jane Shore*'

(*MLQ*) leads him to the assertion that Rowe's 'acknowledged debt to Shakespeare' was not only a matter of blank verse and Elizabethan idiom but was more importantly manifested in departures from the rules of neo-classic tragedy. A different kind of indebtedness is the subject of R. K. Kaul, who compares *The Fatal Secret* with *The Duchess of Malfi* to show 'What Theobald did to Webster' (*Indian Journal of English Studies*). In 'A Forgotten Chapter in English Eighteenth-Century Opera' (*Music and Letters*) J. Merrill Knapp describes two early operas 'after the Italian manner', *Rosamond* (1707) and *Calypso and Telemachus* (1712); and Stanley Wells, in 'A Shakespearean Droll?' (*Theatre Notebook*), gives reasons for supposing that the droll *Dorastus and Fawnia* was based on *A Winter's Tale*. John Harold Wilson claims, in 'Thomas's "Life of Jo. Hayns" ' (*NQ*), that the biography of the famous comedian (1701) was written, not by Tom Brown, but by the actor Tobyas Thomas. Kalman A. Burnim finds in 'Aaron Hill's *The Prompter*: An Eighteenth Century Theatrical Paper' (*Educational Theatre Journal*) information about theatrical politics and styles of acting and production; and some details about actors and theatres in the early years of the century are published by John Harold Wilson in 'Theatre Notes from the Newdigate Newsletters' (*Theatre Notebook*).

(*e*) There are two books on Fielding to be noticed this year. Henry Knight Miller's *Essays on Fielding's 'Miscellanies'*[33] is a volume of much greater general interest than its title would suggest. Its first purpose is to present a detailed analysis of the poems, essays, and translations found in the first

---

[32] *Prologues and Epilogues of the Eighteenth Century*, by Mary E. Knapp. (Yale Studies in English, vol. 149.) Yale U.P. pp. xi+350. $6.

[33] *Essays on Fielding's 'Miscellanies': A Commentary on Volume One*, by Henry Knight Miller. Princeton U.P. pp. xv+474. $10. £4.

volume of the *Miscellanies*, and these comparatively minor works are discussed with great thoroughness in terms of their literary and ideational background, their relationship to the major works, and their intrinsic literary quality. But Miller is never lost in the minutiae of the subject. His study is guided by two assumptions: first, that 'comedy is among the most profound of human activities', and that the book should contribute to an understanding of Fielding's comic view of life. He concludes that 'the measure of his comedy is that it could embrace [the sadder truths of human nature] and yet remain a yea-saying acceptance of life and of the fascinating, pathetic, amusing and damnable nature of man'. Secondly, Miller assumes that 'Fielding holds a high place amongst the world's major writers', and that this justifies—indeed makes imperative—a scrupulous attention to his total output. When one realizes 'the care with which his minor pieces were constructed and the attention to technique that marked them . . . the implications for his larger and greater works are surely obvious'. The volume is a valuable introduction, not only to the *Miscellanies*, but to Fielding's whole moral and literary world.

In *Fielding's Art of Fiction*[34] Maurice Johnson uses the method of close textual analysis to examine Fielding's technique in *Shamela* and the major novels. He is particularly interested in Fielding's use of parody and structural analogy, and he provides excellent commentaries on, for example, the Dedication of *Shamela* compared with that of Middleton's *Life of Cicero*, or, on a broader scale, the relationship between *Amelia* and the *Aeneid*. There is a useful examination of some recurrent motifs—for example, the

various uses to which Sophia's muff is put in *Tom Jones*—and Johnson does a good deal to show how successful Fielding is in his handling of detail. But the book suffers from patchiness: the chapter on Fielding's theory of the novel is somewhat pedestrian, while, at the opposite extreme, the attempt to establish Tom as 'a comic Hamlet' remains high-flown when all has been said. There are many good things in the book, but it does not completely live up to the promise of its title.

Claude E. Jones has edited two separate volumes of Fielding's minor works during the year. *The Female Husband*,[35] a sensational account of a notable case of Lesbianism, together with *The Masquerade* and four Epilogues, appears in the English Reprints Series, and *The Lovers Assistant, or, New Art of Love*[36] is edited for the Augustan Reprint Society. The choice of copy text for the latter volume is severely criticized in *PQ*.

There have been several articles on Fielding, and they may conveniently be taken in the order of the canon. In 'Joseph Andrews: Clothing and Concretization of Character' (*Discourse*) William A. Freedman discusses Fielding's deft exploitation of 'the dubious convention that clothes make the man'. Miriam Allott argues, in 'A Note on Fielding's Mr. Square' (*MLR*), that Cross and Homes Dudden's identification of Square with the Salisbury deist Thomas Chubb is inadequate. 'In *Tom Jones* . . . Fielding epitomizes the main arguments in the deist controversy . . . and he seeks,

[34] *Fielding's Art of Fiction: Eleven Essays on 'Shamela', 'Joseph Andrews', 'Tom Jones', and 'Amelia'*, by Maurice Johnson. Pennsylvania U.P. and O.U.P. pp. 182. $5. 40s.

[35] *The Female Husband and Other Writings*, ed. by Claude E. Jones. (English Reprints Series, 17.) Liverpool U.P. pp. xi+54. 12s. 6d.
[36] *The Lovers Assistant, or, New Art of Love (1760)*, ed. with an Introduction by Claude E. Jones. (Augustan Reprint Society, No. 89.) Los Angeles: Clarke Memorial Library, University of California. pp. iii+36. For members.

through the positive and salutary human values of his story, to combat the aridity and moral confusion which the depressing controversy left in its wake.' In this design Square's role is important, and more complex than the conventional assumption would suggest. Earl Tannenbaum has 'A Note on *Tom Jones* and the Man of the Hill' (*College Language Association Journal*) in which he explores the relationship between the Man of the Hill episode and the rest of the novel. There is an extraordinary article on 'Summer, Winter, Spring, and Autumn in *Tom Jones*' (*MLN*) in which Peter B. Murray attempts to track down seasonal symbolism through the surnames and imagery of the book. Tom emerges unexpectedly as 'the natural son of the unnatural mating of summer and winter'. In a note on Fielding's continental reputation, 'Was There a Temporary Suppression of *Tom Jones* in France?' (*MLN*), B. P. Jones argues that the importance of the *Arrêt* against the book ought not to be exaggerated. 'It certainly does not appear to have held up the sale of two large editions of the novel, or in any way to have affected its reputation in France.' In a long and valuable paper on '*Vanity Fair* and *Amelia*: Thackeray in the Perspective of the Eighteenth Century' (*MP*) E. D. H. Johnson estimates the extent of Thackeray's debt to *Amelia*, and provides an extended comparison of the two novels, particularly in relation to the treatment of character and the moral basis of the satire on society. William G. Lane has studied 'Relationships Between Some of Fielding's Major and Minor Works' (*BUSE*). In an article dealing with *The True Patriot, The Covent-Garden Journal, A Journey from this World to the Next*, and *The Journal of a Voyage to Lisbon*, he shows how 'certain elements of Fielding's work are illuminated and enlarged by a reading of various repre-

sentative minor pieces'. New light on a facet of Fielding's biography is provided by William B. Coley in 'Henry Fielding's "Lost" Law Book' (*MLN*). Evidence from advertisements for *An Institute of the Pleas of the Crown* by Henry Fielding suggests that the novelist's account of his law labours in the preface to *David Simple* is accurate, and that the 'train of Melancholy Accidents' said to have succeeded his wife's death was not so overwhelming as has been believed. Also to be noted is 'Fielding and Mandeville: The "War Against Virtue" ' (*Criticism*), by Leroy W. Smith.

Finally *Joseph Andrews* and *Shamela* have been edited in an extremely useful paperback by Martin C. Battestin.[37] There is a long introduction which describes the clash between Richardson and Fielding and discusses Fielding's moral and literary standards. The notes are well selected and helpful for the student.

Richardson has not provoked any major criticism this year but there are some articles to report. In 'Richardson and Wit' (*Books*) Charles Peake argues for 'recognition of the powerful intelligence displayed in the novels'. This intelligence is examined in passages where Richardson 'distinguishes and evaluates the varieties of wit, and examines the social, temperamental, and purposive factors which produce and condition them'. J. Chalker's ' "Virtue Rewarded": the Sexual Theme in Richardson's *Pamela*' (*The Literary Half-Yearly*) discusses the literary implications of the novelist's Puritan ethic; and William White's 'Samuel Richardson' (*ABC*) examines the psychological realism of his female characters. In ' "Richardsoniana" ' (*SB*)

[37] *Joseph Andrews* and *Shamela*, ed. with an Introduction and Notes by Martin C. Battestin. Boston: Houghton Mifflin Company; Cambridge: The Riverside Press. pp. xliv+370. $1.15.

T. C. Duncan Eaves and Ben D. Kimpel provide notes on a volume of printed Richardsoniana in the Forster Collection. It is established that McKillop's attribution of *Remarks on Clarissa* (1749) to Sarah Fielding is correct, and the authors point out that the volume contains a copy of Richardson's pamphlet, *Answer to the Letter of a Very Reverend and Worthy Gentleman, Objecting to the Warmth of a Particular Scene in the History of Clarissa.* Susie I. Tucker notes six 'Predatings from Samuel Richardson's "Familiar Letters"' (*NQ*); C. Pons has a note on the influence of *Pamela* and *Sir Charles Grandison* on Rousseau: 'Richardson et la *Nouvelle Héloise*' (*Ea*). Also to be mentioned is Elsbeth Nachtigall's *Die 'Memoires' der Marguerite de Valois als Quelle zu Samuel Richardsons 'Clarissa'*.[38]

The most important work on Sterne to appear for many years is Henri Fluchère's monumental study *Laurence Sterne, de l'homme à l'œuvre*.[39] Fluchère is completely at home with the contents of a bibliography which extends to thirty-six very closely printed pages; he feels an immense affection for his subject, and he sets out with the straightforward purpose of describing as clearly as he can first the author and then his work. *Tristram Shandy* is exhaustively analysed in terms of its structure, its themes, and its style, and the special problems of time and causality are given the attention they merit. The picture of Sterne's book that emerges is the reverse of 'nasty trifling', to recall a phrase that has

been applied to it. Sterne's technical innovations are all seen as serving the author's central purpose of presenting reality in all its complexity and strangeness. The cheerfulness of Sterne, Tristram, and Yorick is not irresponsible; it is a kind of *pantagruélisme* which is grounded on an unshakeable faith in human nature—not a Rousseauistic belief in natural goodness, but the certainty that life in its totality is good and that it may be truly apprehended through the comic mode of Shandeism which 'makes the wheel of life run long and cheerfully round'. This view of the book is not revolutionary, but it receives here a solidity of support which will be welcome to everyone who values Sterne's achievement.

Articles on Sterne are also numerous, and many writers have been concerned with linguistic aspects of *Tristram Shandy*. In 'Satire and *Tristram Shandy*' (*Studies in English Literature*) J. M. Stedmond sees the novel as 'one more engagement in the perpetual war between wits and dunces', and as depicting a world 'in which the mechanical means of communication are becoming ever more and more efficient—while at the same time the articulateness, the ability to communicate, is steadily declining'. Sigurd Burckhardt argues in '*Tristram Shandy*'s Law of Gravity' (*ELH*) that 'the vast system of indirections, circuitous approaches—of parables driven to the point of hyperbole' illustrates the fact that language can never communicate directly, but can only 'by indirections find directions out'. Robert J. Griffin suggests in 'Tristram Shandy and Language' (*CE*) that Tristram implicitly criticized Locke's plea for precision and careful definition by showing that 'men do not communicate just by words, or even primarily by words. Men communicate best through rapport, instinctive appreciation,

[38] *Die 'Memoires' der Marguerite de Valois als Quelle zu Samuel Richardsons 'Clarissa'*, by Elsbeth Nachtigall. (Romanistische Versuche und Vorarbeiten, 5.) Bonn: Romanishches Seminar an der Universität, 1960. pp. 140.
[39] *Laurence Sterne, de l'homme à l'œuvre: Biographie critique et essai d'interprétation de 'Tristram Shandy'*, by Henri Fluchère. Paris: Gallimard. pp. 734. 25 F.

inarticulate sensings—sympathy and sentiment.' Dealing with the same problem William Bowman Piper writes on 'Tristram Shandy's Digressive Artistry' (*Studies in English Literature*), and concludes that the 'digressions are the result of [Tristram's] great concern for his audience. He has produced virtually all of them to fulfil his different communicative obligations—to explain, to instruct, and to amuse . . . to accommodate his private life to his public situation.' The same writer's 'Tristram Shandy's Tragi-comical Testimony' (*Criticism*) is also to be noted. Charles Parish discusses 'The Nature of Mr. Tristram Shandy, Author' (*BUSE*). Sterne's problem is to write about a man writing, to present 'the mind of a man re-creating its individuality so that we may know it'. The effects of this on the conduct of the story are considered. In 'New Light on Sterne' (*MLN*) L. P. Curtis prints Sterne's earliest known letter (to John Dealtary). This shows Sterne 'dejected by a frustrating love-affair—at a time when he was supposedly courting his future wife'. The article also contains two letters from Dr. Thomas Newton to Dealtary on the early reception of *Tristram Shandy*, especially amongst the clergy.

There are only two articles on Smollett to be noted this year. 'Fire-Scenes in Richardson's *Clarissa* and Smollett's *Humphrey Clinker*: A Study of a Literary Relationship in the Structure of the Novel' (*TSE*), by Philip Mahone Griffith, suggests that Smollett both parodied Richardson and learnt from his practice. Sheridan Baker's '*Humphrey Clinker* as Comic Romance' (*Papers of the Michigan Academy of Science, Arts, and Letters*) is also to be listed.

Winifred Gérin's *The Young Fanny Burney*[40] is written, according to the publisher, 'principally for the girl in

her late teens'. It is based on the *Diaries* and is designed to show how Fanny Burney 'set about becoming a successful novelist against countless odds'. In a palpitating style a dramatic re-creation of the Burney household and the conditions under which *Evelina* was written is attempted, and the story of Fanny's career is carried up to the point where she acknowledges her authorship. The book is attractively illustrated.

Oscar Sherwin's *Goldy*[41] gives us an enthusiastic account of Goldsmith's career. Sherwin's method is to provide a narrative liberally interspersed with extracts from Goldsmith's writings: 'I have quoted, paraphrased, and included in the body of the text the most winning part of his writing. Scholars will know where, and others may not. But does it matter?' In accordance with this somewhat cavalier attitude we are given a present-tense narrative in the feverish, larger-than-life style of modern popular biography. The result is undoubtedly vivid—and the book uses so much contemporary material that it is bound to give a very immediate picture of the eighteenth-century literary scene—but the danger is that the great figures of the age so often seem little more than eccentric popular entertainers.

There are only two articles on Goldsmith. Michael E. Adelstein writes on 'Duality of Theme in *The Vicar of Wakefield*' (*CE*), arguing that Goldsmith changed his theme from prudence to fortitude in the course of writing the novel, and that in this process 'the central character was transformed from an innocent simpleton to a courageous, resolute hero'. Dr. Primrose, Part I, is not the same individual as Dr. Primrose, Part II. Morris Golden discusses 'The Time

[40] *The Young Fanny Burney*, by Winifred Gérin. Nelson. pp. xi+132. 12s. 6d.

[41] *Goldy: The Life and Times of Oliver Goldsmith*, by Oscar Sherwin. New York: Twayne Publishers Inc. pp. 367. $6.

of Writing of the *Vicar of Wakefield*' (*BNYPL*). He attempts, 'by citing plot devices, verbal parallels, and ideas which are unmistakably the same in the *Vicar* and in other works by Goldsmith whose dates are known, to arrive at some stable chronology for the novel', and he concludes that Goldsmith worked steadily on the book from about 1759 to the autumn of 1762, and that he probably did some touching up in 1763.

Beckford studies are pausing after the appearance of Parreaux's fine book last year, but there are three items to report. Alexander Boyd's 'William Beckford of Fonthill' (*Yale University Library Gazette*) is concerned with Beckford's non-literary achievements, the building of Fonthill and his activities as a collector, particularly his liberal recognition of contemporary talent. Karl F. Thompson in 'Beckford, Byron, and Henley' (*Ea*) puts forward the unexpected point of view that Henley, usually presented as a 'dingy, malevolent figure', was partially justified, by Beckford's dilatoriness and the amount of work that he himself had put into the translation and notes, in publishing *Vathek* anonymously. Some of Thompson's points are answered by André Parreaux in a Note. For Rayner Heppenstall Henley committed a 'reverberating . . . enormity'.[42] He discusses the Episodes of *Vathek* and their relation to the novel itself in 'The Palace of Subterranean Fire', and offers a biographical interpretation.

But the year's major studies on gothic writing appear when one turns to Walpole and 'Monk' Lewis. In the A. W. Mellon Lectures, now beautifully printed, Wilmarth Sheldon Lewis gives us the distillation of his lifetime

interest in Horace Walpole.[43] The six lectures deal with 'Family', 'Friends', 'Politics', 'Strawberry Hill', 'Lord Orford's Works', and 'The Letters'. Lewis's complete command of the vast amount of material available, and his perfectly adjusted sympathy for the subject, give his work an authority which is sustained with perfect lucidity and ease of manner. There are his definitive thoughts on Walpole. 'I don't expect', he tells us, 'to write a longer book on Horace Walpole.' The volume is copiously illustrated with portraits, manuscripts, and prints, and these lend excellent support to the text. The whole book is a notable achievement.

During the year two more volumes of the Yale edition of Walpole's *Correspondence* have appeared.[44] They show the variety of his friendships (from Lord Lincoln to Hannah More), and are particularly valuable in throwing light on his twenties, during the period after his return from the Grand Tour. A very vivid picture emerges of the wealthy social circle in which he moved, but, as Lewis says, 'although his quickness and gaiety and flair for political intrigue might have made him well suited for the life they led, he was too thin-skinned and emotionally

[42] *The Fourfold Tradition: Notes on the French and English literatures with some ethnological and historical asides*, by Rayner Heppenstall. Barrie and Rockliff. pp. 280. 25s.

[43] *Horace Walpole*, by Wilmarth Sheldon Lewis. *The A. W. Mellon Lectures in the Fine Arts, 1960*. Hart-Davis and Pantheon Books. pp. xxvii+215. 63s. $6.50.

[44] *Horace Walpole's Correspondence with George Selwyn, Lord Lincoln, Sir Charles Hanbury Williams, Henry Fox, Richard Edgcumbe*, ed. by W. S. Lewis and Robert A. Smith; being vol. 30 of the Yale Edition of *Horace Walpole's Correspondence*. Yale U.P. and O.U.P. pp. xlviii+479. $15. £6. *Horace Walpole's Correspondence with Hannah More, Lady Browne, Lady George Lennox, Lady Mary Coke, Anne Pitt, Lady Harvey, Lady Suffolk, Mary Hamilton (Mrs. John Dickenson)*, ed. by W. S. Lewis, Robert A. Smith, and Charles H. Bennett; being vol. 31 of the Yale Edition of *Horace Walpole's Correspondence*. Yale U.P. and O.U.P. pp. xl+528. $15. £6.

vulnerable for it'. The letters to Lord Lincoln are printed for the first time, and show that he was one of Walpole's most intimate early friends. The second volume is devoted to correspondence with women, and here, especially in the letters to Hannah More, we see his good nature and wit in their most attractive form.

Louis F. Peck has written the first full-length biography of 'Monk' Lewis to appear since Mrs. Cornwall Baron-Wilson's *Life and Correspondence* of 1839.[45] Using diaries, memoirs, contemporary correspondence, and letters by Lewis that have appeared since that time, Peck gives a sympathetic account of his subject, dealing not only with his literary career, but also at some length with his humanitarian reforms in the treatment of slaves when he inherited two estates in Jamaica. There is an admirable account of *The Monk*'s contemporary reception and a discussion, both descriptive and critical, of Lewis's work for the theatre (mainly important in the history of taste) and his ballad collection. The volume also contains selected letters, including some previously unpublished.

Three more items complete this account of work on the novelists. In 'Two English Editions of *La Nouvelle Héloïse*, 1761' (*MLR*) G. G. Barber concludes that four editions of this work were available in England by the end of March 1761, two French and two English. D. S. Bland discusses the function of scene description in the novel in 'Endangering the Reader's Neck: Background Description in the Novel' (*Criticism*). Finally should be listed the appearance (noticed more fully in Chapter I) of Andrew Block's *The English Novel, 1740–1850*.[46]

(*f*) The most important article on Boswell is Mary Margaret Stewart's 'Boswell's Denominational Dilemma' (*PMLA*). Boswell objected to the services, traditions, and doctrines of the Presbyterian denomination, and received more satisfaction from Anglican and Catholic forms of worship. But he supported the Presbyterians from patriotic and filial motives. A study of his religious attitudes shows his loyalty to the traditions of his country, and also why he 'found life in Scotland irritating and confining'. Harlan W. Hamilton points out in 'Boswell's Suppression of a Paragraph in *Rambler* 60' (*MLN*) that, in quoting from this number of the *Rambler* at the beginning of the *Life*, Boswell omitted Johnson's strictures against the accumulation of unimportant detail, an omission that is significant in relation to his own practice. H. A. Morgan's 'Boswell on the Grand Tour' (*New Rambler*) describes Boswell's meetings with Rousseau and Voltaire; Frederick S. Kiley writes on 'Boswell's Literary Art in the *London Journal*' (*CE*), and Clyde E. Dankert discusses, in a necessarily hypothetical manner, the probable relationship between 'Adam Smith and James Boswell' (*QQ*). Sister M. Victorine Verosky's 'John Walker's One Clergyman' (*NQ*) identifies the clergyman that John Walker told Boswell he had taught as John Milner, a Catholic priest. Some details of Walker's life are added. Finally, there is to be noted Arthur R. Huseboe's 'Boswell's Broken Resolutions' (*North Dakota Quarterly*).

The year saw the appearance of the third volume of *The Correspondence of Edmund Burke*,[47] which deals with the

[45] *A Life of Matthew G. Lewis*, by Louis F. Peck. Harvard U.P. pp. ix+331. $7.75.

[46] *The English Novel, 1740–1850: A Catalogue Including Prose Romances, Short Stories, and Translations of Foreign Fiction*, by Andrew Block, with Introductions by John Crow and Ernest A. Baker. New and Revised Edition. Dawson's. pp. xv+349. £7. 10s. (See Chapter I, note 33.)

[47] *The Correspondence of Edmund Burke*, Vol. III: July 1774–June 1778, ed. by George H. Guttridge. C.U.P. and Chicago U.P. pp. xxvi+479. 84s. $12.

period from July 1774 to June 1778. The volume contains over 300 letters, of which nearly half are printed for the first time, and of which 228 are by Burke. As in the second volume, the correspondence with Rockingham is of great importance: 'their relationship was a subtle one of mutual respect and affection tinged with careful observance of differences in rank and authority'. The Duke of Portland also appears frequently, and a new theme enters with the development of Burke's connexion with Bristol. The correspondence with Champion is a main source for the development of Burke's relationship—a rather aloof one on his part—with his new constituents.

This relationship forms the subject of a monograph by P. T. Underdown, *Bristol and Burke*,[48] in which the story of his gradual estrangement and final rejection is clearly told. Another book to be listed is Stephen R. Graubard's *Burke, Disraeli, and Churchill: The Politics of Perseverance*,[49] a popular work containing a brief life of Burke and concerned particularly with his political activities and ideas.

Several articles deal with Burke's thought. Russell Kirk in 'Burke, Providence, and Archaism' (*Sew*) argues that it is wrong to see Burke as what Toynbee calls an *archaist*, a man 'obdurately devoted to a past or passing mode of life'. On the contrary, 'the just and prudent statesman, in any era, must deal with prevailing opinions and customs as he finds them—though he ought to act in the light of enduring *principles*'. John C. Weston, Jr., has a long article on 'Edmund Burke's View of History' (*Review of Politics*). He considers Burke's view of history in relation to the concepts of Progress, the Divine Will, and 'the status of human nature', and then applies general conclusions on these topics to the discussion of Burke's attitude to the Constitution and the French Revolution. In 'The Basis of Burke's Political Conservatism' (*Modern Age*) Peter J. Stanlis stresses the importance of the idea that 'the principles of true politics are those of morality enlarged'; and in 'Burke and the Sensibility of Rousseau' (*Thought*) the same author discusses Burke's attitude to the concept of universal benevolence. Sensibility might lead to love of man in general without extending to the imperfect individual.

Burke's reputation is dealt with in a chapter of *Historical Studies of Rhetoric and Rhetoricians*.[50] 'The Contemporary Reception of Edmund Burke's Speaking', by Donald Cross Bryant (a reworking for this volume of the author's contribution to *Studies in Honour of Frederick W. Shipley*, 1942), is based on 'two hundred or so different critiques and observations, formal and casual, from over fifty persons'. Burke's faults as a speaker—inopportune long-windedness—are balanced against 'the magnitude of his materials and the fire of his imagination'. In 'Edmund Burke and Thomas Wilkinson' (*NQ*) H. Rossiter Smith prints letters from Thomas Wilkinson which discuss Burke and describe a visit to the trial of Warren Hastings. Finally three items are to be recorded from *Burke Newsletter*: J. S. Ross Hoffman writes on 'Tocqueville and Burke'; William B. Todd on 'The Burke Bibliography: Unresolved Problems'; and John C. Weston, Jr., on 'Burke Manuscripts in the Osborn Collection at Yale'.

[48] *Bristol and Burke*, by P. T. Underdown. Bristol University: Bristol Branch of the Historical Association. pp. 20. 2s.

[49] *Burke, Disraeli, and Churchill: The Politics of Perseverance*, by Stephen R. Graubard. Harvard U.P. and O.U.P. pp. 262. $5. 40s.

[50] *Historical Studies of Rhetoric and Rhetoricians*, ed. by Raymond F. Howes. Cornell U.P. and O.U.P. pp. xiv+446. $6.75. 54s.

With the appearance of *Gibbon's Journey from Geneva to Rome*[51] the publication of Gibbon's Journals, begun in 1929 by D. M. Low and continued since the war by Georges A. Bonnard, is complete. On this part of his tour Gibbon was accompanied by William Guise, and the editor has been able to use Guise's *Journal* to fill in occasional gaps in Gibbon and to provide valuable comparative material. The detailed but unobtrusive commentary adds greatly to the value of the text. The volume gives a very clear picture of Gibbon's tastes and interests, particularly in the fine arts. It is a well-illustrated volume. Also to be noted is D. M. Low's 'Edward Gibbon and the Johnsonian Circle' (*New Rambler*, 1960).

Two items are to be noticed on Adam Smith. In 'Adam Smith—Man of Letters' (*TSLL*) Clyde E. Dankert discusses the range of Smith's literary interests and his critical opinions which were conventionally neo-classical. Erik Erämetsä is concerned with Smith's influence on German in *Adam Smith Als Mittler Englisch–Deutscher Spracheinflüsse*.[52]

James Noxon's 'Hume's Opinion of Critics' (*Journal of Aesthetics and Art Criticism*) is misleadingly titled. It is an analysis of Hume's essay *Of the Standard of Taste* intended to show that in aesthetic matters Hume avoided the extreme subjectivist position sometimes attributed to him by the modern critic. Hugh Trevor-Roper, in 'David Hume as a Historian' (*Listener*), gives a lively account of the controversies

that the *History of England* aroused. Three articles of a predominantly philosophical interest can be simply noted: Antony Flew's 'Did Hume Ever Read Berkeley?' (*Journal of Philosophy*); Philip P. Wiener's 'Did Hume ever Read Berkeley?' (ibid.)—a comment on Flew; and E. J. Furlong's 'Imagination in Hume's *Treatise* and *Enquiry concerning the Human Understanding*' (ibid.).

Several articles on critical ideas and the history of taste can be conveniently grouped at this point. John L. Mahoney's 'Akenside and Shaftesbury: The Influence of Philosophy on English Romantic Theory' (*Discourse*) suggests that Akenside took certain doctrines from Shaftesbury—the theory of benevolence, the identification of truth, goodness, and beauty, and the concept of the moral sense—and shaped them into the beginnings of Romantic theory. Robert Marsh writes on 'Akenside and Addison: The Problem of Ideational Debt' (*MP*). Whereas Addison claims no 'moralistic' purpose for his essays on 'The Pleasures of the Imagination', Akenside regards his poem as 'an instrument of moral and religious, as well as "aesthetic" education'. There is also a fundamental difference of philosophic method. Addison 'works with simple literal terms and definitions'. Akenside's method is 'dialectical and hierarchical', and he attempts to relate the pleasures of the imagination to 'the ultimate, higher forms of reality'.

George B. Schick demonstrates, in 'Joseph Warton's Critical Essays in his *Virgil*' (*NQ*), that in all four essays Warton shows 'a considerable use of the precise words of others'—Addison, Le Bossu, Rapin—to set forth his own critical position.

John Waite Bowers provides 'A Comparative Criticism of Hugh Blair's Essay on Taste' (*Quarterly Journal of Speech*), and suggests that

---

[51] *Gibbon's Journey from Geneva to Rome: His Journal from 20 April to 2 October 1764*, ed. by Georges A. Bonnard. Nelson. pp. xxiv+268. 50s.
[52] *Adam Smith Als Mittler Englisch–Deutscher Spracheinflüsse* (*The Wealth of Nations*), by Erik Erämetsä. (Annales Academiae Scientiarum Fennicae: Series B 125, 1.) Helsinki: Tiedeakatemia. pp. 116. 5.50 mk.

Blair's weakness is his 'failure to commit himself to any specific origin for taste'. He denies the importance of sensory experience and the supernatural, and falls back on an ill-defined *sensus communis*.

In the Arundell Esdaile Memorial Lecture for 1960 Sir Sydney Roberts gives an account of *Richard Farmer (1735–1797)*.[53] His work as a university teacher, librarian, and book-collector is surveyed, and there is a discussion of his *Essay on the Learning of Shakespeare*. 'Farmer's contribution to Shakespearian scholarship lay in his unique knowledge of the literary background against which Shakespeare worked . . . in 1767 the work was a landmark and it still remains as something more than an antiquarian exercise.'

'Colin against Art Again' (*NQ*), by Jim Corder, shows that Spenser was used in Mason's *Essay on Design in Gardening* as an authority to support an informal landscaping style. Two other articles on general aesthetic topics are relevant here: Paul Zucker's 'Ruins—An Aesthetic Hybrid' (*Journal of Aesthetics and Art Criticism*), and 'Le premier renouveau gothique et la sensibilité anglaise au milieu du dix-huitième siècle' (*Ea*), by M. Lévy.

Turning to questions of moral taste, Magdi Wahba's 'Madame de Genlis in England' (*CL*) may be noted. Translations of Madame de Genlis's works into English are surveyed and her reputation discussed. She achieved popularity because she adopted 'the paraphernalia of Rousseau's educational methods but attacked his principles'. This is an interesting essay in the history of manners and educational ideas. Finally there is Mrs. A. M. D. Henderson-Howat's 'Christian Litera-

ture in the Eighteenth Century' (*Historical Magazine of the Protestant Episcopal Church*), which provides notes on devotional writers who were associated with the early years of the S.P.C.K.

There has been little work on periodical literature this year, but there is a substantial article by Edward A. Bloom on 'Neoclassic "Paper Wars" for a Free Press' (*MLR*). He gives an account of the struggle for a free press from the expiration of the Licensing Act (1694) to the Junius affair, with particular emphasis on events in the later period—the prosecution of Wilkes following the publication of *North Briton* 45, the Junius prosecutions, and the 'public interest in individual liberties' and the advancement of free expression which these cases brought about. He concludes that the 'sensationalism and abuse' of the pamphleteers was a 'small price to pay for the ultimate ideal'. Jack W. Marken's 'William Godwin and the *Political Herald and Review*' (*BNYPL*) gives a full description of the *Political Herald and Review*, discusses Godwin's connexion with it and his contributions to it, and attempts to identify the contributions of others to the magazine. In 'The Politics of the *Critical Review*, 1756–1817' (*DUJ*) Derek Roper writes on changes in the political outlook of the *Review*. Roger Lonsdale writes on 'William Bewley and The *Monthly Review*: a Problem of Attribution' (*PBSA*). On the basis initially of a letter from William Bewley to Dr. Burney, Lonsdale corrects attributions to Bewley in Nangle's *The Monthly Review . . . Indexes of Contributors and Articles*. Three other bibliographical items may be noted: William B. Todd's 'A Bibliographical Account of *The Annual Register*, 1758–1825' (*Lib*); Sidney Roberts's 'Bibliography of "Estimate Brown"' (*BC*); and D. G. Neill's 'Samuel Parr's "Notes on Rapin's *Dissertation on Whigs and*

[53] *Richard Farmer (1735–1797)*, by Sir Sydney Roberts. A public lecture delivered at The Library Association, Chaucer House, Malet Place, London, W.C.1, on 12 Oct. 1960. The Library Association. pp. 16. 2s. 6d.

Tories" ' (*BC*). To be entered here also is R. D. Harlan's 'William Strahan's American Book Trade, 1744–76' (*Library Quarterly*), an interesting article on the export of books in the period. There is only a single item on 'Junius' this year: 'The Twistleton Junius: A Suppressed Passage of Junius Restored' (*NQ*), by Francesco Cordasco.

Three items which are primarily of interest to historians can be mentioned very briefly at this point. L. M. Angus-Butterworth's *Ten Master Historians*[54] includes chapters on Hume, Adam Smith, Goldsmith, and Gibbon. D. B. Horn discusses 'Some Scottish Writers of History in the Eighteenth Century' (*Scottish Historical Review*); and Kent R. Newmyer writes on 'John Andrew's *History of the War with America*: A further Note on Eighteenth-Century Plagiarism' (*PBSA*).

(*g*) Work on the drama this year is dominated by Kalman A. Burnim's *David Garrick, Director*,[55] an extremely lively and well-documented account of the Drury Lane theatre during Garrick's long management. In the first five chapters copious quotation from contemporary sources is used to give a general picture of Garrick's aims and methods—his financial arrangements, his choice of plays, methods of casting, rehearsal and theatrical discipline, developments in the use of costume, scenery and staging technique. Here a great deal of varied material is successfully reduced to order, and a very clear picture emerges of the theatre in Garrick's day. This general account is followed by detailed analyses, depending on the evidence of prompt-books and contemporary journalism, of four Shakespearian productions, *Macbeth*,

Romeo and Juliet, *King Lear*, and *Hamlet*; and finally, to balance the account with a comedy, there is a chapter on *The Provoked Wife*. The book is admirably illustrated.

The Letters of David Garrick and Georgiana, Countess Spencer, 1759–1779[56] have been edited for the Roxburghe Club. Virtually all the letters belong to Garrick's retirement, so that they contain little about the stage or the literary world. But they are informative about Garrick himself and about his gay and exuberant relationship with his correspondent.

Four articles have to do with the theatre. David G. Spencer's 'Gentleman John and Jack Plausible' (*NQ*) distinguishes between two actors called John Palmer, one of whom figures in Churchill's *Rosciad*. In 'Mrs. Frances Brooke: Dramatic Critic' (*Theatre Notebook*) Gwendolyn B. Needham describes the dramatic criticism which Mrs. Brooke published in *The Old Maid* under the pseudonym of Miss Mary Singleton. Garrick and Spranger Barry are compared as Lear, and Mrs. Brooke complains at their use of Tate's 'wretched alteration' of the play. Brocard Sewell's 'George Anne Bellamy' (*Wiseman Review*) is a brief life of the actress based mainly upon her own *Apology*, and designed particularly to do justice to her adherence to the Catholic faith in which she was brought up. John Hall Stewart uses contemporary periodicals and newspapers to give an account of 'The French Revolution on the Dublin Stage, 1790–94' (*Journal of the Royal Society of Antiquaries of Ireland*).

As regards the plays themselves there is little to report. Thomas B. Stroup has, for the first time, edited *The Cestus: A Mask*. It is an imitation,

[54] *Ten Master Historians*, by L. M. Angus-Butterworth. Aberdeen U.P. and Dufour. pp. x+182. 30s. $6.

[55] *David Garrick, Director*, by Kalman A. Burnim, with a Foreword by Geo. Winchester Stone, Jr. Pittsburgh U.P. pp. xiv+234. $5.

[56] *Letters of David Garrick and Georgiana, Countess Spencer, 1759–1779*, ed. by Earl Spencer and Christopher Dobson. The Roxburghe Club. pp. 175.

of modest literary value, of Milton and Spenser. The editor dates it between 1783 and 1791 on the evidence of the hand, and suggests that Thomas Warton may have been concerned in writing it, but there is no decisive evidence of authorship. Edgar V. Roberts writes on 'Eighteenth-Century Ballad Opera: The Contribution of Henry Fielding' (*Drama Survey*). J. R. de J. Jackson discusses 'The Importance of Witty Dialogue in *The School for Scandal*' (*MLN*). He analyses draft material of the play in order to show that 'Sheridan constructed his plays around witty sayings, that he was prepared to ignore flaws of plot or character in order to preserve favourite aphorisms intact—in short, that his eye was upon dialogue rather than action'. Finally may be noted: 'A Newly Discovered Play of Robert Merry, Written in America' (*Manuscripts*), and 'The Wonders of Derbyshire: A Spectacular Eighteenth-Century Travelogue' (*Theatre Survey*).

(*h*) From Japan there is to be recorded a volume of *Essays on Thomas Gray* by Rintaro Fukuhara.[57] Most of them are in Japanese, but there are five in English, including a discussion of the three extant manuscripts of the *Elegy* and 'Thomas Gray's Elegy: Its Scheme of Composition', which develops a theory that the poem may have been radically revised, and perhaps to some extent spoilt, during the long period between its inception and publication.

J. Raymond Hendrickson and H. W. Starr make three brief contributions on Gray to *NQ*. 'Two Poems Attributed to Gray' argues that *The Poetical Rondeau* ought not to be attributed to Gray, and discusses the dating of *Lines on Dr. Robert South*. 'The Final Couplet of Gray's *Candidate*' offers anonymity to anyone who can offer an

appropriately bawdy rhyme for the final omitted word of that poem; and, finally, there is a discussion of 'A Mistaken Reading in Gray's "Vah, Tenero" '. In 'Thomas Gray's Christmas Piece, 1727' (*Princeton University Library Chronicle*) Charles Ryskamp describes and comments on a Christmas broadside penned by Gray at Eton and exhibiting already something of his moral preoccupations. Also to be listed is 'Gray's Cat and Pope's Belinda' (*TSL*), by Eleanor N. Hutchens.

There is a substantial article 'On William Collins' *Ode to Evening*' (*EC*) by Merle E. Brown. She argues that for Collins evening 'is the poetic moment, it is the moment of contemplative creative activity, in which the most violent emotion still quivers under the intense gaze of the innocent eye of the poet'. The *Ode* is analysed from this point of view. Winifred Lynskey's 'Collins' *Ode on the Poetical Character*, 60' (*Ex*) is a brief explication of the opening of the antistrophe of Collins's poem.

Yvor Winters provides a long discussion of 'The Poetry of Charles Churchill' (*Poetry*). Winters first attempts a general survey of Churchill's work and a definition of his historical position. He inherits both the strictly rational poetic method of the Renaissance and also the associative method derived from Milton. A detailed analysis of *The Dedication* then shows how Churchill makes use of most of the best elements in preceding tradition, and avoids nearly all the worst. Elements of association are 'carefully controlled by a plan which is rationally apprehensible, and the transitions are never obscure'. The poem presents a 'unified exhibition of the psychology of evil'. In 'Charles Churchill as Man of Feeling: a Forgotten Poem by Mackenzie' (*MLR*) Richard E. Quaintance, Jr., reprints verses by Henry Mackenzie in defence of Churchill published in

[57] *Essays on Thomas Gray*, by Rintaro Fukuhara. Tokyo: Kenkyusha, 1960. pp. 280. Yen. 480.

the Edinburgh *Advertiser*, and discusses their biographical significance.

H. J. Haden, in 'A Shenstone Draft Letter' (*NQ*), shows how much care Shenstone took over letter-writing.

Smart has attracted a good deal of criticism this year. Most important is *Poor Kit Smart*[58] by Christopher Devlin, a sensitive and sympathetic biography. Taking as his starting-point the fact that Smart was dominated by the force of religion, Father Devlin attempts, in the role of 'spiritual adviser after the fact', to analyse 'his ideas and impulses, mystical or maniacal or whatever they were'. He discusses Smart's spiritual life in terms of the classical divisions of spiritual experience, the Purgative Way, the Illuminative Way and the Unitive Way, and, although this approach may seem antipathetic to many readers when applied to so wayward a man as Smart, it enables Father Devlin to give a very clear account of the preoccupations (including the implications of the fact that his wife was a Catholic) which made Smart allow himself 'to be driven out in a loud and turbulent manner to preach to others and to assume the guises of an arrogant pseudo-prophet'. The book has the great merit of concentrating on the central problems of Smart's life, and the picture that emerges is a convincing one.

Geoffrey Grigson's *Christopher Smart*,[59] in the 'Writers and their Work' series, gives a useful and very clear introduction to the poetry, including much perceptive analysis of individual passages. Grigson stresses Smart's affinities with seventeenth-century religious poets, especially Traherne.

Also to be recorded is an edition of

A Song to David prepared by J. B. Broadbent.[60]

In an article on 'Christopher Smart's Knowledge of Hebrew' (*SP*) Charles Parish concludes, from a close study of punning in *Jubilate Agno*, that 'there is no doubt about Smart's knowledge of Hebrew', and that the poem contains a good deal of as yet unrecognized wit. K. M. Rogers has a highly recondite paper, 'The Pillars of the Lord: Some Sources of *A Song to David*' (*PQ*), in which possible sources discussed include the *Talmud*, the Cabala, and Masonic lore. Roger Lonsdale contributes to our bibliographical knowledge in 'Christopher Smart's First Publication in English' (*RES*). He establishes *To Idleness* (*Gentleman's Magazine*, May 1745) as the earliest publication, and also notes texts of two poems previously thought to have remained unpublished in Smart's lifetime—*To Lyce* and *On a Dull Malignant Poet*. There is correspondence by Reginald Horrox and W. H. Bond in *TLS* on a crux in *Jubilate Agno*, 'X Equals —?', and by Geoffrey Grigson on 'Three Lines in *A Song to David*'.

There are only two items to record on Crabbe. W. K. Thomas contributes a general appreciation of the poetry, 'The Flavour of Crabbe' (*DR*); and Thomas B. Brumbaugh prints a sermon, dating probably from 1814 during the poet's residence at Trowbridge, Wiltshire: 'George Crabbe: An Unpublished Sermon' (*NQ*).

A. B. Friedman contributes a major study of a predominantly eighteenth-century subject in *The Ballad Revival: Studies in the Influence of Popular on Sophisticated Poetry*.[61] The centre of

---

[58] *Poor Kit Smart*, by Christopher Devlin. Hart-Davis. pp. 200. 16s. $3.75.

[59] *Christopher Smart*, by Geoffrey Grigson. Longmans for the British Council and the National Book League. pp. 44. 2s. 6d.

[60] *A Song to David*, ed. by J. B. Broadbent. Rampant Lions Press. Distributors Bodley Head. Limited Edition, 1960. pp. 40. £2. 12s. 6d.

[61] *The Ballad Revival: Studies in the Influence of Popular on Sophisticated Poetry*, by A. B. Friedman. Chicago U.P. and C.U.P. pp. vii+376. $6. 48s.

this widely ranging book lies in the chapters on attitudes to the ballad before and after the publication of Percy's *Reliques*. The author is firmly opposed to the romantic-precursor line of thought and is concerned to show, for example, how Addison used classical arguments to champion popular poetry. Similarly he stresses the ambiguity of the word *ballad* itself. The modern tendency is 'to emphasize the ballad's mediaeval character. For this reason, in virtually all standard bibliographies and literary histories, the entire ballad revival is treated as a sub-head of Augustan mediaevalism.' But for Burke, no less than for Addison, the remarkable fact about the ballad was its hold on the common people, and, accordingly, it was in relation to such topics as the unity of taste or the appeal to the natural and simple that the ballad figured in neo-classical literary criticism. From this critical basis Friedman discusses Percy's selection of ballads and his presentation of the text. Despite the book's sub-title it is this account of the ballad revival itself that is of the greatest value. The chapters on 'Ballad Imitations' and 'The Difficulties of Imitation' are comparatively thin.

The Correspondence of Thomas Percy and George Paton[62] is the final volume of *The Percy Letters* edited by D. N. Nicol Smith and Cleanth Brooks. The volume deals with a period when Percy, having published the *Reliques*, was trying to increase his collection of early Scots poetry, and the letters consist largely of bibliographical queries and discussions.

Two cognate items may be mentioned here. J. A. Lavin discusses 'The Source of Ramsay's *Nanny-O*' (*NQ*)

to show that the poem 'is an insipid rewriting of a ballad to suit polite eighteenth-century tastes'. Donald S. Taylor writes about 'The Authenticity of Chatterton's *Miscellanies in Prose and Verse*' (*PBSA*), and claims that 'the appearance of a poem in the *Miscellanies* is no criterion of authenticity for pieces published after 24 April 1770, when Chatterton left Bristol for London'.

Before listing work specifically devoted to Burns, David Craig's *Scottish Literature and the Scottish People, 1680–1830*[63] may conveniently be noticed. Craig's approach is sociological: 'the approach and period of this book have been framed so as to form a "social" history of literature ... always the aim has been to find the particular facts and particular passages of poetry or fiction in which the life of the people seems to reveal itself most genuinely'. The social condition of Edinburgh during the early eighteenth century is described, for example, a condition which 'recalls, not contemporary London but the London of Shakespeare and Ben Jonson'. In contrast the mid-century Edinburgh *literati* belong to the new 'polite' and fragmented culture which gradually emerged, and they were ill at ease, aware of the claims of London's more complex and integrated culture which they could neither ignore nor re-create in their own terms. From this basis of sociological analysis Craig discusses the strengths and weaknesses of Scottish vernacular poetry with particular reference to Burns. It is an independent and stimulating study.

'Narrative Irony in Robert Burns's *Tam O'Shanter*' (*MLQ*), by Richard Morton, discusses the control of ironic distance in the poem. The reader must be constantly aware of the

[62] *The Correspondence of Thomas Percy and George Paton*, ed. by A. F. Falconer. (*The Percy Letters*, ed. by D. N. Nicol Smith and Cleanth Brooks, vol. VI.) Yale U.P. and O.U.P. pp. xxvi+198. $6. 48s.

[63] *Scottish Literature and the Scottish People, 1680–1830*, by David Craig. Chatto and Windus. pp. 340. 30s.

distinction between the parts of the poem devoted to the story and the parts principally devoted to an ironic portrayal of the speaker's personality; 'the placing of a comic narrator between the events and the reader succeeds effectively in distancing and diminishing the narrative'. J. C. Maxwell notes a slightly doubtful echo in 'Burns: An Echo of *Tristram Shandy*' (*NQ*); Allan H. MacLaine discusses 'Some Echoes of Robert Fergusson in Burns's *A Mauchline Wedding*' (*NQ*), and Lucyle Werkmeister gives 'Some Account of Robert Burns and the London Newspapers, with Special Reference to the Spurious *Star* (1789)' (*BNYPL*).

There is one new edition to be recorded, *The Love Songs and Heroines of Robert Burns*,[64] in which the love-songs are interspersed with brief biographical notes about the various heroines.

As usual Blake has attracted a great deal of work. There are two book dealing primarily with his ideas. In a beautifully lucid study of *The Neoplatonism of William Blake*[65] George Mills Harper is concerned both with Blake's thought and with the broader development of ideas in the late eighteenth century. His starting-point is the work of Thomas Taylor, whose translations and commentaries made Plato and the Platonists accessible in the period. Taylor's work is discussed in the first two chapters, and Harper then suggests that 'Blake and Taylor knew so many people in common and Taylor was so widely known and talked of', that the philosopher and the poet were extremely likely to have known each other personally. The most important aspect of Taylor's work, from the poetic point of view, was his championing of 'the obscurity of the myth,

the symbol and the metaphor', and his repeated assertion that Plato 'had delivered the abstruse dogmas of his philosophy obscurely in order to conceal from the profane and vulgar eyes certain sublime truths'. Blake's essential metaphysical ideas are then discussed in chapters on 'Innate Ideas and the Theory of Reminiscence', 'The Ideal Forms', and 'The Absence of Form', and finally there are sections on specific symbols and myths. These final sections contain much detailed analysis of an extremely illuminating kind. The whole work is one to be warmly welcomed.

The Valley of Vision[66] by Peter F. Fisher (which has been edited by Northrop Frye following the author's early death in a sailing accident) attempts to place Blake in an intellectual context, 'to outline the historical background in which he lived with special reference to the history of thought as he saw it'. Blake's judgements of his age were not merely perverse, and Fisher sets out to show what Blake's standpoint was, to analyse the cultural forces in western civilization that led him to assume that 'the true creative artist or poet must also be an inspired prophet; that the social order, by its very nature, tends to restrict, and even destroy, the freedom of expression —both in life and thought—necessary for him; that this restriction takes the form of a bondage to reasonable rules of thought and conduct, ostensibly for the preservation of the civilized arts and sciences from unregulated self-interest, but actually for the defence of established authority in church and state; that such an attitude of defence produces the very disintegration it is supposed to prevent'. Blake is considered, for example, in relation to the Church,

[64] *The Love Songs and Heroines of Robert Burns*, compiled by Rev. John C. Hill. Dent. pp. xiv+155. 18s. $3.75.

[65] *The Neoplatonism of William Blake*, by George Mills Harper. North Carolina U.P. pp. xvi+324. $7.50.

[66] *The Valley of Vision: Blake as Prophet and Revolutionary*, by Peter F. Fisher, ed. by Northrop Frye. Toronto U.P. and O.U.P. pp. xi+261. $6. 48s.

Newtonian science, Platonism, and revolutionary politics. It is a densely packed but rewarding study.

Peter Fisher also contributes an article to *PQ* on 'Blake's Attacks on the Classical Tradition'. He seeks here to answer the question, 'Where and how did [Blake] think classicism had broken with the prophetic tradition or what he called "the everlasting Gospel"?' It is shown that Blake considered the art and literature of the Greeks to suffer from the subordination of imaginative perception, the source of original invention, to 'illustrating the conceptions of the rational understanding and imitating nature'.

Three other articles on general aspects of Blake's work may be dealt with next. E. D. Hirsch, Jr., argues in 'The Two Blakes' (*RES*) that it is misleading to assume that Blake's thought is essentially unified in the sense that his opinions remained basically unchanged throughout his life. A crucial change occurs in 1802 in Blake's attitude to this world. In the nineties his view is that 'Eternity is in love with the productions of time', and that happiness is possible on earth. After 1802 he is convinced that 'This Earth breeds not our happiness.' This new mood reaches its climax in 1804 with the visit to the Truchessian Gallery. Now temporal existence as such is unredeemable; it is only in Eternity that happiness is possible. The early work is discussed in 'The Difficult Innocence: Blake's Songs and Pastoral' (*ELH*) by Donald A. Dike. He shows that the celebrations of innocence 'are distanced by an effect of precarious vulnerability which anticipates and leads towards the disasters of *Songs of Experience*'. The poems are therefore seen as 'another and convincing reminder that pastoral, as a way of relating the human realities, can be toughly honest'. In 'Plato's *Statesman* Myth in Shelley and Blake' (*CL*) Irene

H. Chaynes is concerned with the appearance of the myth of the Golden Age and of recurrent cycles of experience in, among other poems, *The Mental Traveller*. Blake, like Shelley, conceives 'of the span of human life as only the arc of a vast cosmic circle'. William Powell Jones writes on 'The Idea of the Limitations of Science from Prior to Blake' (*Studies in English Literature*). Even in the early years of the century (in Prior) poets show distrust of scientific pride. The appearance of this distrust in Pope, Henry Brooke, Smart, and Cowper is examined, and Jones shows how their mild protest became in Blake a 'belligerent hostility' because he believed that the mechanistic spirit 'throttled the imagination and stifled the creative spirit of poetry'.

Three articles are devoted to particular poems. In 'William Blake and the Human Abstract' (*PMLA*) Robert F. Gleckner provides a very concentrated study of the relationship between *A Divine Image*, 'I heard an Angel Singing', and *The Human Abstract*. Joseph X. Brennan analyses 'The Symbolic Framework of Blake's *The Tyger*' (*CE*) to show that 'the poem not only affirms the tiger's unmitigated fearfulness throughout, but even moves . . . from a consideration of profound and dreadful import in the first four stanzas, to another, more profound and more dreadful yet, in the last two'. Leo Kirschbaum gives a detailed newcritical account of 'Blake's *The Fly* (*EC*); the article contains some good points, but is spoilt by the unearthing of some extremely fanciful ambiguities. There is a postscript by F. W. Bateson and a reply by John E. Grant.

Other contributions may be simply listed: Paul Miner's ' "Newton's Pantocrator" ' (*NQ*) and 'William Blake's *Divine Analogy*' (*Criticism*); Giorgio Melchiori's 'William Blake and Michelangelo' (*Art and Ideas*); and, finally, a bibliographical item: Kerrison

Preston's *Notes for a Catalogue of the Blake Library at the Georgian House, Merstham.*[67]

There are three items to be recorded dealing with Sir William Jones, the orientalist. A selection of his poems has been edited by Jonathan Benthall;[68] and Garland Cannon contributes two articles. 'The Literary Place of Sir William Jones (1746–94)' (*Journal of the Asiatic Society*) is largely concerned with Jones's reputation and

with his influence on Romantic writers. 'Sir William Jones and Benjamin Franklin' (*University College Record*) discusses the friendship between these two men, a friendship which was 'based on a love for America and England, a government of free men, a deep appreciation of the classics and a keen interest in science'.

To complete this section two short articles may be briefly mentioned: Christopher Ricks's 'The Resurrection Men' (*Listener*), which deals with the revival of dead metaphor; and R. P. Draper's 'Style and Matter' (*Revue des langues vivantes*), which touches on poetic diction.

[67] *Notes for a Catalogue of the Blake Library at the Georgian House, Merstham*, by Kerrison Preston. Cambridge: Golden Head Press, 1960. pp. 47. 20s.

[68] *Poems*, selected by Jonathan Benthall. Cambridge: Sebastian Carter. pp. 16. 5s.

XIII. THE NINETEENTH CENTURY

By P. M. YARKER and SHEILA M. SMITH

THIS chapter comprises the following sections: (a) Social and Intellectual Background; (b) Poetry and Drama; (c) Novels and Novelists; (d) Selected Prose Writers. Of these the first two are by P. M. Yarker, and the last two by Sheila M. Smith.

(a) Social and Intellectual Background

Although the title seems to suggest a generation, *Fathers of the Victorians*[1] is mainly about one man, Wilberforce. The wider reference is a tribute to the success of his efforts to propagate the Evangelical doctrine in nineteenth-century England. All the numerous activities of his crowded life were subservient to this end; even the abolition of the slave trade, his greatest achievement, was only an aspect of this central zeal. His failure to grasp this point was, according to the author, the only error in Hazlitt's assessment of Wilberforce in *The Spirit of the Age*. Wilberforce's philanthropy, said Hazlitt, was 'not so ill-bred as to quarrel with his loyalty or to banish him from the first circles'. This was true; but Wilberforce guarded his reputation only in the Evangelical interest. By retaining the respect of the eminent he had far more influence on the trend of opinion than would otherwise have been the case; and in fact it was for this reason that Evangelicalism became such a power in the Victorian period. Numerous subscription-lists of prominent names indicate how judiciously Wilberforce planned his canvassing. The book is crammed with detailed information, not all of equal significance, providing an ample account of how the Evangelical movement developed.

Queen Victoria published two volumes of *Leaves from a Journal*, and was preparing a third when Randall Davidson ventured to advise against it. Consequently the third volume was printed 'for strictly private circulation'. It dealt with the state visit of Napoleon III and the Empress Eugénie to England in the spring of 1855, and the return visit paid by the Queen and Prince Albert the following year. Although material from this Journal has been included in other books, it has not hitherto been published in full. It now appears with an introduction by Raymond Mortimer giving the historical background, and filling in missing details.[2]

A life of Feargus O'Connor, the Chartist, by Donald Read and Eric Glasgow,[3] gives details of his early life in Ireland, and his association with Daniel O'Connell, with whom he soon came in conflict; there is also much information on the history of Chartism.

'The wide claims made by Mill's new biographers for Harriet's intellectual ascendancy cannot be substantiated', says H. O. Pappe in *John Stuart Mill and the Harriet Taylor Myth*.[4] Throughout his 'lifelong adolescence' Mill needed an object of veneration, and

[1] *Fathers of the Victorians*, by Ford K. Brown. C.U.P. pp. 569. 55s. $9.50.

[2] *Leaves from a Journal*, by Queen Victoria. With an Introduction by Raymond Mortimer. Deutsch. pp. 160. 21s.

[3] *Feargus O'Connor: Irishman and Chartist*, by Donald Read and Eric Glasgow. Arnold. pp. 160. 21s.

[4] *John Stuart Mill and the Harriet Taylor Myth*, by H. O. Pappe. Melbourne U.P. and C.U.P. pp. 51. 9s. 6d.

Harriet Taylor succeeded Carlyle in this role. Her essay on 'Toleration' (1832) has been thought to have influenced *On Liberty*, but Pappe shows that its argument does not foreshadow Mill's, and is, in fact, 'inadequately imitative of Mill's thought throughout'. Her influence on Mill's attitude to Socialism has been similarly exaggerated. In his lecture on *John Stuart Mill and the Ends of Life*[5] Sir Isaiah Berlin shows that *On Liberty* contains stresses and implied inconsistencies that derive from its 'attempt to fuse rationalism and romanticism'. This lecture, and an essay by J. C. Rees in *Political Studies*, are discussed in a leading article in *TLS* (10 Mar.). Two analyses of Mill's thought appear in *JHI*: K. E. Miller writes on 'John Stuart Mill's Theory of International Relations', and H. Spiegelberg on ' "Accident of Birth": A Non-Utilitarian Motif in Mill's Philosophy'.

The first volume of a biography of James Anthony Froude[6] tells the story of his appalling childhood and subsequent persecution by his elder brother Hurrell, and traces the effects of these, and of his determination to survive them, down to 1856.

Some 24,000 pamphlets, besides other material concerned with the religious controversies of the nineteenth century, have been collected at Pusey House. These have now been carefully catalogued, and are readily accessible, through cross-references, from a variety of lines of approach. A description of this catalogue[7] has been prepared, with an indication of the nature of the different collections and suggestions of their possible uses.

The manuscript of *The Origin of Species* in the University Library, Cambridge, is described by R. C. Stauffer in '*On the Origin of Species*: An Unpublished Version' (*Science*). The Cambridge University Press have issued *The Handlist of Darwin Papers at the University Library, Cambridge*, compiled by R. V. C. Bailey and J. S. Gosse. E. A. Osborne contributes a note on 'The First Edition of *On the Origin of Species*' (*BC*). G. K. Plochmann, in 'Darwin and Spencer' (*Science*), discusses the posthumous reputations of the two, and considers why that of Spencer has declined.

In *Godliness and Good Learning*[8] David Newsome has written an informative book on these twin ideals of Victorian Education, illustrated, on the masters' side, from the career of James Prince Lee, headmaster of King Edward's, Birmingham, and on the pupils', from the diary of Martin, Archbishop Benson's eldest son, who died at seventeen.

Although dealing with all periods and places, W. H. G. Armytage's *A Social History of Engineering*[9] has an obvious relevance to nineteenth-century Britain. The book gives in detail, and in an attractive manner, an account of the stages of technical development in its many forms. John Gloag's massive report on *Victorian Comfort*[10] suggests that comfort was the first preoccupation of the Victorian mind. Mr. Pickwick's house at Dulwich was 'fitted up with every attention to substantial comfort', and these words, Gloag suggests, 'became the theme song of the Victorian Age'. He interprets the word 'comfort' very liberally,

[5] *John Stuart Mill and the Ends of Life*, by Sir Isaiah Berlin. Council of Christians and Jews. pp. 34. 2s.

[6] *James Anthony Froude, 1818–1856*, by W. H. Dunn. O.U.P. pp. xiv+261. 35s.

[7] *Nineteenth-Century Pamphlets at Pusey House*, compiled by Fr. Hugh, S.S.F. Faith Press. pp. 98. 15s.

[8] *Godliness and Good Learning: Four Studies on a Victorian Ideal*, by David Newsome. Murray. pp. xii+291. 28s.

[9] *A Social History of Engineering*, by W. H. G. Armytage. Faber. pp. 378. 42s.

[10] *Victorian Comfort: A Social History of Design from 1830–1900*, by John Gloag. Black. pp. xvi+252. 50s.

however, and explores many aspects of Victorian life to which neither that term nor his sub-title, 'A Social History of Design', seems particularly applicable. The book, which is profusely illustrated, is a useful reference work, although its tone is hardly that of a disinterested catalogue. Two books recall vanished scenes of London streets. O. J. Morris, in *Grandfather's London*,[11] reproduces a series of photographs taken by Charles Spurgeon, son of the famous revivalist, in South London in 1884 and 1885, and William Stewart's *Characters of Bygone London*[12] is a collection of drawings by the author of once-familiar London types, each with a page of letter-press commenting on its subject.

A new edition of *Studies in Mid-Victorian Imperialism*,[13] by C. A. Bodelsen, first published in 1924, is introduced by H. L. Beales, who says: 'What he was concerned to analyse was the historical origins and basic ideas and aims of the "new" imperialists of the 1880's, those who articulated the "classical expressions" of imperialism, especially Seeley, Froude and the Imperial Federation League.' Violently opposed to these aims was Wilfrid Scawen Blunt, whose life by Lord Lytton[14] gives a vivid account of his activities as a champion of freedom in Egypt, Ireland, and India, as well as presenting an intimate picture of the life of a remarkable family. Little is said, however, of Blunt's literary output.

Some publications of a general nature may be mentioned here. *Earnest Victorians*, by Robert A. Rosenbaum,

Jr.,[15] is an anthology of extracts by or about Shaftesbury, Newman, Elizabeth Barrett, Dante Gabriel Rossetti, Darwin, and Gordon, designed to illustrate a central theme in the life of each. Austin Wright has collected twenty-eight notable essays on Victorian literature[16], including those of F. L. Lucas on Matthew Arnold, Logan Pearsall Smith on Carlyle, Virginia Woolf on Hardy's novels, A. L. Rowse on Macaulay, and T. S. Eliot on Arnold and Pater. The new *Studies in English Literature* devotes an issue to the nineteenth century, containing essays on 'The Wit in Shelley's Poetry', by Newell F. Ford; '*Lady Susan*: Jane Austen's Character of the Merry Widow', by J. A. Levine; 'Arthur Hugh Clough: A Hundred Years of Disparagement', in which Walter E. Houghton suggests that the time has come to ask, 'Was Clough a success?'; a discussion of 'Wordsworth's Final Phase: Glimpses of Eternity', by Seymour Lainoff; and 'Hardy's *The Woodlanders*: Inwardness and Memory', by George S. Fayen, Jr. John Lewis Bradley prints some new letters from Ruskin to Lady Waterford, Patrick G. Hogan and Joseph O. Baylen write on Shaw's relations with W. T. Stead, and G. Robert Stange reviews 'Recent Studies in Nineteenth-Century Literature'.

KSJ includes the following items: 'Keats and the Bible', by Lloyd N. Jeffrey; 'The Reynolds-Hood Commonplace Book: A Fresh Re-appraisal', by Paul Kaufman; and 'The Context of Keats's Fairy's Song', by Jack Stillinger; 'Christmas Day, 1818', in which Aileen Ward differs from Robert Gittings as to the meaning of Keats's visit to Fanny Brawne on that

---

[11] *Grandfather's London*, by O. J. Morris, with an Introduction by John Pudney. Putnam. pp. 127. 25s.

[12] *Characters of Bygone London*, by William Stewart. Harrap. pp. 142. 15s.

[13] *Studies in Mid-Victorian Imperialism*, by C. A. Bodelsen. Heinemann, 1960. pp. 226. 25s.

[14] *Wilfrid Scawen Blunt*, by the Earl of Lytton. Macdonald. pp. 368. 30s.

[15] *Earnest Victorians*, by Robert A. Rosenbaum, Jr. Heinemann. pp. 383. 25s.

[16] *Victorian Literature: Modern Essays in Criticism*, edited by Austin Wright. O.U.P. pp. vi+377. 13s. 6d.

occasion. Neville Rogers and Mabel A. E. Steele print '*I Stood Tip Toe upon a Little Hill*: A Hitherto Uncollated Fragment'; Elizabeth Nitchie writes on 'Mary Shelley, Traveller': B. A. Park discusses 'The Indian Elements of the *Indian Serenade*'; and J. E. Staveson looks at parallels with Byron in 'Shelley's *Julian and Maddalo*'.

(b) Poetry and Drama

This has been a by-year for Wordsworth studies; only a few items of interest are to be listed. In 'Wordsworth's *Descriptive Sketches* and the Growth of a Poet's Mind' (*PMLA*) G. H. Hartman finds evidence in the poem of a necessary crisis in a poet's development, 'a defect of the eye which eventually leads him *through* nature *beyond* it'. Hanspeter Schelp, in 'Wordsworth's "Daffodils" Influenced by a Wesleyan Hymn?' (*ES*), suggests Charles Wesley's *When Quiet in My House I Sit* as a possible source. 'Wordsworth and *Don Quijote*', by Edward Sarmiento (*Bulletin of Hispanic Studies*), sees Wordsworth's dream in *The Prelude*, book v, as a revealing commentary on the novel. A parallel with Vaudracour's 'imbecile mind', in *The Prelude*, book ix, is suggested by Chester L. Shaver in 'Wordsworth's Vaudracour and Wilkinson's *The Wanderer*' (*RES*). Despite its 'atypical treatment of typical elements', the poem is 'a remarkable synthesis of Wordsworth's two great imaginative visions', says Alan Grob in 'Process and Permanence in "Resolution and Independence"' (*ELH*). R. L. Cox examines 'Wordsworth's "*Ode*: Intimations of Immortality"' (*Ex*), and H. Rossiter-Smith writes on 'Wordsworth and Pre-existence' (*Hibbert Journal*). In 'An Incomplete Wordsworth Essay upon Moral Habits' (*REL*) Geoffrey Little gives the text of the essay from a notebook at Grasmere. G. Joyce Padwick, in 'A Tour of

Scotland, 1805' (*Litera*), compares Dorothy Wordsworth's account of the tour with Coleridge's. R. H. Wolfe has a note on 'De Quincey, Wordsworth and *Hamlet*' in *NQ*. In 'Wordsworth and the Copyright Act of 1842: *Addendum*' (*PMLA*) Russell Noyes gives an account of Wordsworth's activities in support of Talfourd's Copyright Bill in 1837 and 1838.

Two different approaches are made to *The Eolian Harp*. Albert Gérard writes on 'Counterfeiting Infinity: *The Eolian Harp* and the Growth of Coleridge's Mind' (*JEGP*), and in 'The Structure of Coleridge's *The Eolian Harp*' (*MLN*) W. H. Marshall shows that the poem is 'constructed upon the interaction of two motifs'. Lucyle Werkmeister discusses 'The Early Coleridge: His "Rage for Metaphysics"' (*HTR*), and Leonard W. Deen examines 'Coleridge and the Sources of Pantisocracy: Godwin, the Bible, and Hartley' (*BUSE*). In *BNYPL* D. V. Erdman describes 'Lost Poem Found: The Cooperative Pursuit and Recapture of an Escaped Coleridge "Sonnet" of 72 Lines'; and in the same journal Carl R. Woodring describes 'Two Prompt Copies of Coleridge's *Remorse*', and Charles S. Bouslog reprints 'Coleridge's Marginalia in the Sara Hutchinson Copy of *Remorse*'. In 'Coleridge's "Spectre-Bark": A Slave Ship?' (*PQ*) Malcolm Ware discloses a reference to *The Ancient Mariner* in connexion with a superstition that slavers were condemned to spectral voyages in Nathan Drake's *Winter Nights, or Fireside Lucubrations* (1820). John A. Stuart finds parallels between St. 'Augustine and *The Ancient Mariner*' (*MLN*), and Stewart C. Wilcox discusses 'The Arguments and Motto of *The Ancient Mariner*' (*MLQ*). George Watson sees 'The Meaning of *Kubla Khan*' (*REL*) in terms of literary criticism, suggesting that it is 'probably the most acute poem about poetry in English'. Three essays discuss related subjects in 'Coleridge's "True and Original Realism"' by Nicholas Brooke (*DUJ*), 'Coleridge: Vision and Actuality' by Vincent Buckley (*Melbourne College Review*), and 'Coleridge's "Time, Real and Imaginary"' by John R. Byers, Jr. (*Ex*).

Coleridge's critical, theological, and political writing receives more attention than his poetry. Carl R. Woodring, in *Politics in the Poetry of Coleridge*,[17] seeks to connect the two sides, but is forced to admit that, although 'political passion was one major impulse through all his life and work', it was not a principal inspiration of Coleridge's poetry. Except, therefore, in the minor poems, Woodring approaches his subject by way of overtones and imagery. The study begins with an account of Coleridge's vicissitudes of political thought, making full use of recent identifications of his newspaper contributions. An examination follows of his use of words with political implications, such as 'nation', 'people', and the synonyms of 'despot'. Poems dealing directly with political matters are divided into two classes: 'Poems for pay and party', such as *Fire, Famine and Slaughter*, and verses printed in the *Morning Post*, the occasions for which are closely examined; and 'Poems of Elevation', such as the *Ode on the Departing Year*, and *France: An Ode*, of which an interesting and informative analysis shows that 'political decisions, extraneous and in the aesthetic view wholly accidental, contributed to the final shape of the poem'. These studies show Coleridge's 'irregular transit from hesitant republican to independent Tory', and the same progress is to be seen in his plays, with an examination of which this shrewd and often revealing study ends.

Three articles by W. Schrickx are of interest. 'Coleridge and Friedrich Heinrich Jacobi' appeared in the *Révue belge de philologie et d'histoire* (1959), and this has been followed by 'Coleridge Marginalia in Kant's *Metaphysische Anfangsgrunde der Naturwissenschaft*' and 'Unpublished Coleridge Marginalia on Fichte', in *Studia Germanica Gandensia*, I and III respectively. Schrickx points out that a full study of Coleridge's relation to post-Kantian German thought is still lacking. These articles publish some of the material that such a study would require. D. B. Schneider contributes 'A Note on Coleridge's Notebooks', and J. B. Beer one on 'Coleridge's *Watchman*', to *NQ*. The *Proceedings and Transactions of the Royal Society of Canada* include papers by George Whalley on 'Coleridge on the *Prometheus* of Aeschylus', and by Kathleen Coburn on 'Poet into Public Servant'. In 'Coleridge's Apologetic Prefaces' (*TSE*) Max F. Schulz notes the complex tone of these 'sententious and offensive, and at the same time, apologetic and ingratiating' exercises in the art of puffing. D. V. Erdman writes on 'Coleridge on Coleridge: The Context (and Text) of His Review of "Mr Coleridge's Second Lay Sermon"' (*Boston Studies in Romanticism*).

In a book on Coleridge's religious thought[18] James D. Boulger, after showing Coleridge's relation in this sphere to his contemporaries and the nineteenth century as a whole, discusses the central question of the 'higher reason', and with it the problem of whether (as Wellek said) Coleridge's utterances on this subject were pervaded by 'a pernicious teaching of double truth', or (as Fairchild maintained) he was never able 'to extricate himself from the traps of self'.

[17] *Politics in the Poetry of Coleridge*, by Carl R. Woodring. Wisconsin U.P. pp. xi+270. $6.

[18] *Coleridge as Religious Thinker*, by James D. Boulger. Yale U.P. pp. xii+224. 42s. $5.

Disagreeing with both, Boulger claims that 'what he offers is an authentic example of the religious mind reporting a variety of experiences in relation to religious dogma'. This discussion involves some comment on Coleridge's 'semi-rejection' of Kant's distinction between pure and practical reason, and the relation of his own ideas to those of the seventeenth-century Platonists. In the later chapters the implications of the doctrines advocated in *Aids to Reflection* and associated works are considered in relation to orthodox theology and to Coleridge's own earlier concepts of Immanence and Pantheism. A chapter on 'Religion and Poetry' considers the effect of the change in his opinions on his later poems, when 'he has become conscious of the "pathetic fallacy", a condition unthinkable in . . . "Frost at Midnight" '.

George Whalley adds Coleridge to the 'Portrait of a Bibliophile' series in *BC*. Lucyle Werkmeister shows a glimpse, or rather three glimpses, of Coleridge in later life, in ' "High Jinks at Highgate" ' (*PQ*), summarizing three accounts of a dinner party that Coleridge attended, given by Frederick Mansell Reynolds in 1828.

Giles Barber looks at '*Poems, by Robert Southey*, 1797' in *The Bodleian Library Record* (1960), and R. Baird Shuman prints 'Southey to Dyer: An Unpublished Letter' (*NQ*).

'Byron's separation from his wife and subsequent exile supplied him with material and stimuli for a new creative phase, and in this respect the rights and wrongs of the affair are unimportant,' says Andrew Rutherford in a study of the poetry[19] that thus resolutely avoids the area of much recent controversy. Yet Byron the man must always occupy a large part of such a study, and

speculation about his character and motives are by no means absent from this one. For example, 'it is quite likely that a sensitive and emotional boy like Byron, with his . . . grounds for feeling insecure, would develop a *façade* . . . as a protection against being hurt'. This inner conflict and outward indifference resulted in Byron's equivocal attitude and changing moods. They resolved themselves into his 'attempt to be both poet and dandy', his aristocratic affinities making him half-ashamed of his poetry, which he sought to efface 'by sneering and laughing at himself, and momentarily discrediting the values which he . . . himself established'. Thus, only in the *ottava rima* satires was he able to speak 'as his normal aristocratic self'. Against this introductory background Rutherford examines the poems in some detail, although of the plays only *Manfred* receives individual treatment at some length. Not unnaturally, *Don Juan* occupies the major portion of the critical commentary, and the chapters concerned with it, together with that on *The Vision of Judgment*, form the most useful part of this very handy guide.

Two essays by W. H. Marshall appear in *MLN*. In 'The Accretive Structure of Byron's *The Giaour*' he says that 'the poem derives its structural complexity from the fact that what is regarded as the complete work is really the original poem covered with several layers of accretion'; and in 'A Reading of Byron's *Mazeppa*' he suggests that the poem is 'a dramatic monologue of which the emotional intensity becomes the object of satire'. He also supplies a note on 'Reference to a Popular Tradition in *Don Juan* and *Mazeppa*' (*NQ*). Andrew Rutherford supplements his informative chapters on the poem by suggesting that 'The Influence of Hobhouse on *Childe Harold's Pilgrimage*, Canto IV' (*RES*) was less than has been supposed. Mario

[19] *Byron: A Critical Study*, by Andrew Rutherford. Oliver and Boyd. pp. xiii+253. 25s.

Praz discusses 'Byron e Foscolo' (*Rivista di letterature moderne e comparate* [Florence]), and in 'Guilt and Retribution in Byron's Sea Poems' (*REL*), Bernard Blackstone considers the symbolism in relevant parts of *Don Juan* and in *The Island*.

Cuthbert Graham writes on 'The Boyhood of Byron' (*Listener*). L. H. Kendall, Jr., prints 'An Unpublished Letter to Shelley' (*MLN*), probably dated 30 July 1821.

When Byron died, his fame and notoriety put a premium on any sort of disclosure of his life and character, and those who had known him, however slightly, scrambled to convert their experience into cash, often not scrupling to exaggerate their acquaintance or 'to tint the picture with colours the reading public would find congenial'. Thus many false legends were born which have proved remarkably resilient. Doris Langley Moore, sifting a vast amount of unpublished material in the John Murray collection, the Lovelace papers, and Hobhouse's diaries, has sought to isolate the truth in the welter of anecdotes, reminiscences, accusations, and innuendo that rapidly multiplied after his death.[20] The most portentous event was the folly of Hobhouse in arranging the destruction of the manuscript of Byron's memoirs, in order to frustrate calumny and preserve his fame. Exactly the opposite effect was achieved. Hobhouse, as Byron's executor, and because of the continuity supplied by his journals, is a central figure in this book. However, his mishandling of Byron's affairs, the timidity or ineptitude of Augusta Leigh, and even the malevolence of Lady Byron's party, did not so effectively traduce his reputation as did the industry of those who sought their own advantage in the circumstances of his death. Trelawney,

although here drawn in the blackest of ink, was only one of many. Leigh Hunt is another upon whose actions Mrs. Moore places the worst possible interpretation, representing him as jealously attacking Byron's good name while battening on his good nature. She admits to partiality, and Byron is certainly represented as the honest and well-intentioned victim of an appalling conspiracy of defamation and lies. Proposing a study never hitherto pursued in detail, and making use of much fresh material, this book appeared to open more lines of inquiry than were closed by it. Following the review in *TLS* (21 July), a correspondence began in that journal, in which the most important letters were from G. Wilson Knight (28 July), Malcolm Elwin (4 Aug., 20 Oct.), Lord Lytton (26 Aug., 22 Sept.), C. H. Gibbs-Smith (29 Sept.), and Keith Walker (1 Sept.). Mrs. Moore replied on 4 August, 8 September, and 27 October.

The Shelley collection in the Carl H. Pforzheimer Library comprises some 1,500 manuscripts, chiefly letters, of which more than 200 are by Shelley himself. Others represented are Godwin, Mary Wollstonecraft, Leigh Hunt, Peacock, Byron, Hogg, Trelawney, Mary Shelley, Sir Timothy Shelley, Harriet Grove, and Edward and Jane Williams. These manuscripts are to be published, probably in eight volumes, of which the first two, covering the period from 1773 to 1811, have appeared under the editorship-in-chief of Kenneth Neil Cameron.[21] The first volume is concerned mainly with Mary Wollstonecraft, Godwin, and Peacock, and contains, besides letters, items such as the first draft of *Fleetwood* and the proof corrections of *Political Justice*. The second opens with Harriet Grove's

---

[20] *The Late Lord Byron*, by Doris Langley Moore. John Murray. pp. viii+542. 42*s*.

[21] *Shelley and His Circle, 1773–1822*. Vols. I and II, ed. by Kenneth Neil Cameron. Harvard U.P. and O.U.P. Vol. I, pp. xlviii+474. Vol. II, pp. xiv+545. £8. 8*s*. the two.

diary for 1809 and 1810, edited by F. L. Jones, and includes thirty-six of Shelley's letters, as well as transcripts of three of his early literary manuscripts. The strictly chronological presentation involves difficulties of organization (Peacock, for example, makes his début far too soon), but the whole scheme is, nevertheless, admirably conceived, and the material arranged in a most accessible order. Each writer and principal correspondent is introduced by a biographical essay placing him well within the setting of the documents, and explaining the circumstances and giving references necessary to his incorporation in the general picture. Shelley is given a main essay in two parts, one biographical and one on him as 'Poet and Thinker', but this is supplemented by many shorter entries. Among the more interesting of these is that on the tampering by Hogg with Shelley's early letters to him. Hogg's aim in this was the suppression of all reference to his atheism and the minimizing of his attachment to Shelley's sister Elizabeth. Thirty-four of the forty-four letters so treated are printed here, collated with Hogg's versions. Several essays deal with contingent matters, such as the provenance of the papers, the value of postmarks as a guide to date, and an account of the divorce proceedings against Shelley's sister Mary in 1829. Although some of the material in these two volumes has appeared before, there is ample new material to make their publication a major event where Shelley studies are concerned, and the prospect of their successors is even brighter.

Two notes by R. R. Pelletier appear in *NQ*, 'Shade and Bower Images in Milton and Shelley', and 'Shelley's Debt to Milton in *The Wandering Jew*'. M. L. Ranald and R. Arthur comment on *Prometheus Unbound*, i. 191–222, in 'Shelley's Magus Zoroaster and the

Image of the Doppelgänger' (*MLN*), pointing out that the superstition is unknown in Zoroastrian writings. Elizabeth Nitchie discusses 'Shelley's *Prometheus Unbound* II, v, 109–110' (*Ex*), and W. H. Marshall links Prometheus with Christ in 'The Father-Child Symbolism in *Prometheus Unbound*' (*MLQ*). C. C. Clarke writes on 'Shelley's "Tangled Boughs" ' (*DUJ*), and M. M. Bhalla discusses 'The Myth of the Two Shelleys' in *The Indian Journal of English Studies* (Calcutta). In 'Cold and Heat in *Adonais*' (*MLN*) Eleanor N. Hutchens comments on a passage in *The Subtler Language* by E. R. Wasserman (*YW* xl. 227). D. J. Hughes suggests, in 'Coherence and Collapse in Shelley, with Particular Reference to *Epipsychidion*' (*ELH*), that the pattern of the poem is one of 'continued aspiration and deprivation', consciously designed 'to mirror in its progress the very process of the mind as it creates the poem'. G. M. Matthews discusses a new text of *The Triumph of Life* at length in *SN* (1960). In 'Shelley and Jane Williams' (*RES*) he suggests that a study of the fragmentary manuscript called 'Lines written in the Bay of Lerici' indicates that Shelley's relations with Jane Williams caused an emotional crisis in June 1822, and that this has a direct bearing on the interpretation of *The Triumph of Life*. Matthews contributes some brief 'Comments on Recent Shelley Studies' to *REL*.

In 'The Keats–Hazlitt–Hunt Copy of *Palmerin of England* in relation to Keats's Poetry' (*JEGP*), C. I. Patterson brings forward additional reasons to those given by Amy Lowell for supposing that Keats had this copy of Southey's translation in 1819. In the same journal Bernice Slote writes on 'La Belle Dame as Naiad', pointing out that Lemprière's *Classical Dictionary* (which Keats knew) gives attributes of naiads reminiscent of Keats's 'faery's child'. Francis Scarfe discusses 'Keats's Use of the Negative' (*Ea*); H. Heinen investigates 'Interwoven Time in Keats's Poetry' (*TSLL*); J. C. Maxwell has a note on 'A Lost Keats Letter' (*NQ*); and J. D. Boulger (*ELH*) makes a general study of 'Keats' Symbolism' in relation to the 'tension between spirit and matter' in his poetry. In 'Keats and Burton: A Reappraisal' (*PQ*) Aileen Ward examines the marginalia on Keats's copy of *The Anatomy of Melancholy*, again differing from Gittings in her conclusions. B. L. Reid writes on 'Keats and the Heart's Hornbook' (*Massachusetts Review*). Edward A. Bloom considers 'Keats' *The Eve of St Agnes* 1–9' (*Ex*). The poem is the subject also of two articles presenting rather different attitudes to Keats from those that are usual: Roger Sharrock argues in 'Keats and the Young Lovers' (*REL*) that the narrative poems reveal Keats as 'supremely the adolescent poet'; and, with more ingenuity, Jack Stillinger, in 'The Hoodwinking of Madeline: Scepticism in *The Eve of St Agnes*' (*SP*), casts Porphyro in the role of cynical seducer, representing 'the ordinary cruelties of life', and suggests that Madeline must blame her superstition for facilitating his task. The theme of the 'hoodwinked dreamer' is traced in other poems. A Letter from Keith Hollingsworth (*TLS*, 27 Oct.) finds a point of contact between '*Vathek* and the *Ode to a Nightingale*'. V. Hutton discusses the *Ode on a Grecian Urn*, (*Ex*), and W. R. Manierre writes on 'Versification and Imagery in *The Fall of Hyperion*' (*TSLL*).

The inventory of *The Tennyson Collection Presented to the University of Virginia in Honor of Edgar Finley Shannon, Jr.*,[22] lists many interesting items, including the manuscripts of *Tears, Idle Tears* and *The Charge of the*

Light Brigade. W. D. Paden prints 'Twenty New Poems Attributed to Tennyson, Praed, and Landor' (*VS*), of which eleven are given to Tennyson, eight to Praed, and one to Landor. C. R. Sanders gives a detailed account of the friendship of 'Carlyle and Tennyson' (*PMLA*). David Daiches writes on 'Imagery and Mood in Tennyson and Whitman' (*English Studies Today*). R. L. Collins gives some new facts and queries concerning 'Clara Tennyson-D'Eyncourt's Copy of *Poems, Chiefly Lyrical*' (*NQ*). G. O. Marshall, Jr., points out, in 'Tennyson's *The Poet*: Mis-seeing Shelley Plain' (*PQ*), that the poem can owe nothing directly to Shelley's *Defence of Poetry*, which was not published until 1840. John Britton discusses '*The Palace of Art*, 1–16' (*Ex*), and Malcolm MacLaren writes on 'Tennyson's Epicurean Lotos-Eaters' (*Classical Journal*). In 'A Neglected Theme in Tennyson's *In Memoriam*' (*MLN*) J. L. Kendall discusses the theme of failure and capitulation. R. C. Schweik adds a note on 'The "Peace or War" Passages in Tennyson's *Maud*' (*NQ*).

The centenary of Elizabeth Barrett Browning's death brought with it many tributes to the poet. A Commemorative Exhibition was mounted in London, and reported in *TLS* (2 June). Naomi Lewis spoke on 'The Genius of Elizabeth Barrett Browning' (*Listener*). J. M. S. Tompkins's Fawcett Lecture at Bedford College was on *Aurora Leigh*. 'All the scenes of *Aurora Leigh*, real, romantic and fantastic, are held together by the questions they ask and the answers they examine,' says Dr. Tompkins, showing how clearly the poem reflected the poet's own experience and opinions. David Bonnell Green prints 'Elizabeth Barrett to Hugh Stuart Boyd: An Additional Letter' (*PMLA*), and Y. Barbery reviews 'La Critique moderne face à Elizabeth et Robert Browning' (*Ea*).

[22] *The Tennyson Collection Presented to the University of Virginia in Honor of Edgar Finley Shannon, Jr.* Virginia U.P. pp. 52. $5.

A selection of Browning's poems made by Edward Shanks has now been published,[23] although without an introduction, since Shanks died before this could be completed. By focusing attention on one aspect of Browning's poetry, the 'character revealing' intention of his monologues, Park Honan has produced an illuminating study of their technical aspects.[24] His examination of the early poems and plays shows what each failure taught the poet, and how he utilized the lesson later. In *Sordello*, for example, 'Browning not only worked himself out of the lyric style of Shelley, but made great strides in developing a blank-verse line that could "imitate" or suggest human speech'. The main portion of the book is a discussion of twenty dramatic monologues (including *The Ring and the Book*), stressing the importance of the situation of the speaker, and his relation to his 'audience', and examining the imagery and diction of the individual poems. The result is to demonstrate the methods by which Browning gave individuality to his personages. This useful book is reviewed by Robert Langbaum in *VS*.

In *Three Essays on Robert Browning's Theory of the Poet*[25] Charles Rivers discusses *Pippa Passes*, the *Essay on Percy Bysshe Shelley*, and 'Robert Browning's Existential Humanism', suggesting that 'Browning's aim as a poet is to achieve a balance between inner and outer life . . . maintaining that the poet's loyalty to truth is the magnetic force guiding mankind towards . . . a perfection which it is not

in his nature to possess'. E. D. H. Johnson offers 'Robert Browning's Pluralistic Universe: A Reading of *The Ring and the Book*' (*Texas Quarterly*). R. W. S. Mendl writes on 'Robert Browning the Poet-Musician' (*Music and Letters*). Boyd A. Litzinger contributes 'A Note on Browning's Defence of Chatterton' (*VNL*). 'Robert Browning and George Smith', by L. P. Kelley, appears in *The Quarterly Review*, giving some unpublished letters. On individual poems, Edward C. McAleer discusses 'Browning's *Nationality in Drinks*' (*Ex*), Litzinger writes on 'The Prior's Niece in *Fra Lippo Lippi*' (*NQ*), T. J. Assad challenges established ideas on 'Browning's *My Last Duchess*' (*TSE*), and P. E. Kilburn also discusses this poem in *Ex*. F. J. Chiarenza examines 'Browning's *The Bishop Orders his Tomb at St Praxed's Church*' in the same journal. T. P. Harrison writes on 'Browning's *Childe Roland* and Wordsworth' (*TSL*). 'Browning: "Mage" and "Maker"—A Study in Poetic Purpose' (*VNL*), by Roma A. King, Jr., is an analysis of *Cleon*. J. V. Hagopian, in 'The Mask of Browning's Countess Gismond' (*PQ*), says that 'Browning has structured the Countess's monologue to suggest that she is lying and that Gautier is indeed the rejected lover'. George R. Wasserman suggests that 'The Meaning of Browning's Ring-Figure' (*MLN*) is most apparent if the analogy is not carried too far.

In a letter to *TLS* (19 May) W. E. Freedman draws attention to Wise's printing of *The Ballad of Jan Van Hunks*, by Dante Gabriel Rossetti, and he writes on 'D. G. Rossetti's *Early Italian Poets*' in *BC*. A. J. Sambrook writes on 'D. G. Rossetti and R. W. Dixon' in *Ea*. 'Christina Rossetti, Almsgiver', by S. Gorley Putt (*English*) deals with her replies to begging letters.

Two more volumes of Swinburne's *Letters* have appeared, covering the

---

[23] *Poems of Robert Browning*, selected by Edward Shanks. Macmillan. pp. xii+327. 10s. 6d.

[24] *Browning's Characters: A Study in Poetic Technique*, by Park Honan. Yale U.P. pp. xiv+327. 60s. $6.50.

[25] *Three Essays on Robert Browning's Theory of the Poet*, by Charles Rivers. Northwest Missouri State College. pp. 40. 50c.

period from 1875 to 1882.[26] Bonamy Dobrée's selection of the poems[27] is designed 'to exemplify as far as may be every aspect of his poetry', so that the range is wide. The poems are printed in chronological order, and the emphasis falls on the early works, for 'there was very little development in Swinburne'. In 'Swinburne's Greek Plays and God, "The Supreme Evil" ' (*MLN*) H. A. Hargreaves gives a Biblical background to passages in *Atalanta* and *Erechtheus*. W. D. Paden gives 'A Few Annotations by Swinburne' (*NQ*) in a copy of *The Oxford and Cambridge Magazine* for 1856, and T. J. Brown adds Swinburne to the 'English Literary Autographs' series in *BC*.

The Voices of Matthew Arnold, by W. Stacey Johnson,[28] examines Arnold's poetry from the point of view of Eliot's *The Three Voices of Poetry*, although one of Eliot's categories is here divided. A preliminary chapter on 'Arnold as a Victorian Poet' suggests that the 'vitiating uncertainty of tone' characteristic of the period did much to mute one of Arnold's voices, the Oracular. This book does not pursue its stated aim very closely, and resolves itself into a commentary on individual poems. D. G. James further examines the 'vitiating uncertainty' in *Matthew Arnold and the Decline of English Romanticism*.[29] By temperament Arnold was a 'pseudo-romantic', casting himself in the role of the lonely sufferer, and this gave a weakness to his poetry, which needed 'a development and extension in him of the high Romanticism manifested in an earlier generation'. But the influence of his father, and of Newman, prevented this. 'High Romanticism' is defined as an aspiration to 'muteness', or a Keatsian freedom from palpable designs. But this 'fundamental doctrine' of Romanticism was denied by Arnold in his criticism, where he 'judged to be necessary, and sought, an intellectual authority to set over poetry'.

Roger L. Brooks contributes a series of notes on Arnold, in 'Matthew Arnold and the *London Review*' (*PMLA*), 'Matthew Arnold and the National Eisteddfod' (*NQ*), 'Matthew Arnold and the *Pall Mall Gazette*' (*MP*), 'A Neglected Edition of Matthew Arnold's Poetry and a Bibliographical Correction' (*PBSA*), and 'An Unrecorded American Edition of the Selected Poems of Matthew Arnold' (*Lib*). R. H. Super adds a note on 'The First Publication of *Thyrsis*' (*NQ*). S. M. B. Coulling gives an account of the conflict between 'Matthew Arnold and the *Daily Telegraph*' (*RES*). J. M. Wallace writes on 'Landscape and "The General Law": the Poetry of Matthew Arnold' (*BUSE*), and A. J. Lubell discusses 'Matthew Arnold: Between Two Worlds' (*MLQ*). In 'The Quest for the Genuine Self: Matthew Arnold and the Modern World' (*Studies in English Literature*, Japan) Takashi Kato says that 'it is Arnold's interest in Senancour that furnishes the key to his inner disharmony'. T. J. Truss, Jr., discusses 'Arnold's "Shakespeare" ' (*Ex*).

Michael Timko discusses Clough's '*Amours de Voyage*: Substance or Smoke?' (*English*).

Metaphor in Hopkins,[30] by Robert Boyle, S.J., is a series of eight images from different poems, each exhaustively analysed as typical of Hopkins's imagination. Boyd A. Litzinger

[26] *The Swinburne Letters*, ed. by Cecil Y. Lang. Vol. 3, 1875–1877. Vol. 4, 1877–1882. Yale U.P. and O.U.P. pp. 335, 325. £4. 4s. the two.
[27] *Swinburne. Poems*, selected and introduced by Bonamy Dobrée. Penguin. pp. 240. 3s. 6d.
[28] *The Voices of Matthew Arnold: An Essay in Criticism*, by W. Stacey Johnson. Yale U.P. pp. vi+146. 46s. $5.75.
[29] *Matthew Arnold and the Decline of English Romanticism*, by D. G. James. O.U.P. pp. viii+110. 18s.
[30] *Metaphor in Hopkins*, by Robert Boyle, S.J. North Carolina U.P. pp. xxiv+231. $6.

examines 'Hopkins' *The Wreck of the Deutschland*, Stanza 19' (*Ex*). In ' "Orion" in *The Wreck of the Deutschland*' (*MLN*) J. Hillis Miller shows that the use of the constellation in the twenty-fifth stanza reflects the patristic tradition that associates Orion with storms and disaster, which are in turn analogous of the sufferings of martyrs. *The Windhover* receives attention from J. D. Thomas (*Ex*), and Thomas J. Assad (*TSE*), who argues that symbolical interpretations have obscured the literal meaning of the poem as a series of comparisons between the kestrel, plough, and embers on the one hand, and man on the other, the whole reflecting the Thomist order of created beings. A Letter on 'Bridges's Debt to Hopkins' by Simon Nowell-Smith in *TLS* (12 May) brought replies from Geoffrey Tillotson and J. G. Ritz (30 June), W. H. Gardner (18 Aug.), and Norman Mackenzie (1 Sept.). A. P. O'Brien discusses the 'Structure Complex of Hopkins's Words' (*Indian Journal of English Studies*), and in *CE* John Nist writes on 'Gerard Manley Hopkins and Textural Intensity: A Linguistic Analysis'—of *Spring and Fall*.

Coventry Patmore's *Essay on English Metrical Law* was first published in *The North British Review* in 1857 as a review of three books dealing with related aspects of the subject. A new edition, fully annotated and introduced by Sister Mary Roth, draws attention to the serious preoccupation of mid-Victorian poets and critics with the problems of English rhythms.[31] Patmore's 'own contribution to the theory is not so much an original stream of thought as the result of his supplementing and augmenting ideas in the general ambient of thought about prosody in his time'. The essay was republished several times in his lifetime,

and was the subject of some correspondence with Hopkins in 1883. A. Thomas considers 'Coventry Patmore's Literary Criticism: The Attribution of Articles' (*NQ*).

Patmore's essay was a major influence on one poet at least, namely Francis Thompson, and a study of the latter by Paul van K. Thomson[32] considers the relation between them in some detail. Two recent books on Thompson, by J. C. Reid and Pierre Danchin (*YW* xl. 237 and xli. 229 respectively), have dealt very thoroughly with all aspects of his life and work, including this one; but Thomson brings a fresh sympathy for the poet which throws a new emphasis on his isolation, and reveals Patmore as 'the one man who could understand and interpret' his poetry. This book is reviewed by Peter Butter at length in an essay entitled 'Francis Thompson' (*REL*). D. H. Rieman writes on 'Shelley, De Vere and Thompson's *Hound of Heaven*' in *VNL*.

The centenary of the founding of 'Morris & Co' was celebrated with exhibitions in London and New York, reported in the *Spectator* by Hugh Graham, and also in the *New Yorker*. The year also saw the first issue of *The Journal of the William Morris Society*, with essays on 'Morris and Calligraphy' by Alfred Fairbank, 'News from Iceland' by Hugh Bushell, 'Morris and Bernard Shaw' by E. E. Stokes, Jr., and 'Notes on Morris and Co's Domestic Stained Glass' by A. C. Sewter. Sir Gordon Russell commented on Morris and his associates in 'Design as a Social Problem' (*Listener*).

A short account of *The Aesthetic Movement in English Literature* by Lorenz Eckhoff[33] comments on

---

[31] *Coventry Patmore's 'Essay on English Metrical Law'*, ed. by Sister Mary Roth. Catholic U.P. pp. 114. $2.

[32] *Francis Thompson: A Critical Biography*, by Paul van K. Thomson. Nelson. pp. 280. 36s. (See p. 255.)

[33] *The Aesthetic Movement in English Literature*, by Lorenz Eckhoff. Oslo U.P., 1959. pp. 34. N. kr. 3.50.

Rossetti and Yeats, as well as on the movement generally.

A collection of Wilde's essays and stories and two plays has been published, with an introduction by Richard Ellmann.[34] In 'The Socialist Aesthete' (*Listener*) A. E. Dyson comments on Wilde's ideas. Hesketh Pearson writes on 'Oscar Wilde and His Actors' (*Theatre Arts*).

'Although he thought of himself as for all time, no man was ever more of and for his own time', says J. B. Townsend in his study of John Davidson.[35] He consequently not only sets Davidson in the nineties (where he was never much at home), but traces his affinities with the nineteenth century as a whole. These extend immediately to the 'Spasmodic' poets, and branch out into many different areas of activity. In a sense he brought some of these to a full stop, for 'he ultimately declared his belief that in man the material universe had already achieved the fullest perfection possible'. This book does much to explain T. S. Eliot's opinion that Davidson possessed 'genius, but the incapacity for perfection'. 'Even the most perfervid student of Davidson could hardly ask much more than he has been given', says R. D. Macleod (whose selection from Davidson was noted in *YW* xl. 266) in a review of the book in *VS*.

Although Thomas Hardy used portions of his first wife's manuscript *Recollections* in his autobiography, the complete manuscript has not hitherto been published. The present edition[36] shows that it is, in fact, of singular importance to the study of Hardy's poetry, since his discovery of it, after his first wife's death, resulted in many poems about her. The full text is given, with notes by Evelyn Hardy, together with fourteen of Hardy's poems directly inspired by passages in it. These are annotated by Robert Gittings. Apart from their relevance to Hardy's poems, these *Recollections* have great charm of their own as a personal account of life in the west of England after the period of the Crimean War. *The Pattern of Hardy's Poetry*, according to Samuel Hynes,[37] is that of 'the eternal conflict between irreconcilables, which was for Hardy the first principle, and indeed the only principle, of universal order'. Dealing with Hardy's use of 'philosophy' in his poems, Hynes argues that 'he was weakest when he attempted to find meaning in experience through logical developmental patterns, and strongest when he was intent simply to set life's contrarieties together and let them act on one another'. A chapter on 'Hardy and the Poets' makes a comparison between Hardy and Barnes, and two admirers of Barnes, Patmore and Hopkins. The implications of these comparisons are carried to a consideration of Hardy's style, the roughness of which was intended to convey 'Man's ignorance, and his inability to reduce the universe to a significant order'. Hardy's failure to find an individual verse form reflected the disintegration of tradition that caused him so much concern; and his imagery reflects the 'antinomial' pattern' that was central to his vision. This perceptive and well-written study ends with a discussion of *The Dynasts* as exemplary of Hardy's achievement —'one of the great eccentric works of our time'. Emma Clifford writes on 'The Impressionistic View of History

[34] *Oscar Wilde: Selected Writings*, ed. by Richard Ellmann. O.U.P. (World's Classics.) pp. xiii+361. 7s. 6d.

[35] *John Davidson: Poet of Armageddon*, by J. Benjamin Townsend. Yale U.P. pp. xiv+555. 68s. $8.50.

[36] *Some Recollections*, by Emma Hardy. Ed. by Evelyn Hardy and Robert Gittings. O.U.P. pp. xv+91. 16s. (Cf. n. 61.)

[37] *The Pattern of Hardy's Poetry*, by Samuel Hynes. North Carolina U.P. and O.U.P. pp. ix+193. 25s.

in *The Dynasts'* (*MLQ*), and T. R. Dale on 'The Dynasts and Eduard von Hartmann' (*NQ*).

William Barnes is the subject of a short study by W. T. Levy.[38]

Bulwer's 1832 Committee of the House of Commons to investigate the state of the drama revealed restrictions and anomalies in the fields of monopoly, censorship, and copyright. These findings are examined by Dewey Ganzel in 'Patent Wrongs and Patent Theatres: Drama and the Law in the Early Nineteenth Century' (*PMLA*). Claude R. Flory writes on 'Charles Rogers: Late Victorian Provincial Playwright' (*MD*). Articles in *Theatre Notebook* included 'The Nineteenth-Century Matinée' by W. A. Armstrong (1960), 'The Nineteenth-Century Stage at Piper's Opera House' by Wendell Cole, 'A Sadler's Wells Scene Book' by Sybil Rosenfeld, and 'William Schwenck Gilbert: An Anniversary Survey', in which Reginald Allen gives a list of first performances of his plays, and of printed editions.

Addenda

The early draft of John Stuart Mill's *Autobiography*, now in the University of Illinois Library, has been published in full for the first time.[39] Written mainly during the years 1853–4 and altered and 'improved' by Mill's wife, this is a complete account, as Mill would have given it, of his life up to his marriage in 1851. This publication includes in the notes a selection of earlier readings, and a series of extracts from thirty rejected leaves preserved at the end of the manuscript.

An unusual and interesting publication is the actress Frances Kemble's account of life on a slave plantation in America.[40]

Henry Bulwer-Lytton is the subject of a study by Juliette Decreus.[41]

(c) Novels and Novelists

This year one of the most entertaining studies of the Victorian novel is Margaret Maison's survey of Victorian religious novels.[42] She writes: 'Fiction became the pulpit, the confessional and the battlefield for countless Victorians, and the novel was used by them more than any other form of art to portray the religious movements of their time, to be a vehicle for all manner of theological and ecclesiastical propaganda, to conduct debates and controversies, and to tell the world of their doubts and conflicts, their spiritual travels and phases of faith.' This is an informative work, but it is a pity that it is not well documented. There is a useful bibliography. E. Rosenberg traces the Jewish criminal and the Jewish paragon as they appear in the English novel during the period 1795–1895.[43] He comments on novels by Maria Edgeworth, Scott, Dickens, Trollope, Bulwer-Lytton, George Eliot, and George Du Maurier. D. S. Bland makes reference to Jane Austen, among others, in 'Endangering the Reader's Neck: Background Description in the Novel' (*Criticism*). Other articles on the novel include Edmund Blunden's 'On Regency Fiction: A Fragment' (*E & S*); Myron F. Brightfield's 'The Medical Profession in Early Victorian England, as Depicted in the

[38] *William Barnes: The Man and the Poems*, by W. T. Levy. Longmans (Dorchester). pp. 195. 10s. 6d.

[39] *The Early Draft of John Stuart Mill's 'Autobiography'*, ed. by J. Stillinger. Illinois U.P. pp. 218. $5.50.

[40] *Journal of a Residence on A Georgian Plantation in 1838–1839*, by Frances Anne Kemble. Ed. and Introd. by J. A. Scott. Jonathan Cape. pp. lxx+415+viii. 36s.

[41] *Henry Bulwer-Lytton et Hortense Allart*, by Juliette Decreus. Paris. pp. 161.

[42] *Search Your Soul, Eustace*, by Margaret Maison. Sheed and Ward. pp. ix+360. 12s. 6d.

[43] *From Shylock to Svengali*, by E. Rosenberg. Peter Owen. pp. viii+388. 42s.

Novels of the Period (1840–1870)' (*Bull. Hist. Medicine*); Marion Lockhead's 'Clio Junior: Historical Novels for Children' (*Quarterly Review*); and 'James Hogg und der Roman der englischen Romantik' (*Archiv*) by Teut Riese. There is a collection of modern essays on Victorian literature.[44]

L. F. Peck has produced the first adequate biography of 'Monk' Lewis.[45] He gives a factual account of Lewis's life and traces his literary career, but does not attempt much critical comment on Lewis's writings. Lewis emerges from this biography an attractive personality. This is a valuable and interesting book.

W. C. Booth in 'Point of View and the Control of Distance in *Emma*' (*NCF*) has made a perceptive and sensible analysis of Jane Austen's use of the 'omniscient narrator' technique; Mordecai Marcus demonstrates 'the pattern and effects of the thematic contrasts' among the four young couples in the novel in his essay 'A Major Thematic Pattern in *Pride and Prejudice*' (*NCF*); and R. E. Hughes in 'The Education of Emma Woodhouse' (*NCF*) tries to combine two prevailing critical approaches to Jane Austen's works. There are notes on her novels by Warren Derry in a letter, 'Jane Austen' (*TLS*, 29 Dec.). Other articles on Jane Austen are F. W. Bradbrook's 'Sources of Jane Austen's Ideas about Nature in *Mansfield Park*' (*NQ*); D. R. Fryxell's '*Lovers' Vows* in *Mansfield Park*' (*Midwest Review*); Ian Jack's 'The Epistolary Element in Jane Austen' (*English Studies Today*); J. A. Levine's '*Lady Susan*: Jane Austen's Character of the Merry Widow' (*Studies in English Literature*); Walton Litz's 'The Chronology of *Mansfield Park*'

(*NQ*); B. C. Southam's 'Jane Austen: A Broken Romance?' (*NQ*), and 'The Text of *Sanditon*' (*NQ*) by the same author; C. E. Edge's '*Mansfield Park* and Ordination' (*NCF*); S. M. Chanda's 'The New Vein in *Mansfield Park*' (*Indian Journal of English Studies*, 1960); and '*The Loiterer*: A Reflection of Jane Austen's Early Environment' (*RES*) by Walton Litz.

In his book on Scott,[46] Donald Davie concentrates on those writers who were influenced by Scott rather than on an appraisal of Scott's own novels, although there is a good discussion of *Waverley*. Articles on Scott are: D. Biggins's '*Measure for Measure* and *The Heart of Midlothian*' (*Ea*); D. B. Green's 'New Letters of Sir Walter Scott: 1813–1831' (*NQ*); W. H. Marshall's 'Point of View and Structure in *The Heart of Midlothian*' (*NCF*); W. U. McDonald, Jr.'s 'A Letter of Sir Walter Scott to William Scott on the Jeffrey-Swift Controversy' (*RES*); W. E. Simeone's 'The Robin Hood of *Ivanhoe*' (*Journal of American Folklore*); and Alexander Welsh's 'Sir Walter Scott and Eisenhower' (*New Republic*).

D. B. Green writes on 'Two Letters of Thomas Love Peacock' (*PQ*). The Everyman edition of *Headlong Hall* and *Nightmare Abbey* has been reissued, with a brief but informative introduction by P. M. Yarker.[47]

Paul Bloomfield has made a rather superficial short study of Benjamin Disraeli.[48] There is a short but interesting study of Disraeli's idealization of Bolingbroke.[49] S. R. Graubard discusses

[44] *Victorian Literature: Modern Essays in Criticism*, ed. by Austin Wright. O.U.P. pp. 377. $2.25.

[45] *A Life of Matthew Gregory Lewis*, by Louis F. Peck. Harvard U.P. pp. ix+331. $7.75.

[46] *The Heyday of Sir Walter Scott*, by Donald Davie. Routledge and Kegan Paul. pp. vii+168. 23s.

[47] *Headlong Hall, Nightmare Abbey*, by T. L. Peacock. Introd. by P. M. Yarker. Dent. pp. xv+298. 8s. 6d.

[48] *Disraeli*, by Paul Bloomfield. Longmans. pp. 39. 2s. 6d.

[49] *Beaconsfield and Bolingbroke*, by R. Faber. Faber & Faber. pp. 107. 18s.

Disraeli together with Burke and Churchill as critics of their times.[50] A. H. Frietzsche examines Disraeli's treatment of religion in his novels.[51] R. W. Stewart makes a shrewd comment (*TLS*, 13 Jan.) on the *TLS* review of B. R. Jerman's *The Young Disraeli* (1960). There is an illuminating study of Disraeli's political career by C. J. Lewis, 'Theory and Expediency in the Policy of Disraeli' (*VS*). C. H. Kegel's 'Lord John Manners and the Young England Movement: Romanticism in Politics' (*Western Political Quarterly*) can be mentioned here.

Following close on Daphne du Maurier's biography of Branwell Brontë comes Winifred Gérin's.[52] The later biography is more scholarly and more objective than the earlier, and is based on a careful scrutiny of the considerable number of manuscripts to which Winifred Gérin has had access. The 'key word' of which C. Burkhart writer in 'Another Key Word for *Jane Eyre*' (*NCF*) is 'nature'. W. H. Marshall has an essay on 'The Self, the World, and the Structure of *Jane Eyre*' (*Revue des langues vivantes*).

J. B. Priestley has made an original contribution to the writings on Charles Dickens in the form of 'a pictorial biography'.[53] He has gathered together all kinds of pictorial material to illustrate a summary of Dickens's life. Obviously this is not a scholarly work, but it is a readable and interesting book. A. O. J. Cockshut studies the combination of public entertainer and literary artist in Dickens.[54] He tries to discover how a man with a commonplace mind, attuned to the public taste, could develop into a master of his art. He considers Dickens to have been a man of limited sensibility and intellect, and concludes that as the novelist's creative mind worried the themes of money, squalor, and violence with which he was obsessed, so his literary art developed. In C. G. L. Du Cann's gossipy book on Dickens,[55] not only are there minor inaccuracies, but the main thesis—that Dickens failed in love, realized it and bitterly felt and expressed the tragedy of that supreme failure—is not very satisfactory. It gives a false perspective of Dickens's life, for, although he might have been the continually disappointed lover, his energies were constantly being absorbed by his other multifarious activities. John Butt and Kathleen Tillotson are nearer the truth when they remark, in *Dickens at Work* (1957), '. . . his life-long love-affair with his reading public . . . when all is said, is by far the most interesting love-affair of his life'.

R. A. Hunter and Ida Macalpine in 'Dickens and Conolly: An Embarrassed Editor's Disclaimer' (*TLS*, 11 Aug.), put in a bad light Charles Reade's attacks on Dickens's medical friend Conolly in *Very Hard Cash*. Far from being the righteously indignant and well-informed social reformer, in this instance Reade appears to have made a malicious and unwarranted attack upon Conolly. In 'Dickens and Conolly' P. A. W. Collins comments on this article and its attribution of anonymous articles in *Household Words* to Dickens (*TLS*, 18 Aug.). W. J. Carlton, in 'Dickens Periodicals' (*TLS*, 22 Sept.), commenting on Collins's remark that the Contributors' Book for *All the Year Round* seems to have disappeared, suggests a clue to its whereabouts. In the Dickens number of *REL* P. A. W.

[50] *Burke, Disraeli and Churchill*, by S. R. Graubard. Harvard U.P. pp. 262. 40s.

[51] *Disraeli's Religion: The Treatment of Religion in Disraeli's Novels*, by A. H. Frietzsche. Utah State U.P.

[52] *Branwell Brontë*, by Winifred Gérin. Nelson. pp. 338. 35s.

[53] *Charles Dickens: A Pictorial Biography*, by J. B. Priestley. Thames and Hudson. pp. 144. 25s.

[54] *The Imagination of Charles Dickens*, by A. O. J. Cockshut. Collins. pp. 192. 16s.

[55] *The Love Lives of Charles Dickens*, by C. G. L. Du Cann. Muller. pp. 268. 30s.

Collins examines 'The Significance of Dickens's Periodicals', and studies Dickens's practices as an editor, and the relationship between his articles and work for periodicals and his novels. 'Much remains to be done', writes Collins, 'on this connection and disparity between Dickens the novelist and Dickens the journalist, public man, and private philanthropist.' Also in this number K. J. Fielding writes on 'The Critical Autonomy of *Great Expectations*', and warns against the dangers of imposing any single interpretation on the novel; Robert Barnard has an essay 'The Choral Symphony: *Our Mutual Friend*'; C. A. Bodelsen discusses Dickens's choice of names in ' "The Physiognomy of the Name" '; John Butt considers 'Dickens's Instructions for *Martin Chuzzlewit*, Plate XVIII'; Douglas Grant comments on 'A Sketch of Charles Dickens'; Arnold Kettle has 'Thoughts on *David Copperfield*'; Sylvère Monod presents 'A French View of Dickens's Humour'; Randolph Quirk makes 'Some Observations on the Language of Dickens'; D. C. Thomson writes on 'Francis Jeffrey: Charles Dickens's Friend and Critic'; and Angus Wilson discusses 'The Heroes and Heroines of Dickens'.

J. K. Gottshall, in 'Devils Abroad: The Unity and Significance of *Barnaby Rudge*' (*NCF*), sees the idiot boy as the centre of this novel, which he considers to be 'the first of Dickens's novels in which the heavenly powers fail to triumph over the forces of darkness'. John Butt makes proposals for an edition of Dickens in 'Editing a Nineteenth-Century Novelist' (*English Studies Today*), and Barbara Hardy discusses 'The Change of Heart in Dickens's Novels' (*VS*). P. A. W. Collins writes on 'Dickens and the Prison Governor George Laval Chesterton' (*Dickensian*), and by means of an account of Chesterton, who was Governor of Coldbath Fields Prison

and who was much admired by Dickens, shows how far Dickens's reputation as a prison reformer is justified. Also in *The Dickensian* are: ' "Captain Holland" Identified', by W. J. Carlton, who also contributes 'More About the Dickens Ancestry'; ' "Wopsle" ' and ' "Snevellicci" ', by V. C. Clinton-Baddeley; 'Dickens on the Education of Girls', by P. A. W. Collins; 'Dickens's Complex Plots', by A. C. Coolidge, Jr.; 'The Uncommercial Traveller and the Royal Commercial Travellers' Schools', by W. H. Drayton; 'Dickens and Miss Burdett-Coutts: The Last Phase', by K. J. Fielding; 'A Note on George Gordon', by F. A. Gibson; 'Dickens in Russia', by B. Gilenson; 'The Modern Tone of Charles Dickens', by Jean M. Kelty; 'The Method of *A Tale of Two Cities*', by W. H. Marshall; ' "The Immortal Memory of Charles Dickens" ', by Sylvère Monod; ' "Messrs. Four, Two and One" ', and 'The Theatrical Ternans', by M. Morley; 'Dickens and the Other Hughes', and 'When the Wine Merchant Wrote to Dickens: The Dickens-Ellis Correspondence', by N. C. Peyrouton; and 'With a Blush Retire'—on Dickens's treatment of death—by A. Walbank.

Other articles on Dickens include: D. D. Anderson's 'Charles Dickens on Lake Erie' (*Inland Seas*); R. Atthill's 'Dickens and the Railway' (*English*); P. A. W. Collins's 'The Middlesex Magistrate in *David Copperfield*' (*NQ*) and 'Queen Mab's Chariot Among the Steam Engines: Dickens and "Fancy" ' (*ES*); C. R. Forker's 'The Language of Hands in *Great Expectations*' (*TSLL*); C. Izzo's 'Charles Dickens' (*Cultura e scuola*); A. Kettle's 'Dickens and the Popular Tradition' (*ZAA*); G. McCelvey's '*A Tale of Two Cities* and Gin Drinking' (*NQ*); R. D. McMaster's '*Little Dorrit*: Experience and Design' (*QQ*); M. H. Miller's 'Charles Dickens at the English Charity Dinner'

(*Quarterly Journal of Speech*); Sister M. C. Sharp's 'The Archetypal Feminine: *Our Mutual Friend*' (*University of Kansas City Review*); R. M. Vande Kieft's 'Patterns of Communication in *Great Expectations*' (*NCF*); and G. J. Worth's 'The Genesis of Jo the Crossing-Sweeper' (*JEGP*).

Arthur Pollard's essay on Mrs. Gaskell, whom he considers to be 'a major minor novelist', is sound and perceptive—'The Novels of Mrs. Gaskell' (*BJRL*). He adds a descriptive list of the Gaskell manuscript material in Manchester. Miriam Allott writes on 'Mrs. Gaskell's "The Old Nurse's Story": A Link between *Wuthering Heights* and *The Turn of the Screw*' (*NQ*).

A study of Charles Reade published this year has not been available for notice.[56]

There are several articles on Anthony Trollope: 'The Road to Hiram's Hospital: A Byway of Early Victorian History' (*VS*), by G. F. A. Best; 'Some New Facts about the Beginning of Trollope's *Framley Parsonage*' (*Studia romanica et anglica Zagrabiensia*, 1960), by Sonia Bićanić; 'The World of Anthony Trollope' (*Texas Quarterly*), by G. W. Brace; 'Trollope's Political Novels (Chronicles of Parliamentary Life)' (*Indian Journal of English Studies*, 1960), by R. Mohan; and 'Trollope's Style' (*Ball State Teachers College Forum*), by Geoffrey Tillotson.

G. J. Worth traces the increasing maturity of Thackeray's Henry Esmond in 'The Unity of *Henry Esmond*' (*NCF*)—in the choices which Esmond has to make in the novel 'he comes to accept the less exciting and glamorous but more stable and solid alternative in each case'. W. H. Marshall studies 'Dramatic Irony in *Henry Esmond*' (*Revue des langues vivantes*) and J.

Hagan has 'A Note on the Napoleonic Background of *Vanity Fair*' (*NCF*). In 'Becky Sharp and Lord Steyne—Thackeray or Disraeli?' (*NCF*) D. J. Greene suggests that Thackeray was indebted for these two characters to Disraeli's creations, Mrs. Guy Flouncey and Lord Monmouth, in *Coningsby*. E. D. H. Johnson, in '*Vanity Fair* and *Amelia*: Thackeray in the Perspective of the Eighteenth Century' (*MP*), makes use of the present fashionable contrast between Fielding and Thackeray which is detrimental to Thackeray, and concludes, 'It is because its negations are so much more convincing than its affirmations that *Vanity Fair* betrays Thackeray into sentimentality whenever he tries to go beyond satire.' Other articles on Thackeray are: C. Comorovski's 'W. M. Thackeray: Aspecte ale măiestrèi artistice (en aplicaţii la problemele de traducere)' (*Revista de filologie romanicà şi germanicà*, 1960); P. G. Davies's 'The Miscegenation Theme in the Works of Thackeray' (*MLN*); and N. A. Salerno's '*Catherine*: Theme and Structure' (*American Imago*).

This year the most important study of George Eliot's work is W. J. Harvey's book.[57] He examines the methods of George Eliot's art and stresses the formal characteristics of her work. He makes an intelligent attempt to see the Victorian novelist's aims and methods in an historical context, and to provide a critical apparatus for judging the Victorian novel not wholly dependent upon an uncritical acceptance of the critical theories of Henry James. There is also a book dealing with Edith Simcox, the Victorian spinster and writer, and her infatuated worship of George Eliot, whom she met in 1872.[58]

---

[56] *Charles Reade: A Study in Victorian Authorship*, by Wayne Burns. N.Y.: Bookman Associates. pp. 360. $6.

[57] *The Art of George Eliot*, by W. J. Harvey. Chatto and Windus. pp. 254. 21s.

[58] *Edith Simcox and George Eliot*, by K. A. McKenzie. Introd. by G. S. Haight. O.U.P. pp. 146. 18s.

The main part of the book consists of Miss Simcox's autobiography, the manuscript of which was acquired by the Bodleian Library in 1958. F. C. Thomson in 'Felix Holt as Classic Tragedy' (NCF) attempts 'to re-examine the Transome plot in the context of classic tragedy'. J. Hagan in 'Middlemarch: Narrative Unity in the Story of Dorothea Brooke' (NCF) scrutinizes the workmanship of the story of Dorothea in the novel. There are several other articles dealing with George Eliot: 'George Eliot in the 1860's' (VS), by Miriam Allott; 'The Heritage of Will Ladislaw' (NCF), by R. A. Greenberg; 'A Missing Month in Daniel Deronda' (TLS, 3 Feb.), by G. Handley; 'Innocence in the Novels of George Eliot' (English Studies Today), by Irène Simon; 'The Metaphorical Texture of Daniel Deronda' (Books Abroad), by W. R. Steinhoff; and 'Lydgate and the Heroic Aspiration in Middlemarch' (Prague Studies in English), by Ian Milner.

Norman Kelvin writes on George Meredith as the artist-moralist,[59] and examines his ideas of nature and society and the ways in which they influenced both the form and the content of his novels and poems. F. R. Karl in 'Beauchamp's Career: An English Ordeal' (NCF) makes a lively study of a neglected novel. I. H. Buchen considers 'The Importance of the Minor Characters in The Ordeal of Richard Feverel' (BUSE); and K. S. Prichard discusses 'Contrasts: Meredith and Marchesi' (Meanjin, University of Melbourne).

Catharine Firman writes on 'Lewis Carroll, Oxford Satirist' (Claremont Quarterly, 1960), and Patricia M. Spacks examines 'Logic and Language in Through the Looking Glass' (ETC.: A Review of General Semantics).

R. L. Wolff has produced a sympathetic and sound study of the work of a neglected novelist, George MacDonald.[60]

Elsie N. Caldwell writes on Robert Louis Stevenson: 'Requiem: Gem of Archives' (Manuscripts). There is a note on the publication of the autograph draft of a preface by Stevenson to Travels with a Donkey—E. Mehew's 'A Stevenson Manuscript' (TLS, 14 July).

Emma Hardy's recollections of her early years which she wrote shortly before her death, and which were discovered and corrected by Hardy, have been published this year.[61] The book contains some lively sketches made by Hardy and Emma. R. E. C. Houghton writes on The Return of the Native and King Lear in 'Hardy and Shakespeare' (NQ), and John Patton prints 'An Unpublished Hardy Letter to Millay' (Colby Library Quarterly). John Hagan has 'A Note on the Significance of Diggory Venn' (NCF). Other articles on Hardy include 'Two Rare Birds in Hardy's The Return of the Native' (NQ), by C. J. P. Beatty; 'Thomas Hardy and the Old Masters' (BUSE), by R. C. Carpenter; 'A Half-open Door' (Listener), by C. Day Lewis; 'A Laodicean; A Note on a Minor Novel' (PQ), by R. Y. Drake, Jr.; 'Tess and the Local Cerealia' (PQ), by L. Elsbree; 'Hardy's The Woodlanders: Inwardness and Memory' (Studies in English Literature), by G. S. Fayen; 'A Reading of Tess of the D'Urbervilles' (Essays in Literary History), by H. E. Hamilton; 'Two Letters of Thomas Hardy to P. W. Bunting' (NQ), by R. L. Lowe; and 'Blind Will or Blind

[59] A Troubled Eden: Nature and Society in the Works of George Meredith, by Norman Kelvin. Oliver and Boyd. pp. ix+250. 25s.

[60] The Golden Key: A Study of the Fiction of George MacDonald, by Robert Lee Wolff. Yale U.P. pp. 425. $6.
[61] Some Recollections by Emma Hardy, with Notes by Evelyn Hardy. Together with Some Relevant Poems by Thomas Hardy, with Notes by Robert Gittings. O.U.P. pp. xv+ 91. 16s. (Cf. note 36.)

Hero: Philosophy and Myth in Hardy's *Return of the Native*' (*Criticism*), by Eleanor McCann.

The correspondence between George Gissing and H. G. Wells has been edited by R. A. Gettmann.[62] The *TLS* review of this book occasioned two letters, one from Anthony Curtis (*TLS*, 28 July), who makes some factual corrections to the review, and one by J. R. Hammond (*TLS*, 4 Aug.). Gissing's letters to his German friend Eduard Bertz, whom he first met in London in 1878, have been edited by A. C. Young.[63] These letters cover the years 1887–1903 and give a clear picture of Gissing's life and personality at that time, of the ways in which he developed ideas for his books, and of the methods by which he wrote them. Storm Jameson has written a biography of Morley Roberts, the friend of Gissing and of W. H. Hudson, and author of the fictionalized life of Gissing, *The Private Life of Henry Maitland*.[64] Jacob Korg has edited 'George Gissing's Commonplace Book: A Manuscript from the Berg Collection of the New York Public Library' (*BNYPL*); and A. C. Young writes on 'The Death of Gissing: A Fourth Report' (*Essays in Literary History*).

U. C. Knoepflmacher has an essay ' "Ishmael" or Anti-Hero? The Division of Self: *The Way of All Flesh*' (*English Fiction in Transition, 1880–1920*), and Anselm Schlösser discusses 'Der viktorianische Gulliver: Betrachtungen über Samuel Butlers *Erewhon* und *Erewhon Revisited*' (*ZAA*).

The following are publications on the minor novelists of the period: an edition of Maturin's *Melmoth the Wanderer*, with a good introduction which 'places' the book in the tradition of the Gothic novel;[65] J. I. Fradin's essay ' "The Absorbing Tyranny of Every-day Life": Bulwer-Lytton's *A Strange Story*' (*NCF*), in which he sees Bulwer's novels as the attempts of the novelist 'to record his reactions to the complex Victorian experience', and relates his purpose in *A Strange Story* to that behind the symbolist movement—'to re-establish the intimate connection between the physical and the spiritual'; D. J. Barr's comment on 'A Misquotation in Lytton' (*NQ*); Marion Lockhead's article 'Margaret Oliphant; A Half-Forgotten Victorian' (*Quarterly Review*); Margaret Maison's amusing and informative comments on Mrs. Henry Wood and the moral sensational novelists, 'Adultresses in Agony' (*Listener*); Horst Drescher's book on Surtees,[66] which is a biography combined with a study of the novels, together with a useful bibliography; Gerald Weales's article on Rider Haggard, 'Reader to Rider' (*Commonweal*); H. J. Francis's essay on George Borrow, 'Borroviana' (*Journal of the Gypsy Lore Society*); and two attractively produced monographs for young readers, one on Mrs. Molesworth,[67] and one on Mrs. Ewing.[68]

(d) Selected Prose Writers

A selection of prose written by the major English Romantic poets and essayists, together with 'Political and Social' and 'Critical and Imaginative' passages from other writers of the period, has been published this year.

[62] *George Gissing and H. G. Wells: Their Friendship and Correspondence*, ed. by R. A. Gettmann. Hart-Davis. pp. 285. 25s.
[63] *The Letters of George Gissing to Eduard Bertz*, ed. by A. C. Young. Constable. pp. xl+337. 30s.
[64] *Morley Roberts*, by Storm Jameson. Unicorn Press. pp. 64. 10s. 6d.
[65] *Melmoth the Wanderer*, by C. R. Maturin. Ed. by W. F. Axton. Nebraska U.P. pp. xxii+412. $2.40.
[66] *Robert Smith Surtees: Ein frühviktorianischer Erzähler*, by Horst Drescher. Marburg. pp. 205.
[67] *Mrs. Molesworth*, by R. Lancelyn Green. Bodley Head. pp. 80. 7s. 6d.
[68] *Mrs. Ewing*, by Gillian Avery. Bodley Head. pp. 80. 7s. 6d.

The book has an informative critical introduction and notes.[69]

E. J. Moyne has an article on Hazlitt's father, 'The Reverend William Hazlitt and Dickinson College' (*Pennsylvania Magazine of History and Biography*), and W. P. Albrecht discusses 'Liberalism and Hazlitt's Tragic View' (*CE*). Other essays on Hazlitt are B. Dobrée's 'William Hazlitt, 1778–1830' (*REL*); W. H. Marshall's 'An Addition to the Hazlitt Canon: Arguments from External and Internal Evidence' (*PBSA*); and H. M. Sikes's 'Hazlitt, the *London Magazine*, and the "Anonymous Reviewer" ' (*BNYPL*).

Elizabeth Nitchie, in 'Mary Shelley, Traveler' (*KSJ*), studies Mary's writings, particularly the *History of a Six Weeks' Tour* (1817) and *Rambles in Germany and Italy* (1844), to give a picture of her as a traveller.

H. M. Sikes writes on 'William Hone: Regency Patriot, Parodist, and Pamphleteer' (*Newberry Library Bulletin*).

Clifford Leech has an article 'De Quincey as Literary Critic' (*REL*), and Geoffrey Carnall, in 'De Quincey on the Knocking at the Gate' (*REL*), considers that De Quincey, typical of his time, felt a 'tremor of exhilaration' at murderers who were free from moral inhibitions.

J. I. Ades writes on 'Charles Lamb, Romantic Criticism, and the Aesthetics of Sympathy' (*Delta Epsilon Sigma Bulletin*); Wallace Nethery discusses 'Eliana Americana 1838–1848' (*ABC*); and J. R. Barker comments on 'The First Mrs. Hazlitt: and Some New Lamb Letters' (*Charles Lamb Society Bulletin*).

There is an article by F. R. Hart, 'Proofreading Lockhart's *Scott*: The Dynamics of Biographical Reticence' (*SB*).

W. U. McDonald, Jr., writes on 'H. D. Inglis (1795–1835): Some Additions and Corrections to *D.N.B.*' (*NQ*).

The first volume of the exhaustive edition of J. H. Newman's letters has appeared.[70] It is the eleventh volume in the series planned, and covers the crucial period in Newman's life from October 1845 until December 1846, that is at the time of, and immediately after, his conversion to the Roman Church. This series of volumes should prove invaluable to all who are interested in Newman as a man, or as a writer, or as a theologian.

'The Newman–Kingsley Dispute Continues' and can be followed in *TLS*, 17 Feb., 24 Feb., 3 Mar., 10 Mar., and 17 Mar. The combatants are D. E. Pett and C. S. Dessain. E. E. Kelly makes a comment on the dispute (10 Mar.).

W. H. Dunn has published a painstaking biography of James Anthony Froude.[71]

C. R. Sanders has an essay, 'Carlyle and Tennyson' (*PMLA*), on the relationship between the two writers, and suggests something of the nature of the impact of Carlyle's mind upon Tennyson's poetry. Saburo Ota writes on 'Thomas Carlyle's Relation with Modern Japanese Literature' (*Studies in English Literature*, Tokyo), and C. R. Sanders on 'Retracing Carlyle's Irish Journey' (*Studies*). There is also a small but attractive selection of Carlyle's written judgements about the age in which he lived, together with an essay on Carlyle by his younger contemporary and fellow-historian, William Lecky.[72] This essay originally

---

[69] *Prose of the Romantic Period*, ed. by Carl Woodring. Boston: Houghton Mifflin. pp. 600.

[70] *Letters and Diaries of John Henry Newman*, Vol. XI, ed. by C. S. Dessain. Nelson. 63*s*.

[71] *James Anthony Froude*, by Waldo Hilary Dunn. O.U.P. pp. xiv+261. 35*s*. (Cf. note 6.)

[72] *These Days*, ed. by J. E. Longhurst. Coronado Press, New Mexico. pp. xxv+91. $1.25.

appeared in *The Contemporary Review* in 1891.

D. G. James has published his Gregynog Lectures (1953) on Matthew Arnold.[73] James describes Arnold's temperament, and then illustrates the decline of Romanticism in England by discussing Arnold's critical writings. James is a stern critic of Arnold the thinker, and maintains that the 'Failure of decisiveness, commitment and steadfastness shows itself . . . throughout his intellectual life; and indeed, he made it one of the themes of his poetry.' A. J. Lubell, in 'Matthew Arnold: Between Two Worlds' (*MLQ*), maintains that 'Arnold's shedding of Christian dogma determined the whole course of his intellectual and spiritual development', and examines 'his lifelong attempt to infuse fresh meaning into the ideals of the old faiths for his own day'. The following are essays and comments on Matthew Arnold: 'Matthew Arnold and the *London Review*' (*PMLA*) and 'Matthew Arnold and the National Eisteddfod' (*NQ*), by R. L. Brooks; 'Matthew Arnold and the *Daily Telegraph*' (*RES*), by S. M. B. Coulling; 'Significant Points of Comparison Between the Biblical Criticism of Thomas and Matthew Arnold' (*PMLA*), by E. L. Williamson, Jr.; and 'Godliness and Good Learning' (*TLS*, 8 Dec.), by Alan Harris.

M. J. Jackson and J. Rogan have an article on 'Thomas Arnold' (*Church Quarterly Review*), and E. L. Williamson, Jr., discusses 'Dr. Arnold as a Literary Critic: Two Uncollected Essays' (*NQ*).

Fernando Luciani writes on 'Macaulay nel centenario della morte' (*Idea*).

J. D. Rosenberg has published a study of Ruskin.[74] One hundred and twenty-four of the letters which Ruskin sent his goddaughter have been acquired by the John Rylands Library. Margaret E. Spence discusses them, and Constance Oldham's sympathy for, and understanding of, her godfather, in 'Ruskin's Correspondence with His God-Daughter Constance Oldham' (*BJRL*). Other articles on Ruskin are: 'Ruskin's Advice to an Amateur Artist: Some New Letters to Louisa, Marchioness of Waterford' (*Studies in English Literature*), by J. L. Bradley; 'English Literary Autographs XXXVIII: John Ruskin, 1819–1900' (*BC*), by T. J. Brown; 'Ruskin's Apologia' (*Downside Review*), by V. A. McClelland; and 'Poetic Truth and Pathetic Fallacy' (*TSLL*), by J. D. Thomas.

A comprehensive study of Walter Pater's life and works has been published by Germain d'Hangest.[75] There is an essay, 'Pattern in Walter Pater's Fiction' (*SP*), by R. T. Lenaghan; and M. Shinski writes on 'The Unfinished Sculptures of Michelangelo' (*Essays in English and American Literature*).

R. H. Tener comments on two articles by Bagehot which have hitherto escaped notice—'Bagehot, Jeffrey and Renan' (*TLS*, 11 Aug.).

[73] *Matthew Arnold and the Decline of English Romanticism*, by D. G. James. O.U.P. pp. viii+110. 18s. (Cf. note 29.)

[74] *The Darkening Glass: A Portrait of Ruskin's Genius*, by J. D. Rosenberg. Columbia U.P. pp. 274. $5.

[75] *Walter Pater l'homme et l'œuvre*, by Germain d'Hangest. Didier: Paris. 2 vols. pp. 371; 404. 60 N.F.

XIV. THE TWENTIETH CENTURY

By Marjorie Thompson *and* B. C. Southam

Sections 1–5 relate to books published during the year, and are by Marjorie Thompson. Sections 6–10, covering articles, are contributed by B. C. Southam.

1. *General*

Martin Green[1] sketches in the background to the literature of today from a provocative angle. He is young and angry, and presents an England which is 'no longer a gentleman's country'. With all traditional images disdainfully dismissed, his estimate is that of a young man who has chosen the American way of life. Amongst a good deal that is superficial and showy, there is some justice in the selection of Lawrence, Orwell, and Leavis as the 'essential' Englishmen of the present day, in that they not only transmit the Victorian heritage, but are the forerunners of the contemporary generation of writers.

A more dispassionate and considered account comes from John Mander,[2] who examines the implications and applications of the term 'commitment', now degenerated into indeterminate vagueness and taken up as the 'rallying cry of those who deplore the artist's unconcern with the political realities of England'. Mander questions whether lack of commitment prevents a man from being a great writer, analysing the work of Orwell, Auden, Thom Gunn, Ted Hughes, and the 'angry young men'. The assessment of John Osborne is particularly shrewd; his historical importance is recognized, but he is described as basically noncommittal. The conclusion is that 'a

working-class novel or play may well be as muddled and at bottom as noncommittal as any West End drawing-room drama'.

A further study of the problems of the contemporary writer is provided in a volume of essays[3] introduced by Stephen Spender. He points out that contemporary conditions are so adverse that they may even prevent the writer from writing, and mentions in particular the shadow of the destruction of civilization, shifting terms of reference, rapid changes—all of which make for difficulty of communication; indeed the air is 'pregnant with impossibilities'. The question is whether the artist 'can continue to function as a source of fresh images of life'. Essays are contributed by Arnold Toynbee, John Bowen, Lawrence Durrell, Gerald Heard, Nathalie Sarraute, and William Golding. Hope is not altogether abandoned, several writers being convinced of the artist's ability to assert his individual judgement, to make a choice, to recognize that freedom will not be extinguished, even in conditions where 'human beings are dwarfed by human society'.

The 'dilemma' of the modern artist had already been foreseen nearly thirty years ago by Cyril Connolly, whose study of contemporary writing[4] is

---

[1] *A Mirror for Anglo-Saxons*, by Martin Green. Longmans. pp. 178. 18s.

[2] *The Writer and Commitment*, by John Mander. Secker & Warburg. pp. 215. 25s.

[3] *The Writer's Dilemma*: Essays first published in *The Times Literary Supplement* under the heading 'Limits of Control' with an Introduction by Stephen Spender. O.U.P. pp. xxi+88. 12s. 6d.

[4] *Enemies of Promise*, by Cyril Connolly. Penguin Books. pp. 283. 3s. 6d.

reissued in the 1949 revised edition. In 1938 he had contemplated the possibility of culture disappearing altogether, the need for 'writing against the current', and had analysed the 'forces that militate against the production of great writing'. When he revised his book in 1949 he was surprised that he had had to make so few alterations in judgement. At this still later date, they stand with equal validity, and at least one of his prophecies has been fulfilled —that of the possibility of a revival in the drama.

The literature of a more settled age is presented for revaluation in a collection of essays edited by Richard Ellmann.[5] The Edwardians and late Victorians are the subjects of a determined attempt to dispel the misconception that they were 'doomed and rather silly'. The writers of the 1890's are shown to anticipate the moderns, and to form the transition from the Victorians. Yeats and Wells are given special attention, Yeats's progress from the ivory tower to responsibility being representative of the whole trend of modern literature. For Wells it is claimed that he cannot be regarded as a mere journalist, since he developed serious attitudes to the novel as an art-form, and in *Tono-Bungay*, for example, was capable of portraying a doomed society in an utterance as prophetic as Shaw's in *Heartbreak House*. Wells is described as the last novelist 'to write from a sense of society as a whole', and is ranked 'just below Conrad, James, Yeats and Shaw'. The Edwardian theatre is rescued from the shadow of Shaw, and given full credit for its independent achievement, with Granville Barker placed as its most noteworthy playwright. The general claim is that the Edwardian

period has been discounted, and that the turning-point towards the modern world came as early as 1900, when a new self-consciousness emerged, a search for self in a period that was 'staring towards the atomic age'.

Rayner Heppenstall's study of the relationship between French and English literature[6] includes two sections on the twentieth century, in which he surveys Catholic writing, and in particular considers Joyce's treatment of Edouard Dujardin. He then proceeds to show how later novelists, since Joyce had 'made further literature impossible', have reverted to an insular form owing nothing to French culture—special attention being given to C. P. Snow, John Wain, and Kingsley Amis.

2. *The Novel*

The operation of one of the 'enemies of promise' detected by Cyril Connolly is carefully observed by Irving Howe,[7] who looks into what happens to the novel 'when subjected to pressures of politics and political ideology'. He deals largely with Continental writers, but devotes a chapter to George Orwell. *1984*, that 'graphic vision of totalitarianism', is said to 'speak for our time'; it cannot be regarded merely as a political study or treatise, yet it must be approached through politics, and the conclusion is that 'the last thing [Orwell] cared about was literature', and that in his work 'politics achieves total dominion'.

The reinstatement of H. G. Wells in the ranks of literature is furthered by Bernard Bergonzi's scholarly study of the scientific romances[8] which covers

---

[5] *Edwardians and Late Victorians: English Institute Essays 1959*. Ed. with a Foreword by Richard Ellmann. Columbia U.P., 1960. pp. 245. 40s.

[6] *The Fourfold Tradition*: Notes on the French and English literatures, with some ethnological and historical asides, by Rayner Heppenstall. Barrie & Rockliff. pp. 280. 25s.

[7] *Politics and the Novel*, by Irving Howe. Stevens (New Left Books). pp. 251. 12s. 6d.

[8] *The Early H. G. Wells: A Study of the Scientific Romances*, by Bernard Bergonzi. Manchester U.P. pp. 226. 21s.

Wells's early period up to 1901. It is convincingly demonstrated that Wells did not merely write 'entertaining yarns', but that his work exhibits the 'intellectual components' of the *fin de siècle* trends of the 1890's, and at the same time looks forward to the twentieth century in its ambivalent attitude towards science which at this early period was sceptical and even pessimistic. The difference between Wells and Jules Verne is well brought out, as also is the influence of Nathaniel Hawthorne. Symbolic significances are traced and defined. There are useful reference notes, a select bibliography, and an appendix which reprints two early stories from the *Science Schools Journal* of 1887-8.

Graham Hough's study of D. H. Lawrence[9] is issued in a new edition. The preface notes the changes in Lawrence's reputation that have taken place in the five years since the book first appeared. That Lawrence is now warmly accepted is clearly demonstrated by the *Lady Chatterley* trial, in which it was obvious that 'many witnesses had absorbed Lawrence as part of their classic literary experience'. Yet, it is felt, the 'daemonic element' in Lawrence and his work will never be absorbed by bourgeois society. In spite of the changes Hough has left his book as it was first written.

Martin Jarrett-Kerr also brings out a second edition of his study of Lawrence,[10] which he first published in 1951 under the pen-name of 'Father William Tiverton' (see *YW* xxxii. 263). In his introduction he too notes the change in Lawrence's reputation, a change which necessitates the omission from T. S. Eliot's original foreword of

the observation that 'after being misunderstood he [Lawrence] is in danger of being ignored'. Otherwise the writer finds that in general his original assessment of Lawrence 'remains precisely what it was'. The section of the original preface which stated the necessity of a study that approached Lawrence from the Christian point of view is reprinted. A review of the major critical works on Lawrence published since the first edition brings the work up to date, and there is added a discussion of the *Lady Chatterley* trial which deals with it from the theological point of view, making a sensible stand against the confusion of prudery with Christian standards and providing an admirably just summary of Lawrence's case. The writer concludes with the insistence that Christians should acknowledge a debt of gratitude to Lawrence, while making it clear that he does not accept Lawrence as a Christian, but merely seeks to establish certain parallels.

Anthony Beal provides a fresh, straightforward interpretation of Lawrence.[11] He gets away from the now familiar established criticisms, and in his analysis of the novels frequently reveals new significances. Again the *Lady Chatterley* case is considered, briefly but soundly, and again an account of the changes in Lawrence's reputation is offered. The main thesis is that, having escaped the 'death rattle' of Proust and Joyce, Lawrence is no innovator in technique, but is of the highest importance for the new range of subject-matter which he brings to the novel.

C. H. Rolph, who was secretary of the Herbert Committee set up by the Society of Authors to reform and rationalize the criminal law of censorship, edits the transcript of the trial of

[9] *The Dark Sun: A Study of D. H. Lawrence*, by Graham Hough. Penguin Books. pp. 305. 5s.
[10] *D. H. Lawrence and Human Existence*, by Martin Jarrett-Kerr. Foreword by T. S. Eliot. S.C.M. Press. pp. 157. 8s. 6d.

[11] *D. H. Lawrence*, by Anthony Beal. (Writers & Critics Series.) Oliver & Boyd. pp. 128. 3s. 6d.

Lady Chatterley.[12] His introduction reveals that the first step towards prosecution was taken, not by the Government, but by the Director of Public Prosecutions; he traces the history of the new Obscene Publications Act of 1958, and outlines the provisions of the Act. His interpolated comments throw light on the whole course of the trial, particularly on the evidence given by Roy Jenkins, M.P., who was chief sponsor of the Obscene Publications Bill. The final comment is that 'it was words that had caused all the trouble', 'putting her ladyship on trial as an adulteress where a more conventionally-spoken gamekeeper might have lent her the immunity of Emma Bovary and Anna Karenina'.

The revised edition of Harry Levin's study of James Joyce[13] carries a preface in which the writer points out that his book was first published in 1944, when the controversy around the living Joyce had just ended. He notes the extraordinary swiftness with which Joyce passed from ostracism to canonization. He has found it necessary to make 'no more than thirty-odd revisions'; the bibliography has been discarded, and in its place a postscript added which provides a commentary on important studies that have appeared since the first edition. 'Brief and selective mention' is made of newly published Joycean documents and of the trends of interpretation and revaluation. Joyce's relevance and significance are admirably assessed, and his development traced as he moved from naturalism to symbolism, and subsequently changed in status 'from contraband to scripture'. Levin was the first to deal at the proper length and with due respect with *Finnegans Wake*, and now at a

further distance in time he sees Joyce in perspective, recognizes the difficulty of writing prose fiction after Joyce, but nevertheless links him with Flaubert as a 'mandarin'.

An important new study of Joyce comes from A. Walton Litz.[14] In spite of its minute examination of detail it never loses sight of main issues, nor of Joyce's achievement and significance in the history of literature. The intention is 'to record and assess Joyce's artistic development between 1914 and 1939', presuming a reader who 'knows Joyce's work and some of the major critical positions'. The evolution of Joyce's technique, the details of his technical methods, and the essential unity of his total achievement are examined. In the composition of *Ulysses* Joyce's debt to Charles Lamb's *Adventures of Ulysses* is noted, and his intention to make it a sequel to *A Portrait of the Artist*, the structural method being to begin at both ends and work towards the centre, where all motifs are united and transformed in the Circe episode. Joyce's notebooks and 'coloured pencil technique' are described, revealing his passionate concern for accuracy of detail, particularly the topographical. His revision was a matter of elaboration, of imposing patterns of analogy, his notes keeping him reminded of his motifs. Joyce's place in modern literature is well defined. His technique as a whole is seen as a response to the 'revolution in sensibility' which occurs when 'traditional ways of knowing the world collapse'. The growth of *Finnegans Wake* through manuscript drafts and galley proofs is traced, and again the structural process is shown to have been double-ended, 'boring into a mountain from different sides'; but throughout all his elaborate expansions, Joyce never lost sight of the

[12] *The Trial of Lady Chatterley: Regina* v. *Penguin Books Ltd.* The Transcript of the Trial, ed. by C. H. Rolph. Penguin Books. pp. 250. 3s. 6d.
[13] *James Joyce: A Critical Introduction*, by Harry Levin. Faber. pp. 207. 21s.

[14] *The Art of James Joyce: Method and Design in 'Ulysses' and 'Finnegans Wake'*, by A. Walton Litz. O.U.P. pp. xi+152. 21s.

central family situation, his method of composition being likened to that of a mosaic artist working upon a pre-determined pattern. It is significantly observed that Joyce never assimilated any further experience after leaving Dublin, but repeatedly, from *Dubliners* onwards, 'treated the same body of experience by a variety of modern techniques'. He may be said to 'recapitulate three generations of literary experience', and therefore must be defined as 'not a seminal force but the terminator of a tradition'. Appendixes include lists of manuscripts consulted, drafts and fragments of *Ulysses*, and a chronology of *Work in Progress*, 1914–39.

One of the many notebooks referred to in the above study is examined in detail by Thomas E. Connolly.[15] The notebook, for which the title 'Scribbledehobble' is taken from the first word entered in it, is reproduced in full, with detailed indication of the use Joyce made of it. It is one of a collection 'rescued' from Joyce's flat by Paul Leon, offered for sale in Paris in 1949, and now part of the Wickser Collection housed in the Lockwood Memorial Library, Northwestern University, U.S.A. It dates from 1922–3 and represents the first stage in the assembly of material for *Finnegans Wake*. The division into forty-seven sections, each headed with a title drawn from one or other of Joyce's earlier writings, e.g. *Circe, Grace, Eumeus*, indicates that Joyce proceeded by way of association rather than logic; it is also proof of the peculiar organic unity of his whole output, *Finnegans Wake* being an extension of all that he had previously written. His method was to 'harvest' entries from the notebook, crossing

them out as he did so in coloured crayons. Some entries never got into the finished work, and these in themselves offer interesting glimpses behind the scenes in Joyce's mind. Scholarship of this kind, so admirably industrious and illuminating, concentrates on the mind of the artist rather than on the nature of his art.

S. L. Goldberg examines the work of art itself. He judges *Ulysses*[16] in the light of Joyce's definition of the 'classical temper' in *Stephen Hero*. After a brief but comprehensive survey of Joycean criticism, the writer proposes to approach the meaning of *Ulysses* as a whole, and particularly to demonstrate its central value as 'the imaginative illumination of the moral and ultimately spiritual experience of representative human beings'. He sees the 'classical temper' as providing 'the ground of Joyce's finest inspiration'. This involves a moral as well as an artistic ideal, and while contemplating the immediate, penetrates to the universal. This approach, with *Ulysses* treated as the novel that it is, produces a profound and illuminating analysis that adjusts many false emphases. It is particularly enlightening in the consideration of Joyce's controlling irony, which results in the complex ambiguities in the character of Bloom, and is often achieved by juxtaposing and shifting the 'point of view'. Joyce's handling of character, making his three central persons complementary to each other, is considered from the standpoint of its total effect, as is also the operation of the Homeric myth. The result is a recognition of *Ulysses* as a narrative, a transcription of experience, tracing the ultimate design, whatever methods of mosaic or lacquer work be employed to achieve it. Joyce's limitations are squarely faced: his

[15] *James Joyce's 'Scribbledehobble': The Ur-Workbook for 'Finnegans Wake'*, ed., with Notes and an Introduction, by Thomas E. Connolly. Northwestern U.P. and O.U.P. pp. 187. 30s.

[16] *The Classical Temper: A Study of James Joyce's 'Ulysses'*, by S. L. Goldberg. Chatto & Windus. pp. 346. 30s.

presentation of the 'nightmare of history' is 'unimpressive'; he offers no 'encyclopaedic criticism of our age'; he omits many vital aspects of modern life, such as industrialization; the range of his sympathetic insights is limited; and he tends to intellectualize vital intuitions. Yet it is amply demonstrated that *Ulysses* satisfies Joyce's definition of the 'classical temper', in that it 'accepts the ordinary world of humanity as the primary object of its attention, and endeavours to see it and present it steadily and whole'.

The psychological complexities of George Orwell and his work are perceptively analysed by Richard Rees,[17] who knew him well during the last twenty years of his life. Rees's portrait is of a man with a constitutional chip on the shoulder carried on behalf of humanity. He finds it misleading to regard Orwell as deeply moral and earnest, seeing him rather as a man who viewed life with remorseless honesty and was profoundly 'conscience-stricken', working out his ideals under the motto, 'All or Nothing'. His socialism was a matter not so much of compassion as of disgust with the life of the worker. He was no political theorist, but in all political matters it was his grasp of fundamentals that counted; yet his books were lifeless when they lacked political purpose, and he was most himself in *The Road to Wigan Pier*. He shared with Dickens the 'gift of disinterested partisanship', and was most closely akin to Dickens in his belief in the goodness and sanity of the common man, though he came to see the common man as rendered inert and imbecile under the enormous pressure of technological bureaucracy. Like Dickens again, he was 'generously angry'; angry not for himself but for all underdogs, yet he is in the direct

line of descent from Wells to Osborne. At the same time he is close to D. H. Lawrence and Middleton Murry in the revival of a religious attitude, though he possessed more of the common touch. For all his importance as the prophet of an industrial machine-civilization that will ultimately destroy itself, the question arises whether Orwell did not defeat his own ends by 'writing for a purpose'. Some valuable personal reminiscences conclude the book, which also carries a bibliographical note.

In his *Collected Essays*[18] Orwell's justification of himself is to be found. 'All art is propaganda', he says. In this volume are assembled all the essays except the short pieces contributed to *Tribune* under the title 'I write as I please'. They tempt the speculation that Orwell is more likely to be remembered as an essayist than as a novelist.

Orwell had regarded P. G. Wodehouse as dated and as displaying the moral outlook of a public schoolboy. Now Richard Usborne[19] gives Wodehouse full and serious attention as a creator of characters 'durable across sixty years . . . in spite of his timeless disregard of changes in social attitudes'. He claims that at his best Wodehouse achieves 'a sort of poetry' and successfully reveals the art behind the artlessness. Though his attitudes were 'steadfastly lowbrow', Wodehouse the scholar lies behind Wodehouse the comedian, as is shown in his use of language, his parodies of cliché in word, situation, and attitude. And his comedy is no mere farce, for it irreverently debunks 'every sacred cow' in England. Another reason for his survival is the datelessness of his stories; stories in which everybody remains the same age

[17] *George Orwell: Fugitive from the Camp of Victory*, by Richard Rees. Secker & Warburg. pp. 160. 18*s*.

[18] *Collected Essays*, by George Orwell. Secker & Warburg. pp. 434. 30*s*.
[19] *Wodehouse at Work: A study of the books and characters of P. G. Wodehouse across nearly sixty years*, by Richard Usborne. Jenkins. pp. 224. 21*s*.

and in which the settings do not change. (A study of revisions for later editions reveals Wodehouse's skill in bringing his slang up to date.) As a divergence from the classical family theme Wodehouse presents the 'state of nepotism', the state of being an orphan nephew, with aunts representing authority and interference. He is well contrasted with W. S. Gilbert, in that he is never unkind, and Gilbert's unwanted middle-aged females are 'gloriously translated into Aunts'. Wodehouse's respectable literary ancestry is traced, and includes not only Anstey and Conan Doyle, but Homer himself. The immortal Jeeves, the 'godlike prime mover' of the plot, is shown to operate the 'nemesis of Bertie's hubris'; but Bertie is also a modern Don Quixote—'aligned with the literary dreamers who have absorbed bilge'. The school stories are given full consideration and this attractive analysis of the nature of Wodehouse comedy is completed with an examination of French and German translations, and a bibliography of books, plays, and films.

Wodehouse's ability to keep up with the times by being timeless is demonstrated by his last novel,[20] which sets its farcical action in the world of crime unavoidable in modern fiction.

Henry Green is an elusive novelist who provokes personal interpretations. A. Kingsley Weatherhead[21] stresses that he offers neither a neutral nor a complete assessment, but a 'reading'— and only one reading. Henry Green stands in some ways apart from the contemporary trend of the novel. He is not interested in sociological themes, but in the 'private movements of individuals'. His repeated theme is that of self-creation, which is here examined in each novel, taken in chronological order. A companion theme, and one which is wholly in keeping with modern trends, is the conflict between dream and reality, the ways in which the ideal is brought to terms with the real world.

The first full-length critical study of Elizabeth Bowen[22] comes from William Heath, who acclaims her as 'the most distinguished woman of letters now writing in English'. After a biographical introduction the writer proceeds to a critical analysis of the novels, indicating their place in the tradition of Chekhov and Katherine Mansfield, and their affinities with those of Jane Austen, Henry James, E. M. Forster, Virginia Woolf, and—though unacknowledged—of George Eliot. The recurrent theme is defined as the presentation of the 'romantic will'. *The House in Paris* is said to be most successful in 'making the novel work as a series of dynamic propositions about the romantic will and society', while *The Death of the Heart* is commended for its greater subtlety, and reckoned as Elizabeth Bowen's finest novel. It is pointed out that in her work 'the most positive solutions are found only by the least complex characters'— the same being true of George Eliot, whose Dorotheas and Maggies are obvious anticipations of Elizabeth Bowen's heroines, without their sophistication. Most noticeable in this connexion is the portrayal of the romantic girl's love of a cad. The poetic element is stressed, and it is made clear that when social interests are considered, as in *The Heat of the Day*, the purpose is to show the effects of social acts on the individual personality. The general picture is of people 'trying to find meaning in a world where they move like fish in shoals'.

[20] *Ice in the Bedroom*, by P. G. Wodehouse. Jenkins. pp. 223. 13s. 6d.
[21] *A Reading of Henry Green*, by A. Kingsley Weatherhead. Seattle: Washington U.P. pp. 170. $4.50.
[22] *Elizabeth Bowen: An Introduction to Her Novels*, by William Heath. Wisconsin U.P. pp. viii+180. $4.50.

J. B. Priestley is the subject of a study that comes from Switzerland, Ladislaus Löb examining his treatment of the individual and society.[23]

G. K. Chesterton's *The Man Who Knew Too Much*,[24] first published in 1922, is well worth reprinting, and indicates that Chesterton holds his important position in the history of detective fiction, not only for his powers of characterization, but for the skilfully suggested social and cultural background—'old Picasso and some of the cubists' mentioned in passing—and for the genial but pointed satire.

Difficulty has always been experienced in classifying and placing Ronald Firbank. The Café Royal Impressionism of his poetic satires combines all the streams of twentieth-century fiction, but remains something entirely individual. His hopes of survival are now regarded as sure. This year three of his best novels are reissued,[25] and the first complete collection of his work appears.[26]

The reissue of Malcolm Lowry's one published novel[27] is a forcible reminder that this writer, little heard of in England, but greatly admired in France, is one of the most powerful and original of modern novelists, who can paint the 'dark night of the soul' with appalling grandeur.

Victoria Sackville-West's last novel,[28] which covers the last few weeks of a dying man, explores values that will survive many more up-to-date social themes, and preserves a traditional grace and clarity of prose style.

Ivy Compton-Burnett with complete success presents another of her stylized studies of family life,[29] unique in their blend of sharp individualization of character and uniformity of idiom; young and old, masters and servants, male and female, all speak alike, with the dual awareness of their own consciousness and that of their creator. Freed from the fussy preoccupations of much modern fiction, these novels move in a timeless sphere of human relationships, and human error.

Evelyn Waugh's third volume[30] completes the story of Guy Crouchback's efforts to find his particular place when confronted with 'the Modern Age in arms', and thus makes up a trilogy that would seem to be the most significant work of fiction to come out of World War II.

Roy Fuller,[31] in a story full of external action and nagging mystery, reveals the complexities of the father-son relationship and the continual flow of the inner life beneath the trivialities or agonies of the external. The background of army and office life as presented by this poet-novelist serves as a reminder that the novel appears to have moved out of the lyrical, feminine, prose-poem phase, into a strongly masculine, professional, bowler-hatted one.

Angus Wilson is in the same tradition. His latest hero[32] is a man of sense,

[23] *Mensch und Gesellschaft bei J. B. Priestley*, by Ladislaus Löb. (Swiss Studies in English.) Bern: Francke Verlag. pp. 221. Sw. fr. 15.

[24] *The Man Who Knew Too Much*, by G. K. Chesterton. Darwen Finlayson. pp. 190. 12s. 6d.

[25] '*Valmouth*', '*Prancing Nigger*', '*Concerning the Eccentricities of Cardinal Pirelli*', by Ronald Firbank. Penguin Books. pp. 251. 3s. 6d.

[26] *The Complete Ronald Firbank*. Preface by Anthony Powell. Duckworth. pp. 766. 42s.

[27] *Under the Volcano*, by Malcolm Lowry. Penguin Books in association with Jonathan Cape. pp. 376. 5s.

[28] *No Signposts in the Sea*, by V. Sack-ville-West. Michael Joseph. pp. 156. 13s. 6d.

[29] *The Mighty and Their Fall*, by I. Compton-Burnett. Gollancz. pp. 221. 16s.

[30] *Unconditional Surrender*, by Evelyn Waugh. Chapman & Hall. pp. 311. 18s.

[31] *The Father's Comedy*, by Roy Fuller. Deutsch. pp. 192. 13s. 6d.

[32] *The Old Men at the Zoo*, by Angus Wilson. Secker & Warburg. pp. 352. 18s.

sensibility, and professional enthusiasm caught up in external events and forced to make a choice of loyalties. Wilson's zoologists and administrators, in an England at war with Europe in 1970, indicate his subtle understanding of the ambitions, frustrations, obsessions, and shams of professional life.

Gerald Brenan looks back, on the other hand, to the early thirties.[33] In his novel the social, the psychological, and the poetic trends meet. His hero suffers the personal restlessness and dissatisfaction of one beset by all the problems now familiar in modern literature—questions of reality and escape, of keeping the spirit alive against the pressures of a material, mechanized, technological world. The motif of the sea recurs throughout the book, symbol of freedom and eternity, and adding the poetic dimension.

Alan Sillitoe's novel[34] is in another tradition. It is a record of youth in working-class Nottingham. It is too long, not because it is wordy—the style is taut and spare—but because he puts in too much indiscriminate detail. D. H. Lawrence inevitably comes up for comparison, and reveals, in his impressionistic selection of detail, the whole difference between a record and an interpretation.

A. J. Smith and W. H. Mason edit an anthology of short stories[35] designed for senior tutorial work in the training of discrimination and critical appreciation. The foreword recommends it as likely to break down the barriers between specialists in the united enjoyment of good writing. Each story is introduced by a biographical note, and carries a commentary offering the 'necessary background and equipment for independent enquiry'. The selection is an excellent one, including amongst others Henry James, James Joyce, D. H. Lawrence, and Dylan Thomas.

Muriel Spark's collection[36] contains short stories and radio plays. Her stories are masterly examples of the handling of long periods of time, of developing human relationships and building up character.

L. P. Hartley[37] has a particular gift of suggesting the strange, the sinister, and the macabre in the short story, but he does so with grace and elegance. These two writers encourage the view that there is a revival in the art of the short story.

3. *Poetry*

An illuminating study of contemporary poetry is provided by Thomas Blackburn.[38] He concentrates on what the poems have to say and avoids technical analysis of how it is said. He regards the function of poetry as being to bridge the gap between the internal and the external worlds in its exploration of human nature. Poets are treated individually, chapter by chapter. Yeats stands as the voice of the 'Great Dream of an age', whose total vision is of immense importance, particularly because of his belief in spiritual existence and in his view of human nature as a 'process' in the universal plan. T. S. Eliot's poetry speaks of man's relations with God; it presents man cut off from God, affirms the fallen condition of the soul, but reaffirms a way of liberation. Edith Sitwell does not stand up very well to Blackburn's scrutiny. He cannot help feeling that there is in her work a theatrical quality, that it is an elaborate

[33] *A Holiday by the Sea: A Novel of the Early Nineteen-Thirties*, by Gerald Brenan. Hamish Hamilton. pp. 254. 16s.

[34] *The Key to the Door*, by Alan Sillitoe. W. H. Allen. pp. 446. 18s.

[35] *Short Story Study: a Critical Anthology*, compiled by A. J. Smith and W. H. Mason, with a Foreword by Lord James of Rusholme. Edward Arnold. pp. 191. 10s. 6d.

[36] *Voices at Play*, by Muriel Spark. Macmillan. pp. 248. 16s.

[37] *Two for the River*, by L. P. Hartley. Hamish Hamilton. pp. 223. 15s.

[38] *The Price of an Eye*, by Thomas Blackburn. Longmans. pp. 170. 18s.

façade, a personal gesture, though he acknowledges that it makes a profound comment at times. Robert Graves speaks with consummate understanding and immediacy of 'the meeting between man and woman'. The poets of the thirties are held up for severe judgement. Auden in particular puzzles and appears to defy definition; Blackburn says at one point that 'the man seems stronger than the poet', but later that 'Auden the man has never grown up to Auden the poet'. 'An odd lack of participation' is noted between Auden and his poetry; he seems to belittle its function. Spender is said to deal best with personal life, whilst MacNeice deals with 'the flux of life itself'. Betjeman, though 'over-estimated', yet speaks 'for the British Middle Class'. Dylan Thomas with his incantatory element appeals to the unconscious and explores the self. Blackburn's would appear to be a romantic conception of poetry and he urges the necessity for the critic to achieve an 'emotional development' to match his academic knowledge. He deplores the 'deflation' of literary criticism into a science. The reasons for Empson's influence on contemporary poetry are expounded, and the poets of the fifties shown to be in danger of narrowing the scope and significance of poetry.

Blackburn himself won the principal Guinness Award for poetry in 1960, and this year he publishes a collection of his poems[39] dating from 1957. His poetry stands up well to his own theories, and he has the gift of exploring human nature and searching out its fundamentals in the familiar setting of café, street, and park.

Elizabeth Jennings's study[40] is concerned with 'the making of poems, the nature of mystical experience and the relationship between the two'. Of the modern poets she discusses Edwin Muir, T. S. Eliot, and David Gascoyne. Muir gives new dramatic life to Christian dogma, even though his poetry is 'rooted in the earth'. Time itself is one of his great themes; its cycles, returns, renewals. He saw life as 'drama continually repeating itself'. An interesting comparison is made between Muir's treatment of time and T. S. Eliot's, and Eliot's treatment of character is proof that 'only *poetry* is an adequate vehicle to convey mystical experience'. Indeed it is suggested that for Eliot poetry is an experience of a mystical kind in itself. Apart from Eliot, David Gascoyne is found to be the 'only living English poet . . . in the true mystical tradition'. His work is 'profoundly Christian', but he has brought new life to the old conventional religious symbols 'in an entirely contemporary setting'. (Cf. Chapter I, note 17.)

In the introduction to her anthology of modern verse[41] Elizabeth Jennings considers contemporary poetry in relation to its background. Her volume covers twenty years (1940–60) of 'suffering, restlessness and uncertainty'. The paradox is that the most marked characteristic of the poetry is its sense of order, clarity, and formal perfection, for which the influence of William Empson is said to be largely responsible. It is interesting to see the poets of the thirties turning to personal expression in line with the younger poets, and leaving politics alone. The general aim of contemporary poets appears to be to create order out of chaos, but it is well said that this is 'not a lofty Augustan interest in mere formal beauty, but a passionately intelligent gesture against chaos'. The academic background of most poets of the fifties is noticed, and

[39] *A Smell of Burning*, by Thomas Blackburn. Putnam. pp. 32. 10s. 6d.
[40] *Every Changing Shape*, by Elizabeth Jennings. Deutsch. pp. 240. 25s.
[41] *An Anthology of Modern Verse, 1940–1960*, chosen and edited with an Introduction by Elizabeth Jennings. Methuen. pp. 299. 11s. 6d.

their independence—they do not really form a Movement, they utter no manifesto, but there is everywhere clear evidence of the vitality of the poetry of today.

Elizabeth Jennings also publishes a volume of her own verse[42] which includes poems that have already appeared separately. The poems are divided into four groups according to theme: the family; religious experience; clowns; love, death, and saints. She is herself a poet profoundly stirred by the search for truth in human experience, and she writes with the simplicity and clarity of her generation.

Maynard Mack is the general editor of an anthology[43] which covers poets who 'exerted most influence since about the time of the First World War', the most recent being W. H. Auden. Hopkins, Yeats, Frost, and Eliot are also given substantial representation as major poets, whilst others appear with a few examples, each under the heading 'Selected Modern Poems'. The editorial introduction provides an admirable background to the study of modern poetry. It discusses the 'modern temper', the influence of psychology, of insecurity and anxiety, of 'doubt about the authenticity of values'. The passing of the romantic concept of nature is observed, and the development of the obsession with time. From the point of view of style a gulf presents itself between the iambic and the non-iambic form. There are useful notes, bibliographical and biographical.

The P.E.N. Anthology[44] includes 'characteristic poems by poets already known and poems of varying distinction by others less well known'. The editors point out that many poets 'are moved to write by the open or implied threat of long-distance genocide', and that this does not necessarily prove a satisfactory inspiration. In contrast, others are driven to concentrate on domestic themes.

W. Eastwood's anthology of science verse[45] ranges from Lucretius to John Wain. He points out that the mistaken notion that science and poetry are mutually exclusive is of quite recent origin. Both 'originate in intense imaginative experience'. It would seem that particularly in this day and age poets should find it impossible to ignore 'what is the western world's most important contribution to civilization'. There can be no future for a culture 'which cannot reconcile the poetic and the scientific impulses'. An appendix entitled 'Some Views on the Relations of Science and Poetry' includes contributions from A. B. Whitehead, I. A. Richards, C. Day Lewis, and J. Bronowski. (Cf. Chapter I, note 53.)

Francis Thompson, as presented by Paul van K. Thomson,[46] earns the right to inclusion in a consideration of twentieth-century poetry, for he not only contended with the problem of 'finding his place and function in the modern world', but anticipated contemporary techniques and ideas. This definitive study is based on the notebooks and manuscripts retrieved by Wilfrid Meynell after Thompson's death and now housed in the Thompson-Patmore Collection of the library of Boston College. Rejected as both

[42] *Song for a Birth or a Death, and Other Poems*, by Elizabeth Jennings. Deutsch. pp. 63. 10s. 6d.

[43] *Modern Poetry*, ed. by Maynard Mack, Leonard Dean, and William Frost. English Masterpieces, Vol. VII, 2nd edition. Prentice-Hall. pp. xi+383. 15s.

[44] *New Poems 1961: A P.E.N. Anthology of Contemporary Poetry*, ed. by William Plomer, Anthony Thwaite, Hilary Corke. Hutchinson. pp. 135. 18s.

[45] *A Book of Science Verse: The Poetic Relations of Science and Technology*, selected by W. Eastwood. Macmillan. pp. xvi+279. 21s.

[46] *Francis Thompson: A Critical Biography*, by Paul van K. Thomson. Nelson. pp. 280. 36s. (See p. 234.)

priest and medical student, always ill and driven to drugs to relieve pain and conscience, Thompson is shown to have been doomed from youth upwards to become one of the world's great outsiders. His career is traced with profound sympathy and understanding. He is firmly detached from the 'Art for Art's Sake' school, their widespread aestheticism conflicting with his own 'deeply religious outlook'. It is in his bold exploration into symbolism, into the creation of new metres, a new poetic language, in his feeling for the Metaphysical poets that Thompson anticipates the twentieth century. Paul Thomson's authoritative study is written with vivid simplicity and skilful handling of material. A select bibliography includes a description of manuscript sources.

The image of Yeats—as he saw himself and as others saw him—and the images, frequently visual, the living material upon which his imagination worked, are presented in the excellent little volume[47] for which D. J. Gordon is chiefly responsible, with the assistance of Frank Kermode, Ian Fletcher, and Robin Skelton. It is an expanded version of the guide to the Yeats Exhibition shown in Manchester and Dublin in 1961, each section introduced by an essay explaining the relevance and significance of the exhibits. Photographs and portraits of Yeats himself, and his own reactions to them are shown to reveal much of his conception of himself as a poet; the poetic costume he was in the habit of wearing makes it understandable that he should be 'worried' by Augustus John's vision of him and should prefer Sargent's romantic study. A discussion of the persons and places that deeply moved him illustrates the way in which these took on a further dimension of meaning for him, and contains a moving

account of Lady Gregory and her influence and significance; also of Robert Gregory and J. M. Synge. The section on the theatre reveals the strong influence of the Bedford Park community and its experimental theatre group, points out the amateurishness of the costumes for Yeats's plays, and comments on the 'sadness' of his part in the Irish Theatre, *Cathleen ni Houlihan* being his one popular success. The inspiration of the Japanese *No* dancer, Ito, is strikingly visible in his portraits. Perhaps most remarkable of all is the revelation of the development of Yeats's interest in Byzantine art which led to the conception of Byzantium as a symbol of Art itself—'the Holy City, the soul out of nature'. Yeats's Pre-Raphaelite tastes are demonstrated in the display of the kind of pictures he liked, and finally the exhibition has examples that illustrate Yeats's interest in dancing, which represented for him 'the surrender to objectified emotion'.

A. G. Stock analyses the thought in Yeats's poems.[48] She begins with his preoccupation with Irish literature, and shows how he harmonized Eastern philosophy with pre-Christian European thought. His 'temperamental aloofness' is stressed; not only did he 'train his genius' on his difference from the English, but in Ireland itself, a Protestant in a Catholic country, he stood apart, and, though feeling part of the Irish civilization, was most himself when aloof and alone. The development from serious preoccupation with faeryland, through the Rose-symbolism period, from sheltering behind dreams to 'daring to come out, dreams and all, and live in the world without capitulation', is traced with much perceptive comment and exposition. Miss Stock is particularly illuminating in her

[47] *W. B. Yeats: Images of a Poet.* Manchester U.P. pp. 151. 18s.

[48] *W. B. Yeats: His Poetry and Thought*, by A. G. Stock. C.U.P. pp. xii+255. 27s. 6d.

treatment of Yeats's mysticism. She declares that he was 'looking not so much for a faith as for the formulation of a faith born in him'. As Yeats enters on his later phase the inevitable comparison with Eliot presents itself. Miss Stock sees the great difference between them as being that Eliot sees all ending in Christ, whereas in Yeats there is no surrender—'Christian civilization is only an episode'. The remarkable and outstanding characteristic of Yeats's genius is given full consideration—his continued and organic development, his 'sustained power of song'. 'As he aged his thought grew lonelier and more recondite but his power of song increased.' This is throughout a most satisfying and at times moving study of the development of Yeats's poetic art and temperament.

Norman Jeffares[49] provides critical studies of individual poems of Yeats 'which are widely read in universities and the upper forms of schools'. In common with the rest of the series, 'Studies in English Literature', edited by David Daiches, of which it is the fourth volume, it emphasizes clarification and evaluation, and 'concentrates on the work of literary art rather than on its historical background or cultural environment'. The individual volumes of poems are discussed chronologically. An admirably compressed and scholarly picture of Yeats's poetic development is provided in the commentaries, which amount to a complete miniature guide to the study of Yeats. Though the personal background is clearly sketched in, this is subject to the reminder that 'what we see is the poem and if it is to be judged successful it must act on us as a poem per se'. The possibility of recognizing symbolic significance implicitly is stressed. Effective use is made of Yeats's own guides to his aims and interpreta-tions, including many references to his unpublished Autobiography. There is a masterly summary of A Vision, and the central themes and significances of Yeats's art are presented in a way that will make this book helpful to many who imagine they know much more about Yeats than the members of the 'upper forms of schools' for which it is intended.

A counterblast comes in a small pamphlet on Yeats by Ivor Winters,[50] who declares that 'the better one understands him, the harder it is to take him seriously'. He spreads nets of logic and common sense in order to entrap and expose Yeats's poetic achievement, but Yeats flies by those nets, and the assault does not reduce his poetic stature. The main charges are self-dramatization, and a sentimental and anti-intellectual view of the nature of his art. The writer is unmoved by Yeats's 'dream of the noble and the beggarman', finds In Memory of Major Robert Gregory a very bad poem, thinks the worst fault of Easter 1916 is its refrain, and sums it up as 'pure Yeatsian fustian'. His ideas are said to be contemptible, and he is emphatically declared not to be a great poet, his readers merely 'overwhelmed by the bardic tone'.

Donald R. Pearce has done Yeatsian studies a great service by collecting and editing Yeats's Senate speeches,[51] which have hitherto been buried in the columns of the official report of the Senate. These throw light on Yeats's growth and development as a poet. It is no doubt in his experience of public debate that he 'achieved the syntax of public speech found in his later work'. The text is based on the official version and Yeats's personal copies. All his

[49] The Poetry of W. B. Yeats, by A. Norman Jeffares. Arnold. pp. 63. 6s.

[50] The Poetry of W. B. Yeats, by Ivor Winters. Swallow Pamphlets 10. Denver: Alan Swallow. pp. 24.

[51] The Senate Speeches of W. B. Yeats, ed. by Donald R. Pearce. Faber. pp. 183. 21s.

speeches are included, and some debates given in their entirety. Yeats's appointment to the Senate in 1922 to advise on matters concerning education, literature, and the arts involved him in what he called 'the slow exciting work of creating institutions' in the first few troubled years of the Irish Free State. Yeats's political sympathies are discussed, and in making the inevitable comparison with Milton it is found that Yeats suffered 'no contraction of personality' by his public work. His wisdom is apparent in his remark on film censorship, 'I think you can leave the arts, superior or inferior, to the general conscience of mankind', his common sense in his objection to the proposal to put up all public signs in Irish, and his discrimination and foresight in his defence of James Joyce's *Ulysses*: he was not sure whether it was great literature, but it was 'the work of an heroic mind'.

The collection of Yeats's *Essays and Introductions*[52] consists mainly of his previous collections, *Ideas of Good and Evil* and *The Cutting of an Agate*. It also includes the introductions he wrote to certain books published between 1931 and 1936, and three unpublished pieces: the Introduction he wrote for his Collected Essays, his General Introduction to his Works, and his Introduction for his Plays, all written in 1937. The first of these three summarizes his beliefs in respect of myth, tradition, and the arts, and his own development as a poet. The General Introduction stresses his debt to John O'Leary, who gave him his theme, and is particularly interesting for his explanation of his attitude to religion and mythology. Looking to the future of poetry, he sees the young writers of the thirties as rejecting dream and personal emotion, involved in politics, and employing an intricate

psychology—'action in character, not as in the ballads character in action'. As an introduction to his Plays he gives a simple, straightforward account of the aims and origins of his theatre, and his own ideals of rejecting needless movement on the stage, making his appeal to the ear and not to the eye, and turning his back on 'all that modish curiosity, psychology'.

Kristian Smidt's study of T. S. Eliot,[53] first published in 1949 (see *YW* xxx. 226), is reissued in a thoroughly revised edition, incorporating a chapter on 'Point of View in Eliot's Poetry' which has already appeared in *Orbis Litt.* xiv. 1 (1959). In this the identity of the 'I' in Eliot's poetry is examined. In his early poetry Eliot used the 'I' as a disguise, but it is observed that as his philosophical certainty increased the point of view in his poetry became correspondingly stable. This still remains one of the most helpful analyses of Eliot, particularly in its treatment of the biographical and cultural background. The revisions include references in footnotes to the immense body of criticism that has accumulated since first publication.

Grover Smith examines the sources and meaning of Eliot's poetry and plays.[54] This is the third impression of a book first published in 1950. It includes an additional chapter on *The Elder Statesman*. In the new chapter the writer comments on Eliot's frequent use of ghosts, and finds analogies with *The Turn of the Screw*, but with a 'Jamesian concern for understanding' Eliot 'blends a Puritan anxiety about guilt'. When Claverton has exorcized his own past, his uneasy ghost, he is free. Comparisons are also made with

[52] *Essays and Introductions*, by W. B. Yeats. Macmillan. pp. xi+530. 36s.

[53] *Poetry and Belief in the Work of T. S. Eliot*, by Kristian Smidt. Routledge & Kegan Paul. pp. xiii+258. 30s.
[54] *T. S. Eliot's Poetry and Plays: A Study in Sources and Meaning*, by Grover Smith. Phoenix Books. Chicago U.P. pp. xii+342. $2.45.

Oedipus at Colonus. It seems tempting to add that this is surely the most Ibsenite of Eliot's plays.

Elder Olson's study of Dylan Thomas,[55] first published in 1954 (see *YW* xxxv. 221), goes into a paperback edition. It remains the most helpful and perceptive guide to Thomas, with its prose paraphrases, and its full, informative notes and glossary.

John Betjeman, as a 'best-selling' poet, is the subject of a study by Derek Stanford.[56] After a biographical chapter the writer analyses the poetry and its popularity. The 'best-selling' quality is easily seen to derive from Betjeman's being in touch with 'mass media man'. He is 'an Edwardian backwater' to the Wasteland, and therefore pleases without disturbing. His is the poetry of 'small intense loyalties'. For him there is none of the questioning and questing of Eliot, but the religious element in his poetry is the common man's affair of choristers and candlelight. It is claimed that he can show 'instances of power' and he is defended from his self-inflicted association with Ella Wheeler Wilcox. In sum, it is Betjeman's 'well-tailored shape and traditional background' that account for his 'fashionableness'.

The *Collected Poems* of Ralph Hodgson, edited by Colin Fenton,[57] reproduces the contents of his three published collections of 1907, 1917, and 1958, together with two other poems. The very dates of these volumes are significant. Hodgson covers almost exactly the same period as T. S. Eliot, but seems to reach back into an earlier age. Though he appears independent of modern trends and clings to a traditional manner, his work shows a pro-gressive development in strength and a grasp of the world's predicament. Though the world may pass him by, he proclaims that 'Truth is great, By Jove! and will prevail'. Nature too prevails, and in spite of bitterness and darkness Hodgson urgently preaches a message of faith and hope. A bibliographical note records the first publication of all the poems except those which first appeared in the collections. The text follows the latest revisions.

Louis MacNeice's latest volume of poems[58] includes some which have already appeared in magazines, and two which have already been printed in 'Eighty-Five Poems'. His work retains its personal immediacy, the response to familiar objects, and sometimes he writes with striking power, as in 'The Wiper', using a favourite image of a car journey—'And yet we hold the road.'

I. A. Richards's preface to his new volume of poems[59] points out that there should be no connexion discernible between the critic's theories and his poetry. Critical theory should not indicate how a poet should write, but it may illuminate the meaning of certain details. His poems are supplemented with full notes explaining his references. An appendix carries a recently delivered lecture on 'The Future of Poetry', which advocates a return to the anonymity of the poet. The nature of poetry is analysed in scientific terms with special reference to the advance in linguistics, which offers new promise to poetry. An improvement in the audience is also advocated, to be based on a better teaching of the art of reading. It is emphatically urged that poetry must 'wake up to what is happening around'.

[55] *The Poetry of Dylan Thomas*, by Elder Olson. Phoenix Books. Chicago U.P. pp. 120. 8s. 6d.

[56] *John Betjeman: A Study*, by Derek Stanford. Neville Spearman. pp. 159. 16s.

[57] *Collected Poems*, by Ralph Hodgson. Macmillan. pp. x+185. 21s.

[58] *Solstices*, by Louis MacNeice. Faber. pp. 78. 12s. 6d.

[59] *The Screens, and Other Poems*, by I. A. Richards. Routledge & Kegan Paul. pp. 127. 18s.

Robert Graves publishes thirty-five poems hitherto unpublished in book form, and four earlier poems revised.[60] It is refreshing to find a poet who makes it his business to make poetry after the classical fashion: clear, fine-drawn, restrained, and totally lacking in fuss.

A very different kind of poetry is written by Samuel Beckett. His collection of poems[61] ranges in date from 1930 to 1948, and includes some that were written first in French and then translated into English by the writer himself. The dramatic monologue 'Whoroscope' is supplied with notes. This sets up discordant echoes of Browning. The publisher claims that Beckett takes his place in the main stream of English poetry, and he has certainly travelled some way with Eliot; specific locations and phenomena—Meath, Dieppe, Ken Wood, Guinness's barges, a sodden packet of Churchman's—are his symbols, but they are symbols of despair. Life itself becomes a 'hiddenness' among 'voices voiceless'. Beckett indeed 'brings novelty to things of everyday', and dislocates language in a manner that reflects the dislocation of life and needs no adjustment to grip the imagination of the reader.

John Montague, born in Ireland, now works in Paris, thus following the course of famous predecessors. His first volume of poems[62] covers the work of the last ten years, some of which has already appeared. The poems are arranged according to theme rather than chronology. Notes explain obscure Irish references. Irish rain drizzles over his poems, yet they are powerful and vigorous, deal with people, have a strong sense of reality, and present the underside of Yeats's Ireland. In 'Old Mythologies' Yeats's legendary heroes are laid low in death—'a whole dormitory of heroes', 'regretting their butchers' days', the valley cradling their 'archaic madness'.

More poetry of the last ten years is to be found in Oliver Bernard's collection,[63] which follows the trend of personal, simple expression. He is quoted as saying, 'The poems are to enjoy. Anything else they do is up to them. . . . Don't pay too much attention to what they say.'

Peter Champkin writes thoughtful, smooth-surfaced poetry,[64] seeking the realities behind forms and institutions, celebrating enduring things.

Thom Gunn conveys, perhaps more than any of his contemporaries, a sense of potential development.[65] Beneath the quiet surface he possesses, as do his 'Sad Captains', a 'hard energy', and at times he attains a grandeur that has almost vanished from contemporary poetry.

4. The Drama

Hesketh Pearson produces the first complete edition of his biography of Bernard Shaw.[66] The first part of the book was published in 1942, and in this section Pearson had Shaw's close co-operation. Pearson then compiled a Boswell-like record of Shaw's conversations which was published as a postscript to the first part in 1951. The two are now brought together in the present volume, with the addition of some passages omitted in the 1942 edition because of paper shortage. Shaw is recorded as saying to Pearson: 'I give you full marks as a Boswell,' and he

[60] More Poems 1961, by Robert Graves. Cassell. pp. 45. 10s. 6d.

[61] Poems in English, by Samuel Beckett. John Calder. pp. 53. 13s. 6d.

[62] Poisoned Lands and Other Poems, by John Montague. MacGibbon & Kee. pp. 59. 12s. 6d.

[63] Country Matters, by Oliver Bernard. Putnam. pp. 32. 8s. 6d.

[64] The Enmity of Noon, by Peter Champkin. Robert Hale. pp. 51. 10s. 6d.

[65] My Sad Captains, by Thom Gunn. Faber. pp. 51. 12s. 6d.

[66] Bernard Shaw: His Life and Personality, by Hesketh Pearson. Methuen. pp. 480. 50s.

told Archibald Henderson that he might be able to improve on Pearson's book critically, but as biography, no.

It is good to see at last a scholarly study of Granville Barker as a playwright. Margery Morgan[67] does full justice to this important and neglected aspect of this many-sided man of the theatre. Her detailed analyses and expositions of the plays provide strong argument for his revival on the stage. Shaw apart, Barker is the most original playwright of his time, and his 'unique and individual vision' still holds a strong appeal, his plays partaking of the elusive, appealing quality of his own temperament. Much manuscript material, including early drafts and notes and five early unpublished plays, are used with advantage to give a full picture of Barker's purpose and achievement.

From Calcutta comes an interpretation of the plays of John Galsworthy. A. D. Choudhuri[68] approaches his subject directly with close study of the texts, and accurately assesses Galsworthy's achievement—his 'patient and sensitive observations . . . critical awareness of the finer aspects of personalities and situations . . . keen sense of the theatre . . . architectural quality of dramatic craftsmanship and . . . highly developed moral tone'. He discusses Galsworthy in relation to Shaw and Barker and to contemporary theatrical tradition.

James Bridie is the subject of a study by Ursula Gerber in the 'Swiss Studies in English' series.[69]

Gerald Weales supplies the first comprehensive account of the development of the modern religious drama.[70] He finds its origins to lie some eighty years back, and traces two streams of tradition, the one commercial, dating from Henry Arthur Jones's *Saints and Sinners*, and the other ecclesiastical, dating from William Poel's revival of *Everyman* in 1901. The two streams meet in the work of Eliot and Fry, but Bernard Shaw was before that 'the most aware of the use of religion in the theatre', and indeed saw the theatre as taking the place of the church. After tracing earlier experiments in verse drama, it becomes clear that religious verse drama only came to its full flowering when an adequate verse form had been evolved—Masefield and Eliot and the distance between them demonstrating this. The important contribution of amateur groups and the church festivals, of Martin Browne, the Pilgrim Players, and the Mercury Theatre is fully acknowledged. Of the dramatists themselves Charles Williams is found to be the 'most exciting', but Eliot and Fry stand as the central figures. An analysis of their work brings out the distinction that, where 'Fry finds God in the world, Eliot finds Him in withdrawal'. In conclusion the whole problem of Christian tragedy is introduced, and it is observed that the modern religious playwrights are not interested in damnation—which, as Dorothy Sayers pointed out, is the only possible Christian theme for tragedy. An appendix provides a list of further significant plays, with brief synopses.

Kaspar Spinner contributes a study of three Irish dramatists, Lennox Robinson, Sean O'Casey, and Denis Johnston.[71]

[67] *A Drama of Political Man: A Study in the Plays of Harley Granville Barker*, by Margery M. Morgan. Sidgwick & Jackson. pp. viii+337. 30s.
[68] *Galsworthy's Plays: A Critical Survey*, by A. D. Choudhuri. Orient Longmans, Calcutta. pp. viii+191. Rs. 9.
[69] *James Bridies Dramen*, by Ursula Gerber. Bern: Francke Verlag. pp. 114. Sw. fr. 9.
[70] *Religion in Modern English Drama*, by Gerald Weales. Pennsylvania U.P. and O.U.P. pp. xvi+318. 60s.
[71] *Die Alte Dame Sagt: Nein!: Drei Irische Dramatiker, Lennox Robinson, Sean O'Casey, Denis Johnston*, by Kaspar Spinner. (Swiss Studies in English.) Bern: Francke Verlag. pp. vi+210. Sw. fr. 15.

J. M. Synge's work is considered not only in relation to his Irish traditions but to the whole European literary tradition in Alan Price's book.[72] The central aspect of Synge's work is defined as the 'tension between dream and actuality' (as basic a theme, surely, for modern literature as the nineteenth-century tension between good and evil). Price begins with a useful survey of existing criticism, and is of the opinion that, now that the definitive biography has arrived, the time is ripe for a full-length critical study. Of all Synge's critics Yeats is found to be the most satisfying. Synge's idiom, the way in which he fulfilled and transcended Yeats's vision for the Irish theatre, his own critical theory and his attitude to Ibsen, his relation to Romantic criticism—all these are fully considered. The Isle of Aran takes its place as the symbol of dream, with the rest of the world mere actuality. The prose works, translations, and poems are examined and related to the plays. Synge, it is well brought out, is in the tradition of the modern poets in his desire to 'bring back poetry into the interests and activities of the majority of people,' and he anticipates Eliot in his observation that the seventeenth-century poets 'used the whole of their personal life as their material'. The homogeneity and unity of his work are indicated, and the plays are analysed in detail. On the whole this section does not prove so illuminating as the general exposition, but Synge is interestingly presented as a blend of the Ibsenite, the near Romantic, and the Jacobean.

Sean O'Casey at the age of eighty produces three new plays.[73] They are plays full of ebullient satire, the affirmation of boisterous life, much movement, people dancing, fiddles playing, rhetoric in full flood, and Kathleen Mavourneen still at large.

Christopher Fry writes again for the theatre after some years of silence.[74] His play is a study of the character of Henry II, a 'search for his reality', bound up with the theme of the interplay of different laws. His Becket does not in any way trespass upon T. S. Eliot's. He is involved in the 'dialectic between the Church and the state', but the tragedy is Henry's, victim of 'the unattended moment'.

John Osborne adds his contribution to the saints and priests who, alongside tramps and beggars, become the heroes of modern drama. His portrait of Luther[75] is painted by a man who lives in this century, as contrasted with Christopher Fry's approach. His play, like the age it is written in, has power without poetry, while Fry's has poetry without power.

John Osborne's television play[76] has the same direct contact with his audience. The satire is directed against the audience as much as against those who prosecuted George Holyoake for blasphemy when he declared, 'Are we not too poor to have God?'

Harold Pinter publishes a collection of one-act plays,[77] one of which was written for the stage, one for television, and one for sound radio, the last five being revue sketches. Much of the technique of the revue sketch goes into his plays, and he has exploited this medium for the subtlest psychological studies of human beings embroiled in the predicament of life today.

---

[72] Synge and Anglo-Irish Drama, by Alan Price. Methuen. pp. xii+236. 25s.

[73] 'Behind the Green Curtains', 'Figuro in the Night', 'The Moon Shines on Kylenamoe', Three Plays, by Sean O'Casey. Macmillan. pp. 157. 12s. 6d.

[74] Curtmantle. A Play, by Christopher Fry. O.U.P. pp. ix+99. 10s. 6d.

[75] Luther: A Play, by John Osborne. Faber. pp. 102. 10s. 6d.

[76] A Subject of Scandal and Concern: A Play for Television, by John Osborne. Faber. pp. 47. 5s.

[77] A Slight Ache and Other Plays, by Harold Pinter. Methuen. pp. 134. 12s. 6d.

Shelagh Delaney's new play [78] deals with three generations of a family and their personal problems in love and marriage. Such a portrait of Lancashire life appears on the surface a far cry from *Hindle Wakes*, but though times may have changed the Lancashire people have not, and Shelagh Delaney's characters have the same toughness. She uses dialogue with a power that expresses the essence of her characters in their idiom, after the manner of Sean O'Casey with his Dubliners.

5. *Miscellaneous*

John Carter's little selection of A. E. Housman's prose[79] amply demonstrates, as he intends, that Housman 'was just as much an artist in prose as he was in verse'. It is felt that this part of Housman's work has been neglected, perhaps because it was buried in learned journals or in out-of-print publications. Though tempted to choose from passages which illustrate Housman's deadly shafts of critical wit, Carter has taken care to choose 'passages or paragraphs . . . both representative . . . of Housman's stance as a scholar and critic, and also characteristic examples of his powers as a prose stylist'. Latin and Greek quotations are here and there omitted, but the review of Schulze's edition of Baehrens's Catullus is printed in full as an example of Housman's minute care for detail in criticizing a text. His inaugural lecture as Professor of Latin at Cambridge in 1911 is here printed for the first time. In addition to reviews and letters to the press, there is included in an appendix a paper on Matthew Arnold which is one of several on English authors read to the Literary Society at University College, London. Housman had desired these to be destroyed after his death, and this is the one survivor.

Raymond Postgate is responsible for the revised edition of H. G. Wells's 'monumentally solid' world history.[80] Reading Wells's introductory chapter on his 'story and aim', the nobility of the common man is powerfully impressed on the mind. Wells may be no Gibbon, but he is the Gibbon of the twentieth century. As with Gibbon, the book may be opened anywhere and read with extraordinary satisfaction, and it becomes unbelievable that it should have been fashionable until a few years ago to deplore Wells's lack of prose style. For the literary scholar this is the background to the twentieth-century conception of the world, indeed to the twentieth-century world-order. Wells left a copy of his work in which he had made preliminary corrections, crossing out 'everything after about 1930' in the Table of Contents. These corrections have been incorporated in the present edition, and reveal interesting modifications in his views upon the Russian revolution. Before the date of Wells's revising, very little has been changed in the present edition. In later years some sections which Wells had only sketched out have been rewritten. The chapters on Apes and Neolithic Man have been revised by G. P. Wells, Wells's son. In the chapter on post-First World War history Raymond Postgate has contributed the sections concerned with the Far and the Near East, the 'Great Crash of 1929', and the Second World War. The last chapter, concerned with the post-Second World War period is entirely his.

Anne Ridler has compiled a selection

[78] *The Lion in Love: A Play*, by Shelagh Delaney. Methuen. pp. 104. 10s. 6d.

[79] *A. E. Housman: Selected Prose*, ed. by John Carter. Cambridge U.P. pp. xv+204. 21s. $3.75.

[80] *The Outline of History: Being a Plain History of Life and Mankind from Primordial Life to Nineteen-sixty*, by H. G. Wells, revised by Raymond Postgate, with Maps and Plans by J. F. Horrabin. Cassell. pp. xviii+1270. 36s.

of the writings of Charles Williams[81] which is intended as an introduction to his work, representing him 'at his best and most characteristic in all the forms in which he wrote except that of fiction'. It therefore covers literary criticism, dramatic work, religious essays, and poems. In all these forms Williams reveals the penetrating originality of his mind, in the sensitive discrimination of values, the revaluation of outworn beliefs, the direct, fresh approach to old truths. The poetry section is introduced by his two illuminating essays on the Arthurian legend, which reveal the reasons of his choice of this myth to express the heart of his mystical experience; for him the tale of the Grail was 'the tale of the mystical way: but also . . . the tale of the universal way'.

Frank O'Connor's account of his childhood and youth[82] in Ireland to some extent describes the raw material out of which were fashioned the plays of Sean O'Casey. His father joins the ranks of touching, comic, endearing, feckless fathers, his mother is one of the noble, courageous, self-sacrificing angels. His childhood was deprived of material advantages such as are handed out by the welfare state, but the 'education' he so earnestly sought and found for himself was a hard-won possession for life, not a mere status symbol. But the value of life was impressed upon him by familiarity with death and prison and the futilities of the Civil War.

Eleanor Farjeon[83] and Noel Streatfeild[84] are the subjects of monographs in a series of studies 'of the lives and work of eminent writers for children'. Noel Streatfeild, brought up in a parsonage, secure yet unhappy, remembers her childhood with acute vividness and can appeal directly to her child readers. In accordance with trends of fashion in children's books, she deals not only with family life, but with the professional training of children for careers. It is interesting to find in her books the values and standards of the professional middle class; assured but not affluent, and eminently nice.

Eleanor Farjeon had a more intellectual, unconventional upbringing, one of a gifted family, in a circle of writers and musicians. Her stories are distinguished by their folk-tale element, their poetic sensitiveness and skilled craftsmanship. The variety of her achievement in writing for children covers poems, plays, and tunes, and the retelling of legends and of Chaucer's *Tales*. Fantasy is 'the perfect medium for Eleanor Farjeon's genius'.

Sacheverell Sitwell[85] records his travels through Peru observing landscapes and works of art. Yet Peru has not only Lima with its lovely gardens, it has not only splendid crafts and architecture. It has its Indian slums, with the problem of finding work for the thousands of Indians who flock into the towns from the country. For one reflecting on such problems, 'even the flowers of Lima lose their loveliness'.

Virginia Woolf's reputation as a novelist would appear now to be in the trough of the wave, but the new edition of her posthumously published collection of essays[86] is a reminder that it is possible that for some time to come she

[81] *Charles Williams: Selected Writings*, chosen by Anne Ridler. O.U.P. pp. viii+244. 8s. 6d.

[82] *An Only Child*, by Frank O'Connor. Macmillan. pp. 276. 21s.

[83] *Eleanor Farjeon*. A Bodley Head Monograph, by Eileen H. Colwell. Bodley Head. pp. 94. 7s. 6d.

[84] *Noel Streatfeild*. A Bodley Head Monograph, by Barbara Ker Wilson. Bodley Head. pp. 61. 7s. 6d.

[85] *Golden Wall and Mirador: From England to Peru*, by Sacheverell Sitwell. Weidenfeld and Nicolson. pp. 286. 36s.

[86] *The Death of the Moth and Other Essays*, by Virginia Woolf. Penguin Books. pp. 212. 3s. 6d.

may be regarded more highly as a critic.

From Australia comes A. D. Hope's first volume of poems[87] to be published in England. He is a powerful, memorable satirist, who, though his own country is 'without songs, architecture, history', returns there gladly from 'the lush jungle of modern thought', from 'the chatter of cultured apes, Which is called civilization over there'.

Patrick White's latest novel[88] is planned on a vast scale, and presents a central problem of our times—the struggle to preserve inner visions in a world of material values. Four vividly drawn characters, an eccentric old lady, a Jew escaped from Germany, a poor laundress with a drunken husband, and an aborigine painter, represent the visionaries, and their lives are drawn together at various points, being at the same time involved in the daily commonplace or evil of contemporary Australian society. The book is the only modern novel to offer something of the labyrinthine infinities of James Joyce.

The publishers have drawn attention to a collection of essays by Canadian specialists[89] on the culture of their country. It is edited by Julian Park, who points out the 'sense of Canadian consciousness' brought out in the essays.

Two volumes of verse come from New Zealand. Louis Johnson's collection[90] is published in Christchurch. In his introductory essay he reviews the present state of poetry with some apprehension. He is deeply disturbed by the possible effects of television on cultural activity. He notes that poetry is 'entrenched in fairly traditional values'.

The second collection, published in England and selected by Allen Curnow,[91] is the 'first really comprehensive anthology' of New Zealand poetry. The editor points out that the poetry belongs, uniquely, to New Zealand, is 'marked or moulded everywhere' by the pressures of the country. The poets see things differently from others. The selection represents the whole history of New Zealand from the nineteenth century onwards, including something from the Maori tradition, and the introduction supplies a useful survey of this history and also considers the present state of poetry. It is to be noted that here too the present trend of culture and society appears 'ominous'. Yet there is hope that young poets will come forward who will achieve the 'difficult orientation of self and art' necessary before they can 'speak to any purpose before an English-speaking audience at large'. A note on New Zealand verse and the Maori tradition, including a section on pronunciation, is compiled with the help of Roger Oppenheim.

Africa and its vastness and darkness and mystery are the subjects of Raymond Tong's poems.[92] Drums beat ominously. 'Dance, Africa, dance, for the night is coming' is a foreboding glimpse into the future.

Africa is also the subject of an unusual book of Graham Greene's.[93] He publishes two journals recording his

[87] Poems, by A. D. Hope. Hamish Hamilton. pp. 120. 15s.

[88] Riders in the Chariot: A Novel, by Patrick White. Eyre & Spottiswoode. pp. 552. 21s.

[89] The Culture of Contemporary Canada, ed. by Julian Park. Cornell U.P. and O.U.P. (1957). 45s. $5.75.

[90] New Zealand Poetry Yearbook, ed. by Louis Johnson. Vol. IX, 1960. Christchurch: Pegasus Press. pp. 101. 10s. 6d.

[91] New Zealand Verse, selected with an Introduction and Notes by Allen Curnow. Penguin Books. pp. 339. 5s.

[92] Fabled City: West African Poems, by Raymond Tong. Glasgow: William Maclellan (1960). pp. 40. 6s.

[93] In Search of a Character: Two African Journals, by Graham Greene. Bodley Head. pp. 123. 10s. 6d.

266   THE TWENTIETH CENTURY

experiences and impressions in the
Congo and in West Africa, and thus
performs a task which many a Graham
Greene scholar would have delighted
in, for the journals represent the raw
material, dating back to 1959 and 1942
respectively, of his two novels, *A
Burnt-Out Case*, and *The Heart of the
Matter*. Footnotes explain references,
and, in some cases, indicate the way
in which the material was used in the
novels.

6. General

In 'The Calendar to Modern Letters'
(*Lond Mag*) Malcolm Bradbury reviews the high level of criticism and
creative writing achieved in that
periodical during its short life between
March 1925 and July 1927. Looking
back two decades, C. L. Mowat
examines 'The Mood of the Thirties'
(*CQ*), considering the nature of literary
engagement with the social, political,
and economic circumstances of the
time, in particular the pressures arising
from the emergence of Nazism and the
Spanish Civil War. John Lehmann
comments upon the period 1945–61 in
'English Letters in the Doldrums' (*TQ*),
offering the reflections of a literary
editor and publisher who finds that the
'real interests of this generation lie
rather in sociology, in critical theory,
and in discussion than in creative
writing'. Another trend is recognized
by Bernard Williams in 'A Changing
Social History of English Writing'
(*Audience*); Williams notes the pre-
dominant influence of D. H. Lawrence
and Orwell rather than of Eliot and
Pound in literature now directed towards a new working-class audience
instead of the traditional middle-class
public. Closely related to this thesis is a
note by Henry Popkin on the emergence of a distinct and recognizable
group of novelists and dramatists,
'Jewish Writers in England: A Tradition Begins' (*Commentary*). Lionel

Trilling, in 'On the Modern Element in
Modern Literature' (*PR*), characterizes
this element as a hostility to civilization, contrasted with the faith in sanity
and civilized order which was possible
for Arnold. A less pessimistic but
equally radical view is presented by
Graham Hough, 'The Nature of a
Revolution' (*Audience*), who mentions
that for the contemporary writer the
creative sources of literature are to be
found in a national rather than in the
cosmopolitan subject-matter treated by
Pound and Eliot. One particularly
national element is discussed by Martin
Green in 'British Comedy and the
British Sense of Humour' (*TQ*), an
essay analysing the distinctive brilliance
of Shaw, an inventor of comic situations, not a rebel; of Evelyn Waugh, a
satirist; and of Amis, whose humour
is that of the ordinary middle-class
Englishman.

7. The Novel

David Garnett provides an important reminiscence, 'Some Writers I
have known: Galsworthy, Forster,
Moore, and Wells' (*TQ*), in which he
records a personal acquaintance with
these men, and passes some acute and
sympathetic comments on the authors
and their works. 'The Novelist's
Responsibility' (*English*) is considered
by L. P. Hartley, who contends that
the modern writer must restore to his
characters their responsibility for
action, and reintroduce to his work
standards of justice and judgement.
Three novelists are concerned with the
problems of criticizing the novel: John
Wain examines the concept of 'character' and the view of the novel as
'dramatic poem', in a review article
(*Encounter*); John Bayley takes exception to the current application of the
term 'life' as a standard of evaluation
and judgement in 'The Novel and the
Life Standard' (*Lond Mag*); and in
'Science, Politics and the Novelist:

Or the Fish and the Net' (*KR*), C. P. Snow discusses a question pertinent to his own fiction—the shortcomings of modern criticism in dealing with the themes of science and politics in the novel. The artistic problem of matching the eloquence of prose to the fullness of human personality is discussed by Iris Murdoch in 'Against Dryness' (*Encounter*).

Beerbohm's marginal literary work is described by David Cecil in 'The Man Who Never Stopped Playing' (*Horizon*); this tells of his private addenda—inscriptions, notes, and portraits—which add a further dimension of satire to many of his books.

Bennett's art is examined by James Hepburn in 'The Two Worlds of Edwin Clayhanger' (*BUSE*). He tests the conventional view of Bennett as a realistic novelist, and suggests rather that his representation of the external world is a means to shadowing forth the inner world of human character.

A hitherto unpublished short story by Joyce Cary, 'The Ball', is provided with an introductory note by James Meriwether (*TQ*) in which the editor gives his opinion that this piece, the original inspiration for *A Fearful Joy*, 'unquestionably deserves to be ranked with Cary's most brilliant short stories'.

In 'Dramatization of Conrad's *Victory*: And a New Letter' (*NQ*) Robert Evans shows that in 1916 the author approved a proposal to dramatize the novel, but there is no evidence of his having assisted in the change. In 'Conrad's *Nostromo*: A Source and its Use' (*TCF*) Rosemary Freeman surveys the possible historical sources of this novel, in particular the 1860 translation of Garibaldi's autobiography by Alexandre Dumas. Interpretations of Conrad's novels include 'The Essential Jim' (*NCF*), by Ann Gossman and George Whiting. Opposing Guerard, they read the hero as a noble, fallible, romantic youth, with whom

the reader is invited to identify himself. Leo Gurko writes of the 'Death Journey in *The Nigger of the Narcissus*' (*NCF*), a drama of death and the Fall in Conrad's earliest masterpiece.

E. M. W. Tillyard, in '*The Secret Agent* Reconsidered' (*EC*), classifies this piece between the novel in the grand manner and the long short story, with the theme of ends miscarrying. John Wills analyses 'Conrad's *The Secret Sharer*' (*UKCR*), pointing out the elements of caricature, the imagery, the point of view, and the symbolic overtones, and identifying the theme as that of the leader and society.

Durrell studies will be considerably furthered by the contribution of Anthony Knerr, 'Regarding a Checklist of Laurence Durrell' (*PBSA*), which gives 162 entries, and extends the Thomas-Powell list down to the end of 1960. There are two notable articles on the Alexandrian Quartet: 'Durrell's Way to Alexandria' (*CE*), in which Carl Bode identifies sex as the central subject, and investigates the author's use of the Tarot pack in symbolic characterization; and Bonamy Dobrée, in 'Durrell's Alexandrian Series' (*Sew*), acknowledges 'the splendidly coloured, vivid experience', yet suggests that the novelist notes 'the sadness of *la condition humaine* without suffering any escape from the depths either of the spirit or the body'.

'Ronald Firbank and an Amateur World' (*Listener*) is the title of a broadcast talk by W. H. Auden, in which the critic discusses the 'amateur activity' in Firbank, the absence of necessity, of care, or dedication in the moral world of his fiction, and the nature of his private Eden. The discovery of an exercise-book containing the autograph fair copy of *The New Rhythum*, which Firbank was working upon at the time of his death in 1926, is recorded by Lord Horder, in 'More Ronald Firbank' (*TLS*). The interest in Ford

Madox Ford continues to grow. Two important bibliographies compiled by Frank MacShane appear in *EFT*: 'Ford Madox Ford: An Annotated Bibliography of Writing about Him: Supplement, with Additions and Emendations by Helmut and Helga Gerber' (this supplements the previous bibliographies in *EFT*); and 'Ford Madox Ford: Collections of His Manuscripts, Periodical Publications by Him, Prefaces and Miscellaneous Contributions to Books by Others.' To *EFT*, MacShane also contributes 'Ford Madox Ford and His Contemporaries: The Techniques of the Novel', where he describes Ford's achievement of an artistic *via media* between excessive subjectivism and more technical accomplishment. There are two further articles by the same critic: 'A Conscious Craftsman: Ford Madox Ford's Manuscript Revisions' (*BUSE*), based upon the opening of *Professor's Progress*, the last unfinished novel, and the original ending to *Some Do Not*; and 'The *English Review*' (*SAQ*), tracing the influence of Ford's editorship from 1908 until its decline by 1913, and surveying the contributors and the general nature of its literary achievement. Richard Ludwig, in 'The Reputation of Ford Madox Ford' (*PMLA*), argues for a fairer judgement upon Ford's relationship with Conrad, and finds a prevalent unwarranted denigration of the writer's personal and literary reputation. A fresh view of the narrator's status is offered in 'The Epistemology of *The Good Soldier*' (*Sew*), by Samuel Hynes, who sees no position of knowledge within the story superior to the narrator's own; the irony stems from the narrator, and is turned upon himself. Another discussion of this topic is contained in 'Ford's Passion for Provence' (*ELH*), by James Cox, which notes the range of critical disagreement over the narrator's reliability in *The Good Soldier*, and points out Ford's technique of ironic allusion to the conventions of the courtly love tradition.

The most important item of E. M. Forster material this year is the 'Indian Entries' (*Encounter*), three groups of notes, dated between October 1912 and April 1913, made in his journal on the occasion of his first visit to India. The Autumn number of *MFS* is devoted to Forster. It includes 'Criticism of E. M. Forster: A Selected Checklist', by Maurice Beebe and Joseph Brogunier, to be used in conjunction with Helmut Gerber's 'Annotated Checklist, 1959'; and 'Theme and Symbolism in *Howard's End*', by George Thomson. The same critic contributes two other articles elsewhere: 'Symbolism in E. M. Forster's Earlier Fiction' (*Criticism*); and 'Thematic Symbol in *A Passage to India*' (*TCL*), which shows the structure to be symbolic of the situation of the individual and of mankind. Another study of this novel is provided by David Shusterman, 'The Curious Case of Professor Godbole' (*PMLA*), refuting the common view of Godbole as a man of genuine goodwill, and the reading of the novel as a tract for Hinduism. In 'Forster's Many-Faceted Universe' (*C*) Frederick McDowell acknowledges the technical flaws in *The Longest Journey*, but claims it to be the most intellectually provocative of the novels, and treats appreciatively the range of the hero's function and presentation.

Earle Labor, in 'Henry Green's Web of Loving' (*C*), observes that the brilliance of the social comedy conceals a tragic seriousness of theme in the grotesque and destructive forms, not of love, but of loving. Opposing this view, Thomas Churchill describes the work in his title '*Loving*: A Comic Novel' (*C*), viewing the serious element of the work not as tragedy, but as contained in the high comedy of manners.

'Graham Greene's Theological Thrillers' (*QQ*), by A. J. M. Smith, discusses his work in the traditional drama of Christian redemption where man's depravity is cleansed by the working of grace. The question of human failure and the possibilities of redemption are also treated by Charles Rob in 'Graham Greene: The Man and the Message' (*Atlantic Monthly*). 'Graham Greene, Master of Melodrama' (*Tamarack Review*) is considered by Philip Stratford, who points to an increasing note of comic absurdity closely related to the melodrama of despair.

In 'The Novels of L. P. Hartley' (*C*) Harvey Webster selects the *Eustace and Hilda* trilogy, *The Boat*, and *The Go-Between* as the author's most significant works, and examines the 'unity and variety' of their vision.

'Books and Manuscripts by James Joyce' (*Library Chronicle of the University of Texas*), by Weldon Thornton, is a brief account of the Joyce collection in the University Library; this includes the schema of *Ulysses* and over two dozen letters and notes by Joyce, most of which have never been published. An interesting view of the writer in Paris during the 1930's is given in 'James Joyce: A First Impression' (*Listener*), by James Stern. The biographical basis of the writer's art is examined by William Noon, in 'James Joyce: Un-facts, Fiction and Facts' (*PMLA*); personal papers and letters in the Cornell Joyce collection are drawn upon in discussing the problem of distinguishing the 'moral history' of Dublin from the artist's self-portrait. This question is also raised by Bernard Benstock, 'A Portrait of the Artist in *Finnegans Wake*' (*Bucknell Review*), who sees self-portraiture and self-caricature in certain aspects of Shem, Penman, and H. C. Earwicker. Florence Walzl, in 'Pattern of Paralysis in Joyce's *Dubliners*: A study of the Original Framework' (*CE*), divides the

original fourteen stories into four groups, each exhibiting paralysis on a different range or level of human activity. In 'Joyce's Irish Politics: The Seventh Chapter of *Ulysses*' (*Massachusetts Review*) Stanley Sultan reveals the chapter's subject: 'the political character of the Irish nation, its theme self-deception, paralysis, futility'. Another study of *Ulysses* is 'Joyce and the Artist's Fingernails' (*RES*), where S. L. Goldberg considers the use made of analytic realism and images of myth to explore Bloom, and, overall, Joyce's concern with 'dramatic' art. Of the later work, Helmut Bonheim considers the pejorative weight of the word 'Tory' in *Finnegans Wake* (*NQ*); and Bernard Benstock, in 'Anna Livia and the City Builder' (*NQ*), argues the association of Anna Livia with Earwicker and Finnegan in the theme of city building. The same author reviews Joyce's 'conclusively negative' religious experience, his 'antitheism', in 'The Final Apostacy: James Joyce and *Finnegans Wake*' (*ELH*). Notes on Joyce's verbal usage are contributed by J. B. Bamborough, 'Joyce and Jonson' (*REL*), reviewing what is known of the writer's acquaintance with Jonson, and suggesting the possibility of influence in matters of diction, prose, and, more especially, with regard to Jonson's concern for the position of the artist. Influence from another direction is traced by Haskell Black, in 'Theory of Language in Gustave Flaubert and James Joyce' (*RLC*); Black finds both writers 'in a common literary tradition'.

Further information is forthcoming about the life of D. H. Lawrence. Some hitherto unknown details about his movements in September 1913 and November 1925 are given by Arnold Armin, 'In the Footsteps of D. H. Lawrence in Switzerland: Some New Biographical Material' (*TSLL*). The degree and extent to which Egbert is a 'portrait' of Percy Lucas is re-examined by Barbara Lucas in 'Apropos of *England, My England*' (*Twentieth Century*), where she corrects the account of sources given in *The Intelligent Heart* by Henry Moore. Michael Sharpe analyses 'The Genesis of D. H. Lawrence's *The Trespasser*' (*EC*), and shows that the novel was based on part of the material from which Helena Corke wrote *Neutral Ground* (1933), and influenced by the sonnets of Rachel Annand Taylor and the criticisms of Ford and Edward Garnett. The aftermath of the *Lady Chatterley* trial is to be found in articles and correspondence in *Encounter*, and in 'The New Orthodoxy' (*Spectator*), by F. R. Leavis, who questions whether the novel's present high repute can be justified on literary grounds. S. L. Goldberg, in '*The Rainbow*: Fiddle-Bow and Sand' (*EC*), judges the artistic power to decline in the second part, where dramatic exploration gives way to a mode of social fable. A comparison among 'Lawrence, Joyce and Powys' (*EC*) by G. Wilson Knight shows all three writers to have been concerned with abnormal sexuality.

As Frank Tuohy remarks, in 'Day of a Dead Man' (*Spectator*), there seems to be an international campaign afoot to promote the reputation of Malcolm Lowry. The Spring issue of *Canadian Literature* is devoted to this author: the most interesting article, 'More than Music: Glimpses of Malcolm Lowry', by Kirk Downie, quotes from letters to suggest the width of the author's intellectual interests.

Helmut Gerber has compiled 'George Moore: An Annotated Bibliography of Writings About Him; Supplement II' (*EFT*). This should be used in conjunction with the original Bibliography (*EFT*, 1959), and Supplement I (*EFT*, 1960).

'The Progress of Iris Murdoch' (*ESA*) from *Under the Net* to *The Bell* is described by Olga Meidner, who considers questions of prose style and fictional technique, of achievement and failure.

Ronald Bottrell writes of 'L. H. Myers' (*REL*) as a philosophical thinker whose religious convictions enabled him to meet no difficulty in what are usually considered to be the problems of personality and communication.

'George Orwell: A Selected Bibliography' (*Bulletin of Bibliography*), by Zoltan Zeke and William White, comprises, in Part I, a list of Orwell's writings (including juvenilia, poems and reviews), and, in Part II, works about Orwell (including chapters, periodical articles, and reviews). In 'My Brother, George Orwell' (*Twentieth Century*) Avril Dunn gives her reminiscences from about 1914 until his death; the last period is treated more fully. *Encounter* prints 'Some letters of George Orwell to Cyril Connolly, Richard Rees, Stephen Spender, T. R. Fyvel and others'; these are dated between 1936–49, and include references to his own writing during this period. John Wain, in 'Here Lies Lower Binfield' (*Encounter*), examines the socialist dislike of Orwell's anti-modernism, especially as displayed in *Coming Up for Air*.

In '*Du côté de chez* Waugh' (*REL*) Peter Green observes that Evelyn Waugh's 'first serious novel' is *A Handful of Dust*, 'an extended illustration of *The Waste Land* in fictional terms'.

Working on the H. G. Wells papers at the University of Illinois, Gordon Ray provides an account of 'H. G. Wells's Contributions to the *Saturday Review*' (*Lib*), listing 111 items, some of them previously unattributed, published between November 1894 and February 1898. Kenneth Newell discusses 'The Structure of H. G. Wells' *Tono-Bungay*' (*EFT*) in terms of the principle of change and the accompanying metaphorical ideas.

'Virginia's Web' (*Chicago Review*), by Geoffrey Hartman, a study of *A Room of One's Own*, emphasizes how Virginia Woolf attempts to solve her problems in the structure of fiction through style and realistic plot. Her use of language is also examined by Ramsay Warren in 'The Claims of Language: Virginia Woolf as Symbolist' (*EFT*). John Graham, 'The "Caricature Value" of Parody and Fantasy in *Orlando*' (*UTQ*), indicates that there is a growing seriousness in her use of these literary devices, though not consistently maintained.

8. Poetry

In 'Break-through in Modern Verse' (*Lond Mag*) Cyril Connolly sees the critical stage in English poetry as the period between the end of the First World War and the publication of *The Waste Land*, with Eliot and Pound as the prime figures. A. Alvarez also looks back to Eliot and Pound in 'English Poetry Today' (*Commentary*), yet he finds no continuation of their achievements in *vers libre* and calls for a new seriousness, not a new programme. G. S. Fraser surveys 'English Poetry in the 1950's' (*Audience*), identifying groups of innovators, reactionaries, and, in a middle position, the Movement poets, characterized by their insularity, their avoidance of political issues, and their strength in ineloquence. The Movement is treated in more detail by Allan Rodway, in 'A Note on Contemporary English Poetry' (*TQ*); he examines its origins and its trends, and describes its members as 'competent and sane (and technically immensely influential)'. A further stage is described by Bernard Bergonzi, in 'After "The Movement" ' (*Listener*), following the course of twentieth-century English poetry up to Movement anthology, *New Lines* (1956), and then considering its legacies and latest developments.

'The Poetry of Auden' (*Lond Mag*), by Nathan Scott, argues that the poet's achievement is to be reckoned with *now*, that he shows a deep concern with the immediate age, and that his achievement is largely in having arrived at a traditional religious faith amidst the confusions of our time. Monroe Spears, in 'Auden in the Fifties: Rites of Homage' (*Sew*), relates the definition of poetry advanced in Auden's inaugural lecture as Professor of Poetry at Oxford ('Making, Knowing and Judging') with his recent work, in particular the volume *Homage to Clio* (1960).

The possibility of Eliot's authorship of eight contributions to the *Criterion* between 1924–5 is discussed by Gwenn Boardman in 'T. S. Eliot and the Mystery of Fanny Marlow' (*MFS*). Herbert Howarth, in 'T. S. Eliot and the "Little Preacher" ' (*AQ*), remarks on the influence of the poet's grandfather, the St. Louis Unitarian minister, William Greenleaf Eliot. 'Sweeney Among the Nightingales' is placed beside 'Tradition and the Individual Talent' by Stanley Hyman, in 'Poetry and Criticism: T. S. Eliot' (*AS*), to exemplify the relationship between these two fields of writing. Merrel Clubb, in following 'The Heraclitean Element in Eliot's *Four Quartets*' (*PQ*), finds the work heavily dependent upon Heraclitean concepts, especially the 'dialectic of paradox'. A severely critical note is struck in 'An Individual Talent' (*TLS*), which suggests limitations to the poet's achievement.

'David Gascoyne: A Check-List' (*TCL*), 200 items, compiled by Ann Atkinson, 'is an attempt to record all the published work . . . in books and periodicals', together with a select list of criticism.

'Robert Graves and the Decline of Modernism' (*EC*), delivered as Professor D. J. Enright's inaugural lecture at the University of Malaya (an occasion with some political repercussions), remarks upon the writer as poet, novelist, and critic, and notes that the rise in his reputation has coincided with the decline of modernism. Ronald Gaskell, in 'The Poetry of Robert Graves' (*CQ*), identifies the importance of the poet's war experiences, and examines the quality and limitations of his technical power.

G. S. Fraser discusses 'The Poetry of Thom Gunn' (*CQ*), its spareness and strength, its wit that of the thirties rather than the fifties.

In 'Poet Without a Mask' (*CQ*) V. de S. Pinto recounts that D. H. Lawrence turned from the traditional poetic forms, seeing them as a pretence or game, and sought 'to create an organic or expressive form to express his naked, passionate experience'.

'Edwin Muir: An Appreciation' (*TQ*), by Kathleen Raine, explores the meaning of the term 'Fable' as used by the poet, and as exemplified in the subject-matter and symbolism of his poetic vision. Joseph Summers, in 'The Achievement of Edwin Muir' (*MR*), surveys his range and development as poet and critic, and considers the pressures of life and circumstance upon the artist.

'The Poetic Roles of Edith Sitwell' (*Chicago Review*), by Ralph Mills, presents the poet's development from ironist to judge of society, and more recently, to prophet, with an accompanying change in modes of expression and technique.

The *Colby Library Quarterly* (March) is dedicated to James Stephens. 'James Stephens at Colby College', by Richard Cary, is a classified bibliography of the Stephens holding in the James A. Healey collection of modern Irish literature. This provides details of his contributions to newspapers and periodicals, his manuscripts and letters, and biographies and criticism. Birgit Bramsbäck contributes 'James Ste-

phens: Dublin–Paris–Return', revealing what is not generally known, that Stephens wrote a good deal of poetry and some prose in Paris, 1913–15; this period is documented by his letters to Dr. Thomas Bodkin; and we are able to follow closely the stages in the growth of his two collections of verse, *Songs from the Clay* and *The Adventures of Seumas Beg*. There is also an appreciation and reminiscence, 'James Stephens', by Oliver St. John Gogarty.

In 'Dylan Thomas' *Collected Poems*: Chronology of Composition' (*PMLA*), Ralph Maud points out that this volume brings together in sequence and with little change the contents of the five separate volumes previously published; however, the notebooks, and other sources of evidence, reveal an order of composition altogether different. Taking as his example 'Vision and Prayer', John Nist, in 'Dylan Thomas: Perfection of the Work' (*Arizona Quarterly*), argues that 'the less perfection in the life, the more perfection in the work'.

There is a wide range of Yeats studies. Curtis Bradford establishes that 'The Order of Yeats' *Last Poems*' (*MLN*) is largely that of the poet's own decision. In 'Vestiges of Creation' (*Sew*) Thomas Parkinson analyses the varieties of the poet's creative experience as revealed in the writing of a number of the poems. 'Yeats and Pound in England' (*TQ*), by Patricia Hutchins, gives details of the correspondence and meetings between the two men, in particular as these refer to their opinions of each other's writing. 'A Source for Yeats's "The Black Tower" ' (*NQ*) in Standish O'Grady's *Finn and his Companions* is suggested by Patrick Diskin. T. K. Dunseath, in 'Yeats and the Genesis of Supernatural Song' (*ELH*), examines the artistic concepts underlying the early 'Baile and Aillinn', to trace the mature development of these ideas in 'Ribh at the Tomb of

Baile and Aillinn', and to outline the structural order of the *Supernatural Songs*. In 'The Human Image in Yeats' (*Lond Mag*) Denis Donoghue compares 'The Wild Swans at Coole' with the later works, many of which are flawed by shrillness and distortion, faults consequent upon the poet's strained role. The same critic, in 'Tradition, Poetry, and W. B. Yeats' (*Sew*), considers the use and meaning of 'tradition' to the poet, and scrutinizes some of the recent critical approaches to Yeats. Norman Jeffares, in 'Yeats as Public Man' (*Poetry*), discusses the polemical and 'public speech' elements in his verse. 'Fine Manners, Liberal Speech: A Note on the Public Poetry of W. B. Yeats' (*EC*), by Graham Martin, discusses a shift (in *Responsibilities* and the later volumes) of the poet's attitude towards Anglo-Irish culture, 'from idealisation through critical examination to nostalgia'; the critical and nostalgic poems convince, not those which make claims for that culture. Thomas Whitaker, in 'Yeats's "Dove or Swan" ' (*PMLA*), analyses a section of *A Vision*, which illustrates the writer working at an intermediate stage between the facts of history and the symbolism of his poetry; it is 'a typically romantic achievement: a vision of history as art'.

9. *The Drama*

The February issue of *Twentieth Century* is a Theatre Number with contributions from the following dramatists: Harold Pinter, Christopher Fry, Arnold Wesker, John Whiting, John Arden, Alan Sillitoe, and John Osborne. The socially conscious drama of Clifford Odets, and the work of Osborne, Logue, Wesker, and Delaney, is surveyed by Albert Hunt in 'Only Soft-Centred Left' (*Encore*). In the same periodical appears 'Beyond Naturalism Pure', by Stuart Hall, a study of the present contest between ideas

and naturalism. An anonymous contributor to *TLS*, in 'The Reaction Against Realism', sees the need for the modern dramatists (he mentions Arden, Wesker, Alun Owen, Osborne, Pinter, Delaney) to widen their techniques in dealing with the new subject-matter of working-class life. This question is also taken up by Bernard Kops in 'The Young Writer and the Theatre' (*Jewish Quarterly*); Kops sees a popular theatre evolving, with young writers engaged on contemporary themes, in current regional dialects, requiring a new approach from actors, designers, and producers.

In 'Un théâtre poétique intérieur' (*Cahiers du Sud*) Henri Fluchère traces the development of T. S. Eliot's drama, where, initially, there is the theme of man's view of man and the difficulty of mutual understanding; in his last work, *The Elder Statesman*, human love has come close to divine love. Jack Winter finds ' "Prufrockism" in *The Cocktail Party*' (*MLQ*), with characters who cherish dreams of salvation and delusions of unattainable love, although they far exceed Prufrock in attaining the contentment of resignation.

Christian Pons, in 'De Shakespeare à Christopher Fry' (*Cahiers du Sud*), writes appreciatively of *The Dark is Light Enough*, translating portions of the work, and providing a critical summary of the writer's achievement here and in his other plays.

Modern Drama IV is devoted to Irish dramatists, including Sean O'Casey. Robert Hogan gives an account of 'O'Casey's Dramatic Apprenticeship', referring to a number of unproduced and now unavailable one-act plays written prior to *The Shadow of the Gunman*, and showing the development of the later plays to stem from his experience of this early form. W. Armstrong treats 'The Sources and Themes of *The Plough and the Stars*', relating the play to the dramatist's experiences in the Easter Rising of 1916, political speeches of the period, and the Communist Manifesto. This play is also at the centre of a discussion by Vincent De Baun, 'Sean O'Casey and the Road to Expressionism'. Katherine Worth follows the evolution of 'O'Casey's Dramatic Symbolism' from the realistic action and settings of the early plays. David Krause identifies Ossianic myths as a source and motivation for a recurrent theme, in ' "The Rageous Ossean"; Patron-Hero of Synge and O'Casey'.

'John Osborne: A Bibliography' (*TCL*), from 1956 to the third quarter of 1960, is compiled by Shirley Bailey.

Daniel Leary and Richard Foster contribute 'Adam and Eve: Evolving Archetypes in *Back to Methuselah*' to the *Shaw Review*; they trace the continuity of the author's ideas on creative evolution from *Back to Methuselah* to *Man and Superman*. Samuel Butler's influence upon the writer is followed in 'The Butlerian Inheritance of G. B. Shaw' (*DR*), by Claude Bissell. Stephen Stanton reveals the extent of 'Shaw's Debt to Scribe' (*PMLA*), a writer whom Shaw criticized severely, yet to whose plays, *Bataille de dames* in particular, he was considerably indebted for the tricks and devices of stagecraft put to use in his early works. A score of further articles on Shaw are published in *The Shavian* and the *Shaw Review*.

In 'Synge and the Celtic Revival' (*MD*) David Greene uses the evidence of the writer's notebooks to show his regard for Gaelic sources, and the extent to which they were drawn upon in his work. 'The Making of the *Play-*

boy' (*MD*), by Patricia Spacks, argues that the meaning of 'playboy' is defined in the action, and in the hero, who controls his bodily strength, his emotions, and his words. Under the title 'Synge's Last Play: *And a Story Will be Told Forever*' (*MD*) Harold Orel reveals that there survive more than a dozen manuscript versions of *Deirdre of the Sorrows*, and he maintains that, had the dramatist lived to produce a synthesis of the variants, the outcome might have been his greatest play.

Peter Ure contends that in 'Yeats's *Deirdre*' (*ES*) theory and practice conflict; intended by Yeats as an expression of his anti-naturalist views, it is 'surely more full of character and artifice than the theory'. In 'The Anti-Theater of W. B. Yeats' (*MD*) Anna Sandberg recounts Yeats's attempt to use legend symbolically in the *Plays for Dancers*, where he achieves a 'theatre in which action revealed not character, but pure emotion'.

10. *Miscellaneous Prose*

In a review-article, 'John Middleton Murry' (*CQ*), J. B. Beer judges him a fine but not great critic, often prolix and inconsistent, yet armed with seriousness, discrimination, and integrity.

Franklin Parker has compiled 'Alfred North Whitehead (1861–1947): A Partial Bibliography' (*Bulletin of Bibliography*), listing works by and about Whitehead.

A 'Checklist of Reviews by Charles Williams' (*PBSA*) is supplied by Lawrence Dawson, Jr.; this mentions 280 reviews written between 1918 and 1945.

XV. AMERICAN LITERATURE

By GEOFFREY MOORE

1. General

THE expectations aroused by Roy Harvey Pearce's essays on American poetry which have been appearing in *NEQ*, *HR*, and other publications (see *YW* xli. 277) are amply fulfilled by the appearance of *The Continuity of American Poetry*.[1] This rather special kind of history, covering American poetry from the seventeenth century to the present, is concerned, not 'with the history of the making of poems, but rather with the history which poems have made'. However, Pearce's book is not only a study in cultural history, but also a collection of acute analyses of individual poems. In the chapter devoted to Wallace Stevens, for example, one finds a rewritten version of Pearce's pioneering critique of 'Notes Toward a Supreme Fiction' which appeared originally in *PMLA*. Perhaps the most interesting section is that which is concerned with the American epic. Here, with reference to 'The Columbiad', 'Song of Myself', 'The Cantos', 'The Bridge', and 'Paterson', Pearce considers the attempts which American poets have made since the eighteenth century to define their sense of America and their relationship to the world. Although not all students of American poetry will be in agreement with all of Pearce's strongly expressed views, it is a relief to find an American critic who does not hide what he feels under an umbrella of jargon talk.

John Henry Raleigh's study of Matthew Arnold and American cul-

ture[2] deals in the main with Arnold's influence on five writers: Henry James, William Brownell, Stuart P. Sherman, T.S. Eliot, and Lionel Trilling. Between 1865 and 1950, Raleigh believes, no other foreign critic exercised such an influence in the United States. Arnold was well received to begin with because much of what he had to say had been anticipated or hinted at by American critics. His influence remained because he provided just that sense of a critical tradition which a later generation of Americans felt that they lacked.

In *American Literature: Traditions and Talents*[3] Warner Berthoff considers the felt lack of a tradition in America from another angle. He is concerned with American provinciality, disconnectedness, and preoccupation with self-judgement. Many transatlantic themes and mannerisms, he believes, may be attributed to the evangelical and sectarian legacy of the Reformation. The fixation upon loneliness and moral isolation derives in part from the protestant stress on the individual conscience. Can Americans, Berthoff asks, expect some decisive new turn for the literary life in the future? He is hopeful of a positive answer only if American writers forsake Eliot's attempt to get the feeling of the whole order of past literature in their bones. 'Personal examples and case histories' must be the order of the day. Americans

---

[2] *Matthew Arnold and American Culture*, by John Henry Raleigh. California U.P. and C.U.P. pp. x+301. $1.95. 17s.

[3] *American Literature: Traditions and Talents*, by Warner Berthoff. Oberlin, Ohio: Press of the Times, 1960. pp. 23.

[1] *The Continuity of American Poetry*, by Roy Harvey Pearce. Princeton U.P. pp. xv+442. $7.50.

must make literary capital out of 'the whole character of the life they have found themselves committed to'.

In 'American Letters' (*Yale Review*) R. W. B. Lewis is also concerned with 'the current intensive guessing about out literary future'. He proceeds to do some guessing of his own, his conclusion being that the best hope for the coming years is that the age that has started will present the writer with 'something worth the dignity of resistance'. The more vigorous and coherent the age, the more energetically the writer will be able to honour it by his own mode of rebellion.

Earl H. Rovit covers much the same ground in 'American Literature and "The American Experience"' (*AQ*). He points out—as others have done before him, but with refreshing intelligence—that it was natural for American writers to take over English forms, and with them an assumption of English experience, at the beginning. The typical American hero is isolated, the typical American form abstract or symbolic. Americans have attempted poetic definitions of ambiguous subjective experience rather than analyses of society. The best American art— *Moby-Dick*, *Leaves of Grass*, *Walden*, Emerson's 'oral essays', *The Education of Henry Adams*—has forged its own unique forms. The American artist and thinker, Rovit considers, is better qualified to face the stresses of our modern condition than is his European contemporary.

In an article in *Encounter* Marcus Cunliffe examines 'images' of America from the time of Duhamel and Crêvecoeur to the present. Today, he believes, European images of America almost coincide with American self-images. America will continue to be blamed excessively when something goes wrong; that is her punishment and privilege for being an imaginary as well as a real country.

Charles L. Sanford's topic[4] is what, since R. W. B. Lewis's *The American Adam*, has usually been called the 'Adamic' myth. Sanford retitles it the 'Edenic' myth, however, and surveys a much broader field than Lewis. His emphasis is on the myth itself rather than the 'cultural dialogue' which developed round the figure of Adam. He assembles a considerable amount of evidence to show how the pursuit of 'an idea of paradise' gave shape to a number of popular images of the roles of Americans and America. Chief among these he places the sense of mission, the idea of progress, the success story, and the concept of the frontier. In tracing the development of the 'Edenic' myth Sanford surveys a large sector of Western history. He believes that the myth has been at different times a way of interpreting history, an effect of history, and a contributing factor to history. The discovery of America removed the Edenic dream from its religious context. Migration from Europe symbolized a moral regeneration, a rebirth out of the hell of Europe into the Eden of America. None of this, of course, is original to Sanford, but what is valuable about his book is its documentation and ordering of the evidence. The chapters on Franklin and Jefferson, on Henry James, and on 'Diplomacy in Eden, 1900–1950' are particularly interesting.

Edwin T. Bowden[5] considers twelve great American novels which reflect the continuing concern in American life with the problem of human isolation. After an introduction by way of *Of Plymouth Plantation* he groups his selected novels under the following

[4] *The Quest for Paradise: Europe and the American Moral Imagination*, by Charles L. Sanford. Illinois U.P. pp. x+282. $5.

[5] *The Dungeon of the Heart: Human Isolation and the American Novel*, by Edwin T. Bowden. New York and London: Macmillan. pp. xi+175. $1.75. 13s. 6d.

headings: 'The Frontier Isolation' (*The Deerslayer, Huckleberry Finn, My Antonia, The Catcher in the Rye*), 'The Mighty Individual' (*Look Homeward, Angel, The Scarlet Letter, The Portrait of a Lady*), 'The Commonplace and the Grotesque' (*The Rise of Silas Lapham, Winesburg, Ohio, Light in August*, and *The Grapes of Wrath*), and 'The Monkey-Rope' (*Moby-Dick*). Like so many of the books which yearly seek to 'explain' the American novel, Bowden's is an essay in cultural history. It is certainly true, as more than one critic has noted, that there runs through the history of the American novel the theme of the isolated man who, tortured by his loneliness, searches for some point of contact with his fellow men. Bowden documents this theme very adequately and to this extent his study is useful. But this kind of book merely adds a few more facts to our knowledge of the American writer's relationship to his society. It does not tell us whether the literature which is dwelt on at such length is good as literature.

Daniel G. Hoffman's *Form and Fable in American Fiction*[6] does not help us in this way either, though from the point of view of the reader interested in the stuff of literature it is more helpful than Bowden's. It shows how folk-lore, myth, and ritual were used by three major American authors—Hawthorne, Melville, and Mark Twain—and by a number of lesser writers, among them Crèvecoeur, Franklin, Irving, and Paulding. Hoffman believes that folk traditions and myth have been peculiarly appropriate to the poetic, non-realistic character of American romance-fiction. For example, the typical American hero has sought to discover his identity by rebelling against father, ruler, society, or God.

Hawthorne's work seems to interest Hoffman more than that of his other chosen writers. He explores the implications of Hawthorne's 'Moral Picturesque', ' "My Kinsman, Major Molineux" and the "Yankee Bumpkin" theme', ' "The Maypole of Merry Mount" and the Folklore of Love', 'The "Village of Witches" ("Young Goodman Brown")', 'The Scarlet Letter and the Green', 'Paradise Regained at Maule's Well', and 'May-Day in a Cold Arcadia (*The Blithedale Romance*)'. Hoffman writes with a poet's sensibility. One could wish for another book from him in the field of 'pure' literary criticism.

Hoffman also contributes an article on 'The Deaths and Three Resurrections of Davy Crockett' to the *Antioch Review*. This interesting account of the Crockett myth covers an area in which American literature, history, and sociology meet.

In *The Idea of an American Novel*[7] Louis D. Rubin and John Rees Moore document the pronouncements of a wide range of American writers and critics on the subject of 'the Great American Novel'. In the early days of the Republic Americans talked in terms of a national epic, for did not Rome have the *Aeneid*, England the Arthurian legends, and France the *Song of Roland*? In the nineteenth century, however, attention switched to the concept of defining the national character in the novel, and it is here, more than in any other literary form, that America has sought her own image. Rubin and Moore collate their findings under the headings of: 'The Call for a National Literature', 'The Scope of "The Great American Novel" ', 'The American Novel and "Reality" ', 'The American Character', 'Ideals for the American Novel', and

---

[6] *Form and Fable in American Fiction*, by Daniel G. Hoffman. New York and London: O.U.P. pp. xvi+368. 50s.

[7] *The Idea of an American Novel*, ed. by Louis D. Rubin, Jr., and John Rees Moore. New York: Crowell. pp. xxii+394. $5.75.

'American Art and American Experience'. They end with a chronological list of novelists and the remarks that critics and other novelists have made about them. One could describe their book as a ragbag of quotation or a mine of information. Whichever way one looks at it, however, it shows very clearly how intimately the American novel has been bound up with the American experience. In so doing, it explains in part the proliferation of 'interpretations' of the American novel which have been appearing since the Second World War.

Some sense of the variety and detail of these interpretations emerges from *The American Novel, 1789–1959: A Checklist of Twentieth-Century Criticism*.[8] The major proportion of this book is devoted to listings under authors. For each author the listing is made under three headings: for each novel, then general studies of the author, and finally bibliographies. There are also listings of general studies of the American novel arranged by centuries. Gerstenberger and Hendrick also include a bibliography of sources consulted. Theirs is an invaluable book, supplementing and bringing up to date the bibliography of the *Literary History of the United States*.

Edwin W. Gaston, Jr., and Irwin R. Blacker survey the fiction of the American West from different points of view. Gaston's critical history[9] deals with novels about the South-West during the period 1819–1918. It begins with *L'Héroine du Texas*, published by an anonymous Frenchman in 1819, and ends with *The Desire of the Moth* (1916), by the cowboy novelist Eugene

Manlove Rhodes. Forty representative novels are chosen, synopses of which are supplied in an appendix. Although much of the material commented on is of little interest except to a regional literary historian, Gaston's book is not without its value. From the days of the Dime Novels and Zane Grey to the present, the American West has captured the imagination of several generations of readers. Blacker's book[10] is not a history but an anthology, and although it deals with the 'Old West' the writing is more than half in the twentieth century. It contains one complete novel, *Grant of Kingdom*, by Harvey Fergusson, excerpts from three others—A. B. Guthrie's *The Big Sky*, Alan Le May's *The Searchers*, and Stewart White's *The Long Rifle*—and eleven stories, including Steinbeck's *The Leader of the People* and Stephen Crane's *The Bride Comes to Yellow Sky*.

In *The American Short Story*[11] Danforth Ross undertakes to cover the whole history of his subject in forty-seven pages. He says very little in a general way, but plunges from the first page into an account of the writers who are in his opinion the most important in the field of the short story. These include Irving, Poe, Hawthorne, Melville, Mark Twain, Bret Harte, Ambrose Bierce, Howells, Henry James, Hamlin Garland, Frank Norris, Dreiser, Willa Cather, Sherwood Anderson, William Carlos Williams, Steinbeck, Stephen Crane, Hemingway, Fitzgerald, Faulkner, Lardner, Eudora Welty, J. F. Powers, R. V. Cassill, and Jack Kerouac. There is very little fault to find with this list, except that Ross has omitted some

[8] *The American Novel, 1789–1959: A Checklist of Twentieth-Century Criticism*, by Donna Gerstenberger and George Hendrick. Denver: Alan Swallow. pp. 333. $4.75.

[9] *The Early Novel of the Southwest*, by Edwin W. Gaston, Jr. New Mexico U.P. pp. xiii+318. $5.

[10] *The Old West In Fiction*, ed. by Irwin R. Blacker. New York: Obolensky. pp. 471. $7.50.

[11] *The American Short Story*, by Danforth Ross. (Minnesota Pamphlets on American Writers, No. 14.) Minnesota U.P. and O.U.P. pp. 47. 65c. 5s.

important figures, like O. Henry, and included one or two novelists, like Norris and Dreiser, who wrote very few short pieces. With the method, perhaps, one could have more quarrel. In so small a space it might have been wiser to concentrate on, say, ten major short-story writers who have made outstanding and original contributions to the form—for example, Poe, Hawthorne, Mark Twain, James, Crane, Anderson, Hemingway, Faulkner, Fitzgerald, and Steinbeck.

American Literary Manuscripts: A Checklist of Holdings in Academic, Historical and Public Libraries in the United States[12] is a most important new work of reference compiled over a period of ten years by the American Literature Group of the Modern Language Association of America. The Committee appointed by this group investigated the manuscript holdings in American literature of over 270 American libraries and emerged with notations concerning 2,350 American writers. Authors are listed alphabetically, and under each author-heading there is a further alphabetical list showing holdings by states. For example, if one takes Mark Twain, listed under 'Clemens, Samuel Langhorne', one finds that the first entry is 'CCS L6', which means that in California (C), in Claremont (C), at Scripps College (S), there are six Mark Twain letters. The only drawback about this kind of listing—and it arises from the fact that the book is so comprehensive—is that it is not specific. One could not tell where to go to find the manuscript of *Huckleberry Finn*, for example. It would presumably be necessary to start with libraries listed

as having very large and unspecified collections (+), then work back through 'SC' (special collections relating to the author) to 'MS' (manuscripts of creative works).

A useful bibliography in *AQ* lists writings on the theory and teaching of American Studies. The categories used are 'The Philosophy of American Studies', 'Courses and Programs in American Studies', 'Subjects and Methods of Teaching', and 'Bibliography'.

Finally, in the general category of books, we have another kind of collection,[13] this time of literary 'examples' chosen by the well-known anthologist Louis Untermeyer. Untermeyer's book is, in fact, a two-volume anthology of American literature ranging from Captain John Smith in the seventeenth century to Richard Wilbur in the twentieth. Its great merit is that it does not attempt to be original for the sake of originality. Here one can find within four covers all the pieces one wants for instruction or illustration without having to search in a hundred individual books. There is Crèvecoeur's 'What is an American?', Freneau's 'The Wild Honeysuckle', Hawthorne's 'The Maypole of Merry Mount', Frost's 'The Witch of Coös', and O'Neill's *The Emperor Jones*. Since this collection represents Untermeyer's individual choice, the notes on each author are agreeably personal. This is an ideal book for the reader who does not seek overmuch for critical evaluation or bibliographical information.

2. Colonial

In 'The "Whens" of Mary Rowlandson's Captivity' (*NEQ*) Douglas Edward Leach sympathetically analyses

[12] *American Literary Manuscripts: A Checklist of Holdings in Academic, Historical and Public Libraries in the United States*, compiled and ed. by Joseph Jones, Ernest Marchand, H. Dan Piper, J. Albert Robbins, and Herman E. Spivey. Texas U.P., 1960. pp. xxviii+421. $5.

[13] *The Britannica Library of Great American Writing*, ed. with historical notes and a running commentary, by Louis Untermeyer. 2 vols. Chicago: Britannica, 1960. pp. xvii+ix+1764. $30.

Mrs. Rowlandson's seventeenth-century narrative. He believes that previous editors have been in error about the date of her Fourteenth Remove.

In *AL* Donald E. Stanford describes a manuscript which the Reverend Roderick Terry, great-great-great-grandson of Edward Taylor, purchased in 1905, and which was passed on by his son to the Redwood Library and Athenaeum of Newport, Rhode Island. Stanford believes, with Terry, that this manuscript was written by Taylor. He has entitled it *A Metrical History of Christianity*, and finds in it a number of verbal similarities to *Preparatory Meditations* and *God's Determinations*. In bulk it corresponds to about half Taylor's poetic output, and is written for the most part in rhymed decasyllabic couplets. It may not add to Taylor's poetic reputation, but it increases our knowledge of his language and outlook.

Typical of the collections of complete writings and correspondence of American worthies which are now pouring from the University presses are *The Papers of Benjamin Franklin*, Volumes Three[14] and Four[15] (see *YW* xli. 277). Volume Three continues Franklin's story from 1 January 1745 to 30 June 1750 inclusive, and Volume Four from 1 July 1750 to 30 June 1753 inclusive. In the former we find Franklin leading a movement to create a volunteer militia to protect Philadelphia from incursions by French and Spanish privateers. In 1749 he sets on foot a scheme for establishing The Academy of Philadelphia, later to become the University of Pennsylvania. There are several pieces showing Franklin's wit, including 'The Speech of Miss Polly Baker', a parody never before published ('Verses on the Virginia Capitol Fire') and extracts from the *Poor Richard Almanacs* and the *Pennsylvania Gazette*. In the period covered by the latter volume Franklin helped to found the Pennsylvania Hospital and was elected a member of the state Assembly. Correspondence with his English friend William Strahan is included, and with colleagues in other colonies on scientific and educational topics. The book ends with a letter from Aaron Burr asking for Franklin's observations on the approaching transit of the planet Mercury. 'I add but my hearty Wishes', says Burr, 'that the general Design of promoting useful Knowledge in the World may be still attended with desired Success.'

In his book on Jonathan Edwards,[16] Douglas J. Elwood considers some of the contradictions of Edwards's life. He preached hell-fire and damnation from the pulpit, yet he was an apostle of divine love. He was a Calvinist, yet he had a pronounced mystic strain; a theist, yet he expressed views that seem to us pantheistic. Elwood believes that these apparent contradictions can be resolved. He suggests that Edwards be judged not so much by the climate of the New England in which he lived as by his contribution to philosophical theology. To meet the problems of his day Edwards constructed a new system of thought which followed a middle course between traditional Calvinism and pantheism. This course, which Elwood calls Edwards's 'third way', he examines in some detail. It amounts, in effect, to a liberalization of Calvinism in order to meet the challenge

[14] *The Papers of Benjamin Franklin*. Vol. III, 1 Jan. 1745 through 30 June, 1750. Ed. by Leonard W. Labaree and Whitfield J. Bell, Jr. Yale U.P. and O.U.P. pp. xxv+513. $10. 80s.

[15] *The Papers of Benjamin Franklin*. Vol. IV, 1 July, 1750 through 30 June, 1753. Ed. by Leonard W. Labaree and Whitfield J. Bell, Jr. Yale U.P. and O.U.P. pp. xxvii+544. $10. 80s.

[16] *The Philosophical Theory of Jonathan Edwards*, by Douglas J. Elwood. Columbia U.P., 1960. pp. xii+220. $3.75. 30s.

of Newton and Locke. Despite his circumlocutory approach, Elwood's book is another step on the way to our comprehension of why Edwards should be estimated so highly by American scholars.

3. Early Nineteenth Century

In the early nineteenth century—as Perry Miller, Howard Mumford Jones, and other authorities on American thought agree—the Scottish philosophy of Common Sense held a persistent attraction for American thinkers. In *The Instructed Vision: Scottish Common Sense Philosophy and the Origins of American Fiction*[17] Terence Martin establishes the patterns of this appeal and shows how the Common Sense commitment to actuality worked with the ethic of puritanism to make it doubly difficult for the creative writer in America to find an audience. The philosopher taught what the novelist learned from the attitudes of society. Martin analyses what he calls 'the strategies of creation' which allowed fiction to be written at all in such an intellectual milieu. He attempts to show how the creative artist in nineteenth-century America failed. His contention is that, in teaching Americans how to think about reality, Scottish Common Sense philosophy may have 'constrained the writer of romance to think otherwise about the nature of fictional creation'.

Adelheid Staehelin-Wackernagel's monograph[18] considers various attitudes towards puritanism in American novelists from McHenry to Cooper

(1820–30), Lee to Motley (1840–50), and Hawthorne to Thompson (1850–60). She also examines literary theories in the period she has chosen, and the selection and treatment of historical material. Her detailed and painstaking study would be more rewarding if it were written in a less impenetrable style. It ends with an account of the way in which typical Puritan figures and features were treated in the American novel before the Civil War.

Thomas Philbrick's book on Fenimore Cooper[19] is concerned with the novelist as a writer of sea stories. The book grew, says Philbrick, out of a conviction that *Moby-Dick* was too often regarded as the first sea book in American fiction. He considers the theme of the sea in American literature before 1820, Cooper's early nautical romances, the work of Cooper's contemporaries from 1820–35, the sea novels of Cooper's middle period, and contemporary novels from 1835–50. There is a concluding chapter on Cooper's last sea fiction, and an epilogue on his high place in writing of this genre. Philbrick believes that Melville's inheritance from the sea fiction which Cooper and his contemporaries created was as essential to the making of *Moby-Dick* as the Bible, Shakespeare, the seventeenth-century metaphysical writers, and the nineteenth-century writers of cetological treatises.

In an article in *AQ* Robert H. Zoellner quotes William Cooper's belief that 'wherever men's minds are uncontrolled they will in a short time discover what is for their interest better than strangers can instruct them'. Zoellner believes that this shows William's intellectual superiority over his son Fenimore. The novelist's criticisms of American society sprang

---

[17] *The Instructed Vision: Scottish Common Sense Philosophy and the Origins of American Fiction*, by Terence Martin. Indiana U.P. pp. viii+197. $4.50.

[18] *The Puritan Settler in the American Novel before the Civil War*, by Adelheid Staehelin-Wackernagel. (No. 7 of The Cooper Monographs on English and American Language and Literature, ed. by H. Lüdeke, Basel.) Bern: Francke Verlag. pp. 165. Sw. fr. 18.

[19] *James Fenimore Cooper and the Development of American Sea Fiction*, by Thomas Philbrick. Harvard U.P. pp. xi+329. $6.25.

from psychic apostasy and emotional alienation, not from faith and conviction.

Vincent Buranelli's book on Poe[20] in the Twayne United States Authors Series is concerned with Poe as a thinker rather than as a literary figure. Buranelli analyses Poe's stories, poems, and criticism in an attempt to discover a coherent philosophy. He is particularly concerned with Poe's ideas concerning art, science, and philosophy, maintaining that Poe drew upon Pascal's theory of imaginative intuition as a unifying principle. His book is interesting for its discussion of 'Eureka', a work which until recent years has been considered seriously only in France. On the whole, however, Buranelli may be said to have attempted too much in too small a space. The drawback of this kind of study is that it is altogether too earnest, and misses entirely the fact that with half of his mind a writer of Poe's type is, perfectly legitimately, playing a game both with himself and the reader.

Die Todesszene und ihre Funktion im Kurzgeschichtenwerk von Edgar Allan Poe[21] is, by contrast, almost too literary. It examines in detail 'death scenes' and their function in Poe's short stories from 1832–5 ('Metzengerstein' to 'Morella'), from 1836–9 ('Ligeia' to 'The Conversation of Eiros and Charmion'), from 1840–2 ('The Murders in the Rue Morgue' to 'The Pit and the Pendulum'), and from 1843–9 ('The Tell-Tale Heart' to 'Hop-Frog'). Lubbers's thesis is thorough and, within its limits, extremely informative. The last chapter, which relates Poe's work to the general theory of the grotesque, is of particular value.

In 'A Misreading of Poe's "Ligeia" ' (*PMLA*) James Schroeter analyses two groups of interpretations: those by older critics like Woodberry and Clayton, and those by such modern commentators as D. H. Lawrence, Marie Bonaparte, Roy Basler, and Clark Griffith. Schroeter disagrees with most of the later critics, particularly Basler.

Another of Poe's stories is analysed in *PMLA* by E. Arthur Robinson under the heading of 'Order and Sentience in "The Fall of the House of Usher" '. Robinson considers that Madeline and Roderick represent, not separate elements of human nature, but differing manifestations of the same tendency towards dissolution.

Edwin R. Marks (*AL*) thinks that it is time that Poe was reappraised as a literary theorist. Although he finds grave deficiencies in Poe's work, he agrees with Edmund Wilson that Poe wrote 'the most remarkable body of criticism ever produced in the United States'. He was one of those 'on whom nothing is lost', and was therefore able to extract sound criticism from tawdry material.

Another ante-bellum Southern writer, William Gilmore Simms, is the subject of a monograph[22] by Edd Winfield Parks. Simms was something of a critic as well as a novelist. Parks devotes chapters to Simms's opinions 'On Novels and Novelists', 'On Poetry and Poets', and 'On Dramas and Dramatists'. He sees Simms's preface to *The Yemassee* as his most influential critical work.

Edward Wagenknecht's book on Hawthorne[23] is neither a biography nor a critical evaluation, but a 'psycho-

[20] *Edgar Allan Poe*, by Vincent Buranelli. (Twayne's United States Authors Series.) New York: Twayne. pp. 157. $3.50.

[21] *Die Todesszene und ihre Funktion im Kurzgeschichtenwerk von Edgar Allan Poe*, by Klaus Lubbers. Munich: Max Hueber. pp. 178. DM. 13.80.

[22] *William Gilmore Simms as Literary Critic*, by Edd Winfield Parks. (No. 7 of The University of Georgia Monographs.) Georgia U.P. pp. viii+152. $2.75.

[23] *Nathaniel Hawthorne: Man and Writer*, by Edward Wagenknecht. O.U.P. pp. x+233. 35s.

graph', which, Wagenknecht is careful to point out, means that it seeks to establish traits and characteristics by direct reference to the evidence. The result is one of the most interesting accounts of Hawthorne the man that we have had for a long time. One's only qualification might be that Wagenknecht is almost too careful to exclude his own opinions. We are left wanting more. What really led to the early death of so apparently healthy a man? Was it cancer, as his last conversation with Dr. Holmes might imply, or was the cause psychosomatic? By integrating all the available material on Hawthorne's personality, Wagenknecht is able to shed light on such things as Hawthorne's attitudes to sex and the Civil War. What emerges is a full-length, revealing portrait of a complex and fascinating man.

M. L. Allen (*Studi Americani*) writes on 'Hawthorne's Art in his Short Stories'. He agrees with Mrs. Q. D. Leavis about the high importance of the 'ritual drama' of 'My Kinsman, Major Molineux'.

In 'Hawthorne and the Gothic Style' (*NEQ*) Maurice Charney asserts that Gothic architecture was the only art which could arouse Hawthorne to enthusiasm. His impressions of gothic cathedrals are filled with religious awe and romantic rapture. Hawthorne used 'gothic' and 'romantic' as synonyms. Charney believes that he tried to achieve in his romances the qualities that moved him so deeply in gothic churches.

The publication of the second volume of *The Journals and Miscellaneous Notebooks of Ralph Waldo Emerson*[24] is marred by the death of one of the three editors, Merrell R.

Davis, Professor of English at the University of Washington. The current volume covers the years 1822–6. During this time Emerson stopped dedicating his Journals to some ideal, and substituted letters and numbers for the more pretentious heading of 'Wide World'. Although he was coming to the end of his 'reading period', much of the experience of which he speaks continues to be bookish. One can see him trying his hand at being a moral essayist after the manner of Bacon or Sir Thomas Browne, but his essays are as yet 'private', not intended for publication. During these years Emerson was teaching, an occupation which he disliked, and his Journals represented an escape. They were his 'ancient friend & consoler'. Biographically, they are illuminating, for Emerson was coming to a critical decision about his career. His sickness is shown in the handwriting which is reproduced in one of the four plates. In this excellently edited and copiously footnoted book, the editors keep to the techniques laid down in Book I, except that they have been somewhat bolder in the matter of editorializing.

Emerson is also, in part, the subject of an account of the Brook Farm community.[25] This Corinth Press reprint of Lindsay Swift's admirable little book of 1899 describes the Transcendental Club and the practical details of its earthly home at West Roxbury, Massachusetts. There is an account of the School and its Scholars, the Curtises, Isaac Thomas Hecker, the Members, George Ripley and his wife, Charles Dana, John Dwight, Hawthorne (for a time), John Orvis, John Allen, and the Visitors, who included Margaret Fuller, William Ellery Channing, Emerson, Orestes Brownson, and

[24] *The Journals and Miscellaneous Notebooks of Ralph Waldo Emerson.* Vol. II, 1822–1826, ed. by William H. Gilman, Alfred R. Ferguson, and Merrell R. Davis. The Belknap Press of Harvard U.P. pp. xvi+438. $10.

[25] *Brook Farm: Its Members, Scholars, and Visitors,* by Lindsay Swift, with an Introduction by Joseph Schiffman. New York: Corinth. pp. x+303. $1.95.

Amos Bronson Alcott. In a sympathetic introduction, Joseph Schiffman points out that Swift's book has a particular poignancy arising from the date of its publication. Writing when it had at last become clear that Transcendentalism had finally succumbed to 'the Great American Dream', Swift was celebrating a lost cause of 'noble illusions'.

In a well-documented account of 'Emerson's Revisions of *Essays: First Series*', Paul Lauter (*AL*) shows that, in cutting the text, Emerson not only eliminated repetitions and theoretical passages but also carefully revised his early work in the light of his later philosophy. The revisions indicate indisputably that Emerson was not content to remain 'a passive organ of his initial promptings'.

In another article on Emerson in the same periodical (*AL*), William White presents 'Thirty-Three Unpublished Letters of Ralph Waldo Emerson' which he discovered while cataloguing the manuscripts in the Feinberg Collection, Detroit.

A fellow-traveller of the Transcendentalist movement was William Ellery Channing the Elder, who so impressed the young Emerson by his Dudleian lecture at Harvard in 1821. Channing is the subject of a concise and workmanlike study[26] by Arthur W. Brown, which is No. 7 in the Twayne United States Authors Series. Dr. Channing, who is not to be confused with William Ellery Channing the poet, played a quite considerable role as a leader of early nineteenth-century causes. Although he was never closely associated with the Transcendentalist Club, it was a suggestion of his which started the movement going. Emerson, although he was disappointed in Channing's unwillingness to commit

himself, told Elizabeth Peabody that he was 'our Bishop, and we have not done with him yet'.

Two new editions of Thoreau's *Walden* indicate the steadily growing interest in this author. The New American Library version[27] reprints *On the Duty of Civil Disobedience* as well. A typically pungent Afterword by Perry Miller points out that Thoreau simply demanded of American democracy a right to go his own way at his own gait. He refused to conduct himself according to standards which were not his. Larzer Ziff's edition[28] in the Holt, Rinehart, and Winston 'American Classics' series is unusual in that it is designed for college students of writing. Ziff points out that prose works like *Walden* do not come mysteriously into being without some of the pangs and labour which attend the birth of stories, poems, and novels. For all students, whether of 'writing' or of literature, this beautifully printed edition, with its full notes and questions on the text, will be most welcome.

In 'The Movement of Thoreau's Prose' (*AL*) John C. Broderick sees the geometric design of Thoreau's life to be a thing of loops and curlicues. Concord was his base for a series of forays into an alien world. His writings mirror the rhythms of his life. In style as well as in structure, in language as well as in idea, Thoreau recapitulates the archetypal Romantic theme of rebirth.

Perry Miller's paper presented to the Thoreau Society in the autumn of 1960 is reprinted in *NEQ* as 'Thoreau in the Context of International Romanticism'. This is a most important piece of criticism, not only for its insights into

[26] *William Ellery Channing*, by Arthur W. Brown. (Twayne's United States Authors Series.) New York: Twayne. pp. 172. $3.50.

[27] *Walden, or Life in the Woods* and *On the Duty of Civil Disobedience*, by Henry David Thoreau, with an Afterword by Perry Miller. New York: Signet, 1960. pp. 256. 50c.

[28] *Walden*, by Henry David Thoreau, with commentaries and notes by Larzer Ziff. New York: Holt, Rinehart and Winston. pp. xiv+332. $1.75.

Thoreau's mind and art, but also for the direction which it takes. Too much work by students of American literature reads as if America and her writers developed in a vacuum. Miller compares the thought of Thoreau and Wordsworth. The former, he believes, was both a Transcendentalist and a Natural Historian. He did not surrender on either front, though the last years of his *Journal* show how desperate were his efforts to 'keep both standards aloft'.

In another article in the same periodical Lawrence Willson considers Thoreau's compelling interest in the Pilgrims and his five visits to Cape Cod between 1849 and 1857.

A comparison of Thoreau and Whitman in terms of their 'esthetics' is the subject of a book[29] by Charles R. Metzger. Metzger's previous book was a study of Emerson and Horatio Greenough in the same terms. He believes that all four writers are intimately connected in their attitudes towards Transcendentalism. Metzger analyses Thoreau's views on economy, the communicant, poetics, and architecture. In the case of Whitman, he concentrates on 'key' concepts and terms: the Soul, the Self, democracy, the 'divine literatus'. Whitman he sees to be a Quaker version of Thoreau. They were both principally concerned with salvation—at once spiritual and material.

Richard Chase's essay on Whitman in the University of Minnesota 'Pamphlets on American Writers' series[30] is an interesting document, coming as it does six years after his *Walt Whitman Reconsidered*. In this brief but rewarding account, Chase forsakes his former

extreme view and tackles some of the central problems in Whitman criticism. Without mentioning the word 'symbol', he conveys succinctly how symbolic of the mid-nineteenth-century predicament Whitman's epic of 'One's-self' actually was. Whitman was a 'spokesman for the tendencies of his country'.

Gay Wilson Allen's contribution to the 'Evergreen Profile Book' series[31] is between three and four times as long as Chase's booklet. Allen can therefore afford to spend more time on biography and background. The book is excellently illustrated, as is the custom in this series. There are photographs of Whitman's birthplace, of Whitman in his various poses, a facsimile of the opening of Emerson's famous letter, a page of the 1860 edition of *Leaves of Grass* as revised by the author, and many other fascinating and informative 'visual aids'. Allen's text, as might be expected of the author of *The Solitary Singer*, is clear and accurate. There are also extracts from Whitman's chief works.

Allen has also published a selection of his essays on Whitman under the title of *Walt Whitman as Man, Poet, and Legend*.[32] There are three sections. Part One, 'The Man', is a concise exposition of Whitman's character and personality. Part Two contains critical interpretations of the poet's themes, motifs, and methods. In a significant essay in this section, 'Mutations on Whitman's Art', Allen answers Malcolm Cowley's contention that the first edition of *Leaves of Grass* contains all of Whitman's great poetry. Part Three consists of fourteen letters by friends of Whitman which have never before

[29] *Thoreau and Whitman: A Study of their Esthetics*, by Charles R. Metzger. Washington U.P. pp. iv+113. $4.25.
[30] *Walt Whitman*, by Richard Chase. (Minnesota Pamphlets on American Writers, No. 9.) Minnesota U.P. and O.U.P. pp. 48. 65c. 5s.
[31] *Walt Whitman*, by Gay Wilson Allen. New York: Grove Press. London: Evergreen Books. pp. 192. $1.35. 6s.
[32] *Walt Whitman as Man, Poet, and Legend*, by Gay Wilson Allen, with a checklist of Whitman Publications 1945–1960, by Evie Allison Allen. Southern Illinois U.P. pp. xii+260. $6.50.

been published. There is also a checklist of Whitman publications from 1945 to 1960 compiled by Evie Allison Allen.

In his long and detailed introduction to the facsimile edition of the 1860 text of *Leaves of Grass*,[33] Roy Harvey Pearce reminds us of the superb letter from the former publisher's clerks, Thayer and Eldridge, in which they proclaim their interest in 'a true poem ... writ by a *true* man'. A month after its receipt Whitman was in Boston with his manuscript and, in April 1860, the new edition was announced. The Whitman of the 1860 edition, says Pearce, is a 'humanist'. In a typically sympathetic and informative piece Pearce supports his preference for the 1860 version. The text itself is beautifully printed. It is a delight to be able to get the 'feel' of the original at so cheap a price.

In 'Walt Whitman and the "New Poetry"' (*AL*) Clarence A. Brown considers the vicissitudes of Whitman's reputation. It is improbable, Brown believes, that Whitman was the father of all the new schools of verse in early twentieth-century America, but that he was one of the most powerful influences during that time of revolt is borne out by the evidence.

James M. Cox points out in 'Whitman, Twain, and the Civil War' (*Sew*) that of all the great American writers in the nineteenth century only Whitman and Mark Twain directly participated in the Civil War. In a most interesting account he shows the difference between the two men and their attitudes to the war. For Whitman it was a transforming ordeal; for Mark Twain an evasion.

Leon Howard's University of Minne-

sota pamphlet on Melville[34] is, like all the booklets in this series, too brief to be of much use to any but the general reader. In the customary forty-odd pages, however, Howard does his best. He spends little time on purely biographical details, but concentrates instead on the chief novels. The section on *Moby-Dick* is especially good.

No. 5 in the Yale Publications in American Studies series[35] takes its title from Media's cry in *Mardi*: 'Reverence we render thee, old Orienda, original of all empires and emperors!' It is an account of Melville's preoccupation with the Near East and of its profound influence on his work. Miss Finkelstein investigates Melville's interest in Belzoni, a pioneer of Egyptian antiquities, and analyses the Islamic elements in Melville's symbolism with precise reference to Melville's known reading in Oriental literature. She establishes an important distinction between the Near Eastern and Polynesian elements in Melville's Orientalism. She believes that his feeling for the Near East was an expression of conscious historical awareness and not of romantic longing. Miss Finkelstein writes gracefully as well as accurately.

A welcome addition to the 'Premier World Classics' series in the Fawcett Publications Paperbacks is *The Shorter Novels of Herman Melville*,[36] welcome both for its astonishingly cheap price of fifty cents and for its long introduction by Raymond Weaver. Of the four pieces printed, however, one—'Bartleby the Scrivener'—might be more properly described as a short story, and

---

[33] *Leaves of Grass*, by Walt Whitman. A facsimile edition of the 1860 text with an Introduction by Roy Harvey Pearce. Cornell U.P. and O.U.P. pp. li+467. $2.25. 18s.

[34] *Herman Melville*, by Leon Howard. (Minnesota Pamphlets on American Writers, No. 13.) Minnesota U.P. and O.U.P. pp. 48. 65c. 5s.

[35] *Melville's Orienda*, by Dorothee Metlitsky Finkelstein. Yale U.P. pp. x+317. 52s.

[36] *The Shorter Novels of Herman Melville*, with an Introduction by Raymond Weaver. Greenwich, Conn.: Fawcett, 1960. pp. 272. 50c.

the other three—'Benito Cereno', 'The Encantadas, or Enchanted Isles', and 'Billy Budd, Foretopman'—as 'novellas' or 'tales'.

In 'The Serious Functions of Melville's Phallic Jokes' (*AL*) Robert Shulman asserts that although Melville's phallic jokes and images are typically playful and good-natured on the surface, beneath the surface they are characterized by hostility and defiance. Through Ishmael, Melville repeatedly used deceptively understated phallic references in order to satirize conventional religious, economic, and social values.

The subject of 'Something in Emblems: A Reinterpretation of *Moby-Dick*' (*NEQ*) is Charles H. Foster's disagreement with Luther S. Mansfield and Howard P. Vincent. In their edition of *Moby-Dick* Mansfield and Vincent support the usual contention that—to use Whitman's words about Emerson—it was Hawthorne who 'brought Melville to the boil'. Foster believes, rather, that it was the issues facing America in the Civil War and, in particular, Melville's feelings about Chief Justice Shaw and Daniel Webster, which affected him most.

In an exploration of the Biblical sources of *Moby-Dick* entitled 'Moby-Dick: Jonah's Whale or Job's?' (*Sew*) Daniel G. Hoffman comes to the conclusion that Melville's novel is the greatest work of the American imagination for the same reasons that Dante's, Shakespeare's, and Cervantes's are the greatest works of European Christendom. *Moby-Dick* expresses the aspirations and limitations of the culture out of which it sprang as much as it does the thoughts of the individual genius who produced it.

Leon S. Roudiez (*Symposium*) discusses the influence of *Moby-Dick* on Albert Camus. Taking a remark of Roger Quilliot ('Il prépara *La Peste* sous l'influence de *Moby-Dick*') as his guide, Roudiez deduces that the French novelist read Melville before the writing of *La Peste* but after that of *L'Étranger*.

The theme and structure of *The Confidence Man* are the subject of an article by Walter Dubler in *AL*. Dubler finds it a penetrating artistic critique of American attitudes and *mores*. Melville's most characteristic image, the microcosmic boat, is, in *The Confidence Man*, cast on the waters of the Mississippi, the date is April Fool's day, and the characters typify the American scene. In this novel Melville created a dramatic framework by means of which he could survey and comment on the America of his day.

4. Later Nineteenth Century

The Innocent Eye[37] is a most interesting and well-written study of Mark Twain's use of the theme of childhood. In tracing his development of this motif from the time of his early stories to the days of Nook Farm, Albert E. Stone, Jr., reviews nearly all of Mark Twain's published writings, as well as much new unpublished material. He compares his cast of characters— the bad boy, the precocious infant, the virginal maiden—both with their literary forebears and with their counterparts in the work of Hawthorne, Aldrich, and Howells. Stone also draws upon his knowledge of contemporary dime novels and the *St. Nicholas Magazine for Boys and Girls*. He believes that the 'Romantic image of the child as natural saint and natural aristocrat' is reflected in Mark Twain's fiction. Stone concludes with a chapter on 'Mark Twain's Tradition'.

It is good to have a revised edition of *Mark Twain: The Man and His Work*.[38] Edward Wagenknecht has modified

[37] *The Innocent Eye: Childhood in Mark Twain's Imagination*, by Albert E. Stone, Jr. Yale U.P. pp. xi+289. $5.

[38] *Mark Twain: The Man and his Work*, by Edward Wagenknecht. Oklahoma U.P. (1935, revised 1961.) pp. xiii+272. $4.50.

some of his original opinions and strengthened others. He appears to have read all the historical and critical studies of Mark Twain since his book first appeared in 1935, so that the current volume presents as adequate a summary of Mark Twain knowledge as did the previous one.

Kenneth S. Lynn has produced an extremely useful text of *Huckleberry Finn*, together with a list of sources and criticism.[39] In printing the novel he includes the 'raftsmen passage' which was originally part of *Huckleberry Finn*, but which was later printed as Chapter Three of *Life on the Mississippi*. It is possible to quarrel with the section on sources, since there is nothing from Artemus Ward or any of the other Western humorists. However, the section on criticism is all that one could wish for. It includes an unsigned review from *Life* of 1885, Lionel Trilling's essay on 'The Greatness of *Huckleberry Finn*', T. S. Eliot's introduction to the novel, and Leo Marx's 'Mr. Eliot, Mr. Trilling, and *Huckleberry Finn*'. An essay by Lynn himself, entitled 'Huck and Jim', completes the selection.

In '*Huckleberry Finn* and the Whole Truth' (*CQ*) A. E. Dyson asserts that the much maligned ending of *Huckleberry Finn* is 'the final twist of [Mark Twain's] technique towards truth'. He feels that it is right that Tom Sawyer should come into the ascendant again, because he is a natural leader. Dyson's point of view is tenable, although not easily defensible. He seems wilfully to misinterpret the sense of Hemingway's remark about Mark Twain 'cheating' in the end.

The Pattern for Mark Twain's Roughing It[40] consists of letters from

Nevada by Samuel and Orion Clemens from 1861 to 1862. These were directed to the Keokuk *Gate City* and the St. Louis *Missouri Democrat*. Franklin R. Rogers believes that *Roughing It* was based on the letters he prints. The *Gate City* letters are most important, not only as an early indication of Mark Twain's craftsmanship, but also as one of the major sources of his most successful and distinctive structural pattern. This pattern was used almost without change in 'Old Times on the Mississippi', and, with modifications, in the central parts of *The Prince and the Pauper* and *Huckleberry Finn*.

Mark Twain's only regular 'humorous department in a magazine' is made available for the first time in *Contributions to The Galaxy 1868–1871*.[41] This facsimile reproduction, edited by Bruce R. McElderry, Jr., has full notes and a bibliography. The illustrations include a portrait of Mark Twain, his 'Map of Paris', and samples of a cover and of a table of contents.

Mark Twain's friendship with Captain Edgar Wakeman is described by Ray B. Browne in *AL*. The influence of this sea captain, whom Twain met while sailing by way of Nicaragua to New York in 1866, is seen in the letters and notebooks. A teller of tall tales, this colourful character must have inspired many Mark Twain anecdotes, Browne thinks, the most obvious example being 'Captain Stormfield's Visit to Heaven'.

Curtis Dahl (*AQ*) cites evidence to show that much of Mark Twain's work parallels in content and flavour the

It: Letters from Nevada by Samuel and Orion Clemens 1861–1862, collected and ed. with an Introduction by Franklin R. Rogers. California U.P. pp. viii+72. $1.50.

[41] *Contributions to The Galaxy 1868–1871*, by Mark Twain. A facsimile reproduction ed. and with an Introduction and Notes by Bruce R. McElderry, Jr. Gainesville, Fla.: Scholars' Facsimiles & Reprints. pp. 157. $6.

[39] *Huckleberry Finn: Text, Sources, and Criticism*, ed. by Kenneth S. Lynn. New York: Harcourt, Brace and World. pp. vi+218. $1.95.

[40] *The Pattern for Mark Twain's Roughing*

moving 'panoramas' that were so popular in the mid-nineteenth century.

Coleman O. Parsons (*Antioch Review*) gives an account of 'Mark Twain in Australia'. Mark Twain, as he said in reply to a toast by Sir Richard Baker, was received as 'a member of the family'.

Spanish literature, says Ivan A. Schulman (*Symposium*), obviously had some effect on Mark Twain, but Mark Twain had much more effect on Spanish literature. He gives an account of the leading popularizer of Mark Twain's work in the Spanish-speaking world, José Martí.

Mrs. Ward's book on Emily Dickinson[42] is arranged in two parts of three chapters each. Part One, 'To Live is Endowment', deals directly with elements of Emily Dickinson's inner life at different periods: first in the formative years of childhood and youth, then in the crucial period that occurred when she was about thirty and at the time of her greatest creative energy, and finally as a mature woman living for the most part in seclusion. Part Two, 'My Friends Are My "Estate" ', contains the stories of three of her most important friendships. The friends chosen—Dr. and Mrs. Josiah Gilbert Holland, Samuel Bowles, and Thomas Wentworth Higginson—are those to whom she wrote the letters that make up the most substantial part of her correspondence as it appears in *The Letters of Emily Dickinson*.

In ' "Compound Manner": Emily Dickinson and the Metaphysical Poets' (*AL*) Judith Banzer asserts that, although Emily Dickinson's genius and poetry are unique, her inner vision and unifying style link her with Donne, Marvell, Vaughan, and Herbert, poets who argued the community of 'all that which God doth touch and own'.

In a most welcome account of Hamlin Garland's early work and career[43] Donald Pizer interprets the material in the Hamlin Garland Collection at the University of Southern California. He discusses Garland's development of a literary creed in the early eighties, his stories of the 'Middle-Border', his desire to reform the theatre and the arts in general, and his part in the 'Populist Revolt 1891–1892'. The paradox of Garland's career, Pizer considers, was that he was 'an evolutionist with a closed mind'. It was not Garland who changed, but the times. Garland's later career illustrates his failure to adapt his permanent principle—the need for freedom of the individual in social, political, and artistic life—to the changing modes of expressing that principle. It is the early career which is important; Garland's later life was a tragic failure.

Between November 1892 and September 1894 William Dean Howells wrote twenty-three 'Altrurian' essays for the *Cosmopolitan*. The first twelve were reprinted as *A Traveller from Altruria* in 1894; the other eleven have never been republished in full until now. Clara M. Kirk and Rudolf Kirk's facsimile reproduction of these eleven *Letters of an Altrurian Traveller (1893–94)*[44] is of great interest today since it provides Howells's candid comments on the America of his time. The letters, purporting to be from one Aristides Homos to a friend in 'Altruria', show Aristides (Howells) to be deeply concerned with the growth of American 'plutocracy'.

In *TSLL* Elaine Hedges writes about

[42] *The Capsule of the Mind: Chapters in the Life of Emily Dickinson*, by Theodora Ward. The Belknap Press of Harvard U.P. pp. x+205. $4.50.

[43] *Hamlin Garland's Early Work and Career*, by Donald Pizer. California U.P., 1960. pp. ix+220. $4.75.

[44] *Letters of an Altrurian Traveller (1893–94)*, by William Dean Howells. A facsimile reproduction with an Introduction by Clara M. Kirk and Rudolf Kirk. Gainesville, Fla.: Scholars' Facsimiles & Reprints. pp. 127. $5.

'Howells on a Hawthornesque Theme'. She quotes a passage from Hawthorne's *American Notebooks* which she considers to be a 'strikingly accurate' summary of the situation on which Howells based *The Shadow of a Dream*. Miss Hedges makes a good case for the presence of other Hawthorne-like tendencies in the apparently realistic writing of Howells.

Albert Mordell's *Discovery of a Genius*[45] is an account of the friendship between Howells and Henry James. Mordell claims that Howells was the first to recognize James's genius. His book is a collection of articles and reviews written by Howells about James's novels and short stories. Part One consists of Howells's earlier reviews of James, from *The Passionate Pilgrim and Other Tales* to *Hawthorne*. Part Two contains articles and reviews written between 1881 and 1888, and Part Three, comments by Howells on the later writing of James from 1890 to 1903. In an interesting introduction Sylvia Bowman considers that this testimony of Howells's perspicacity will add another dimension to his stature as writer and critic. It certainly provides evidence of Howells's understanding and sympathy for his more famous friend.

Henry James's preoccupation with evil is the subject of *The Imagination of Disaster*.[46] J. A. Ward considers that the fact that James took evil seriously and absolutely is probably one of the reasons why twentieth-century critics have shown such a great interest in his work. He disagrees with the view that James is a 'pure' novelist. On the contrary, he was a man profoundly aware of the crisis of civilization. James's novels and tales dramatize not only the timeless conflicts of good and evil, but also the unique form that these conflicts assume in the modern world. After a section on James's 'Consciousness of Evil', Ward turns to 'Evil and the International Theme', 'Evil in London', and 'Evil and the Major Phase' (*The Ambassadors, The Wings of the Dove*, and *The Golden Bowl*). A final section is devoted to the 'Last Tales'. Ward's is a rewarding line of investigation. His choice of theme alone—one which is at the heart of James's consciousness of the world—would put his study ahead of those peripheral theses which have been appearing in such numbers during the past few years.

Oscar Cargill's *The Novels of Henry James*[47] is a most useful volume. Working through the great mass of commentary on James, says Cargill, he was struck by the fact that 'nobody apparently reads anybody else'. There existed no accumulated wisdom in the field of James criticism, no 'body' of appreciation. Such a body Cargill attempts to create. Although he says modestly that his own contribution has been 'the journeyman job of elementary synthesis', his book represents a major effort. In the process of examining the opinions of other critics, fresh patterns 'emerged of themselves'. He is particularly good in Chapter One, 'The Drive to Distinction', which deals with the novels from *Watch and Ward* to *The Portrait of a Lady*, and in Chapter Four, 'The Major Phase', which is devoted to the last three great novels.

The Background of 'The Princess Casamassima'[48] is an account of the

[45] *Discovery of a Genius: William Dean Howells and Henry James*, compiled and ed. by Albert Mordell with an Introduction by Sylvia E. Bowman. New York: Twayne. pp. 207. $4.

[46] *The Imagination of Disaster: Evil in the Fiction of Henry James*, by J. A. Ward. Nebraska U.P. pp. xi+185. $3.

[47] *The Novels of Henry James*, by Oscar Cargill. Macmillan. pp. xviii+505. 60s.

[48] *The Background of the Princess Casamassima*, by W. H. Tilley. University of Florida Monographs: Humanities No. 5, 1960. Florida U.P. pp. 61. $2.

materials which Henry James knew and probably used in writing his novel. W. H. Tilley is only in part interested in tracking down James's sources, for example, accounts of revolutionists in *The Times*, and elsewhere. He is more concerned with the problem of 'artistic credibility'. Since 1920 *The Princess Casamassima* has been criticized as a serious treatment of a silly theme; but in its own day it was thought of as a 'dainty dabbling among matters of profound importance'. Tilley attempts to show that James's book is serious both in subject and in style, and he succeeds very well.

Edward Stone's book[49] is very good value indeed. It consists of seven of James's stories—'The Marriages', '"Europe"', 'The Liar', 'The Real Thing', 'The Pupil', 'The Beast in the Jungle', and 'The Jolly Corner'—each followed by a series of commentaries. The names which occur most often are those of F. O. Matthiessen and Kenneth Murdock for their edition of *The Notebooks of Henry James*. James himself, Quentin Anderson, Christof Wegelin, Marius Bewley, Philip Rahv, F. W. Dupee, and Miriam Allott are among the other critics quoted.

James's revisions of the style of *The Reverberator* are the subject of an article by Sister Mary Brian Durkin in *AL*. She finds the most notable stylistic change in the New York edition to be in the emphasis placed on figurative language. In detailing James's many emendations, she hopes to convince the doubters that it is James's revised work which reveals the true art of the master.

In 'The Sacred Fount: The Narrator and the Vampires' (*PMLA*), Norma Phillips claims that the novel she discusses, although narrow because of the restricted nature of its 'focal speaker',

has dimensions with which it is rarely credited. It contains bizarre comedy as well as irony.

George W. Johnson's article on 'Frank Norris and Romance' (*AL*) follows Richard Chase in considering it 'a useful strategy . . . to neglect provisionally [Norris's] obvious realism and emphasize his programmatic plea for the revival of that "really honest and noble formula" of romance'.

An edition of *Stephen Crane's Letters*[50] compiled by R. W. Stallman and Lillian Gilkes adds greatly to our knowledge of the novelist's method and background. The editors reprint all of the Stephen Crane letters which are known to exist, together with a selection of letters from Cora Crane. From them one can learn something of Crane's attempt to develop a new form of literature. However, these letters are much more revealing of the man himself. Crane emerges as a most likeable and sympathetic personality.

5. Twentieth Century

The Inaugural Lecture[51] by the Irving Babbitt Professor of Comparative Literature at Harvard is a typically urbane and civilized piece of writing. After paying a graceful tribute to Babbitt, whose student he was, Harry Levin goes on to speak of him as an exemplar of the American Scholar. Babbitt's approach to the cultural crisis of modernity, he considers, was adapted from Arnold's. Culture, for both critics, was a certain type of education, and nearly everything else was anarchy. More than fifty years ago Babbitt could refer nostalgically to the 'almost lost art of reading'. He could not have foreseen a technological

[49] *Henry James: Seven Stories and Studies*, ed. by Edward Stone. New York: Appleton-Century-Crofts. pp. x+310. $1.95.

[50] *Stephen Crane: Letters*, ed. by R. W. Stallman and Lillian Gilkes with an Introduction by R. W. Stallman. New York U.P., 1960. pp. xxx+366. $6.50.

[51] *Irving Babbitt and the Teaching of Literature*, by Harry Levin. Harvard U.P. pp. 28.

revolution such as we have today. Babbitt's terrain was basically the history of ideas, the middle ground between literature and philosophy. Against the mounting pressures that encroach from all sides upon the autonomy of the individual, the single stratagem Babbitt would have recommended was the exercise of 'the ethical imagination': the will to resist what seems evil in the name of what seems good.

Under the title of *American Perspectives*,[52] Robert E. Spiller and Eric Larrabee print ten essays by specialists in American Studies. Although these essays cover the fields of history, literature, philosophy, politics, economics, sociology, art, music, the popular arts, and the mass media, they all discuss a common theme: what image of the American national character is reflected in these various aspects of American culture, and what changes can be noted in it during the period 1900 to 1950? The consensus of opinion is that the first fifteen years constituted a period of debunking. Between the wars there was an explosion of creative energy, but in more recent years Americans have sought a more stable national image. The essays on 'History and the American Past' by Ralph H. Gabriel, 'Literature and the Critics' by Robert E. Spiller, and 'The Public Image: Politics' by John M. Blum are especially welcome.

Daniel Aaron's *Writers on the Left*[53] is a social chronicle of the Left Wing writer in America from 1912 to the early 1940's. It describes the response of a selected group of writers to the idea of Communism, and deals with

the particular issues and events during the first forty years of this century which helped shape their opinions. Radicalism of the Russian variety was a glorious crusade to many intellectuals of the thirties. Aaron's book is an attempt to show why this was so, and why most of its sympathizers had, by the forties and fifties, become disenchanted. Since Aaron has an artist's eye for colour and background, the mood of the Depression period comes alive in his book. He makes it clear why the guilt-ridden writers of the thirties should have decided that politics and art were inseparable. His book is divided into three parts. Part One, 'Patterns of Rebellion', deals with the period before and immediately after the First World War, the heyday of Floyd Dell, Randolph Bourne, and John Reed. Part Two, 'The Appeal of Communism', documents the hysteria of the twenties and thirties, and Part Three, 'Disenchantment and Withdrawal', the aftermath during and after the Second World War.

In *Strangers to This Ground*[54] W. M. Frohock expresses his sharp disagreement with the social critics who currently describe American culture as one of increasing uniformity. He contends that contemporary American writing reveals the great cultural differences which are present under the apparent conformity of American life. In support of his thesis, Frohock discusses Ezra Pound, Scott Fitzgerald, Edna St. Vincent Millay, James Gould Cozzens, Jack Kerouac, and others. It is not merely for their diversity that he examines the work of these authors, however. Frohock is a literary critic of originality and liveliness. His book is a worthy successor to *The Novel of Violence in America*.

[52] *American Perspectives: The National Self-Image in the Twentieth Century*, ed. by Robert E. Spiller and Eric Larrabee. Harvard U.P. pp. vii+216. $4.75.
[53] *Writers on the Left: Episodes in American Literary Communism*, by Daniel Aaron. New York: Harcourt, Brace and World. pp. xvi+460. $7.50.
[54] *Strangers to this Ground: Cultural Diversity in Contemporary American Writing*, by W. M. Frohock. Southern Methodist U.P. pp. x+180. $4.50.

R. W. Stallmann's collection of literary studies[55] takes its title from his essay on *The Portrait of a Lady*. In Part One he also analyses works by Hardy, Stephen Crane, Conrad, Fitzgerald, Hemingway, and Faulkner. Part Two consists of an account of 'the New Criticism' of poetry, and an essay on 'Fiction and its Critics'. The extraordinary thing about Stallman's work is that it is at once so sympathetic and so alien—sympathetic because he uses his intelligence and gets down to the business of analysing each work without frills, and alien because he lapses into a jargon which, to the English ear at least, is quite unacceptable. If it were not for the evidence of such excellent American stylists in criticism as Edmund Wilson, Lionel Trilling, and Harry Levin, one would be tempted to exclaim, with Oscar Wilde, 'We are divided by a common language!'

It is paradoxical that, having said this, the next book for review should be a beautifully written pamphlet on Edith Wharton by Louis Auchincloss.[56] This brief study is a model of how to write criticism which is both elegant and telling. Auchincloss, whose talents in the novel are somewhat similar to those of Mrs. Wharton, has captured the spirit of her writing admirably.

By contrast, Frederick J. Hoffman's pamphlet[57] in the same series, is brisk and workmanlike. Hoffman's subject is Gertrude Stein, but his style is in no sense like hers. Although not a brilliant writer, Hoffman is an experienced and talented critic. In a very short space, he tells us more about Gertrude

Stein's contribution to literature than many full-length books that have appeared in the last few years. His discussion of her 'nonrepresentational writing' is lucid and succinct.

The same can hardly be said of Hilary Corke. Corke has little sympathy for Gertrude Stein, and says so with considerable force and not a little vulgarity. 'Reflections on a Great Stone Face' (*KR*) is amusing up to a point, but much of the effect it might have had is destroyed by Corke's overstatement of his case. The result is that, although one might originally have felt, with Corke, that Donald Sutherland had overstated *his* case in his book on Gertrude Stein, one ends by feeling sympathy for Sutherland and not for his detractor. Subsequent correspondence by Sutherland and Corke gets us nowhere, since they argue from different points of view. The only significant point to emerge is how well-mannered the American is compared with the Englishman.

In an article in *AL* Richard Bridgman contends that Miss Stein relied heavily on *Things as They Are* for her story 'Melanctha' in *Three Lives*. He concludes that no more justification exists for considering the story 'an achieved stylistic enquiry' than for praising it as a tribute to the Negro.

In *Studi Americani* Michael Millgate writes on 'Theodore Dreiser and the American Financier'. Although Millgate admires the power of Dreiser's work, he considers his novels 'the raw material of the art of fiction' rather than the art itself.

Dreiser is one of the chief correspondents in *Letters of H. L. Mencken*.[58] This excellently printed and annotated selection by Guy J. Forgue brings to light the fact that, although Mencken

[55] *The Houses that James Built and Other Literary Studies*, by R. W. Stallman. Michigan State U.P. pp. xii+254. $5.

[56] *Edith Wharton*, by Louis Auchincloss. (Minnesota Pamphlets on American Writers, No. 12.) Minnesota U.P. and O.U.P. pp. 46. 65c. 5s.

[57] *Gertrude Stein*, by Frederick J. Hoffman. (Minnesota Pamphlets on American Writers, No. 10.) Minnesota U.P. and O.U.P. pp. 48. 65c. 5s.

[58] *Letters of H. L. Mencken*, selected and annotated by Guy J. Forgue, with a personal note by Hamilton Owens. New York: Knopf. pp. xxxviii+506+xxii. $7.95.

was an immensely busy man, he was a much busier correspondent. He apparently made it a practice to answer every letter addressed to him within twenty-four hours—sometimes at great length. Fifty thousand letters from him are said to exist. Forgue has selected over 400, running from 1900, when Mencken was twenty, to 1956, the year of his death. Among the correspondents, other than Dreiser, are James Joyce, Carl Van Vechten, Sinclair Lewis, Scott Fitzgerald, Edgar Lee Masters, and James T. Farrell.

In an amusing article entitled 'Criticism with Vine Leaves' (*TSLL*) William Nolte appraises Mencken as a literary critic. He ends by quoting the 'Three American Immortals' section of *Prejudices: First Series* as an example of 'the sort of thing that helped induce the rebellion of the 1920s'.

It is good to have William Carlos Williams's *The Farmers' Daughters*[59] in a paperback edition. Although Williams is an important novelist and short-story writer as well as a poet, and has had all kinds of honours in America, no English publisher has ever seen fit to publish his work. The importation of his collected stories at such a relatively cheap price might do something to remedy the deficiency. *The Farmers' Daughters* contains stories from *The Knife of the Time*, *Life Along the Passaic River*, and *Beer and Cold Cuts*, together with the story which gives the volume its title.

Mildred R. Bennett has revised her study of Willa Cather[60] originally published in 1951. As a Nebraskan herself, Miss Bennett is especially well qualified to write about Willa Cather's background. She weaves her comments on the novels into a sympathetic account of the Cather family and the farming people among whom they lived. There is now a full apparatus of notes and a very comprehensive index.

MFS publishes a symposium on Scott Fitzgerald. Robert F. McDowell and A. E. Dyson both write about *The Great Gatsby*, but whereas McDowell dwells at tedious length on the symbolism of Dr. Eckleburg's eyes, which he equates with East Egg and West Egg, Dyson writes sensibly and moderately about the place of Fitzgerald's most highly praised novel in the Anglo-Saxon canon. Eugene White writes on 'The "Intricate Destiny" of Dick Diver', and Kent and Gretchen Kreuter on 'The Moralism of the Later Fitzgerald'. There is also a checklist of Fitzgerald criticism by Maurice Beebe and Jackson R. Bryer.

Sinclair Lewis is the subject of a monumental study by Mark Schorer.[61] Schorer covers Lewis's life and work in six sections: 'Small Town', 'College', 'Climb', 'Success', 'Decline', and 'Fall'. His book is immensely detailed and does not attempt to gloss over the horrors and disasters of Lewis's life. There is also much comedy and happiness, however, for Lewis was a man with a great gusto for life. Although Schorer is an excellent literary critic, he has not attempted in this book to make an evaluation of Lewis's contribution to literature. Rather, he has located Lewis in the American literary scene, and contrasted and compared him with his contemporaries. He sees Lewis to be a prime example of that characteristic phenomenon of American literature—the man who enjoys great early success and then suffers through a long period of decline and deterioration.

[59] *The Farmers' Daughters: The Collected Stories of William Carlos Williams*, with an Introduction by Van Wyck Brooks. New York: New Directions Paperbook. pp. xix+374. $1.95.

[60] *The World of Willa Cather*, by Mildred R. Bennett. A new edition with notes and index. Nebraska U.P. pp. xvi+285. $1.50.

[61] *Sinclair Lewis: An American Life*, by Mark Schorer. New York, Toronto, and London: McGraw-Hill. pp. xxiii+867. $10.

Rex Burbank's book on Thornton Wilder[62] shows how Wilder's work has been enriched by his reading of Plato and Berdyaev, Aeschylus and Sartre, Sophocles and James Joyce. It places him with Walt Whitman in his attempt to identify the facts of everyday American life with the destiny of mankind. Burbank analyses Wilder's five novels and four full-length plays in terms of his efforts to find in the lives of his characters qualities which affirm the dignity of the individual and the value of life. *Thornton Wilder* is a work of interpretation and evaluation. Burbank's approach is closely analytical but not narrow. There emerges from it a sense of Wilder as a true humanist and a far greater writer than he is nowadays generally considered.

Hemingway, by Stewart Sanderson,[63] is a worthy addition to the Writers and Critics Series. Sanderson is a commonsense critic, who has read his material carefully. While one might not agree with all his conclusions, particularly his high estimate of *The Old Man and the Sea*, his book may be recommended as a good general guide.

In '"The Snows of Kilimanjaro": A Revaluation' (*PMLA*) Oliver Evans explores the emotional and personal undertones of Hemingway's short story.

Hemingway's 'iceberg' theory of literature is discussed with reference to *The Old Man and the Sea* by Robert O. Stephens in *MFS*.

Michael Millgate's study of Faulkner[64] is an intelligent piece of work. After a brief chapter on Faulkner's background and relationship to Missis-

sippi Millgate discusses the chief novels and stories with care. Although the space allowed him does not permit the detailed kind of analysis which Faulkner calls for, his comments always strike the right note. Millgate is very well acquainted with the critical literature on Faulkner, and his last chapter is devoted to an examination of the chief books and articles in this genre.

Warren Beck's criticism of Faulkner has been noticed before (*YW* xli. 301). *Man in Motion*[65] includes some of the material previously published in periodicals on the subject of Faulkner's trilogy, *The Hamlet*, *The Town*, and *The Mansion*. Beck makes a close study of the interwoven structure of the three novels, differentiates between their narrative modes, and analyses the main characters and their conflicts. His title is derived from his conviction that a central theme of Faulkner's art is 'his vision of life as motion'. He finds Faulkner to be magnificently ingenious in devising artistic techniques to represent 'a multi-dimensioned reality'. If one can spend the time unravelling Beck's close-packed, obfuscatory style, there is much that is rewarding in this study.

Frederick J. Hoffman's book on Faulkner in the Twayne United States Authors Series[66] offers several new perspectives upon Faulkner's work. The study of his uses of time is important since Hoffman employs it, by implication, in order to analyse Faulkner's style. Following this general opening Hoffman devotes five chapters to discussion of the novels in order of their publication. Chapter Two considers Faulkner's apprentice work, ending with a consideration of *Sartoris*.

[62] *Thornton Wilder*, by Rex Burbank. (Twayne's United States Authors Series.) New York: Twayne. pp. 156. $3.50.

[63] *Hemingway*, by Stewart Sanderson. (Writers and Critics Series.) Oliver & Boyd. pp. 120. 5s.

[64] *Faulkner*, by Michael Millgate. (Writers and Critics Series.) Oliver & Boyd. pp. 120. 3s. 6d.

[65] *Man in Motion: Faulkner's Trilogy*, by Warren Beck. Wisconsin U.P. pp. viii+203. $6 cloth. $1.75 paper.

[66] *William Faulkner*, by Frederick J. Hoffman. (Twayne's United States Authors Series.) New York: Twayne. pp. 134. $3.50.

Chapter Three is a study of *The Sound and the Fury* and *As I Lay Dying*. Chapter Four makes particular reference to Faulkner's several ways of treating the problem of evil. Chapter Five is concerned with 'The Negro and the Folk'. In the final section Hoffman deals with the last ten years of Faulkner's writing. Faulkner is here seen to be struggling with 'the problems of rhetoric and forceful moral statement'—and presumably their reconciliation. While Hoffman's book is intended for the general reader, and draws upon his considerable experience of teaching Faulkner, it can be read with profit by those for whom Faulkner's novels are not closed books.

In *CQ* Brian Way considers aspects of *Sanctuary*, *The Sound and the Fury*, *Light in August*, and *The Wild Palms*. His discussion of the last, although brief, is unusually perceptive. He does not make the mistake of most critics in relegating this passionate and moving love story to an inferior place.

Joseph Gold writes on 'Delusion and Redemption in Faulkner's *A Fable*' in *MFS*.

In 'Call Me Ishmael: The Hagiography of Isaac McCaslin' (*TSLL*) Stanley Sultan considers some of the intricacies of *Go Down, Moses*. He believes that it embodies Faulkner's most comprehensive pronouncement on the subject of race, the South, and human nature. Sultan's discussion of 'The Bear' gains considerably from analysis in the context of the book as a whole—an interesting critical discovery.

In another article on *Go Down, Moses* printed in *PMLA* and entitled 'The Wilderness and the Negro in Faulkner's "The Bear"', Melvin Backman maintains that the story he discusses is the heart of the book. It voices the concern of conscience over the Negro's plight in a white-man's world, but it voices also the concern of conscience over its own helplessness.

In the early chapters of John H. Wrenn's *John Dos Passos*[67] there is a considerable amount of biography, much of it derived from the 'Camera Eye' sections of *U.S.A.* and *Chosen Country*. The middle chapters are devoted to criticism. The later chapters, like Dos Passos's later works emphasize history. *U.S.A.* Wrenn sees to be a 'central work of artistic fulfillment—the complete integration of biography, autobiography, criticism, and history'. With this synthesis, Wrenn thinks, Dos Passos found himself, established his identity in time and space, and became a major writer of his time.

Blanche H. Gelfant (*PMLA*) considers the major novels of Dos Passos in 'The Search for Identity in the Novels of John Dos Passos'. She finds them evidence of Dos Passos's attempts to trace his 'generic hero's response to the socio-political scene'. This gradually changes as he loses perspective and objectivity.

The purpose of Warren French's *John Steinbeck*,[68] says the author, is to get people to read Steinbeck's deceptively lucid works as carefully as possible. He believes that the general reader's attention should be called to three tendencies which shape Steinbeck's fiction. The first of these is his interest in allegory. Steinbeck is not merely a reporter. He 'looks for a pattern in the event around which an account of it may be organized'. The second most important thing about Steinbeck, according to French, is his preoccupation with 'non-teleological' thinking, which 'concerns itself primarily not with what should be, or could be, or might be, but rather with

[67] *John Dos Passos*, by John H. Wrenn. (Twayne's United States Authors Series.) New York: Twayne. pp. 208. $3.50.

[68] *John Steinbeck*, by Warren French. (Twayne's United States Authors Series.) New York: Twayne. pp. 190. $3.50.

what actually *is*'. Steinbeck's theology—the third important thing to remember about him—is of a pattern with nineteenth-century American transcendentalism. French believes that some insight into Steinbeck's work may be gained by reading Emerson and Thoreau.

In *The Fiction of John O'Hara*[69] Edward Russell Carson concentrates on O'Hara's 'Gibbsville' or 'Lantenengo County' novels and stories—that is, *Appointment in Samarra, A Rage to Live, Ten North Frederick, From the Terrace*, and *Ourselves to Know*. What sets these works apart from O'Hara's other novels and collections of short stories is that the 'Gibbsville' novels comprise a more noticeably autobiographic outlet for the author's personal experience. His method is the 'photographic precision of the still-life painter'. Considering its briefness, Carson's account is very thorough, although he tends to overrate his subject.

James F. Light's 'interpretative' study of Nathanael West[70] is the most extensive treatment of West's life to appear in print. Light's book is not merely a biography, however. He analyses the novels with some care. West's universe, he admits, is a limited one, but as the novelist himself pointed out, to introduce the normal into it would be to destroy its very fabric. Though limited, and nightmarish, it is a valid universe. For more and more readers, West's vision has the honesty, the seriousness, and the power to ensure that it will not be forgotten. Josephine Herbst, who knew West, writes feelingly about him in *KR*. His novels she sees to be 'dark parables',

embodying West's vision of what it means to be a human being in this world. There are no heroes.

A whole number of *MFS* is devoted to 'Theories and Trends of Modern Fiction'. John Graham has some original things to say about Hemingway's style, and Daniel J. Hughes compares *Lolita* and *Henderson the Rain King* under the heading of 'Reality and the Hero'.

In 'The Southern Muse: Two Poetry Societies' (*AQ*) Louis D. Rubin, Jr., ironically quotes H. L. Mencken's 'Down there, a poet is almost as rare as an oboe-player, a dry-point etcher, or a metaphysician.' He is concerned to prove Mencken wrong by detailing the poetic activities of the South in Mencken's time.

In the autumn of 1916, magazine editors and reviewers of poetry found on their desks a volume of verse of sixty-odd pages. It bore the title *Spectra* in large black letters and below it, in smaller letters, the words 'New Poems'. Underneath were the names of two previously unknown poets, Emanuel Morgan and Anne Knish. The book was respectfully received. Emanuel Morgan was thought to be an expatriate painter-turned-poet and Anne Knish a Hungarian beauty whose only previous work was a volume of poems in Russian. After a few years suspicion began to grow that the whole thing might be a hoax. Finally Witter Bynner admitted that he was 'Emanuel Morgan' and Arthur Davison Ficke 'Anne Knish'. William Jay Smith tells the story with admirable moderation in *The Spectra Hoax*.[71] It is not without its moral for those who care to ponder over it.

Samuel Hynes discusses the technique of Ezra Pound in an article entitled 'Pound and the Prose Tradition' (*Yale Review*). He approaches

[69] *The Fiction of John O'Hara*, by E. Russell Carson. (Critical Essays in English and American Literature Series.) Pittsburgh U.P. pp. 73. $1.25.

[70] *Nathanael West: An Interpretative Study*, by James F. Light. Northwestern U.P. pp. 220. $4.75.

[71] *The Spectra Hoax*, by William Jay Smith. Wesleyan U.P. pp. ix+158. $3.50.

the subject by way of a remark of T. E. Hulme's, and goes on to describe Pound's attempt to establish a 'prose tradition' in poetry. Hynes concludes with some salutary words on current attempts to write off the Pound–Eliot revolution in diction as an aberration and a perversity.

In *KR* Roy Harvey Pearce quotes Robert Frost's remark that he owed more to Emerson than anyone else 'for troubled thoughts about freedom'. He considers that Frost puts the Emersonian doctrine of freedom to his own special use, managing in his poems to create nothing less than an orthodoxy— as against Emerson's heterodoxy—of the self.

William Y. Tindall's pamphlet on Wallace Stevens[72] is so agreeably written that one is almost lulled into an unquestioning state of acceptance. It is a shock, therefore, to realize that some of his judgements are far from accurate. For example, he calls 'Le Monocle de Mon Oncle' one of the most precious poems of *Harmonium* and shows an almost complete lack of awareness of the high seriousness of this apparently dandified poem. The first part of the study, however, which deals with Stevens's career as business-man and poet, may be thoroughly recommended.

In 'Wallace Stevens' *Ideas of Order*: The Rhetoric of Politics and the Rhetoric of Poetry' (*NEQ*) Joseph N. Riddell shows that Stevens was much more alive to the bitter social tensions of the early 1930's than is generally supposed.

In *MLN* the same writer disputes the authorship of 'On Poetic Truth', found by Samuel French Morse among Wallace Stevens's papers and included in *Opus Posthumous*. The piece is, in fact, a series of extracts from an article with this title by H. D. Lewis which appeared in the July 1946 issue of *Philosophy*.

Ever since its appearance in 1930 *The Bridge* has been a subject of controversy. Almost every critic of importance who has commented on it has considered the poem to be a failure. In *Hart Crane's Sanskrit Charge*[73] L. S. Dembo considers that their objections can be met. *The Bridge* has both meaning and form, but neither has been properly appreciated because the kind of experience that the poem presents has never been understood. *The Bridge* is not a naïve attempt to set up a national myth based on technology for its own sake, but an account of 'the exiled poet's quest for a logos in which the Absolute that he has known in his imagination will be made intelligible to the world'. Dembo amply justifies his reference to *The Bridge* as 'a romantic lyric with epic implications'. It is not concerned with America in the same way as *Leaves of Grass*. Rather, it tries to present American history as an enlarged or collective version of a romantic poet's biography.

William White has compiled a useful bibliography of Karl Shapiro.[74] He lists books, poems in periodicals, articles in reviews, anthologies containing material by Shapiro, reviews, biography, and criticism, and manuscripts and other material in the Feinberg Collection, Detroit.

In his University of Minnesota pamphlet[75] Alan Downer deals with

[72] *Wallace Stevens*, by William York Tindall. (Minnesota Pamphlets on American Writers, No. 11.) Minnesota U.P. and O.U.P. pp. 47. 65c. 5s.

[73] *Hart Crane's Sanskrit Charge: A Study of 'The Bridge'*, by L. S. Dembo. Cornell U.P. and O.U.P., 1960. pp. xii+137. 22s. 6d.
[74] *Karl Shapiro: A Bibliography*, by William White, with a note by Karl Shapiro. Wayne State U.P., 1960. pp. 113. $4 cloth. $3 paper.
[75] *Recent American Drama*, by Alan Downer. (Minnesota Pamphlets on American Writers, No. 7.) Minnesota U.P. and O.U.P. pp. 46. 65c. 5s.

plays which have appeared since the Second World War. He points out that the difficulty in evaluating recent drama in the United States is that the critic has to deal with 'experience first and the larger questions of art second'. Although the theatre has contracted physically it has grown increasingly complex as a vehicle for the dramatist. Whereas O'Neill refused furiously to allow a single line of his plays to be changed, Tennessee Williams rewrote the final act of *Cat on a Hot Tin Roof* at the request of his director. This awareness gives some indication of Downer's general grasp of the current American dramatic scene. His comments on Arthur Miller, Tennessee Williams, William Inge, Paddy Chayefsky, Arthur Laurents, and Archibald MacLeish are concise and to the point.

In *Encounter* Mary McCarthy also writes about the contemporary American theatre. Under the title of 'Americans, Realists, Playwrights' she asks whether it is true that there is a school of realists in the American theatre, or whether the notion is a critical fiction. For the purposes of discussion she takes it for granted that Arthur Miller, Tennessee Williams, William Inge, Paddy Chayefsky, and the Elmer Rice of *Street Scene* do constitute such a school. She comes to the conclusion that no dramatist today can accept—as O'Neill did—the full implications of being a realist.

The Theme of Loneliness in Modern American Drama[76] is one of those odd books to which one cannot take exception because it is so thoroughly and devotedly written but which one cannot feel was really necessary. For example, one could just as easily examine the theme of loneliness in the American novel, the American short story, American poetry, or American *belles lettres*, and it would have just as much, or just as little, point. Miss Dusenbury organizes her thesis under the headings of 'Personal Failure', 'Homelessness', 'An Unhappy Family', 'The Failure of a Love Affair', 'Socioeconomic Forces', 'In the South', 'Conflict between the Material and the Spiritual', and 'The Lonely Hero'. There are full notes, a bibliography, and an index.

Although some of S. K. Winther's *Eugene O'Neill*[77] has an out-of-date air (he takes V. F. Calverton to task, for example, in his chapter entitled 'This Sickness of Today'), the book still stands as a thorough discussion of the basic principles of O'Neill's art. It was first published in 1934, and is now reissued with an additional chapter entitled 'O'Neill and Modern Tragedy'. This seems hardly adequate to cover the last thirty years, however. A larger section on this period and a more complete revision would have been welcome. Nevertheless, for such chapters as 'The Destructive Power of the Romantic Ideal', 'The Anathema of Puritanism', 'Religion', 'Pessimism and Tragedy', and 'Optimism and Comedy' Winther's book is still useful.

Two books on Tennessee Williams adopt different methods of treating his work. Signi Lenea Falk's study[78] starts with the words on the page, Benjamin Nelson's[79] with the playwright's life. Miss Falk's book is free from the extremes of adulation or excoriation. In an intelligent and well-written analysis of Williams's

[76] *The Theme of Loneliness in Modern American Drama*, by Winifred L. Dusenbury. Florida U.P., 1960. pp. vi+231. $6.50.

[77] *Eugene O'Neill: A Critical Study*, by Sophus Keith Winther. New York: Russell & Russell. pp. 319. $7.50.

[78] *Tennessee Williams*, by Signi Lenea Falk. (Twayne's United States Authors Series.) New Haven: College and University Press. pp. 224. $1.65.

[79] *Tennessee Williams: His Life and Work*, by Benjamin Nelson. London: Peter Owen. pp. 262. 25s.

contribution to the drama, she deals first of all with his place in the 'Southern Renaissance'. Her theory is that Williams searched for the best medium in which to express his poetic apprehension of the modern Southern sensibility. He came to the drama only after trying poetry and the short story. Miss Falk examines the major plays under the headings of 'The Southern Gentlewoman', 'Southern Wenches', 'The Desperate Heroes', and 'The Degenerating Artist'. In her final chapter, entitled 'The Literary World of Tennessee Williams', Miss Falk points out that, although Williams seems to be writing about the South or contemporary society, he is more often writing about himself. Yet although his plays may fall apart upon analysis, in his best work something of importance remains—an insight into character and motivation, an understanding of the lack of communication between people, and an awareness of the emptiness and cruelty of 'many well-fed Americans'.

Nelson's account is much more biographical since it is his belief that the plays can best be understood within the context of the playwright's life. It is perhaps unfortunate that his chapters have such titles as 'It was a tragic move', 'The Parlour was uncomfortable as the cellar', and 'Jack be nimble, Jack be quick, Jack jump over, Arithmetic!', but one ought not to be put off by such apparent archness. Nelson's comments on the plays themselves are also sometimes quite illuminating.

In 'Tendenzen in der amerikanischen Literaturgeschichtsschreibung der letzten zwanzig Jahre' (*Jahrbuch für Amerikastudien*) Franz H. Link records the changes which have taken place during the past twenty years in the interpretation of American literary history. Commentators have with much more frequency asked how American literature differed from other literatures. Link begins with *The Spirit of American Literature* (1913). The chief documents after that he sees to be Parrington's *Main Currents in American Thought*, H. M. Jones's *Theory of American Literature*, *The Literary History of the United States*, Matthiessen's *American Renaissance*, Feidelson's *Symbolism and American Literature*, and Lewis's *The American Adam*.

Finally, Francis J. Rigney and L. Douglas Smith present us with a 'sociological and psychological study of the "Beats"'. *The Real Bohemia*[80] is a clinical account of the San Francisco North Beach community. It is, none the less, of interest to the literary- as well as the medically-minded. Between October 1958 and March 1959 the authors organized a 'project'. Rigney obtained the material; Smith tested the 'subjects'. In twelve chapters they reveal the case histories of the Beat poets and artists who consented to answer their questions. What interested the investigators as much as the Beats themselves was the public's reaction against them. Theirs is a sympathetic—sometimes a pathetic—account which, without intending to do so, goes some way towards explaining why so much Beat art fails to carry conviction.

[80] *The Real Bohemia*, by Francis J. Rigney and L. Douglas Smith. New York: Basic Books. pp. xi+250. $5.

INDEX I. AUTHORS

INDEX II. AUTHORS
AND SUBJECTS TREATED

Wise, Thomas J., 132.
Wither, George, 163, 164.
Wodehouse, P. G., 250–1.
Wolfe, Thomas, 10, 277.
Wood, Anthony à, 186.
Wood, Mrs. Henry, 242.
Wood, Margaret, 30.
Woodward, Hezekiah, 165.
Woolf, Virginia, 17, 251, 264, 271.
Worde, Wynkyn de, 87.

Wordsworth, William, 16, 18, 23, 29, 121, 127, 225, 226, 232, 285.
Wright, David, 28.
Wright, Judith, 11.
Wright, Thomas, 137.
Wulfstan, 60.
Wyatt, Sir Thomas, 83, 98, 99, 100, 101, 102, 144.
Wycherley, William, 183, 187.

Wycliffite New Testament, the, 70–71.
Wylde, A. E., 28.

Yeats, W. B., 10, 27, 235, 246, 253, 255, 256–8, 260, 262, 272–3, 274.
Yeoman, the, 140–1.
Young, Andrew, 27.
Young, Bartholomew, 142.

PRINTED IN GREAT BRITAIN
AT THE UNIVERSITY PRESS, OXFORD
BY VIVIAN RIDLER
PRINTER TO THE UNIVERSITY